COMPOSING A CIVIC LIFE

COMPOSING A CIVIC LIFE

A Rhetoric and Readings for Inquiry and Action

MICHAEL BERNDT

Normandale Community College

AMY MUSE

University of St. Thomas

PEARSON

Longman

New York San Francisco Boston
London Toronto Sydney Tokyo Singapore Madrid
Mexico City Munich Paris Cape Town Hong Kong Montreal

Senior Vice President/Publisher: Joseph Opiela
Acquisitions Editor: Lynn Huddon
Executive Marketing Manager: Ann Stypuloski
Media Supplements Editor: Nancy Garcia
Senior Supplements Editor: Donna Campion
Production Manager: Eric Jorgensen
Project Coordination, Text Design, and Electronic Page Makeup: Electronic Publishing
Services Inc., N.Y.C.
Cover Designer: Nancy Danahy
Cover Illustration: Peg Baldock
Manufacturing Manager: Dennis J. Para
Printer and Binder: R.R. Donnelley & Sons, Co.
Cover Printer: Coral Graphic Services

For permission to use copyrighted material, grateful acknowledgment is made to the copyright
holders on pp. 567–570, which are hereby made part of this copyright page.

Library of Congress Cataloging-in-Publication Data

Berndt, Michael
    Composing a civic life: a rhetoric and readings for inquiry and action/Michael Berndt,
Amy Muse
        p. cm.
    Includes bibliographical references and index.
    ISBN 0-321-08641-4
    1. Readers—Community Life. 2. Community life—Problems, exercises, etc. 3. English
language—Rhetoric—Problems, exercises, etc. 4. Report writing—Problems, exercises, etc.
5. College readers. I. Muse, Amy. II. Title.

PE1127.S6 B47 2002
808'.0427—dc21

Please visit our Web site at http://www.ablongman.com/berndt

ISBN: 0-321-08641-4

1 2 3 4 5 6 7 8 9 10—DOC—05 04 03 02

To Mike Carls, my American government teacher,
for modeling good teaching and a dedicated civic life.

To Suzanne, my wife, for offering encouragement and time.

To Reid, who was born at the project's beginning,
and Paige, who was born at the end,
for putting all things into perspective.

Michael Berndt

To my parents, Bill and Marlene Muse,
for setting the example of a life engaged in
and enriched by community and learning.

Amy Muse

To our students—past, present, and future—who inspire us
with their curiosity and empathy.

BRIEF CONTENTS

DETAILED CONTENTS

Preface xv

Acknowledgments xviii

4   Arguing: Action as Inquiry 116

6 Negotiating Community: Living a Civic Life 189

11   Communities of Faith 439

12   Virtual Communities 503

PREFACE

"Democracy cannot succeed," wrote Franklin D. Roosevelt, "unless those who express their choice are prepared to choose wisely. The real safeguard of democracy, therefore, is education." In the last several years, Americans have expressed a growing concern about the quality of their civic lives. These concerns have come from social and religious leaders, from educators and activists, and from politicians at all points on the political spectrum. They have asked citizens to reaffirm their membership in various communities by getting informed and involved. They have also called on educators to prepare young people to be good citizens of the twenty-first century—not just by providing them with knowledge, but by developing their ability to think critically, communicate effectively, and live wisely.

The writing classroom is an ideal place to cultivate a healthy civic life. Here you can learn critical thinking, reading, and writing—the civic skills central to both academic success and effective democratic participation. You can learn how to research an issue, argue your views to academic and public audiences, and reflect on your experiences—key components of citizen action and community learning. You can study the people of different communities and the frameworks they use for making sense of the world. You can even test those frameworks, examining social issues that challenge the values and beliefs of these communities. The work you do in this course can prepare you to live what philosophers call an *examined life*, but it isn't the only way you can learn. The model of community you establish in the classroom can also shape the quality of your civic life.

We imagine the writing classroom as a potential model of rigorous, ethical inquiry and action, one that could set a standard for the work you do in other classes and communities. This vision is based on several assumptions about students and instructors.

We believe that you, as students, have a genuine desire to learn and to participate more actively in your communities. We also believe that you can rise to the intellectual level of whatever material you are given, and that the quality of your thinking and writing will improve if you are asked to work with meaningful, challenging material. Your greatest assets in this work are your energy, your idealism, and your access to the experts and resources of a college community. We encourage you to give all of your work in this course a good-faith effort. At the same time, we encourage you to inquire into the wisdom and intent of your instructors and the ideas and exercises in this text. You should get involved actively in your own learning by understanding more fully why you are participating in these classroom activities.

We believe that you, as instructors, come into the classroom with energy, commitment, and expertise. The last thing we want is to discourage you from using those strengths. Instead of writing a text so comprehensive that you feel like you are a supplement in your own classroom, we have favored an interactive approach that sets up you, your students, and the text as equal partners in the creation of classroom knowledge. For example, much of the writing instruction in this textbook consists of a series of inquiries. We give students just enough instruction to set up individual or in-class exercises. These exercises encourage them to work with you in creating classroom knowledge. Our students who went through this process created much of the instruction in this textbook. For this interactive process to work, however, we encourage you to communicate actively with your students, helping them understand the intellectual and ethical reasons for all classroom activities.

To realize our vision of the writing classroom and of teaching critical thinking, reading, and writing in the context of students' civic lives, we have written a text that is exciting and unique. Here are some of the book's more outstanding features:

- *A first-week unit on citizenship that introduces the book's main subjects.* The first chapter sets the tone for the entire book; it is interactive, dynamic, and progressive. It immerses you in a series of short inquiries that will deepen your understanding of citizenship. You can create Mind Maps to assess what you know. Then, you can compare dictionary definitions, consult excerpts from the U.S. Constitution, complete part of the Immigration and Naturalization Service's naturalization process, and read three personal narratives, comparing what you have learned with the lived experiences of other citizens. All of these exercises introduce the main subjects of the book, from critical thinking to community.

- *A creative approach to critical thinking and reading.* We introduce critical thinking by asking you to wrestle with several ethical dilemmas. We then ask you to read and respond to the Declaration of Independence. If such a revered document can be read critically, then any document can be questioned, analyzed, and viewed from multiple perspectives. At the end of each section, we encourage you to offer your own suggestions for thinking and reading critically.

- *An accessible, adaptive writing process.* We present writing as a process of looking inside ourselves: we can use writing to clarify our thinking and to teach ourselves the truth of what we want to say. We also present writing as a process of looking outside ourselves: we can use writing to communicate our ideas effectively and ethically. These two perspectives, internal and external, reinforce each other as writers go through the steps of creating, clarifying, and crafting their essays. Because the writing process varies with individuals and with assignments, we present it as an accessible series of strategies that you can adapt to different circumstances. To illustrate this point, we weave in the experiences of Thomas Jefferson in writing the Declaration of Independence, encouraging you to compare your process with his.

- *A fresh, common-sense approach to research.* To introduce research, we invite you to explore inquiry more generally, treating it as a natural expression of our curiosity. Using Socrates's famous question, "How should one live?" and passages from Henry David Thoreau's *Walden*, we frame inquiry first as individual exploration, then as participation in larger conversations. We invite you to respond to Thoreau creatively, seeing in your own poems, essays, songs, or plays the idea that how we write shapes the kind of inquiry we can conduct. Building on this idea, we then teach methods of library, media, and field research, including observing, interviewing, and surveying.

- *An approach to arguing that emphasizes inquiry.* The strategies of arguing effectively are presented as a natural expression of our empathy, our capacity to anticipate and shape how people respond to our ideas. Because arguing strategies can be used unethically, to discourage critical thinking and break down community ties, we treat arguing as inquiry, our effort to test our ideas by introducing them into the conversations going on around us.

- *A multidisciplinary approach to the research essay.* To apply the more general principles of inquiry and arguing to work in academic disciplines—like history, sociology, biology, or business—we take you through the process of writing a research paper. Using the stories of several different students, we help you discover a research question, set up a research plan, and write up the results in a format appropriate to different academic disciplines. Because each discipline has its own standards for good research and research papers, we include exercises to help you discover those standards for yourself and compare them. Learning to be a savvy college writer means learning how to identify and meet an instructor's expectations, regardless of the discipline.

- *Writing instruction based on the genres of public debate.* To help you communicate with public audiences effectively, we encourage you to first consider the ethics of social action and the avenues through which people communicate to community members—what we call the genres of public debate. We then provide guidelines for selecting an appropriate genre and advice that is tied to examples in the readings. In addition to covering common genres like newspaper stories, editorials, and letters, we also cover posters, pamphlets, Web discussion groups, and zines.

- *Readings chapters organized around real communities.* In addition to local and national communities, we have included communities organized around family, education, spirituality, the environment, and technology. We have included a wide range of communities because citizens view themselves and their actions from many perspectives. These communities also have their own standards for rigorous and ethical communication that you will need to learn if you want to participate in them effectively.

- *Substantive case studies.* The case studies in this book usually begin with one or two works that provide detailed information about the issues or events involved. We have found that all of us can participate more rigorously and intelligently when we have information on which to build our opinions. We then provide argumentative works, including editorials, government documents, letters to the editor, and so on that model the way community concerns get framed into social issues, and we invite you to articulate your own views in relation to the public conversations already taking place. To help you develop your own case study, we have included prompts for a case study on the environment that is built entirely on your own inquiry and action.

- *Dialog boxes to encourage you to think critically and read as writers.* In each chapter you will find two types of dialog boxes. Stop and Think boxes prompt you to connect what you are reading to other issues and to your own experiences. Writing Style boxes offer additional writing tips, and they discuss the conventions of academic and public writing. These style boxes connect the writing instruction of the beginning chapters with the readings, asking you to think about the readings as crafted texts.

- *A companion Website to further your inquiries.* Throughout the book we have included our Web site **http://www.ablongman.com/berndt** that invite you to contribute your knowledge to the community of students and instructors formed around this book. The site also encourages you to inquire further using the links and readings provided. You can even critique aspects of the book, telling us what readings and case studies appealed to you or what works you would like us to include in future editions.

- *An instructor's manual.* This manual will assist instructors in using the unique features of *Composing a Civic Life*, accessing the Companion Website, building syllabi, as well as offering different assignment sequences.

When we sent this book to our editor, the United States had just declared war on terrorism and was attacking Afghanistan. The need for critical thinking and civic education is more urgent than ever. We hope you will continue the conversation with us.

ACKNOWLEDGMENTS

Over the three years we've been developing this book, we have accumulated many debts it is now our pleasure to acknowledge. The project began as a response to the University of Minnesota's freshman writing courses on citizenship and public ethics. For help in conceiving the project and crafting the manuscript, we thank our colleagues from the University of Minnesota, especially Tim Gustafson, Ilene Alexander, Lillian Bridwell-Bowles Patrick Bruch, Anne Carter, Pat Crain,

Elaine Cullen, Eric Daigre, Piyali Nath Dalal, Tom Reynolds, John Wallace, and Jonathan Cullick. We're also grateful to those students in three semesters of classes who gave us honest feedback on what works and what doesn't.

In our new scholarly communities we have found allies as well. At the University of St. Thomas, English department chair Michael Mikolajczak has been a warm supporter, and colleagues Andy Scheiber, Marty Warren, and Kanishka Chowdhury have shown particular interest in the project with their challenging questions and smart reading suggestions. At Normandale Community College, Jack Miller, Linda Tetzlaff, and David Pates kindly lent us their attention as we talked through ideas. Paula Backscheider and Richard Graves of Auburn University supported the project from its inception; and Keith Abney, California Polytechnic State University–San Luis Obispo, cheerfully answered e-mails on questions of teaching ethics from the point of view of a philosopher.

In the Twin Cities we are fortunate to have a number of communities that serve as our models of civic life. We would like especially to thank D'Ann Urbaniak Lesch and all the folks at the Jane Addams School for Democracy in St. Paul, where questions of citizenship were honed, and the staff of the Riverview Café in Minneapolis, where much of this book was drafted. And here and beyond we are always grateful for the interest, sustenance, and good ideas of friends and family, including Van and Lori Muse, Larry Lindeman and Ellen Muse-Lindeman, Peter Shea and Nathan Kuhlman.

In the Longman community, we would like to thank Sandy Lindelof, who was our local representative and an early and enthusiastic proponent of the project, as well as Linda Schlesinger and Leslie Hill, former and current Longman representatives. Sandy introduced us to our editor, Lynn Huddon, who, along with our development editor, Katharine Glynn, generously lent expertise to shape the manuscript and patiently encouraged us along the way. We would also like to acknowledge Kristi Olson, Editorial Assistant; Eric Jorgensen, Production Manager; and Shannon Egan, Project Editor. Our tireless permissions editor Pam Foley, has endured our many revisions with remarkable forbearance and good humor.

Finally, we would like to thank the reviewers whose enthusiastic and strong responses, both positive and negative, showed how deeply instructors feel about civics as a part of writing instruction: Greg Beatty, North Carolina State University; Martha D. Bone, Maysville Community College; Margaret Baker Graham, Iowa State University; Glenn Hutchinson, University of North Carolina–Charlotte; Katherine Kessler, James Madison University; Megan Knight, University of Iowa; Jeff Koloze, Lorain County Community College; Robin Morris, Cape Fear Community College; Marshall Myers, Eastern Kentucky University; Carole Clark Papper, Ball State University; Steve Parks, Temple University; Sheryl Stevenson, University of Akron; Jan Strever, Spokane Community College; Deborah Coxwell Teague, Florida State University; and Eve Wiederhold, East Carolina University–Greenville.

Michael Berndt
Amy Muse

CHAPTER 1

What Does It Mean to Be a Citizen?

"An idea is a feat of association."
Robert Frost

GETTING STARTED: Picturing Citizenship

When you hear the question "What does it mean to be a citizen?" what ideas come first to your mind? If you imagine concepts like freedom or duty, or actions like voting, try to visualize them; are there objects, persons, or events that help you picture these ideas? Hold one of those images in your mind, then take out a piece of clean paper and draw that image in the paper's center.

Some images, such as flags, will be easy to draw, but others, like a group of people living together in harmony, will not, so you might symbolize that idea with two stick figures holding hands. The image does not have to be drawn well, but it should be kept relatively small to give you room on the paper for further drawing. As you introduce yourselves to your classmates, describe what image you drew and why. Then compare the images; are there significant differences or similarities?

FIRST INQUIRY: USING MIND MAPS TO ASSESS WHAT YOU KNOW ABOUT CITIZENSHIP

The pictures you drew in the Getting Started exercise are the first step in creating a Mind Map of citizenship. Created by Tony Buzan and based on the notebooks of great thinkers like Leonardo da Vinci, Mind Maps help us create and examine our ideas. Writers begin with a central image and expand outward, writing down additional words or images that they associate with the central image. From these new words and images, writers can see new connections, creating more ideas and expanding the map further.

1

While Mind Maps can be used in a variety of ways, from planning an activity to taking class notes, the map of citizenship included below demonstrates how writers can use maps to brainstorm, or generate ideas, about citizenship. Created by several freshmen at the University of Minnesota, this Mind Map represents only one of thousands of possible maps. As you analyze it, describe how the Mind Map helped you create or examine ideas about citizenship. Then assess whether the map achieves three common goals of brainstorming: 1) to assess what we already know, 2) to alert us to what we don't know, and 3) to suggest directions for further inquiry.

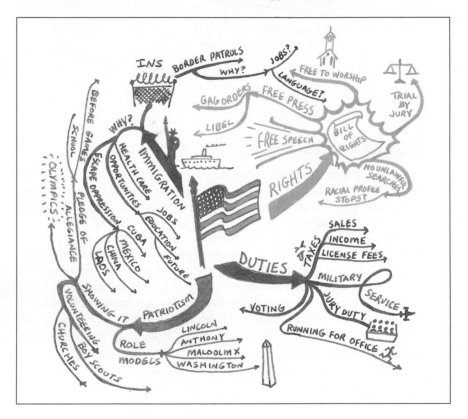

As you examined the Mind Map, did you think of other ideas or images associated with citizenship? Now assess your own ideas about citizenship by creating your own Mind Map.

EXERCISE 1.1   Creating Your Own Mind Map

1. *Place the paper with your image of citizenship in front of you.* Starting a Mind Map with a picture or symbol encourages creativity because we associate many ideas and feelings with visual images. Placing the image in the center of your paper will free you to expand in any direction.

2. *Write down any words suggested by the image.* In different locations around the central image, write down any words, phrases, or images inspired by the central image. You shouldn't second-guess any of your ideas by worrying about what others will think. Next, connect the words and images to your central image with arrows that point outward from the center. These arrows can help you organize your thoughts by showing the direction of your thinking.

3. *Continue expanding on the secondary words and images.* Using each new word, phrase, or image as your starting point, expand your ideas, connecting those ideas with new arrows. As you expand outward, include specific ideas and examples that clarify the elements in your map. A completed Mind Map often resembles a spider's web because each new word or image suggests additional ideas that radiate outward from it. Finish your Mind Map only when you've exhausted your ideas. Even though you may not use every item in a Mind Map, having an abundance of ideas can offer more possible directions for further inquiry.

Once you have finished your Mind Map, meet in small groups and compare your ideas. Do some of your words and images parallel those of your classmates? Do other words or images suggest conflicting ideas about citizenship? As a follow-up exercise, you might do a class Mind Map, beginning with the most commonly used image from the Getting Started exercise.

CONTINUING THE INQUIRY: DICTIONARY DEFINITIONS

Your Mind Maps may have suggested many common ideas among your classmates. At the same time, the maps may have highlighted differences in your definitions of citizenship that are hard to reconcile. One student may associate citizenship with social protests while another may associate it with law, order, and social harmony. One student may see citizenship primarily as our civil rights, while another may focus on our civic duties. To reconcile these differences, we might turn to an outside authority like a dictionary. Consulting a dictionary about unfamiliar words becomes natural for college students; perhaps you even looked up the words *citizen* and *citizenship* in the dictionary before beginning your Mind Map.

Dictionaries guide readers on a word's pronunciation and usage and trace its etymology (its earliest introduction into the language). Dictionaries also provide several features useful to understanding a word's meaning. Each dictionary's editorial board identifies the alternative meanings of a word, using numbers to differentiate them and letters to note differences within a particular meaning. Some dictionaries even provide examples, called *citations*, of how the word is used in a sentence. *The Oxford English Dictionary*, for example, provides citations from writers of different historical periods, showing how a word can gain new meanings over time. Finally, dictionaries occasionally provide synonyms, which are words with similar meaning. To further explore how dictionaries work, try the following exercise:

EXERCISE 1.2 Comparing Dictionary Definitions

Look up the words *citizen* and *citizenship* in your own dictionary, compare them with the following definitions, and then—either individually or in small groups—respond to the questions that follow the definitions.

1. There are a number of differences in the dictionary definitions. The variety might be a result of writing for different audiences. Who might be the probable audiences and what might be the likely purposes for each definition, based on each definition's features?
2. Consider your needs as a college writer. Which of the dictionary definitions would be most useful to you, and why?
3. To communicate their ideas effectively, writers choose precisely worded statements over vague, generally worded statements. Do the dictionary definitions help to clarify your ideas of citizenship by giving you more precisely worded descriptions?

The American Century Dictionary:

> **cit·i·zen** /sit′əzən/ *n.* member of a country,
> state, city, etc. —**cit′i·zen·ry** /-rē/ *n.*; **cit′i·**
> **zen·ship′** *n.* [OFr. rel. to CITY]

Webster's Ninth New Collegiate Dictionary:

Definition of "Citizen" from *Merriam-Webster's Collegiate® Dictionary, 10th Edition*
©2001 by Merriam-Webster, Incorporated, by permission of Merriam-Webster, Inc.

> **cit·i·zen** \'sit-ə-zən *also* -sən\ *n* [ME *citizein,* fr. AF *citezein,* alter. of OF *citeien,* fr. *cité* city] (14c) **1 :** an inhabitant of a city or town; *esp* : one entitled to the rights and privileges of a freeman **2 a :** a member of a state **b :** a native or naturalized person who owes allegiance to a government and is entitled to protection from it **3 :** a civilian as distinguished from a specialized servant of the state — **cit·i·zen·ly** \-zən-lē *also* -sən-\ *adj*
> **syn** CITIZEN, SUBJECT, NATIONAL mean a person owing allegiance to and entitled to the protection of a sovereign state. CITIZEN is preferred for one owing allegiance to a state in which sovereign power is retained by the people and sharing in the political rights of those people; SUBJECT implies allegiance to a personal sovereign such as a monarch; NATIONAL designates one who may claim the protection of a state and applies esp. to one living or traveling outside that state.
> **cit·i·zen·ess** \-zə-nəs *also* -sə-\ *n* (1796) : a female citizen
> **cit·i·zen·ry** \-zən-rē *also* -sən-\ *n, pl* **-ries** (1819) : a whole body of citizens
> **citizen's arrest** *n* (1952) : an arrest made not by a law officer but by a citizen who derives his authority from the fact that he is a citizen
> **citizens band** *n* (1965) : a range of radio-wave frequencies that in the U.S. is allocated officially for private radio communications
> **cit·i·zen·ship** \'sit-ə-zən-ˌship\ *n* (1611) **1 :** the status of being a citizen **2 a :** membership in a community (as a college) **b :** the quality of an individual's response to membership in a community

The Oxford English Dictionary (see p. 5):

> © Oxford University Press 1989. Definition reprinted from **The Oxford English Dictionary** (2nd edition 1989) by permission of Oxford University Press.

citizen ('sɪtɪzən). Forms: 4 citisein, -sain, -seyn(e, citesayne, -ceyn, -zeyn, citizein, 4-5 citeseyn, -zein(e, 4-6 -sen, 5 cita-, citiesyn, cetisen, cytezane (Sc.), -eyn, -ein. sitesyn, sytizin, (setsayne), 5-6 citesyn, -zen, 6 cytezyn, cityzen, -sen, cittesen, cytiezin, cytyzyn, 7 cittizen, 6-citizen. [ME. citesein, etc., a. Anglo-Fr. citeseyn, -zein, sithezein, altered form of OF. citein, citehain, citein, citeen, citien, citain, later citeyen, citoyen:—L. type *civitātān-um, f. civitāt-em city (cf. oppidān-um, villān-um): Romanic type civitáno, -dano, whence Pr. ciutaaan, Sp. ciudadano, Pg. ciudadão; and Pr. ciptadan, It. cittadano, now cittadino. OF. cite(ñ)ain. The intercalation of s (z) in Anglo-Fr. citesain has not been explained: association with dainzain denizen, which was often an equivalent term, has been suggested.

The suggestion that z was a mistaken reading of ȝ, meaning y, on the part of a 13th or 14th c. scribe or scribes, is in every respect untenable.]

1. An inhabitant of a city or (often) of a town, esp. one possessing civic rights and privileges, a burgess or freeman of a city.

c1314 Guy Warw. (A.) 5503 þe citiseins of þat cite wel often god þonkeden he. c1330 Arth. & Merl. 5000 To London..thai come. The citisains fair in hem nome. 1382 Wyclif Acts xxi. 39, I am a man..of Tarsus..a citeseyn or burgeys, of a citee not unknown. c1400 Destr. Troy 3263 (MS. after 1500] Sum of the Citizens assemblit with all. Ibid. 11879 Citisyns. 1480 Caxton Chron. Eng. ccvi. 187 The cytezeyns of london. c1480 Pol. Poems (1859) II. 281 He thonckyd the cetisence of thayre fidelite. 1512 Act 4 Hen. VIII. c. 9. §2 Citeezens of Cities and Burgeys of boroughes and Townes. 1556 Chron. Gr. Friars (1852) 16 The kynge [Hen. VI.] came to London, & there was worshuppfully reseved of the cittezens in whytt gownes & redde whoddes. 1596 Shaks. Tam. Shr. iv. ii. 95 Pisa renowned for graue Citizens. a1674 Clarendon Hist. Reb. (1704) III. xv. 471 You, the Knights, Citizens, and Burgesses, of the House of Commons. a1699 Lady Halkett Autobiog. (1875) 20 Furnished by an honest Cittisen. 1782 Cowper Gilpin i, John Gilpin was a citizen Of credit and renown. 1848 Macaulay Hist. Eng. I. 352 The chiefs of the mercantile interest are no longer citizens. They avoid, they almost contemn, municipal honours and duties.

b. Used also as feminine. (Cf. citizeness.)

1605 Lond. Prodigal III. i. 243, I'll have thee go like a citizen, in a guarded gown and a French hood. 1655 Francion VI. 20 She who was the most antient of the two Citizens.

c. A townsman, as opposed to a countryman.

1514 Barclay Cyt. & Uplondyshm. Prol., Faustus accused and blamed cytezyns, Amyntas blamed the rurall men agayne. 1845 S. Austin Ranke's Hist. Ref. II. 209 Both citizens and peasants are tired of it. 1860 Ruskin Mod. Paint. V. i. i. 4 The words 'countryman..villager', still signify a rude and untaught person, as opposed to the words 'townsman' and 'citizen'.

d. A civilian as distinguished from a soldier; in earlier times also distinguished from a member of the landed nobility or gentry. Johnson says 'a man of trade, not a gentleman'.

1607 Shaks. Cor. III. iii. 53 When he speakes not like a Citizen You finde him like a Soldier. 1871 [see citizenhood].

e. With reference to the 'heavenly city', the New Jerusalem.

1340 Hampole Pr. Consc. 8925 bis cetè of heven..ilka citesayne þat wonned þare. 1526 Pilgr. Perf. (W. de W. 1531) 1 b, Amonge yᵉ citezyns of heuen. 1665 Boyle Occas. Refl. v. x. (1675) 338 A Citizen of the Heavenly Jerusalem, and but a Stranger and a Sojourner here.

2. A member of a state, an enfranchised inhabitant of a country, as opposed to an alien; in U.S., a person, native or naturalized, who has the privilege of voting for public offices, and is entitled to full protection in the exercise of private rights.

1382 Wyclif Sel. Wks. II. 69 [He] clevede to oon of þe citizeins of þat countre. 1538 Starkey England 46 The nombur of cytyzyns, in euery commynalty, Cyty, or cuntrey. 1633 Massinger Guardian v. iv. To save one citizen is a greater prize Than to have killed in war ten enemies. 1752 Hume Ess. & Treat. (1777) I. 281 A too great disproportion among the citizens weakens any state. a1799 Washington (Webster), If the citizens of the United States should not be free and happy, the fault will be entirely their own. 1843 Penny Cycl. XXVI. 11/1 A pledge, both to American citizens and foreign states. 1875 Jowett Plato (ed. 2) V. 79 The object of our laws is to make the citizens as friendly and happy as possible. 1884 Gladstone in Standard 19 Feb. 2/4 A nation where every capable citizen was enfranchised. Mod. Arrest of an American citizen.

b. as a title, representing Fr. citoyen, which at the Revolution took the place of Monsieur.

1795 Argus Dec. 26 Letter from the Minister for Foreign Affairs to Citizen Miot. 1799 Med. Jrnl. I. 155 He was called to the female citizen [= citoyenne] Dangviller, whom he found in a miserable situation. 1801 Ibid. V. 359 Such

Citizen Mayor, are the motives of the propositions which the Committee have the honour of laying before you. 1837 Carlyle Fr. Rev. III. II. i.

c. phr. citizen of the world: one who is at home, and claims his rights, everywhere; a cosmopolitan; also, citizen of nature. (Cf. Cicero De Leg. i. xxiii. 61 civem totius mundi.)

1474 Caxton Chesse 31 Heide hvm bourgeys and cytezeyn of the world. 1625 Bacon Ess. Goodness, etc. (Arb.) 207 If a Man be Gracious, and Courteous to Strangers, it shewes, he is a Citizen of the World. 1760 Goldsm. (title), The Citizen of the World: or, Letters from a Chinese Philosopher. 1762-71 H. Walpole Vertue's Anecd. Paint. (1786) III. 148 An original genius, a citizen of nature.

3. transf. = Inhabitant, occupant, denizen. (Of men, beasts, things personified.)

c1384 Chaucer H. Fame 930 (Fairf. MS.) In this Region certeyn Duelleth many a Citezeyn Of which that seketh Daun Plato These ben evrys bestes. 1508 Fisher Wks. (1876) 235 Who ben the cytezyns of this regyon, truly none other but deuylles. 1593 Shaks. Lucr. 465 His hand..—Rude ram, to batter such an ivory wall!—May feel her heart—poor citizen!—distress'd Wounding itself to death. 1603 Dekker Grissil (1841) 5 Let's ring a hunter's peal..in the ears Of our swift forest citizens. c1630 Drumm. of Hawth. Poems i. xxvi. Wks. (1711) 5 A citizen of Thetis christal floods.

4. adj. = citizenish, city-bred, nonce-use.

1611 Shaks. Cymb. iv. ii. 8, I am not well: But not so Citizen a wanton, as To seeme to dye, ere sicke.

5. attrib. and Comb., chiefly appositive,' as citizen-king, -magistrate, -prince, -soldier, -sovereign; also, citizen-life; citizen-like adj. Citizens' Advice Bureau, any of a network of local offices where members of the public may obtain free and impartial advice, esp. when experiencing difficulties with authorities or other individuals; citizen's arrest Law (orig. U.S.), an arrest carried out without a warrant by a private citizen' (allowable in certain cases); Citizens(') Band orig. U.S., a short-wave band made available for private radio communication; abbrev. C.B.

1830 Hobhouse in T. Juste S. Van de' Weyer (1871) App. iii. 268 He [Leopold] may do very well for a *citizen-king. 1851 Ht. Martineau Hist. Peace (1877) III. iv. xiii. 113 All eyes were fixed on the citizen-king [Louis Philippe]. 1874 Mahaffy Soc. Life Greece viii. 254 *Citizen life was too precious to be poured out in wrath. 1598 Florio, Cittadinesco, *Citizen-like. 1847 Emerson Repr. Men, Plato Wks. (Bohn) I. 303 He [Socrates] affected a good many citizen-like tastes. 1837-9 Hallam Hist. Lit. I. iii. §59 A republican government that was rapidly giving way before the *citizen-prince. 1939 Times 5 Oct. 11/1 The Queen.. visited Branches of the 'Citizens' Advice Bureau of the Charity Organisation Society at Fulham, Chelsea, Battersea and Clapham. 1969 Guardian 20 July 5/5 There is already a citizens' advice bureau just down the road. 1984 Metro (Auckland) Mar. 103/3 A phone call to the central Citizens' Advice Bureau soon put me in touch with experts in. 1941 Rep. Cases Supreme Court Calif. XVI. 659 Defendant concedes that he intended to make a *citizen's arrest — upon a charge of perjury. 1978 Daily Tel. 9 Nov. 1/7 A citizen's arrest..ended the nationwide hunt... He pinned her arms behind her and said: 'I am taking no chances on you, lady. I am making a citizen's arrest.' 1986 Guardian 20 Aug. 1/5 Joseph Hanson..was detained after a private detective made a citizen's arrest on a double-decker bus. 1948 Radio & TV News Dec. 44 (heading) *Citizens Band oscillator. Ibid. 44/3 It has been possible to obtain greater output at higher efficiencies with less heating power in cathode types than in filamentary types at the Citizens Band frequency. 1958 Ibid. Nov. 37/1 There are many needs for radio, in delivery vehicles, on farms, and in small business. The Citizens Band has been a convenient catch-all for these groups. Ibid. 38/2 Under Citizens Band rules power was limited and eligibility requirements were simple. 1976 Perkowski & Stral Joy of CB ii. 13 As originally established in 1948, there were three classes of Citizens' Band licenses available. 1981 Times 4 Mar. 16/3 The messy compromise which Ms Whitelaw..announced over the introduction of Citizens Band radio was in the end forced on the Government. 1843 Prescott Mexico I (1850) II. 310 The *citizen-soldiers of Villa Rica.

Hence **citizen** v., to address as 'citizen'.

1871 Daily News 19 Apr. 5 Now the sentinel 'citizens' me, and I 'citizen' him.

citizenship ('sɪtɪzənʃɪp). [f. as citizen + -ship.] The position or status of being a citizen, with its rights and privileges.

1611 Cotgr., Citoyennerie, a Citizenship, the freedome of a Citie. a1792 Br. Horne Occas. Serm. 158 (T.) Our citizenship, as saith the apostle, is in heaven. a1832 Sir J. Sinclair Corr. II. 13 General laws, relative to naturalization and citizenship. 1864 City Chamberlain to Garibaldi in Times 21 Apr., The City of London invites you to-day to accept the highest honour at her disposal, placing your distinguished name upon the list of worthies inscribed upon the roll of honorary citizenship. 1869 Seeley Lect. & Ess. i. 5 The Italian allies..had not yet been admitted to the Roman citizenship. 1881 N. T (Rev. Vers.) Phil. iii. 20 Our citizenship [Wyclif living, 16th c. vv. conversation] is in heaven.

Black's Law Dictionary:

Definition of "citizen" from *Black's Law Dictionary*, 6th edition. Reprinted with permission of the West Group.

> **Citizen.** One who, under the Constitution and laws of the United States, or of a particular state, is a member of the political community, owing allegiance and being entitled to the enjoyment of full civil rights. All persons born or naturalized in the United States, and subject to the jurisdiction thereof, are citizens of the United States and of the state wherein they reside. U.S.Const., 14th Amend. See Citizenship.
>
> "Citizens" are members of a political community who, in their associated capacity, have established or submitted themselves to the dominion of a government for the promotion of their general welfare and the protection of their individual as well as collective rights. Herriott v. City of Seattle, 81 Wash.2d 48, 500 P.2d 101, 109.
>
> The term may include or apply to children of alien parents born in United States, Von Schwerdtner v. Piper, D.C.Md., 23 F.2d 862, 863; U. S. v. Minoru Yasui, D.C.Or., 48 F.Supp. 40, 54; children of American citizens born outside United States, Haaland v. Attorney General of United States, D.C.Md., 42 F.Supp. 13, 22; Indians, United States v. Hester, C.C.A.Okl., 137 F.2d 145, 147; National Banks, American Surety Co. v. Bank of California, C.C.A.Or., 133 F.2d 160, 162; nonresident who has qualified as administratrix of estate of deceased resident, Hunt v. Noll, C.C.A.Tenn., 112 F.2d 288, 289. However, neither the United States nor a state is a citizen for purposes of diversity jurisdiction. Jizemerjian v. Dept. of Air Force, 457 F.Supp. 820. On the other hand, municipalities and other local governments are deemed to be citizens. Rieser v. District of Columbia, 563 F.2d 462. A corporation is not a citizen for purposes of privileges and immunities clause of the Fourteenth Amendment. D. D. B. Realty Corp. v. Merrill, 232 F.Supp. 629, 637.
>
> **Citizenship.** The status of being a citizen. There are four ways to acquire citizenship: by birth in the United States, by birth in U.S. territories, by birth outside the U.S. to U.S. parents, and by naturalization. See Corporate citizenship; Diversity of citizenship; Dual citizenship; Federal citizenship; Naturalization; Jus sanguinis; Jus soli.

The dictionary definitions give us more ideas to associate with citizenship, such as being an inhabitant of a city. They may also give us a clearer idea of what citizen and citizenship mean by providing more precisely worded descriptions. For example, we may not have differentiated between "native" and "naturalized" citizens in our understanding of citizenship. Nevertheless, the different dictionaries, like the preceding Mind Maps, still define the words in slightly different ways. For example, the first meaning given for *citizen* in the *American Century Dictionary* does not mention entitlement to civic rights or privileges, as do the others. If dictionaries are supposed to be our authorities for a word's meanings, why don't they all define words in exactly the same way?

The most obvious answer for the differences between the dictionaries is that, like any form of written communication, each has its own *purpose* and *audience*. For example, the range of the *American Century Dictionary* is broad but each entry is brief; it is also inexpensive, appealing to general readers who want a guide useful for looking up unknown words but don't need to distinguish between a word's different senses. The *Oxford English Dictionary,* on the other hand, has a different purpose and audience. First proposed by the Philological Society in England in 1857, the dictionary took more than seventy years to complete and occupies twelve large volumes. The second edition, which came out in 1989, defines over half a million words and occupies twenty volumes. The dictionary is so large because its purpose is to demonstrate, through the use of citations, the full range of the word's various meanings. Because the cost of producing such an exhaustive work is high, few general readers can afford to buy it. Consequently, its audience tends to be researchers and library patrons.

Dictionaries like *Webster's Ninth New Collegiate Dictionary* are more common for college students who may need a rigorous but affordable guide. Finally, some dictionaries like *Black's Law Dictionary* are specialized for a particular audience. The use of precise legal language (e.g., "All persons born or naturalized in the United States, and subject to the jurisdiction thereof") and the references to relevant court cases (e.g., *Herriott v. City of Seattle*) make the definitions more useful to lawyers, law students, and legal scholars.

Dictionary definitions are not the only writing situations shaped by the writer's purpose and audience. All forms of writing, from personal diaries to business memos, are shaped by the writer's subject, purpose, and audience. This is an important point to consider, because knowing what restrictions your subject places on your writing, what goals you have for writing about the subject, and what your audience knows or wants to know about the subject will help you communicate more effectively. As a follow-up exercise, you might list different writing types or situations, and then discuss how the writer's subject, purpose, and audience shape each of these examples.

CONTINUING THE INQUIRY: OFFICIAL DOCUMENTS

Dictionary definitions describe how English speakers and writers use concepts like citizenship. To learn how these concepts are defined in the context of American political and social institutions, we might examine official documents. Official documents like laws, court opinions, and organization policies—even mission statements, press releases, and the published speeches of public officials—offer definitions closely tied to the visions and practices of actual businesses, government agencies, and public interest groups. In this section we will examine two sets of documents fundamental to American citizenship: the Immigration and Naturalization Service's naturalization requirements, and the Constitution of the United States.

INS Naturalization Requirements

According to the U.S. Immigration and Naturalization Service (INS), 849,807 immigrants arrived legally in the United States in 2000. Many of these immigrants applied for U.S. citizenship. The Immigration and Nationality Act (INA) of 1952 and its many amendments serve as the basis for existing immigration law. Because the law is complex, the INS offers guides to assist immigrants in applying for citizenship. A candidate for citizenship must satisfy a number of different criteria and successfully complete several forms and exams. The process outlined in those guides has been simplified in this chapter to illustrate some of the ideas about citizenship that form the basis of the process. After you complete each stage, consider the follow-up questions individually or in groups.

In order to even apply to become a U.S. citizen, a candidate must first pass several naturalization requirements. A candidate for citizenship must

- Be at least eighteen years old.
- Have been "lawfully admitted for permanent residence" according to immigration laws, which means that the person has been registered as an immigrant and has filled out certain forms (for census and tax purposes, for example); this is in contrast to a person who arrives as an "illegal alien" and does not have registration papers (who is, in other words, "undocumented").
- Have been a lawful resident for at least five years and have been physically present in the United States for at least thirty months out of those previous five years.
- Have resided in a state or district for at least three months.

In short, the person must be an adult who has entered the country through the standard legal channels and has lived here most of the last five years. In small groups or as a class, consider the following questions:

1. Why do you think it is so important for citizenship candidates to be lawful residents for at least five years?
2. Why must they have stayed in one state or district for three months?
3. What do these requirements suggest about the INS definition of citizenship?

If candidates meet the above requirements, they must still meet additional eligibility criteria. Complete part ten of the Request for Naturalization form (Form N-400), which appears on pages 9–10; as you answer the questions, consider what these criteria have to do with U.S. citizenship

Part 10. Additional Questions

Please answer questions 1 through 14. If you answer "Yes" to any of these questions, include a written explanation with this form. Your written explanation should (1) explain why your answer was "Yes," and (2) provide any additional information that helps to explain your answer.
------------------------------------ // ------------------------------------

B. Affiliations

8. a. Have you **EVER** been a member of or associated with any organization, association, fund, foundation, party, club, society, or similar group in the United States or in any other place?   ☐ Yes   ☐ No

b. If you answered "Yes," list the name of each group below. If you need more space, attach the names of the other group(s) on a separate sheet of paper.

Name of Group	Name of Group
1.	6.
2.	7.
3.	8.
4.	9.
5.	10.

9. Have you **EVER** been a member of or in any way associated *(either directly or indirectly)* with:

a. The Communist Party?   ☐ Yes   ☐ No

b. Any other totalitarian party?   ☐ Yes   ☐ No

c. A terrorist organization?   ☐ Yes   ☐ No

10. Have you **EVER** advocated *(either directly or indirectly)* the overthrow of any government by force or violence?   ☐ Yes   ☐ No

11. Have you **EVER** persecuted *(either directly or indirectly)* any person because of race, religion, national origin, membership in a particular social group, or political opinion?   ☐ Yes   ☐ No
------------------------------------ // ------------------------------------
D. Good Moral Character

For the purposes of this application, you must answer "Yes" to the following questions, if applicable, even if your records were sealed or otherwise cleared or if anyone, including a judge, law enforcement officer, or attorney, told you that you no longer have a record.

15. Have you **EVER** committed a crime or offense for which you were NOT arrested?   ☐ Yes   ☐ No

16. Have you **EVER** been arrested, cited, or detained by any law enforcement officer (including INS and military officers) for any reason?   ☐ Yes   ☐ No

17. Have you **EVER** been charged with committing any crime or offense?   ☐ Yes   ☐ No

18. Have you **EVER** been convicted of a crime or offense?   ☐ Yes   ☐ No

19. Have you **EVER** been placed in an alternative sentencing or a rehabilitative program (for example: diversion, deferred prosecution, withheld adjudication, deferred adjudication)?   ☐ Yes   ☐ No

20. Have you **EVER** received a suspended sentence, been placed on probation, or been paroled?   ☐ Yes   ☐ No

21. Have you **EVER** been in jail or prison?   ☐ Yes   ☐ No

Part 10. Additional Questions *(Continued)*

Write your INS "A"- number here:
A _ _ _ _ _ _ _ _ _

If you answered "Yes" to any of questions 15 through 21, complete the following table. If you need more space, use a separate sheet of paper to give the same information.

Why were you arrested, cited, detained, or charged?	Date arrested, cited, detained, or charged *(Month/Day/Year)*	Where were you arrested, cited, detained or charged? *(City, State, Country)*	Outcome or disposition of the arrest, citation, detention or charge *(No charges filed, charges dismissed, jail, probation, etc.)*

Answer questions 22 through 33. If you answer "Yes" to any of these questions, attach (1) your written explanation why your answer was "Yes," and (2) any additional information or documentation that helps explain your answer.

22. Have you **EVER**:

   a. been a habitual drunkard? □ Yes □ No

   b. been a prostitute, or procured anyone for prostitution? □ Yes □ No

   c. sold or smuggled controlled substances, illegal drugs or narcotics? □ Yes □ No

   d. been married to more than one person at the same time? □ Yes □ No

   e. helped anyone enter or try to enter the United States illegally? □ Yes □ No

   f. gambled illegally or received income from illegal gambling? □ Yes □ No

   g. failed to support your dependents or to pay alimony? □ Yes □ No

23. Have you **EVER** given false or misleading information to any U.S. government official while applying for any immigration benefit or to prevent deportation, exclusion, or removal? □ Yes □ No

24. Have you **EVER** lied to any U.S. government official to gain entry or admission into the United States? □ Yes □ No

F. Military Service

29. Have you **EVER** served in the U.S. Armed Forces? □ Yes □ No

30. Have you **EVER** left the United States to avoid being drafted into the U.S. Armed Forces? □ Yes □ No

31. Have you **EVER** applied for any kind of exemption from military service in the U.S. Armed Forces? □ Yes □ No

32. Have you **EVER** deserted from the U.S. Armed Forces? □ Yes □ No

H. Oath Requirements *(See Part 14 for the text of the oath)*

Answer questions 34 through 39. If you answer "No" to any of these questions, attach (1) your written explanation why the answer was "No" and (2) any additional information or documentation that helps to explain your answer.

34. Do you support the Constitution and form of government of the United States? □ Yes □ No

35. Do you understand the full Oath of Allegiance to the United States? □ Yes □ No

36. Are you willing to take the full Oath of Allegiance to the United States? □ Yes □ No

37. If the law requires it, are you willing to bear arms on behalf of the United States? □ Yes □ No

38. If the law requires it, are you willing to perform noncombatant services in the U.S. Armed Forces? □ Yes □ No

39. If the law requires it, are you willing to perform work of national importance under civilian direction? □ Yes □ No

Unlike the first set of criteria, the eligibility factors relating to political party involvement, military service, and personal moral character seem less clear. For example, Section D—designed to assess what the INS calls *good moral character*—may seem insufficient for assessing candidates' characters. A candidate might meet the criteria and still be a poor citizen morally. In addition, Question 22 might seem an invasion of individual privacy. Should the government be able to learn, for example, if you are an alcoholic? Keep these larger questions in mind as you complete the next stage of the application process: the United States history and government exam.

The U.S. history and government exam consists of twenty questions chosen randomly from a set list. Because candidates respond to questions orally or in writing, INS officers can assess another eligibility requirement, the candidates' ability to speak, read, write, and understand the English language. Reprinted below are twenty questions selected randomly from one hundred samples provided by the INS to help candidates prepare for the exam.

1. What are the colors of the American flag?
2. How many states are there in the union?
3. Can the Constitution be changed?
4. For how long do we elect the president?
5. How many branches are there in the American government?
6. How many senators are there in Congress?
7. What is the Bill of Rights?
8. Who said, "Give me liberty or give me death?"
9. Which countries were our enemies during World War II?
10. Who elects the President of the United States?
11. Why did the pilgrims come to America?
12. Who wrote "The Star-Spangled Banner"?
13. Who was the main writer of the Declaration of Independence?
14. What special group advises the president?
15. What is the minimum voting age in the United States?
16. When was the Declaration of Independence adopted?
17. What kind of government does the United States have?
18. In what year was the Constitution written?
19. Where is the White House located?
20. What is the introduction to the Constitution called?

After you have answered the questions, check your answers at the end of the chapter. To pass this portion of the test, candidates need to get twelve or more correct. The exam can give each of us insight into our own knowledge of U.S. history and government; when joined with the other naturalization requirements, it can also tell us something about how Congress, which establishes naturalization laws, defines citizenship. If you recall that all of the dictionary definitions of citizenship refer to membership in a community, you can see that the naturalization requirements make assumptions about the nature of our national community.

A community is usually defined as a group of people living in the same place and sharing the same government, but the definitions also carry the sense of having common rights and claims that bond individual members together. Reread the naturalization requirements and U.S. history and government exam; then consider the following questions.

1. These requirements assume a common set of values. How would you describe these values? Should the U.S. government set minimum moral standards for naturalization candidates? What might be the social consequences of not setting such standards?

2. Do these requirements assume a common U.S. history, or a view of what is most important in U.S. history? Could Question 11, asking why the pilgrims came to America, be replaced with "Why did the Spanish conquistadors come to the Americas?" Assuming that INS officers must select those questions they consider most important for U.S. history—because they can only ask twenty questions in all—would the new question suggest a new version of U.S. history?

3. Should INS officers require citizens to demonstrate competence in English? What is the value to a community of having a common language?

4. Do these requirements assume a common political ideology (a set of ideas about how a society should be run)? Should a candidate who believes in a different political ideology, like communism, be allowed to gain U.S. citizenship?

5. Should INS officers require citizens to take an oath of allegiance? Many immigrants who are naturalized continue to maintain familial and political ties with their countries of origin. Do you see any benefits or drawbacks to citizens having dual loyalties?

In answering the above questions, you may discover that not everyone has the same ideas about the nature of our national political community. Disagreements on issues of public ethics, which we will explore in later chapters, are often based on just such competing ideas. For example, the conflict in states like California over bilingual education—teaching students in more than one language—involves larger disagreements over the place of non-English languages in the United States. As you read the next official source of ideas on citizenship, the U.S. Constitution, consider how it does or does not anticipate the issues raised in the above questions.

The U.S. Constitution

The United States existed for just over ten years without a written constitution. The Constitution was written in 1787 because the previous effort at constitutional government, the Articles of Confederation, failed to adequately define the power and responsibility of the federal government and its relationship with the states. Under a federal system, power is shared between a national government and state governments, with each having clearly established powers. Although citizens are subject to both national and state laws, their rights and powers are also recognized in the Constitution. As you will discover in later chapters, American society has often struggled to balance the competing interests of the national government, individual states, and individual citizens.

The U.S. Constitution is made up of a preamble, a statement of the document's purpose; seven articles outlining the makeup, responsibilities, and procedures of the government; and twenty-seven amendments, or changes, that have been made to those articles. Here is an index of the Constitution:

Included below are selected passages from the U.S. Constitution; the complete text can be accessed from this book's accompanying Web site **http://www. ablongman.com/berndt**. After you've read the selections, consider the questions that follow.

The Constitution of the United States

We the People of the United States, in Order to form a more perfect Union, establish Justice, insure domestic Tranquillity, provide for the common defence, promote the general Welfare, and secure the Blessings of Liberty to ourselves and our Posterity, do ordain and establish this Constitution for the United States of America.

Article. I.

Section. 1.

All legislative Powers herein granted shall be vested in a Congress of the United States, which shall consist of a Senate and House of Representatives.

Section. 2.

The House of Representatives shall be composed of Members chosen every second Year by the People of the several States, and the Electors in each State shall have the Qualifications requisite for Electors of the most numerous Branch of the State Legislature.

No Person shall be a Representative who shall not have attained to the age of twenty five Years, and been seven Years a Citizen of the United States, and who shall not, when elected, be an Inhabitant of that State in which he shall be chosen.

Representatives and direct Taxes shall be apportioned among the several States which may be included within this Union, according to their respective Numbers, which shall be determined by adding to the whole Number of free Persons, including those bound to Service for a Term of Years, and excluding Indians not taxed, three fifths of all other Persons. The actual Enumeration shall be made within three Years after the first Meeting of the Congress of the United States, and within every subsequent Term of ten Years, in such Manner as they shall by Law direct. The Number of Representatives shall not exceed one for every thirty Thousand, but each State shall have at Least one Representative; and until such enumeration shall be made, the State of New Hampshire shall be entitled to chuse three, Massachusetts eight, Rhode-Island and Providence Plantations one, Connecticut five, New-York six, New Jersey four, Pennsylvania eight, Delaware one, Maryland six, Virginia ten, North Carolina five, South Carolina five, and Georgia three.

Article. IV.

Section. 1.

Full Faith and Credit shall be given in each State to the public Acts, Records, and judicial Proceedings of every other State. And the Congress may by general Laws prescribe the Manner in which such Acts, Records and Proceedings shall be proved, and the Effect thereof.

Section. 2.

The Citizens of each State shall be entitled to all Privileges and Immunities of Citizens in the several States.

A Person charged in any State with Treason, Felony, or other Crime, who shall flee from Justice, and be found in another State, shall on Demand of the executive Authority of the State from which he fled, be delivered up, to be removed to the State having Jurisdiction of the Crime.

No Person held to Service or Labour in one State, under the Laws thereof, escaping into another, shall, in Consequence of any Law or Regulation therein, be discharged from such Service or Labour, but shall be delivered up on Claim of the Party to whom such Service or Labour may be due.

Section. 3.

New States may be admitted by the Congress into this Union; but no new State shall be formed or erected within the Jurisdiction of any other State; nor any State be formed by the Junction of two or more States, or Parts of

States, without the Consent of the Legislatures of the States concerned as well as of the Congress.

The Congress shall have Power to dispose of and make all needful Rules and Regulations respecting the Territory or other Property belonging to the United States; and nothing in this Constitution shall be so construed as to Prejudice any Claims of the United States, or of any particular State.

Section. 4.

The United States shall guarantee to every State in this Union a Republican Form of Government, and shall protect each of them against Invasion; and on Application of the Legislature, or of the Executive (when the Legislature cannot be convened) against domestic Violence.

Article. V.

The Congress, whenever two thirds of both Houses shall deem it necessary, shall propose Amendments to this Constitution, or, on the Application of the Legislatures of two thirds of the several States, shall call a Convention for proposing Amendments, which, in either Case, shall be valid to all Intents and Purposes, as Part of this Constitution, when ratified by the Legislatures of three fourths of the several States, or by Conventions in three fourths thereof, as the one or the other Mode of Ratification may be proposed by the Congress; Provided that no Amendment which may be made prior to the Year One thousand eight hundred and eight shall in any Manner affect the first and fourth Clauses in the Ninth Section of the first Article; and that no State, without its Consent, shall be deprived of its equal Suffrage in the Senate.

Article. VI.

All Debts contracted and Engagements entered into, before the Adoption of this Constitution, shall be as valid against the United States under this Constitution, as under the Confederation.

This Constitution, and the Laws of the United States which shall be made in Pursuance thereof; and all Treaties made, or which shall be made, under the Authority of the United States, shall be the supreme Law of the Land; and the Judges in every State shall be bound thereby, any Thing in the Constitution or Laws of any state to the Contrary notwithstanding.

The first ten amendments to the Constitution, the Bill of Rights, were proposed to Congress on September 25, 1789, and ratified on December 15, 1791. (Originally there were twelve amendments proposed; the first two, in regard to compensating members of Congress and the number of constituents for each Representative, were not ratified. Numbers 3–12 became the first ten amendments.)

Amendment I.

Congress shall make no law respecting an establishment of religion, or prohibiting the free exercise thereof; or abridging the freedom of speech, or of the press; or the right of the people peaceably to assemble, and to petition the Government for a redress of grievances.

Amendment II.

A well regulated Militia, being necessary to the security of a free State, the right of the people to keep and bear Arms, shall not be infringed.

Amendment III.

No Soldier shall, in time of peace be quartered in any house, without the consent of the Owner, nor in time of war, but in a manner to be prescribed by law.

Amendment IV.

The right of the people to be secure in their persons, houses, papers, and effects, against unreasonable searches and seizures, shall not be violated, and no Warrants shall issue, but upon probable cause, supported by Oath or affirmation, and particularly describing the place to be searched, and the persons or things to be seized.

Amendment V.

No person shall be held to answer for a capital, or otherwise infamous crime, unless on a presentment or indictment of a Grand Jury, except in cases arising in the land or naval forces, or in the Militia, when in actual service in time of War or public danger; nor shall any person be subject for the same offence to be twice put in jeopardy of life or limb; nor shall be compelled in any criminal case to be a witness against himself, nor be deprived of life, liberty, or property, without due process of law; nor shall private property be taken for public use, without just compensation.

Amendment VI.

In all criminal prosecutions, the accused shall enjoy the right to a speedy and public trial, by an impartial jury of the State and district wherein the crime shall have been committed, which district shall have been previously ascertained by law, and to be informed of the nature and cause of the accusation; to be confronted with the witnesses against him; to have compulsory process for obtaining witnesses in his favor, and to have the Assistance of Counsel for his defence.

Amendment VII.

In Suits at common law, where the value in controversy shall exceed twenty dollars, the right of trial by jury shall be preserved, and no fact tried by a jury, shall be otherwise re-examined in any Court of the United States, than according to the rules of the common law.

Amendment VIII.

Excessive bail shall not be required, nor excessive fines imposed, nor cruel and unusual punishments inflicted.

Amendment IX.

The enumeration in the Constitution, of certain rights, shall not be construed to deny or disparage others retained by the people.

Amendment X.

The powers not delegated to the United States by the Constitution, nor prohibited by it to the States, are reserved to the States respectively, or to the people.

Amendment XIII.

Section 1.

Neither slavery nor involuntary servitude, except as a punishment for crime whereof the party shall have been duly convicted, shall exist within the United States, or any place subject to their jurisdiction.

Section 2.

Congress shall have power to enforce this article by appropriate legislation.

[Passed by Congress January 31, 1865. Ratified December 6, 1865.]

Amendment XIV.

Section. 1.

All persons born or naturalized in the United States and subject to the jurisdiction thereof, are citizens of the United States and of the State wherein they reside. No State shall make or enforce any law which shall abridge the privileges or immunities of citizens of the United States; nor shall any State deprive any person of life, liberty, or property, without due process of law; nor deny to any person within its jurisdiction the equal protection of the laws.

Section. 2.

Representatives shall be apportioned among the several States according to their respective numbers, counting the whole number of persons in each State, excluding Indians not taxed. But when the right to vote at any election for the choice of electors for President and Vice President of the United States, Representatives in Congress, the Executive and Judicial officers of a State, or the members of the Legislature thereof, is denied to any of the male inhabitants of such State, being twenty-one years of age, and citizens of the United States, or in any way abridged, except for participation in rebellion, or other crime, the basis of representation therein shall be reduced in the proportion which the number of such male citizens shall bear to the whole number of male citizens twenty-one years of age in such State.

Section. 3.

No person shall be a Senator or Representative in Congress, or elector of President and Vice President, or hold any office, civil or military, under the United States, or under any State, who, having previously taken an oath, as a member of Congress, or as an officer of the United States, or as a member of any State legislature, or as an executive or judicial officer of any State, to support the Constitution of the United States, shall have engaged in insurrection or rebellion against the same, or given aid or comfort to the enemies thereof. But Congress may by a vote of two-thirds of each House, remove such disability.

Section. 4.

The validity of the public debt of the United States, authorized by law, including debts incurred for payment of pensions and bounties for services in suppressing insurrection or rebellion, shall not be questioned. But neither the United States nor any State shall assume or pay any debt or obligation incurred in aid of insurrection or rebellion against the United States, or any claim for the loss or emancipation of any slave; but all such debts, obligations and claims shall be held illegal and void.

Section. 5.

The Congress shall have power to enforce, by appropriate legislation, the provisions of this article.

[Passed by Congress June 13, 1866. Ratified July 9, 1868.]

Amendment XV.

Section. 1.

The right of citizens of the United States to vote shall not be denied or abridged by the United States or by any State on account of race, color, or previous condition of servitude.

Section. 2.

The Congress shall have power to enforce this article by appropriate legislation.

[Passed by Congress February 26, 1869. Ratified February 4, 1870.]

Amendment XIX.

Section. 1.

The right of citizens of the United States to vote shall not be denied or abridged by the United States or any State on account of sex.

Section. 2.

Congress shall have power to enforce this article by appropriate legislation.

[Passed by Congress June 4, 1919. Ratified August 18, 1920.]

Amendment XXVI

[Note: Amendment 14, section 2, of the Constitution was modified by Section 1 of the 26th amendment.]

Section. 1

The rights of citizens of the United States, who are eighteen years of age or older, to vote shall not be denied or abridged by the United States or by any State on account of age.

Section. 2.

The Congress shall have power to enforce this article by appropriate legislation.

[Passed by Congress March 23, 1971. Ratified July 1, 1971.]

Here are some questions that may help you reflect on what you've read. The questions encourage you to consider the Constitution as a *written* document and to recall the other documents on citizenship that you have studied so far.

1. What impressions of American citizenship do you get from the Constitution? How do these impressions compare with those you got from your Mind Map, the dictionary definitions, and INS naturalization requirements?

2. The majority of the Constitution deals with the makeup, procedures, and authority of the federal government. Is this what you expected when you began reading the Constitution? Why do you think the rights of individual citizens were not addressed until the amendments?

3. How would you describe the language of the Constitution? Consider the kinds of words used, the words' specificity or vagueness, the length and complexity of the sentences, and so on. Does this language fit the authors' purpose and audience?

While the U.S. Constitution provides the framework for the citizens' relation to their government, it is only one of many laws defining how citizens ought to live. There are rules for driving automobiles, for operating a business, and for running political campaigns. There are laws protecting individuals within families, protecting groups within society, and for taking affirmative action against past injustices. Take a few minutes to brainstorm other laws that define what individuals can or cannot do as citizens. You might also consult your library, the Internet, or government agencies to examine the laws themselves.

Then, consider the fact that all of these laws are written. What advantages do written laws offer for a community? Are there disadvantages? Finally, create a list of other instances where writing helps to define your communities or the issues your community is facing. How significant is writing to citizens' lives?

CONTINUING THE INQUIRY: VISUAL MESSAGES

In addition to government documents, you might examine the many messages about citizenship that circulate in our communities. Advertisements, public service messages, works of art, flags, memorials, the credos and mission statements of civic organizations—citizens are exposed to thousands of messages every day, each seeking to affect how we view our community membership. These messages may complicate—or oversimplify—the definitions of citizenship that we find in official documents.

Many of these messages are conveyed to us using visual themes. Recognizing that these messages seek to shape our understanding of citizenship, we can respond to them more thoughtfully. In Chapter Four, you will study how writers seek to persuade us using written and visual texts. To get some initial practice analyzing visual messages, examine the following messages. The first is an advertisement for a consumer affairs organization that appeared in the *US News & World Report* on May 27, 2002 (p. 20). The second is a cartoon that appeared in the *New Yorker* on October 15, 2001 (p. 21). Here are some questions to help you begin your analysis.

1. What is the central message of each visual text? What associations does each piece make between being a good citizen and a consumer? Note when the pieces were published; e.g., the cartoon appeared one month after the September 11, 2001 attacks. Why is this significant?

2. Who is the audience for these messages? What do you know about *U.S. News & World Report* and the *New Yorker*? Why would these particular images by printed in those individual magazines?

3. Read the two images side by side, as if they were in a conversation with one another, each conveying a message to you. In what ways could the cartoon by read as a critique of or commentary upon the advertisement?

4. Do you think the pieces are effective? Why or why not?

5. Do you think the pieces are ethical? Why or why not?

"This isn't for me—it's for the economy."

Your analysis of the visual texts may have illustrated just how complex these messages can be. They often use sophisticated strategies to communicate, and they raise important questions about what it means to be a "good" citizen. To continue your inquiry into how visual messages shape our understanding of citizenship, you might bring additional examples into your classroom: more advertisements or public service announcements from magazines and billboards, for instance, or even bumper stickers and t-shirts.

CONTINUING THE INQUIRY: NARRATIVES OF CITIZENSHIP

In the preceding sections, you inquired further into the definition of citizenship. Yet the definitions you examined are collective and general; consequently, they don't illustrate how individual citizens experience their citizenship. For example, the Fourteenth Amendment guarantees citizens "equal protection of the laws," but our history has repeatedly shown that some groups—whether because of race, class, gender, age, sexual orientation, or ability—have not experienced the same privileges and immunities as other citizens. To learn about citizenship as it is lived by individuals, we can turn to their stories.

In this section, you will find the narratives of politicians, fiction writers, and fellow citizens. The insights these writers provide about their civic lives are tied to the narrative as a form of writing. Unlike dictionary definitions and legal documents, narratives can teach us about citizenship in unique ways. Narratives can:

- *Dramatize ideas.* Writers can show a character's actions and the consequences, encouraging readers to discover the writers' ideas or arguments for themselves.
- *Show us other viewpoints.* We can better appreciate how individual citizens think or feel by seeing, for ourselves, how they interpret events around them.
- *Appeal to our emotions.* Using vivid descriptions of people, places, and events, writers can inspire us, encourage us to empathize, even anger us into taking action.
- *Generate interest.* Stories intrigue us as human beings. Writers can catch and hold our attention by appealing to our imaginations.

As you read the following narratives, underline lines or passages that illustrate the qualities outlined above. In addition, explore other ways in which these narratives, as forms of writing, teach you about citizenship. Then, after you've read the narratives, read the suggestions for writing your own narrative of citizenship.

BENJAMIN FRANKLIN From *Autobiography*

> *Benjamin Franklin (1706–1790) is considered one of the founding fathers of the United States. He worked as a printer in Philadelphia, where he became deeply involved in the civic life of that city and the developing nation. Later in life he served in the Continental Congress, on the committee to draft the Declaration of Independence, and as America's ambassador to France. A great believer in living a civic life, he set up one of the earliest libraries, organized a fire company, updated the U.S. Post Office, helped found the American Philosophical Society, and invented the Franklin stove and the lightning rod. The following passages are excerpted from his* Autobiography *(The Library of America, 1993), which he worked on from 1771 until his death in 1790, when it was left unfinished.*

It was about this time that I conceiv'd the bold and arduous Project of arriving at moral Perfection. I wish'd to live without committing any Fault at any time; I would conquer all that either Natural Inclination, Custom, or Company might lead me into. As I knew, or thought I knew, what was right and wrong, I did not see why I might not *always* do the one and avoid the other. But I soon found I had undertaken a Task of more Difficulty than I had imagined: While my Care was employ'd in guarding against one Fault, I was often surpriz'd by another. Habit took the Advantage of Inattention. Inclination was sometimes too strong for Reason. I concluded at length, that the mere speculative Conviction that it was our Interest to be compleatly virtuous, was not sufficient to prevent our Slipping, and that the contrary Habits must be broken and good Ones acquired and established, before we can have any Dependance on a steady uniform Rectitude of Conduct. For this purpose I therefore contriv'd the following Method.—

In the various Enumerations of the moral Virtues I had met with in my Reading, I found the Catalogue more or less numerous, as different Writers included more or fewer Ideas under the same Name. Temperance, for Example, was by some confin'd to Eating & Drinking, while by others it was extended to mean the moderating every other Pleasure, Appetite, Inclination or Passion, bodily or mental, even to our Avarice & Ambition. I propos'd to myself, for the sake of Clearness, to use rather more Names with fewer Ideas annex'd to each, than a few Names with more Ideas; and I included under Thirteen Names of Virtues all that at that time occurr'd to me as necessary or desirable, and annex'd to each a short Precept, which fully express'd the Extent I gave to its Meaning.—

These Names of Virtues with their Precepts were

1. TEMPERANCE.
   Eat not to Dulness.
   Drink not to Elevation.
2. SILENCE.
   Speak not but what may benefit others or your self. Avoid trifling Conversation.

3. ORDER.
Let all your Things have their Places. Let each Part of your Business have its Time.

4. RESOLUTION.
Resolve to perform what you ought. Perform without fail what you resolve.

5. FRUGALITY.
Make no Expence but to do good to others or yourself: i.e. Waste nothing.

6. INDUSTRY.
Lose no Time.—Be always employ'd in something useful.—Cut off all unnecessary Actions.—

7. SINCERITY.
Use no hurtful Deceit.
Think innocently and justly; and, if you speak; speak accordingly.

8. JUSTICE.
Wrong none, by doing Injuries or omitting the Benefits that are your Duty.

9. MODERATION.
Avoid Extreams. Forbear resenting Injuries so much as you think they deserve.

10. CLEANLINESS
Tolerate no Uncleanness in Body, Cloaths or Habitation.—

11. TRANQUILITY
Be not disturbed at Trifles, or at Accidents common or unavoidable.

12. CHASTITY.
Rarely use Venery but for Health or Offspring; Never to Dulness, Weakness, or the Injury of your own or another's Peace or Reputation.—

13. HUMILITY.
Imitate Jesus and Socrates.—

My intention being to acquire the *Habitude* of all these Virtues, I judg'd it would be well not to distract my Attention by attempting the whole at once, but to fix it on one of them at a time, and when I should be Master of that, then to proceed to another, and so on till I should have gone thro' the thirteen. And as the previous Acquisition of some might facilitate the Acquisition of certain others, I arrang'd them with that View as they stand above. *Temperance* first, as it tends to procure that Coolness & Clearness of Head, which is so necessary where constant Vigilance was to be kept up, and Guard maintained, against the unremitting Attraction of ancient Habits, and the Force of perpetual Temptations. This being acquir'd & establish'd, *Silence* would be more easy, and my Desire being to gain Knowledge at the same time that I improv'd in Virtue, and considering that in Conversation it was obtain'd rather by the Use of the Ears than of the Tongue, & therefore wishing to break a Habit I was getting into of Prattling, Punning & Joking, which only made me acceptable to trifling Company, I gave *Silence* the second Place. This, and the next, *Order*, I expected would allow me more Time for attending to my Project and my Studies; RESOLUTION once become habitual, would keep me firm in my Endeavours to obtain all the subsequent Virtues; *Frugality* & *Industry*, by freeing me from my remaining Debt, & producing Affluence & Independance would make

more easy the Practice of *Sincerity* and *Justice,* &c. &c.. Conceiving then that agree-
able to the Advice of Pythagoras in his Golden Verses,* daily Examination would
be necessary, I contriv'd the following Method for conducting that Examination.

5   I made a little Book in which I allotted a Page for each of the Virtues. I rul'd
each Page with red Ink so as to have seven Columns, one for each Day of the
Week, marking each Column with a Letter for the Day. I cross'd these Columns
with thirteen red Lines, marking the Beginning of each Line with the first Letter of one of the Virtues, on which Line & in its proper Column I might mark
by a little black Spot every Fault I found upon Examination, to have been committed respecting that Virtue upon that Day.

Form of the Pages

TEMPERANCE.						
Eat not to Dulness. *Drink not to Elevation.*						
S	M	T	W	T	F	S
							T
••	•		•		•		S
•	•	•		•	•	•	O
		•		•			R
	•			•			F
		•					I
							S
							J
							M
							Cl.
							T
							Ch
							H

Let not the stealing God of Sleep surprize,
Nor creep in Slumbers on thy weary Eyes,
Ere ev'ry Action of the former Day,
Strictly *thou dost, and* righteously *survey.*
With Rev'rence at thy own Tribunal stand,
And answer justly to thy own Demand.
Where have I been? In what have I transgrest?
What Good or Ill has this Day's Life exprest?
Where have I fail'd in what I ought to do?
In what to GOD, *to Man, or to myself I owe?*
Inquire severe whate'er from first to last,
From Morning's Dawn till Ev'nings Gloom has past.
If Evil were thy Deeds, repenting mourn,
And let thy Soul with strong Remorse be torn:
If Good, the Good with Peace of Mind repay,
And to thy secret Self with Pleasure say, }
Rejoice, my Heart, for all went well to Day.

I determined to give a Week's strict Attention to each of the Virtues successively. Thus in the first Week my great Guard was to avoid every the least Offence against Temperance, leaving the other Virtues to their ordinary Chance, only marking every Evening the Faults of the Day. Thus if in the first Week I could keep my first Line marked T clear of Spots, I suppos'd the Habit of that Virtue so much strengthen'd and its opposite weaken'd, that I might venture extending my Attention to include the next, and 'for the following Week keep both Lines clear of Spots. Proceeding thus to the last, I could go thro' a Course compleat in Thirteen Weeks, and four Courses in a Year.—And like him who having a Garden to weed, does not attempt to eradicate all the bad Herbs at once, which would exceed his Reach and his Strength, but works on one of the Beds at a time, & having accomplish'd the first proceeds to a second; so I should have, (I hoped) the encouraging Pleasure of seeing on my Pages the Progress I made in Virtue, by clearing successively my Lines of their Spots, till in the End by a Number of Courses, I should be happy in viewing a clean Book after a thirteen Weeks daily Examination.

This my little Book had for its Motto these Lines from *Addison's Cato;*

Here will I hold: If there is a Pow'r above us,
(And that there is, all Nature cries aloud
Thro' all her Works) he must delight in Virtue,
And that which he delights in must be happy.

Another from *Cicero.*

O Vite Philosophia Dux! O Virtutum indagatrix, expultrixque vitiorum! Unus dies bene,
& ex preceptis tuis actus, peccanti immortalitati est anteponendus.[1]

Another from the Proverbs of Solomon speaking of Wisdom or Virtue;

Length of Days is in her right hand, and in her Left Hand Riches and Honours; Her Ways
are Ways of Pleasantness, and all her Paths are Peace. III, 16, 17.

And conceiving God to be the Fountain of Wisdom, I thought it right and necessary to solicit his Assistance for obtaining it; to this End I form'd the following little Prayer, which was prefix'd to my Tables of Examination; for daily Use.

O Powerful Goodness! bountiful Father! merciful Guide! Increase in me that Wisdom which
discovers my truest Interests; Strengthen my Resolutions to perform what that Wisdom dic-
tates. Accept my kind Offices to thy other Children, as the only Return in my Power for
thy continual Favours to me.

10   I us'd also sometimes a little Prayer which I took from *Thomson's* Poems. viz

Father of Light and Life, that Good supreme,
O teach me what is good, teach me thy self!
Save me from Folly, Vanity and Vice,

---

[1]*A paraphrased translation (with several lines omitted): "O, Philosophy, guide of life! O teacher of virtue and corrector of vice. One day of virtue is better than an eternity of vice."* Tusculan Disputations 5.2.5

From every low Pursuit, and fill my Soul
With Knowledge, conscious Peace, & Virtue pure,
Sacred, substantial, neverfading Bliss!

The Precept of *Order* requiring that *every Part of my Business should have its allotted Time,* one Page in my little Book contain'd the following Scheme of Employment for the Twenty-four Hours of a natural Day,

The Morning Question, What Good shall I do this Day?	5	Rise, wash, and address *Powerful Goodness*; contrive Day's Business and take the Resolution of the Day; prosecute the present Study; and breakfast.—
	6	
	7	
	8	Work.
	9	
	10	
	11	
	12	Read, or overlook my Accounts, and dine.
	1	
	2	
	3	Work.
	4	
	5	
	6	
	7	Put Things in their Places, Supper, Musick, or Diversion, or Conversation, Examination of the Day.
Evening Question, What Good have I done to day?	8	
	9	
	10	
	11	
	12	
	1	Sleep.—
	2	
	3	
	4	

I enter'd upon the Execution of this Plan for Self Examination, and continu'd it with occasional Intermissions for some time. I was surpriz'd to find myself so much fuller of Faults than I had imagined, but I had the Satisfaction of seeing them diminish. To avoid the Trouble of renewing now & then my little Book, which by scraping out the Marks on the Paper of old Faults to make room for new Ones in a new Course, became full of Holes: I transferr'd my Tables & Precepts to the Ivory Leaves of a Memorandum Book, on which the Lines were drawn with red Ink that made a durable Stain, and on those Lines I mark'd my Faults with a black Lead Pencil, which Marks I could easily wipe out with a wet Sponge. After a while I went thro' one Course only in a Year, and afterwards only one in several Years; till at length I omitted them entirely, being employ'd in Voyages & Business abroad with a Multiplicity of Affairs, that interfered. But I always carried my little Book with me. My Scheme of ORDER, gave me the most Trouble, and I found, that tho' it might be practicable where a Man's

Business was such as to leave him the Disposition of his Time, that of a Journey-man Printer for instance, it was not possible to be exactly observ'd by a Master, who must mix with the World, and often receive People of Business at their own Hours.—*Order* too, with regard to Places for Things, Papers, &c. I found extreamly difficult to acquire. I had not been early accustomed to it, & having an exceeding good Memory, I was not so sensible of the Inconvenience attending Want of Method. This Article therefore cost me so much painful Attention & my Faults in it vex'd me so much, and I made so little Progress in Amendment, & had such frequent Relapses, that I was almost ready to give up the Attempt, and content my self with a faulty Character in that respect. Like the Man who in buying an Ax of a Smith my Neighbour, desired to have the whole of its Surface as bright as the Edge; the Smith consented to grind it bright for him if he would turn the Wheel. He turn'd while the Smith press'd the broad Face of the Ax hard & heavily on the Stone, which made the Turning of it very fatiguing. The Man came every now & then from the Wheel to see how the Work went on; and at length would take his Ax as it was without farther Grinding. No, says the Smith, Turn on, turn on; we shall have it bright by and by; as yet' tis only speckled. Yes, says the Man; but—*I think I like a speckled Ax best.*—And I believe this may have been the Case with many who having for want of some such Means as I employ'd found the Difficulty of obtaining good, & break-ing bad Habits, in other Points of Vice & Virtue, have given up the Struggle, & concluded that *a speckled Ax was best.* For something that pretended to be Reason was every now and then suggesting to me, that such extream Nicety as I exacted of my self might be a kind of Foppery in Morals, which if it were known would make me ridiculous; that a perfect Character might be attended with the Inconvenience of being envied and hated; and that a benevolent Man should allow a few Faults in him-self, to keep his Friends in Countenance. In Truth I found myself incorrigible with respect to *Order;* and now I am grown old, and my Memory bad, I feel very sensi-bly the want of it. But on the whole, tho' I never arrived at the Perfection I had been so ambitious of obtaining, but fell far short of it, yet I was by the Endeavour made a better and a happier Man than I otherwise should have been, if I had not attempted it; As those who aim at perfect Writing by imitating the engraved Copies, tho' they never reach the wish'd for Excellence of those Copies, their Hand is mended by the Endeavour, and is tolerable while it continues fair & legible.—

And it may be well my Posterity should be informed, that to this little Arti-fice, with the Blessing of God, their Ancestor ow'd the constant Felicity of his Life down to his 79th Year in which this is written. What Reverses may attend the Remainder is in the Hand of Providence: But if they arrive the Reflection on past Happiness enjoy'd ought to help his Bearing them with more Resignation. To *Temperance* he ascribes his long-continu'd Health, & what is still left to him of a good Constitution. To *Industry* and *Frugality* the early Easiness of his Circum-stances, & Acquisition of his Fortune, with all that Knowledge which enabled him to be an useful Citizen, and obtain'd for him some Degree of Reputation among the Learned. To *Sincerity* & *Justice* the Confidence of his Country, and the honourable Employs it conferr'd upon him. And to the joint Influence of the whole Mass of the Virtues, even in their imperfect State he was able to acquire them, all that Evenness of Temper, & that Chearfulness in Conversation which makes his Company still sought for, & agreable even to his younger Acquaintance. I hope therefore that some of my Descendants may follow the Example & reap the Benefit.—

  It will be remark'd that, tho' my Scheme was not wholly without Religion there was in it no Mark of any of the distinguishing Tenets of any particular Sect.—I had purposely avoided them; for being fully persuaded of the Utility and Excellency of my Method, and that it might be serviceable to People in all Religions, and intending some time or other to publish it, I would not have any thing in it that should prejudice any one of any Sect against it.—I purposed writing a little Comment on each Virtue, in which I would have shown the Advantages of possessing it, & the Mischiefs attending its opposite Vice; and I should have called my Book the ART *of Virtue,* because it would have shown the *Means & Manner* of obtaining Virtue; which would have distinguish'd it from the mere Exhortation to be good, that does not instruct & indicate the Means; but is like the Apostle's Man of verbal Charity, who only, without showing to the Naked & the Hungry *how* or where they might get Cloaths or Victuals, exhorted them to be fed & clothed. *James* II, 15, 16.—

15 But it so happened that my Intention of writing & publishing this Comment was never fulfilled. I did indeed, from time to time put down short Hints of the Sentiments, Reasonings, &c. to be made use of in it; some of which I have still by me: But the necessary close Attention to private Business in the earlier part of Life, and public Business since, have occasioned my postponing it. For it being connected in my Mind with a *great and extensive Project* that required the whole Man to execute, and which an unforeseen Succession of Employs prevented my attending to, it has hitherto remain'd unfinish'd.—

  In this Piece it was my Design to explain and enforce this Doctrine, that vicious Actions are not hurtful because they are forbidden, but forbidden because they are hurtful, the Nature of Man alone consider'd: That it was therefore every ones Interest to be virtuous, who wish'd to be happy even in this World. And I should from this Circumstance, there being always in the World a Number of rich Merchants, Nobility, States and Princes, who have need of honest Instruments for the Management of their Affairs, and such being so rare, have endeavoured to convince young Persons, that no Qualities were so likely to make a poor Man's Fortune as those of Probity & Integrity.

  My List of Virtues contain'd at first but twelve: But a Quaker Friend having kindly inform'd me that I was generally thought proud; that my Pride show'd itself frequently in Conversation; that I was not content with being in the right when discussing any Point, but was overbearing & rather insolent; of which he convinc'd me by mentioning several Instances;—I determined endeavouring to cure myself if I could of this Vice or Folly among the rest, and I added *Humility* to my List, giving an extensive Meaning to the Word.—I cannot boast of much Success in acquiring the *Reality* of this Virtue; but I had a good deal with regard to the *Appearance* of it.—I made it a Rule to forbear all direct Contradiction to the Sentiments of others, and all positive Assertion of my own. I even forbid myself agreable to the old Laws of our Junto,[2] the Use of every Word or Expression in the Language that imported a fix'd Opinion; such as *certainly, undoubtedly,* &c. and I adopted instead of them, *I conceive, I apprehend,* or *I imagine* a thing to be so or so, or it so appears to me at present.—When another asserted something that I thought an Error, I deny'd my self the Pleasure of contradicting him abruptly, and of showing immediately some Absurdity in his Proposition; and in answering I began by observing that in certain Cases or Circumstances his Opinion would be right, but that in the present case there *appear'd* or *seem'd* to me some Difference, &c. I soon found the Advantage of this Change in my Manners. The Conversations I engag'd in went on more pleasantly. The modest way in which I propos'd my Opinions, procur'd them a readier Reception and less Contradiction; I had less Mortification when I was found to be in the wrong, and I more easily prevail'd with others to give up their Mistakes & join with me when I happen'd to be in the right. And this Mode, which I at first put on, with some violence to natural Inclination, became at length so easy & so habitual to me, that perhaps for these Fifty Years past no one has ever heard a dogmatical Expression escape me. And to this Habit (after my Character of Integrity) I think it principally owing, that I had early so much Weight with my Fellow Citizens, when I proposed new Institutions, or Alterations in the old; and so much Influence in public Councils when I became a Member. For I was but a bad Speaker, never eloquent, subject to much Hesitation in my choice of Words, hardly correct in Language, and yet I generally carried my Points.—

In reality there is perhaps no one of our natural Passions so hard to subdue as *Pride.* Disguise it, struggle with it, beat it down, stifle it, mortify it as much as one pleases, it is still alive, and will every now and then peep out and show itself. You will see it perhaps often in this History. For even if I could conceive that I had compleatly overcome it, I should probably be proud of my Humility.—

Thus far written at Passy 1784

QUESTIONS FOR FURTHER INQUIRY

1. Americans often identify Franklin as one who achieved the American Dream: he became wealthy, and powerful in local and state governments. How does his search for moral perfection fit with achieving the American Dream?

---

[2]*Junto was an organization that Franklin, a printer, formed in 1727 with a group of other tradesman in Philadelphia. In his biography* Franklin of Philadelphia *(Harvard UP, 1986), Esmond Wright describes it as "part mutual aid society, part social fraternity, part academy. Its organization was modeled on Mather's neighborhood Benefit Societies, but it was touched also by Masonic principles: it was intended to be secret and exclusive. The questions the members set themselves included 'queries on any point of Morals, Politics or Natural Philosophy,' but the real motivation was self-improvement, the 'wish to do good' that would also bring them advantages, or even profit" (37–38).*

2. Working from the details Franklin gives us about the way he lives his life, what does he value as both a private person and as a public citizen? How much do you think he distinguishes between the two? What might be his definition of citizenship?

3. Franklin's ideas about living a successful, moral life still influence the plans of many self-improvement advocates. Create your own written plan for successful living, live by it for at least a week, and then compare your plan and your experiences with Franklin's. Did you become a better person when following your plan? Will you continue to follow it in the future?

Writing Style

CRAFTING A PERSONA

In Chapter Four, you will learn how to craft your *persona*, the image your writing projects to others of your ability as a thinker, writer, and researcher; your attitude towards your subject and readers; and your personality. Franklin presents a very distinctive persona in his *Autobiography*.

At one point in his narrative, he says that while he may not have acquired genuine humility, he had succeeded "a good deal with regard to the *Appearance* of it." To guard against complaints that the *Autobiography* is a boastful record of his many accomplishments, Franklin works hard to create the appearance of humility in his writing. He records his mistakes and failures as well as his successes and he often pokes fun at himself. For example, in the beginning of the *Autobiography*, he lists his reasons for writing about his life. The last of his reasons, he states, is to "gratify my own Vanity. Indeed I scarce ever heard or saw the introductory Words, *Without Vanity I may say*, etc. but some vain thing immediately followed. Most People dislike Vanity in others whatever Share they have of it themselves, but I give it fair Quarter wherever I meet with it. . . ." In what other ways does Franklin seek to create a more humble persona?

Review your own writing. What kind of persona do you think it shows to readers? What features of your writing would lead them to this conclusion? How might you change your persona to meet new writing situations, e.g., a cover letter for a job application, a letter to a friend, or a research paper?

RALPH ELLISON Prologue from *Invisible Man*

Ralph Ellison was born in Oklahoma in 1914. In 1933, he won a state scholarship to study music at the Tuskegee Institute; while there he met Richard Wright, who encouraged him to become a writer. Ellison then moved to New York, where he eventually worked for the WPA's federal Writer's Project. His novel Invisible Man *(1952) won the 1953 National Book Award. Considered a classic of American literature,* Invisible Man *follows an African-American antihero's efforts to*

define himself and his place in American society. In a 1955 interview for The
Paris Review, *Ralph Ellison offered this explanation for why he writes:*

> I feel that with my decision to devote myself to the novel I took on one
> of the responsibilities inherited by those who practice the craft in the
> United States: that of describing for all that fragment of the huge diverse
> American experience which I know best, and which offers me the possi-
> bility of contributing not only to the growth of the lIterature but to the
> shaping of the culture as I should like it to be.

*Literary critics in the 1960s often criticized Ellison for not trying more
actively to shape American culture. Specifically, they criticized his unwill-
ingness to use his fiction to protest against racism. In "The World and the
Jug" (in two parts, 1963 and 1964), he responded that "protest is an element
of all art, though it does not necessarily take the form of speaking for a political or social program."*

Prologue

I am an invisible man. No, I am not a spook like those who haunted Edgar Allan
Poe; nor am I one of your Hollywood-movie ectoplasms. I am a man of substance,
of flesh and bone, fiber and liquids—and I might even be said to possess a mind.
I am invisible, understand, simply because people refuse to see me. Like the
bodiless heads you see sometimes in circus sideshows, it is as though I have been
surrounded by mirrors of hard, distorting glass. When they approach me they
see only my surroundings, themselves, or figments of their imagination—indeed,
everything and anything except me.

Nor is my invisibility exactly a matter of a biochemical accident to my epi-
dermis. That invisibility to which I refer occurs because of a peculiar disposition of the eyes of those with whom I come in contact. A matter of the
construction of their *inner* eyes, those eyes with which they look through their
physical eyes upon reality. I am not complaining, nor am I protesting either. It
is sometimes advantageous to be unseen, although it is most often rather wearing on the nerves. Then too, you're constantly being bumped against by those
of poor vision. Or again, you often doubt if you really exist. You wonder whether
you aren't simply a phantom in other people's minds. Say, a figure in a nightmare which the sleeper tries with all his strength to destroy. It's when you feel
like this that, out of resentment, you begin to bump people back. And, let me
confess, you feel that way most of the time. You ache with the need to convince
yourself that you do exist in the real world, that you're a part of all the sound
and anguish, and you strike out with your fists, you curse and you swear to make
them recognize you. And, alas, it's seldom successful.

One night I accidentally bumped into a man, and perhaps because of the
near darkness he saw me and called me an insulting name. I sprang at him, seized
his coat lapels and demanded that he apologize. He was a tall blond man, and

as my face came close to his he looked insolently out of his blue eyes and cursed me, his breath hot in my face as he struggled. I pulled his chin down sharp upon the crown of my head, butting him as I had seen the West Indians do, and I felt his flesh tear and the blood gush out, and I yelled, "Apologize! Apologize!" But he continued to curse and struggle, and I butted him again and again until he went down heavily, on his knees, profusely bleeding. I kicked him repeatedly, in a frenzy because he still uttered insults though his lips were frothy with blood. Oh yes, I kicked him! And in my outrage I got out my knife and prepared to slit his throat, right there beneath the lamplight in the deserted street, holding him in the collar with one hand, and opening the knife with my teeth—when it occurred to me that the man had not *seen* me, actually; that he, as far as he knew, was in the midst of a walking nightmare! And I stopped the blade, slicing the air as I pushed him away, letting him fall back to the street. I stared at him hard as the lights of a car stabbed through the darkness. He lay there, moaning on the asphalt; a man almost killed by a phantom. It unnerved me. I was both disgusted and ashamed. I was like a drunken man myself, wavering about on weakened legs. Then I was amused: Something in this man's thick head had sprung out and beaten him within an inch of his life. I began to laugh at this crazy discovery. Would he have awakened at the point of death? Would Death himself have freed him for wakeful living? But I didn't linger. I ran away into the dark, laughing so hard I feared I might rupture myself. The next day I saw his picture in the *Daily News,* beneath a caption stating that he had been "mugged." Poor fool, poor blind fool, I thought with sincere compassion, mugged by an invisible man!

Most of the time (although I do not choose as I once did to deny the violence of my days by ignoring it) I am not so overtly violent. I remember that I am invisible and walk softly so as not to awaken the sleeping ones. Sometimes it is best not to awaken them; there are few things in the world as dangerous as sleepwalkers. I learned in time though that it is possible to carry on a fight against them without their realizing it. For instance, I have been carrying on a fight with Monopolated Light & Power for some time now. I use their service and pay them nothing at all, and they don't know it. Oh, they suspect that power is being drained off, but they don't know where. All they know is that according to the master meter back there in their power station a hell of a lot of free current is disappearing somewhere into the jungle of Harlem. The joke, of course, is that I don't live in Harlem but in a border area. Several years ago (before I discovered the advantages of being invisible) I went through the routine process of buying service and paying their outrageous rates. But no more. I gave up all that, along with my apartment, and my old way of life: That way based upon the fallacious assumption that I, like other men, was visible. Now, aware of my invisibility, I live rent-free in a building rented strictly to whites, in a section of the basement that was shut off and forgotten during the nineteenth century, which I discovered when I was trying to escape in the night from Ras the Destroyer. But that's getting too far ahead of the story, almost to the end, although the end is in the beginning and lies far ahead.

5   The point now is that I found a home—or a hole in the ground, as you will. Now don't jump to the conclusion that because I call my home a "hole" it is damp and cold like a grave; there are cold holes and warm holes. Mine is a warm hole. And remember, a bear retires to his hole for the winter and lives until spring; then he comes strolling out like the Easter chick breaking from its shell. I say all this to assure you that it is incorrect to assume that, because I'm invisible and live in a hole, I am dead. I am neither dead nor in a state of suspended animation. Call me Jack-the-Bear, for I am in a state of hibernation.

My hole is warm and full of light. Yes, *full* of light. I doubt if there is a brighter spot in all New York than this hole of mine, and I do not exclude Broadway. Or the Empire State Building on a photographer's dream night. But that is taking advantage of you. Those two spots are among the darkest of our whole civilization—pardon me, our whole *culture* (an important distinction, I've heard)—which might sound like a hoax, or a contradiction, but that (by contradiction, I mean) is how the world moves: Not like an arrow, but a boomerang. (Beware of those who speak of the *spiral* of history; they are preparing a boomerang. Keep a steel helmet handy.) I know; I have been boomeranged across my head so much that I now can see the darkness of lightness. And I love light. Perhaps you'll think it strange that an invisible man should need light, desire light, love light. But maybe it is exactly because I *am* invisible. Light confirms my reality, gives birth to my form. A beautiful girl once told me of a recurring nightmare in which she lay in the center of a large dark room and felt her face expand until it filled the whole room, becoming a formless mass while her eyes ran in bilious jelly up the chimney. And so it is with me. Without light I am not only invisible, but formless as well; and to be unaware of one's form is to live a death. I myself, after existing some twenty years, did not become alive until I discovered my invisibility.

That is why I fight my battle with Monopolated Light & Power. The deeper reason, I mean: It allows me to feel my vital aliveness. I also fight them for taking so much of my money before I learned to protect myself. In my hole in the basement there are exactly 1,369 lights. I've wired the entire ceiling, every inch of it. And not with fluorescent bulbs, but with the older, more-expensive-to-operate kind, the filament type. An act of sabotage, you know. I've already begun to wire the wall. A junk man I know, a man of vision, has supplied me with wire and sockets. Nothing, storm or flood, must get in the way of our need for light and ever more and brighter light. The truth is the light and light is the truth. When I finish all four walls, then I'll start on the floor. Just how that will go, I don't know. Yet when you have lived invisible as long as I have you develop a certain ingenuity. I'll solve the problem. And maybe I'll invent a gadget to place my coffee pot on the fire while I lie in bed, and even invent a gadget to warm my bed—like the fellow I saw in one of the picture magazines who made himself a gadget to warm his shoes! Though invisible, I am in the great American tradition of tinkers. That makes me kin to Ford, Edison and Franklin. Call me, since I have a theory and a concept, a "thinker-tinker." Yes, I'll warm my shoes; they need it, they're usually full of holes. I'll do that and more. . . .

Please, a definition: A hibernation is a covert preparation for a more overt action. . . .

Meanwhile I enjoy my life with the compliments of Monopolated Light & Power. Since you never recognize me even when in closest contact with me, and since, no doubt, you'll hardly believe that I exist, it won't matter if you know that I tapped a power line leading into the building and ran it into my hole in the ground. Before that I lived in the darkness into which I was chased, but now I see. I've illuminated the blackness of my invisibility—and vice versa. And so I play the invisible music of my isolation. The last statement doesn't seem just right, does it? But it is; you hear this music simply because music is heard and seldom seen, except by musicians. Could this compulsion to put invisibility down in black and white be thus an urge to make music of invisibility? But I am an orator, a rabble rouser—Am? I *was,* and perhaps shall be again. Who knows? All sickness is not unto death, neither is invisibility.

10   I can hear you say, "What a horrible, irresponsible bastard!" And you're right. I leap to agree with you. I am one of the most irresponsible beings that ever lived. Irresponsibility is part of my invisibility; any way you face it, it is a denial. But to whom can I be responsible, and why should I be, when you refuse to see me? And wait until I reveal how truly irresponsible I am. Responsibility rests upon recognition, and recognition is a form of agreement. Take the man whom I almost killed: Who was responsible for that near murder—I? I don't think so, and I refuse it. I won't buy it. You can't give it to me. *He* bumped *me, he* insulted *me.* Shouldn't he, for his own personal safety, have recognized my hysteria, my "danger potential"? He, let us say, was lost in a dream world. But didn't *he* control that dream world—which, alas, is only too real!—and didn't *he* rule me out of it? And if he had yelled for a policeman, wouldn't *I* have been taken for the offending one? Yes, yes, yes! Let me agree with you, I was the irresponsible one; for I should have used my knife to protect the higher interests of society. Some day that kind of foolishness will cause us tragic trouble. All dreamers and sleepwalkers must pay the price, and even the invisible victim is responsible for the fate of all. But I shirked that responsibility; I became too snarled in the incompatible notions that buzzed within my brain. I was a coward . . .

But what did *I* do to be so blue? Bear with me.

QUESTIONS FOR FURTHER INQUIRY

1. Ellison's narrator admits, "I am one of the most irresponsible beings that ever lived. Irresponsibility is part of my invisibility; any way you face it, it is a denial. But to whom can I be responsible, and why should I be, when you refuse to see me?" What are the consequences to a democratic society if certain groups or individuals are marginalized?

2. Compare this narrative to the Black Panthers' Ten-Point Plan in Chapter Four. How do their responses to injustice differ? Is the Black Panthers' response better or worse than the invisible man's?

3. In a 1955 interview for *The Paris Review*, Ralph Ellison argued that "One function of serious literature is to deal with the moral core of a given society. Well, in the United States the Negro and his status have always stood for that moral concern. He symbolizes among other things the human and social possibility of equality." What is the prospect for equality represented in this narrative? What are the prospects now, over four decades later?

Writing Style

WRITING AS A PERFORMANCE ART

Ellison's wonderful "music of invisibility" should remind us that writing can be a performance. When readers begin a written work, they are agreeing to be led by the writer. This gesture puts responsibility on the writer to perform well, giving readers what they want and need. Everything we select from our ideas to our specific words shapes the readers' experience.

In practical terms, this might mean withholding information to create some suspense. It might mean including the actual speech of interesting characters. It might even mean mixing realistic and fantastic situations, like a basement room with 1,369 lights in it. The point is that writers' imaginations can be infinitely creative if they can learn to expand their ideas about what makes a proper essay.

To help themselves get into a role, actors often exaggerate some feature of their characters. For example, if an actor needs to play a wily, slithering character, she might practice by pretending to be a snake. Then, she can tone it down to where she exhibits the qualities she wants without the exaggeration. This exercise is good for writing as well. Identify some quality you want to emphasize in your own writing. Perhaps you want to project an angry tone or make your readers laugh. Exaggerate that quality; have fun with it. Then, if you need to, you can tone down your performance to make it fit your subject, purpose, and audience. Hopefully, enough of that quality will remain to enliven your writing style.

ANZIA YEZIERSKA "America and I"

Anzia Yezierska (c. 1885–1970) was born near Warsaw and immigrated with her family to New York City. She wrote novels about Jewish-American life, including Salome of the Tenements *(1923) and* Bread Givers *(1925), and worked for the Works Progress Administration's Writers Project in Manhattan. "America and I" was originally published in 1922. Immigration laws changed in 1924 and restricted access to those not from northern or western Europe. How would that fact have changed Yezierska's narrative?*

As one of the dumb, voiceless ones I speak. One of the millions of immigrants beating, beating out their hearts at your gates for a breath of understanding.

Ach! America! From the other end of the earth from where I came, America was a land of living hope, woven of dreams, aflame with longing and desire.

Choked for ages in the airless oppression of Russia, the Promised Land rose up—wings for my stifled spirit—sunlight burning through my darkness—freedom singing to me in my prison—deathless songs tuning prison-bars into strings of a beautiful violin.

I arrived in America. My young, strong body, my heart and soul pregnant with the unlived lives of generations clamoring for expression.

5   What my mother and father and their mother and father never had a chance to give out in Russia, I would give out in America. The hidden sap of centuries would find release; colors that never saw light—songs that died unvoiced—romance that never had a chance to blossom in the black life of the Old World.

In the golden land of flowing opportunity I was to find my work that was denied me in the sterile village of my forefathers. Here I was to be free from the dead drudgery for bread that held me down in Russia. For the first time in America I'd cease to be a slave of the belly. I'd be a creator, a giver, a human being! My work would be the living joy of fullest self-expression.

But from my high visions, my golden hopes, I had to put my feet down on earth. I had to have food and shelter. I had to have the money to pay for it.

I was in America, among the Americans, but not of them. No speech, no common language, no way to win a smile of understanding from them, only my young, strong body and my untried faith. Only my eager, empty hands, and my full heart shining from my eyes!

God from the world! Here I was with so much richness in me, but my mind was not wanted without the language. And my body, unskilled, untrained, was not even wanted in the factory. Only one of two chances was left open to me: the kitchen, or minding babies.

10   My first job was as a servant in an Americanized family. Once, long ago, they came from the same village from where I came. But they were so well-dressed, so well-fed, so successful in America, that they were ashamed to remember their mother tongue.

"What were to be my wages?" I ventured timidly, as I looked up to the well-fed, well-dressed "American" man and woman.

They looked at me with a sudden coldness. What have I said to draw away from me their warmth? Was it so low from me to talk of wages? I shrank back into myself like a low-down bargainer. Maybe they're so high up in well-being they can't any more understand my low thoughts for money.

From his rich height the man preached down to me that I must not be so grabbing for wages. Only just landed from the ship and already thinking about money when I should be thankful to associate with "Americans."

The woman, out of her smooth, smiling fatness assured me that this was my chance for a summer vacation in the country with her two lovely children. My great chance to learn to be a civilized being, to become an American by living with them.

15   So, made to feel that I was in the hands of American friends, invited to share with them their home, their plenty, their happiness, I pushed out from my head

the worry for wages. Here was my first chance to begin my life in the sunshine, after my long darkness. My laugh was all over my face as I said to them: "I'll trust myself to you. What I'm worth you'll give me." And I entered their house like a child by the hand.

The best of me I gave them. Their house cares were my house cares. I got up early. I worked till late. All that my soul hungered to give I put into the passion with which I scrubbed floors, scoured pots, and washed clothes. I was so grateful to mingle with the American people, to hear the music of the American language, that I never knew tiredness.

There was such a freshness in my brains and such a willingness in my heart that I could go on and on—not only with the work of the house, but work with my head—learning new words from the children, the grocer, the butcher, the iceman. I was not even afraid to ask for words from the policeman on the street. And every new word made me see new American things with American eyes. I felt like a Columbus, finding new worlds through every new word.

But words alone were only for the inside of me. The outside of me still branded me for a steerage immigrant. I had to have clothes to forget myself that I'm a stranger yet. And so I had to have money to buy these clothes.

The month was up. I was so happy! Now I'd have money. *My own, earned money.* Money to buy a new shirt on my back—shoes on my feet. Maybe yet an American dress and hat!

20   Ach! How high rose my dreams! How plainly I saw all that I would do with my visionary wages shining like a light over my head!

In my imagination I already walked in my new American clothes. How beautiful I looked as I saw myself like a picture before my eyes! I saw how I would throw away my immigrant rags tied up in my immigrant shawl. With money to buy—free money in my hands—I'd show them that I could look like an American in a day.

Like a prisoner in his last night in prison, counting the seconds that will free him from his chains, I trembled breathlessly for the minute I'd get the wages in my hand.

Before dawn I rose.

I shined up the house like a jewel-box.

25   I prepared breakfast and waited with my heart in my mouth for my lady and gentleman to rise. At last I heard them stirring. My eyes were jumping out of my head to them when I saw them coming in and seating themselves by the table.

Like a hungry cat rubbing up to its boss for meat, so I edged and simpered around him as I passed them the food. Without my will, like a beggar, my hand reached out to them.

The breakfast was over. And no word yet from my wages.

"Gottuniu!"[1] I thought to myself. "Maybe they're so busy with their own things they forgot it's the day for my wages. Could they who have everything know what

---

[1] *Oh, my God!*

I was to do with my first American dollars? How could they, soaking in plenty, how could they feel the longing and the fierce hunger in me, pressing up through each visionary dollar? How could they know the gnawing ache of my avid fingers for the feel of my own, earned dollars? *My* dollars that I could spend like a free person. *My* dollars that would make me feel with everybody alike!"

30   Breakfast was long past.

Lunch came. Lunch past.

Oi-i weh! Not a word yet about my money.

It was near dinner. And not a word yet about my wages.

I began to set the table. But my head—it swam away from me. I broke a glass. The silver dropped from my nervous fingers. I couldn't stand it any longer. I dropped everything and rushed over to my American lady and gentleman.

35   "*Oi weh!* The money—my money—my wages!" I cried breathlessly.

Four cold eyes turned on me.

"Wages? Money?" The four eyes turned into hard stone as they looked me up and down. "Haven't you a comfortable bed to sleep, and three good meals a day? You're only a month here. Just came to America. And you already think about money. Wait till you're worth any money. What use are you without knowing English? You should be glad we keep you here. It's like a vacation for you. Other girls pay money yet to be in the country."

It went black for my eyes. I was so choked no words came to my lips. Even the tears went dry in my throat.

40   I left. Not a dollar for all my work.

For a long, long time my heart ached and ached like a sore wound. If murderers could have robbed me and killed me it wouldn't have hurt me so much. I couldn't think through my pain. The minute I'd see before me how they looked at me, the words they said to me—then everything began to bleed in me. And I was helpless.

For a long, long time the thought of ever working in an "American" family made me tremble with fear, like the fear of wild wolves. No—never again would I trust myself to an "American" family, no matter how fine their language and how sweet their smile.

It was blotted out in me all trust in friendship from "Americans." But the life in me still burned to live. The hope in me still craved to hope. In darkness, in dirt, in hunger and want, but only to live on!

There had been no end to my day—working for the "American" family.

45   Now rejecting false friendships from higher-ups in America, I turned back to the Ghetto. I worked on a hard bench with my own kind on either side of me. I knew before I began what my wages were to be. I knew what my hours were to be. And I knew the feeling of the end of the day.

From the outside my second job seemed worse than the first. It was in a sweat-shop of a Delancey Street basement, kept up by an old, wrinkled woman that looked like a black witch of greed. My work was sewing on buttons. While the morning was still dark I walked into a dark basement. And darkness met me when I turned out of the basement.

Day after day, week after week, all the contact I got with America was handling dead buttons. The money I earned was hardly enough to pay for bread and rent. I didn't have a room to myself. I didn't even have a bed. I slept on a mattress on the floor in a rat-hole of a room occupied by a dozen other immigrants. I was always hungry—oh, so hungry! The scant meals I could afford only sharpened my appetite for real food. But I felt myself better off than working in the "American" family, where I had three good meals a day and a bed to myself. With all the hunger and darkness of the sweatshop, I had at least the evening to myself. And all night was mine. When all were asleep, I used to creep up on the roof of the tenement and talk out my heart in silence to the stars in the sky.

"Who am I? What am I? What do I want with my life? Where is America? Is there an America? What is this wilderness in which I'm lost?"

I'd hurl my questions and then think and think. And I could not tear it out of me, the feeling that America must be somewhere, somehow—only I couldn't find it—*my America,* where I would work for love and not for a living. I was like a thing following blindly after something far off in the dark!

"Oi weh!" I'd stretch out my hand up in the air. "My head is so lost in America! What's the use of all my working if I'm not in it? Dead buttons is not me."

50   Then the busy season started in the shop. The mounds of buttons grew and grew. The long day stretched out longer. I had to begin with the buttons earlier and stay with them till later in the night. The old witch turned into a huge greedy maw for wanting more and more buttons.

For a glass of tea, for a slice of herring over black bread, she would buy us up to stay another and another hour, till there seemed no end to her demands.

One day, the light of self-assertion broke into my cellar darkness.

"I don't want the tea. I don't want your herring," I said with terrible boldness. "I only want to go home. I only want the evening to myself!"

"You fresh mouth, you!" cried the old witch. "You learned already too much in America. I want no clock-watchers in my shop. Out you go!"

55   I was driven out to cold and hunger. I could no longer pay for my mattress on the floor. I no longer could buy the bite in the mouth. I walked the streets. I knew what it is to be alone in a strange city, among strangers.

But I laughed through my tears. So I learned too much already in America because I wanted the whole evening to myself? Well America has yet to teach me still more: how to get not only the whole evening to myself, but a whole day a week like the American workers.

That sweat-shop was a bitter memory but a good school. It fitted me for a regular factory. I could walk in boldly and say I could work at something, even if it is was only sewing on buttons.

Gradually, I became a trained worker. I worked in a light, airy factory, only eight hours a day. My boss was no longer a sweater and a blood-squeezer. The first freshness of the morning was mine. And the whole evening was mine. All day Sunday was mine.

Now I had better food to eat. I slept on a better bed. Now, I even looked dressed up like the American-born. But inside of me I knew that I was not yet an American. I choked with longing when I met an American-born, and I could say nothing.

60   Something cried dumb in me. I couldn't help it. I didn't know what it was I wanted. I only knew I wanted. I wanted. Like the hunger in the heart that never gets food.

An English class for foreigners started in our factory. The teacher had such a good, friendly face, her eyes looked so understanding, as if she could see right into my heart. So I went to her one day for an advice:

"I don't know what is with me the matter," I began. "I have no rest in me. I never yet done what I want."

"What is it you want to do, child?" she asked me.

"I want to do something with my head, my feelings. All day long, only with my hands I work."

65   "First you must learn English." She patted me as if I was not yet grown up. "Put your mind on that, and then we'll see."

So for a time I learned the language. I could almost begin to think with English words in my head. But in my heart the emptiness still hurt. I burned to give, to give something, to do something, to be something. The dead work with my hands was killing me. My work left only hard stones on my heart.

Again I went to our factory teacher and cried out to her: "I know already to read and write the English language, but I can't put it into words what I want. What is it in me so different that can't come out?"

She smiled at me down from her calmness as if I were a little bit out of my head. "What *do you want* to do?"

"I feel. I see. I hear. And I want to think it out. But I'm like dumb in me. I only feel I'm different—different from everybody."

70   She looked at me close and said nothing for a minute. "You ought to join one of the social clubs of the Women's Association," she advised.

"What's the Women's Association?" I implored greedily.

"A group of American women who are trying to help the working-girl find herself. They have a special department for immigrant girls like you."

I joined the Women's Association. On my first evening there they announced a lecture: "The Happy Worker and His Work," by the Welfare director of the United Mills Corporation.

"Is there such a thing as a happy worker at his work?" I wondered. "Happiness is only by working at what you love. And what poor girl can ever find it to work at what she loves? My old dreams about my America rushed through my mind. Once I thought that in America everybody works for love. Nobody has to worry for a living. Maybe this welfare man came to show me the *real* America that till now I sought in vain.

75   With a lot of polite words the head lady of the Women's Association introduced a higher-up that looked like the king of kings of business. Never before in my

life did I ever see a man with such a sureness in his step, such power in his face, such friendly positiveness in his eye as when he smiled upon us.

"Efficiency is the new religion of business," he began. "In big business houses, even in up-to-date factories, they no longer take the first comer and give him any job that happens to stand empty. Efficiency begins at the employment office. Experts are hired for the one purpose, to find out how best to fit the worker to his work. It's economy for the boss to make the worker happy." And then he talked a lot more on efficiency in educated language that was over my head.

I didn't know exactly what it meant—efficiency—but if it was to make the worker happy at his work, then that's what I had been looking for since I came to America. I only felt from watching him that he was happy by his job. And as I looked on this clean, well-dressed, successful one, who wasn't ashamed to say he rose from an office-boy, it made me feel that I, too, could lift myself up for a person.

He finished his lecture, telling us about the Vocational-Guidance Center that the Women's Association started.

The very next evening I was at the Vocational-Guidance Center. There I found a young, college-looking woman. Smartness and health shining from her eyes! She, too, looked as if she knew her way in America. I could tell at the first glance: here is a person that is happy by what she does.

80   "I feel you'll understand me," I said right away.

She leaned over with pleasure in her face: "I hope I can."

"I want to work by what's in me. Only, I don't know what's in me. I only feel I'm different."

She gave me a quick, puzzled look from the corner of her eyes. "What are you doing now?"

"I'm the quickest shirtwaist hand on the floor. But my heart wastes away by such work. I think and think, and my thoughts can't come out."

85   "Why don't you think out your thoughts in shirtwaists? You could learn to be a designer. Earn more money."

"I don't want to look on waists. If my hands are sick from waists, how could my head learn to put beauty into them?"

"But you must earn your living at what you know, and rise slowly from job to job."

I looked at her office sign: "Vocational Guidance." "What's your vocational guidance?" I asked. "How to rise from job to job—how to earn more money?"

The smile went out from her eyes. But she tried to be kind yet. "What *do* you want?" she asked, with a sigh of last patience.

90   "I want America to want me."

She fell back in her chair, thunderstruck with my boldness. But yet, in a low voice of educated self-control, she tried to reason with me:

"You have to *show* that you have something special for America before America has need of you."

"But I never had a chance to find out what's in me, because I always had to work for a living. Only, I feel it's efficiency for America to find out what's in me so different, so I could give it out by my work."

Her eyes half closed as they bored through me. Her mouth opened to speak, but no words came from her lips. So I flamed up with all that was choking in me like a house on fire:

95   "America gives free bread and rent to criminals in prison. They got grand houses with sunshine, fresh air, doctors and teachers, even for the crazy ones. Why don't they have free boarding-schools for immigrants—strong people—willing people? Here you see us burning up with something different, and America turns her head away from us."

Her brows lifted and dropped down. She shrugged her shoulders away from me with the look of pity we give to cripples and hopeless lunatics.

"America is no Utopia. First you must become efficient in earning a living before you can indulge in your poetic dreams."

I went away from the vocational-guidance office with all the air out of my lungs. All the light out of my eyes. My feet dragged after me like dead wood.

Till now there had always lingered a rosy veil of hope over my emptiness, a hope that a miracle would happen. I would open up my eyes some day and suddenly find the America of my dreams. As a young girl hungry for love sees always before her eyes the picture of lover's arms around her, so I saw always in my heart the vision of Utopian America.

100   But now I felt that the America of my dreams never was and never could be. Reality had hit me on the head as with a club. I felt that the America that I sought was nothing but a shadow—an echo—a chimera of lunatics and crazy immigrants.

Stripped of all illusion, I looked about me. The long desert of wasting days of drudgery stared me in the face. The drudgery that I had lived through, and the endless drudgery still ahead of me rose over me like a withering wilderness of sand. In vain were all my cryings, in vain were all frantic efforts of my spirit to find the living waters of understanding for my perishing lips. Sand, sand was everywhere. With every seeking, every reaching out I only lost myself deeper and deeper in a vast sea of sand.

I knew now the American language. And I knew now, if I talked to the Americans from morning till night, they could not understand what the Russian soul of me wanted. They could not understand *me* any more than if I talked to them in Chinese. Between my soul and the American soul were worlds of difference that no words could bridge over. What was that difference? What made the Americans so far apart from me?

I began to read the American history. I found from the first pages that America started with a band of Courageous Pilgrims. They had left their native country as I had left mine. They had crossed an unknown ocean and landed in an unknown country, as I.

But the great difference between the first Pilgrims and me was that they expected to make America, build America, create their own world of liberty. I wanted to find it ready made.

105   I read on. I delved deeper down into the American history. I saw how the Pilgrim Fathers came to a rocky desert country, surrounded by Indian savages on all sides. But undaunted, they pressed on—through danger—through famine, pestilence, and want—they pressed on. They did not ask the Indians for sympathy, for understanding. They made no demands on anybody, but on their own indomitable spirit of persistence.

And I—I was forever begging a crumb of sympathy, a gleam of understanding from strangers who could not sympathize, who could not understand.

I, when I encountered a few savage Indian scalpers, like the old witch of the sweat-shop, like my "Americanized" countryman, who cheated me of my wages— I, when I found myself on the lonely, untrodden path through which all seekers of the new world must pass, I lost heart and said: "There is no America!"

Then came a light—a great revelation! I saw America—a big idea—a deathless hope—a world still in the making. I saw that it was the glory of America that it was not yet finished. And I, the last comer, had her share to give, small or great, to the making of America, like those Pilgrims who came in the *Mayflower*.

Fired up by this revealing light, I began to build a bridge of understanding between the American-born and myself. Since their life was shut out from such as me, I began to open up my life and the lives of my people to them. And life draws life. In only writing about the Ghetto I found America.

110   Great chances have come to me. But in my heart is always a deep sadness. I feel like a man who is sitting down to a secret table of plenty, while his near ones and dear ones are perishing before his eyes. My very joy in doing the work I love hurts me like secret guilt, because all about me I see so many with my longings, my burning eagerness, to do and to be, wasting their days in drudgery they hate, merely to buy bread and pay rent. And America is losing all that richness of the soul.

The Americans of to-morrow, the America that is every day nearer coming to be, will be too wise, too open-hearted, too friendly-handed, to let the least last-comer at their gates knock in vain with his gifts unwanted.

QUESTIONS FOR FURTHER INQUIRY

1. Yezierska begins her narrative optimistically, saying, "I arrived in America. My young, strong body, my heart and soul pregnant with the unlived lives of generations clamoring for expression." How does her attitude toward America change as she begins making a life for herself? Her title "America and I" suggests some kind of relationship. How does this relationship change as her attitude toward the country changes?

2. Yezierska says that learning English helped her see "American things with American eyes." Does learning English help one become an American? Do other Americans see her as a fellow countryman once her English improves?

3. Were Yezierska's expectations of life in America accurate? Do you think immigrants still see America as "a land of living hope, woven of dreams"?

Writing Your Own Narrative of Citizenship

Like dictionary definitions and legal documents, narratives follow their own writing conventions, strategies of presentation that, over time, readers have come to expect. When writers violate these conventions, they usually do so strategically. In other words, they discover those strategies that will help them most effectively achieve their purpose. Here are several strategies common in narratives:

- *Focus on a main idea or dominant impression.* Knowing what idea, attitude, or feeling you want to communicate through your story can help you decide which parts of the story to emphasize. Ralph Ellison includes many details in his story, but they all contribute to his main point: The invisible man is not recognized by the white citizens of the United States and New York City. Although he doesn't directly comment on what this means in terms of social justice, racial equality, or the place of African Americans in our national community, his details dramatize these issues, letting us discover our own insights.

- *Organize events for effect.* As long as you provide clear transitions, your plot (the sequence of events that make up your story) can begin and end just about anywhere. What strategy you choose depends on the point you want to convey to your readers. You could start at the beginning and move to the end; you could drop readers into the action, pause to give background information, and then return to the action; or you could, as Ralph Ellison does, begin at the end and then return to the beginning to explain how the ending situation came about.

- *Choose a perspective that complements your purpose.* Individuals see the same events in different ways. Writers can use this fact to achieve their purpose. They might tell a story from their own perspective, from the perspective of another participant, or even from the perspective of an objective narrator, someone not involved in the story's events. For instance, Franklin tells the story of his self-improvement plan as an example for others to follow. At the same time, he includes doubts he felt and mistakes he made, which gives his tale of moral perfection a more human quality.

- *Use specific details, sensory descriptions, and actual dialog.* Writers can make their stories seem more real for readers by using specific details. For example, the woman who cheats Anzia Yezierska out of her wages speaks to her out of "her smooth, smiling fatness." This sensory description not only creates a mental picture, it also suggests Yezierska's attitude toward the woman.

Narratives offer extraordinary opportunities for communicating our ideas of citizenship as it is lived. As you write your own citizenship narratives, go back to the qualities that narratives offer. Does your narrative dramatize or show your ideas, expose the reader to particular viewpoints, appeal to a reader's emotions, and engage the reader's imagination?

ASSESSING THE PROGRESS OF OUR INQUIRIES

Before turning to the final chapter exercises, we should assess how far we have come in answering the central question of this chapter: What does it mean to be a citizen? Past students have made the following observations in answering this question:

- *Being a citizen means having both a private and public life.* Even if we don't participate actively in politics or follow social issues, the laws, values, and beliefs of our communities shape our private lives. Private citizens can shape a community's laws, values, and beliefs by getting involved. Benjamin Franklin affected the quality of his public life by becoming a party leader in the Pennsylvania Assembly and later serving in the Continental Congress.

- *Being a citizen means testing our ideas and values against experience.* For example, Anzia Yezierska learned the hard way that our ideas about America may differ from reality. Her struggles as a new immigrant trying to escape factory life caused her to abandon her rosy view of America. She then used her writing to urge Americans toward that ideal society she had realized was still in the making.

- *Writing can help us think through our ideas about citizenship.* In writing about what citizenship means we can find the words that clarify our own ideas. In writing about his daily activities and long-term goals, Benjamin Franklin gained insights into his own responsibility as a citizen of Philadelphia and the new United States. Shaping his thoughts throughout his life into a narrative helped him to see the importance of critically examining his own choices and effecting change in the community around him.

- *Writing can let us share our ideas about citizenship with others.* Although Ralph Ellison's story is fictional, it lets him show what citizens can experience when they aren't acknowledged as full members of the community. Because citizens saw Ellison's character only as a threatening abstraction, they didn't see him as a real individual. However, by writing this story, Ellison makes the community's racism real for other citizens. Reading Ellison's narrative encourages us to rethink our own ideas about race, identity, and the kind of community we want to build in America.

In the first chapter, thinking, reading, and writing represent both opportunities to ask questions (inquiry), and to exchange ideas (action). In the chapters that follow, we will expand this process of inquiry and action to some of the most pressing questions facing our communities. Through these questions, we will explore our civic lives, our experiences as members of various communities. This exploration will also cultivate within us what the ancient Greek philosopher Socrates called the *examined life.* The civic life is an examined life when we consciously reconsider the choices we make in our education, our friendships, our government, and our planet. Socrates once told his students that "the unexamined life is not worth living." While we might not go that far, we do believe that an examined life is better for ourselves and our communities.

In Chapter Two, we will explore the examined life further by learning the strategies for thinking, reading, and writing critically that make such a life possible. Because our private and public lives are intertwined, these strategies will help us to live more thoughtful lives, and they will also serve as civic skills, tools we can use to participate more effectively in the community.

Chapters Three and Four take inquiry and action to a more rigorous level, one consistent with the kind of work you will do as college students. As we have already discovered in Chapter One, inquiry can be a form of action; performing research using dictionaries, government documents, and personal narratives actively challenges our thinking, and the act of research is itself a form of social action. In the same way, presenting our ideas to others can be a form of inquiry. The responses we get push us to reshape or refine these ideas.

Finally, Chapter Five helps us recognize that inquiry and action occur within specific social conditions. Our ability to research and argue is influenced by the parameters set within a classroom; our access to libraries, research facilities, and experts; and the routes available to us for communicating with the larger public. These conditions will become real for us as we work through the writing assignments in each chapter.

QUESTIONS FOR INQUIRY AND ACTION

1. Tell a personal story that illustrates a point you want to make about what citizenship means to you. Use the story to set up a further discussion of your point or integrate your comments within the story itself.

2. Compare and contrast experiences as a member of different communities. These communities might be national, international, local, or unofficial, like a political organization, a student group, a religious group, or a social club. Your community might also be defined by a shared ethnic identity, sexual identity, class, or subculture. Whatever communities you decide to compare, show us with relevant, specific examples what it is like to be a member of more than one community. Do these communities complement one another? Do they conflict? Do they encourage you to be a different person within each group?

3. Analyze a recent event to show how it exemplifies some point about citizenship. In writing your analysis, use specific details from the event and specific discussion of how those details illustrate your point.

4. Pick a social issue that interests you, then look around campus for any groups or resources that can help you research that issue and advocate a particular position. Write a guide to other students explaining how they can use campus resources to participate in public debate over the issue you selected.

5. Talk with your instructors, examine the syllabi from your courses, and review the classes you need for your degree; are there opportunities for you to do coursework that also benefits other communities? Write an essay that shows how students within your major can also be good citizens.

6. Prepare an extended etymology of the word *citizenship* to show how its meaning has been shaped over time. You might also write an essay that compares your own experiences as a citizen with a definition from the dictionary or official government documents.

7. Prepare your own Code of Citizenship that outlines the principles of participation in a particular community. Then, explain in detail why you created each principle.

Answers to the U.S. History and Government Exam

The complete list of one hundred questions that the Immigration and Naturalization Service uses as part of the U.S. citizenship exam can be found at <http://www.ins.usdoj.gov/graphics/services/natz/require.htm>. The INS Web site also includes an interactive self-test visitors can use to test their knowledge of U.S. history and government.

1. Red, white, blue

2. 50

3. Yes

4. Four years

5. 3

6. 100

7. The first 10 amendments

8. Patrick Henry

9. Germany, Italy, Japan

10. The Electoral College

11. For religious freedom

12. Francis Scott Key

13. Thomas Jefferson

14. The cabinet

15. 18

16. July 4, 1776

17. Republican

18. 1787

19. Washington, D.C. (1600 Pennsylvania Avenue, NW)

20. The Preamble

CHAPTER 2

Critical Literacy: The Skills to Live an Examined Life

Thought is activism, discussion is activism, education is activism every bit as much as licking stamps at campaign headquarters.

Paul Rogat Loeb, Soul of a Citizen

GETTING STARTED: Critical Thinking as Examining Life

Read the following scenarios. Try acting them out in class in groups, letting people try out different strategies and make different decisions in each case. Consider how you would define the dilemma posed in each, and how you would you begin to resolve it. What steps would you take? What resources would you draw upon?

- You have just learned in one of your classes that Thomas Jefferson, founding father and author of the Declaration of Independence, a person you've been taught was a hero and role model for all Americans, owned slaves, fathered children with one of his slaves, and then refused to acknowledge those children. What do you do?

- An outspoken member of a neo-Nazi organization has moved in next door to you and holds group meetings at his house. You don't agree with his beliefs, but he and his family are always pleasant to you. You notice that his 13-year-old daughter, who looks up to you, has been wearing swastika earrings. She thinks they are really cool. What do you do?

- One of the company employees you supervise has been wearing a button pinned to her lapel. The button shows a photograph of an aborted fetus with the words "Stop Abortions Now" above the picture. Other employees have complained about it to you, but when you suggest that she not wear it to work, she states that the button expresses her religious beliefs. She claims you cannot suppress her expression so long as she is not harming anyone else. What do you do?

49

- A close friend has emailed you a message that she received through an international listserv. The message warns Americans living in large metropolitan cities against drinking tap water, citing reports of a terrorist plot to contaminate city reservoirs with dangerous biological agents. The message is quite detailed and identifies specific persons and news organizations as sources of these reports. Anyone receiving the email is urged to forward it to as many people as possible. What do you do?

Discuss how each of these situations poses a dilemma of *ethics* as well as of *critical thinking*. How are intellectual and ethical decision-making intertwined?

Compare the strategies you used to think critically, both intellectually and ethically, and make decisions in each scenario. For instance, critical thinkers tend to:

- *Ask questions.* They even question their own assumptions and beliefs, wanting to know *why* they think what they think.
- *Look at issues from multiple perspectives.* They can put themselves in the place of others and recognize that individuals with different opinions can be equally sincere but may be basing their opinions on different beliefs, values, or experiences.
- *Resist the talk-show mindset.* While they recognize differences, they refuse to model their responses after talk shows which often celebrate all opinions as equally valid or provoke people with different views to attack one another. Instead, they seek ways to evaluate opposing ideas and to learn from disagreements.
- *Uncover hidden assumptions and prejudices.* In order to understand arguments, they go under them to reveal the underlying values and beliefs. People tend to assume that their values and beliefs are natural and shared by others, and thus may not even be aware of how these assumptions shape their viewpoints.
- *Refuse to oversimplify situations.* They see that situations are generally more complicated than they may appear, and so they examine the contexts—social, cultural, historical, personal—in which the situations occur.
- *Research to expand their perspectives.* They seek more information from sources such as printed materials, broadcast media, and other people. Instead of reaching decisions by consulting their own feelings only, they reach out and consult the ideas of others. Instead of blindly accepting information, they approach it from different perspectives and analyze where it is coming from.

Critical thinking is an approach to life, not just a tool for academic work. In our daily lives as well as in our academic studies we are faced with situations that ask us to think carefully and act wisely. Critical thinkers are those who meet these situations with sharp powers of discrimination, active imaginations, and the ability to empathize with others. These are people who live, as Socrates said, examined lives.

Critical thinking is also a civic skill. As Paul Rogat Loeb states in the opening quotation, thinking, talking, and educating ourselves and others are activities just as important to our civic lives as campaigning or voting. They are essential elements of critical literacy. The term literacy means our ability to read and write. Critical literacy-takes those abilities further: reading carefully to understand; writing to think. As critically literate people we think, read, and write with greater awareness, precision, and complexity. We need critical literacy not just for success in college, but for a genuine, vital democracy. Citizens need to be able to distinguish worthy information from deceptive advertising, biased media reports, slanted political rhetoric, get-rich-quick schemes, pseudo-academic studies, and hoaxes such as the contaminated water urban legend. (You can read more about this urban legend on this book's Web site **http://www.ablongman.com/berndt.**)

Becoming critically literate, however, means more than just protecting ourselves from misinformation. It also means attending to our own roles as speakers and writers, paying attention to the impact our thoughts and words have on others. In other words, we need to be aware of our ethical responsibilities as communicators and to develop what philosophers call a moral imagination. Critical literacy helps us to imagine greater futures and to relate to others and know ourselves in deeper ways. In short, it helps us live an examined life. In this chapter we continue practicing critical literacy by reading and responding to Thomas Jefferson's Declaration of Independence, and by developing our own writing processes, which we will compare to the process Jefferson used in drafting the Declaration.

FIRST INQUIRY: CRITICAL READING AS ACTIVE CONVERSATION

"Books are to be called for and supplied on the assumption that the process of reading is not a half-sleep; but in the highest sense an exercise, a gymnastic struggle; that the reader is to do something for himself."

Walt Whitman

"What really knocks me out is a book that, when you're all done reading it, you wish the author that wrote it was a terrific friend of yours and you could call him up on the phone whenever you felt like it."

Holden Caulfield, The Catcher in the Rye

When you read other parts of this textbook, you probably didn't think much about *how* you read it. Concentrating on the book's ideas, you may have taken for granted the process by which you experienced those ideas. Yet reading is a fascinating process. Reading opens new subjects to us, connects us to other beings, and frees us to enter new worlds. Reading is a powerful tool for expanding the boundaries of our private and public lives. But what is *critical reading*?

Usually we think of critical reading as defensive or practical. We read other people's claims skeptically, to defend ourselves against the exaggerated promises of advertisers and propaganda writers. We might also read carefully, using the practical tools of critical reading to retain more information from written sources, like textbooks. Both of these definitions share the assumption that readers have responsibilities toward themselves and the texts they are reading. In this sense, critical reading is like engaging writers in a conversation. Without our participation, a written work is nothing but ink and paper. When we read, we bring the work's ideas to life in our minds; consequently, we are obliged to read carefully, recreating the writer's ideas with accuracy. At the same time, we are obliged to reflect on what we read. The writer's ideas will become part of our knowledge, part of who we are, so we should make sure that what we retain is truly valuable. Critical reading, like critical thinking, is part of living an examined life.

Critical reading takes longer than simply reading, but it has several advantages. First, it saves us time by focusing our attention. If you have ever read to the bottom of a page, only to discover you don't remember what you just read, then you can appreciate the importance of reading actively. Second, critical reading makes our research more efficient. If you have ever had to page through a book or reread an article to find some quote you vaguely remember, then you can appreciate the value of underlining passages and taking notes. Third, critical reading helps us get more from the reading experience. If you have spent hours reading works that you can't remember a week later, then you can appreciate techniques like previewing, summarizing, and responding.

Try developing your own critical reading practice using Thomas Jefferson's Declaration of Independence, a significant historical document and a model of clear prose. If you can engage thoughtfully in conversation with such a revered text, you can read any text critically.

1. Before you begin reading, write down what you already know about the Declaration. What expectations, attitudes or preconceived notions do you have?

2. Read the first paragraph and stop. Describe *how* you read it.

3. Go back and read it again. Do you notice yourself doing anything differently now that you're thinking about how you read?

4. Read the entire text and write down how closely the actual text met your expectations and preconceived notions. Do you still have the same attitudes toward the text? Then, discuss what you wrote with your classmates. Finally, discuss what strategies you used to read effectively.

The Declaration of Independence

IN CONGRESS, July 4, 1776.

The unanimous Declaration of the thirteen united States of America,

When in the Course of human events, it becomes necessary for one people to dissolve the political bands which have connected them with another, and to assume among the powers of the earth, the separate and equal station to which the Laws of Nature and of Nature's God entitle them, a decent respect to the opinions of mankind requires that they should declare the causes which impel them to the separation.

We hold these truths to be self-evident, that all men are created equal, that they are endowed by their Creator with certain unalienable Rights, that among these are Life, Liberty and the pursuit of Happiness. —That to secure these rights, Governments are instituted among Men, deriving their just powers from the consent of the governed, —That whenever any Form of Government becomes destructive of these ends, it is the Right of the People to alter or to abolish it, and to institute new Government, laying its foundation on such principles and organizing its powers in such form, as to them shall seem most likely to effect their Safety and Happiness. Prudence, indeed, will dictate that Governments long established should not be changed for light and transient causes; and accordingly all experience hath shewn, that mankind are more disposed to suffer, while evils are sufferable, than to right themselves by abolishing the forms to which they are accustomed. But when a long train of abuses and usurpations, pursuing invariably the same Object evinces a design to reduce them under absolute Despotism, it is their right, it is their duty, to throw off such Government, and to provide new Guards for their future security. —Such has been the patient sufferance of these Colonies; and such is now the necessity which constrains them to alter their former Systems of Government. The history of the present King of Great Britain is a history of repeated injuries and usurpations, all having in direct object the establishment of an absolute Tyranny over these States. To prove this, let Facts be submitted to a candid world.

He has refused his Assent to Laws, the most wholesome and necessary for the public good.

He has forbidden his Governors to pass Laws of immediate and pressing importance, unless suspended in their operation till his Assent should be obtained; and when so suspended, he has utterly neglected to attend to them.

He has refused to pass other Laws for the accommodation of large districts of people, unless those people would relinquish the right of Representation in the Legislature, a right inestimable to them and formidable to tyrants only.

He has called together legislative bodies at places unusual, uncomfortable, and distant from the depository of their public Records, for the sole purpose of fatiguing them into compliance with his measures.

He has dissolved Representative Houses repeatedly, for opposing with manly firmness his invasions on the rights of the people.

He has refused for a long time, after such dissolutions, to cause others to be elected; whereby the Legislative powers, incapable of Annihilation, have returned to the People at large for their exercise; the State remaining in the mean time exposed to all the dangers of invasion from without, and convulsions within.

He has endeavoured to prevent the population of these States; for that purpose obstructing the Laws for Naturalization of Foreigners; refusing to pass others to encourage their migrations hither, and raising the conditions of new Appropriations of Lands.

He has obstructed the Administration of Justice, by refusing his Assent to Laws for establishing Judiciary powers.

He has made Judges dependent on his Will alone, for the tenure of their offices, and the amount and payment of their salaries.

He has erected a multitude of New Offices, and sent hither swarms of Officers to harrass our people, and eat out their substance.

He has kept among us, in times of peace, Standing Armies without the Consent of our legislatures.

He has affected to render the Military independent of and superior to the Civil power.

He has combined with others to subject us to a jurisdiction foreign to our constitution, and unacknowledged by our laws; giving his Assent to their Acts of pretended Legislation:

For Quartering large bodies of armed troops among us:

For protecting them, by a mock Trial, from punishment for any Murders which they should commit on the Inhabitants of these States:

For cutting off our Trade with all parts of the world:

For imposing Taxes on us without our Consent:

For depriving us in many cases, of the benefits of Trial by Jury:

For transporting us beyond Seas to be tried for pretended offences:

For abolishing the free System of English Laws in a neighbouring Province, establishing therein an Arbitrary government, and enlarging its Boundaries so as to render it at once an example and fit instrument for introducing the same absolute rule into these Colonies:

For taking away our Charters, abolishing our most valuable Laws, and altering fundamentally the Forms of our Governments:

For suspending our own Legislatures, and declaring themselves invested with power to legislate for us in all cases whatsoever.

He has abdicated Government here, by declaring us out of his Protection and waging War against us.

He has plundered our seas, ravaged our Coasts, burnt our towns, and destroyed the lives of our people.

He is at this time transporting large Armies of foreign Mercenaries to compleat the works of death, desolation and tyranny, already begun with circumstances of Cruelty & perfidy scarcely paralleled in the most barbarous ages, and totally unworthy the Head of a civilized nation.

He has constrained our fellow Citizens taken Captive on the high Seas to bear Arms against their Country, to become the executioners of their friends and Brethren, or to fall themselves by their Hands.

He has excited domestic insurrections amongst us, and has endeavoured to bring on the inhabitants of our frontiers, the merciless Indian Savages, whose known rule of warfare, is an undistinguished destruction of all ages, sexes and conditions.

In every stage of these Oppressions We have Petitioned for Redress in the most humble terms: Our repeated Petitions have been answered only by repeated injury.

A Prince whose character is thus marked by every act which may define a Tyrant, is unfit to be the ruler of a free people.

Nor have We been wanting in attentions to our Brittish brethren. We have warned them from time to time of attempts by their legislature to extend an unwarrantable jurisdiction over us. We have reminded them of the circumstances of our emigration and settlement here. We have appealed to their native justice and magnanimity, and we have conjured them by the ties of our common kindred to disavow these usurpations, which, would inevitably interrupt our connections and correspondence. They too have been deaf to the voice of justice and of consanguinity. We must, therefore, acquiesce in the necessity, which denounces our Separation, and hold them, as we hold the rest of mankind, Enemies in War, in Peace Friends.

We, therefore, the Representatives of the united States of America, in General Congress, Assembled, appealing to the Supreme Judge of the world for the rectitude of our intentions, do, in the Name, and by Authority of the good People of these Colonies, solemnly publish and declare, That these United Colonies are, and of Right ought to be Free and Independent States; that they are Absolved from all Allegiance to the British Crown, and that all political connection between them and the State of Great Britain, is and ought to be totally dissolved; and that as Free and Independent States, they have full Power to levy War, conclude Peace, contract Alliances, establish Commerce, and to do all other Acts and Things which Independent States may of right do. And for the support of this Declaration, with a firm reliance on the protection of divine Providence, we mutually pledge to each other our Lives, our Fortunes and our sacred Honor.

You may discover in talking to your classmates that you all had different experiences reading the Declaration; these differences illustrate how actively we participate in the creation of the works we read. We bring our own values, beliefs, experiences and interests into conversation with the authors'. Similarly, we bring different reading skill levels and strategies to these texts. Compare the strategies your class discussed with the following list we created with our students. Add your class's strategies in the margin or on our Web site **http://www.ablongman.com/berndt.**

Good critical readers tend to:

- *Preview the whole piece.* Critical readers use these strategies to get an overview of the work as a whole, picturing it in their minds and forming expectations about the work's content and its historical and social context. Testing these expectations out as they read encourages them to read the work itself more actively.

  1. Give the reading a once-over. Read the title, the table of contents, any subheadings or section titles within the body, and any pictures, graphs, or visuals.

  2. Examine the author's biographical information, the place of publication (e.g., academic journal, popular magazine, etc.), and any bibliographic information (e.g., date of publication).

3. Skim the first few paragraphs for the thesis or a statement of the author's purpose; the introductory and concluding paragraphs for the overall argument; and the summary on the book's jacket (if it has one).

4. Look for textual clues. Are some words listed in bold or italics, or printed in the margin? How does the text give you clues as to what is most important to remember?

- *Read interactively.* Critical readers use these strategies to get more out of the reading experience. The strategies focus their attention, record their ideas while reading, help them analyze a writer's assumptions and evidence, and even help them articulate their own arguments.

  1. Circle unfamiliar words or concepts and look them up in a dictionary or encyclopedia.

  2. Underline key points, striking passages, or interesting arguments. What you underline will vary with your purpose for reading a work (e.g., if you are looking for good writing techniques or ideas about a particular subject).

  3. Annotate the text by jotting notes like "good," "no way," or "proof?" in the margins. You can also note references to other works or events, your own rebuttals, and the like.

  4. Mark the writer's definitions of key terms and evidence of his or her assumptions.

- *Internalize the writer's ideas.* Critical readers use these writing strategies to sharpen their understanding of a text and preserve an accurate record of the writer's ideas for later use.

  1. Paraphrase the writer's main idea, or thesis. Sometimes the thesis is actually written in the essay—usually in the first few paragraphs—and sometimes it is implied, meaning it isn't actually stated but everything in the essay leads readers to realize that main idea. To ensure you've internalized that idea and will be able to remember it, you should paraphrase it. In other words, you should write the thesis using your own words. If it takes you several sentences to identify the author's main idea, that is fine.

  2. Summarize the work. A summary is generally a short overview of the author's thesis and the main supporting arguments or ideas. To write a summary, go back through your annotations, identify the main supporting ideas—those which served as the main idea of a particular chapter, section, or cluster of paragraphs—and paraphrase them in a smooth, coherent paragraph. More advice on writing summaries can be found in Chapter Four.

- *Go beyond the text.* The real work of critical reading is done in our own creative response to what we read. We need to go beyond underlined passages, one-word comments, and questions to more sustained conversations with the writer's ideas. The nature of this conversation can vary, depending on what qualities or ideas in the text attract our attention. The following prompts encourage a wide range of creative responses.

1. Can you extend the author's main argument, applying it to new subjects?
2. What might be the consequences of public policies based on the author's ideas?
3. Can you find a personal experience to support the author's main argument?
4. Can you find a personal experience that challenges the author's main argument?
5. What do the author's arguments say about his or her values and beliefs?
6. Who might disagree with the author's arguments and why?
7. How would people from a different time period view the author's arguments?
8. How would people of a different culture view the author's arguments?
9. Can you imagine situations in which the author's main argument would be unethical?
10. Why had people not made the author's arguments before?

Not all of these prompts will apply to particular texts; they are, rather, general frameworks for seeing an author's ideas from different perspectives. Trying several different prompts on the same text can encourage new ways of seeing the same material.

To test these critical reading strategies, practice them on the Declaration of Independence. You might also exercise them on your course syllabus or your college's mission statement.

SECOND INQUIRY: USING A WRITER'S NOTEBOOK TO CONNECT THINKING, READING, AND WRITING

I write entirely to find out what is on my mind, what I'm thinking, what I'm looking at, what I'm seeing, and what it means.

Joan Didion, "Why I Write"

What sort of diary should I like mine to be? Something loose knit and yet not slovenly, so elastic that it will embrace any thing, solemn, slight or beautiful that comes into my mind. I should like it to resemble some deep old desk, or capacious hold-all, in which one flings a mass of odds and ends without looking them through.

Virginia Woolf, A Writer's Diary

The thinking, reading, and writing we have done so far have often overlapped; we used one civic skill to help us master another. For example, consider the complex ways these skills interact in reading critically:

- As we read a text, we relate the author's ideas to our experiences and to other texts. Reading provides us with new ideas and challenges our current ways of thinking.
- To help our reading, we annotate the text, paraphrase the author's ideas, and write critical responses. Writing focuses our attention and helps us remember more; it also encourages good critical thinking.
- If we want to respond more extensively, we might use brainstorming strategies like Mind Maps to generate ideas. In this case, we write to actually start our thinking.
- At the same time, we write our ideas down to remember them. We might even reread them later and consider them more critically, expanding or clarifying our ideas further.

In each of these examples, we use one skill to help us perform another; the skills are interconnected. One of the best—and easiest—ways to appreciate the ways thinking, reading, and writing assist one another is to keep a writer's notebook. A notebook is a place where you can exercise these skills and record your efforts for later use. The notebook itself does not have to be anything formal: a spiral notebook, a sketchbook, or perhaps a bound journal with an inspiring cover. The notebooks of Leonardo Da Vinci, for example, are made up of over 5000 pages, many of which are notes written on loose-leaf paper. One sample page is shown on page 59.

As we can see from the sample page, Da Vinci brought together words and pictures, often without any formal order. In working through his many inquiries on art, physics, health, or engineering, he created a method in his notebooks that worked for him. In our own notebooks, we can write down great quotations, notes from our reading, or questions we would like to answer. We can paste in cartoons, news clippings, or photographs. We can plan out our projects, reflect on the day's experiences, or draw our own pictures. The whole point of the notebook is to provide ourselves with a place where we can work on our thoughts or record interesting ideas. Notebooks should inspire our creative and analytical thinking by giving our minds material on which to work. How we construct these notebooks will ultimately depend on what strategies help us think, read, and write most effectively. Another, different example from one of the authors' notebooks appears on page 60.

As this example illustrates, writers' notebooks vary. People don't read, think, or write in the same ways, so their notebooks will reflect those differences. Those who are visually oriented, for instance, might have notebooks with a lot of pictures, Mind Maps, and drawings. Those who are technologically savvy might create personal Web sites that serve as notebooks, where they can post statements, pictures, or questions; link up to interesting Web sites; or host online discussions. However these notebooks are created, they provide writers with a record of their learning and of their interests at a given time. Professor Susan Miller informs us

that past writers often thought of keeping a notebook as "making a portable memory" or an "index of yourself."

Keeping a writer's notebook as you go through your composition course and through college can help you experience the way your thinking, reading, and writing develop. These skills usually develop slowly, yet your experience at college will shape them strongly. Having a record of your progress can help you

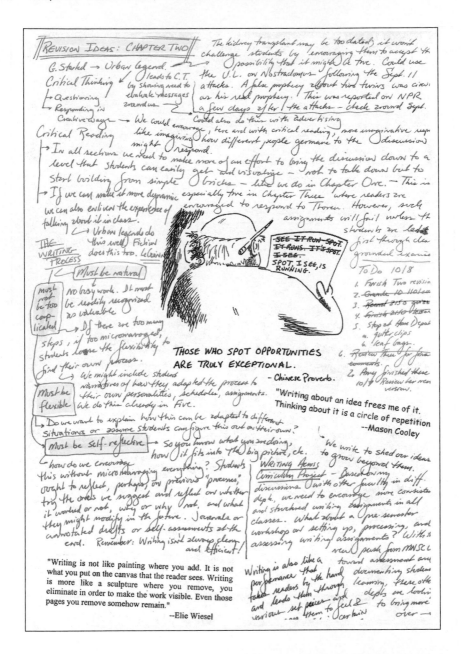

recognize the ways you will be changed by this experience. You may also find that keeping a writer's notebook will benefit your writing by inspiring you to write, by giving you ideas to write about, and by preserving your thinking, reading, and writing for later use.

Here's a way to get started: In your writer's notebook, write down one hundred questions you want to know the answer to. They can range from abstract to concrete, serious to trivial: "What's the meaning of life?" "Why is the sky blue?" "What should I major in?" "What is a comma splice?" "Do cats have long-term memory?" At first, the questions will come easily, but it's important to keep thinking of and writing down questions even when you think you can't think of any more. One hundred questions is a lot, but it will push you to consider more than you might have if you had settled for the first twenty at the top of your head. It will also push you out of the mindset that only certain questions are appropriate ones to explore in writing. Some of the questions may be variants of one another; in fact, it's expected, for you are drawn to particular subjects and themes. When you are in the habit of using your writer's notebook to record ideas and questions, you will create a reservoir of writing ideas, so that when you need a research question or paper topic, you'll be ready to go.

Asking questions is one of the strongest signs of our curiosity. The practice of asking questions cultivates the inquiring mind. It exercises our creativity, for asking questions encourages us to see things from new or various perspectives. When you get into the habit of asking and writing down questions, you will find it easier to bring them up for closer examination in academic assignments. In that way, college assignments become exercises in investigating the questions you want most to answer. Perhaps most important at this time in your life, asking questions can help you direct your education. Rather than passively accepting the expectations of others, you should embrace the possibilities open to you as a student. Exploring the questions you are most interested in helps you to command and shape your education.

THIRD INQUIRY: FINDING YOUR WRITING PROCESS

We may be bored by the phrase "the writing process," but it is a wonderful process. When you have written some inspired draft, it has found a home *outside* you—*on paper*. Having that draft *outside* your head gives the brain new perspective. Your brain, behind your eyes, looks at what you've written. It sees ways to deepen or to contradict the text. Let it. Let the brain do this wonderful work.

Carol Bly, Beyond the Writers' Workshop

You may not consider yourself a "writer" in any classic sense. You may not see yourself as a warbling poet, a slick and savvy copy writer, or a tormented soul hunched over an old, clackety typewriter. But all college students are writers; writing is an essential part of the college experience. You will write to demonstrate your knowledge, to record your inquiries, and to develop your mind, learning how to think with more rigor, focus, and subtlety.

Of course, having to write doesn't make writing seem less daunting. How does one get from the jumble of half-baked ideas and vague intentions to a clear, focused document that communicates our insights to others? The answer is to see writing as a process. If we try to create a perfect piece of writing the first time, we will be daunted; we will stare dumbly at our computer screens, we will procrastinate, we will curse the instructor who brought this writing assignment into our lives. On the other hand, if we break up a writing project into smaller, more manageable steps, we can empower ourselves. We can give ourselves specific, achievable goals; we can better visualize where we are in the project; we can better manage our time; and we can build momentum as we complete steps successfully. The following inquiry breaks the writing process into three general stages: conceiving, clarifying, and crafting. Here is an overview of the activities writers go through in each stage:

1. *Conceiving:* This stage is made up of three intertwining steps: planning, prewriting, and drafting.
   - *Planning:* Writers explore their writing situation.
   - *Prewriting:* Writers generate ideas and discover their focus.
   - *Drafting:* Writers explore and expand upon those ideas and discover the essay's thesis and direction.
2. *Clarifying:* This stage is made up of three intertwining steps: re-seeing, reviewing, and revising.
   - *Re-seeing:* Writers take time to evaluate their initial ideas and opinions, and to re-envision the work as a whole.
   - *Reviewing:* Writers test their work on readers to see how effectively they have communicated their ideas and intentions.
   - *Revising:* Writers reshape their work with a clearer understanding of their purpose and audience: what they want to say and how they want to say it to readers.
3. *Crafting:* This stage is made up of two intertwining steps, editing and proofreading.
   - *Editing:* Writers reread their work, revising for clarity, smoothness, and style.
   - *Proofreading:* Writers reread their work to ensure proper spelling and usage, and to polish the final work.

As we go through this process, keep the following points in mind.

First, the writing process is as much intellectual revision as writing revision. Much of our thinking relies on language; our ideas take shape through words. As we revise our writing, we improve the clarity, strength, and sophistication of our ideas.

Second, writing processes are not absolutes. Although our writing will be better if we develop it through a process, the process itself will vary between individuals and between writing situations. To illustrate this point, we will examine, at each stage of the writing process, the process Thomas Jefferson used to write the Declaration of Independence. Although his writing process parallels the one described here, he altered, shortened, or collapsed different steps to fit his situation. As a beginning writer, you might give each stage a good faith effort. Then, in future writing assignments, you can adapt the process to your own style—not necessarily what is easiest for you, but what lets you produce a quality final draft most effectively.

Third, although we've laid it out here as a sequence of steps, the process is not really linear. In real writing situations, we don't completely "finish" one step and move to the next. Instead, we return frequently to earlier steps, each time engaging our ideas and clarifying and refining them.

Finally, the writing process asks us to look both inward and outward. As we go through each step, we think critically about our subject and about our own values and beliefs. In an intensive way, we live an examined life when we write. We also look outward to our audience, crafting our writing to reach them most effectively. In this way, writing is activism; it helps us to forge relationships with others in our community, seek ways to resolve disagreements, and forward our common interests.

Conceiving: The Early Stage of Writing

Imagine yourself sitting in front of an empty computer screen or a blank sheet of paper. Your assignment is to write a six-page essay with a clear focus, an easy-to-follow structure, specific details, and smooth transitions. Not knowing quite how to begin, you had procrastinated until now, the night before it is due. You have twelve hours left. Begin.

Does such a task seem insurmountable?

It may seem less time consuming to begin directly with a final draft—conceiving, clarifying, and crafting as you go along. You will probably discover, however, that the time you waste trying to start, to generate clear and polished thoughts, and to unify ideas that don't fit together naturally will nearly equal the time you would have spent in preparing, prewriting, and drafting. In addition, by taking the time to work through these early stages in the writing process, your essay will likely avoid the faults common in essays written at the last minute. It will avoid the bland introductions, the vague theses, and the wandering structure—a patchwork of ideas held loosely together with transition words. It will also avoid the irrelevant details, the bits of rejected sentences that the writer forgot to erase, and the conclusion that either trails off at the end into an incoherent whimper or serves up a simplistic platitude.

Taking time early in the process to understand your writing situation will make the entire project easier and less stressful; it will also improve the quality of your work dramatically.

Planning: Exploring Your Writing Situation

Jefferson's Writing Situation

Realizing that their efforts at compromise had failed, the Congress of the American colonies decided on June 11, 1776 to declare independence from Great Britain. To prepare a draft of that declaration, they formed a committee that consisted of Thomas Jefferson, Benjamin Franklin, John Adams, Roger Sherman, and Robert R. Livingston. Since Jefferson was known as an excellent writer and was from the key political state of Virginia, he was delegated the task of writing the first draft. He knew that not all of the colonies believed that declaring independence was wise; therefore, this document he was about to draft had to convince the rest of the Congress to form a united front, as well as announce to the English government that the colonies were declaring themselves independent.

When Jefferson was assigned to write the Declaration of Independence, he was given his subject, the purposes of his document, and American and British audiences who each held different values and beliefs. To successfully achieve his purposes with these audiences, he had first to understand his writing situation. When we too get a writing assignment, we should take a moment to understand what is expected of us. Whether we write for instructors or the public, knowing our audience's expectations, both for what we should write about and how we should write about it, can help us reach such readers more successfully. Here are some questions we should always know the answers to, even before we begin writing.

- When are the drafts and final essay due?
- Does the essay have a designated subject matter or topic?
- Does it have to be written in a particular genre or format (e.g., a critical essay, a lab report, a narrative)? If so, what are the conventions of that genre that we will need to follow?
- Has the essay's purpose been established by the instructor (e.g., a narrative that shows readers what it means to live as a member of a particular community)? If not, what might be our purpose (e.g., to inform, to persuade, to entertain, or all three)?
- Has the instructor issued other instructions (e.g., include at least four sources, include a separate title page)?
- Will the essay be written to audiences outside of class? If so, how will they need to be addressed?
- How will the work be evaluated (e.g., more weight on a clear focus than on correct spelling)?

You might also talk to your instructor more generally about the assignment, and you might request to see models of successful work, not to mimic them but to better visualize the sort of product that is expected of you. What topics have students chosen in the past? Why did the instructor choose to give this particular assignment? The more you know, the more effectively you can anticipate readers' expectations.

Prewriting: Generating Ideas

Jefferson's Prewriting

Because he was busy with congressional matters during the day, Jefferson set aside the early morning and late evening hours for writing the Declaration of Independence. He was in Philadelphia and didn't have time to go home to his study in Virginia on the weekends, so he wrote in his room on an eighteenth-century version of a "laptop"—a portable lap desk that he had made to his specifications.

When he began drafting the Declaration, Jefferson had already been thinking about the ideas in it. For years he had been reading works about human rights and recording his thoughts in his notebook. Among the authors he had read were the English philosopher John Locke, who advocated for the rights of individuals, and the Scottish philosopher Francis Hutcheson, who emphasized group values. You can see some of their ideas competing in Jefferson's work.

Since writing is a creative endeavor, much of the process of writing consists of generating ideas. We need to generate ideas at all stages of the writing process; for instance, to get started we generate ideas for essay topics. Later, we write to explore new perspectives on our subject and to clarify our thinking. We also write to work through problems we encounter with our writing; for example, we might try several different methods to explain a difficult concept before we find one we like. You'll remember that in Chapter One we used brainstorming techniques to discover what we know and how well we know it, to open new avenues for inquiry, and to find a way into an essay (e.g., whether we want to tell a story or analyze a current event). At each stage of writing you can use a range of strategies to help yourself find the ideas or the clarity you need for that specific stage. Learning how to use a number of strategies allows you to choose the one you need in the particular situation, just as knowing how to work with a number of tools allows you to select the most effective one for the job. For example, listing ideas would work if you had only the back of your checkbook to write on, and freewriting ideas on a computer would work if the ideas are coming to you faster than you can handwrite them.

The primary goal of the stage of prewriting is to generate a critical mass of ideas and, out of that mass, to find a focus for your piece of writing. The term *prewriting* is somewhat of a misnomer, because you write to generate those ideas and find that focus: you write in preparation for writing. Below is a list of common strategies for generating ideas; these are often called *invention strategies*. We encourage you to try all of the invention strategies in order to discover which work best for you under particular conditions and at different stages in the writing process. We also urge you to push your brainstorming or idea generating. Often we see students obediently going through the process because they have to, but abandoning it after only a cursory effort and moving on to the drafting stage before they've had a chance to really let the invention strategies work. Keep working with the strategy until you feel you have a lot to say and a sense of direction for your piece of writing.

- *Talking.* Talk with others about your topic, and work out and test your ideas with them. You can use a tape recorder in order to preserve any great insights.
  Talking is a natural, comfortable way to discover ideas; it can, however, distract you from getting started if the talking wanders from the subject into regular conversation.

- *Freewriting.* Write your initial idea or topic at the top of a blank page. Then write, without stopping or lifting your pen, for ten minutes. Don't stop to edit yourself; keep writing even if you run out of things to say. This helps you dislodge ideas from the back of your mind and discover new ones.

     Freewriting has the advantage of pushing you to discover insights you might not have thought of otherwise; it has the disadvantage of producing a lot of work that is less focused, so you often have more material to toss out.

- *Reading.* Read about your topic on the Internet, in magazines, newspapers and books. You'll deepen your knowledge of the subject and also discover connections to other subjects, which will give you ideas for fresh angles for writing.

     Reading is one of the most useful modes of generating ideas; however, it has the disadvantage of being time-consuming and it can encourage procrastination by keeping you from deciding upon a point of focus.

- *Questioning.* Ask yourself questions the journalist's questions (who, what, when, where, why, and how) as well as "what is the significance of this issue?" and "who would care?"

     A formal strategy of questioning can help you to develop a good sense of purpose and appropriate audience, as well as to be thorough in your coverage. Sticking too closely to just the questions can keep you from exploring and deepening your project, however.

- *Listing.* Write your topic at the top of a sheet of paper, and then make a list of your thoughts about it—directions you might take it, related ideas, and such. These don't have to be full sentences, just a few words. Or, if you have no topic yet, write your assignment guidelines at the top of the page and list all the possible topics you can think of. Listing works on free association, so don't stop to edit yourself, even if some of your ideas sound stupid.

     As with freewriting, listing is useful for dislodging ideas when you feel you have no ideas. Its disadvantage is that, because it does not make you articulate your ideas in full sentences, it does not make you develop your ideas as full thoughts; thus, you can be left with somewhat disjointed ideas.

- *Treeing* or *Mapping.* These strategies give you a visual representation of your ideas, and can help you structure them and connect them. Write your topic or main idea in the center of the page. Make a Mind-Map of it, following the instructions in Chapter One. Or, to use the Treeing strategy, draw a line extending from that center idea, and write a related idea on that line or branch, and then ideas related to that branch as various extended twigs. Continue in this way, connecting ideas to the trunk or various branches. You might draw the lines and write the ideas in different colors or different styles.

     Mapping techniques have the advantage of allowing you to visualize the whole of your project and provide clear relationships between the various parts;

they have the disadvantage of sometimes taking longer to produce, and, because they produce images rather than sentences, you do not generate as much immediately useable text to incorporate into your writing project.

- *Outlining.* Start with your main point or working thesis. Then list and detail the various points you want to make to support that thesis. The outline can be made in paragraphs, Roman numerals, bullet points—whatever works best for you. The point is for you to be able to get a sense of the whole essay, the point you want to make, and some sense of how you will get there.

     Outlines have the advantage of getting you quickly organized and allowing you to experiment with arranging your ideas before you attempt to work out a full draft; they have the disadvantage of occasionally encouraging you to narrow your thoughts and settle on a format too quickly. For this reason, outlining is a strategy that often works best after you've already thought through your project and are ready to organize and structure your argument's main points. Many writers find that outlining works well *after* they've completed a draft, because it helps them re-see what they've written and organize points more clearly and logically.

Drafting

Jefferson's Drafting

The Library of Congress still has Jefferson's "official Rough Draught" of the Declaration of Independence. This is the draft he took to Franklin and Adams for their comments. Although Jefferson called it a rough draft, it was carefully thought out, and evidence indicates that it was not by any means his *first* draft; he wrote and rewrote it to clarify his thinking. Like all writers, Jefferson began his drafting from his own thinking. We see earlier versions of his argument in documents he had written previously, such as "A Summary View of the Rights of British America" and the preamble to the Virginia Constitution. In the draft of the Declaration of Independence, Jefferson tried to work out his thoughts on human rights and to find the words that would capture his vision of the new independent United States. Later, in the revision stages, he reshaped paragraphs and points of the Declaration to meet the needs of the specific audiences.

Up to this point, you wrote, talked, read, or researched to generate ideas, a critical mass of material that would impel you forward into the next stage of the writing process: drafting. The goal of drafting is to give this material a focus and shape. Of course, this task isn't easy. Your materials hold so many possibilities that you may feel like any essay you write must explode into a thousand different directions at once. Unfortunately, essays don't unfold this way for readers. They receive your ideas linearly, sentence by sentence and paragraph by paragraph. If you tried to write your final essay at this early stage you would likely wander from point to point, repeat your ideas, or lead readers down intellectual dead ends. To effectively communicate your ideas to readers, you need to focus those ideas and give to them a shape that readers will recognize.

Sometimes you finish prewriting with a clear working thesis, that is, a recognizable sense of what you want to communicate to your readers. Often, however, you still need to figure out what you think about your topic and what you want to focus on; in this case you might write an *inquiry draft* or *zero draft*. This is a more focused stage of freewriting in which you dive in and write about your subject without a clear sense yet of where it will lead you. You don't worry about introductions, organization, or grammar. You don't worry that you're repeating yourself or developing ideas in a mishmash fashion. You let the act of writing help you discover what you want to say about the topic. Of course, bells won't go off and confetti won't fall from the ceiling when you happen across a good working thesis. As you write, be alert to any statements about your topic that excite you, that you could write about for several more pages; chances are, you have a good candidate for your working thesis. Remember that any mass of prewriting could probably lead you to dozens of different theses.

Another way you'll know you have a potentially good working thesis is if it helps you to get an intellectual handle on the material. You'll not only get a sense of direction, you'll also be able to visualize what shape the essay will take. For example, a thesis like "The Big Mac is, layer for layer, the finest sandwich ever created" suggests analysis. The writer will analyze each layer of the Big Mac to show why it is so wonderful. The structure, then, might move from two all-beef patties, special sauce, lettuce, and cheese to pickles, onions, and a sesame-seed bun. On the other hand, a thesis like "Preparing a Big Mac requires skill and grace under pressure" promises to explain an activity. The thesis suggests the writer will organize chronologically from beginning to end: from heating the two pucks of beef to lathering on the sauce to wrapping it all up in a box. In both examples, the writer could use the thesis to visualize, or to see in his or her mind, what the essay might look like. The thesis and structure are intertwined; the structure is how you will lead readers to see the truth of your thesis.

To fully develop the visualization suggested by your working thesis, you might try the invention strategy of *outlining*. Imagine the thesis as the destination you want your readers to reach. You have a general sense of direction from your visualization, but if you want to lead other people to your destination, you'll need to offer more explicit directions. Outlining pushes you to be explicit, clarifying the purpose of each step and how it helps readers to see the truth of your thesis. In other words, outlining pushes you to be more intellectually honest. At the same time, outlines encourage creativity. They are quick and relatively painless to create, so you can play around with different strategies, as you might map out different routes, imagining which would be the most the interesting or practical for your guests.

Having a working thesis and some idea of the structure does make drafting the actual essay easier. Where you go from here may vary, however, because the drafting process itself varies from writer to writer. The precise content, direction, shape, and tone of each essay you write will differ, but each will have a main point or thesis of some sort, and each piece of writing will have a beginning, a middle, and an end. Writers, in many creative and varied ways, lead readers into their writing, make an impression or an argument, and escort them out of the writing. Understanding the function and particular qualities of each of these parts of an essay will help you create the most appropriate and effective ways of communicating your thoughts to your readers.

Beginning Your Essay: Introductions

Introductions are essential to any piece of writing because they establish subject matter, focus, direction, pace, argument, point of view, tone, and persona. Readers depend heavily upon introductions to draw them into the essay, provide them with information, and give them direction as to the content, the author's perspective, and the significance of what is to come in the rest of the essay. The introduction is the make-or-break point of many essays, for it is the point at which readers will decide whether they want to read on or to toss the paper aside; they tend to prejudge the whole essay based on their impressions of the introduction.

For these reasons, an introduction can be daunting to write, especially if you think you have to know everything from your subject matter to tone and point of view, all at once. However, you do not need to enter your draft with a completed introduction. The process of working out your introduction will help you focus, organize your thoughts, determine your direction, and get you involved in and excited about your argument; and the process of working out your entire draft will help you develop your introduction. Many professional writers first sketch out a working introduction that looks very much like their earlier outline and that will guide them through their drafting process. This is meant to be a crutch to help them get going. Then, after they've completed the draft and have a better idea of what they want to say, they return to the opening and carefully craft an introduction that leads readers into the essay.

To figure out what strategy will best lead readers into their essay, writers consider their subject matter, their thesis, and how they want to present themselves to and converse with their readers. You have many choices for beginning a piece of writing, which include but are not limited to the following:

- Pose a question.
- Present dialogue between characters or figures.
- Tell an anecdote or story, or relate a case study.
- Describe a scene, event, or item.
- Offer a statistic or fact (generally a surprising or startling one).
- Quote a text or person.
- Provide background or contextual material to prepare readers for your thesis.

Note the ways the various authors in this book introduce their works. Skim through one community chapter, reading only the introductions. Which ones stand out to you? Why? In which essays is the thesis not placed in the introduction? What effect(s) does this have on you as a reader? What does the author do instead to draw you in and prepare you for the essay to follow?

Developing Your Essay: Body Paragraphs

The body of your essay is where you do most of the explicit work of leading readers to see the truth of your thesis. That is, the body paragraphs develop and support your thesis, whether the thesis has been formally announced in the introduction, will be revealed later, or remains implied throughout. In most—but not all—cases, each body paragraph will focus on explaining one aspect, or supporting point, of the thesis, which will be announced in the topic sentence of the paragraph. Each paragraph will provide evidence to support the thesis, and transitions will connect the paragraphs to one another and will advance the thesis throughout the essay.

Topic sentences hold a paragraph together. They are the main points to which all of the other sentences in the paragraph are connected. While you are drafting, topic sentences help you organize your thoughts; then, in the finished product, they provide guidance and direction for the readers. As Stephen King says in *On Writing*, "Topic-sentence-followed-by-support-and-description insists that the writer organize his/her thoughts, and it also provides good insurance against wandering away from the topic."

Topic sentences are generally either the first or last sentence in a paragraph. At the beginning of a paragraph, topic sentences announce the paragraph's topic or point. Because we indent or add white space to indicate the beginnings of new paragraphs, the reader's eye is drawn to the beginnings of paragraphs; therefore, the first sentence of a paragraph carries a lot of weight and can be a good spot to place your strongest claims. However, you can also organize the paragraph by introducing readers to examples that let them recognize an overall point for themselves. This point gets reinforced in a topic sentence that closes the paragraph.

Body paragraphs provide the evidence that supports your thesis. As you will learn in Chapter Four, each paragraph should contain reasoning and/or specific evidence to explain or prove the claim that is stated in the topic sentence of the paragraph. Depending upon your purpose and audience, you might supply evidence from:

- Your own logical reasoning
- Your or others' personal experience
- Observations and experiments
- Research studies and professional opinions of authorities and experts
- Data and statistics

If you receive a comment from your instructor or a peer that your paper lacks depth, it does not mean that you are a shallow person and incapable of thinking deeply; it probably means that your paper lacks support. The support you provide for each claim is the real core or the substance of your argument; without it you're just asserting a claim and asking readers to believe you.

Transitions create continuity, or flow, between one idea and the next. They do this by showing the relationship between the point you just made and the point you're about to make. For instance, "furthermore" tells the reader you are continuing to develop the point you just made, adding evidence to it; but "however" suggests that you're about to move in a different direction, probably disagreeing with your previous point. You can find whole lists of transitional words and phrases in writing handbooks. Providing smooth transitions that clearly show the relationship between the supporting points of your thesis will advance the thesis step by step. Transitions also provide the flow that is essential to readability and enjoyment and keeps an essay from sounding choppy.

Transitional paragraphs can help you signal a move from one idea to the next. You can also use an entire paragraph to provide a transition. For example, when you are moving from one fairly complex point to another, just a phrase or sentence may not provide enough direction for readers, and you may want to use a paragraph to wrap up the first point, signal your move, and prepare readers for the next point.

Ending Your Essay: Conclusions

Conclusions are the paragraph or paragraphs that wrap up the loose ends of your essay. They are memorable when readers are led smoothly out of your argument but are motivated to continue thinking about it and learning from the essay's insights. Think of enlarging the world of your essay as you narrow it to a close: the audience should feel a sense of closure, but should also feel that they can continue the conversation on this topic beyond your essay.

Student writers have often been taught to reiterate their thesis statements in the concluding paragraph. Academic essay assignments in lower-division undergraduate courses are generally short enough, however, that readers have not had time to forget your introduction and thesis, so mere reiteration can be condescending or just plain boring—for you as well as the reader. Do reaffirm your thesis, to pull the essay together, but then go beyond it. To conclude in the most appropriate and effective manner for your specific writing project, consider your subject matter, the tone and seriousness of your argument, your specific audience, and, most important, your purpose—what you want readers to do as a result of reading your essay. As with introductions, you have a number of choices for how to do this, which include but are not limited to the following:

- Circle back to your introduction: its opening anecdote or story or quotation or dialogue or question.
- Present the implications of your argument in a wider context.
- Pose a question that has arisen as a result of exploring your thesis.
- Make a suggestion to readers as to where to go next, what action they can take.
- Make a connection with readers by noting ways your argument might affect them personally.

Note the ways the various authors in this book conclude their works. As you did with the introductions, skim through one community chapter reading only the conclusions. Which ones do you find most effective, and why? What is the effect they have on you as a reader? What do the authors do to give you a sense of closure? What do they do to let you make your own conclusions and to continue the work of the essay on your own?

Clarifying: The Middle Stage of Writing

Peer-Reviewing Jefferson's Draft

After working out the first draft, Jefferson presented his "original Rough Draught" to Franklin and Adams. (See a copy of it on the following page.) Both were trusted readers, experienced writers, and statesmen, and they had the good of the overall document foremost in their minds. Both of them read and wrote their suggestions for revision on Jefferson's draft; Jefferson then took those suggestions and incorporated them into a clean copy for the whole committee. Members Sherman and Livingston made minor suggestions, which he also incorporated. Historians have noted that forty-seven alterations, three new paragraphs among them, were made to the document before it was presented to the Congress for their revisions on June 28, 1776.

When we've completed a first draft of our work, we enter a middle stage of the writing process in which we look inside ourselves and outside to readers in order to deepen and clarify our thoughts. This happens long before we attempt to make stylistic improvements or correct grammar. As writer Carol Bly observes, this stage is more *psychological* than it is artistic because we are closely examining our own ideas and convictions. We want to intensify and develop those ideas for ourselves before we submit them to critique. Thus, in *re-seeing* we reacquaint ourselves with what we have written and evaluate how well it expresses what we really want to say. Then, by *reviewing* we discover how effectively our draft is engaging readers and communicating our intentions, and by *revising* we reshape the whole piece with new attention to our own intentions and our readers' needs and desires.

Re-seeing: Rethinking Your Premises

[E]xperienced writers describe their primary objective when revising as finding the form or shape of their argument. Although the metaphors vary, the experienced writers often use structural expressions such as "finding a framework," "a pattern," or "a design" for their argument. When questioned about this emphasis, the experienced writers responded that since their first drafts are usually scattered attempts to define their territory, their objective in the second draft is to begin observing general patterns of development and deciding what should be included and what excluded.

Nancy Sommers, "Revision Strategies of Student Writers
and Experienced Adult Writers"

A Declaration by the Representatives of the UNITED STATES OF AMERICA, in General Congress assembled.

When in the course of human events it becomes necessary for one people to dissolve the political bands which have connected them with another, and to assume among the powers of the earth the separate and equal station to which the laws of nature & of nature's god entitle them, a decent respect to the opinions of mankind requires that they should declare the causes which impel them to the separation.

We hold these truths to be self-evident, that all men are created equal, that they are endowed by their creator with inherent & inalienable rights, that among these are life, liberty, & the pursuit of happiness; that to secure these rights, governments are instituted among men, deriving their just powers from the consent of the governed; that whenever any form of government becomes destructive of these ends, it is the right of the people to alter or to abolish it, & to institute new government, laying it's foundation on such principles & organising it's powers in such form, as to them shall seem most likely to effect their safety & happiness. prudence indeed will dictate that governments long established should not be changed for light & transient causes: and accordingly all experience hath shewn that mankind are more disposed to suffer while evils are sufferable, than to right themselves by abolishing the forms to which they are accustomed. but when a long train of abuses & usurpations [begun at a distinguished period & pursuing invariably the same object, evinces a design to subject reduce them under absolute Despotism,] it is their right, it is their duty, to throw off such government & to provide new guards for their future security. such has been the patient sufferance of these colonies; & such is now the necessity which constrains them to expunge their former systems of government. the history of the present king of Great Britain is a history of unremitting injuries and usurpations, [among which appears no solitary fact to contradict the uniform tenor of the rest, but all have] in direct object the establishment of an absolute tyranny over these states. to prove this, let facts be submitted to a candid world, [for the truth of which we pledge a faith yet unsullied by falsehood.]

Whereas most student writers tend to view the revision process as a matter of *correcting*, experienced writers tend to view it as a time to sit back and *re-see* the work in its entirety and to *rethink* the premises of the thesis and the overall shape of the piece. This can sound overwhelming to student writers because it is more time-consuming than merely correcting errors, and few students have had training and experience in substantive revision. Rethinking the premises of your thesis may well mean changing your mind, and consequently changing your thesis and the entire direction of your paper. Sometimes this will be the case. At other times, you will just refine what you've already got in draft form.

First, allow yourself to take a step back and re-see the whole. Reread your draft. Reacquaint yourself with what you've written. One reason for doing this is that writers often continue to think about their subjects, consciously or unconsciously, after the draft is completed. As a result, the essay you have in your mind is sometimes clearer and more developed than the essay you have on paper. Rereading the draft reacquaints you with what you had actually written.

Rethink the premises of your argument. To deepen and refine your initial ideas, when you come to claims, ask yourself whether what you have said is what you truly believe, or whether you're just going along with what everyone else says, or repeating things you've heard but haven't really experienced for yourself. What is *underneath* what you have said? What are you not saying yet? It may be something you haven't discovered yet, or it may be something you're afraid you can't say, because it's an unpopular idea. Grant yourself the courage to rethink your thoughts, to complicate them, and to change them.

Visualize the overall shape of the piece of writing. As you read the entire piece again and again, is there an image or phrase that stands out to you, that seems to work like a magnet to hold the essay together? Often such images and phrases, your best insights, are buried in the body of the paper because they were discoveries you made in the process of drafting. Find those insights, excavate them, and move them to more prominent sections of the paper. One of those insights might make a better thesis than your working thesis, for instance. It may even give you a great title. Reading for these magnetic words or phrases will help you to find the framework, pattern, or design that Sommers refers to in the passage quoted above.

Reviewing: Getting Feedback from Readers

Feedback from someone I'm close to gives me confidence, or at least it gives me time to improve. Imagine that you are getting ready for a party and there is a person at your house who can check you out and assure you that you look wonderful or, conversely, that you actually do look a tiny tiny tiny bit heavier than usual in this one particular dress or suit or that red makes you look just a bit like you have sarcoptic mange. Of course you are disappointed for a moment, but then you are grateful that you are still in the privacy of your own home and there is time to change.

Anne Lamott, Bird by Bird: Some Instructions on Writing and Life

Writing is about forging a connection of minds through language. If you want to communicate effectively you need to know, at various points in the writing process, whether your language is successfully conveying your ideas. While you let your mind and body recover from the drafting and re-seeing processes, you can give your work to trusted others to read to see how they respond to your ideas and whether those ideas are understandable and engaging. Feedback can come from many different sources. Here are just a few suggestions:

- Make an appointment and discuss the draft with your instructor.
- Work with a tutor in your school's writing center.
- Give it to your parents to read. They can often provide good insights, and you will create an opportunity to reconnect with them now that you are in college.
- Find trusted classmates or friends who have already had composition courses or who are taking the class with you.
- Visit your high-school English teacher. They are usually overworked, but they know how to give feedback and might appreciate the respect you are showing for their expertise.

As you pass around your drafts, keep several points in mind. First, let your readers see the assignment sheet. If they don't know the context in which you are writing and your intended audience, they may give you misleading advice. Second, encourage them to respond to the larger issues; the goal is not to correct spelling errors or mechanical problems, but to discover whether you have made your points as clear and substantive and appealing as they can be. Third, encourage them to give feedback freely. You are the one who must ultimately decide what advice to take or leave. Many of your readers will be, like you, learning how to think and talk about writing. If they worry about misleading you, they won't want to discuss the larger revision issues.

Admittedly, working with others can be difficult, and the process of subjecting your work to the critique of others can be psychologically painful because we tend to see our writing as an intimate extension of ourselves. Like most authors, Thomas Jefferson was also sensitive to changes made to his writing.

Historians tell us that evidently Jefferson sat in Congress and fumed while his text was cut and changed. He wrote later that during the revising Ben Franklin sat next to him and tried to comfort him by telling him the story of a young hatmaker who had made an advertising sign that first read "John Thompson, Hatter, makes and sells hats for ready money." After he asked his friends to critique it for him, however, the sign was reduced to just the words "John Thompson," and a picture of a hat.

Jefferson held a grudge about the group's revision for years, insisting that his original draft was better. He even sent copies of both versions to his friends for them to judge whether his was not the stronger version. Ultimately, though,

> he was proud of his work on this important document. For the epitaph on his gravestone, he composed a list of his greatest accomplishments: "Author of the Declaration of Independence [and] of the Statute of Virginia for religious toleration & Father of the University of Virginia." (Interestingly, he omitted President of the United States.)

As Anne Lamott stated above, a trusted reader can save us from later embarrassment, frustration, or even failure. In order to be a trusted reader yourself, use your critical reading strategies to converse with the author's work. As with any essay you read, read interactively, responding in the margins and marking the text when you find passages that are striking, vivid, persuasive, vague, ineffective, and so on. In addition, keep in mind that your goal is to help the author develop his or her *own* thoughts as clearly and precisely as possible. While reviewing the work can provide a great opportunity to argue about the subject—pushing the author to think more deeply and clearly about his or her views—you shouldn't, as a reviewer of the writing, try to change the author's views to your own.

And, to get feedback on the specific criteria on which you'll be evaluated, ask pointed questions about the piece of writing. Here are some basic questions and suggestions that pertain to most essays; revise them and add others as needed for your specific writing situation.

- *Look at the assignment and evaluation criteria.* Does the essay fulfill the assignment? Does it meet all the requirements imposed by the instructor?
- *Look at the thesis.* When you read the draft, what one thing draws everything in the essay together? Write out this main point or thesis in your own words. Is it clear, concrete, and intriguing? Is the thesis not simply repeated but actually developed and enhanced throughout the body of the essay?
- *Look at the introduction.* Is the choice of an introduction strategy the most compelling and accurate one for the author's purposes? Does the introduction clearly set up the argument and lead you into it? Do you feel well prepared for the essay that will follow, and engaged so that you *want* to read it?
- *Look at the structure of the argument.* Remember that essays are like guided tours or classroom lectures; authors need to lead readers clearly from one point to the next to see the truth of the thesis. Does the author need to reorganize the order of the argument's points? Does the author need to focus on clearer and more precise topic sentences? Do transitions explain the relationship between various points and guide readers more explicitly from point to point?
- *Look at the evidence given as support for the argument.* The argument will be stronger if readers can see the argument's truth for themselves. Has the author sufficiently developed the supporting arguments, using specific details, so that you can visualize for yourself his or her point? Is the support that is given relevant to the overall thesis? Are there holes or weaknesses that leave you confused as to how the author came to his or her conclusion? Is more evidence or explanation needed to make the argument clearer or more compelling?

- *Look at the conclusion.* By the conclusion, has the thesis been effectively developed? Does its truth now seem self-evident? How does the author leave you? Does he or she provide closure? Does the author connect with readers in the conclusion? Does the conclusion encourage you to continue thinking about the subject beyond the author's thesis?

As you learned in the previous section, writing can help us think through our ideas about a piece of writing. The same is true for readers; they can use the writing of comments to you to clarify their feedback. At the same time, readers should not stop with writing a response. They should also talk with the writer. Talking, as another form of brainstorming, will help both reader and writer to discover new ideas that could help the writer revise.

Once you've gotten responses from your various readers, bring them together in your writer's notebook by summarizing them. What were the most common concerns? What aspects of the draft did they most like or dislike? Did their paraphrases of your thesis match what you intended? Summarizing their comments can help you internalize your readers' views. You can now use their insights and advice to help you revise.

Revising: Reshaping Your Work

Revising Jefferson's Declaration

From July 2–4, the Congress debated Jefferson's draft and made a large number of changes. Some were stylistic; for instance, they changed "We hold these truths to be sacred and undeniable" to the now-familiar and resonant "We hold these truths to be self-evident." Such revisions resulted in a smoother, more polished draft.

Two large changes were made to Jefferson's content. After the "He has" phrases in the body of the document, Jefferson had directed a paragraph toward the English people, the "British brethren," criticizing them for not supporting the colonies. Congress softened that paragraph substantially, not wanting to incur the wrath of the Britons, many of whom were relatives and friends.

Jefferson also included, as the last of the "He has" phrases, a sharp indictment of George III for waging "cruel war against human nature itself"—that is, for permitting the slave trade. A slave owner himself, Jefferson was highly ambivalent about the institution of slavery and wanted to phase it out. However, purely in terms of argumentation, George III was not to blame for the colonies' use of slaves; many of the colonies were still willingly participating in and/or benefiting from the slave trade. Therefore, the paragraph did not fit Jefferson's thesis. It is often the case that a writer must relinquish a cherished idea or statement because it does not fit smoothly into the thesis of the essay. (Of course, the Continental Congress also deleted the paragraph because they knew not all the colonies would agree to sign the Declaration if they would have to give up slavery. Congress needed everyone to sign for the former colonies to become the *United* States.)

Throughout this revision process you have looked inward to your increasingly clear sense of what you want to say and how you want to say it and outward to your readers' advice. Now you can take your insights and their advice and reshape your essay with a heightened sense of *audience*. Student writers often find the idea of shaping their work for a specific audience to be at best a hassle and at worst a censoring of their own expression. However, there's an important distinction to make between changing your *content* for readers—having controversial stances suppressed or being coerced into saying the same thing everyone else is saying—and revising your *form*, in which your stance becomes more firmly and clearly communicated as a result of making your thesis more straightforward and precise, reordering paragraphs, or clarifying sentence structure. The latter, not the former, is what instructors are almost always requesting when they ask for revision.

Reshaping with readers in mind reminds us that writing is an ethical as well as an intellectual act. Revising gives us a chance to pay close attention to being clear, engaging, and honest at each point of the essay, from its introduction through its conclusion. For instance, the thesis is a promise or commitment you make to your readers. You give your word that, over the course of your essay, you will *show* the truth of your thesis to your readers; it is assumed, then, that your thesis should require demonstration. Your readers will find your thesis more effective and interesting if they can learn from it and if there is room for disagreement and discussion, as opposed to a thesis that presents a fact that does not need proving, an obvious statement, or a merely subjective judgment.

Although it is conventional in academic essays to announce the thesis at the end of the introductory paragraph, you can also do so in a separate introductory paragraph, as a turning point in the middle of your essay, or as a revelation at the end of your essay. Consider where your readers will need that information most and where they will respond to it best. Wherever you place your thesis, however, it is an ending of sorts: it is what you have resolved (however tentatively) about your argument. The rest of the essay serves as a space for you to show the readers how you came to that resolution.

As you revise the body of the essay, particularize your argument by adding details and qualifying your points. When you come to claims, ask whether they are *really* and *always* true, or whether they are *somewhat* and *sometimes* true. If they are only true under certain circumstances, then admit that, and name the circumstances. This process will make you a subtle, more generous thinker and communicator as well as a better, more precise writer.

Of course, making these decisions is generally much easier if we know who our readers are. Our understanding of the audience's needs and expectations is often intuitive—we make reasonable guesses as to what will best teach them, inspire them, or persuade them. Nevertheless, we should consciously attend in the revision process to how much we think our audience knows or cares about our subject, where the common ground is between us and them, and what values or beliefs we share with them that we can draw upon in addressing them.

Crafting: The Later Stage of Writing

Writing is a recursive process; this means that you continually return to the beginning of the piece and work through the stages of the process again, each time tightening your focus and adding the knowledge you have gained from your last time through the process. At the crafting stage you are ready to adopt the mindset of an artisan, looking to the sentences and words themselves—the style, precision, and grace of your language. The care you give these items reveals the seriousness and professionalism of your work.

At this crafting stage, think first of editing for clarity, style, and grace of expression, and then proofreading for correctness. Grammar is more an aid to communication than a series of hard and fast rules that indicate whether or not an essay is "correct." This stage is when your writing handbook will be of most use to you. Now that you've got a deepened draft, your writing handbook will help you shape and refine it because it provides advice on improving your style of expression as well as instruction on correct usage of grammar, punctuation, and mechanics. Work closely with it and look things up as you have questions.

Editing

Although you may think that editing means skimming an essay to catch grammar or spelling mistakes, you should see it as an opportunity to further refine your thinking by reflecting carefully on the words and sentences that convey that thinking. At this stage, writers can focus on the clarity, grace, and style of their expression. They can check whether their words are clear and precise. They can check whether their sentences are varied in length, reach an appropriate level of complexity for readers, and emphasize the more important information. They can also make sure their tone and diction, or word choice, communicate effectively with a desired audience. Some of these qualities, such as clarity and precision, are essential to all good writing; other qualities, such as tone, will vary with different purposes and readers.

The following strategies instruct you on editing your own work, taking you step by step through different editing tasks.

- Repeating the same sentence structure and length can make writing sound choppy. Read your sentence aloud to see if your writing is falling into such a pattern.
- Look in the style section of your writing handbook for advice on sentence structure and variety. Experiment with combining sentences or varying the structure of sentences both to convey your thoughts precisely and to engage readers.
- Check to see that your title accurately conveys the focus of your essay and will attract your readers' interest.
- Rewrite the introduction to reflect what you discovered while drafting (rather than what you first thought you would write about). Lead readers methodically into the essay, and, in many cases, into your thesis.
- Rewrite the last sentences of your conclusion so that you lead readers out of your essay clearly and powerfully.

- When you are working with source materials, read carefully to make sure all of your quotations and paraphrases are accurate, and that you have cited all of the sources you have used and have provided precise page numbers or URLs for Web pages. Also make sure that you've documented all sources fully according to the style manual that's been assigned, e.g., MLA or APA. (See Chapter Five for more information on using quotations and citing and documenting sources.)

Proofreading for Correctness

Proofreading is the final step in preparing your writing for submission. It is the time at which you polish your text and ready it for presentation. This involves correcting the grammar, punctuation, and mechanics, and formatting the essay according to your audience's expectations. This stage should not be hurried through because even minor matters such as uncorrected typos and apostrophe errors indicate carelessness and can affect how seriously readers take your ideas.

- Read through carefully and correct typos. Watch for missing words and word errors that the spell checker program doesn't catch because the words are not misspelled (such as *where* and *were*, or *woman* and *women*), and words that were left out. Reading aloud will help you catch these errors.
- Read for common grammatical errors such as run-on sentences, comma splices, or sentence fragments. Double check that each sentence you split in half while editing doesn't get left as a sentence and a sentence fragment and that the words you bracketed to come back to later don't remain bracketed.
- Read for mechanical errors involving usage of commas, semicolons, and apostrophes. Pay particular attention to the correct use of apostrophes to indicate possession (e.g., the dog's bone or the dogs' bone), and the incorrect use of apostrophes with plural nouns (e.g., the dog's ran down the street together). If you are unsure of what to do in a particular situation, consult your handbook for an example.
- Correct uses of commonly confused words, such as it's/its, your/you're, there/their/they're, to/too/two; as well as effect vs. affect, and conscious vs. conscience.
- Correct uses of common misspellings or misunderstandings of words, such as "could of" for "could've," the contraction of "could have."
- Overall, know your own weak points and check for them. What aspects of grammar or mechanics have you consistently been corrected on or consistently been confused about? Consult your handbook, instructor, or a writing center tutor for guidance.
- Ready the presentation of the text for submission. Double check your format. How are you to do the page numbering, heading, title, margins, font size, and such?
- Ready the whole package for submission. Are you supposed to include earlier drafts or other work with it? Are you supposed to submit the essay in a folder? Are you supposed to staple the pages together, or to use a paper clip?

FINAL INQUIRY: CRITICAL LITERACY AND CITIZENSHIP

> ### The Critical Compromise of the Declaration of Independence
> Representatives of the American colonies struggled to decide on the details of the Declaration of Independence. Jefferson especially could not understand why Congress could keep slavery to preserve the colonies' "greater good": their union. Historians have argued that we could just as easily have had a smaller version of the Civil War at this time, and indeed the founders were planting the seeds of that war in this critical compromise. Susan B. Anthony and the Black Panthers show in their critiques (printed in Chapter Four) that all the universal goods and rights proclaimed in the Declaration were not being experienced by many Americans.

This final inquiry encourages you to practice critical thinking, reading, and writing in an environment of democratic collaboration. Many situations today require us to compose and revise documents with others; nearly all governmental, institutional, educational, and business work includes some collaborative writing. Working with other writers can be hard on egos, and, significantly, hard on ideals. We all need to learn when and how to negotiate and compromise, and when and how to concede smaller points to win larger ones.

As an exercise in democratic collaboration, you might discuss whether the country needs to officially apologize for the past enslavement of African Americans. In recent years, American leaders have issued apologies and offered reparations for the country's past human rights violations. In 1988, Ronald Reagan formally apologized to Japanese Americans for their internment in U.S. prison camps during World War II, offering $20,000 to each Japanese American who had been interred. In 1993, the U.S. Congress officially apologized to native Hawaiians for overthrowing the Kingdom of Hawaii. In 1997, Bill Clinton apologized to survivors of the Tuskegee syphilis experiment, offering $10 million to the surviving victims and their families. In 2000, Kevin Gover, Assistant Secretary–Indian Affairs, Department of the Interior, apologized for the agency's history of inhumane treatment of Native Americans. In the same year, Ohio Democrat Tony Hall introduced a resolution calling for the U.S. government to apologize for the slavery of African Americans. In the following exercise, discuss whether we need an official, written apology for slavery and whether we need to offer reparations for it.

1. Divide into several small groups of about 4–5 people each. Discuss whether we should have an official, written apology for the history of slavery in the United States; and, furthermore, if we should make reparations to African Americans for the years of slavery.
   a. If you decide the United States should apologize, draft the apology (just one good paragraph will do for this assignment) and a plan for any reparations, along with your reasons justifying it.
   b. If you decide the country should not apologize, write a memo (again, a paragraph is fine) stating why there should be no official apology or reparations, along with your reasoning justifying it.

2. Each group then reads its document aloud and passes around a written copy of it. Then, the entire class can debate these documents and collaborate on drafting one good paragraph that communicates the class's opinion whether there should be an official apology, and if so, what it should look like, and if not, why not.

In nearly every case, members of the class will express a number of opinions—not just for or against opinions, but a full spectrum of nuanced responses. For example, some may want an apology but no reparations; others may want reparations but only a certain amount. Your task is to give everyone a chance to air their views and to find a way to incorporate as many views as possible, into the final document. Afterward, reflect on the process of writing collaboratively. What worked well? What was particularly difficult? Did anything new arise as a result of working collaboratively?

QUESTIONS FOR INQUIRY AND ACTION

1. Reflect in your notebook on the work you've done over the course of this chapter. Have you sensed yourself becoming a more critical thinker? How might your thinking, reading, and writing critically help you to develop an examined life?

2. Do you think that all people read in the same way? How might our different experiences affect the ways we read a text? For instance, do women read differently from men? You might begin your inquiry with Jonathan Culler in "Reading as a Woman" and Pat Schweikert in "Reading Ourselves." (See the bibliography for where to find these essays.)

3. Why are you in college? What does "higher education" mean to you?

4. What connections are there are between liberty and education?

5. What is the relevance of the Declaration of Independence today? Does it still speak to us individually and as a nation? If so, how? If not, how and why not?

6. Citizens composed the United States, in part, through writing: the Declaration of Independence and the Constitution provided cohesion for the colonies. Do we still construct our national identity through writing today? If so, how? What pieces of writing have helped to shape American identity? If we no longer construct our national identity through writing, why do we not? How do we construct our identity then, if not through writing?

7. What kind of world are we constructing through our writing? What values would you like to see our country (or some other community) develop? How, realistically, can you help in the construction?

CHAPTER 3

Researching: Inquiry as Action

For apart from inquiry, apart from the praxis [practice or action], individuals cannot be truly human. Knowledge emerges only through invention and re-invention, through the restless, impatient, continuing, hopeful inquiry human beings pursue in the world, and with each other.

Paulo Freire, Pedagogy of the Oppressed

GETTING STARTED: Inquiring in Our Communities

In Plato's *Republic*, the character Socrates reminds his companions that one question lies at the heart of their discussion of justice and the ideal society: "How should one live?" This introductory section asks you to begin to answer Socrates's question. The question is practical (e.g., "What career should I choose?") and ethical (e.g., "Should I become a vegetarian?"). It is also private (e.g., "Should I cheat on tests?") and public (e.g., "Should my country intercede in the wars of other countries?"). As you explore the full range of this question use each of these four methods of inquiry:

- *Think.* Take some time to reflect on the question. You might take a walk, stare out the window, or shoot hoops as you think.
- *Talk.* Discuss the question with two other people—e.g., your friends, minister, parents, teachers, or people you see each day on the bus.
- *Write.* In your notebook, record your experiences thinking and talking with others. Then, expand your thoughts using the invention strategies you learned in Chapter Two, such as freewriting and Mind Mapping.
- *Read.* Seek answers to the question from books, magazines, newspapers, Web sites, billboards, bumper stickers, t-shirts—from any printed source.

After you've tried these different methods of inquiry, discuss your discoveries with your classmates. Then, discuss your experiences with the different methods. Try using the following questions to guide your discussion:

1. Did the different methods of inquiry provoke different answers to the question? If so, in what ways?
2. Which methods of inquiry gave you the most insight? Why?
3. Which methods of inquiry were the most enjoyable to pursue? Why?

When students in our classes discussed how it felt to work with various methods of inquiry, they expressed different preferences:

- Some students preferred *talking* because they connected with others while they learned. One student related the insights of his great uncle who had fought in World War II and had discussed the war with former president Harry Truman. The student's conversations with his great uncle helped him understand why his uncle had been willing to fight in the war.
- Some students preferred *reading* because they could explore the question at their leisure, without having to respond to someone else's statements. One student actually read Plato's *Republic* after learning of the assignment; he extracted several thoughtful quotes, which he shared with the class.
- Some students found *writing* most useful because they could build on the ideas they had in front of them. One student created her own personal code, a list of core beliefs she could refer to whenever she wanted to know how she ought to live.

In each of these instances, students found themselves more engaged in the process of inquiry when they could draw from a variety of research methods. They also found new opportunities to connect with others both in doing their research and in sharing their results. As Brazilian educator Paulo Freire says in the opening quotation, inquiry is an essential part of being human. When we reflect on the events, people, and issues surrounding us, we shape our sense of the world, defining who we are as members of different communities. In this sense inquiry is also a form of social action, the action of an examining citizen. By getting us to talk with other people and read other people's thoughts, inquiry connects us with citizens who are conducting searches of their own.

Inquiry, in other words, is not just for research papers. Inquiry, or research, is a natural response to the questions that come up in our lives. We research when figuring out which school to attend, what scholarships to apply for, what buses to take, and what stereo to buy. Even when we are not focused on some specific task, we research to enrich our lives. We research to understand the natural world, to express our spirituality, or to give meaning to the experiences in our lives. Researching, then, is a process of discovery that helps us understand a situation, a text, or a person more clearly and fully. In short, researching is a way of thinking through issues, of examining life, and of connecting with others.

You have already been researching in your work with this book. In Chapter One you worked through methods of inquiry in order to develop answers to your questions about the meanings of citizenship: you consulted reference works, examined legal and historical documents, and read narratives of people's lived experiences. The methodical process you followed and the variety of sources you consulted allowed you to gradually deepen your understanding of citizenship. You discovered that our citizenship extends far beyond our basic duties of voting, paying taxes, and obeying laws. It extends to living an examined life. In Chapter Two, you experienced what it means to live an examined life when you worked critically through ethical dilemmas, read and responded to others' words, and created a process for yourself that should enable you to enter any writing situation with confidence. Essential to this examining process is the writer's notebook, which gives you a space in which you can ask and explore the questions that most perplex and fascinate you.

Developing an inquiring mindset and learning how to ask the questions that inspire innovation and unlock mysteries are critical to academic success and to advancement in our world. This chapter uses questions to lead us into examining life more rigorously and systematically. It takes our natural curiosity, our inborn inclination to inquire, and gives it greater structure and discipline by introducing new methods for inquiring and by making those methods we already know more sophisticated. Throughout the chapter, Socrates's fundamental question, "How should one live?" will guide us through a series of methods of inquiry. These methods will help us to test, complicate, and thereby deepen the research questions we ask, the answers we discover, and the actions we take in the world.

FIRST INQUIRY: WRITING TO INQUIRE AND CONVERSE WITH OTHERS

We write to think through our answers to questions such as those in the Getting Started section. The starting point for all inquiries is ourselves. We begin with our curiosity and concern, our experiences and prior knowledge, and we write to examine those and ascertain what our thoughts and feelings are. When we begin an inquiry and write about our own views, it may feel as if we are acting entirely on our own. However, we are actually responding to things we have read and experienced. Thus, our process takes us from ourselves to reading and talking with others in order to widen our inquiry and broaden our knowledge.

Other writers ponder the same questions we do. When we read and respond to their works, we create conversations. As in face-to-face conversations, we join our thoughts with others' and seek to advance knowledge on a particular subject. Writers converse over time and across cultures, interacting with people they will never meet but who explore the same ideas and contribute to the same discussions. As active inquirers we have an ethical obligation to search out other people's discoveries, and to acknowledge the contributions they've made to our thinking. We converse with other writers not only because we want to be thorough and conscientious researchers and because we can benefit from their insights, but because they are fellow human beings calling out to us through their writing.

The nineteenth-century American writer Henry David Thoreau provides a good example of someone who asked how one should live; his answers still call out to us for response. Thoreau used his notebooks to think, he read the works of other thinkers, he talked with others in his community, and he acted upon his ideas for how one should best live life. In late March of 1845, Thoreau left his home in Concord, Massachusetts and moved to a wooded area near Walden Pond. The land was owned by his friend Ralph Waldo Emerson, the famous writer and public intellectual. Thoreau used his time at Walden Pond to continue reading and to test the tentative answers he had gained from his conversations. He recorded and reflected upon his experiences in his journals; some of this material he revised into his book *Walden*. Read the following short excerpts from the book, and compare Thoreau's thoughts with the answers you generated for the Getting Started section on how one should live.

> I went to the woods because I wished to live deliberately, to front only the essential facts of life, and see if I could not learn what it had to teach, and not, when I came to die, discover that I had not lived. I did not wish to live what was not life, living is so dear; nor did I wish to practise resignation, unless it was quite necessary. I wanted to live deep and suck out all the marrow of life, to live so sturdily and Spartan-like as to put to rout all that was not life, to cut a broad swath and shave close, to drive life into a corner, and reduce it to its lowest terms, and, if it proved to be mean, why then to get the whole and genuine meanness of it, and publish its meanness to the world; or if it were sublime, to know it by experience, and be able to give a true account of it in my next excursion. For most men, it appears to me, are in a strange uncertainty about it, whether it is of the devil or of God, and have somewhat hastily concluded that it is the chief end of man here to "glorify God and enjoy him forever."

> No method nor discipline can supersede the necessity of being forever on the alert. What is a course of history or philosophy, or poetry, no matter how well selected, or the best society, or the most admirable routine of life, compared with the discipline of looking always at what is to be seen? Will you be a reader, a student merely, or a seer? Read your fate, see what is before you, and walk on into futurity.
>
> I did not read books the first summer; I hoed beans. Nay, I often did better than this. There were times when I could not afford to sacrifice the bloom of the present moment to any work, whether of the head or hands. I love a broad margin to my life. Sometimes, in a summer morning, having taken my accustomed bath, I sat in my sunny doorway from sunrise till noon, rapt in a reverie, amidst the pines and hickories and sumachs, in undisturbed solitude and stillness, while the birds sing around or flitted noiseless through the house,

until by the sun falling in at my west window, or the noise of some traveller's wagon on the distant highway, I was reminded of the lapse of time. I grew in those seasons like corn in the night, and they were far better than any work of the hands would have been. They were not time subtracted from my life, but so much over and above my usual allowance. I realized what the Orientals mean by contemplation and the forsaking of works. For the most part, I minded not how the hours went. The day advanced as if to light some work of mine; it was morning, and lo, now it is evening, and nothing memorable is accomplished. Instead of singing like the birds, I silently smiled at my incessant good fortune. As the sparrow had its trill, sitting on the hickory before my door, so had I my chuckle or suppressed warble which he might hear out of my nest. My days were not days of the week, bearing the stamp of any heathen deity, nor were they minced into hours and fretted by the ticking of a clock; for I lived like the Puri Indians, of whom it is said that "for yesterday, today, and tomorrow they have only one word, and they express the variety of meaning by pointing backward for yesterday forward for tomorrow, and overhead for the passing day." This was sheer idleness to my fellow-townsmen, no doubt; but if the birds and flowers had tried me by their standard, I should not have been found wanting. A man must find his occasions in himself, it is true. The natural day is very calm, and will hardly reprove his indolence.

One young man of my acquaintance, who has inherited some acres, told me that he thought he should live as I did, *if he had the means*. I would not have any one adopt *my* mode of living on any account; for, besides that before he has fairly learned it I may have found out another for myself, I desire that there may be as many different persons in the world as possible; but I would have each one be very careful to find out and pursue *his own* way, and not his father's or his mother's or his neighbor's instead.

Thoreau's words have become part of the ongoing conversation about how we should live our lives that has taken place over centuries and in many different forms, or *genres*, of writing. Plato tackled the question by constructing a philosophical dialogue in which the main character, Socrates, questioned the other characters, examined their answers, and provoked them to refine their thinking. Thoreau responded with *Walden*, a series of autobiographical essays filled with close observations of nature, descriptions of everyday life, and candid commentary. Many writers have been moved to respond to Thoreau's words, and they have done so in different genres—that is, not just in essays.

Different genres, like poetry, short stories, sermons, or plays allow us to explore a subject and express our views in unique ways. For instance, during the Vietnam War and the protests against it, the playwrights Jerome Lawrence and Robert E. Lee joined the larger conversation, responding directly to Thoreau's ideas about civil disobedience with their play, *The Night Thoreau Spent in Jail* (1970). At its center is the story of how Thoreau, while living at Walden Pond, refused to pay his poll tax. He didn't want to contribute money to a government that supported slavery and, later, the Mexican-American War. He was arrested and thrown in jail for a night (a friend then bailed him out). This experience inspired Thoreau's most famous essay, "Civil Disobedience" (which we excerpt in Chapter Six), and that essay inspired Lawrence and Lee to dramatize the thoughts of its writer.

In your class, act out or read aloud the following scene from the play, in which Thoreau (Henry) is in conversation with his mentor, Ralph Waldo Emerson (Waldo), and is trying to make Emerson stand up for what he believes. Within the play, they debate the question of how one should live, whether to live purely according to one's ideals away from the common society, as Thoreau does, or to live within the society and slowly, imperfectly work toward improving it, as Emerson does. As you read the scene, note how Thoreau's ideas and Socrates's original question get developed, refined, or changed by the form of this modern play.

> **Henry:** Listen to me. . . . Can you lie in bed every morning? Have your breakfast brought to you—your soft-boiled egg, your toast and tea? Can you lift your right hand to your mouth while your left hand—which is also you—your government—is killing men in Mexico? How can you swallow, Waldo? How can you taste? How can you breathe? You cast your ballot with your right hand—but has your left hand killed Henry Williams, running to be free! [Williams was a fugitive slave whom Thoreau befriended; in the play they had just heard of his assassination.]
>
> **Waldo:** Because I don't rant like Jeremiah, do you think I'm not outraged? I do what *can* be done!
>
> **Henry:** That's not enough. Do the impossible. That's what you tell people in your lectures. But you don't really believe any of it, do you? You trundle up and down New England, stepping to the lectern with that beneficent smile, accepting the handshake of mayors and the polite applause of little old ladies. You go on singing your spineless benedictions.
>
> **Waldo:** What I say is not spineless!
>
> **Henry:** Well, occasionally you've sounded a battle-cry. But you—you yourself—refuse to hear it.
>
> **Waldo:** You are a very difficult man!
>
> **Henry:** Good. The world is too full of *easy* men.
>
> **Waldo:** Do you want me to go out and advocate violence and rebellion?
>
> **Henry:** I ask you to *stop* violence. As for rebellion, do you think this country was hatched from a soft-boiled egg???
>
> *(Gesturing.)* Look around Concord; what do you see? We have *become* everything we protested against!
>
> **Waldo:** And what are you doing about it, young man? You pull the woods up over your head. You resign from the human race. Could your woodchucks, with all their wisdom, have saved Henry Williams? Are your fish going to build roads, teach school, put out fires?

(For a moment, Henry is caught without a ready reply.) Oh, it's very simple
for a hermit to sit off at a distance and proclaim exactly how things should
be. But what if everybody did that? Where would we be?

Henry: Where *are* we, Waldo?

Waldo: We are at war. I am aware of it.

Henry: Are you aware of the reasons—slave-holders grasping for more slave territory? *More* slavery and less freedom, is that what you want?

Waldo: Henry, we must work within the framework of our laws. The end to
this war—the condition of the blacks—this is the business of the President.
And the Congress.

Henry: Do you really believe that? Then I guess I'm wrong. I thought you had
the same disgust that I have for what the military is doing. But if it doesn't
trouble you, then I must've made a mistake.

(With acid sarcasm.) You're right to keep still. I'll go back to the woods—and
leave you at peace with your war.

(Waldo is in genuine pain.)

Waldo: *(After a pause.)* All right, my young conscience. What shall I do?

Henry: Declare yourself!

Waldo: *(After another pause.)* I will. Absolutely. The next time the occasion
arises—

Henry: *(Fiercely.)* NOW! A year ago was too late! I'll get you an audience. This
afternoon. At Concord Square!

(Runs offstage.)

Many writers have been moved to respond to Thoreau's thoughts through
poetry, as well. The Thoreau Reader Web site has collected "Poetry on Henry:
Poems about or inspired by Thoreau" <http://eserver.org/thoreau/poetry.html>.
One of the poets published there is Amy Belding Brown, who has written a lot
of "Thoreauvian Poetry," as she refers to it, on her Web page <http://www.psy-
mon.com/walden/amy/index.html>. This one, "Thinking About Thoreau," from
January 26, 2000, connects directly to his experiences as described in *Walden*.
Read it aloud in your class; notice similarities and differences between the fig-
ure of Thoreau presented in the excerpts from *Walden* and *The Night Thoreau
Spent in Jail.*

Thinking About Thoreau

Tending his bean plants
by the pond,
tracking the waywardness
of lichens,
5   measuring the crystal concentration

of spring ice—
he tries so hard to pay
attention,
but his mind is always
10   leaping off
in new directions, as if
the whole point
is to cross life's river of confusion
on the stones
15   of metaphor—though careful observation
will reveal
he never seems entirely sure he
wants to go.

Discuss the excerpt from *Walden*, the scene, and the poem with your class. Did you respond differently to the voice and ideas of Thoreau as presented in the three works? If so, what it is that made you respond differently? Reading conversations that take shape in different genres can teach us that there are many ways to inquire into the same subject. For instance, when we discussed the play in class, we noticed:

- Dramas advance through dialogue, which allows us to imagine Emerson and Thoreau talking to one another, to put ourselves in their shoes and continue their debate.
- Dramas center on conflict, and dramatize it—that is, they exaggerate differences, but, because there is no narrator directing our view and commenting on the situation, a play can often present both sides of an argument vividly and get the audience to consider more than one perspective at once.

When we discussed the poem, on the other hand, we noticed:

- Poetry is often more introspective. Because it presents its situation in concentrated language, often with the use of imagery or other figurative language, it asks us to imagine, to re-create the situation in our minds, and to reflect upon it. The verse form tends to slow our reading and to cause us to observe details more closely.
- Poetry tends to transform the ordinary and to ask us to look at everyday events or people in fresh ways. We can take Thoreau's descriptions of his day and imagine ourselves walking with him, as him, and convey the experience of seeing the world with such wonder.

What if you wrote a stand-up comedy sketch about Thoreau—or *as* Thoreau? Or what if you performed a Thoreauvian rap? Or drew a cartoon of Thoreau at home on Walden Pond? How might each of those forms allow you to explore something different about Thoreau and to express your own thoughts differently?

The following exercise asks you to deepen your response to Thoreau, and to the original question on how one should live, by writing in different forms.

Respond to Thoreau's words, as Lawrence and Lee and Brown did, in any form that is appropriate for what you want to say. The point of this exercise is not so much that you compose a polished piece of writing, but that you reflect on yourself as an inquirer when you write. Notice how the path of your inquiry is directed by the form, or genre, you choose. What aspects of the question does one genre allow you to explore that another does not? How does the form challenge and hone your thinking?

EXERCISE 3.1 Joining the Conversation

1. Write a short reflection upon the excerpts from *Walden* in which you respond to Thoreau's views on how one should live. What form feels like a natural way for you to respond? A poem? A lab report? A business memo? A song? A stand-up comedy sketch? A journal in Thoreau's own style?

2. After your class has drafted responses, compare your experiences of writing in different genres. How does writing in a particular genre change the nature of your inquiry?

3. Read the reflections aloud and notice how you respond to others' choice of genre and style. How does our status or position change when we write in different styles? Do we tend to respect the inquiries of one genre and writer more than we do another? Do some seem more serious than others, for example?

With your class, reflect on how this writing has helped you to inquire. Writing itself is a method of inquiry, since it dislodges thoughts; and writing in different forms, with different constraints and conventions, focuses our questions and shapes the direction and expression of our thoughts, so that as a result of the writing, we know more than when we began. However, it is not so much that we end with answers. On the contrary, we are probably left with more questions, and with a desire to inquire further.

Where would you go next, what would you do next, to deepen and develop the line of inquiry you have begun? Would you build a cabin in the woods? Read Plato? The second inquiry of this chapter encourages you to develop a plan. All inquiries that are methodical or disciplined need more formal and comprehensive planning, and even casual searches can benefit from a quick sketch that provides direction. Nearly all writers, from scholars to poets, agree that you will aid your creativity by planning the process of your projects. The planning process is not only a matter of efficiency and thoroughness; it is an intellectual process. It makes us think through the course of action and refine our questions before we even begin consulting resources. It helps us focus our thinking and consider creative and alternative ways of finding information so that we are not limited to the most obvious sources.

SECOND INQUIRY: DEVELOPING A RESEARCH PLAN

It may not have seemed, upon first reading, that Thoreau had a particular plan or even that he was conducting research at all, since he did not adhere to traditional academic research paper format in building his argument in *Walden*. Yet he went into the woods with philosophical and practical goals in mind—to build a cabin and live as naturally and independently as possible—and his conclusions stem from extensive reading and from his field research, which included taking meticulous notes on his observations and experiments. His researching process, with discoveries, expenditures, thoughts, is recorded in his notebook. *Walden* reflects his initial questions that inspired him to live outside the mainstream society, how he thought he would find what he was seeking out at Walden Pond, how he planned this experiment in living, and how he changed and refined it as he made discoveries.

The plans for your inquiries may be more or less involved than Thoreau's. All research plans, though, help writers visualize what kind of research they want to do, how they want to do it, and where they will go for information. For example, if we go back to the Getting Started question, "How should one live?," what related questions does it raise for you? What did it make you curious to know more about? The first step for the plan is to focus your larger question into one that interests you in particular. For instance, a few types of questions that might come out of reading Thoreau could include:

- Should we get rid of all our possessions and build a cabin in the woods?
- Should I quit college and educate myself?
- Should we reject the influence of the fashion industry by becoming nudists?

The question should be a true expression of your curiosity. Do not worry yet about having to phrase it in the form it would take as your "research question" in an academic research paper. If you are working on such a project, you can refine and revise the question later, as you discover the direction in which your project is going. Begin with what intrigues you most—with what you really want to know—and leave yourself open to finding things you might not have considered otherwise.

What kind of research do you want to do? Define what kind of search this will be. For example, Neil Postman, a professor of communications at New York University, makes an important distinction among a search primarily for information, one for knowledge, and one for wisdom. Sometimes, when your issue is not well-known to your readers, you will want first to gather information and let others know about it—a sort of fact-finding mission. Perhaps you want to inform readers about the range of Thoreau-reading nudist colonies that are springing up around the country. At other times, when an issue is discussed but is not well understood, or needs to be looked at more closely and carefully, you will want to use your inquiry to create new knowledge—to sort through information, analyze a situation, and explain it. Maybe perceptions of nudist colonies have been skewed and we need to investigate what draws people to them. At still other times, especially when it seems that a situation has been misunderstood and people are acting thoughtlessly, you will want to find the wisdom in a situation—to assess and judge it and advise others on courses of action. It may be that living in nudist colonies is the way to undermine a consumer culture that puts so much stock on the clothes people wear that their minds and hearts are ignored. In some projects, of course, you'll want to do all of this. In our so-called information age, too often the "news" or "knowledge" we are presented with is nothing more than unexamined information, and we have to learn how to interpret and understand it. In rigorous and ethical inquiry, we examine the sources and contexts of information and seek to generate knowledge and, even more, wisdom from it. This inquiry is always grounded in the context of our examined life, in what concerns us.

How do you want to conduct your research? This is a question about methodology. Your methods will need to match your goals and questions. Do you think your best answers will come from *quantitative* research (that is, answers that can be expressed in terms of quantity, or numbers, such as statistics), or from *qualitative* research (that is, answers that can be expressed in terms of their qualities, or individual characteristics, such as narratives of people's experiences)? Do you want to focus on reading textual sources from electronic or print media? Do you want to search in historical archives? Or to interview people and get their opinions on a subject? Or to build a cabin in the woods and plant a garden?

Where will you go for information? Where, physically, should you search for information? Some projects may start and end in the college library, but others will need you to research in other places and ways. Consider where the conversations around your questions take place, both in terms of the settings of such conversations—e.g., your hometown city council meetings, sports bars, an Internet chat room—and the general contexts for such conversations—e.g., formal religious debates, teenagers' casual conversations, cyberspace. When you answer those questions, determine where you might go to educate yourself. What kinds of sources would probably be most useful and reliable? Try the following exercise to help you focus your question and frame your inquiry.

EXERCISE 3.2   Developing a Research Plan

1. In your writer's notebook, write down what you already know about your subject, and list any questions you would like to have answered. Choose a question that you like and feel capable of answering. Freewrite on why the question concerns you, why you're obsessing about it, how it affects you or others you care about. What experience do you have with the questions that you could draw upon?

2. What kind of inquiry will this primarily be? A search for information, knowledge, or wisdom? Why? If it is a combination of kinds, which will need to predominate, and why?

3. How do you want to conduct your research? Will it be mostly quantitative or qualitative? What kind of material will you need to find, and how will you keep track of it?

4. In what settings and contexts does your question get explored? Where are you most likely to find information that will help you examine and explore this question and begin to develop some answers to it?

All of this planning helps you to frame your inquiry. With your plan in hand, you can begin what is generally thought of as the inquiry itself: the search for those sources that can help you answer your questions and support your views. You will probably feel more creative and confident when you have a variety of ways to conduct your research, and you know how to select the best one(s) for your needs, as well as knowing a range of strategies for inquiring effectively and ethically. The third inquiry introduces you to basic research methods that will help you to generate and test answers to your questions. While we have arranged them in order from electronic and printed textual sources to out-in-the-field sources, this is not necessarily the order you will follow for all your inquiries; for example, in some cases library research will follow experimentation or field research rather than precede it.

THIRD INQUIRY: INQUIRING EFFECTIVELY USING RESEARCH METHODS

When we research we have a number of methods available to use, each of which will be most useful in particular circumstances and communities. We need to become familiar with a range of methods, when to use them, and how to use them rigorously and ethically. This means we want to research in a way that uncovers information thoroughly and accurately, and that builds alliances rather than excludes others or robs them of their dignity, their confidence, or their knowledge. To do this conscientiously we need to learn the conventions of inquiry for particular communities and situations. In this next section, we present each of the most basic research methods. We also discuss under what circumstances we might choose that method, and we offer strategies students have discovered to use that method effectively. Finally, we invite you to experiment with the method and discuss its merits and challenges with your classmates.

Becoming Information Literate: Researching Electronic, Print, and Broadcast Media

We often think of the intellectual work of researching as simply the reading of the information we find. However, a large part of the intellectual work of researching lies in the actual searching itself; the sheer abundance of information in our age demands that we become information literate. We must learn the skills needed to find material pertinent to our needs and discern what will hold value for our inquiries. *Information literacy* is the new term used to describe how our perspectives on and practices of researching have changed. Researching is a much wider field of endeavor than it used to be. We now need to be conversant with new forms of technology and in using electronic sources as well as traditional print resources. But this is not just a matter of knowing how to operate the latest machines or software programs. Some principles of information literacy include:

- Knowing how to find and use the latest electronic sources
- Knowing how to interpret and skeptically evaluate sources, including statistics
- Critically reflecting on the social and cultural contexts of information
- Knowing how to publish work of our own using the media channels and technologies available to us

In sum, acquiring information literacy means not just learning a skill, but learning how to access information in a democratic society, how to read critically for yourself, and how to obtain the materials you need to live your life well. One of the ideals of the American Revolution was that people would be able to govern themselves. So that we can advance our knowledge as citizens, we want to take advantage of the resources available to us, and use our freedom responsibly.

Different communities and societies come up with ways to manage and organize their information and make it accessible to others. Today we have the Internet as one of our primary sources for gathering and disseminating information. From our computer terminals we can enter a whole world of information. What we find through that terminal, though, depends upon how well we can access the various storehouses of information. One dimension of becoming information literate is learning to visualize how the various channels of information are entered. For instance, simply searching the general World Wide Web will not bring us to databases of articles and books and many of the materials that will be most useful for our academic studies. For those, we need to enter sites through specific portals. Other materials are only available on subscription-based listservs, or on CD-ROM technology that needs to be accessed from a specific Web site or library.

Computer-based Searching with the World Wide Web

We begin this discussion of basic research methods with those that use your computer to do research. As teachers and library lovers we of course encourage you to work in your library. However, your library's catalog is most likely accessed through the Web, and you will need knowledge of how to use the Web in order to use the catalog. In addition, you can often use your time more efficiently by searching from your computer terminal first, then going to your library with a list of call numbers and specific titles.

Using the World Wide Web for research allows you, from one location, to do a fairly thorough review of the published material on your subject. It is a good method for fast inquiry, too; it is the fastest form of inquiry we have right now. You can find information on just about any topic and you can get up-to-the-minute discoveries, whereas most printed research takes a year or more from writing to publication. Much of what you will find is just surface material, rather than in-depth knowledge. On a subject like Thoreau, for example, you might find news articles about Walden Pond, lists of quotes from Thoreau's works, or an ecology project put together by Mr. Smith's fourth grade science class. Still, you can generally find an overview of your topic almost immediately.

The Internet may also be our most democratic form of information distribution. You can find information from all kinds of sources, professional and credentialed and otherwise, that can give you a wider range of voices than can often be found in print media. Not all of these voices are reliable, however. In addition to the International Thoreau Society, you might find sites by ecoterrorists or complete nuts. For this reason you should examine material you've found on the Web carefully.

How do you find information online? By using a search engine, you can connect to the World Wide Web sites of organizations, institutions, corporations, offices of the government, some listserv and USENET discussions, and individuals' professional and personal sites, among other sources. There are a number of them, e.g., Google, Yahoo, or Lycos. Search engines such as Ask Jeeves let you type in a whole question, for example, "Should we become nudists?" Information sites such as about.com are fine for initial inquiry and for quick overviews on a subject. However, when you're searching for material to use as evidence of conversation on a topic, these are not strong sources because most of the pieces are unsigned. They're the equivalent of an encyclopedia; they can provide general grounding on a subject, but you should move beyond them to get involved in specific discussions.

Searching the Internet is done either by subject-based or keyword-based inquiries. The subject-based searches, on engines such as Yahoo, are best when you do not know yet exactly what you are looking for, but just know the general subject area. You can search through the given categories of subject headings and try to focus your search.

When you know more clearly what your issue or topic is, the most effective method for generating material through Internet search engines is by using keywords. Keywords are the words or phrases used most often when people converse about your topic. Try conducting a search for "nudist colony," for instance; you might find advertisements for vacation spots or seminars, organizations for and against them, crank manifestoes, chat rooms, testimonials on personal Web pages, online journals, porn sites, and a host of other sources, some of which will be useful and others not.

Consider what keywords you'll use before you conduct your search. Write down all the words that come up when you think of that issue, of what concerns you have about it, and/or what interests you most about it. What "key" words or phrases keep coming up? Write down synonyms of your keywords, too; for instance, if you're investigating the benefits of a nudist lifestyle, you could write down both "nudist" and one of its synonyms, "clothing-optional."

Most search systems use the Boolean system of search logic in which placing an AND between keywords will bring up only references with both words, an

OR will bring up references with either word, and a NOT will bring up the references with the first word but not the second, helping you pare away associated topics that you don't want. You can also truncate words by using a question mark or an asterisk, depending upon the specific search engine. Truncating a word indicates that the search engine should pull up all the variations on the word; for example, vot? or vot* will bring up vote, voter, voting, etc. (Some search engines or databases have different rules. For instance, Yahoo uses + and − signs rather than AND and OR. Read the searching tips for each search engine or database; this is often found under labels of "advanced search" or "help").

As you become a skillful researcher you will develop a set of practices that work well for you. If you work online on a home computer, keep track of the best sites for your inquiries by bookmarking them for easy reference. You might also bookmark a collection of reference sites like these so you can reach them quickly:

> The Internet Public Library: <http://www.ipl.org/>
>
> Librarians' Index to the Internet: <http://www.lii.org/>
>
> The Voice of the Shuttle: Web Page for Humanities Research:
>   <http://vos.ucsb.edu/>
>
> The Library of Congress: <http://www.lcweb.loc.gov>
>
> The National Archives and Records Administration: <http://nara.gov>
>
> Merriam-Webster Dictionary: <http://www.m-w.com/>
>
> New Encyclopedia Britannica: <http://www.britannica.com>
>
> Public information research sites: <http://Refdesk.com/> and
>   <http://libraryspot.com/>

EXERCISE 3.3   Using the World Wide Web for Research

1. Choose an issue or topic of interest to you and conduct a search on the World Wide Web, tracing your topic through at least three search engines. Record in your notebook what kinds of material you find in each place, especially the sites found on one search engine but not another.

2. Report back to your class what resources are available on your topic, and from what different kinds of sources. Compare the kinds and quality of material you found. How much of it is substantive and useful?

3. Compare your experiences of inquiring on the Web. What do you like and dislike about it? In what ways is it easy and in what ways is it challenging? In what ways is it enlightening and in what ways is it banal or even offensive?

If you want to discuss a subject in more depth and detail than is often found in public chat rooms, you will probably want to subscribe to a listserv that discusses that subject, whether it is nudist colonies or pinball machines or eighteenth-century literature. And if you want to find articles from newspapers, magazines, or academic journals, you will need to enter a database, which is where most of them are cataloged. Your school's library will most likely subscribe to several databases, and you will probably need to enter the databases through your college's or public library's Web site. Go to their address, and look for a listing of magazine or journal databases.

The various databases contain different kinds of information. For instance, the Lexis-Nexis Academic Universe is one database. It includes abstracts and many full-text articles on a wide range of subjects from general news to legal and political matters, and health and medical information. Through it you can also find online texts of about fifty U.S. newspapers, including campus newspapers; transcripts of many radio and TV programs, especially NPR, PBS, and CNN; Associated Press news stories; Congressional records (voting records, bills on the House and Senate floor, ways to contact members of Congress); legal information; state and country profiles; and biographical information. Other databases include Expanded Academic Index, Newspaper Index, Ethnic Newswatch, Alternative Press Index, and the AP (Associated Press) Photo Archive, just to name a very few. There are also specialized databases for nearly every discipline, such as business, agriculture, literature, psychology, history, physics, physiology, and education. Ask your librarians which databases would be most useful for your inquiry.

Many full-text articles are available through online databases, but they are not the majority, and you don't want to limit yourself to only those articles you can get online. When you find an article of interest to you, you will need to write down the periodical title, volume and/or date, and page numbers, because you will then need to find the title in your library's online catalog. The database won't always tell you whether your library carries the periodical. When you enter your library's catalog online, look up the periodical title (*not* the article title), and note whether the library carries the periodical itself and the specific volume number you need, and, if so, where in the library you can locate it (e.g., in current periodicals, the bound periodicals, or in microforms or CD-ROM). For example, if you wanted to find the article, "Why I No Longer Live in the Woods: A Refutation of Thoreau," from the journal *Urban Life Quarterly*, volume 14, number 2, 1993, you would do a title search in your library's catalog under "Urban Life Quarterly." If your library does not carry the periodical you seek, talk to your librarian, because you can often order articles through Interlibrary Loan (ILL) and sometimes you can receive them electronically and quickly.

EXERCISE 3.4   Finding Articles in Databases

1. From your library's Web page, search in four databases for journals and other kinds of information on Thoreau or a topic of your choice. Choose a variety of databases, if you can.
2. Determine which articles you can read in your own library, where they are located, and which you would need to order from Interlibrary Loan.

3. Compare your findings with those of your classmates. Discuss the different kinds of material found in the different databases. Under what circumstances would you use particular databases for your research? Which ones do you think you'll use most often in your major field?

Library-based Research

Not all of your sources will be available via electronic media, and at some point you will need to get into the library itself to read materials and ask questions of the experts: the librarians. Your academic work will require you at some time to become familiar with how to access materials in a library system, and your professors will expect you to be familiar with the books and journals in your field of study; it is the way you enter the conversation of your field. When the material you need will probably be found in books and more serious magazines, newspapers, and journals, the library is your best resource. Published printed materials are still our most consistently reliable form of information, as most of them have to go through a more rigorous process of review before they are published. Your institution's library (and your local public library) is also the repository for all kinds of local information that will not be available elsewhere, such as locally produced and published materials, pamphlets, letters, news items, historical and rare materials.

Maybe you want to find a copy of David Sedaris's *Naked*, which includes an account of his visit to a nudist colony; or Jack Kerouac's *On the Road* for a more serious recounting of getting out of mainstream society and examining life; or read the archives of the local utopian society that built a commune in your hometown in the 1880s; or sociological research into current utopian societies. Where would you look for them?

You want to get acquainted with all aspects of your library and the resources it has to offer you. Begin with a library tour. There are almost always tours scheduled at the beginning of semesters and you can also usually arrange for one at any time during the term if you ask. In addition, get instruction on the catalog system; libraries often have short guided sessions for this, too. Learning the cataloging system your library uses, whether Library of Congress, Dewey Decimal System, or both, is essential.

Walk around the library and familiarize yourself with the stacks (the areas where books are shelved), including the folio and quarto size books, which are oversized and often shelved in a separate section. What are the common call numbers for the books in your fields of interest? Where are they located in the library stacks? Where are the current periodicals shelved? The bound periodicals (those prior to the current year)? Reference works (including those available on CD-ROM)? The visual arts, including video and audio recordings? Investigate the special collections department to see what local or rare materials and collections are housed there.

When navigating your library, keep in mind the following tips:

- Look up your materials in the catalog first. Don't wander around the stacks trying to find sources without call numbers. It will take forever. However, when you do have time, wander around the stacks and browse. You'll find interesting things you might not ever have discovered otherwise. In both cases you will be using your time wisely.

- Have three or four alternatives when you head to the stacks to find a book, because a book is often not there exactly when you need it. Since books are cataloged by subject matter, browse the books in the same section as the book you seek to see what else has been written on the subject.
- When you're looking for good sources, check the bibliography of the books and articles you've found. You'll see some names repeatedly cited; these are often the authorities on the topic and you'll want to consult their work.

EXERCISE 3.5   Inquiring in Your Library

1. Learn the library and its cataloging system. Paste a map of the library in your notebook, and make a list of the kinds of resources available there.
2. Using the library's catalog, explore an issue of interest to you. Find at least four different sources of information on it that will require you to visit different sections of the library and locate different kinds of materials, e.g., a reference work, a book, a periodical, and another work, perhaps a dissertation or film or government document or rare manuscript.
3. Discuss with your class the resources in the library, what is available on your topic and from what different kinds of sources, the best study areas, and other interesting things you've found. Generate a list of suggestions for improving the library, especially things that were confusing or needlessly complicated. You could compile these into a whole class list and give them to a librarian.

   Throughout your research process, consult your reference librarians. They are terrific resources. They can help you refine your searches and think of sources you may not have thought of. And if your school doesn't have a book or article you're looking for, they can show you how to order a copy through Interlibrary Loan.

So, what do you do with all the information you find through electronic and print media resources? You pull the best sources into a critical conversation on your topic by evaluating each one carefully, reading critically as you learned in Chapter Two, considering the source, the timeliness, the credentials of the author, and the tone and attitude of the author. Sources on the Internet should be read with particular skepticism because there are no standards that an author has to meet to have his or her work published there. When you pull up a Web site, look at its address. Note the differences between .com (commercial establishment), .edu (educational institution—four-year college or university), .cc (educational institution—community college), .gov (governmental organization), .org (generally nonprofit organization), or .mil (military organization). The information on .com sites should be read with special care and skepticism since they are generally trying to sell you something. Check the date of publication of your sources, and the dates of statistics, figures, graphs, and such that they use. When you're trying to decide whether to trust a source, pay attention to the author's credentials, especially in relation to the subject matter. If a Web site does not list an author's name or credentials, you might need to look at it more skeptically. But not everyone will be famous or have impressive credentials to their names; don't dismiss a source simply because the author is not well known. Consider whether the issue is addressed in a thoughtful manner. For instance, does the source provide and consider more than one perspective on the subject? Does the author appear to be in conversation with other sources by citing and documenting other studies?

Gathering information and discovering the conversation on a topic makes us aware of the other people who are working or have worked on these same issues. When we're working with others' ideas and words, plagiarism becomes a concern. Plagiarism, the passing off of someone else's work (including their words and ideas) as your own, is considered unethical in our culture, especially in academic culture. You know from your own experience that researching material and thinking critically is hard work. We believe in giving people credit for the hard work they do and the things they discover; and we also care about individual intellectual property and consider that people, in a sense, "own" their ideas. This is why plagiarism is considered unethical, because you are stealing someone else's hard work and not giving him or her the credit for it. In most academic settings plagiarism is grounds for failure of the assignment, failure of the course, or, in the most egregious cases, expulsion from the school. It is a hard charge to recover from; it is hard to be trusted again if it is known you have cheated. Talk with your instructor whenever you have questions or doubts about the ways you are working with your sources.

Most students' plagiarism is unintentional, a result of careless notetaking or of copying out passages that are part paraphrase and part direct quotation, without the quotation marks to indicate which is which. Consequently, the distinction between the source's words and ideas and the writer's own words and ideas gets blurred in the writer's essay. Therefore, avoid plagiarism or carelessness and inaccuracy by learning how to take notes clearly and carefully.

One of the most remarkable aspects of the World Wide Web is that so much material is freely shared. However, this can make it easy to take for granted someone else's hard work and not give him or her credit for it; it can be hard to see who "owns" what knowledge or who began a train of thought. And it can make it seem easier to take someone's ideas or even an entire work and pass it off as your own. You know when you've plagiarized from a book or magazine; you've had to work harder to do it. Pasting together bits and pieces from various Web sites, without documenting all the borrowed material, is also plagiarism. Effective note taking is especially important when researching on the Internet because it is easy to get careless and to cut and paste whole chunks of text from a piece and then forget to put quotation marks around it in our own work, and to mark carefully what site, URL, and author it came from.

Researching Using Broadcast Media

Being information literate also means knowing how the broadcast media operate. Knowing when stations or media outlets are owned by individuals or, increasingly, corporations that have ties to other corporations will help you to discern the outlets' possible biases and priorities. What counts as "news" on the news programs? What subjects do and do not get covered in the mainstream media? How many perspectives, and which perspectives, are given air time? You can get more information on media literacy from the Media Literacy Online Project at the University of Oregon: <http://interact.uoregon.edu/MediaLit/HomePage>. In addition, there are "media watchdog" Web sites that work to hold the media accountable for their reporting. One conservative site is the Media Research Center: <http://www.mediaresearch.org>. A liberal choice is the organization FAIR: Fairness and Accuracy in Reporting, at <http://www.fair.org>. These sites, because they represent a spectrum of political perspectives, reveal how our ideas of what is fair and accurate are based on our own experiences, contexts, and ideological stances.

You may want to consult broadcast media for your research when your inquiry needs to go beyond or outside the bounds of published written texts. This will be the case when others have not yet analyzed and written about your subject, when your issue is particularly timely, or when your issue emerges from contemporary popular culture that is transmitted through these media more than others.

Part of the research into broadcast media can be conducted just as you would a search for any print materials. A number of transcripts of television and radio programs (particularly news programs) are available through TV and radio stations' Web sites and databases such as Lexis-Nexis. However, you can also conduct research by watching or listening to TV or radio programs and recording your discoveries. One common method for doing so is called a *content analysis*.

To do a content analysis, decide first what your purpose will be—what you will be looking at, and looking for. For example, you might watch primetime TV shows to discover whether they provide us with any examples of ideal communities that can help us live our lives more ethically. You will look for specific examples that teach you about your question; e.g., what kinds of communities do you find on *The Simpsons, Friends,* or *The Sopranos?* Watch or listen to particular programs over a set period of time and record the elements you're looking for. Designing a chart for your content analysis will remind you to collect the same information each time, because the most important aspect of doing this effectively is recording data precisely. Details matter in this analysis. Note carefully exactly what you see and hear. Don't exaggerate just to get the result you want. Others will need to rely on your findings, so you need to be sure to be especially vigilant, accurate, and honest.

EXERCISE 3.6 Inquiring in Broadcast Media

1. Determine your purpose and how you will carry out your experiment, i.e., which shows you will watch or listen to, what exactly you will be looking for, and how long your project will last. Draw up a chart that covers all of the elements you want to record. Form a hypothesis; what do you expect to find?

2. Each week (or day, if you choose a daily program), tune into your program and faithfully record all of the details in your chart. At this point, do not worry about analyzing what you are finding; just record all of the information, whether or not it fulfills your expectations.

3. At the end of the project period, bring your chart to class and discuss your findings with your classmates. Discuss the experience of conducting a content analysis as well as the information you found. In what ways is it enjoyable and in what ways is it challenging research? How did the analysis affect the way you watch TV or listen to the radio? Are you more aware now when you watch or listen to any program? What are you more aware of? What do you notice that you didn't before?

By researching in broadcast media we start to notice the effect such media have on our lives, and can enter those conversations. Because more people get their news (and often their knowledge and wisdom, too) from broadcast media, particularly TV, than from any other source, it has been the focus of scrutiny and often of blame for the destructive and unappealing aspects of our society. To explore this conversation in more detail, see the case study in Chapter Six and the readings in Chapter Twelve.

Getting the Lived Experience: Inquiring Through Field Research

There is research you do by sitting at computer terminals, watching TV and films, listening to the radio, and combing through libraries; it includes a lot of reading of text and processing words and images. Then there is research you do out in the "field," by talking with people and observing their behavior. This section discusses the nature of field research and how its ethical concerns and researcher preparation vary from text-based forms of inquiry. Then we introduce you to three basic methods of field research: observing, interviewing, and surveying, and offer an exercise at the end that you can practice individually or with your class.

You may want to conduct field research in circumstances where you will be inquiring into a subject that is not yet heavily talked about or documented in written sources, or that is happening on a local level and has not had much, or any, written investigation or formal analysis. In addition, you may quite often find that the best sources of information on a subject are those who are directly experiencing it—those who are living in cabins in the woods, or who are organizing nudist colonies. This can personalize your research and allow you to get more meaningfully involved and active in it, because you'll be meeting the people who are living it.

In field research we should remind ourselves not to go into the situation with an argument already decided, but to go in open-minded, and open-eyed, as the most interesting findings will likely come from mundane, everyday details. You might not see these details if you go into the research with a thesis already decided. Good field research takes time: you must work on others' schedules; be there, present, watching, talking; and be patient. You do have time to do some field research for term papers; you just need to plan your project carefully.

Whereas much of the ethics of text-based research concerns plagiarism, the ethics of field research concerns working directly with people, their words, their actions, and treating them honestly, openly, and respectfully. With text-based research, when you read and view works, they are already interpreted by others; with field research, you are the interpreter of your subjects' words and therefore you want to be as accurate and unbiased as you can to avoid distorting their perspective.

The preparation for text-based research and field research is different as well. The process of searching textual materials can be more forgiving. If you are not as organized as you would like, if you missed something the first time you searched, you can return to the books, articles, Web sites, and, often, transcripts of broadcasts, and reread them. It is not so easy with live subjects, who may find it annoying or insulting. (This does not mean you cannot return to people for fact checking, for follow-up to your projects, to deepen what you've found, and to stay in contact with them as friends. Those are all important and rewarding parts of this research methodology.) "Conversation" is not always used figuratively in field research. You are often conducting a live conversation and should follow the etiquette necessary for any situation in which you work with people.

Observation

We begin the field research methods with observation, because, as Kristine Hansen points out in *A Rhetoric for the Social Sciences*, "observing is really the basis of all methods" of research. Observing ourselves and others is a core part of an examined life. Probably the first way you learned to inquire into how one should live, for instance, was by observing your parents' and friends' lives. We observe informally all the time, including when we're using other methods such as reading materials and interviewing and surveying people. We've learned about formal observation from anthropologists, who conduct ethnographic research when they write (*-graphy*) about people (*ethno-*).

You might want to live at a utopian society for a few weeks, or go out into the woods yourself and observe your own behavior and the environment you're in. You might want to attend meetings, or watch how people treat each other on the street. You can perform an *unobtrusive observation* by watching people on the street or other open setting. You can also do this by attending theater performances, lectures, protests, political rallies, or meetings and taking careful notes about what transpires there. Or you can perform a *participant observation*, as Margaret Talbot did for her essay "A Mighty Fortress," which you can read in Chapter Seven. In this kind of observation you actually participate in the environment, interacting with others in the particular situation you observe. You especially want to do this when you will gain the greatest understanding of the situation by experiencing it or living it yourself, rather than just observing others doing so. You also can perform a *structured observation* by setting up an environment and watching people who know they are part of an observation experiment. You can do this "live," by observing and taking notes in the setting, or you can videotape the situation and take notes on it later.

Whatever form of observation you conduct, take close and extensive notes. You can write out questions you want to answer through your observation so that you can focus your attention. But don't be limited by these questions and don't disregard contradictory behavior. And record your own responses are well. Observe yourself in the situation and take notes, as objectively and in as much detail as you can, of your own reactions without interpreting or judging. Ethnographers use the term *thick description* to describe the practice of taking very detailed notes of everything you observe, as Talbot did with the kind of toys the Scheibner children played with, and the expressions on their faces when discussing religion or dating or household chores. In *The Interpretation of Cultures*, anthropologist Clifford Geertz argues that observing in close detail is a way toward understanding others: "We must . . . descend into detail, past the misleading tags, past the metaphysical types, past the empty similarities to grasp firmly the essential character of not only the various cultures but the various sorts of individuals within each culture, if we wish to encounter humanity face to face" (53).

When you are taking notes, don't sort through the information while you are recording it—that is, don't categorize or judge or interpret it, just write down everything you see and hear and experience. Anthropologists make a distinction between *realistic details* and *status details*. Realistic details are plain and simple recording description that do not advance our understanding or reveal meaning about the person or object or event. Status details reveal habits and morals, or inform us as to themes, relationships, and such. (See the opening paragraph of Talbot's "A Mighty Fortress" for an excellent use of status details.)

Interviewing

In other cases you will want to conduct an interview for your research. Interviews are generally good for getting the words of an authority on a subject, or for getting the personal opinion of people affected by a certain situation. You can get individuals' perspectives firsthand and, if you maintain a safe and trustworthy environment for the discussion, you can ask the questions that don't get asked by mainstream media sources. Interviews are also a way of sharing information and building community. You are not just taking information from your sources, you are having a conversation with them.

You could talk with someone who argues that we should live apart from mainstream society and has set up her own community. You could also talk with the leader of a local political party who argues we need to live side by side and meet frequently to air our differences. In any case, you will want to prepare well in advance, because you are asking the person or persons to give up some of their time for you. Interviewing is also a very personal form of research. While it has the potential for deep insight, it also can cause hurt feelings or misunderstandings.

Determine your purpose and make sure you're interviewing the best person or persons for the perspective or knowledge you need. Contact the person, explain your project, ask whether he/she has the information you need, and request permission to talk with him or her for a certain amount of time (e.g., a few minutes, or half an hour). If the subject is willing, make an appointment. *Ask at this time, when you are making the appointment, if the subject will allow you to tape record the interview.* Don't insist on it, however, if the person is uncomfortable with it.

If you can, do background reading on the person and the subject matter, so that you can ask more substantial questions and not have to take up a lot of the interview time asking basic questions. Prepare a list of clear questions before the interview, and be familiar with them so you don't have to look down at your questions often.

But don't be afraid to ask "stupid" questions. Don't assume you know how he or she will define a term or see a situation, even if it seems obvious. Ask for an explanation; you may be surprised at what you hear.

Above all, *listen.* This may seem like a silly reminder, but often we get nervous and forget just to have a conversation with the interview subject and to listen to what she or he is saying. Don't be so tied to your prepared questions that you hold onto them even if the interview takes a new and interesting direction. Write down the main details of the interview in your notebook while you are there. Put quotation marks around exact words so that you can represent them accurately later. Don't be afraid to ask the person to repeat something so that you can get it all down in your notes. (In fact, don't be afraid to call back later if you need to check the accuracy of a quote; experts especially will appreciate your desire to represent them fairly and precisely.)

Immediately after the interview, take time to go through your notes and fill in information you weren't able to get down during the interview. Record the parts of the conversation you might have missed, and go over your quoted material to fill in any gaps. Also, this is the time to note the context for the interview, the environment in which it took place, the tone of the conversation. Record your own response to the interview.

Send a thank-you note afterward. It's the polite thing to do, and it will make contact smoother if you need to talk to the person again. Often you'll want to provide the person with a copy of your finished or published interview or essay. This is courteous, and it keeps you honest because you'll be especially careful to represent your interview accurately if you know the interviewee is going to read it.

STOP AND THINK

INTERVIEWING: LARRY KING ON ASKING THE GOOD QUESTIONS

The secret to a successful interview is asking good questions, the ones that will invite your interview subject to speak openly. Watch and listen to skilled interviewers such as Barbara Walters, Ray Suarez, Terry Gross, or Larry King. What kinds of questions do they ask, and how do they ask them? How do they approach asking sensitive questions?

In *How to Talk to Anyone, Anytime, Anywhere*, Larry King writes:

I have never been afraid to ask what others might consider a dumb question, if it's one I think my viewers will be curious about . . . . I asked President Bush during the 1992 campaign, "Do you dislike Bill Clinton?" Many professional journalists would argue that the question didn't have a thing to do with the campaign, yet the case could be made that it had everything to do with it because it brought out the human element—one man's attitude toward another—in a person who held the highest office in the land.

We're human beings, even those who become president, and that was a question the human beings watching on TV would ask, so I asked it.

I asked Richard Nixon, "When you drive by the Watergate, do you feel weird?" The last time I interviewed President Reagan, I asked him what it was like to be shot. Maybe a reporter would ask him something else about John Hinckley's attempt on his life on March 30, 1981, but I bet a lot of people wondered just what I did.

One special kind of interview is an *oral history*. Usually in an oral history you are interviewing ordinary people rather than experts, and are asking them for their personal experiences with a particular historical event, or for stories of their life in a particular region or time period. These can be truly valuable and meaningful forms of knowledge. For your own personal purposes, you might want to interview your grandparents or other older relatives or friends, or other special people in your life. It's a great way to get to know them better and to discover aspects about their lives and about earlier eras, as well. Because you want to preserve their words as much as possible, it may be best to record these on audio or video tape, in which case you will need to get permission, probably written permission. You will also probably need to make this person or persons feel more at ease, and assure them that their story is worth hearing.

Edward Ives, in *The Tape-Recorded Interview: A Manual for Field Workers in Folklore and Oral History*, recommends beginning the interview by speaking into the microphone yourself, recording your name and the date and the name of the person you are interviewing and the subject of the interview. Then you can ask the person if he or she will give you permission to interview, and if so, then it is recorded on tape. As in any interview, listen carefully, let the person talk, ask questions that you've prepared but be flexible enough to follow interesting subjects that come up. About one hour is usually sufficient, as you don't want to wear out the interviewee; if you find that there's much more to be said, you can make an appointment for another session or so. As always, send a thank you note, and send a copy of your interview when it's finished—the print copy or tape.

Surveys

In some inquiries you will want responses from a number of people and may want to conduct a survey. This is particularly effective when your inquiry will not be answered by reading other people's research, or when you have very specific information you need to gather, especially local, very current, or personal information, in order to answer questions, make a decision, or develop a program. You might, for example, survey people at a local nudist colony to see what it is that draws them to that life. You might survey people in your neighborhood to see if they want to develop a communal area for playing and gardening on the old school lot. Surveys, especially when they are written rather than oral, can be the best way to learn what people's real attitudes or practices are, because people will tend to be more truthful and less likely to try to answer as they think you expect them to.

Like interviews, surveys can be very sensitive forms of research, so you want to prepare carefully before approaching people. First, determine your purpose: what you want to find out with this survey, and what you want to do with the information you gather. Then decide whom it would be best to survey. What kinds of people? What age or ethnicity or neighborhood or gender or occupation or interest group? How many people will you need to survey to get a good sampling? Can you find them by just walking around or going to a certain location, or will you need to set up a survey-taking time and invite people? You can also do surveys in your composition or other courses, as you tend to have a captive and interested audience who can also provide feedback on the effectiveness of the survey.

Then draw up your list of questions. Spend time crafting these, as they matter most of all to the success of your project. Consider the formality of your inquiry: if it's more informal and you know the people well, you can be somewhat more casual in your phrasing of the questions, as you can assume shared knowledge and concerns.

What kind of questions should you ask? This depends on what kind of information you need. You can write quantitative *fixed-response* questions, where the survey-taker is given the question and a selection of answers from which to choose. Multiple-choice and true/false questions fall under this category. This kind of question allows you to control the responses and get a more focused outcome. For example:

How often, in any given year, do you take a walk in the woods or other wild place?

1. Nearly every day.
2. About once a week.

3. Maybe once a month.
4. A few times a year.
5. Never.

Or you can write qualitative *open-ended* questions, in which the survey-taker is free to construct his or her own answer to the question. This kind of question allows you to get a fuller, more specific and personalized response. For example:

What does it mean to you to be able to walk in the woods?

Ask yourself whether it is more important to get a range of personal responses, or to be able to group responses into distinguishable categories, perhaps for the sake of taking specific action on an issue. Some fixed-response questions can be too restrictive (which may force people to choose answers they wouldn't normally and not give you their candid, individual answers to the question), while some open-ended questions can keep you from getting any overlap or focus from respondents. You may want a combination of questions.

You may want to begin the survey with demographic questions (asking them about their age, race, nationality, gender, occupation, income, education, political affiliation, religion, specific group memberships, and so forth), depending on what you want to measure. Usually these questions can be fixed; you can just ask participants to check off answers in boxes.

STOP AND THINK

WHAT SURVEYS CAN TELL US: ROBERT PUTNAM ON CRAFTING QUESTIONS

In his book, *Bowling Alone: The Collapse and Revival of American Community*, Robert Putnam relies heavily on evidence from surveys. Although surveys certainly have their limitations, which he acknowledges, they can provide us with information that we get no other way. For instance, Putnam found that "A well-designed poll can provide a useful snapshot of opinions and behavior. Even better, a series of comparable surveys can yield a kind of social time-lapse photography. Just as one snapshot a day from a single camera pointed unvaryingly at the same garden patch can yield a marvelous movie of botanical birth and growth, so a single survey question, if repeated regularly, can produce a striking image of social change. Moreover, if the question has been formulated deftly enough, it can encompass a more diverse and changing social landscape than the study of any single organization."

Be aware of how you ask the questions. For instance, are you assuming that your survey takers are just like you—that they share your race and ethnicity, gender, class, educational background, taste, and such? Are you unintentionally setting up an us vs. them situation if you refer to white men, or children, or

African-Americans, or Muslims as "them" in a question? Are your questions phrased in a way that leads the survey-takers toward one particular answer?

Most of all, your subjects must be able to trust you. When you ask people to answer personal questions about their intimate lives, their opinions or prejudices, their criminal backgrounds—anything that could be held against them— you have a strict obligation to preserve their anonymity. You need to set up the survey questions and the survey-taking environment and survey interpretation in such a way that will maintain confidentiality.

EXERCISE 3.7   Practicing Field Research Techniques

Do some brainstorming on a research question that you and your classmates want to explore, one that will accommodate a variety of research methods. Divide the class into groups who want most to conduct an observation, an interview, or a survey. The individuals in each group can conduct their own individual studies, or groups could plan one together. You may find it educational to have three groups, each of which begins with the same research question, and to compare the different kinds of answers you get when using different research methods.

1. In each case, set your purpose and goals first and then follow the guidelines above for conducting observations, interviews, and surveys.
2. Record your own responses to your field research. Observe yourself as a researcher and take notes, as objectively and in as much detail as you can, of your own reactions without interpreting or judging.
3. Discuss your findings with your class. What different kinds of responses did you get from your different kinds of methods? What kinds of conclusions can you draw? Make sure to discuss the experience of doing the field research. How did you feel? What did you think? How did people respond to you? Did you feel self-conscious? Did you encounter any difficult intellectual or ethical dilemmas? If so, how did you address or resolve them? What was particularly interesting or difficult or surprising about the process? In what ways was it enjoyable and in what ways was it challenging research?

Your field research may be a one-time venture into interviewing or surveying or observing people or events; in other words, you may contact people solely for your immediate researching purposes and may not have future contact with them. However, your field research may develop out of—or may lead into— your work in a service learning course or from other experience as a participant in a community program. Often field research, because it tends to involve us more personally than does textual research, can make us want to continue working with communities or individuals, or with certain ongoing projects or causes, even if we don't have a particular assignment.

STOP AND THINK

ETHICS OF FIELD RESEARCH: KNOWING YOUR IRB

If you are working with human subjects you may need to submit a formal proposal to your college's Institutional Review Board for the Protection of Human Participants (IRB) stating that you will receive the informed consent of your participants and that your study will not cause harm to them. Your IRB can give you full information about the ethics of your research. It is often a lengthy process requiring a lot of paperwork, so if you are doing field research for a school project you will want to get started early.

It is self-evidently important not to harm others in the course of your research. However, go beyond the basics prescribed by your IRB. Go beyond informed consent. Don't use people. Especially when you are conducting research in communities, share the project with those you're interviewing or surveying, and discuss it with them. For years, it was assumed that university-affiliated researchers were those with the knowledge, and community members were information for studies, or were there to be taught the knowledge of the researchers. University researchers have gone into communities and gathered information, often without ever getting to know the people of the community, and without sharing the analysis and decision-making power with them. Find ways to get yourself and others involved so that you can avoid simply taking information from the community or individuals.

WEAVING TOGETHER INQUIRY AND ACTION IN COMMUNITY-BASED SERVICE LEARNING

At the opening of this chapter we emphasized that inquiry is a form of social action. All inquiry contributes to our education and the action we take in the world. Some inquiry connects directly with action and is itself a form of action. As students you can participate in what are often called *service-learning* activities through your institution and make your academic inquiry directly connect with and have an impact on local communities.

Community-based service learning is an experiential approach to education that integrates classroom theory with real-world experience and reflective practice; it takes classroom reading, thinking, and writing and puts it into conversation with real-world situations. It is based on the philosophy that we learn by doing. Students, instead of being passively lectured to, take responsibility for their own learning and learn in interaction with others. Professors, instead of being the bearers of knowledge, are the facilitators of knowledge and learn alongside their students. Because you learn as much—or more—from the community members as they do from you, many educators prefer the term *community learning* to service learning, to avoid the implication that those in the campus community are doing those in the local community a one-way service.

Community-based service learning programs are guided by the belief that institutions of higher education should be preparing students for their whole civic lives, not just their professions (although community learning experience is excellent for developing leadership skills and gaining contacts for future internships and jobs). Through community experience you tend to gain a deeper understanding of civic life and participation because you are actually working with others on specific projects rather than just reading about them in theory.

How does it work? Students and faculty members generally spend part of their semester hours off campus working with the members of a nonprofit community organization, or with students in a school. This collaboration is a way for the campus and local communities to share their resources and to learn from one another's experiences. Service learning gives you the opportunity to research and get involved in issues that might seem too huge to tackle if you were considering doing so all by yourself. When you conduct field research through your service learning, you are doing so in conjunction with community members, and your inquiring can be aimed not just at gathering the information you need, but toward strengthening ties between people in the various communities.

Service learning can also be an excellent mode of inquiry because it allows you to experience how research changes you, the researcher. You discover what you really think by acting on your beliefs every day. You build models based on your real-world experience and compare them with the theories you read in the classroom. Reflective writing is therefore a critical component of service learning. The experience of working in the community is intellectually, politically, and personally challenging and sometimes frustrating or distressing, and you need the space and time to think through your experiences and express them to others. Recording your thoughts in a journal allows you to see how, over time, the community work contributes to your personal, intellectual, and civic development. It helps you gain an awareness of your whole environment, in and out of college. Though it is often difficult, it can be the most rewarding part of your college education.

In English department courses, especially composition courses, service learning opportunities often involve tutoring adults or children in developing English literacy skills, and sometimes in test preparation. This is a good opportunity for you to reflect on your own literacy, its meaning to you, and its place in your world. And, importantly, you can reflect critically upon the ways we educate people—our educational strategies and priorities. In this situation you will be both a teacher and a learner. Teaching others helps us become more aware of how we ourselves have been taught.

Many colleges and universities now have offices dedicated to service learning. Ask on your campus how you can get involved. If you are interested in getting involved in service learning, you'll want to prepare yourself first. Before you go out into the community, consider why you want to do so, and what you expect the experience to be like, to do for you, and to do for those you'll be working with. In short, examine your motives, because most communities aren't interested in having someone come in who wants to "save" them, even if the person means well. Try this exercise, adapted from one developed by the organization Campus Compact, in your class as a way of discussing attitudes toward community service.

EXERCISE 3.8 Examining Our Motives

1. Designate one wall of the classroom as the "continuum." (The blackboard wall is good for this.) At one end, write "charitable volunteer"; at the other end, write "radical social activist." Have everyone in class choose a spot along the wall, according to where you'd place yourself along the continuum, and stand there.
2. Let each person discuss why he or she chose that specific spot. Discuss what the words "charitable volunteer" and "radical social activist" mean to you. What do they imply about the attitudes toward and purposes of the action you will perform in the community?
3. Ask those at each end to describe the people at the other end. On what points do you agree and disagree?

Often those who are at one end of the spectrum find it difficult to understand those at the other end, because they have contradictory approaches to solving the same problems. What are your assumptions about the work you'll be doing? What do you believe is the best way to achieve a just society? Do you think of yourself, for instance, as trying to help individuals one by one, or are you trying to change an entire system? How will this affect the way you approach service learning activities?

CONCLUSION: INQUIRY AS ARGUMENT

Although it may not have seemed like it to you, as you inquire you are developing an argument, a way of seeing the situation or issue that you are inquiring into. Chapter Four introduces you to a number of strategies for recognizing and developing that argument and presenting it to an audience. We argue to learn; in fact, the act of presenting your argument becomes another form of inquiry, a way of thinking itself.

QUESTIONS FOR INQUIRY AND ACTION

1. In what ways do you now notice yourself "inquiring" more consciously in everyday life? Do you notice a difference if you or other people do *not* research the issues you discuss and debate?

2. What does *inquiry* have to do with *citizenship*? Do you need research skills and knowledge to be a productive, reflective citizen? If so, what kinds of skills and knowledge do you need? Write out all the ways you can imagine inquiry—however you conceive of that right now—being part of a citizen's life. Imagine specific scenarios from your own life and others' experiences.

3. As you start to pursue a specific major field or academic discipline, do some research for yourself to see how interested you are in the way that discipline thinks about and creates "knowledge." For instance, what is the history of your discipline? When did it become an academic discipline, included in college curricula? What changes has it gone through? Why are you interested in it? What about the way that people in that discipline "think" is interesting to you, or matches the way you think? What are the methods of inquiry in your discipline? Why are those methods considered the most reliable and desirable?

4. How can you get involved in community service learning on your campus? Investigate what resources exist for you.

CHAPTER 4

Arguing: Action As Inquiry

What democracy requires is public debate, not information. Of course it needs information too, but the kind of information it needs can be generated only by vigorous popular debate. We do not know what we need to know until we ask the right questions, and we can identify the right questions only by subjecting our own ideas about the world to the test of public controversy . . . . When we get into arguments that focus and fully engage our attention, we become avid seekers of relevant information. Otherwise, we take in information passively—if we take it in at all.

Christopher Lasch, Revolt of the Elites

GETTING STARTED: Arguing in Our Communities

In Chapter Three you learned how to use available sources to answer Socrates's question, "How should one live?" This section asks you to consider a more specific version of that larger question: "What can we do to improve our communities?" In your writer's notebook, write down five specific suggestions you would like to see your local or national communities implement to improve the quality of their citizens' lives. Here are a few suggestions from previous students:

- "Encourage civic-mindedness by requiring one year of military or civil service for all students as they come out of high school."
- "We need to enrich our spiritual lives. We should encourage each other to go to church. It doesn't matter what religion, just go."
- "Prisoners should have more opportunities to work while in prison. The state's profits from the prisoners' labor can be used to pay for the prisons and prisoners can learn a useful trade."

After you've written down your suggestions, get into small groups and try to convince the other group members that your suggestions are the most practical, ethical, or effective. Each group should use its debates to reduce the members' recommendations to a list of three that they can then present to the rest of the class. The class can then debate the merits of each list. After the debates, answer the following questions in your writer's notebook:

1. How did participants try to convince others that some arguments were more practical, ethical, or effective?
2. How did their persuasive efforts work on others in the class? Did their efforts encourage or discourage critical thinking?
3. Did you learn something more about these subjects through the debates? Why or why not?

The eighteenth-century satirist Jonathan Swift once said that arguments are the "worst sort of conversation." You might agree with Swift if the debates you helped to create in the Getting Started exercise resembled these examples we have witnessed in our classes:

- A student was silenced when several others accused him of sucking up to the instructor. He had been participating in class discussion actively, but after the accusation he withdrew, fearing his participation would be viewed as insincere.
- Students stubbornly avoided debate, prefacing every sentence with "I think" or "This is just my opinion." As a result, no one felt challenged enough to critique other positions or defend their own. Instead, the students congratulated themselves on their tolerance for other people's opinions.
- Two students tried to railroad consensus by arguing that the other side's position contradicted biblical teachings. Not wanting to get into a discussion of religious beliefs, most people stopped talking.

On each of these occasions, students afterwards expressed dissatisfaction with the debates; the debates, they said, were entertaining but not very instructive.

If we accept Christopher Lasch's view of arguing, as expressed in the opening quotation, then the above examples do indeed represent the worst sorts of conversation. Lasch defines arguments as engaged conversations that push us to think more deeply and critically about issues that affect our communities. Citizens present their views on issues so that others can bring their own values, beliefs, and experiences into dialog with them. The hope is that such conversations push all participants to clarify their ideas, to account for disagreements, and to discover intelligent, practical solutions to social issues. In this sense, arguing becomes a form of active inquiry.

Students in the above examples discouraged such conversations by turning them into quarrels or shutting them down. The arguers attacked other students' characters to discredit the students' views, they framed their arguments as opinions to avoid controversy, or they suppressed opposition by making the other arguers uncomfortable. None of these examples encouraged active inquiry. The purpose of arguments, Lasch would argue, is not to harm the other arguer or even to win, but to achieve mutual understanding, compromise, a willing consensus, or at least a deeper knowledge of other views. Arguments like these become the *best* sorts of conversation for achieving democratic solutions to our communities' problems.

If we wish to learn from our arguments or to think through community problems, then we need to learn how to inquire through arguing. The Getting Started activity showed that you already know how to argue. This chapter builds upon that knowledge, encouraging you to adopt an arguing-to-inquire mindset and to internalize strategies that will make your arguments more rigorous and ethical.

FIRST INQUIRY: WHAT IS ARGUING TO INQUIRE?

Disagreements are an inevitable aspect of community life. They develop around different political, economic, or religious beliefs. They develop between members of different nations, regions, cultures, generations, sexes, and sexual orientations. Even members of the same community view common issues through their own unique values, experiences, and visions of community life. All of these opportunities for disagreement can create conflict, testing our ability as members to live together in harmony.

How we deal with these disagreements says a lot about our communities. If we fight, cheat, or threaten each other, we create a very different quality of life than if we compromise, build agreement, or submit to acceptable laws. In situations where we want to learn or where our choices really matter, we need ways of arguing that push us to clarify our views, test our opinions, and strengthen community ties.

We learned in Chapter Three to begin an inquiry by asking questions. Not only is this a natural way to begin, questions can also free us from the temptation to research only to prove what we already believe. Because most questions don't presume only one answer, we can consult many different views. We need to consider each of these views sincerely and rigorously if we are to inquire ethically. This doesn't mean we should agree with everyone's views. Rather, we should try to understand why, for example, someone would promote vegetarianism, private gun ownership, affirmative action, or any number of views similar to or different from our own. Understanding *why* people would argue particular positions on some social issue helps us go under their arguments, appreciating the experiences, values, beliefs, visions, or missions that have caused them to adopt those positions.

When we read an argument, especially one we disagree with, we are often tempted to judge it immediately. Students in our classes have often responded to readings by saying, "This essay is boring," "That arguer is such an idiot," or "This writer kicks butt." Although responses like these can be a good place to start critical thinking, they shouldn't represent the end of our response. This is especially true if we want to create communities that treat disagreements as opportunities to learn, not as occasions to bully our neighbors.

Taking the time to understand what arguers are saying and why they are saying it encourages us to inquire more deeply into the conversations circulating around particular social issues. Instead of exchanging arguments and just criticizing one another, arguers seek to go under each other's arguments to understand why they disagree and how they might proceed despite their differences. For example, people opposing handgun ownership might criticize organizations like the National Rifle Association (NRA) for supporting handgun ownership. Calling NRA members redneck vigilantes, however, probably won't advance the argument on the issue. What would succeed is trying to understand how supporters view gun ownership, the government's role in legislating personal safety, and so on. Going under other people's arguments can also make us more effective respondents. Instead of responding only to their arguments, we can challenge the very beliefs and visions that support those arguments, encouraging a more rigorous conversation. For example, instead of simply battering handgun advocates' arguments with arguments of their own, opponents to handgun ownership could challenge the very vision of gun ownership on which the supporters' arguments are based.

Summarizing an Argument

To reach this deeper response to other people's arguments, we first need to understand thoroughly what an arguer is saying. When faced with written arguments, we can develop this level of understanding by summarizing them. A summary is usually a short paragraph that presents the thesis and main supporting points of a work. It condenses the work's content so other readers can learn what the original writer is arguing and how that argument is supported. Summaries have value for readers because the readers get a sense of the work before they read it, and summaries have value for writers because the writers must master the original work's ideas enough to teach them to others. Here is an example summary of Jefferson's Declaration of Independence, which you read in Chapter Two:

> The Declaration justifies the colonies' decision to break off from England. First, it presents the assumptions on which the colonies' argument is based, namely, that people have the inherent rights to live, to be free, to shape their own destinies, and to throw off any government that limits these rights. Second, it presents the many ways England has imposed on the colonists' rights. Third, it argues that England has continually rejected the colonists' efforts to correct these impositions, and therefore the colonists are forced to declare their independence.

We might summarize Jefferson's argument in the Declaration differently, adding or reducing the number of details depending on how thoroughly we want readers to understand Jefferson's work. Yet, regardless of how long our summaries are, we should keep several points in mind if we want to learn from writing them.

First, we should write the summary in our own words. Translating an arguer's ideas into language we feel comfortable with pushes us to better grasp those ideas. As a result, we will understand them more fully and remember them longer.

Second, we should focus on the significant points. To give readers some sense of how the writer's argument develops, so they can better comprehend the argument as a whole, we should exclude any details or examples that might distract us from the main points. We should also revise the summary so it comes together as a clear, unified paragraph. In the above example, we can see how Jefferson's argument proceeds because the summary writer organized the paragraph logically. The writer reinforced this organization by using transition words like *first, second,* and so on.

Analyzing an Argument

After writing the summary, readers are in a better position to analyze what they've read. To analyze is to take something apart to understand how it works. In this case, however, the goal is not to tear an argument apart so we can criticize it, saying it is poorly written, unconvincing, or immoral (although an argument might be all three). Rather, we analyze the argument to explain where the arguer is coming from and why he or she uses particular strategies to convince us. In other words, we summarize to understand *what* an arguer is saying; we analyze to understand *why* he or she says it.

Unlike summaries, analyses of a work take no particular form. We could write multiparagraph essays or record insights in our writer's notebooks. In any case, we should keep several points in mind as we analyze a written argument. First, we need to examine the text as writers. Usually, we respond to an arguer's ideas, not paying much attention to how those ideas are presented. Yet, if we really want to understand what values and beliefs shape an arguer's viewpoint, then we need to look at the writing itself. The arguer is usually not available to us to explain why they chose a particular viewpoint, so we have to infer their values and beliefs from the writing itself. We do this by identifying distinguishing features of a written argument, asking questions about those features, and speculating on why the arguer chose those features over others.

In the next section of this chapter, we will discuss different arguing strategies. Knowing how arguers seek to persuade readers can help us identify the strategies they use on us. For example, in the Declaration, Jefferson lists England's transgressions against America. He might have listed three or four examples, instead of almost thirty. A good analyzer would ask what this writing decision says about Jefferson's views of England, its relationship with the American colonies, and the situation in which he was writing. A good analyzer would ask questions about all of an argument's distinguishing features. He or she would assume those features were chosen by the writer deliberately, and, as a result, those choices express the writer's values, beliefs, and purposes for arguing.

Of course, the Declaration—and any text, for that matter—probably won't tell us why the arguer has shaped his or her text in a particular way, but we can speculate based on what we know about writing, arguing, and human nature. We can also speculate based on the arguer's biography, time, place, circumstances, and audience. Because written works usually come out of specific writing situations, we can understand them more fully if we know more about those situations. For example, we can make an educated guess why Jefferson listed so many British transgressions. We know that many Americans felt strong political, social, even familial ties to England. Perhaps one of Jefferson's motives was to persuade these reluctant colonists to become revolutionaries by overwhelming them with evidence. Formulating possible explanations, like this one, for why Jefferson supported American independence can help us understand his values and beliefs, making our responses to the Declaration more rigorous.

In the following exercise, we can examine two such responses, one by Susan B. Anthony and the other by the Black Panthers organization. Each writer responds to the Declaration, arguing that its promises of life, liberty, and an equal chance at happiness were not being extended to all citizens. At the same time, each writer uses Jefferson's arguments in making her or his own argument.

EXERCISE 4.1   Critically Responding to the Declaration of Independence

1. Read the declarations by Susan B. Anthony and the Black Panthers and summarize each of them in your writer's notebook so that readers who have not read the declarations will have a general understanding of what each writer is arguing.
2. Analyze each declaration and write your analyses in your writer's notebook. Writing can be a tool for generating thoughts as well as expressing them, so try to push each analysis to two pages. To help you learn about the background of these writers and of their writing situations, follow the inquiry strategies suggested in Chapter Three.
3. Once you have finished writing your own analyses, compare them with those of your classmates. Then discuss the following questions:
   a. Did you find it hard to resist attacking the writers' arguments?
   b. Did you learn more about the declarations by taking the time to summarize and analyze them, instead of jumping to evaluation?
   c. Did you learn persuasive strategies from the works that you can use in your own arguments?

SUSAN B. ANTHONY Women's Right to Vote

Susan B. Anthony (1820–1906) was an early activist, participating in the anti-slavery and temperance movements. Along with Elizabeth Cady Stanton, she joined the women's rights movement in 1852, and eventually became president of the National American Woman Suffrage Association. Beginning in 1868, she published a newspaper, The Revolution, *from Rochester, New York; its masthead read, "Men their rights, and nothing more; women, their rights, and nothing less," and had the aim of establishing "justice for all."*

In 1872, a presidential election year, she decided to test the Fourteenth Amendment to the Constitution. The first section of that Amendment states that "all persons born or naturalized in the United States" are citizens, and are therefore entitled to equal protection under the law. It was written primarily to secure citizenship rights for African Americans after the Civil War, but Anthony took the opportunity to challenge its argument. Anthony, three of her sisters, and other women attempted to register and cast their votes, but were arrested. In 1873, before her trial, Anthony traveled around, giving a speech that has come to be called "Women's Right to Vote." The full text can be found in Elizabeth Cady Stanton, Susan B. Anthony, and Matilda Joslyn Gage, eds., History of Woman Suffrage, *Vol. 2 (Salem, NH: Ayer, 1985) 630–47.*

Women gained the right to vote by the Nineteenth Amendment in 1920, fourteen years after Anthony's death.

I stand before you under indictment for the alleged crime of having voted at the last presidential election, without having a lawful right to vote. It shall be my work this evening to prove to you that in thus doing, I not only committed no crime, but instead simply exercised my citizen's rights, guaranteed to me and all United States citizens by the National Constitution beyond the power of any State to deny.

Our democratic-republican government is based on the idea of the natural right of every individual member thereof to a voice and a vote in making and executing the laws. We assert the province of government to be to secure the people in the enjoyment of their inalienable rights. We throw to the winds the old dogma that government can give rights. No one denies that before governments were organized each individual possessed the right to protect his own life, liberty and property. When 100 to 1,000,000 people enter into a free government they do not barter away their natural rights; they simply pledge themselves to protect each other in the enjoyment of them through prescribed judicial and legislative tribunals. They agree to abandon the methods of brute force in the adjustment of their differences and adopt those of civilization. . . . The Declaration of Independence, the United States Constitution, the constitutions of the several States and the organic laws of the Territories, all alike propose to *protect* the people in the exercise of their God-given rights. Not one of them pretends to bestow rights.

> All men are created equal, and endowed by their Creator with certain inalienable rights. Among these are life, liberty and the pursuit of happiness. To secure these, governments are instituted among men, deriving their just powers from the consent of the governed.

Here is no shadow of government authority over rights, or exclusion of any class from their full and equal enjoyment. Here is pronounced the right of all men, and "consequently," as the Quaker preacher said, "of all women," to a voice in the government. And here, in this first paragraph of the Declaration, is the assertion of the natural right of all to the ballot; for how can "the consent of the governed" be given, if the right to vote be denied? . . . The women, dissatisfied as they are with this form of government, that enforces taxation without representation—that compels them to obey laws to which they never have given their consent—that imprisons and hangs them without a trial by a jury of their peers—that robs them, in marriage, of the custody of their own persons, wages, and children—are this half of the people who are left wholly at the mercy of the other half, in direct violation of the spirit and letter of the declarations of the framers of this government, every one of which was based on the immutable principle of equal rights to all. By these declarations, kings, popes, priests, aristocrats, all were alike dethroned and placed on a common level, politically, with the lowliest born subject or serf. By them, too, men, as such, were deprived of their divine right to rule and placed on a political level with women. By the practice of these declarations all class and caste distinctions would be abolished, and slave, serf, plebeian, wife, woman, all alike rise from their subject position to the broader platform of equality.

The preamble of the Federal Constitution says:

> We, the people of the United States, in order to form a more perfect union, establish justice, insure domestic tranquility, provide for the common defence, promote the general welfare and secure the blessings of liberty to ourselves and our posterity, do ordain and establish this Constitution for the United States of America.

5   It was we, the people, not we, the white male citizens, nor we, the male citizens; but we, the whole people, who formed this Union. We formed it not to give the blessings of liberty but to secure them; not to the half of ourselves and the half of our posterity, but to the whole people—women as well as men. It is downright mockery to talk to women of their enjoyment of the blessings of liberty while they are denied the only means of securing them provided by this democratic-republican government—the ballot. . . .

For any State to make sex a qualification, which must ever result in the disfranchisement of one entire half of the people, is to pass a bill of attainder, an ex post facto law, and is therefore a violation of the supreme law of the land. By it the blessings of liberty are forever withheld from women and their female posterity. For them, this government has no just powers derived from the consent of the governed. For them this government is not a democracy; it is not a republic. It is the most odious aristocracy ever established on the face of the globe. An oligarchy of wealth, where the rich govern the poor; an oligarchy of learning, where the educated govern the ignorant; or even an oligarchy of race, where the Saxon rules the African, might be endured; but this oligarchy of sex which makes father, brothers, husband, sons, the oligarchs over the mother and sisters, the wife and daughters of every household; which ordains all men sovereigns, all women subjects—carries discord and rebellion into every home of the nation. . . .

It is urged that the use of the masculine pronouns *he, his* and *him* in all the constitutions and laws, is proof that only men were meant to be included in their provisions. If you insist on this version of the letter of the law, we shall insist that you be consistent and accept the other horn of the dilemma, which would compel you to exempt women from taxation for the support of the government and from penalties for the violation of laws. There is no *she* or *her* or *hers* in the tax laws, and this is equally true of all the criminal laws.

Take for example, the civil rights law which I am charged with having violated; not only are all the pronouns in it masculine, but everybody knows that it was intended expressly to hinder the rebel men from voting. It reads, "If any person shall knowingly vote without *his* having a lawful right." . . . I insist if government officials may thus manipulate the pronouns to tax, fine, imprison and hang women, it is their duty to thus change them in order to protect us in our right to vote. . . .

Though the words persons, people, inhabitants, electors, citizens, are all used indiscriminately in the national and State constitutions, there was always a conflict of opinion, prior to the war, as to whether they were synonymous terms, but whatever room there was for doubt, under the old regime, the adoption of the Fourteenth Amendment settled that question forever in its first sentence:

> All persons born or naturalized in the United States, and subject to the jurisdiction thereof, are citizens of the United States, and of the State wherein they reside.

10   The second settles the equal status of all citizens:

> No State shall make or enforce any law which shall abridge the privileges or immunities of citizens of the United States; nor shall any State deprive any person of life, liberty or property without due process of law, or deny to any person within its jurisdiction the equal protection of the laws.

The only question left to be settled now is: Are women persons? I scarcely believe any of our opponents will have the hardihood to say they are not. Being persons, then, women are citizens, and no State has a right to make any new law, or to enforce any old law, which shall abridge their privileges or immunities. Hence, every discrimination against women in the constitutions and laws of the several States is today null and void, precisely as is every one against negroes.

Is the right to vote one of the privileges or immunities of citizens? I think the disfranchised ex-rebels and ex-State prisoners all will agree that it is not only one of them, but the one without which all the others are nothing. Seek first the kingdom of the ballot and all things else shall be added, is the political injunction. . . .

However much the doctors of the law may disagree as to whether people and citizens, in the original Constitution, were one and the same, or whether the privileges and immunities in the Fourteenth Amendment include the right of suffrage, the question of the citizen's right to vote is forever settled by the Fifteenth Amendment. "The right of citizens of the United States to vote shall not be denied or abridged by the United States, or by any State, on account of race, color or previous condition of servitude." How can the State deny or abridge the right of the citizen, if the citizen does not possess it? There is no escape from the conclusion that to vote is the citizen's right, and the specifications of race, color or previous condition of servitude can in no way impair the force of that emphatic assertion that the citizen's right to vote shall not be denied or abridged. . . . If, however, you will insist that the Fifteenth Amendment's emphatic interdiction against robbing United States citizens of their suffrage "on account of race, color or previous condition of servitude," is a recognition of the right of either the United States or any State to deprive them of the ballot for any or all other reasons, I will prove to you that the class of citizens for whom I now plead are, by all the principles of our government and many of the laws of the States, included under the term "previous conditions of servitude."

Consider first married women and their legal status. What is servitude? "The condition of a slave." What is a slave? "A person who is robbed of the proceeds of his labor; a person who is subject to the will of another." By the laws of Georgia, South Carolina and all the States of the South, the negro had no right to the custody and control of his person. He belonged to his master. If he were disobedient, the master had the right to use correction. If the negro did not like the correction and ran away, the master had the right to use coercion to bring him back. By the laws of almost every State in this Union today, North as well as South, the married woman has no right to the custody and control of her person. The wife belongs to the husband; and if she refuse obedience he may use moderate correction, and if she do not like his moderate correction and leave his "bed and board," the husband may use moderate coercion to bring her back. The little word "moderate," you see, is the saving clause for the wife, and would doubtless be overstepped should her offended husband administer his correction with the "cat-o'-nine-tails," or accomplish his coercion with blood-hounds.

Again the slave had no right to the earnings of his hands, they belonged to his master; no right to the custody of his children, they belonged to his master; no right to sue or be sued, or to testify in the courts. If he committed a crime, it was the master who must sue or be sued. In many of the States there has been special legislation, giving married women the right to property inherited or received by bequest, or earned by the pursuit of any avocation outside the home; also giving them the right to sue and be sued in matters pertaining to such separate property; but not a single State of this Union has ever secured the wife in the enjoyment of her right to equal ownership of the joint earnings of the marriage copartnership. And since, in the nature of things, the vast majority of married women never earn a dollar by work outside their families, or inherit a dollar from their fathers, it follows that from the day of their marriage to the day of the death of their husbands not one of them ever has a dollar, except it shall please her husband to let her have it. . . .

15   Is anything further needed to prove woman's condition of servitude sufficient to entitle her to the guarantees of the Fifteenth Amendment? Is there a man who will not agree with me that to talk of freedom without the ballot is mockery to the women of this republic, precisely as New England's orator, Wendell Phillips, at the close of the late war declared it to be to the newly emancipated black man? I admit that, prior to the rebellion, by common consent, the right to enslave, as well as to disfranchise both native and foreign born persons, was conceded to the States. But the one grand principle settled by the war and the reconstruction legislation, is the supremacy of the national government to protect the citizens of the United States in their right to freedom and the elective franchise, against any and every interference on the part of the several States; and again and again have the American people asserted the triumph of this principle by their overwhelming majorities for Lincoln and Grant.

The one issue of the last two presidential elections was whether the Fourteenth and Fifteenth Amendments should be considered the irrevocable will of the people; and the decision was that they should be, and that it is not only the right, but the duty of the national government to protect all United States citizens in the full enjoyment and free exercise of their privileges and immunities against the attempt of any State to deny or abridge. . . .

It is upon this just interpretation of the United States Constitution that our National Woman Suffrage Association, which celebrates the twenty-fifth anniversary of the woman's rights movement next May in New York City, has based all its arguments and action since the passage of these amendments. We no longer petition legislature or Congress to give us the right to vote, but appeal to women everywhere to exercise their too long neglected "citizen's right." We appeal to the inspectors of election to receive the votes of all United States citizens, as it is their duty to do. We appeal to United States commissioners and marshals to arrest, as is their duty, the inspectors who reject the votes of United States citizens, and leave alone those who perform their duties and accept these votes. We ask the juries to return verdicts of "not guilty" in the cases of law-abiding United States citizens who cast their votes, and inspectors of election who receive and count them.

We ask the judges to render unprejudiced opinions of the law, and wherever there is room for doubt to give the benefit to the side of liberty and equal rights for women, remembering that, as Sumner says, "The true rule of interpretation under our National Constitution, especially since its amendments, is that anything *for* human rights is constitutional, everything *against* human rights unconstitutional." It is on this line that we propose to fight our battle for the ballot—peaceably but nevertheless persistently—until we achieve complete triumph and all United States citizens, men and women alike, are recognized as equals in the government.

THE BLACK PANTHERS Ten Point Plan

The Black Panther Party was a revolutionary political organization formed in 1966 in the midst of the Civil Rights movement, soon after the assassination of Malcolm X and the riots in Watts (Los Angeles) in protest to the police beating of a black man. Led by Huey P. Newton, Bobby Seale, and David Hilliard, the Black Panthers fought for black liberation. In contrast to the nonviolent civil disobedience of Martin Luther King, Jr. and the Southern Christian Leadership Conference, whose methods they considered too slow, submissive, and ineffective, the Black Panther Party was committed to a more revolutionary agenda: immediately for blacks to arm themselves against their oppressors, and ultimately to change the structure of inequality in the United States. They also set up local Survival Programs in major American cities to provide services to poor and African-American community members, most famously the Free Breakfast for Children Program. The Ten Point Plan was their manifesto for the end to African-American oppression. You can read more about it at their Web site: <http://www.blackpanther.org/>.

1.   **WE WANT FREEDOM. WE WANT POWER TO DETERMINE THE DESTINY OF OUR BLACK AND OPPRESSED COMMUNITIES.** We believe that Black and oppressed people will not be free until we are able to determine our destinies in our own communities ourselves, by fully controlling all the institutions which exist in our communities.

2.   **WE WANT FULL EMPLOYMENT FOR OUR PEOPLE.** We believe that the federal government is responsible and obligated to give every person employment or a guaranteed income. We believe that if the American businessmen will not give full employment, then the technology and means of production should be taken from the businessmen and placed in the community so that the people of the community can organize and employ all of its people and give a high standard of living.

3.   **WE WANT AN END TO THE ROBBERY BY THE CAPITALISTS OF OUR BLACK AND OPPRESSED COMMUNITIES.** We believe that this racist government has robbed us and now we are demanding the overdue debt of forty acres and two mules. Forty acres and two mules were promised 100 years ago as restitution for slave labor and mass murder of Black people. We will accept the payment in currency which will be distributed to our many communities. The American racist has taken part in the slaughter of our fifty million Black people. Therefore, we feel this is a modest demand that we make.

4.   **WE WANT DECENT HOUSING, FIT FOR THE SHELTER OF HUMAN BEINGS.** We believe that if the landlords will not give decent housing to our Black and oppressed communities, then housing and the land should be made into cooperatives so that the people in our communities, with government aid, can build and make decent housing for the people.

5. **WE WANT DECENT EDUCATION FOR OUR PEOPLE THAT EXPOSES THE TRUE NATURE OF THIS DECADENT AMERICAN SOCIETY. WE WANT EDUCATION THAT TEACHES US OUR TRUE HISTORY AND OUR ROLE IN THE PRESENT-DAY SOCIETY.** We believe in an educational system that will give to our people a knowledge of the self. If you do not have knowledge of yourself and your position in the society and in the world, then you will have little chance to know anything else.

6. **WE WANT COMPLETELY FREE HEALTH CARE FOR ALL BLACK AND OPPRESSED PEOPLE.** We believe that the government must provide, free of charge, for the people, health facilities which will not only treat our illnesses, most of which have come about as a result of our oppression, but which will also develop preventive medical programs to guarantee our future survival. We believe that mass health education and research programs must be developed to give all Black and oppressed people access to advanced scientific and medical information, so we may provide ourselves with proper medical attention and care.

7. **WE WANT AN IMMEDIATE END TO POLICE BRUTALITY AND MURDER OF BLACK PEOPLE, OTHER PEOPLE OF COLOR, ALL OPPRESSED PEOPLE INSIDE THE UNITED STATES.** We believe that the racist and fascist government of the United States uses its domestic enforcement agencies to carry out its program of oppression against black people, other people of color and poor people inside the United States. We believe it is our right, therefore, to defend ourselves against such armed forces and that all Black and oppressed people should be armed for self defense of our homes and communities against these fascist police forces.

8. **WE WANT AN IMMEDIATE END TO ALL WARS OF AGGRESSION.** We believe that the various conflicts which exist around the world stem directly from the aggressive desire of the United States' ruling circle and government to force its domination upon the oppressed people of the world. We believe that if the United States government or its lackeys do not cease these aggressive wars it is the right of the people to defend themselves by any means necessary against their aggressors.

9. **WE WANT FREEDOM FOR ALL BLACK AND OPPRESSED PEOPLE NOW HELD IN U. S. FEDERAL, STATE, COUNTY, CITY AND MILITARY PRISONS AND JAILS. WE WANT TRIALS BY A JURY OF PEERS FOR ALL PERSONS CHARGED WITH SO-CALLED CRIMES UNDER THE LAWS OF THIS COUNTRY.** We believe that the many Black and poor oppressed people now held in United States prisons and jails have not received fair and impartial trials under a racist and fascist judicial system and should be free from incarceration. We believe in the ultimate elimination of all wretched, inhuman penal institutions, because the masses of men and women imprisoned inside the United States or by the United States military are the victims of oppressive conditions which are the real cause of their imprisonment. We believe that when persons are brought to trial they must be guaranteed, by the United States, juries of their peers, attorneys of their choice and freedom from imprisonment while awaiting trial.

10.   **WE WANT LAND, BREAD, HOUSING, EDUCATION, CLOTHING, JUSTICE, PEACE AND PEOPLE'S COMMUNITY CONTROL OF MODERN TECHNOLOGY.** When, in the course of human events, it becomes necessary for one people to dissolve the political bonds which have connected them with another, and to assume, among the powers of the earth, the separate and equal station to which the laws of nature and nature's God entitle them, a decent respect to the opinions of mankind requires that they should declare the causes which impel them to the separation.

We hold these truths to be self-evident, that all men are created equal; that they are endowed by their Creator with certain unalienable rights; that among these are life, liberty, and the pursuit of happiness. That to secure these rights, governments are instituted among men, deriving their just powers from the consent of the governed; that, whenever any form of government becomes destructive of these ends, it is the right of the people to alter or to abolish it, and to institute a new government, laying its foundation on such principles, and organizing its powers in such form as to them shall seem most likely to effect their safety and happiness. Prudence, indeed, will dictate that governments long established should not be changed for light and transient causes; and, accordingly, all experience hath shown that mankind are most disposed to suffer, while evils are sufferable, than to right themselves by abolishing the forms to which they are accustomed. But, when a long train of abuses and usurpation, pursuing invariably the same object, evinces a design to reduce them under absolute despotism, it is their right, it is their duty, to throw off such government, and to provide new guards for their future security.

As Anthony's and the Black Panthers' responses demonstrate, arguing does not mean simply attacking or dismissing an opposing viewpoint. Each of their texts celebrates the ideals that are proclaimed in the Declaration of Independence, even as they critique the way those ideals have been realized in American society. Their responses also demonstrate that arguers use a variety of different strategies to communicate their ideas. Anthony's and the Black Panthers' arguments are radically different in the kinds of arguments they make and in how they make them. Each writer was sensitive to what their audiences did or didn't want to hear and what appeals and stylistic choices would most move them.

In the Second Inquiry, we will discuss how to make our own arguments more convincing, by learning how to assess opportunities to inquire by arguing. An arguing-to-inquire mindset means finding appeals that powerfully affect our audiences while promoting rigorous, ethical conversations. We call this mindset the arguing mind.

SECOND INQUIRY: DEVELOPING AN ARGUING MIND

Just as disciplined curiosity can help us develop an inquiring mind, so we can train our empathy to help us develop an arguing mind. According to psychologist William Ickes, empathy is our capacity to infer the thoughts and feelings of others by drawing on close observations, on our memories, and on our knowledge of the people around us. This ability to imaginatively share in the experiences of others is what binds communities together. Aside from consciousness itself, Ickes argues, it "may be the greatest achievement of which the mind is capable" (10).

Of course, our powers of empathy are limited. While we can't actually read other people's minds, our work in the book so far suggests that we can make credible inferences. In the previous exercise, for example, we used textual clues in Anthony's and the Black Panthers' declarations, information we gathered about the writers' historical and social situations, and our general knowledge and wisdom to infer what the writers believed. We used our empathic imaginations to understand and connect with citizens of two different generations.

In addition to understanding the arguments of others, we also use empathy to anticipate how our audience will respond to arguments of our own. For example, the students who silenced a classmate during one Getting Started exercise used empathy. Based on their knowledge of human behavior, they anticipated that calling him a "suck up" would make him self-conscious, effectively shutting down his participation. Unfortunately, as this example illustrates, empathy can be used unethically, to identify and manipulate the fears of others in order to secure compliance or shut down discussion. We can see this tendency in the worst examples of peer pressure, advertising, and political propaganda.

The arguing mind, however, draws on empathy to promote inquiry. Arguers try to "read" their audience and situation to discern what strategies will be most effective. The goal is to push those involved to defend their views and to respond more rigorously in turn. In other words, the more effectively everyone argues, the more powerfully each participant can inquire. Of course, arguers must balance effectiveness with appropriateness. Many strategies of persuasion are effective but unethical; threatening physical violence is a case in point.

Most communities have their own written or unwritten guidelines for civil, or respectful, arguing. In Chapter Five, we will investigate the standards of civil arguing in academic communities. Here, however, we might begin by identifying some general guidelines for civil arguing in the classroom. As you complete the following exercise, remember that arguing minds seek to use the opportunities afforded by disagreement to inquire, and in the process they try to preserve the ties that bind members together.

EXERCISE 4.2 The Principles of Civil Arguing

1. To help you set guidelines for arguing in the classroom, get into small groups and discuss what makes arguments good or bad (use the goals of promoting inquiry and community as your standards of evaluation).
2. Then, from your observations, generalize a list of five principles you would like to see the class observe when conversing about readings, papers, and so on.
3. After each group has made its list, discuss them as a class. Compile them into an overall class list.

4. Each time your class argues, bring out the list and listen for moments when the conversation seems to violate those principles. After the conversation is over, you can then discuss those infractions and why they happened. Do they represent examples of unethical arguing, principles that are too strict, or even conversations where inquiry is not an appropriate goal?

STOP AND THINK

DEBORAH TANNEN AND THE ARGUMENT CULTURE

In her 1998 book *The Argument Culture: Moving from Debate to Dialogue*, linguistics professor Deborah Tannen shows that arguing in our culture is based on an adversarial model common in Western culture. This model is especially prevalent in education and in fields like law, journalism, and politics. According to this model, people assume that social issues have only two sides, with supporters of each attacking the other side, hoping that their view will win out. We need only look at public debates on abortion, gun control, or the death penalty to see the prevalence of this model.

Unfortunately, this kind of public debate sets a more general model for how individuals in our communities relate to one another. In other words, citizens learn to oversimplify issues and to criticize in their private and public lives any views different from their own.

Tannen suggests we supplement this style of arguing with nonconfrontational alternatives drawn from other cultures and from our own imaginations. We could inquire further into this suggestion by talking to others and by brainstorming. How can we rigorously explore ideas without using an adversarial model? How can we improve the adversarial model to avoid the attacking attitude common to it now?

From previous discussions on civil arguing that our students have done, two principles have emerged that seem central to the arguing mind. First, arguers need to put their ideas out into the public. We can't learn through debate unless we express our views to others. Unfortunately, we often assume that everything we argue is a direct and lasting representation of who we are and what we stand for. We forget that the point of arguing to inquire is to learn. No one is born having the wisest views on all issues. If we discover that our views are inaccurate, or if we modify our views as we gather additional information, knowledge, or wisdom, then we ought to celebrate. We are living an examined life.

Second, arguers need to challenge others directly. Arguers frequently present their evidence and persuasive claims only to be met by other arguers presenting evidence and claims of their own. Unless the evidence and claims directly challenge each other, then the arguers talk past one another. They don't seek to shake up each other's ideas or beliefs. For example, a student who thinks the best way to address cheating in college is to toughen penalties is not necessarily talking to a student who thinks cheating is an overexaggerated issue. To really inquire, they would need to first address the second student's argument. Only if the first student shows that cheating is a genuine problem will the second student be ready to discuss ways to solve it.

Of course, a diverse society like America maintains its unity by respecting differences of opinion. This does not mean, however, that we shouldn't use disagreements as opportunities to talk. In other words, if we really wish to be active citizens living examined lives, then we need to seek out opportunities to argue and to frame our arguments in ways that challenge all participants' views. The alternative is to embrace a talk-show mindset, discussed in Chapter Two, in which we accept the truth of all opinions equally, simply because they are opinions.

Because arguments occur in specific places and times, and involve specific people, we need to first learn how to assess opportunities to argue. In Chapter Two, we learned how to assess writing situations; many of those same questions apply here as well. For example, asking ourselves how our audience thinks and feels about our subject can suggest effective arguing strategies. Asking ourselves about the historical and social background of an opportunity can help us decide if this is a good time and place to inquire through arguing. The more rigorously we understand a situation, the more effectively we can prepare to argue within it. Of course, we often don't know everything about our situation, so we must use our imaginations and draw from our own experiences. To begin to habituate yourself to assessing opportunities to argue, try the following exercise.

EXERCISE 4.3   Assessing Opportunities to Argue

1. Read the initial readings or case study in one of the book's chapters. You might practice your summarizing skills by writing short summaries of each reading.
2. In your writer's notebook, list at least three places in the readings where you would like to respond. Perhaps you agree or disagree with a writer's ideas, or perhaps you want to qualify them. Your goal is to identify opportunities where you might respond with your own arguments.
3. Next, assess how you might argue to inquire by asking questions; you might refer to the questions listed in "Exploring Your Writing Situation" in Chapter Two. Finally, discuss your results with others in the class. Do they agree with your assessments? Are your three places good opportunities to learn by arguing?

In addition to assessing opportunities to argue, we also need to frame our arguments so we can participate in existing conversations. Framing an argument is much like framing a research question. To get into an issue, we seek a frame of reference, a way of seeing the issue that allows us to define what kind of research we want to do. The same process occurs in arguing. We need to decide what kind of an argument we want to make. Here are four common ways in which people disagree, which create the reasons people argue:

- *Definitions.* As we learned in Chapter One, definitions often vary with different audiences and purposes. Because the way we define something can shape our responses to it, arguments often form around the appropriate definition of a word or concept. For example, many of the disagreements over family policies in the United States hinge on conflicting definitions of the family.

- *Facts.* Sometimes citizens argue over whether a thing or issue exists or over whether an event has occurred. Environmental groups, business owners, and government officials have argued vigorously in recent years whether the planet is facing an environmental crisis. Some say global warming exists; others say it merely reflects natural changes in the Earth's temperature. Participants in this conversation won't discuss solutions until they agree that a problem exists.

- *Evaluations.* When we argue whether a movie is good or bad, a policy is practical or impractical, or a particular action is moral or immoral, we are evaluating. Framing an evaluative argument often means setting up criteria we then use to assess the excellence or morality of a particular thing, issue, or event. For example, determining whether the Internet is good or bad, or moral or immoral for American democracy depends on what criteria we use to make that assessment. We might assess the Internet by its ability to offer information or by its ability to encourage face-to-face interaction among community members. Each set of criteria would produce a different evaluation.

- *Actions.* Even if we agree on the facts and an evaluation of those facts, we may disagree on whether to respond and how. For example, most of us would agree that poverty exists in the United States and that it is socially and morally bad. However, we may not agree on the best way to respond. Should we promote more employment by encouraging the development of businesses? Should we offer government-sponsored relief programs, or should we do nothing at all as a nation, relying instead on individuals and private charities?

Of course, many arguments will contain different types of arguments within them. For example, a citizen offering a solution to urban sprawl must first establish that urban sprawl is a problem. Then, he or she can advocate a particular action. Once we know what kind of an argument we want to make, we can consult those people or written works with whom we want to argue. In other words, we can focus on those people or works that more directly support or contend the argument we have framed. In this way, we force ourselves to account for their views, promoting in our own arguments a more rigorous discussion. To practice framing arguments, try the following exercise.

EXERCISE 4.4   Framing Our Arguments

1. Taking the opportunities you discovered in Exercise 4.3, brainstorm in your writer's notebook about which kinds of argument you want to make. Do you want to argue over facts, definitions, evaluations, or actions, or do you want to combine them?

2. Review the initial readings or case study works you read in Exercise 4.3. Which of these works makes arguments that seem in direct conversation with the kinds of arguments you have framed?

Once we have a clearer sense of the arguments we want to make and the conversations we want to join, we need to consider the strategies we will use to make those arguments more rigorous. This is the subject of the next inquiry.

THIRD INQUIRY: ARGUING EFFECTIVELY

Chapter Two reminds us that writing is not just self-expression; it is communication with the goal of affecting readers in real ways. Because of our ability to empathize with readers, we can anticipate, in a limited way, how they will be affected by the arguing strategies we use to persuade them. When we appeal to evidence, to reason, to our reputations as careful researchers or writers, and, to readers' emotions, we already have some sense of how readers will probably respond. Knowing more about these arguing strategies can help us employ them more effectively and more ethically.

Four points about these strategies should be considered before we proceed. First, you already possess the ability to use these arguing strategies. Learning the subtleties of emotional or visual appeals, for example, would be difficult if our cultural upbringing hadn't already taught us how. We have appealed to sympathy to avoid punishment, we have appealed to reason to get our curfews extended, and we have acted appropriately to persuade our employers that we can handle our jobs. In a thousand different instances, we demonstrate our ability to use these appeals. Learning more about them can help us craft these appeals in more savvy and ethical ways.

Second, persuasion is not an exact science. Although these appeals are presented in a particular order, we don't apply them to our writing methodically. Rather, we consider what strategies we will use when we assess an arguing opportunity. We also consider types of appeals as we write, and we sharpen our appeals as we revise. Writing persuasively is tied intimately to writing itself, as much a concern through the writing process as clarity, precision, or coherence.

Third, different types of appeals often work together. Although we present these strategies individually, they often complement one another in actual writing. For example, a story might serve as evidence of a claim, but the story might also elicit emotions that encourage readers to accept the claim's truth. On the other hand, examining the types of appeals individually can sensitize us to those times when different appeals might conflict, as when a story serves as good evidence, but prompts emotions damaging to the writer's credibility.

Fourth, whether our appeals are effective and ethical often depends on the writing situation. For example, appealing to church doctrine as evidence of a claim might be both effective and ethical in a religious community, but it might be considered a *fallacy* in a scientific community, representing a breech of that community's standards for rigorous and ethical arguing.

Usually we think of fallacies as errors in our reasoning, but this view assumes a rationalist perspective. Rationalism is the belief that logic and evidence alone are reliable guides for assessing the truth of a claim. Most academic disciplines base their research methods and arguing standards on rationalism. However, not all communities follow this model, and many of the arguments we participate in will make use of non-rational appeals. As a result, we should know how to detect and use them appropriately. In addition, identifying a fallacy as a violation of an arguer's good faith agreement to inquire rigorously and ethically reminds us of our obligation to learn a community's arguing standards. To test the truth of this fourth point, and of the other three points, try the following exercise as a class:

EXERCISE 4.5 Discovering Types of Appeals

1. Below are three opportunities to inquire through arguing. Choose one of these opportunities as a class and imagine yourself in that situation. Then, in small groups brainstorm what types of appeals or arguing strategies you would use to convince your audience.

   a. The Council to Promote Stronger Families (CPSF) wants you to create a Web site designed to promote family values. What strategies or kinds of appeals can you make to convince Americans to view families as married, heterosexual couples with children? Now, create a Web site that will compete with the CPSF's, convincing Americans to reject the organization's definition of the American family, arguing instead that individuals have the right to establish their own definitions of family. What kinds of appeals would you use in each situation?

   b. Try to convince your parents that they should give you $10,000 (assuming they have it) and let you travel around Europe for a year. What kinds of appeals would you use to persuade them?

   c. Using the case study you read for Exercises 4.3 and 4.4, brainstorm the kinds of appeals you would use to persuade a given audience. (The case studies allow you to frame the issue in different ways and with different arguing strategies that come out of particular arguing situations; consequently, you will first need to narrow the case study's issue to a more specific opportunity, similar to the first opportunity above. That example originates from the family values case study in Chapter Seven.)

2. Next, share your groups' ideas with the class. Write the different appeals on the blackboard and categorize them according to the kinds of appeals you think they make (e.g., to reason, to the emotions, and so on). Then, discuss further whether you think particular appeals are especially effective or potentially unethical.

The preceding exercise should have demonstrated that you already have an intuitive sense of how to argue. It should have also demonstrated that you can turn to a variety of appeals to support your arguments. What follows is a further inquiry into the more common types. As you may discover, however, these categories are only general descriptions; our use of these strategies is more subtle and imaginative than any label can capture.

Appealing to Evidence

In Chapter Three, we learned how to gather information to answer our questions and to develop knowledge and wisdom. The information we gather usually leads us toward particular answers to the questions we have posed. This information is evidence. Normally, we think of evidence as something that we need to prove our points to others. This is true, but when we weave our arguments in with the facts, observations, experimental data, or opinions of knowledgeable people, we are also discovering the truth of these claims for ourselves. The more rigorously we can use evidence as an argumentative strategy, the more sure we can be in our own knowledge and wisdom.

The different research methods we learned in Chapter Three provide us with different kinds of evidence. The first kind, *quantitative*, allows us to generalize about larger populations. Such evidence can come from surveys, experiments, or observations that quantify, or count, particular phenomena. For example, census data on American families might provide evidence about the number of families that divorce, have children, or contain two working parents. At the same time, such evidence would not help us to understand what going through a divorce, having children, or sharing household responsibilities is like. For that kind of inquiry, we would need to gather evidence on individuals' experiences; in other words, we would need *qualitative* evidence.

Qualitative evidence can come from personal narratives, interviews, interpretations of written documents, or observations of individual behavior. Such evidence is rich in details allowing us to support subtle claims about particular phenomena. For example, Margaret Talbot's interviews with and observations of one American family in Chapter Seven help us understand what it is like to live by conservative religious principles in a secular society. On the other hand, Talbot's research would not support general claims about *all* American families. She would first have to show, using statistics, that the family she studied is representative of many or all American families. Because each evidence type has its own unique strengths and limitations, arguers often draw from both quantitative and qualitative evidence to verify the truth of their claims.

EXERCISE 4.6   Assessing Appeals to Evidence

To explore how evidence is used to support arguments, isolate appeals to evidence from your list of arguing strategies or locate ten appeals to evidence in the case study readings. Write down the claim the writer is trying to prove, then write down the evidence he or she uses to support that claim. Consider statistics; statements by authorities or experts; historical, cultural or physical facts; arguers' personal experiences; other people's experiences (e.g., interviews, summarized observations); and so on. For each of your ten examples, answer the following questions:

1. Do the authors have enough evidence to support their claim?
2. How does this evidence work to convince you?
3. How do they present the evidence? (e.g., Do they put the evidence or claim first?)

Then, discuss these questions with others in the class. How do we know when we have enough evidence, or what kind of evidence we ought to use? In how many ways can we present evidence in a work?

The Scottish philosopher David Hume once said, "a wise man proportions his belief to the evidence." This statement is a useful guide for deciding how much evidence we need to support our claims. The more difficult it is for us to accept the truth of a particular claim, the more we would need to surround it with evidence. Consider the following examples, taken from previous discussions. Does each arguer provide enough evidence to support his or her claim?

> Broadening the definition of marriage to include same-sex unions would stretch it almost beyond recognition—and new attempts to expand the definition still further would surely follow . . . . Why on earth would [advocates of same-sex marriages] exclude from marriage a bisexual who wants to marry two other people? . . . Or . . . a father and daughter who want to marry. Or two sisters. Or men who want (consensual) polygamous arrangements.

> Going to Europe would be an educational experience. My friend John went to Italy with his architecture class. He said he learned more about structure and design in two weeks than he did in two semesters at college.

The first example, from William Bennett's "Leave Marriage Alone" in Chapter Seven, is a claim without any evidence. For many of his readers such a claim would need no evidence; it is an obvious truth that fits in with their own sense of American society. For other readers, however, it is a highly biased statement, representing many unexamined assumptions, like the belief that our older institution of marriage is worth protecting. Opponents to Bennett's claim would also consider it a fallacy, an *unsubstantiated claim* that tries to pass itself off as self-evident, or obviously true. Bennett's piece was originally published in *Newsweek*; he may have felt a mainstream audience would not demand support for his claim. On the other hand, to strengthen his own conviction, and to challenge those who might oppose his views, he could have provided evidence showing that broadening the definition of marriage in some areas has caused a weakening of marriage vows and a desire for ever broader definitions.

The second example, from a student eager to travel in Europe, appeals to qualitative evidence. The student cites a friend's experience to support his claim that traveling in Europe would be educational. While the student's example exhibits the strength of qualitative evidence—for example, his parents can visualize the student's friend touring Italy and learning about architecture—it lacks the strength of quantitative evidence. One example isn't enough to support the general conclusion that everyone who travels to Europe will have an educational experience, especially since the friend went only for two weeks and never left Italy. Once again, it depends on the situation. For some parents, a single example like this one might be sufficient. For others, many examples, supported by other forms of evidence, might be necessary.

In the second example, the student might even be accused of a fallacy, of offering *misleading evidence*, if he or she withheld the example of two friends who went to Europe, learned absolutely nothing, and even got into trouble with local officials. Ignoring evidence that disagrees with our claims, presenting evidence in ways that oversimplify complex issues, or misrepresenting evidence by taking it out of its original context are all examples of this fallacy because they diminish the rigor and fair-mindedness of our inquiry.

Here are a few additional suggestions paraphrased from previous students' comments about appealing to evidence rigorously and ethically. Please add your own suggestions to the list on our Web site **http://www.ablongman.com/berndt**:

- Readers probably won't change their beliefs just because we tell them to, no matter how strongly we assert our claims. We need to prove, through evidence, any claims they might disagree with. We can learn which claims are most controversial by reading other works on our subject.

- If we don't have evidence to support a claim—because we think it is self-evident or because we can't find any—we should acknowledge that fact; lacking evidence doesn't necessarily mean that our claim is wrong. Besides, if we are honest and straightforward, readers will think better of us as arguers.

- We should make our assumptions clear and explicit. Defining our terms and exposing beliefs and values that are relevant to our arguments will help readers understand where we are coming from. Even if they don't agree with those assumptions, they will appreciate our effort to be open and sincere.

- If we cop a condescending attitude toward our subject or our readers, we will encourage those who disagree with us to respond in the same way. If we stay positive, even when we disagree, we can encourage inquiry and preserve community ties.

- We should be aware of the limitations of our writing situation. If we are writing an editorial, for example, we don't have the space to include extensive evidence. If we still want to be rigorous and ethical, we may have to reframe our argument to something smaller and more manageable.

Appealing to Reason

When we tell other arguers to be "reasonable" or to talk "rationally," we usually mean that they should be more *cautious* in what they say, more *dispassionate* in how they say it, and more *self-conscious* in how they carry on the conversation. All of these qualities suggest that appeals to reason are appeals to clear away the clutter, to put aside any thoughts or feelings that might bias our decisions. These qualities also suggest we would, as reasonable arguers, pay attention to the way we make our decisions, in other words, to be aware of the patterns of thought we follow to make sense of information and to create knowledge or wisdom. We would have to determine whether we followed these patterns conscientiously.

In this section, we will look more closely at three common patterns of thought: deduction, induction, and analogy. Since these patterns are central to the way we think about ourselves and about the world, we will focus on how to appeal to them more rigorously and methodically.

First, to think *deductively* means to affirm the truth of a specific claim because it fits with larger claims we already accept as true. For example, we see deductive thinking when meteorologists use theories about pressure systems to predict the local weather on any given night. We see it when people criticize some particular action like driving without a seat belt because it violates common sense. We also see it when religious leaders condemn a social practice like prostitution because it offends a community's moral principles. Whether we apply general claims about the physical world, human behaviors, or community moral standards, the pattern of our thinking is similar. We assert the truth of a specific claim (e.g., "I must take composition to graduate") by appealing to a larger claim (e.g., "All students at this college must take composition to graduate").

Second, to think *inductively* means to form general claims by appealing to a number of specific claims. The scientific theories, points of common sense, and moral principles we apply in deductive thinking are often formed through the accumulation of experience and inductive reasoning. If a physics professor asks us to drop a ball and measure its velocity twenty times, he or she is asking us to confirm laws of the physical world, like gravity. If we get bitten every time we try to pet the neighbor's dog, we can probably assume it will bite us the next time as well. Finally, if we continually hurt others by telling lies, we might conclude that we shouldn't lie anymore (assuming we don't want to hurt others). As these examples illustrate, the reliability of our general claims varies, depending on how many specific examples we accumulate, and how carefully we generalize from the examples.

Finally, to think *analogically* means to make sense of something we don't know by comparing it to something we do know. We often use analogies in writing or speaking to explain a complicated or abstract concept; we compare the unfamiliar, abstract concept to something concrete and familiar to our audience. In Chapter Ten, for instance, David W. Orr's essay, "Saving Future Generations from Global Warming," compares global warming to slavery. At first these two things seem too dissimilar to be analogous, but this strange pairing actually hooks the readers' interest. Readers want to know just how global warming and slavery might be related. Orr then develops the analogy by comparing our rationalizations for dismissing the dangers of global warming to earlier generations' justifications for continuing the practice of slavery, which now seem embarrassingly self-serving and indefensible.

Analogies often take the form of metaphors. Writers will use metaphors to describe physical phenomena (e.g., "Mitochondria are the *powerhouses* of the cell"). They use them to visualize complex processes (e.g., "According to Adam Smith, individuals seeking their own economic good are led by *an invisible hand* to benefit their society"). They even use them to reach a moral judgment (e.g., "In the essay "Lifeboat Ethics," researcher Garrett Hardin compares our planet to *a lifeboat* with limited space; if we try to save everyone, everyone will sink). If readers find the metaphor itself persuasive, they are likely to find the entire argument persuasive. Comparisons of all kinds are very common in our arguing, formal and informal. Even arguing itself is talked about through analogies. Whether we talk about arguing as combat, with generals strategizing and going on the offensive, or as diplomacy, with representatives seeking compromise, we still conceive of it in terms of analogy.

EXERCISE 4.7   Assessing Appeals to Reason

To explore how appeals to reason are used to tie claims or evidence into existing knowledge, pull out examples from your list of persuasive strategies or locate ten appeals to reason in the readings. Write down each example, discuss what patterns of thought it follows, and then answer the following questions:

1. Is this appeal to reason convincing? Why or why not?
2. Is it sufficiently careful, rigorous, and systematic to convince members of an academic or civic community?
3. In what ways could the appeal be strengthened, to make the truth of the claim it supports more certain?

Here are three additional examples of different appeals to reason, taken from previous classroom discussions. Each represents one of the common patterns of thought discussed above. As you read them, answer the above questions.

People grow by experiencing new things. I will have all kinds of new experiences in Europe. I could really grow as a person from this trip.

Going to Europe would be an educational experience. My friend John went to Italy with his architecture class. He said he learned more about structure and design in two weeks than he did in two semesters at college.

As one step on behalf of law and order—and on behalf of opportunity as well—the President has initiated the "Weed and Seed" program—to "weed out" criminals and "seed" neighborhoods with programs that address root causes of crime.

In the first example, the writer is appealing to deductive reasoning. The first statement, "People grow by learning about and experiencing new things," is a generalization, a statement expressing the common belief that people mature as human beings by exposing themselves to new experiences. If we accept it as true, then it follows that the arguer, who will learn about and experience new things in Europe, will also grow as a person. In this case, the arguer is asserting the truth of a particular claim—he or she will grow by experiencing new things in Europe— by appealing to the general claim that people grow by experiencing new things.

Of course, we could probably find many examples where people learn about or experience new things but fail to grow. This would suggest that the general statement is not absolutely true, at least not true in the same sense as statements like "All triangles have three sides" or "All human beings are mortal." Most of the general statements we make in life will not be absolutely true; rather, they will be more or less probable. Whether our audience accepts our general claim as likely or unlikely will depend on their experiences. Have they experienced something that would suggest this claim is true? Part of living an examined life is testing our generalized knowledge of the world against lived experience, all of those particular situations in which our generalizations may or may not apply. To always assume that our general knowledge is true, especially when dealing with human behavior, is to fall into *dogmatism*, a fallacy in which beliefs are never subjected to examination.

Previous students have come up with several suggestions for improving the rigor and ethical appropriateness of appeals to deductive reasoning. Please add your own suggestions to the list on our Web site **http://www.ablongman.com/berndt**.

- Readers might be more willing to accept a general claim, and therefore a particular claim that appeals to it, if that general claim is clearly and precisely worded. For instance, the word *things* in the first example is vague; does it mean any kind of experience, like walking around the block, or more significant experiences, like traveling to a new country?

- We should qualify our general claims to express how much faith we have in their truth. We might use words like *often, sometimes, frequently, may, could, in some cases*, and so on to state that our general claim doesn't apply to all particular claims. For example, we could rewrite the general claim in the first example as "People often grow by learning about and experiencing new things," or "Many people grow by learning about and experiencing new things," if we feel confident in its truth.

- We should make sure our particular claim is really an example of our general claim. For example, if we had already seen everything we planned to visit in Europe, then our claim that visiting Europe would help us grow can't appeal to our general claim. After all, the things we plan to see would no longer be new to us.

We have already seen the second example, which illustrates an appeal to inductive reasoning, in the Appealing to Evidence section. This example demonstrates an important point about appeals to reason and evidence: they usually work together. In this case, the arguer is drawing on other particular examples to arrive at the general claim "Going to Europe would be an educational experience."

This claim is much like the general claim in the previous example: "People grow by experiencing new things." Their similarity suggests another important point: We as human beings usually arrive at general knowledge and wisdom inductively, by generalizing from many particular instances. We then apply this knowledge and wisdom deductively, testing its truth against more particular instances.

Of course, the example of inductive reasoning we have here is weak. To move from one example, where a student learned something in Europe, to the general claim that everyone going to Europe would have an educational experience is to commit a *hasty generalization* fallacy, meaning we assert a conclusion that isn't supported by enough evidence. We might also be guilty of this fallacy if we jumped to a conclusion that isn't even suggested by the particular instances we've gathered together. For example, if many students in a course failed, we might assume they didn't work very hard. However, the same particular instances, the students failing, might suggest different conclusions. Perhaps the course was very difficult, the instructor taught badly, or the time of day discouraged learning.

Rigorous arguers look closely at any patterns suggested by evidence so the general claims they reach genuinely represent what was going on in the individual instances. Here are additional suggestions offered by previous students. Again, please add your own to the list on our Web site **http://www.ablongman.com/berndt.**

- If we want readers to believe our general claims, we should show them our evidence. For example, scientists who write reports on their research usually include the raw data so readers can see for themselves whether the scientists reached the correct conclusions.
- We should qualify the conclusions we reach according to how many particular examples we've drawn together and how confident we feel in our inductive reasoning. Using words like *always, never, all, none, certainly,* or *absolutely* may commit us to a fallacy if our evidence doesn't support such sweeping generalizations.

The last example, from Dan Quayle's 1992 speech at the Commonwealth Club of California, illustrates an appeal to analogous reasoning. In this case, Quayle is alluding to someone else's analogy, but his other statements suggest this is an analogy he supports. Something we know about (or at least we can visualize)—lawn care—is used as a metaphor for explaining social policy in inner cities. In this case, former President George Bush's program implies that we can create uniform prosperity in inner cities if we remove those people we don't want—the criminals—and encourage those who we do want—the hard-working, honest citizens—by offering them incentive programs designed to eliminate their poverty. Just as weeds seek to choke off the grass, so criminals seek to destroy the efforts of good people to improve their communities.

Analogies like the one Quayle refers to are hard to create because no two things are exactly the same. Quayle's supporters might believe that this analogy works because they see criminals as different from regular citizens. Criminals are individuals who decide to violate the laws and disrupt their communities. To prevent the rest from being victimized, these criminals must be removed.

On the other hand, readers who don't support Quayle's values and beliefs might accuse him of committing a *false analogy* fallacy, asserting similarities between subjects that are really different. If these critics of Quayle believe that criminals are not essentially different from law-abiding citizens, but are themselves victims of poverty and despair, then they wouldn't accept the weed and seed metaphor as accurate.

Philosopher Mark Johnson argues that moral decision-making is essentially imaginative. We use imaginative structures like analogies as frameworks to make sense of the world around us and to act in ethical ways. Do we see criminals as undernourished grass or noxious weeds? How we answer that question might determine whether we build more prisons or more schools, more courthouses or drug rehabilitation programs. Or, do we abandon this analogy altogether, seeking alternative ways we can get a handle on the complex problems facing inner cities?

Previous students have offered several suggestions for improving the rigor and ethical appropriateness of appeals to analogy. Add your own suggestions to the list on our Web site **http://www.ablongman.com/berndt**.

- An analogy isn't the same as evidence. Just because you call social programs *seeds* doesn't mean they will actually work in "growing" better communities.
- We should work out the consequences of our analogies before we use them. If we call criminals *weeds* does that mean we should rip them out of their communities and kill them? Explaining how far we want our analogies to apply—saying criminals are weeds only because they prey on innocent community members—will set limits to readers' imaginations.
- We should be sensitive to the emotions or ideas readers might associate with the words or images we want to use as analogies. For example, if we say criminals are *pond scum* we will encourage readers to think and feel about criminals negatively. If we say criminals are *lost sheep*, we will encourage very different thoughts and feelings. The important point is that in both cases we have provided no evidence to suggest why readers should think one way or another; the analogies themselves shape our thinking.

Although we already follow patterns of deductive, inductive, and analogous thinking, we can improve our appeals to reason by exercising the suggestions offered above. Included below are four statements on which we can practice. After you read them, discuss how they might be rewritten to represent more cautious, dispassionate, self-conscious reasoning.

1. Al Gore is a Washington insider. You can't trust him.
2. In a 1991 Roper survey, researchers discovered that, out of 6000 respondents, 119 had experienced these five indicators of an alien abduction: 1) unusual lights in their room, 2) a loss of time, 3) physical paralysis, 4) levitation, and 5) unexplainable scars on their bodies. If these results are extrapolated to the entire U.S. population, then over 5 million peo-

ple have experienced alien abduction. Surely the number of people who have experienced such similar events confirms the truth that aliens are among us.

3. The human mind is a *tabula rasa*, a blank slate on which experience writes.

4. "Broadening the definition of marriage to include same-sex marriages would stretch it almost beyond recognition—and new attempts to broaden the definition still further would surely follow. On what principled grounds can [advocates of same-sex marriages] exclude others who most desperately want what [they want], legal recognition and social acceptance? Why on earth would [they] exclude from marriage a bisexual who wants to marry two other people? . . . . [Or] a father and daughter who want to marry. Or two sisters. Or men who want (consensual) polygamous arrangements."

STOP AND THINK

MICHAEL SHERMER AND SKEPTICISM

Michael Shermer, the author of *Why People Believe Weird Things* (1997) and director of the Skeptics Society, defines a skeptic as "one who questions the validity of a particular claim by calling for evidence to prove or disprove it" (17). Skeptics base their beliefs on observation and on clear inductive and deductive reasoning. They also test their knowledge against further observations. Unfortunately, this rational approach to creating knowledge is often short-circuited by the limits of our research tools, by mistakes in our reasoning, or by misunderstandings on what makes for reliable knowledge. Shermer offers several reasons why people believe in alien abductions, ghosts, psychic predictions, and other "weird things" that fail to meet skeptics' criteria for reliable knowledge:

- Our desire for simple, easily understood answers often pushes us to oversimplify complex issues. We need to remember that many issues don't have easy, simple answers; we need to think critically about them.
- We often form a possible solution to an issue and seek evidence to prove it, instead of also seeking evidence to disprove it.
- We frequently mistake rumors for true stories. Just because most of us have heard that alligators roam New York sewers doesn't mean it is true.
- We tend to remember those instances that confirm our beliefs and to forget those that reject our beliefs. For example, if a psychic makes one correct prediction out of five guesses, we shouldn't forget the four predictions that she or he got wrong.

Because critical thinking is so difficult and people make mistakes all the time, Shermer suggests we adopt an inquiring attitude. We should question other people's claims, not to ridicule them, but to better understand the world around us.

Appealing to Character

Evidence and reason appeal strongly to us today but we also value an arguer's character, those intellectual and moral qualities that distinguish the individual arguer and serve as the basis of his or her reputation. Our character can be established in two ways when we argue: by the history of our actions and by the image we present of ourselves in writing and speaking.

The first way, called our *situated character*, refers to our reputation at a given time and within a given community. The history of what we have said or done reveals to other people the kind of person we are. For example, your writing, your participation in class discussion, even your actions during outside conferences have shaped your instructor's and classmates' views on your ability, your seriousness, and your credibility as a critical thinker. You can change your reputation only by changing your behavior, letting community members accumulate a new history of your actions.

The second way, called our *invented character*, refers to our *persona*, the image we project of ourselves by how we write. When we read an essay, we not only digest the content, we also form an opinion of the writer—the writer's knowledge of the subject and his or her ability as a thinker and communicator. This opinion often influences how seriously we consider the writer's ideas. Fortunately, we usually have the leisure to craft our writing carefully, presenting the best possible image of ourselves.

Of course, dismissing someone's argument because of their character, whether situated or invented, can be unethical, what rhetoricians call an *ad hominem* fallacy. This fallacy, which means "to the person," refers to our tendency to dismiss an arguer's claim by dismissing the arguer. Perhaps a writer is known for expressing biased opinions. Perhaps a writer frequently misspells words, adopts a condescending tone toward readers, or uses too many complex words and ideas. Dismissing a speech or written work for these reasons is unethical; critical thinkers believe arguments should be evaluated on their own merit and not on the credibility of the arguer alone. Nevertheless, we often make such judgments in our daily lives, and we ought to guard against them both as readers and writers. While we cannot easily change our situated characters, we can practice strategies that improve our invented characters. Since the people who read our arguments probably don't know us very well, our invented characters become quite important.

EXERCISE 4.8   Assessing Appeals to Character

To explore how situated and invented characters affect our persuasiveness as arguers, review your list of persuasive strategies. Brainstorm additional ways you could impress your audience with your competence, sincerity, or fair-mindedness.

Alternatively, locate two works in the readings that caused you to have a strong positive or negative reaction to the writer. Then, explain why you reacted so strongly. Often our response is intuitive—we aren't aware of the reasoning process we went through to reach our conclusions—so we need to analyze the readings closely. Identify five strategies the two writers used that strengthened or weakened their character in your eyes.

Based on previous discussions, here are several strategies for improving our invented characters. Of course, which strategies we use will depend on our writing situation. Please add your own suggestions to the list on our Web site **http://www.ablongman.com/berndt**.

- We need to know our subject. We show our credibility by engaging others who have written on the subject, by using specific details, and by carefully explaining how our evidence supports our claims.
- We should acknowledge other people's views. Arguers who dismiss or ignore alternative viewpoints can appear manipulative, like they are hiding the truth. Showing we appreciate where other people are coming from, even if we disagree with them, will make us appear fair-minded.
- If we appeal to the values and beliefs of our readers, we show that we are one of them. For example, politicians express rural values when talking with farmers, even if they never grew up on a farm. Of course, drawing on the audience's values and beliefs may backfire if the connection we are trying to make with them is insincere. The best way to decide if we should appeal to shared values and experiences is to put ourselves in the audience's position. How would we view someone making such appeals?
- We should express a tone appropriate to our subject and audience. Experts in business communication like Andrew Carnegie suggest we show a positive attitude even if we disagree with readers. This tone will encourage the audience to hear our arguments more readily than if we were dismissive of or hostile to their views.

Appealing to Emotions

The French mathematician Blaise Pascal once wrote, "The heart has its reasons, which reason does not understand." Pascal's suggestion, that humans are sometimes driven by emotions, might seem an unhappy description of our tendency to act irrationally, against the better judgment of cool, objective reasoning. This view, however, assumes that reason and emotion are separate and opposed. It also assumes that reason alone is the proper guide to our actions.

Recent research in neurology, however, indicates that emotions and reasoning are intimately connected. Antonio Damasio, a professor of neurology at the University of Iowa College of Medicine, suggests we modify Pascal's quote to read, "The organism has some reasons that reason must utilize" (200). Damasio argues that when we are faced with a decision, our emotions direct us in considering our options. Some courses of action may be supported within the individual by negative or positive feelings; these feelings act as aversions or incentives that limit the number of choices the individual must consider. To recognize this idea, we might read Ursula Le Guin's "The Ones Who Walk Away from Omelas" in Chapter Six. Even though the Omelans' decision to base the joy of thousands on the misery of one child may seem a logical choice—the happiness of many requires the suffering of only one—most of us would probably feel a strong emotional aversion to such a decision.

Knowing the role emotion plays in our decision-making process can sensitize us to its positive or negative effects. To explore this idea, and to discover ways we can appeal to readers' emotions in effective and ethical ways, try the following exercise.

EXERCISE 4.9   Assessing Appeals to Emotions

To explore how emotional appeals are used to support arguments, review your list of persuasive strategies or locate five examples in the readings in which writers try to persuade their audience by encouraging an emotional response. Write these examples down in your writer's notebook and then share them with your classmates. Consider the following questions as you discuss them:

1. What kind of an emotional response is the writer encouraging?
2. How is the writer able to encourage an emotional response?
3. Does this emotional appeal assist or diminish readers' critical thinking? In other words, is it ethical?

Here are three examples from previous discussions, followed by several suggestions how to use emotional appeals effectively. Do they support Damasio's argument that emotions play an intimate role in reasoning?

> Families are the people for whom it matters if you have a cold, are feuding with your mate or training a new puppy. Family members use magnets to fasten the newspaper clippings about your bowling team on the refrigerator door. They save your drawings and homemade pottery. They like to hear stories about when you were young . . . . Whether or not they are biologically related to each other, the people who do these things are family.

> All the students in my program are getting international experience. If you don't let me go too, I'll never be able to compete against them in the job market.

> Give me money to go to Europe or I will never speak to you again.

In the first example, from Mary Pipher's *The Shelter of Each Other: Rebuilding Our Families* in Chapter Seven, readers are encouraged to broaden their definitions of family to include those people with whom we share our experiences, both trivial and important. To persuade her audience, Pipher uses emotional examples like "training a new puppy." These examples arouse positive feelings, encouraging us to accept her argument. If she relied only on these emotional images to convince us, she might be accused of committing a *sentimental appeal* fallacy, using emotions like nostalgia to encourage an uncritical response. Emotions can help us reason more constructively, but we need reason and evidence to help ensure that we aren't being manipulated by the writer.

The second example calls on parents to think of their child's future. The arguer tries to get their consent by arguing that other parents are helping their children. If the arguer's parents truly love their child, and are concerned about his or her welfare, they will join the crowd. In other words, the arguer is appealing to the parents' fear that their child might fall behind in the world. If the arguer appealed only to this emotion, he or she would be committing a *bandwagon* fallacy, persuading readers to agree to an idea because everyone else does. The example might be acceptable if the arguer provided evidence that candidates in his or her field do indeed need international experience. Emotions can connect us to others. Just as appeals to common sense testify to the shared experiences of community members, so emotional appeals testify to our shared emotional needs. However, if we use these needs to compel acceptance of our ideas at the expense of evidence and reason, then we argue unethically.

The third example might seem rather weak as an argument. To threaten the audience with silence in order to compel their agreement is to commit a fallacy; *scare tactics*, direct or indirect threats to our audience, discourage readers from thinking critically about the subject and from considering alternative viewpoints. Emotions can move us to take action. As writers, however, we should exercise the emotional intelligence to be aware of our feelings toward our subject and audience. We can move our readers to act, but in communities where willing consensus is valued, we should seek to move our readers by evidence, reason, a credible persona, and emotional appeals appropriate to that community's arguing standards. If we try to win by threats or unethical appeals to emotions, we only undermine our own credibility.

Here are additional suggestions offered by previous students:

- We should assess the situation to see if emotional appeals are appropriate. Is the subject an emotional one for readers? Would expressing your emotions on the subject help or hurt your purpose? Is emotion appropriate in the genre in which you are writing (e.g., in a science report)?

- We can establish common ground with our readers by acknowledging any emotional attitudes toward the subject that exist out there. Readers may respect us more if we acknowledge how they feel about the subject, especially if we plan to argue against their views.

- We can evoke emotions like sympathy or pity or anger by choosing scenes or events that will really resonate with them and then describing them in concrete detail. However, we should remember to appeal also to evidence and reason, in case we risk committing a sentimental appeal fallacy.

- We should evoke emotions by paying careful attention to our language use, especially our word choice. This strategy is difficult to use well without alienating readers so it should be used cautiously. For example, consider the very different emotional responses created by using either of the following pairs of words in an abortion debate: *baby/fetus, kill/abort, rip apart/remove.*

Appealing to Visual Arguments

Visual arguments are all around us. The obvious and most recurrent form they take is in advertising, but we find visual arguments in photojournalism, art, illustrations, TV news programs, cartoons, maps, charts, bar graphs—wherever images are used to demonstrate a point or persuade an audience. Visual arguments are effective because they impact us much more quickly than words do, and they tend to stick with us, to linger in our minds long after we have seen them. This means we should be aware of how visual arguments work, both so we can read them critically and so we can create them effectively.

We often think of photojournalism as presenting us with objective, real images, rather than carefully developed arguments. To analyze the visual arguments present in photojournalism, compare the two family images in Chapter Seven. Mark Seliger's photograph for *Rolling Stone* and Jeff Riedel's photograph for *The New York Times Magazine* represent two different versions of the American family. As you study the images, use the following questions to guide your analysis.

1. Identify the photograph's "thesis" or "message." To identify this, consider what impression it immediately makes on you, what it makes you feel or think. What point does it seem to be making?

2. What seems to be the point of view of the photographer? What vision does he have of this American family? Look closely for subtle hints that might not be obvious on your first few viewings of the photo. Notice the background, the setting, and all of the individuals' positions and facial expressions.

3. What seems to be the point of view of the subjects of the photographs? What do their facial expressions and positions convey to you? What do they seem to be thinking?

4. Notice how the textual elements are also part of the argument. What are the key words used in the headline and the copy? How do they capture our attention quickly and strike a chord with readers? How does the message of the text—the title and subtitle—of each photograph work with or against the message of the image? Are they complementary; i.e., does the image illustrate the text's argument, or the text explain the image? Or are they contrasting; i.e., the image and text seem to give contradictory messages, perhaps to reveal the difference between the appearance and reality of an issue?

Since visual arguments, especially advertisements, are aimed at us on a daily basis and affect the way we choose to live our lives, we need to get in the habit of viewing them critically and with awareness of their goals. Knowing how visual arguments work can also help us use them more effectively in our own work. Although visual arguments work on audiences more immediately than written ones, developing a visual argument follows much the same process as developing a written one. Here are several suggestions for creating your own visual arguments:

- Assess your situation. What is the subject matter, audience, and your purpose?
- How will you use the visual argument to achieve your purpose? For instance, will it illustrate your point? Will it serve as the primary argument itself, and be explained by your text?
- What kind of appeal should the image have? Should it appeal to logic or emotion? Should it strengthen your reputation?
- What kind of image will be most effective? Do you want to use a graph, a table, a photograph, a graphic image, or a work of art?
- How can you avoid misleading or manipulating your audience with your images? Are your graphs, tables, or maps current and accurate? What are the implications of your images; will they convey the message you want and only that message?

Use the previous guidelines to help you complete the following exercise. It gives you an opportunity to practice constructing visual arguments by creating your own print advertisement.

EXERCISE 4.10 Creating Visual Arguments: Adbusters

Adbusters, a Vancouver-based satire magazine, develops spoofs of famous ads in order to make arguments about the ethics of advertising. Their Web site gives you step-by-step advice on how to develop an ad of your own.

1. Go to the Adbusters Web site at <http://adbusters.org/spoofads/printad/> and follow their instructions.
2. When you have finished your advertisements, present them to one another and test their effectiveness.
3. Assess your skill at reading the arguments in one another's advertisements.

CONCLUSION: ARGUMENT AS INQUIRY

In Chapter Three, you learned that an inquiring mind seeks information, knowledge, and wisdom. The arguing mind has the same goals, but whereas inquirers ask questions and exercise disciplined research methods, arguers respond to the ideas of others critically and argue their insights rigorously. In other words, they test out possible answers to their questions by actively arguing with others. Yet, because such arguments often create new questions, and the questions we ask often originate from our existing values and beliefs, we should think of inquiring and arguing as interwoven, complementary aspects of the same thoughtful mind.

QUESTIONS FOR INQUIRY AND ACTION

1. To reinforce your willingness to pause and understand another person's viewpoint, try analyzing an argument you disagree with; this argument might appear in an essay, book, speech, editorial, or Web site. Try not to criticize the arguer's ideas but to objectively summarize what they believe and then explain, based on your analysis of the work itself, what values and beliefs would push the arguer to hold his or her viewpoint.

2. Write a letter to the editor for your local or campus newspaper (see the Writing Style box in Chapter Eight for advice on writing letters to the editor). At the end of the letter, invite responses. Then, collect any responses you get and analyze the kind of conversation you started. How did they respond? What aspects of your letter did they respond to? (If you don't get any responses, you can complete this exercise by discussing why.)

3. Take an issue that means a lot to you and analyze your own reasons why you believe what you believe. What values, beliefs, and experiences have shaped your views on this issue?

4. Over the span of a week, watch different talk shows and news programs that encourage debate (e.g., *Crossfire* and *Donahue*). Take notes on the participants' arguing styles and strategies. Which styles and strategies seem to most encourage inquiry (e.g., from which do you learn the most)? Which seem most persuasive? Are those styles and strategies that you found most persuasive the same as those that promoted inquiry?

CHAPTER 5

Writing in Communities: Academic Research and Social Action

Civic participation is a formula for human happiness, both private and public. It is more than a slogan to be intoned or even a duty to be self-imposed; it is a delight to be savored as the essential quality of life that makes democracy an authentic reality. It will be a pleasure for students to fulfill themselves by applying the principles of justice in a democratic, community forum—complete with debate, dialogue, advocacy, assertion, and implementation.

Ralph Nader, Practicing Democracy

GETTING STARTED: Critical Literacy and Civic Participation

In this opening section, you can use your critical literacy skills—thinking, reading, writing, researching, and arguing—to investigate a case study from this book or a current situation that affects the people in your class. After you have read the case study or researched the current situation, outline, on the blackboard, the main concerns involved in this situation. What happened or is happening? What are the stakes for those involved? Why should or shouldn't you get involved?

Next to your outline, brainstorm a list of projects that you could undertake as students and citizens to investigate this situation and get involved. Push to develop a range of possibilities, no matter how remote they might seem at the moment.

Finally, discuss the following questions as a class:

1. What channels of action and communication are open to you?
2. In what communities could you communicate your ideas?
3. How could you use your knowledge and skills to act?
4. How and why might these actions be fulfilling and pleasurable?

As members of various private and public communities, you can use your critical literacy skills to create and share your knowledge with others.

Unfortunately, college students are not always encouraged to participate fully in academic or public conversations, even though they pay tuition and possess legal citizenship. You usually need some degree of training and expertise to participate in these communities, but you can begin to develop these qualities right now. You can conduct substantive research, investigate the conventions of academic and public writing, and participate in public debate. Even as beginning writers, you have more power and more opportunities than you might think.

The authors experienced students' potential while developing this book. On September 11, 2001, the towers of the World Trade Center in New York City and the Pentagon in Washington, D.C., were attacked by terrorists who hijacked commercial airplanes and flew them into the buildings. The World Trade Center towers were destroyed and thousands of people were killed. The entire country wondered how to respond. The prime suspect was Osama bin Laden, a Saudi dissident who was accused of participating in a movement to terrorize the United States. President George W. Bush threatened to attack Afghanistan if the ruling Taliban government didn't hand bin Laden over. Soon the United States began bombing Afghanistan.

We and our students anxiously watched television, read newspapers, shared e-mail postings, and discussed our feelings in class. We wanted to act as students and citizens to better understand the situation and to reach out to others. Our classes completed the Getting Started suggestions, and we decided we might respond to the attack in many ways. We could:

- Research the Taliban, Al Qaeda, Osama bin Laden, and the history of American foreign policy in the Middle East.
- Research the history and theology of Islam.
- Ask professors to devote class time to discussing politics in the Middle East, the possibilities for action there, and alternatives to military action.
- Modify a class project to focus on ways to understand and connect with Muslim students.
- Write a letter to President Bush supporting his stance on terrorism or urging him to seek peaceful alternatives.
- Write a letter to the local or campus newspaper expressing your views.
- Hold a meeting of concerned students who want more information.
- Join an e-mail petition.
- Join a discussion on a local or national radio talk show (such as NPR's *Talk of the Nation*).
- Organize times for reflective writing, discussion, or group prayer.

This chapter encourages you to pursue projects like those listed above so you can realize your own potential for academic and civic participation. As an undergraduate writer in a college classroom, you are a member of an apprenticeship community, one "in training" to join academic and civic communities.

To that end, you are learning to think critically, read carefully, and write clearly and effectively. You are also learning to research issues and develop sound arguments. These skills will get a workout as you learn how to compose works common to academic and civic communities.

FIRST INQUIRY: WRITING IN AN ACADEMIC COMMUNITY

In the first section of this chapter, you will learn how to develop a research paper. The research paper was chosen because it is one of the most common genres in academic communities, and it is the primary vehicle for developing the skills of inquiry and argument necessary to do college-level work. This is true whether you analyze U.S.-Middle East politics, verify the results of studies on frog populations, or research the historical context of William Shakespeare's *Macbeth*. Learning to develop a researched argument is also good for your career and civic life because the higher-level thinking, organization, and analysis it teaches will improve your ability to participate effectively in these communities.

Re-seeing the Research Paper

Reflect for a moment on your past experiences with writing research papers. What does the term *research paper* bring to mind for you? What kinds of topics do you generally consider appropriate for a research paper?

Previous students, when asked these questions, often described research papers as "boring," "tedious," or "a lot of busy work in the library." These students also tended to list the same subjects over and over: abortion, capital punishment, euthanasia, marijuana legalization, or gun control. These subjects are certainly important, challenging the bonds of our communities in real ways, but the students who selected them often did so because they believed that such issues were the only research topics available to them.

In Chapters Three and Four, we learned that inquiring and arguing can be broad, pulling together many interests from our public and private lives. We should bring this same active, inquiring mindset to academic research, asking questions and developing projects that connect with our real interests and life experiences.

For example, here are a few research projects students in our classes have pursued. We will refer to these projects throughout the chapter to illustrate different aspects of the research process.

- Janette researched the history of tattooing and body piercing to understand why her daughter had tattooed her arms and stuck steel rods through her nose, lip, and belly button. Her essay compared contemporary body mutilation practices in the United States with those in other cultures; her goal was to look at these practices in a larger historical and social context.

- Rick couldn't decide if he should go into mechanical, electrical, or chemical engineering, so he wrote an essay that helped other students match one of these areas to their interests, lifestyle, and career goals. To research the subject, he read career literature and interviewed guidance counselors and two engineers from each field.

- Mia wanted to know why people hold religious beliefs. She looked at the research of psychologists to discover what emotional, physical, and psychological needs religions fulfill. Her research paper summarized psychologists' current understanding of this phenomena and suggested areas where they could do additional research.

- Rico, a student in wildlife biology, set up an experiment to test the effects of road salt runoff on local swamp lands. Working with composition and biology instructors, he tested different concentrations of salt water on plants, recorded the different levels of growth over thirty days, and then wrote up his results in a six-page research report.

- Abby compared samples of neighborhood graffiti with popular works of modern art. She used art historians' definitions of art to assess whether graffiti can be seen as a legitimate form of public art.

- At three professional football games, Jake and Robert observed and categorized the behaviors of ten randomly selected fans who were all drinking beer. Drawing together quantitative and qualitative evidence, they argued that these fans tended to cheer and jeer more actively, even as their actual awareness of the game diminished. Their results were written up in an essay that was aimed at general readers.

The above examples are meant to show that students shouldn't feel compelled to write only on particular topics and only in one particular style. Even professional researchers explore a variety of subjects and write in a variety of styles, as the next exercise should demonstrate.

EXERCISE 5.1 Comparing Research Papers

What are the different ways research can be presented? With your class, analyze several research papers. Here are a few examples from this book:

- In Chapter Seven, Margaret Talbot's "A Mighty Fortress" offers a substantive, researched essay written for the popular audience of *The New York Times Magazine*.
- In Chapter Nine, James L. Watson's "China's Big Mac Attack" is a carefully-researched article that explains the complex concept of globalization to the readers of the journal *Foreign Affairs*.
- In Chapter Twelve, David Bell's "Community and Cyberculture" is a classically-structured, meticulously researched argument that situates itself in a large ongoing conversation on cyberculture by citing and discussing a number of other works.

As you analyze these essays, use the following questions to guide your discussion.

1. What do the authors' essays have in common as research papers? Do you notice the authors adhering to certain conventions and formulas?
2. In what ways do their essays differ? How would you compare their structures, their ways of presenting research, or the authors' relationship with the audience?
3. How do these essays compare with your existing ideas of research papers? What conventions are consistent or different?

As the above projects and essays show, research papers need not be tedious exercises in collecting and regurgitating the ideas of others. Research really can be a meaningful experience if it begins with our genuine interests and concerns. In Chapter Two, you were encouraged to write down one hundred questions to which you would like to know the answer. Many of these questions could serve as excellent research projects if you shed the idea of a typical research topic. For example, Mia was raised as an agnostic, someone who actively questions the existence of a supreme being. Many of her friends, however, were deeply religious. A natural question for her was why? She was inspired to begin her project because the initial question mattered to her; it would help her understand, at least from a psychologist's perspective, why her friends believed.

In addition to being meaningful, research ought to be active. In Chapter Three, we learned that when writers begin an inquiry they often join ongoing conversations. As an apprentice researcher, you might feel inadequate to the task of building on or critiquing the conversations of academics and professional researchers. This is a natural feeling; you have only begun to develop the knowledge and skills needed to become a full and active member of these communities. Nevertheless, this does not mean you should embrace the other extreme, cutting and pasting ideas into a dull, passive summary. Consider the examples of these other students.

- Abby does not have a degree in art history, yet she tested her understanding of modern art by applying definitions of it to a new subject, graffiti. The project not only helped her better understand the difficulty of defining modern art, it also gave her new appreciation for the graffiti covering her neighborhood.
- Rico didn't know the first thing about testing the effects of salt on plants. Even after he got help from a biology professor, he ran into several problems with his experimental method. Nevertheless, the experience taught him a lot about setting up scientific experiments and writing research reports.
- Professional social scientists would have found several problems with the methods Jake and Robert used to observe the effects of alcohol consumption on fan participation. However, Jake and Robert set up their research

project in good faith, trying to be rigorous and methodical within the limits of time and money imposed upon them. The experience taught them better ways to conduct observations, and they learned how to make their research accessible to general readers.

In each of these examples, the writers engaged the works of other researchers. Abby looked up definitions of modern art, Rico followed the methods described in other research reports, and Jake and Robert used their experiment to test previous social scientists' results. In each case, the students took action. On a level appropriate to their knowledge, expertise, time, and resources, they questioned, built upon, or added to the knowledge of various communities. At the same time, they exercised their academic and civic skills.

As you plan out your own research projects, consider ways you can respond more actively.

- *You might apply current ideas to new subjects.* One student applied the definition of a subculture to video gamers, defining them as a unique community.
- *You might bring together different viewpoints in new ways.* One student created a dialog between advocates of creationism and evolution; she wanted to show that these different groups won't be able to really talk until they agree on some basic facts and definitions.
- *You might add to existing research, even if in a small way.* One student interviewed three women who had had abortions; he discovered that the emotional and psychological pain of the procedures had lingered for them, and the clinics these women had visited hadn't prepared them sufficiently to deal with this pain.

Even if your project doesn't contribute significantly to academic conversations, it will, in an inspiring way, fulfill your primary purpose—to learn how to research, argue, and write a research paper.

As you work through the next section, keep this wider understanding of the research paper in mind. You may have to modify your project to fit the limits imposed by your writing situation, but you can still start with a question that excites you, one that will inspire you throughout the project.

Forming a Research Question

In Chapter Three, we learned that research often begins with questions. We learned that questions can make the writing process easier by narrowing our topic's scope. We also learned that questions can give us an ending point to the research process. Our work is finished when we have sufficiently answered the question we posed.

For instance, Rick's first research question was a disaster because it tried to cover too much material, and it offered no end to his research. He had posed the question, "Which engineering field is the best?" When he began his research, his interviewees each told him not only that their engineering field was the best, but that other engineering fields were peopled with dregs and engineering school dropouts. None of his sources gave him the kind of definitive information he needed to compare and rank engineering fields. To make his project work, Rick needed to reshape his question. Eventually, he came up with "What interests, lifestyle preferences, and career goals should a person interested in mechanical, electrical, or chemical engineering have?" This new question not only limited the scope of his research project, it also helped him end the project. As soon as he had gathered enough evidence to answer this question adequately, he wrote his essay.

A research question can also keep our research honest by encouraging us to consult a variety of sources, not just those that confirm our existing values and beliefs. A well-phrased question does not imply one particular answer or viewpoint; it invites us to test many possible answers against one another and against our own experiences. At the same time, however, our question can imply the kind of project we do to answer it.

For example, by asking how road salt runoff from city streets might affect local swamps, Rico committed himself to one of two science projects. He might consult other studies on salt's effects on plants and generalize to his own local community, or he might set up and conduct his own experiment. He had to choose the latter because no one had published a study of salt's effects on the particular marsh plants in his area. He then had to decide whether to write a scientific research report for specialists in his field or a general essay his fellow citizens could understand and appreciate.

On the other hand, Abby's question, "Is the graffiti in my neighborhood art?" permitted her to explore a variety of projects. She could, like an anthropologist, analyze the social purpose of graffiti; does it satisfy the same cultural needs as other works of public art? She could, like a legal scholar, analyze the legal status of graffiti; how is graffiti different from other forms of public art, especially those works of art that really tick people off? Abby could even look at the aesthetic qualities of graffiti to see if they match various definitions of art (e.g., a pleasing unity of expression). When she chose the latter project, she then committed herself to specific research methods. For instance, she had to take lots of photographs of graffiti so she could show the works' aesthetic qualities to her readers.

As Rico's and Abby's experiences suggest, the kind of research project you do will depend in part on the writing situation. Within academic communities, inquiries tend to get divided along disciplinary lines. Biologists, psychologists, literary scholars, historians, business scholars, and so on all approach community issues from their own perspectives, asking questions and practicing research methods that are unique to their fields. They then write up their results in specific formats and styles, publish in particular journals, and evaluate each other's work according to their own intellectual and ethical standards. Learning to write within a particular community empowers you to communicate effectively with its members.

At the same time, the aim of your higher education is not to adopt one way of thinking only, but to appreciate the variety of ways we can inquire and act.

Learning some of the expectations of different academic disciplines can help you write more effectively in a variety of classes, recognize the strengths and limitations of different disciplinary perspectives, and approach issues from multiple perspectives. Even when you want to violate the expectations of a particular community for your own purposes, knowing why they have these expectations can help you anticipate your readers' responses.

In Chapter Four you explored standards of civil or acceptable arguing. The following exercise asks you to explore the standards that academic disciplines use to evaluate civil or acceptable ways to inquire and argue.

EXERCISE 5.2 Inquiring and Arguing in Academic Communities

You might try this exercise individually, interviewing professors from two or three different disciplines to see how they would respond to your research topic. You might also try this exercise as a class, each member interviewing different professors on how they would respond to a common topic like violence, children, or emotion. Use the following questions to guide your interviews:

1. Would scholars in your discipline address this topic? What kinds of questions would they ask?
2. What research methods do scholars use in your discipline? How would they research this topic?
3. How would the results of the scholars' research be presented? Who are the different audiences to whom they would write or speak?
4. What are the guidelines for arguing ethically in this discipline? Are some strategies, like appealing to emotion, discouraged?

In class, have each person go to the board and write down the discipline and some specific answers they got to their questions. Then, as a class, look at the findings and discuss the similarities and differences. What conventions seem fairly standard across all academic disciplines?

Researching the conventions of different disciplines is wise for beginning writers because instructors will appeal to their field's conventions when evaluating your work. Consequently, if you want to succeed, you need to actively discover the conventions of each academic community for which you will write.

Planning the Research Project

In Chapter Three, you learned to think through your inquiries, visualizing as much as possible what you wanted to research, why it was important to you, what methods you wanted to use, what audiences you wanted to reach, and how long you had to inquire. In academic communities, this plan is often formalized into a proposal, a detailed account of a research project. Proposals are valuable because they force researchers to clarify what they are going to do and to test how feasible their methods are given the limits of money, resources, and time. As an apprentice researcher, you might simply think through your project by writing in your writer's notebook. As you read through the following suggestions and examples, consider what general truths are being shown about the research process.

Research the Writing Situation

First, researchers need to get some sense of the writing situation. As you discovered in the previous section, the kind of question you ask will push you toward a particular discipline, each with its own set of conventions. These conventions developed over time to help researchers succeed. For example, scientists often number the steps in their methodology to make each step easier to distinguish from the others. This convention helps the scientist to verify a researcher's results by accurately replicating his or her experiment. Mastering conventions like this one will make you a savvier participant in your academic community. In addition, your instructor may wish to set limits that will affect how you complete your project. For example, he or she might want one kind of research only, a certain number of sources in your bibliography, or a particular documentation style like MLA. To be successful, you should also ask your instructor to explain what he or she will be looking for in the research papers. You might use the writing situation assessment questions listed in Chapter Two to guide your inquiry.

When Jake and Robert planned their research project, they realized that the method they needed to use to create credible evidence—in this case, observation—didn't fit with the lighthearted paper they wanted to write. Consequently, they had to come up with a hybrid—a serious research project described in a casual, conversational style. You can see another example of this hybrid approach in the essay "Tune Out," located in Chapter Twelve. In both cases, the researchers first had to learn the conventions of these different writing situations so their efforts to go against them wouldn't confuse or irritate their readers.

Set the Scope of Your Research

Second, researchers need to clarify what it is they want to research. In addition to writing and revising your research question, you should write out, in your writer's notebook, how you think this question will define the scope and ending point of your research. For example, after brainstorming on just one graffiti selection, Abby realized that she could not cover all the different aesthetic qualities of the graffiti in her neighborhood (it was too diverse), nor could she afford to take dozens of pictures. She decided right away to limit her selections to five. In addition, she decided to focus on one different aesthetic quality with each selection. Had she discussed all she wanted to with each selection, she figured she would never have finished. As Abby's example illustrates, you may need to set additional limits to your project, in addition to those already imposed by your discipline and your writing instructor. Writing out the scope and end of your project in your notebook can help you make these decisions before you get too involved in the research itself.

Clarify Your Purpose

The third step you should take in planning your research project is to remind yourself why you want to answer your research question. Writing about what you hope to learn and teach your readers can give you a clearer sense of your purpose. For example, Janette's purpose was to regain her sanity in light of all her daughter's tattoos and piercings. She sometimes lost that focus while researching, because she became fascinated with all the bizarre body mutilation rituals that humans practice. When she wrote her essay, however, she tried to show how normal such practices were in their respective societies. Emphasizing that normalcy not only kept her research paper focused, it helped her maintain perspective even when her daughter, a few days before the final draft was due, came home with a chain connecting her lips.

Define Your Methods

The fourth step you should take in planning your research project is to write out a more detailed narrative of your research methods. If you plan to do library research, prepare a bibliography of your sources. If you plan to do a survey, identify how many respondents you will need, where you will conduct the survey, and what specific questions you will ask. If you plan to conduct an experiment using people, consult your college's Institutional Review Board for the Protection of Human Participants. Whatever your research methods, take the time to think through how you will answer your research question and whether your methods are appropriate and practical. For example, when Mia did her initial search for literature explaining why people hold religious beliefs, she said she almost swallowed her tongue. There were way too many books and articles on her subject. She decided to focus primarily on what psychologists had written in the last ten years. This decision let her get through all the readings on time and discuss them in greater depth in her paper. Working out your research method in more detail can also help you anticipate any problems and propose alternative methods or sources of information.

Set Your Schedule

The last step is to work out a schedule for finishing your research. Your instructor will give you some of your deadlines, but you may need to set your own to ensure you aren't underestimating how long your work will take. For example, Rico's experiment on the effects of salt water on plants would take six weeks to complete. It would take that long for his plants to germinate and grow. Having thought about it ahead of time, he was able to negotiate new due dates to turn in his work. Jake and Robert didn't plan ahead. When the first draft of their research paper was due, they still had two more football games to attend. Consequently, they lost points on their final grades. If instructors aren't willing to work with you on the schedule for your project, you may need to adjust your research question or methods. It is better to know this ahead of time, if only to save you anxiety during the research process.

Based on the above examples, we might make two points about planning the research process. First, the more detailed you make your plan, the easier it will be to get started and to see potential problems. When Janette first narrated her method for researching body modification, she didn't go into detail. She said she planned to go to her local public library to get some books. She also planned to interview some of her daughter's friends who had gotten their bodies tattooed or pierced. When Janette implemented her plan, however, she discovered that her public library didn't carry books on the body mutilation rituals of other cultures. Janette might have saved herself the trip had she thought more carefully about what resources would most help her project. Eventually, she browsed a university library catalog from her home computer, prepared a bibliography of possible sources, and then went to the library, saving herself time and grief by going into more details on her research plan.

Another point we might make about planning the research process is that these plans are often educated guesses as to what sources and methods will be most useful. You need to remain flexible, always considering alternative methods you might use or alternative sources you might turn to get the information you need. When Janette asked her daughter's friends why they had gotten tattoos, they didn't reply much beyond, "Because they're cool," "Seemed like fun," or "Whatever." Janette decided to use books on the history of tattooing to explain why Americans get tattoos, instead of relying on her daughter's articulate friends. Whenever you do research, remember that things will go wrong—books you need will be checked out, people won't return your surveys, weather will prevent you from observing people's behaviors. This is why you need to plan and start researching early, so you can adjust your methods or select alternative ones when the unanticipated happens. Keep these two points in mind as you complete the following exercise.

EXERCISE 5.3   Writing Up Your Research Plan

To set up your own research process and to test the advice given above, complete the following steps in your writer's notebook.

1. *Get some sense of the writing situation.* What parameters is your instructor setting for the research paper (e.g. particular methods, formats, page lengths, due dates)?
2. *Clarify what you want to research.* Can you narrow your research question or the scope of your essay to make it manageable within the limits of your writing situation?
3. *Explain why you want to pursue this research project.* What do you hope this information will do for you and for your community? How will those concerns shape the final research paper?
4. *Write a detailed narrative of your research methods.* How will you answer your research question? Why are you choosing some research methods over others?

5. *Work out a schedule for completing the project.* Can you complete your project within the due dates set by your instructor? What problems do you anticipate possibly having, and how will you address them?

After you've completed planning your research project, share your plans with other members in the class. Raise concerns about the clarity, appropriateness, or practicality of each other's projects.

Researching

You have many different research methods available to you, from analyzing written texts to observing human behavior. These methods will create different research experiences. For example, with some methods, you will actually craft your research paper as you conduct the research. Once Abby had photographed samples of local graffiti, she began analyzing them, testing the samples' qualities against various definitions of art. She was able to work these analyses directly into her essay, refining her insights as she revised her drafts. Other research methods, however, may require you to complete all the research before writing the paper. Rico was able to write up the methodology section in his scientific research report while planning his project, but he couldn't write up the results or discussion sections until he had collected all of his data.

Most research projects also require that you acknowledge and participate in the conversations already begun around your subject. You have been learning how to do this in the previous chapters. In Chapter Two, you learned how to read works critically, conversing with writers by underlining, annotating, and commenting on their ideas. In Chapter Three, you learned to respond in more depth, exploring how different genres of writing shaped your ideas. Then, in Chapter Four, you learned to summarize and analyze arguments, seeking to understand the writers' underlying values and beliefs. The next step is to use writing to clarify your views *as* they emerge from your conversation with other writers. When we read the works of other writers, our ideas about our topic change. Our ideas might be challenged, strengthened, qualified, or even reversed. We can use writing to preserve a record of those changes. We can also use writing to help us think through those changes, clarifying what other writers tell us and how their ideas relate to our research question, to our own views, and to the views of other participants in the conversation.

EXERCISE 5.4   Telling the Story of Your Research

We learned in Chapter One that good narratives focus events around a main idea or dominant impression. We can apply this idea to our research by writing a story of our progress in answering our research question. As you read each of your books, articles, Web sites, and so on, answer the following questions in your writer's notebook:

1. What are the main ideas in this work?
2. How does this work help you answer your research question?

3. How do this work's ideas relate to your own at this point?
4. How do this work's ideas relate to those of other works you've read?

As you answer these questions with each source, you will begin to create a narrative of your thinking on this topic. Patterns will emerge of the conversation as you see it. Some writers will agree or disagree; some of their points will match or contradict one another. When you start to get a sense of the conversation, you might create a Mind Map of it, starting with your tentative thesis in the middle and drawing in the ideas of other writers around it. Depending on where you locate those writers you can show, visually, who agrees or disagrees with you, who qualifies your arguments, and who argues points unconnected with your thesis. The goal here is to clarify for yourself how your argument fits into the ongoing conversation.

As you complete this exercise, remember to assume the role of a skeptic. In Chapter Four, you learned that skeptics test the truth of their ideas against evidence and the ideas of other researchers. Often we form research questions with some idea of what we already believe. As you research, try to find evidence and ideas that challenge your tentative thesis. If your views on your topic change as a result of the research process, remember that changing our views is part of living an examined life.

Writing the Research Paper

In Exercises 5.1 and 5.2 you compared the formats researchers in different academic fields use to report the results of their research. Some disciplines use pre-established formats to report their results while others use a thesis-driven format, letting the writer's thesis direct the shape of the essay. When you commit to the research conventions of a particular field, you also commit, to some extent, to the field's writing conventions. These conventions assist researchers in working through their methods and sharing their results with others in their field. In other words, you should think of writing a research paper as a continuation of your research; you are presenting your arguments to a community in order to stimulate further discussion. Trying to follow the conventions of your readers' community will encourage them to take your work more seriously, even though, as an apprentice, you are still learning what those conventions are.

For example, Rico learned that researchers in biology follow a pre-established format. Their essays usually begin with an abstract (a short summary of the project and results) and a clear, detailed title. Then, the researcher's question and his or her tentative thesis (called a hypothesis) are introduced, the method of the experiment is described in painstaking detail, and the experiment's results, the raw data, are presented, often in a table or graph format. Finally, the importance of the results are discussed and the initial hypothesis is confirmed, denied, or modified. The writing itself tends to be simple, clear, and direct. Although Rico thought these conventions made his paper sound boring and overly formal, he recognized that readers of his work would not be interested in the pleasure of the reading experience, but in the knowledge he created through his experiment. To access that knowledge, they needed everything in the essay to be clear, straightforward, and highly organized.

Rick, on the other hand, let his thesis direct the shape of his essay. Because he was exploring three different engineering fields, he created three different sections, each one covering a different field. Within each field he further divided the essay into sections addressing how that field would appeal to people's interests, lifestyle, and career goals. At the same time, he realized that he needed to energize his essay if he wanted people to get excited about engineering. So, he shaped the sections on interests, lifestyle, and career goals into small stories, drawing on the qualitative evidence he had gathered from his interviews. His goal was to help readers see for themselves what it would mean to live the life of a mechanical, electrical, or chemical engineer.

Rico's and Rick's experiences should remind us of two points made in earlier chapters. First, we can make the writing process easier if we try to envision the essay as a whole. For Rico, this was easy because the format was already set, but for Rick, imagining three separate sections, each covering the same three types of information, made his twelve-page research paper easier to write. He could work on specific parts while seeing how all those parts fit together.

Second, we should always keep our audience in mind as we write. If our purpose is to win our audience's agreement, we might be tempted to hold back evidence contrary to our thesis or to use appeals that violate the ethical standards of academic communities. Of course, trying to win agreement may or may not promote further inquiry. If we seek to promote inquiry, however, we should use all our relevant evidence and reasoning to assist readers in seeing for themselves the truth of our conclusions.

EXERCISE 5.5   Asking Questions to Revise

As you learned in Chapter Two, writers must look inward and outward when revising. They look inward to clarify their ideas, and they look outward to ensure they are communicating those ideas effectively. Ernest Hemingway once said, "The most essential gift for a good writer is a built-in shock-proof shit-detector." Consider these questions your own detectors for writing a research paper. Ask them continuously as you read your drafts out loud.

1. Have you tried to express your own honest views throughout? Are there any places where you felt false, writing only what you thought others wanted to hear?
2. Have you clarified your arguments by defining your terms, explaining complex ideas, and providing plenty of examples?
3. Do you provide enough evidence for your readers to see the truth of your claims for themselves?
4. Have you reasoned carefully and ethically? Are there any places where you have fudged your thinking?

5. Does your essay seek to foster community? Does it engage readers as companions in your search for knowledge and wisdom?

Detecting those moments when your writing slips from clarity, from rigor or from grace will help you revise your research paper into a more effective instrument for promoting inquiry and community with your readers. At the same time, you should remember the community of other writers you conversed with during the research process. They too should be acknowledged in the research paper.

Citing and Documenting Sources

In *Beyond the Writers' Workshop*, Carol Bly writes, "Civilization is partly about noticing and appreciating what other people are doing" (111). To encourage the kind of ethical inquiry central to strong academic communities, we need to notice and appreciate the work of other researchers, acknowledging it when we present our own. We can do this by citing their ideas in our writing. For example, in the previous statement, Bly taught us, the authors, to see documenting in a fresh way, as a civic duty. We wished to acknowledge her contribution by mentioning, or citing, her work in our text. If you turn to the back of this book, you will see her work documented in our bibliography, the list of works we recognize as contributors to our thinking. This activity of citing and documenting sources not only promotes community in academia, it helps define it. Research papers are one of the primary ways scholars learn about one another and about their work.

Citing and documenting our sources also moves the work in our respective disciplines forward. First, it encourages more rigorous inquiry. Other readers can locate and check our sources, seeing if we have represented other people's ideas accurately and ethically. As an apprentice researcher, you should cite and document your sources so your instructor can verify that you are indeed mastering the skills of research. Second, citing and documenting sources encourages further inquiry by offering additional research opportunities. Someone reading your research paper might be inspired by an idea you borrowed from another source. Knowing the source you used will help the reader begin a new research project or develop a broader understanding of your topic.

Citing and documenting sources is useful and ethical, but not all the information we get from them needs to be acknowledged. Facts like the boiling point of water, the circumference of the Earth, or the founder of Amway do not need to be cited or documented if readers consider them "common knowledge." Common knowledge refers to those facts or bits of information that most people know simply by living as members of a particular community. Even when you have to look up common knowledge, like who the eighteenth president of the United States was, you don't necessarily have to cite and document it. Had Bly told us simply to cite and document sources that contribute to our thinking, we probably wouldn't have cited her work because the idea is common knowledge to anyone who teaches writing.

If Bly's advice had been new to you, however, would you have needed to acknowledge it? Knowing when to cite and document other people's ideas isn't easy, especially when you are an apprentice researcher for whom most of the information you gather is brand new. The Modern Language Association's *Handbook for Writers of Research Papers* gives this advice: "You must indicate the source of any appropriated material that readers might otherwise mistake for your own." If you are still in doubt, go ahead and cite it; instructors probably won't penalize you just for being conscientious. Another way to decide whether to cite and document a source is if you *want* readers to know the source of particular ideas. Here are a few situations when citing and documenting a source is appropriate:

- If you want to strengthen the persuasiveness of your claims by showing that other professional researchers agree with you.
- If you want readers to verify your research or to consult your sources on their own.
- If you want to identify the other researchers with whom you have been conversing throughout the research process.

One of your strongest contributions as a writer will be telling your audience *how to read* the sources, and how to understand the larger conversation of which they are a part. Remember that your readers haven't necessarily read everything that you have, and no one understands the situation in quite the way that you do. Thus, instead of simply inserting a direct quotation from your source to support one of your claims, provide context for the quotation and explain what it means to your overall argument. Put yourself into conversation with the various voices and opinions from your source materials so that you can move beyond simply agreeing or disagreeing with a source, or citing a source as authority.

Using Other Writers' Words and Ideas

We can incorporate other people's words and ideas in two ways, by directly quoting from their works or by paraphrasing, expressing their ideas in our own words. Generally speaking, it is better to paraphrase, because, while we still acknowledge the work of the source, we preserve the flow of our writing by maintaining one person's voice, our own. Paraphrasing is also preferable because, in using our own language, we show readers that we understand the other writer's ideas. In some situations, however, direct quotations are preferable, especially when:

- The original writer's words are especially precise, colorful, or eloquently phrased.
- The exact words are needed to convey the writer's meaning, specific tone, or context for the discussion.
- It would be particularly persuasive to hear the voice of a recognized authority or someone who has experience on the subject.

Make sure to put quotation marks around the author's or speaker's words to distinguish them from your own words, and to cite your source according to the conventions of your writing community, whether parenthetically or in footnotes or endnotes.

When you paraphrase, you put the content of what you've read into your own words, while keeping the sense of the original. If you use any of the original words or phrases, put quotation marks around them. Remember that you will still need to cite your source and document it in your bibliography, even if you never quote directly from it.

It takes a lot of work to incorporate other people's words and ideas smoothly and accurately into your own. It is one of the biggest reasons research papers generally take longer to compose than other essays. However, it will make your thinking and, in the end, your paper, far more sophisticated than if you simply drop in direct quotations here and there. Here are some examples for incorporating sources into your writing.

Incorporating Sources

Introduce your sources. You want to guide your readers through your argument, and you are responsible for helping them understand the sources in the context of the larger conversation on the topic. Therefore, introduce all sources, whether you use them in the form of a direct quotation, paraphrase, or summary.

Take, for example, this passage from Margaret Talbot's "A Mighty Fortress":

> In their 1999 book, *Blinded by Might*, Cal Thomas, a conservative columnist, and Ed Dobson, a Baptist minister, offered a similar analysis, arguing that "religious conservatives have heard sermons that man's ways are not God's ways . . . . In politics they have fused the two, causing damage to both church and state."

Note how Talbot helps her readers understand how to read this source by:

- Introducing the source by title (in this case, a book) and author(s)
- Providing brief introductions to the authors' views and positions
- Helping readers interpret the comments in conversation with her own thoughts and other sources

She does this by:

- Weaving their words into her own sentence
- Providing a transition from a point she'd made previously from another source ("offered a similar analysis")
- Revealing the tone of the original statement ("arguing")
- Providing ellipses to show where she has cut out some words to make the quotation briefer and clearer. We use ellipses, three spaced periods (. . .), leaving a space before the first period and after the third period, too, to indicate words cut from the middle of a sentence. Talbot uses four spaced periods, which indicates that she has eliminated words between the first and second sentences.

(Note: Talbot is writing for a popular magazine that does not require that she provide a bibliography or cite sources parenthetically or in footnotes. In most academic situations you will be required to provide page numbers and other information in the body of your paper or in footnotes, and again on a formal bibliography or Works Cited page.)

Even when you are not directly quoting from your sources, you still want to introduce and explain them to your readers. Take, for example, this passage from David Bell's "Community and Cyberculture":

> In his book on new social movements, *Expressions of Identity*, Kevin Hetherington (1998) revisits Tönnes' work in the context of 'neo-tribes', also drawing on the notion of the *Bund*, or communion—partly because it offers a better way to think through the kinds of groups he's interested in . . . . Given the inaptitude of community as a term to describe online groupings, as noted by both Hetherington and Graham, might Hetherington's revival of the Bund offer us a new way of thinking about what people do together in cyberspace?

Note how Bell helps his readers read and understand this source by:

- Introducing the source by its title or author
- Explaining how the source informs his own argument
- Directly quoting only the exact words he needs, like "neo-tribes"

Bibliographies and Documentation

Research papers in academia include bibliographies, called Works Cited pages in MLA style and References pages in APA style. Each source in your paper must appear on that final bibliography, and the entry must be complete and accurate. Likewise, the page numbers you give in the text of your paper must match the page numbers on which the material will be found when readers follow your lead and look up these sources for themselves. It is a time-consuming process that demands careful attention, but it is crucial.

For every direct quotation, and for every piece of evidence that you provide in paraphrase or summary, provide the source in the body of your paper and again in your bibliography. Different professional fields have different conventions for citing and documenting sources. Here we will discuss two of the most common: those developed by the Modern Language Association (MLA) and the American Psychological Association (APA). More detailed information and guidance can be found in the writers' manuals published by each organization, as well as at theirWeb sites, <http://www.mla.org> and <http://www.apa.org>.

MLA documentation is used in many humanities fields, including English literature, other modern languages, and rhetoric and composition. It is the convention you will probably be asked to follow for your composition courses. It has two main steps. The first is citing sources by author's name or source's title and by page number parenthetically within the body of the paper. The second step is providing full bibliographic information for each source that appears in the text on a Works Cited list at the end of the paper.

Incorporating authors and titles into the body of your sentences is a good practice as it keeps the parenthetical notes short and unobtrusive. Sometimes a parenthetical note would be cumbersome, for instance, when you want to refer to an interview or survey, or the source is an organization rather than a person, or the source is a Web site or a document with a long title. Whenever it would be smoother to mention the source in the body of your essay, do so. The point of the notes is to quickly and accurately identify sources so that readers can find them readily on the Works Cited page and then track them down for future use. The Works Cited page is a separate page, included at the end of your paper, on which you list all the sources you've cited in a parenthetical note in your paper, whether you quoted, paraphrased, or summarized. Unlike some bibliographies, when using MLA documentation you do not list sources you read and gathered general knowledge from but do not actually cite in the paper.

In many of the social sciences (including political science, psychology, sociology, anthropology, and education) you will be asked to use APA conventions in citing and documenting your research papers. It has two main steps: citing sources by author's name, publication date, and page number parenthetically within the body of the paper, and then providing full bibliographic information for each source that appears in the text on a References page at the end of the paper. Authors' first names are not given, only their initials.

Writers often struggle with balancing their own and others' words. For example, we too often either report on others' works by stringing together a lot of quotations with just a topic sentence here and there of our own argument holding the quotations together, or by writing our own essay and simply dropping in a quotation occasionally to back up a claim. There's no magic proportion or number of citations or sources, and how many you use will vary from project to project, but do consider at what points you need more support or others' words, and at what points you need to step forward and lead in the argument.

Research Process in Action: A Student's Story

Here we present Holly Van De Venter's research paper for her first-year composition course at the University of Minnesota. Her marginal comments give us insight into how she decided upon her topic, how she chose her sources, and how she developed her argument.

When deciding upon a topic, I thought about my life and what I would like to change, improve upon, or complete in the future. Then, I came up with reasons why these topics were important to me. To narrow down the topics, I decided on a choice that not only I cared about, but a topic that others could relate to, and perhaps take action on.

Holly Van De Venter

EngC 1014

Dr. Muse

November 16, 2000

Educating the New America

As a nation made up of immigrants, the United States has always been a melting pot of people, languages, ideas, and customs. As we reflect on our country at the close of the year 2000, we must ask ourselves if we are providing a welcoming environment and if we represent and respect the changing face of American society today. Our country is no longer a white, middle-class population; we are a diverse nation and in states such as California, there is no longer a majority ethnic group. Instead of celebrating and exploring the different ways of life, many people are closing their doors, locking the windows, and shutting the curtains on the new society, the real America.

I believe that one way to foster a new generation, open and accepting to all ways of life, is to teach a foreign language in the primary grades. These children will gain people skills, learn about a different culture, and be more accepting to change. We will give our children not only a new perspective on the world, but a skill for life: the ability to communicate with others. As the world becomes more global, our students will have a better chance to succeed in the job market, and American diplomats will better understand the people they are trying to help. The benefits of a multilingual nation will be seen through early childhood development, a better understanding of America's demographic makeup, and more success in the global world.

The thesis was the hardest part because I wanted it to accomplish something.

As a democratic society, we should give everyone an equal chance to succeed. Many studies have been done that show the benefits on brain development when children are challenged to learn two languages concurrently. Studies published in the *Bilingual Educational Series: 5* conclude that bilingual students showed a higher level of intelligence than monolingual students. Specifically, in the Pearl and Lambert study of 1962, it proved that with the bilingual child "wider experiences in two cultures have given him advantages . . . It has left him with a greater mental flexibility, a superiority in concept formation, and a more diversified set of mental abilities" (Ramirez et al.

38). Because the language centers of the brain are still forming in children, learning a second language concurrently with English stimulates thinking from a new angle.

I first looked on Internet search engines such as infoseek.com and yahoo.com with numerous sets of keywords, using different combinations of related search topics. This was used as general background, to help me become more familiar with the topic. I also checked out popular news Web sites, such as CNN.com and abc-news.com to see if there had been any recent reporting on my topic.

While the positive effects on the brain are well documented, we cannot overlook the many positive psychological effects on the mind that one can gain also. As our nation becomes more diverse, it will be necessary to understand the different cultures, so we are able to work together without conflict. It is almost impossible to work together if you don't understand where other points of view are coming from. As found on the Center for Multilingual and Multicultural Research web page, Sabine Ulibarri said:

> In the beginning was the Word. And the Word was made flesh. It was so in the beginning and it is so today. The language, the Word, carries within it the history, the culture, the traditions, the very life of a people, the flesh. We cannot even conceive of a people without a language, or a language without a people. The two are one and the same. To know one is to know the other.

We must remember that how one person views his past, largely determines how he views his future. Today, many children do not have any knowledge of their family tree, and are taught even less about their country's history. Implementing foreign language programs would help the students gain insight about the struggles and victories their ancestors had. A Spanish language curriculum would not only include learning the words and sentence structure, but also include lessons about the history, holiday festivals, music, and traditional foods in the Spanish culture. For a Spanish immigrant in that class, he would learn of his heritage and be given a firm foundation for growth and success. His self-confidence would rise because he would be

proud of his past, and would look to achieve more in the future.
The students who were born in the United States or who do not
have any exposure to another culture, would benefit by realizing
that there are many ways of life, and that one way of doing
something is not the only way. As stated in the <u>Memphis
Business Journal</u>, Barbara Williams, an elementary foreign
language teacher at Christ the King Lutheran School in
Memphis says, "We have a Spanish festival to increase
awareness of the many Spanish cultures. We want them to know
that tacos are not Spanish food but Mexican food, and that all
Spanish-speaking people are not Mexican" (qtd. in Greer 27).

5   The main reason we must change people's way of thinking
is evident in the following graph. America's demographic
makeup will change dramatically in the next fifty years. How we
educate now will determine how our nation will grow in the
future. This mix of people will allow us to offer a rich,
multicultural, melting-pot experience to the young generation,
but we must accept the challenge of educating in a new era.

Incorporating all the sources I wanted to use was at times difficult. I had several points I wanted to stick to, but had other information that I thought was useful and interesting that didn't really pertain to the thesis. You have to narrow down and decide what you will include and what you won't.

When looking at general Web sites, I was skeptical of the information when it didn't contain an author's name or publication information. Since my essay was on education, I trusted resources such as ERIC (Educational Resources Information Center) and the NCBE (National Clearinghouse for Bilingual Education), both of which have been funded in part by grants from the Department of Education. I also found articles in reliable magazines, and when choosing books, I looked at the author's credentials.

U.S. Population by Ethnicity (in percents)

2000		2050
White, non-Hispanic	71.5%	52.8%
Hispanic	11.7%	24.3%
Black/African American	12.2%	13.2%
Asian and Pacific Islander	3.8%	8.9%
American Indian, Eskimo, Aleut	0.7%	0.8%

Source: Lundholm-Leary, Kathryn. <u>Biliteracy for a Global
Society: An Idea Book on Dual Language Education</u>. George
Washington University. August 2000: 11.

In this global job market, American companies are
finding it hard to communicate and compete in this fast-paced

world. We have been called elitists, isolationists, and tongue-tied because so many corporations do not have competent businesspeople who fluently speak foreign languages. As a result, it has reduced our competitiveness in the business world. Millions of dollars have been lost in business deals where the language has been interpreted wrong.

Since America is the world's democracy leader, giving support to those countries that strive for independence, we have often been in the position of negotiating peace treaties between two warring nations. America could gain the respect of the two parties involved first-hand by showing the ability to work together through face-to-face negotiations instead of through interpreters. With knowledge of the history and culture of a nation, the diplomats would be more understanding and able to see both sides of the argument. Knowledge of the past would help us make better plans for the future.

I acknowledge the fact that adding foreign language programs can be costly. One main reason the American educational system does not place learning a foreign language high on its priorities list is that many schools feel that the money would be better spent elsewhere. With technology becoming more and more important, many districts have focused their budget on computer upgrades and new software programs. However, some schools across the nation are implementing these programs on their own. Paul Nikol co-founded the "Foreign Languages in the Community" program because he and others realized that U.S. students are woefully behind in foreign language competency. "We are the only modern industrial nation that doesn't place importance on learning foreign languages and learning them in the primary grades. Here we're isolationists, in a sense, and we're not preparing our kids for the millennium" ("Two Languages" 17). Nine years ago, Nikol teamed with two other teachers to develop

a program to educate students in the Spanish language. The
school district did give administrative approval, but couldn't
afford to hire new teachers. So Nikol turned to high school
students to teach classes. Not only do they get to practice and
become more proficient in the language, but they get to learn
teaching skills and possibly find a career path. Because of many
volunteers, the students are reaping the benefits of this
program, and it's basically costing the school system nothing.

Transitions, I learned, are necessary and a must to have a paper that smoothly moves from one idea to another. You cannot just jump from one idea to the next, or your reader will wonder what happened.

Another argument against teaching multiple languages
in the primary grades is that it would lead to segregation
among the different minorities, and that students would fall
behind in their English language learning. By including all
races in language classes, the children are able to interact
with each other and learn from their peers. This kind of
learning is beneficial because they are able to understand the
benefits of working together. As proved in numerous studies,
the fear of losing English proficiency is an unfounded claim.
The vocabulary of the English language is actually expanded
with exposure to another language.

10   While walking through campus at the University of
Minnesota, I hear many different languages spoken around
me. I am amazed at the diverse background and knowledge
these students have. I was shocked at how different the world
is because I really had no background or history on any other
cultures. Sure, I could take a language class to learn about
another way of life, but I would only be playing catch-up.
Instead of always lagging behind, struggling to become equal,
let's instruct our children in a way so that they are given a
head start in the world.

Our society cannot keep educating our children as
though they live in a white, solely English-speaking country.
It is time we open our eyes to the changing face of America.
Instead of hiding from our shortcomings, let's realize that we

can take suggestions for improvements from others. We must remember that we have much to offer the world, but there is much we can learn from the world also. Instead of giving our children limitations, let's give them opportunities to branch out and explore new ideas, encourage them in different ways of thinking, and support the many different cultures that make America what it is today.

Works Cited

Center for Multilingual Multicultural Research. University of Southern California. 7 Nov. 2000. <http://www-bcf.usc.edu/~cmmr/BEResources.html>.

Green, Jason. "Foreign languages increasingly added to elementary schools." *Memphis Business Journal*, 21 Jan. 2000; 27.

Lundholm-Leary, Kathryn. *Biliteracy for a Global Society: An Idea Book on Dual Language Education*. George Washington University. Aug. 2000: 11. 20 Nov. 2000. <http://www.ncbe.gwu.edu/ncbepubs/ideabook/dual/biliteracy.pdf>.

Ramirez, Manuel, et al. *Bilingual Education Series: 5*. Center for Applied Linguistics: 38.

"Two Languages Come Early." *NEA Today*. May 1999: 17.

SECOND INQUIRY: WRITING IN CIVIC COMMUNITIES

This next part of the chapter provides you with ways to take your researched argument public. There, you can learn about the more common genres of public debate, including letters to the editor, pamphlets, and Web pages. You will probably discover that many of the conventions of classroom writing will have to be modified to meet the requirements of these new genres. However, the deeper understanding and more effective arguments you create by writing a researched argument paper will make your other types of writing much more effective.

In Chapter Three you learned that inquiry can be a form of social action, yet citizens don't necessarily stop at researching the issues, nor do students necessarily stop with writing academic research papers. Consider the following examples from history; they represent only a few of the countless times people have acted on their understanding of a particular issue:

- On December 1, 1955, Rosa Parks refused to give up her seat to a white man on a Montgomery, Alabama bus. She challenged the segregation order in court but lost, so she and others organized a boycott of Montgomery buses that lasted 382 days. Their actions led eventually to the U.S. Supreme Court decision to outlaw segregation on city buses.

- On February 27, 1973, American Indian Movement activists and local Oglala Lakota people occupied a trading post and Catholic church in Wounded Knee, South Dakota. Hoping to attract media attention and voice their grievances, they were instead surrounded by federal agents. The two groups exchanged gunfire during the seventy-one-day standoff.

- On October 25, 1997, fourteen-year-old Adam Chestnut of Toronto, Ohio participated in the annual Make a Difference Day by collecting used clothing from the people on his paper route. He collected fifty bags of clothing and received an award of $2000, given on his behalf to a Goodwill Industries Rehabilitation Center.

- On April 5, 1999, members of the Animal Liberation Front broke into two University of Minnesota buildings, setting over one hundred research animals free and damaging around three million dollars in computers and research equipment. They claimed that these animals were being abused; representatives for the university said the loss of the animals would seriously impede research on Alzheimer's and Parkinson's diseases.

- On November 30, 1999, approximately 50,000 people from around the world convened in Seattle, Washington, to disrupt a meeting of the World Trade Organization (WTO). Many of the protesters were college students; they joined labor union members, environmentalists, and supporters of Third World development in protesting the WTO's record of human rights, environmental protection, and fair trade practices. Most of the protests were peaceful, but isolated skirmishes resulted in hundreds of arrests and injuries. The actions in Seattle prepared the way for protests in New York City, Philadelphia, Calgary, Quebec, Los Angeles, and Minneapolis.

The above examples represent a wide range of responses to social issues, from peaceful civil disobedience to violence. Are these acts equally appropriate responses? How would you evaluate the ethical correctness of these acts as they have been described? You may want to research some of these incidents further to get a fuller understanding of the surrounding circumstances before deciding. Is it ever ethical to break the laws or to commit acts of violence? Could you provide guidelines to help citizens decide when such actions are appropriate?

In truth, some of these examples involve complex ethical questions about the propriety of breaking the law and of using violence that should be discussed. The examples should also remind us that social action can bring positive and negative consequences; consequently, we should make ethical considerations part of our decision how to act.

Of course, ethics is already part of our decision to get involved in the first place. Whether we further research a community issue, write a letter to our Congressperson, or protest against some public policy, we are choosing to act by our own values and beliefs. We are making a moral decision. According to Ralph Nader, an advocate for civic participation, college students are uniquely positioned to advocate democratic solutions to social problems. At the peak of their idealism, they have the energy and commitment to act on their values and beliefs.

Students also represent a powerful education community—14.5 million members in 1998—with access to libraries, expert faculty, laboratories, student organizations, and common places where they can meet and organize. To discover these resources for yourself, you might tour your own campus and identify resources available to students interested in public issues. You might also pick a particular issue that interests you and investigate opportunities for researching and advocating it further.

Student Participation in Public Debate

Within your own writing classroom, you have many opportunities to participate in public debate. As a form of social action, writing is particularly effective. Writers have time to craft their messages carefully, and they can reach a wide audience. Indeed, we usually learn what issues are significant and being discussed in public through the media, including text-based media forms like newspapers, magazines, pamphlets, and posters. In fact, the media often form the conduit through which we exchange opinions and the place where these opinions meet. To see this, try conducting the following exercise.

EXERCISE 5.6   Noticing Conversations in the Public Sphere

Follow local and national events in a newspaper for one week. Then answer the following questions:

1. What events were covered during the week? Which ones received priority in terms of their placement within the paper and the depth and extent of the journalists' coverage? Why do you suppose those particular stories received greater coverage?
2. What are the different types of articles written in the newspaper? Can you group these types into categories depending on who writes them, where they are located in the paper, and how they are written?
3. How do these different types of articles shape our awareness of public issues? To get a different perspective, you might watch television news for the same week. Do these programs cover the same events? How is the coverage similar or different? What do newspapers offer that television news does not?

Newspaper editorials, Web sites, and pamphlets are common forms of public writing, yet they probably differ from the essays you have written in the classroom, especially the academic research paper. Professional researchers do publish their research in academic journals, as you discovered earlier in this chapter, and they follow many of the same conventions you do in your own research papers. They must investigate which subjects people want to read about, conduct research appropriate to their fields, and follow a writing process involving peer review. Nevertheless, the work of professional researchers is typically grander in scope and more rigorous in research methods because they have more training, time, and resources.

To get his article "Jihad vs. McWorld" published in *The Atlantic* magazine, Benjamin Barber put in years of research. He had also selected a topic that people wanted to learn more about. After his article was published, it was widely discussed and Barber became rather famous. He used this opportunity to further encourage global awareness by expanding his article into a book, also titled *Jihad vs. McWorld.*

As an apprentice in a writing community, you probably don't have the same degree of access to academic journals or to mainstream media sources. At the same time, you may feel the need to share your values and beliefs with an audience wider than your classroom. A number of opportunities exist for public writing by students. For instance, Holly Van De Venter reworked the results of her research into a letter to the president of the North Dakota Education Association.

Holly Van De Venter

394 Territorial Hall

417 Walnut St. SE

Minneapolis, MN 55455

December 14, 2000

Max Laird

NDEA

PO Box 5055

Bismarck, ND 58502

Dear Max Laird:

I am writing as a North Dakota high school graduate, concerned about the future of education and the economic well-being of our state. I propose that the State of North Dakota require schools to teach a foreign language in the primary grades. The foreign language curriculum should not only teach verb usage and sentence structure, but also include lessons about the history and traditional celebrations.

The biggest benefit in implementing a foreign language program would be the positive change in our society. America's demographic make-up is becoming more diverse every day. We need to expose our children to different ways of life, teach them about different cultures, and help them realize that the United States is no longer a solely English-speaking country. North Dakota has seen an increase in its immigrant population, and teaching young children about their culture would lead to a higher respect for and understanding of each culture's uniqueness.

It is clearly evident that the business world has changed dramatically in the last two decades. This global marketplace requires that we be able to communicate with all countries efficiently to fully realize all the gains from trade. As you can see, teaching foreign languages would not only give our students better communication and people skills, but a head start for any career. These real-world skills would give our graduates a better chance to succeed.

I am fully aware of North Dakota's declining population. One way to attract newcomers to the state and convince people to stay is with a strong education system. Parents want their children to have a strong academic background so they will be prepared for the challenges ahead. This would be a great new opportunity for our children, giving them insight into the changing face of America.

5 I urge you to consider and discuss implementing foreign language programs with your colleagues, and to make it a priority in your upcoming meetings. I ask that the NDEA lobby school administrators and teachers for support, and take a proposal to the ND State Legislature to get funding for elementary foreign language programs. I would appreciate a response and any ideas that you may have on this subject. This call for action comes only with the concern of the student

in mind, and the belief that we need to promote our state's
educational excellence and build upon it with new programs
for the future.

Sincerely,

Holly Van De Venter

If you compare Van De Venter's earlier academic research paper with this
letter, you can see that she needed to rewrite her research results to meet the
conventions of this form of public writing. To write for the public, you too will
need to learn the conventions of public writing, just as you learned the conventions of writing in your classroom. These conventions may develop as a result
of the genres' publishing constraints. For example, newspaper stories usually have
short paragraphs because the stories are printed in narrow columns on the newspaper page. Long paragraphs would make the columns look too dense and unread-
able. Sometimes these conventions develop to help writers better reach their
audience. Pamphlets, for instance, are usually brief, visually appealing, and well
organized. This format allows people to read the pamphlet quickly.

At the same time, you should also exercise your imagination. In delivering your
message, you should strive for clarity, but you can sharpen your work's persuasiveness by using the argumentative strategies outlined in Chapter Four. For example,
Van De Venter ends her letter to Max Laird by affirming their common goal of
improving education in North Dakota. This strategy sets a tone of cooperation
instead of opposition. You can also exercise your imaginations by finding new
sources and strategies for getting out your message. The growing importance of
the Internet, for instance, has new created writing opportunities. You could share
your view in a chat room dedicated to your issue, you could e-mail fellow citizens, or you could create your own Web site, linking your arguments with other sites
that share your views. In the next section, we will examine several genres of public writing and how readers can decide which genre will be most effective.

The Genres of Public Debate

As with any writing situation, our first task is to analyze the writing situation. Public writing, however, is more sensitive than classroom writing to the effects of time
and place. For example, a poster might fail to reach its audience if a city ordinance
forbids displaying posters in public or if the issue being presented is no longer being
discussed by the public. To decide if the genres of public debate are appropriate for
expressing your message, and to decide which genre will be most effective, answer
the following questions. Then, as you read through brief descriptions of the public
writing genres, select those that best match your answers to the questions.

- Is this issue or event new to the public?
- Is this issue currently being discussed by the public?

- Where would people interested in this issue, and capable of putting your ideas into action, be likely to encounter your message?
- Because you may need to narrow the scope of your research, what aspects of the subject will most interest and move the public?
- What argumentative strategies would persuade your audience most effectively?
- What ethical concerns do you have in communicating your message to the public?

News Articles

News articles appear in newspapers, magazines, and news-oriented Web sites. They inform the public about current events and issues that affect the community. Because they are written primarily by professional journalists, you may need to try local or college newspapers or organization newsletters to get your articles published. You may even want to create a print or online newsletter of your own.

News articles are a good choice for public writing if:

- You want to inform the public of an issue or event that hasn't received enough attention. News articles provide valuable information by answering the journalist's basic questions: who, what, where, when, why and how.
- The issue or event you want to cover represents a current concern for the community.
- You want to reach a wider audience, especially if that audience reads the paper or magazine in which you want to publish the article.

News articles are not the best choice, however, if:

- You want to advocate a particular viewpoint or action. News articles try to remain objective, reporting only on the issues or events themselves and not on what the community ought to do about them.
- You want to analyze your event or issue in depth. While some news articles do go into great depth on a given subject, most cover only the basic information, aiming at those readers who read the articles while commuting, eating, or waiting for a bus.
- The readers of the publication are not in a position to address the issue you raise.

You can read an example of a good news story in Chapter Six's case study, where we print Mark Obmascik's "Massacre at Columbine High" from the *Denver Post*. Another good news story, along with advice on how to write one yourself, is found in Chapter Eight's case study, with George Dohrmann's "U Basketball Program Accused of Academic Fraud" from the *St. Paul Pioneer Press*. Both of these writers won Pulitzer Prizes for their reporting.

Editorials and Opinion Pieces

Editorials and opinion pieces also appear in newspapers, magazines, and Web sites, and like news articles they contain detailed facts. Unlike news articles, however, the writers express strong opinions about the events or issues; their purpose is to stimulate public discussion. The writers are usually professional journalists or editors, so you may need to try local, college, or organization newspapers, or you may try Web sites that encourage public opinion.

Editorials and opinion pieces are good choices for public writing if:

- You want to advocate a position or course of action on an issue being publicly debated, especially if news articles ran previously in the newspaper or magazine in which you want to publish the piece.
- You want to reach a wide audience, especially if that audience reads the paper or magazine in which you want to publish the article.

Editorials and opinion pieces are not the best choices, however, if:

- You want to avoid controversy. Editorials and opinion pieces express strong views in order to stimulate public debate, not avoid it.
- The readers of the publication are not in a position to respond to your position or to follow your recommended actions.
- You want to advocate your position in depth. While some opinion pieces do go into great depth on a given subject, most run only several paragraphs, focusing on one or two significant points.

You can find examples of editorials and opinion pieces throughout the readings chapters. You will find advice on how to write them yourself in Chapter Seven's case study on family values, where you'll find editorials from the *Seattle Times* and the *Christian Science Monitor*.

Letters to the Editor

Like news articles and op-ed pieces, letters to the editor are common features of newspapers and magazines, but unlike the former genres, letters to the editor are written by readers, not professional journalists. Letters give readers the opportunity to express their views about current issues or about ideas expressed in previous news articles, editorials, or opinion pieces. The space allotted for letters to the editor is limited, however, so writers must compete with other citizens to get their letters accepted.

A letter to the editor is a good choice for public writing if:

- You want to advocate a position or course of action on an issue, or if you want to continue a public debate begun by previous news articles, editorials, opinion pieces, or other letters.
- You want to reach a wide audience, especially if that audience reads the paper or magazine in which you want to publish the article.

- You don't have the time to craft a long opinion piece. Letters are usually 150 words or less, so writers must get directly to their point.

Letters to the editor are not a good choice, however, if:

- You want to avoid controversy. Letters to the editor encourage others to respond because they express strong opinions.
- You don't address issues relevant to the publication's readers. If your letter doesn't address an issue currently being covered, the editor will probably not publish the piece.
- You want to advocate your position in depth. Letters that run over 150 words may either be rejected or edited.

You can find examples of letters to the editor and advice on writing them yourself in the case study in Chapter Eight, on the basketball scandal at the University of Minnesota.

Letters to Public Officials

Not all of the genres of public debate need to be published. Citizens concerned about a particular social issue can write directly to their representatives in government. While elections and public opinion polls give government representatives some sense of their constituents' opinions, direct letters are often very effective. Representatives recognize that citizens concerned enough to write will probably take the time to vote for or against them in the next election. Because letters to public officials seek to create a one-on-one relationship with the official, writers need to prepare extensively for their letters to be effective.

A letter to a public official is a good choice for public writing if:

- You want to advocate a specific action or a perspective on an issue that may lead to future actions.
- Your issue can be positively affected by the individual office, governmental body, or political organization to which you write.
- Your opinion matters to the official because you are a constituent, a customer, or a supporter of their cause.

A letter to a public official is not the best choice, however, if:

- The issue is outside their jurisdiction.
- You want to reach a wider audience. Many public officials have their letters read by staff members who compile the information into summaries.
- You want to advocate your position in depth. Because public officials receive so many letters, your letter stands a better chance of being read if it is short and to the point.

Holly Van De Venter's letter in this chapter is an example of a letter to a public official that you can use as a guideline for writing your own letters.

The same conditions that help writers decide whether to write to public officials apply to writing to private individuals. Like government representatives, companies and organizations depend on patronage or public support; consequently, they usually take letters and other forms of public expression seriously.

Pamphlets and Posters

Like other genres, the conventions of pamphlets and posters have evolved to fill specific communication needs. Pamphlets are distributed to people passing on the street, or they are left in public places like libraries, subways, or college student centers. Posters are placed on lampposts, in hallways, even on the sidewalk—wherever people's eyes rest as they are traveling. To get these people to take a pamphlet or examine a poster, writers must grab their attention. Consequently, pamphlets and posters rely heavily on visual elements to enliven, clarify, and argue their points.

Pamphlets and posters are good choices for public writing if:

- You want to reach a wide audience, especially if the event or issue is related to the location where you display the pamphlets and posters. For example, a pamphlet protesting animal research would be more effective in front of an animal research facility.
- Your issue is readily identifiable and your message is easily understood. Because people spend only minutes looking at a pamphlet or poster, they need to receive and understand your message quickly.
- You have visual elements to complement your argument. People will read your poster or pamphlet if their eyes are drawn to interesting or powerful graphics.
- They complement other forms of direct action like boycotts, picketing, or rallies. They can then explain to observers why you are engaging in direct action.

Pamphlets and posters are not the best choices, however, if:

- You want to avoid controversy. People reading the posters or accepting the pamphlets may argue with you, tear down your posters, or ask you to leave the area.
- You don't address issues relevant to the people who read your posters or pamphlets. To reach people who can act on your recommendations, you may need to research where your audience would most likely see the writing.
- You want to advocate your position in depth. To hold your readers' attention, you need to deliver your message very quickly, often in less than a minute.
- The place where you want to present the pamphlets or posters does not permit the public display of private messages.

You can find an example of a substantive pamphlet and advice on creating one yourself in Chapter Nine's case study, where we include *A Citizen's Guide to the World Trade Organization*.

The Internet: Web Sites, Newsgroups, Chat Rooms, and Listservs

The Internet provides tremendous opportunities to communicate with people who share your views on social issues. Posting documents on an existing Web site or creating your own site can help you reach an international audience. Including your e-mail address with the documents can also help readers contact you, encouraging the formation of conversations.

A Web site is a good choice for public writing if:

- You want to reach a wide audience. However, unlike pamphlets or posters, readers must come to the site to get your message. Writers might combine pamphlets or posters with Web sites where the issues are discussed in greater depth.
- You want to alert people about an issue that other media forms have not covered.
- You want to encourage arguments as opportunities to better understand an issue. By including your e-mail address, you can converse with other citizens to better understand your own values and beliefs.
- You want to advocate your position in depth. Web sites allow you to publish documents of considerable length, but to keep readers' attention you may need to make the work visually accessible, using bullet points, hypertext links, and pictures.

Web sites are not the best choices, however, if:

- You want to reach a wide audience in a short period of time, especially if you want to reach people located in a particular area. Even if your site receives 10,000 hits, it won't help your cause if the people you wish to persuade are not among the visitors.
- You can't advertise the site to your audience. Simply posting a document on the Web will not guarantee others will find it.
- You cannot write in HTML (hypertext markup language), the computer code that allows writers to post their work on the Internet. Fortunately, many sites have features allowing people to post messages by typing them into a preselected box. In addition, programs like Adobe PageMill and Microsoft Front-Page permit computer programming novices to create their own Web pages.
- You can't find a university or company willing to host your page, or if the content you wish to publish violates the host's policies regarding Web publications.

You are probably already familiar with many Web sites, but you can see one and discuss its features by examining The Hunger Site: <http://www.thehungersite.com>, which we refer to in the Stop and Think box in Chapter Twelve.

In addition, on the Internet, newsgroups, chat rooms and listservs offer opportunities to share your ideas, to get feedback from other citizens, and to organize other forms of social action. Unlike other forms of public writing, these online forms allow you to follow-up your initial writing to respond to other citizens, further clarifying your arguments or answering their objections.

Newsgroups, chat rooms, and listservs are good choices for public writing if:

- You want to reach a wider audience of people interested in discussing your issue. You can converse with other citizens from all over the world.

- You want to encourage arguments as opportunities to better understand an issue. The diversity of perspectives can help you better understand your own values and beliefs.

- You want to alert people about an issue that other media forms have not covered.

Newsgroups, chat rooms or listservs are not the best choices, however, if:

- You want to avoid controversy. There is a greater degree of anonymity when communicating online, so people who disagree with you may be less civil than if they talked with you face-to-face. Many listservs have moderators, however, who can edit out inappropriate responses.

- Your audience is not in a position to act on your suggestions. Unless the electronic forum has local participants, you wouldn't bring local community problems to them unless they could actually help.

- You want to advocate your position in depth. Participants in chat rooms and listservs generally prefer messages no longer than a paragraph or two, especially if they receive many other messages and emails.

- Your issue is irrelevant or inappropriate for particular audiences. For example, many college-sponsored listservs are created to facilitate research. Members may not appreciate calls to social action no matter how just the cause.

Zines

Zines, short for fanzines, are low-budget, self-produced magazines on a variety of topics that allow writers and artists an outlet for their ideas away from the mainstream media. They are much more personal and idiosyncratic than commercial magazines are, and vary widely in terms of quality and quantity. They tend to be focused on one topic or area of interest, whether that is pinball, motherhood, skateboarding, peaceful alternatives to war, organic gardening, or King Diamond. You can find them photocopied and distributed around your campus or town, or posted on the Web, and they get known mainly by word of mouth. Some that started life as local zines, such as *Bust, Hip Mama,* and *Punk Planet,* have developed into larger-scale magazines with a national following. Although zines rarely speak to large audiences, they are one of the best ways for students to enter the public sphere of debate on topics of particular interest, because instead of having to convince someone else to publish your work, you can create and publish it on your own and distribute it where you want people to read it.

You can find a resource guide for creating and publishing your own zine, as well as recommendations for good zines, at *The Zine and E-zine Resource Guide* site: <http://www.zinebook.com/>.

We suspect you are more knowledgeable about zines than we, the authors of this book, are. We encourage you to inform us about the best zines and to provide links to your own zines by posting the information on our Web site **http://www.ablong.com/berndt**.

QUESTIONS FOR INQUIRY AND ACTION

1. Take a moment to reflect upon the research paper you developed. What excited you most about the project? What did you learn from doing it—both about the subject matter or issue you were exploring, and about the process of researching, developing the argument, and writing the paper?

2. If you had "world enough and time," what would you do with your research project? How could you publish the knowledge in it, whether as a research paper or in one of the genres of public debate?

3. How can you imagine yourself changing or in some way making a difference in the situation you're concerned about? What, realistically, would you have to do? How could you get others involved, too?

4. Envision launching a zine, whether by yourself or with a group of friends or classmates. What subject would you focus on? What is not being talked about enough? How would you present your zine—in paper, online, or both? Where and to whom would you initially distribute it, and why?

CHAPTER 6

Negotiating Community: Living a Civic Life

community n. 1. a. A group of people living in the same locality and under the same government. b. The district or locality in which such a group lives. 2a. A group or class having common interests: *the scientific community; the international business community.* b. A group viewed as forming a distinct segment of society: *the gay community; the community of color.* 3a. Similarity or identity. u *community of interests.* b. Sharing, participation, and fellowship. 4. Society as a whole; the public. 5. *Ecology* a. A group of plants and animals living and interacting with one another in a specific region under relatively similar conditions. b. The region occupied by a group of interacting organisms. [Middle English *communite*, citizenry, from Old French, from Latin *communitas*, fellowship, from *communis*, common.]

American Heritage Dictionary, *fourth edition (2000).*

GETTING STARTED: What Does a Community Look Like?

In the following ethnographic exercise, you are to observe your local community, your neighborhood, and then to examine closely one particular meeting place in that community. (An alternative possibility is to use this exercise as a whole-class field trip, and explore one of your campus's neighborhoods.)

1. Take a walk around your neighborhood. Describe what you see in your writer's notebook.

   Buildings: What kinds of buildings predominate?

   - Residences (mostly single-family, multi-family, or a mix)?
   - Businesses (e.g., retail shops, restaurants, or industrial plants)?
   - Schools (what kinds and levels)?
   - Houses of worship (more than one denomination or religion)?

   Architectual styles: Is there a consistency (or lack thereof) in style? How does that make the neighborhood feel?

"Green spaces": Are there parks, playgrounds, gardens, yards, etc? Are these mostly public or private spaces? Are people welcome to congregate in them? Are people there when you are observing?

Traffic: How much car traffic is there in your neighborhood? Is it on a bus line? Do you see people walking or riding their bikes for transportation as well as for recreation and exercise?

People:

- What kinds of people do you see? Is there a consistency or a diversity in the kinds of people that you see, in terms of race or ethnicity, or socioeconomic class?
- How friendly are the people? Do they greet or talk to one another? Do they greet or talk to you?
- How many of the people do you know: (a) by sight? (b) by name?

2. Stop for a while in one neighborhood gathering spot or meeting place. *Is* there one in your neighborhood? What kind of place is it? What does it feel like? Who comes here? Are these people representative of the neighborhood as a whole?

Discuss your findings with your classmates.

1. The word *community* tends to conjure up warm, fuzzy images of single-family houses on a tree-lined street, where children play outside together and adults borrow cups of sugar from one another. Is that what you observed in your community?

2. Is every group of "people living in the same locality," as the *American Heritage Dictionary* puts it, a community? How would you define community? What are your criteria? Finish this sentence: I feel most in community with others when. . .

3. Do you think that your neighborhood lacks a sense of community? Why or why not? Do you think that your neighborhood—or your city, or country—*suffers* because of a lack of community? Why or why not?

4. In what ways does having a sense of community matter (or not) to the quality of our civic lives?

As we learned in Chapter One, dictionary definitions cannot reveal to us people's lived experiences with community—the ways that community gets created, defined, or destroyed in everyday life. What do we want and expect from our communities? How much emphasis, for instance, do we and should we place on interconnectedness and collective activities, and how much on autonomy and individualism? What responsibilities do we have to others in our communities, and to the flourishing of the community as a whole? Is building strong communities—at all levels—essential to the strength of our civic life? The readings in this chapter raise these questions through a variety of genres.

In our first case study we examine the April 20, 1999 shootings at Columbine High School in Littleton, Colorado. The shootings shocked the community— and the entire nation. People couldn't believe that such a model, safe community could experience such terror and violence. In the aftermath, however, many residents admitted that there hadn't been much *community* in the city of Littleton or at Columbine High School. The media treated the Columbine situation as a national wake-up call to renew communities and our sense of civic values.

Some people criticized media leaders for sensationalizing the event, profiting from a community's anguish and playing into the killers' desires by continuing to present their story as front page, prime time news. Including the shootings as a case study for examination might also seem to be sensationalizing the event by continuing to probe its dark corners. That is not our intention, however. We lead off with this case study because we regard the shootings as an opening to a discussion that needs to be held: a discussion of the daily lives of high school students, which often include student-on-student psychological as well as physical violence. Since most of you are probably recent high school graduates and all of you are members of local communities, you have a voice in planning the kinds of community we need to be forging in high schools as well as in your other communities.

ROBERT FROST Mending Wall

Robert Frost (1874–1963) is a much-loved American poet who has been especially appreciated for his accessible writing style. He wrote often about life in rural New England communities and is well known for classic poems such as "The Road Not Taken" and "Stopping by Woods on a Snowy Evening," but he also wrote words of political protest, including "U.S. 1946 King's X" which describes the nightmare of nuclear holocaust. Frost was awarded the Pulitzer Prize for Poetry in 1924, 1937, and 1943. "Mending Wall" was written in 1914 and is most famous for its line, "Good fences make good neighbors."

Something there is that doesn't love a wall,
That sends the frozen-ground-swell under it,
And spills the upper boulders in the sun;
And makes gaps even two can pass abreast.
5   The work of hunters is another thing:
I have come after them and made repair
Where they have left not one stone on a stone,
But they would have the rabbit out of hiding,
To please the yelping dogs. The gaps I mean,
10   No one has seen them made or heard them made,
But at spring mending-time we find them there.
I let my neighbor know beyond the hill;
And on a day we meet to walk the line
And set the wall between us once again.
15   We keep the wall between us as we go.
To each the boulders that have fallen to each.
And some are loaves and some so nearly balls
We have to use a spell to make them balance:
"Stay where you are until our backs are turned!"
20   We wear our fingers rough with handling them.
Oh, just another kind of outdoor game,
One on a side. It comes to little more:
There where it is we do not need the wall:
He is all pine and I am apple orchard.
25   My apple trees will never get across
And eat the cones under his pines, I tell him.
He only says, "Good fences make good neighbors."
Spring is the mischief in me, and I wonder
If I could put a notion in his head:
30   "*Why* do they make good neighbors? Isn't it
Where there are cows? But here there are no cows.
Before I built a wall I'd ask to know
What I was walling in or walling out,
And to whom I was like to give offense.
35   Something there is that doesn't love a wall,
That wants it down." I could say "Elves" to him,

But it's not elves exactly, and I'd rather
He said it for himself. I see him there
Bringing a stone grasped firmly by the top
40   In each hand, like an old-stone savage armed
He moves in darkness as it seems to me,
Not of woods only and the shade of trees.
He will not go behind his father's saying,
And he likes having thought of it so well
45   He says again, "Good fences make good neighbors."

QUESTIONS FOR INQUIRY AND ACTION

1. Sketch out the action described in the poem. What are the two men, the speaker and his neighbor, doing? How do Frost's descriptions of their actions help you to understand the poem?

2. Frost's narrator seems impatient with walls, yet Frost provides descriptions that encourage us to question the narrator's ideas. For example, how would you interpret the following lives: "I see him there/Bringing a stone grasped firmly by the top/In each hand, like an old-stone savage armed" (ll. 38–40)? Does this threatening image suggest a need for walls? Why or why not?

3. Why do you think Frost explores the idea of barriers in a poem? Try rewriting this meeting between neighbors as a short story, a play, or an essay. How does your new genre change the way you explore Frost's idea?

4. Examine your own living space. Where you live are there clear borders between your own space and your neighbors' space? If so, what kind of form does the border take? How do you feel about borders? Do you like them? Are they necessary?

CAROL BLY Enemy Evenings

Carol Bly is a St. Paul, Minnesota-based essayist, short story writer, and teacher of writing and ethics. She edited the anthology Changing the Bully Who Rules the World: Reading and Thinking about Ethics *(1996), and she is the author of a number of works of fiction and nonfiction, including* The Tomcat's Wife and Other Stories *(1991) and* Beyond the Writers' Workshop: New Ways to Write Creative Nonfiction *(2001). (We include advice from this book in Chapters Two and Five.) "Enemy Evenings" appears in her collection of essays entitled* Letters From the Country *(New York: Harper & Row, 1981).*

In Minnesota towns one sometimes has the feeling of moving among ghosts, because we don't meet and talk to our local opponents on any question. We know, for example, that somewhere in our town of 2,242, there live people who believe that the preservatives sodium nitrite, sodium nitrate, and BHA variously threaten future health, and also in town live the local staff of the Agricultural Extension

Division, who have just published an essay saying the advantages of these preservatives outweigh the disadvantages. Yet these two sets of people don't meet each other on open panels, and scarcely at all even privately, thus providing another major American issue which small-town people are left out of.

The case is always made that to keep a town from flying apart you must discuss only matters in which there is little conflict. That means that whenever a woman physician enters a room in which a few people are urging, intriguingly enough, that the man should be head of the woman (St. Paul), the topic must automatically be changed to whether or not we are getting that hard winter they kept talking about last fall.

There is nothing much wrong with weather talk except that far from preventing people from feeling "threatened" it is in fact the living proof that you don't care about those people: you haven't any interest in their thoughts; you don't want to hear them out.

There is little lonelier than small-town life when small talk is the principal means of peace. Sherwood Anderson illustrated it long ago, but people who still read Anderson seem to do so in a mist of nostalgia rather than for any revelation we can put to use. Also, I'm not content with the usual explanations for small-town citizens' being so uneasy around intense feelings. The question is: why are thousands and thousands of lively and feeling people who live in the countryside willing to give up, for their whole lives, the kind of friendship people enjoy who deliberately, curiously, and civilly draw out one another's views on serious subjects?

5   The reason generally offered, of course, is that airing last night's hassle at the church council will curtail this morning's sale of advertising space in the paper. This reason presupposes that serious exchange is a *hassle,* and must be the result of gaucherie. I don't believe it. Another commonly offered explanation is that less-informed or less-intelligent people will feel unequal to frank self-expression in the presence of more-informed or more-intelligent people. That is abundantly untrue. I have heard extremely strong opinions plentifully and bravely offered by people including myself who could hardly have been less informed or less gifted about the subject.

We simply need experience in taking an interest in the other side and doing so with the proponents of the other side present. If we could get this habit going I think we could reduce one of the most dismal characteristics of small-town life—the loneliness. Of course human loneliness is general, but this particular source of it, exercised in hypocrisy, could be ended.

Therefore, I propose that small community groups develop panels for Enemy Evenings. Obviously some much better word has to be used, but I like the pure madness of this one: it reminds me of that fantastic creation of Nixon, Ehrlichman, and Haldeman—the enemies list. Enemy Evenings would definitely need two things: a firm master of ceremonies in whom general affection for human beings would be paramount, not a chill manner or a childish desire to get the fur flying; second, it would need very just panel representation. An example of unjust panel representation would be a four-person panel to discuss the defense budget made up of a leader of American Writers vs. the Vietnam War; a director of Episcopal Community Services, Minneapolis; Senator Mondale; and (the chump) an American Party spokesman. It would be helpful too, if controversial panels were conducted with humor, but that isn't essential.

In discussing this notion at a Cultural Affairs Committee meeting in my town, we observed with interest the 1974–75 policy of the Minnesota Humanities Commission, emphasizing the relation between private concerns and public policies. Also, the National Endowment for the Humanities (through the Upper Midwest Council) has supported a series of television dialogues this winter, covering controversial subjects. All that is interesting, but for the common viewer what is seen on television is irrevocably "something they had on television." Seeing one's own neighbor speak out passionately (and having the chance to respond) is immediately engaging.

Here is a suggested rough list of seldom-discussed subjects with strongly opposed participants:

1. Additives in commercial food products and the relationship of 4-H instruction materials to the Wheat Institute.
   Suggested participants:
      Home Extension personnel
      Local members, the International Academy for Preventive Medicine
2. Fertilizing methods
   Suggested participants:
      County agent
      Anhydrous ammonia dealers
      Bag fertilizer dealers
      Soil Conservation Service Experiment station personnel
      Members of the Soil Improvement Association
      Local subscribers to Department of Natural Resources publications and
         Organic Gardening, and readers of U.S. Agricultural yearbooks
3. Fall plowing vs. spring plowing
   Suggested participants:
      County agent (The official Ag. stand now is that fall plowing is detrimental, but by far the largest number of farmers still do it when they have time.)
      Farmers committed to both plowing practices
4. Defense Department budget of the United States
   Suggested participants:
      VFW or Legion Auxiliary officers
      VFW or Legion Post officers
      Local members, Women's League for Peace and Freedom
      Local members, Common Cause
      National Guard unit officers
5. St. Paul's stand on man as the head of woman
   Suggested participants:
      Fundamentalist church representatives
      Local Charismatic Christians—who tend to be nicely divided on this, providing an interesting confusion

Local members of Business and Professional Women's Clubs
Local Officers of American Federation of Women's Clubs
Grain elevator managers

6. The growth of shopping malls *around* small towns
   Suggested participants:
   Local promoters of comprehensive plans
   Main Street businessmen
   Members of senior citizens' clubs
   High school Ecology Club members
   The mayor or council members

7. The emphasis on technical training at the high school level
   Suggested participants:
   Local painters, writers, and musicians
   Vocational center director and staff
   Visiting college humanities division members
   Visiting Vo-Tech schools' faculty members

8. Drainage ditches
   Suggested participants:
   County commissioners and engineers holding contracts for ditches
   Soil Improvement Association members
   DNR staff members on loan
   SCS personnel on loan

9. Competition vs. cooperation, as taught in U.S. elementary schools
   Suggested participants:
   Angry parents on both sides
   School counselor
   Fifth- or sixth-grade faculty members
   Psychology faculty from neighboring community colleges

10. The lives of men and women in rural towns
    Suggested participants:
    President of the Jaycees
    President of the Mrs. Jaycees
    Larry Batson or Robert T. Smith of the *Minneapolis Tribune* or anyone
       half so lively
    Very conservative pastors or priests
    Personnel from West Central Mental Health Center

10   A painful fact of American life is that people from small towns are afraid of directness. Small-town kids, unlike suburban kids, can't take much from the shoulder. Example: A suburban Minneapolis child with a first-rate music instructor goes off to her piano lesson. She is working up a small piece of Mozart, she hasn't done her homework, and she smears the counting. The music instructor tells her it's an irresponsible job, sloppy phrasing, whatever she tells her—in any case, it won't do. The child returns home and works the piece up much more conscientiously next time, having learned that music is a disciplined pleasure.

A rural piano student cannot be spoken to so plainly. It is hard for her to be stirred into being responsible to the music at hand because the instant a teacher tries to correct her directly her soul sags into mere self-condemnation. Our style, in the countryside, is not to criticize children at all: we very seldom tell them the plane model was glued carelessly and the sleeve set in without enough easing. (The counterpart of this is that we seldom praise them much for anything either. "You played a real good game against Dawson"; "You did a real good job of that speech contest"—not "I knew you'd do well at the speech thing: I didn't know that I would cry—in fact, I'm *still* moved by what you said!") So the children develop neither stamina about criticism nor the imagination to picture to themselves gigantic praise if they excel. They live lightly handed into a middle world of little comment, and therefore little incitement to devotion. Should a music teacher try to explain Mozart's involvement in the music— what *he* had in mind for this or that phrase—the student wouldn't hear over the ground noise of dismay in her own feelings. "I'm being attacked! I'm being attacked!" is all her inexperienced soul can take in. Piranhas when you're out swimming, mean music teachers when you're taking piano—it's all the same to her. On a psychological ladder, she is rungs below being able to move from self to Mozart.

What we need in rural life is more Serious Occasion. By the time a child is ten, he or she should have heard, at least a few hundreds of times, "I loved that dying cowboy routine. Do it again. Do be quiet, Uncle Malcolm. Noah's going to do his dying cowboy routine." And adults would have shut up, listened, and praised. That moment would have been a Serious Occasion. Then a child is caught lying. It is horrible to lie—the notice of it should be serious and major. Then lying— whether or not one did it—is the subject of a Serious Occasion. Then, after some hundreds of such occasions, one can take in a conversation about music— what does Mozart want out of this piece? Remember: we are not now talking about you or yourself. We are talking about someone *other*—a musician long dead—and he is making a demand on us, and we are going to meet that demand! We are not going to scream and flee, because discipline is not the same thing as piranhas in the river.

I think we will surge into twice as much life through Serious Occasion.

At the same time, Minnesota rural life gives comfort and sweetness. Our young people are always returning home on their college weekends. When they drop out of college they tend to wander back here instead of prowling the streets of San Francisco or St. Paul. Apparently they garner genuine comfort from the old familiarity, the low-intensity social life, and with it a pretty good guarantee of not being challenged. Their ease has been bought, however, at the expense of the others who live here year round. To preserve our low-key manners, they have had to bottle up social indignation, psychological curiosity, and intellectual doubt. Their banter and their observations about the weather are carapace developed over decades of inconsequential talk.

15 The problem isn't like the major psychological phenomena in the United States—the increasing competitiveness and cheating in Ivy League and other

top colleges, the multiplication of spies and counterspies in private corporations, the daily revelations of crookedness and irresponsibility on the part of major corporations, the ominous pursuance of the Law of the Sea conventions regardless of Cousteau's warnings, the overriding of public opinion about strip mining in the West. These are the horrible things that depress everybody. Remembering them, I think we can skip toward solving small-town dilemmas rather cheerfully. I commend frank panel evenings with opponents taking part: let's try that for a change of air, after years of chill and evasive tact.

QUESTIONS FOR INQUIRY AND ACTION

1. Bly proposes that "what we need in rural life is more 'Serious Occasion.'" What does she mean by this? Do you agree with her?

2. We often avoid conversations about controversial subjects because we don't want to threaten people. Bly argues, however, that avoiding debate is "living proof that you don't care about those people: you haven't any interest in their thoughts; you don't want to hear them out." In other words, Bly re-sees a situation that is generally framed as a matter of politeness as one of ethics. Respond to her statement. Does it make you reexamine why you avoid talking about controversial issues?

3. "Enemy Evenings" contains a proposal for improving the quality of conversations and, as a result, the quality of life in Bly's small-town Minnesota community. Compare Bly's proposal with the Black Panthers' Ten Point Plan in Chapter Four. You'll notice how starkly different they are, but begin your comparison by noting their similarities. Then, when you look at their differences, consider the reasons. For instance, how is the context different for each proposal? How is the relationship of the proposers to the audience different in each, demanding a different kind of proposal for action?

4. Try proposing an "enemy evening" in a community you're involved in that needs to discuss difficult issues but tends to avoid doing so. Plan it carefully, and reflect on it afterward, preferably with all of the people there.

HENRY DAVID THOREAU from Civil Disobedience

Henry David Thoreau (1817–1862) was an American writer best known for living life on his own terms and encouraging others to do so as well. He is the author of several books, most famously Walden (excerpts from which are included in Chapter Three). To protest the United States' continuing practice of slavery and its aggression in the Mexican-American War, Thoreau refused for six years to pay his poll tax. This was against the law, and as a result Thoreau was thrown in jail. (He was bailed out the following morning.) He put his protest into words—words that have become his most famous essay. Thoreau titled it "Resistance to Civil Government" and delivered it as a speech to the Concord Lyceum on January 26, 1848; it was first published in May of 1849, in Aesthetic Papers, a short-lived journal. It was posthumously titled "Civil Disobedience."

I heartily accept the motto, "That government is best which governs least"; and I should like to see it acted up to more rapidly and systematically. Carried out, it finally amounts to this, which also I believe—"That government is best which governs not at all"; and when men are prepared for it, that will be the kind of government which they will have. Government is at best but an expedient; but most governments are usually, and all governments are sometimes, inexpedient. The objections which have been brought against a standing army, and they are many and weighty, and deserve to prevail, may also at last be brought against a standing government. The standing army is only an arm of the standing government. The government itself, which is only the mode which the people have chosen to execute their will, is equally liable to be abused and perverted before the people can act through it. Witness the present Mexican war, the work of comparatively a few individuals using the standing government as their tool; for in the outset, the people would not have consented to this measure.

This American government—what is it but a tradition, though a recent one, endeavoring to transmit itself unimpaired to posterity, but each instant losing some of its integrity? It has not the vitality and force of a single living man; for a single man can bend it to his will. It is a sort of wooden gun to the people themselves. But it is not the less necessary for this; for the people must have some complicated machinery or other, and hear its din, to satisfy that idea of government which they have. Governments show thus how successfully men can be imposed upon, even impose on themselves, for their own advantage. It is excellent, we must all allow. Yet this government never of itself furthered any enterprise, but by the alacrity with which it got out of its way. It does not keep the country free. It does not settle the West. It does not educate. The character inherent in the American people has done all that has been accomplished; and it would have done somewhat more, if the government had not sometimes got in its way. For government is an expedient, by which men would fain succeed in letting one another alone; and, as has been said, when it is most expedient, the governed are most let alone by it. Trade and commerce, if they were not made of india-rubber, would never manage to bounce over obstacles which legislators are continually putting in their way; and if one were to judge these men wholly by the effects of their actions and not partly by their intentions, they would deserve to be classed and punished with those mischievious persons who put obstructions on the railroads.

But, to speak practically and as a citizen, unlike those who call themselves no government men, I ask for, not at once no government, but *at once* a better government. Let every man make known what kind of government would command his respect, and that will be one step toward obtaining it.

After all, the practical reason why, when the power is once in the hands of the people, a majority are permitted, and for a long period continue, to rule is not because they are most likely to be in the right, nor because this seems fairest to the minority, but because they are physically the strongest. But a government in which the majority rule in all cases can not be based on justice, even as far as men understand it. Can there not be a government in which the majorities do not virtually decide right and wrong, but conscience?—in which majorities decide only those questions to which the rule of expediency is applicable? Must the citizen ever for a moment, or in the least degree, resign his conscience to the legislator? Why has every man a conscience then? I think that we should be men first, and subjects afterward. It is not desirable to cultivate a respect for the law, so much as for the right. The only obligation which I have a right to assume is to do at any time what I think right. It is truly enough said that a corporation has no conscience; but a corporation on conscientious men is a corporation with a conscience. Law never made men a whit more just; and, by means of their respect for it, even the well-disposed are daily made the agents on injustice. . . .

5　All men recognize the right of revolution; that is, the right to refuse allegiance to, and to resist, the government, when its tyranny or its inefficiency are great and unendurable. But almost all say that such is not the case now. But such was the case, they think, in the Revolution of '75. If one were to tell me that this was a bad government because it taxed certain foreign commodities brought to its ports, it is most probable that I should not make an ado about it, for I can do without them. All machines have their friction; and possibly this does enough good to counterbalance the evil. At any rate, it is a great evil to make a stir about it. But when the friction comes to have its machine, and oppression and robbery are organized, I say, let us not have such a machine any longer. In other words, when a sixth of the population of a nation which has undertaken to be the refuge of liberty are slaves, and a whole country is unjustly overrun and conquered by a foreign army, and subjected to military law, I think that it is not too soon for honest men to rebel and revolutionize. What makes this duty the more urgent is that fact that the country so overrun is not our own, but ours is the invading army. . . .

Practically speaking, the opponents to a reform in Massachusetts are not a hundred thousand politicians at the South, but a hundred thousand merchants and farmers here, who are more interested in commerce and agriculture than they are in humanity, and are not prepared to do justice to the slave and to Mexico, *cost what it may.* I quarrel not with far-off foes, but with those who, near at home, co-operate with, and do the bidding of, those far away, and without whom the latter would be harmless. We are accustomed to say, that the mass of men are unprepared; but improvement is slow, because the few are not as materially wiser or better than the many. It is not so important that many should be good as you, as that there be some absolute goodness somewhere; for that will leaven the whole lump. There are thousands who are in opinion opposed to slavery and to the war, who yet in effect do nothing to put an end to them; who, esteeming themselves children of Washington and Franklin, sit down with their hands in their pockets, and say that they know not what to do, and do nothing; who even postpone the question of freedom to the question of free trade, and quietly read the prices-current along with the latest advices from Mexico, after dinner, and, it may be, fall asleep over them both. What is the price-current of an honest man and patriot today? They hesitate, and they regret, and sometimes they petition; but they do nothing in earnest and with effect. They will wait, well disposed, for other to remedy the evil, that they may no longer have it to regret. At most, they give up only a cheap vote, and a feeble countenance and Godspeed, to the right, as it goes by them. There are nine hundred and ninety-nine patrons of virtue to one virtuous man. But it is easier to deal with the real possessor of a thing than with the temporary guardian of it.

All voting is a sort of gaming, like checkers or backgammon, with a slight moral tinge to it, a playing with right and wrong, with moral questions; and betting naturally accompanies it. The character of the voters is not staked. I cast my vote, perchance, as I think right; but I am not vitally concerned that that right should prevail. I am willing to leave it to the majority. Its obligation, therefore, never exceeds that of expediency. Even voting for the right is doing nothing for it. It is only expressing to men feebly your desire that it should prevail. A wise man will not leave the right to the mercy of chance, nor wish it to prevail through the power of the majority. There is but little virtue in the action of masses of men. When the majority shall at length vote for the abolition of slavery, it will be because they are indifferent to slavery, or because there is but little slavery left to be abolished by their vote. They will then be the only slaves. Only his vote can hasten the abolition of slavery who asserts his own freedom by his vote. . . .

Unjust laws exist: shall we be content to obey them, or shall we endeavor to amend them, and obey them until we have succeeded, or shall we transgress them at once? Men, generally, under such a government as this, think that they ought to wait until they have persuaded the majority to alter them. They think that, if they should resist, the remedy would be worse than the evil. But it is the fault of the government itself that the remedy is worse than the evil. It makes it worse. Why is it not more apt to anticipate and provide for reform? Why does it not cherish its wise minority? Why does it cry and resist before it is hurt? Why does it not encourage its citizens to put out its faults, and do better than it would have them? Why does it always crucify Christ and excommunicate Copernicus and Luther, and pronounce Washington and Franklin rebels?

One would think, that a deliberate and practical denial of its authority was the only offense never contemplated by its government; else, why has it not assigned its definite, its suitable and proportionate, penalty? If a man who has no property refuses but once to earn nine shillings for the State, he is put in prison for a period unlimited by any law that I know, and determined only by the discretion of those who put him there; but if he should steal ninety times nine shillings from the State, he is soon permitted to go at large again.

10   If the injustice is part of the necessary friction of the machine of government, let it go, let it go: perchance it will wear smooth—certainly the machine will wear out. If the injustice has a spring, or a pulley, or a rope, or a crank, exclusively for itself, then perhaps you may consider whether the remedy will not be worse than the evil; but if it is of such a nature that it requires you to be the agent of injustice to another, then I say, break the law. Let your life be a counter-friction

to stop the machine. What I have to do is to see, at any rate, that I do not lend myself to the wrong which I condemn.

As for adopting the ways which the State has provided for remedying the evil, I know not of such ways. They take too much time, and a man's life will be gone. I have other affairs to attend to. I came into this world, not chiefly to make this a good place to live in, but to live in it, be it good or bad. A man has not everything to do, but something; and because he cannot do *everything,* it is not necessary that he should do *something* wrong. It is not my business to be petitioning the Governor or the Legislature any more than it is theirs to petition me; and if they should not hear my petition, what should I do then? But in this case the State has provided no way: its very Constitution is the evil. This may seem to be harsh and stubborn and unconciliatory; but it is to treat with the utmost kindness and consideration the only spirit that can appreciate or deserves it. So is all change for the better, like birth and death, which convulse the body.

I do not hesitate to say, that those who call themselves Abolitionists should at once effectually withdraw their support, both in person and property, from the government of Massachusetts, and not wait till they constitute a majority of one, before they suffer the right to prevail through them. I think that it is enough if they have God on their side, without waiting for that other one. Moreover, any man more right than his neighbors constitutes a majority of one already. . . .

Under a government which imprisons unjustly, the true place for a just man is also a prison. The proper place today, the only place which Massachusetts has provided for her freer and less despondent spirits, is in her prisons, to be put out and locked out of the State by her own act, as they have already put themselves out by their principles. It is there that the fugitive slave, and the Mexican prisoner on parole, and the Indian come to plead the wrongs of his race should find them; on that separate but more free and honorable ground, where the State places those who are not with her, but against her—the only house in a slave State in which a free man can abide with honor. If any think that their influence would be lost there, and their voices no longer afflict the ear of the State, that they would not be as an enemy within its walls, they do not know by how much truth is stronger than error, nor how much more eloquently and effectively he can combat injustice who has experienced a little in his own person. Cast your whole vote, not a strip of paper merely, but your whole influence. A minority is powerless while it conforms to the majority; it is not even a minority then; but it is irresistible when it clogs by its whole weight. If the alternative is to keep all just men in prison, or give up war and slavery, the State will not hesitate which to choose. If a thousand men were not to pay their tax bills this year, that would not be a violent and bloody measure, as it would be to pay them, and enable the State to commit violence and shed innocent blood. This is, in fact, the definition of a peaceable revolution, if any such is possible. If the tax-gatherer, or any other public officer, asks me, as one has done, "But what shall I do?" my answer is, "If you really wish to do anything, resign your office." When the subject has refused allegiance, and the officer has resigned from office, then the revolution is accomplished. But even suppose blood shed when the conscience is wounded? Through this wound a man's real manhood and immortality flow out, and he bleeds to an everlasting death. I see this blood flowing now. . . .

15   I have paid no poll tax for six years. I was put into a jail once on this account, for one night; and, as I stood considering the walls of solid stone, two or three feet thick, the door of wood and iron, a foot thick, and the iron grating which strained the light, I could not help being struck with the foolishness of that institution which treated me as if I were mere flesh and blood and bones, to be locked up. I wondered that it should have concluded at length that this was the best use it could put me to, and had never thought to avail itself of my services in some way. I saw that, if there was a wall of stone between me and my townsmen, there was a still more difficult one to climb or break through before they could get to be as free as I was. I did not for a moment feel confined, and the walls seemed a great waste of stone and mortar. I felt as if I alone of all my townsmen had paid my tax. They plainly did not know how to treat me, but behaved like persons who are underbred. In every threat and in every compliment there was a blunder; for they thought that my chief desire was to stand the other side of that stone wall. I could not but smile to see how industriously they locked the door on my meditations, which followed them out again without let or hindrance, and they were really all that was dangerous. As they could not reach me, they had resolved to punish my body; just as boys, if they cannot come at some person against whom they have a spite, will abuse his dog. I saw that the State was half-witted, that it was timid as a lone woman with her silver spoons, and that it did not know its friends from its foes, and I lost all my remaining respect for it, and pitied it.

Thus the state never intentionally confronts a man's sense, intellectual or moral, but only his body, his senses. It is not armed with superior wit or honesty, but with superior physical strength. I was not born to be forced. I will breathe after my own fashion. Let us see who is the strongest. What force has a multitude? They only can force me who obey a higher law than I. They force me to become like themselves. I do not hear of men being forced to live this way or that by masses of men. What sort of life were that to live?

When I meet a government which says to me, "Your money or your life," why should I be in haste to give it my money? It may be in a great strait, and not know what to do: I cannot help that. It must help itself; do as I do. It is not worth the while to snivel about it. I am not responsible for the successful working of the machinery of society. I am not the son of the engineer. I perceive that, when an acorn and a chestnut fall side by side, the one does not remain inert to make way for the other, but both obey their own laws, and spring and grow and flourish as best they can, till one, perchance, overshadows and destroys the other. If a plant cannot live according to nature, it dies; and so a man. . . .

I have never declined paying the highway tax, because I am as desirous of being a good neighbor as I am of being a bad subject; and as for supporting schools, I am doing my part to educate my fellow countrymen now. It is for no particular item in the tax bill that I refuse to pay it. I simply wish to refuse allegiance to the State, to withdraw and stand aloof from it effectually. I do not care to trace the course of my dollar, if I could, till it buys a man or a musket to shoot with—

the dollar is innocent—but I am concerned to trace the effects of my allegiance. In fact, I quietly declare war with the State, after my fashion, though I will still make what use and get what advantage of her I can, as is usual in such cases.

If others pay the tax which is demanded of me, from a sympathy with the State, they do but what they have already done in their own case, or rather they abet injustice to a greater extent than the State requires. If they pay the tax from a mistaken interest in the individual taxed, to save his property, or prevent his going to jail, it is because they have not considered wisely how far they let their private feelings interfere with the public good. . . .

20   I do not wish to quarrel with any man or nation. I do not wish to split hairs, to make fine distinctions, or set myself up as better than my neighbors. I seek rather, I may say, even an excuse for conforming to the laws of the land. I am but too ready to conform to them. Indeed, I have reason to suspect myself on this head; and each year, as the tax-gatherer comes round, I find myself disposed to review the acts and position of the general and State governments, and the spirit of the people to discover a pretext for conformity. . . .

I believe that the State will soon be able to take all my work of this sort out of my hands, and then I shall be no better a patriot than my fellow-countrymen. Seen from a lower point of view, the Constitution, with all its faults, is very good; the law and the courts are very respectable; even this State and this American government are, in many respects, very admirable, and rare things, to be thankful for, such as a great many have described them; but seen from a point of view a little higher, they are what I have described them; seen from a higher still, and the highest, who shall say what they are, or that they are worth looking at or thinking of at all?

However, the government does not concern me much, and I shall bestow the fewest possible thoughts on it. It is not many moments that I live under a government, even in this world. If a man is thought-free, fancy-free, imagination-free, that which is not never for a long time appearing to be to him, unwise rulers or reformers cannot fatally interrupt him.

I know that most men think differently from myself; but those whose lives are by profession devoted to the study of these or kindred subjects content me as little as any. Statesmen and legislators, standing so completely within the institution, never distinctly and nakedly behold it. They speak of moving society, but have no resting-place without it. They may be men of a certain experience and discrimination, and have no doubt invented ingenious and even useful systems, for which we sincerely thank them; but all their wit and usefulness lie within certain not very wide limits. They are wont to forget that the world is not governed by policy and expediency. . . .

The authority of government, even such as I am willing to submit to—for I will cheerfully obey those who know and can do better than I, and in many things even those who neither know nor can do so well—is still an impure one: to be strictly just, it must have the sanction and consent of the governed. It can have no pure right over my person and property but what I concede to it. The progress from an absolute to a limited monarchy, from a limited monarchy to a democracy, is a progress toward a true respect for the individual. Even the Chinese philosopher was wise enough to regard the individual as the basis of the empire. Is a democracy, such as we know it, the last improvement possible in government? Is it not possible to take a step further towards recognizing and organizing the rights of man? There will never be a really free and enlightened State until the State comes to recognize the individual as a higher and independent power, from which all its own power and authority are derived, and treats him accordingly. I please myself with imagining a State at last which can afford to be just to all men, and to treat the individual with respect as a neighbor; which even would not think it inconsistent with its own repose if a few were to live aloof from it, not meddling with it, nor embraced by it, who fulfilled all the duties of neighbors and fellow men. A State which bore this kind of fruit, and suffered it to drop off as fast as it ripened, would prepare the way for a still more perfect and glorious State, which I have also imagined, but not yet anywhere seen.

QUESTIONS FOR INQUIRY AND ACTION

1. How does "Civil Disobedience" work as both inquiry and action? Do you consider the essay a form of social action? Do you think it is effective action? Why or why not?

2. Paraphrase Thoreau's main argument. Can you imagine situations in which his main argument would be considered unethical? Is it applicable to all cultures and times?

3. What are the distinctions between "civil disobedience" and other forms of social protest?

4. Research the conversation that was started by Thoreau's essay. How many liberation movements and leaders have been influenced by Thoreau's words and his example? You might begin with the works of Gandhi and Martin Luther King, Jr., and Myles Horton's *The Long Haul*, all of whom acknowledged an intellectual debt to Thoreau.

PUBLIC ART

You Belong Here! The Covington Millennium Mosaic

The Covington Millennium Mosaic project of park benches, "You Belong Here!" (also featured on the cover of the book), is an example of *public art*. Public art signifies that the work of art is on display in a public area—often outside—as opposed to being exhibited in a museum or other private location. You are probably familiar with the monuments and other works of art that are common in cities and towns. Increasingly, though, as seen in Covington's "You Belong Here!" project, the "public" aspect of the public art means that the artist does not create the work privately, away from the community, and then bring the work in for display. Instead, the artist conceives the work from the beginning as part of that community; indeed, the work is designed to reflect that specific community and unite it in

continued on next page

some way. Occasionally, as is also the case with the Millennium Mosaic project, people from the community help to create the work of art. In that sense, then, "public art" is that created by and for the public who will look at and experience it daily.

Covington, Kentucky is an old river city located in the greater Cincinnati metropolitan region. Like many urban areas, Covington has experienced a prolonged decline in population, resources, and economic vitality over the past several decades. The 1990's, however, were a time of significant revitalization in the downtown riverfront area. New office towers, hotels, a regional convention center and other new businesses have made the city an entertainment and tourist attraction.

While this commercial development was focused on the riverfront, Covington's urban neighborhoods were largely excluded from the city's economic revival. In response, Covington Community Center, a local nonprofit community development organization, sponsored the Covington Millennium Mosaic—a collaborative public art project designed to literally and figuratively reconnect residents with the Covington riverfront; create an atmosphere of partnership; and increase residents' sense of pride in the city. This was accomplished by bringing together residents from all of Covington's neighborhoods to participate in the design process for a planned riverfront park and create a unified community vision through art.

Covington Community Center hosted artist-in-residence Olivia Gude, Assistant Professor in the School of Art and Design at the University of Illinois at Chicago and visual artist with the Chicago Public Art Group. Through leaps of inspiration and the patient step-by-step placement of over 100,000 tiles, Gude worked collaboratively with hundreds of community residents to design and execute 25 mosaic panels for a bench installation destined for a new downtown plaza.

Work on the project began with eight design sessions with neighborhood associations held throughout the city. Residents were asked to reflect on "where we have been, who we are and what we hope to become." Olivia Gude and a core design

group of Intergenerational Covington residents then incorporated the community's ideas into the project design, which included text and images. The title of the mosaic installation, "You Belong Here," is taken from the text of one of the mosaic panels. A play on the "You are here" that one finds on site maps, the phrase is a statement of what it takes to create community and the recognition of each person's or group's fundamental right to belong.

Over 125 middle school students and adults created homes and significant public buildings in ceramic bas relief. The glazed and painted ceramic buildings were arranged into landscapes which suggested particular features associated with the city created by glass tile mosaic. Volunteers worked six days a week, often ten or more hours a day, for three months in the detailed process of creating the mosaics. The resulting mosaic panels were mounted on five cast-concrete benches.

The Millennium Mosaic project was part of Artists & Communities: America Creates for the Millennium, a national initiative sponsored by the Mid-Atlantic Arts Foundation and National Endowment for the Arts that placed many of the nation's finest artists in residencies in all 56 states and jurisdictions during 2000. The initiative's purpose was to expand public awareness of the benefits of arts to a healthy society. Covington Community Center was selected as the host site for the state of Kentucky. The project won the Inclusion Network's Community Leadership Award 2000 for bringing together so many segments of the community.

Ellen Muse-Lindeman
Director of Program Development
Covington Community Center

How can you imagine public art adding an important dimension to our community life and citizenship, whether locally, nationally, or even internationally? What kinds of projects could you envision for your own communities?

URSULA LE GUIN The Ones Who Walk Away from Omelas

Ursula Le Guin is a prolific author of novels, essays, poems, and, children's books. She is best known as a science fiction writer, although her novels such as The Left Hand of Darkness, *(1969) and* The Dispossessed *(1974) have appealed to many different audiences, challenging their consciences. "The Ones Who Walk Away from Omelas" won the Hugo Award for best short story in 1974.*

With a clamor of bells that set the swallows soaring, the Festival of Summer came to the city. Omelas, bright-towered by the sea. The rigging of the boats in harbor sparkled with flags. In the streets between houses with red roofs and painted walls, between old moss-grown gardens and under avenues of trees, past great parks and public buildings, processions moved. Some were decorous: old people in long stiff robes of mauve and grey, grave master work men, quiet, merry women carrying their babies and chatting as they walked. In other streets the music beat faster, a shimmering of gong and tambourine, and the people went dancing, the procession was a dance. Children dodged in and out, their high calls rising like the swallows' crossing flights over the music and the singing. All the processions wound towards the north side of the city, where on the great water-meadow called the Green Fields boys and girls, naked in the bright air, with mud-stained feet and ankles and long, lithe arms, exercised their restive horses before the race. The horses wore no gear at all but a halter without bit. Their manes were braided with streamers of silver, gold, and green. They flared their nostrils and pranced and boasted to one another; they were vastly excited, the horse being the only animal who has adopted our ceremonies as his own. Far off to the north and west the mountains stood up half encircling Omelas on her bay. The air of morning was so clear that the snow still crowning the Eighteen Peaks burned with white-gold fire across the miles of sunlit air, under the dark blue of the sky. There was just enough wind to make the banners that marked the racecourse snap and flutter now and then. In the silence of the broad green meadows one could hear the music winding through the city streets, farther and nearer and ever approaching, a cheerful faint sweetness of the air that from time to time trembled and gathered together and broke out into the great joyous clanging of the bells.

Joyous! How is one to tell about joy? How describe the citizens of Omelas?

They were not simple folk, you see, though they were happy. But we do not say the words of cheer much any more. All smiles have become archaic. Given a description such as this one tends to make certain assumptions. Given a description such as this one tends to look next for the King, mounted on a splendid stallion and surrounded by his noble knights, or perhaps in a golden litter borne by great-muscled slaves. But there was no king. They did not use swords, or keep slaves. They were not barbarians. I do not know the rules and laws of their society, but I suspect that they were singularly few. As they did without monarchy and slavery, so they also got on without the stock exchange, the advertisement, the secret police, and the bomb. Yet I repeat that these were not simple folk, not dulcet shepherds, noble savages, bland utopians. They were not less complex than us. The trouble is that we have a bad habit, encouraged by pedants and sophisticates, of considering happiness as something rather stupid. Only pain is intellectual, only evil interesting. This is the treason of the artist: a refusal to admit the banality of evil and the terrible boredom of pain. If you can't lick 'em, join 'em. If it hurts, repeat it. But to praise despair is to condemn delight, to embrace violence is to lose hold of everything else. We have almost lost hold; we can no longer describe a happy man, nor make any celebration of joy. How can I tell you about the people of Omelas? They were not naïve and happy children—though their children were, in fact, happy. They were mature, intelligent, passionate adults whose lives were not wretched. O miracle! but I wish I could describe it better. I wish I could convince you. Omelas sounds in my words like a city in a fairy tale, long ago and far away, once upon a time. Perhaps it would be best if you imagined it as your own fancy bids, assuming it will rise to the occasion, for certainly I cannot suit you all. For instance, how about technology? I think that there would be no cars or helicopters in and above the streets; this follows from the fact that the people of Omelas are happy people. Happiness is based on a just discrimination of what is necessary, what is neither necessary nor destructive, and what is destructive. In the middle category, however—that of the unnecessary but undestructive, that of comfort, luxury, exuberance, etc.—they could perfectly well have central heating, subway trains, washing machines, and all kinds of marvelous devices not yet invented here, floating light-sources, fuel-less power, a cure for the common cold. Or they could have none of that: it doesn't matter. As you like it. I incline to think that people from towns up and down the coast have been coming in to Omelas during the last days before the Festival on very fast little trains and double-decked trams and that the train station of Omelas is actually the handsomest building in town, though plainer than the magnificent Farmers' Market. But even granted trains, I fear that Omelas so far strikes some of you as goody-goody. Smiles, bells, parades, horses, bleh. If so, please add an orgy. If an orgy would help, don't hesitate. Let us not, however, have temples from which issue beautiful nude priests and priestesses already half in ecstasy and ready to copulate with any man or woman, lover or stranger, who desires union with the deep godhead of the blood, although that was my first idea. But really it would be better not to have any temples in Omelas—at least, not manned temples. Religion yes, clergy no. Surely the beautiful nudes can just wander about, offering themselves like divine soufflés to the hunger of the needy and the rapture of the flesh. Let them join the processions. Let tambourines be struck above the copulations, and the glory of desire be proclaimed upon the gongs, and (a not unimportant point) let the offspring of these delightful rituals be beloved and looked after by all. One thing I know there is none of in Omelas is guilt. But what else should there be? I thought at first there were no drugs, but that is puritanical. For those who like it, the faint insistent sweetness of *drooz* may perfume the ways of the city, *drooz* which first brings a great lightness and brilliance to the mind and limbs, and then after some hours a dreamy languor, and wonderful visions at last of the very arcana and inmost secrets of the Universe, as well as exciting the pleasure of sex beyond all belief; and it is not habit-forming. For more modest tastes I think there ought to be beer. What else, what else belongs in the joyous city? The sense of victory, surely, the celebration of courage. But as we did without clergy, let us do without soldiers. The joy built upon successful slaughter is not the right kind of joy; it will not do; it is fearful and it is trivial. A boundless and generous contentment, a magnanimous triumph felt not against some outer enemy but in communion with the finest and fairest in the souls of all men everywhere and the splendor of the world's summer: this is what swells the hearts of the people of Omelas, and the victory they celebrate is that of life. I really don't think many of them need to take *drooz*.

Most of the processions have reached the Green Fields by now. A marvelous smell of cooking goes forth from the red and blue tents of the provisioners. The faces of small children are amiably sticky; in the benign grey beard of a man a couple of crumbs of rich pastry are entangled. The youths and girls have mounted their horses and are beginning to group around the starting line of the course. An old woman, small, fat, and laughing, is passing out flowers from a basket, and tall young men wear her flowers in their shining hair. A child of nine or ten sits at the edge of the crowd, alone, playing on a wooden flute. People pause to listen, and they smile, but they do not speak to him, for he never ceases playing and never sees them, his dark eyes wholly rapt in the sweet, thin magic of the tune.

5 He finishes, and slowly lowers his hands holding the wooden flute.

As if that little private silence were the signal, all at once a trumpet sounds from the pavillion near the starting line: imperious, melancholy, piercing. The horses rear on their slender legs, and some of them neigh in answer. Sober-faced, the young riders stroke the horses' necks and soothe them, whispering, "Quiet, quiet, there my beauty, my hope. . . ." They begin to form in rank along the starting line. The crowds along the racecourse are like a field of grass and flowers in the wind. The Festival of Summer has begun.

Do you believe? Do you accept the festival, the city, the joy? No? Then let me describe one more thing.

In a basement under one of the beautiful public buildings of Omelas, or perhaps in the cellar of one of its spacious private homes, there is a room. It has one locked door, and no window. A little light seeps in dustily between cracks in the boards, secondhand from a cobwebbed window somewhere across the cellar. In one corner of the little room a couple of mops, with stiff, clotted, foul-smelling heads, stand near a rusty bucket. The floor is dirt, a little damp to the touch, as cellar dirt usually is. The room is about three paces long and two wide: a mere broom closet or disused tool room. In the room a child is sitting. It could be a boy or a girl. It looks about six, but actually is nearly ten. It is feeble-minded. Perhaps it was born defective, or perhaps it has become imbecile through fear, malnutrition, and neglect. It picks its nose and occasionally fumbles vaguely with its toes or genitals, as it sits hunched in the corner farthest from the bucket and the two mops. It is afraid of the mops. It finds them horrible. It shuts its eyes, but it knows the mops are still standing there; and the door is locked; and nobody will come. The door is always locked; and nobody ever comes, except that sometimes—the child has no understanding of time or interval—sometimes the door rattles terribly and opens, and a person, or several people, are there. One of them may come in and kick the child to make it stand up. The others never come close, but peer in at it with frightened, disgusted eyes. The food bowl and the water jug are hastily filled, the door is locked, the eyes disappear. The people at the door never say anything, but the child, who has not always lived in the tool room, and can remember sunlight and its mother's voice, sometimes speaks. "I will be good," it says. "Please let me out. I will be good!" They never answer. The child used to scream for help at night, and cry a good deal, but now it only makes a kind of whining, "eh-haa, eh-haa," and it speaks less and less often. It is so thin there are no calves to its legs; its belly protrudes; it lives on a half-bowl of corn meal and grease a day. It is naked. Its buttocks and thighs are a mass of festered sores, as it sits in its own excrement continually.

They all know it is there, all the people of Omelas. Some of them have come to see it, others are content merely to know it is there. They all know that it has to be there. Some of them understand why, and some do not, but they all under-stand that their happiness, the beauty of their city, the tenderness of their friend-ships, the health of their children, the wisdom of their scholars, the skill of their makers, even the abundance of their harvest and the kindly weathers of their skies, depend wholly on this child's abominable misery.

10   This is usually explained to children when they are between eight and twelve, whenever they seem capable of understanding; and most of those who come to see the child are young people, though often enough an adult comes, or comes back, to see the child. No matter how well the matter has been explained to them, these young spectators are always shocked and sickened at the sight. They feel dis-gust, which they had thought themselves superior to. They feel anger, outrage, impotence, despite all the explanations. They would like to do something for the child. But there is nothing they can do. If the child were brought up into the sunlight out of that vile place, if it were cleaned and fed and comforted, that would be a good thing, indeed; but if it were done, in that day and hour all the prosperity and beauty and delight of Omelas would wither and be destroyed. Those are the terms. To exchange all the goodness and grace of every life in Omelas for that single, small improvement: to throw away the happiness of thou-sands for the chance of the happiness of one: that would be to let guilt within the walls indeed.

The terms are strict and absolute; there may not even be a kind word spo-ken to the child.

Often the young people go home in tears, or in a tearless rage, when they have seen the child and faced this terrible paradox. They may brood over it for weeks or years. But as time goes on they begin to realize that even if the child could be released, it would not get much good of its freedom: a little vague pleasure of warmth and food, no doubt, but little more. It is too degraded and imbecile to know any real joy. It has been afraid too long ever to be free of fear. Its habits are too uncouth for it to respond to humane treatment. Indeed, after so long it would probably be wretched without walls about it to protect it, and darkness

for its eyes, and its own excrement to sit in. Their tears at the bitter injustice
dry when they begin to perceive the terrible justice of reality and to accept it.
Yet it is their tears and anger, the trying of their generosity and the acceptance
of their helplessness, which are perhaps the true source of the splendor of their
lives. Theirs is no vapid, irresponsible happiness. They know that they, like the
child, are not free. They know compassion. It is the existence of the child, and
their knowledge of its existence, that makes possible the nobility of their architecture, the poignancy of their music, the profundity of their science. It is because
of the child that they are so gentle with children. They know that if the wretched
one were not there snivelling in the dark, the other one, the flute-player, could
make no joyful music as the young riders line up in their beauty for the race in
the sunlight of the first morning of summer.

Now do you believe in them? Are they not more credible? But there is one more
thing to tell, and this is quite incredible.

At times one of the adolescent girls or boys who go to see the child does not
go home to weep or rage, does not, in fact, go home at all. Sometimes also a
man or woman much older falls silent for a day or two, and then leaves home.
These people go out into the street, and walk down the street alone. They keep
walking, and walk straight out of the city of Omelas, through the beautiful gates.
They keep walking across the farmlands of Omelas. Each one goes alone, youth
or girl, man or woman. Night falls; the traveler must pass down village streets,
between the houses with yellow-lit windows, and on out into the darkness of
the fields. Each alone, they go west or north, towards the mountains. They go on.
They leave Omelas, they walk ahead into the darkness, and they do not come
back. The place they go towards is a place even less imaginable to most of us
than the city of happiness. I cannot describe it at all. It is possible that it does
not exist. But they seem to know where they are going, the ones who walk away
from Omelas.

QUESTIONS FOR INQUIRY AND ACTION

1. What effect does the opening description of the community have on you as a
   reader? What is the effect of the narrator's voice breaking in after the first paragraph? What does the narrator seem to need to explain to us?

2. Look up the origins of the word "scapegoat" in the *Oxford English Dictionary*
   and/or an encyclopedia. How does this definition affect the way you read Le
   Guin's story?

3. Le Guin commented that this story is about "the dilemma of the American conscience." What do you think she means by that? Where do you see descriptions
   or points of commentary that seem especially indicative of American culture?

4. How does the story challenge us to think about the foundations of our communities? For example, read Le Guin's story with the WTO case study in Chapter
   Nine. Does the happiness and success of American society rest on the suffering
   of others?

CASE
STUDY

THE COLUMBINE SHOOTINGS MAKE US
QUESTION COMMUNITY

MARK OBMASCIK Massacre at Columbine High

Mark Obmascik is a staff writer at the Denver Post. *He was the lead writer for "Massacre at Columbine High," which won a Pulitzer Prize for Reporting in 1999. On April 20, 2000, a year after the killings, on the* Jim Lehrer News Hour, *Obmascik commented, "The thing that made Columbine touch so many people was that it played to so many universal fears. Everyone's been to high school, everybody's been afraid at some point in high school, everyone's been worried that they didn't quite fit in, so where do we go from now, from there?"*

Bloodbath leaves 15 dead, 28 hurt

April 21, 9:15 A.M. MST—Two students, cloaked in black trench coats and armed with guns and bombs, opened fire Tuesday at Columbine High School, killing 15 people and wounding 28 others in the worst school shooting in U.S. history.

Police found the two suspects shot to death in the library. All the dead remained in the school overnight as police neutralized 30 bombs and booby traps that had been left behind by the suspects. The final toll of dead and wounded wasn't announced until this morning.

The masked shooters first targeted specific victims, especially ethnic minorities and athletes, then randomly sprayed school hallways about 11:30 A.M. with bullets and shotgun blasts, witnesses said. The bloody rampage spanned four hours.

"I saw them shoot a girl because she was praying to God," said Evan Todd, 15, a sophomore. "They shot a black kid. They called him a nigger. They said they didn't like niggers, so they shot him in the face."

5   School hallways were booby-trapped with at least 12 bombs, some on timers, which still were exploding at 10:45 P.M. One suspect's coat was laced with explosive devices, and undetonated pipe bombs were planted around bodies, police said.

Students described the shooters as part of an outcast group of a dozen or so suburban high school boys known as the Trench Coat Mafia who often wore dark trench coats and had German slogans and swastikas on their clothes. The suspects were identified as Eric Harris, 18, and Dylan Klebold, 17.

The murders came on the 110th anniversary of Adolf Hitler's birth. "I've heard numbers as high as 259 deaths," said Jefferson County Sheriff John Stone, adding that 17 were confirmed. "When we did make entry into the library, it was a pretty gruesome scene." He called the murders a "suicide mission."

Byron Kirkland saw the massacre begin: "There was a girl crouched beneath a desk in the library, and the guy came over and said, 'Peekaboo,' and shot her in the neck," said Kirkland, a 15-year-old sophomore. "They were hooting and hollering and getting big joy out of this."

Aaron Cohn, 15, a sophomore, said he was ducking beneath a table when he suddenly felt a gun barrel pressed to his head. A gunman said: "All the jocks stand up. We are going to kill you," Cohn said.

10   Bree Pasquale, a junior, said: "You could hear them laughing as they ran down the hallways shooting people. He put a gun in my face and said, 'I'm doing this because people made fun of me last year.'" She escaped unshot but splattered with a fellow student's blood.

Meanwhile, Brittany Bollerud, 16, hid under a library table and saw only the gunmen's shoes and long trench coats. "They yelled, 'This is revenge,'" she said. "They asked people if they were jocks. If they were wearing a sports hat, they would shoot them."

"I saw (a teacher) on the floor bleeding from everywhere. He was trying to direct kids, but he couldn't talk," said Rachel Erbert, a 17-year-old senior. "It was really scary. Kids were falling, and you'd help them up. I thought I might get shot."

By 3:45 P.M., shots still rang out inside the school. While more than 200 law enforcement officers and four SWAT teams tried to stop the gunmen and evacuate wounded high school students, paramedics frantically treated victims in makeshift triage units on the front lawns of houses outside the suburban Jefferson County school.

At one point, a bloody boy dangled down from a second-floor window and was caught by two SWAT team members. Another person held up a sign in a classroom window: "Help, I'm bleeding to death."

15   "There are some who were killed as they were hiding under desks," said an officer who was inside the school. "Some looked like they were trying to crawl away. They were executed—shot in the head."

With news of the murders being broadcast locally and nationally on live television, Columbine High School looked like a war zone. Medical helicopters landed on nearby athletic fields, then whisked the wounded to six local hospitals. More than 2,000 people across metro Denver waited in line to donate blood. Panicked parents rushed to the school for news about their children. Some talked to their trapped children on cell phones.

At 6:25 P.M., Jefferson County District Attorney Dave Thomas told parents gathered inside Leawood Elementary School that at least 10 bodies could not be removed immediately from the high school because there were bombs near the bodies.

Parents were told to bring their children's dental records. Some parents vomited.

Search warrants were executed Tuesday night at the suspects' homes, the district attorney said. The sheriff said the gunmen used at least one automatic assault rifle and several shotguns in the attack.

20   At 8 P.M., Michael Shoels was still awaiting word on his son, Isaiah, an 18-year-old senior. Shoels feared his son was targeted because he was black.

"This late, it's not looking good at all," Shoels said. "It's like a dream I'm trying to wake up from. . . . I just wish everybody would pray for my family." Shoels' two other children also attend Columbine, and they were safe.

The shootings were the latest in a series of school shootings since 1997 that have shocked the nation and led to calls for tighter security and closer monitoring of troubled students. Two people were killed at a school in Pearl, Miss., three at West Paducah, Ky., five at Jonesboro, Ark., and two at a school in Springfield, Ore.

President Clinton opened a news conference Tuesday by calling for prayers for the students, teachers and staff at Columbine. The murders came as Gov. Bill Owens and the Colorado Legislature have tried to pass a bill to liberalize the state's concealed-weapons laws.

Jenni LaPlante, 18, said one of the suspected shooters was calm Tuesday morning at a before school bowling class. She said the student was extremely smart.

25   "He knew all the answers. If we were reading Shakespeare, he would know the hidden meaning," LaPlante said.

"I've never seen them lash out at anyone," LaPlante said. "But I would say, 'Why do you guys wear all that German stuff? Are you Nazis?' And they would say, 'Yeah, Heil Hitler.'" LaPlante said she never knew whether the suspects were joking.

One shooter was in Michele Fox's creative-writing class.

"They hate our school. They hate everything about it," said Fox, 18, a senior. "In our class, we have to read out loud and stuff, and they would always write about death. They wore black trench coats with combat boots and their pants tucked into them."

Ben Grams, a junior, called the Trench Coat Mafia group "a bunch of unwanted kids who were teased and pushed around a lot."

30   Another student said the group talked often in class about beheading people, and many often sang and quoted songs by shock-rocker Marilyn Manson. Some also wore bands that read, "I hate people."

Students said the bloodshed began when two students—dressed in black trench coats and masks that were taken on and off—hurled at least one bomb onto the school roof during the A-track lunch hour. Another bomb was stashed in a backpack and left by the front door.

John Cook, 16, a sophomore, was eating lunch outside with friends when the violence started.

"These guys opened fire on every thing that looked human," Cook said. "They were shooting at some kids down below, then they pointed at us and started shooting. Bullets were bouncing everywhere. Two guys next to me got hit."

As the gunmen hustled into the school and through the hallways, panic spread. Casey Fisher, 15, was buying his lunch in the cafeteria with a friend. "My friend came out and he was standing 10 feet from the guy, and they shot him and he fell to the ground," Fisher said.

35   Karen Nielson, a cafeteria worker, said, "I tried to help the others, but he just kept firing." Some witnesses reported hearing as many as 15 bomb blasts. At

one point, a bomb exploded and hurt several students, including one girl later hospitalized with eight shards in her chest. "I was running for my life," said Crystal Enney, 18, a senior.

Smoke spread, and the fire alarm blared. In the chaos, some students sprinted to safety. Others were gunned down in the hall. A few tried locking themselves in bathrooms.

In Katie Crona's freshman earth sciences class, students dived under their desks. In the next classroom, students could hear windows being blasted out by gunmen. A few students escaped and told how others had been shot. "We sat there in a circle for four hours. We were huddled together. It was terrifying," Crona said. The students heard someone tugging at their classroom doorknob, but it was locked. The gunmen continued on.

The worst carnage was in the library, where the gunmen terrorized 45 fellow students with bullets—and maniacal laughs.

"They were going around asking people why they should let them live," said Todd, the 15-year-old sophomore. "Once when they shot a black kid, one of them said, 'Oh my God, look at this black kid's brain! Awesome, man!'"

40   "They came up to me, pointed a gun at my head and asked if I was a jock. I said no. Basically I lied. They said, 'It's revenge time on jocks for making us outcasts.'"

Jonathan Vandermark, 16, a sophomore, said he passed three bodies in a stairwell as he and other students were rescued from the biology lab by a SWAT team. Shards of glass were everywhere, he said.

Vandermark was about 20 feet away from one of the shooters when gunfire broke out. He described the weapons as being like Uzis. Other witnesses recalled a sawed-off shotgun and at least one handgun. "A teacher who tried to help us was shot in the arm," said Vandermark, who hid in the biology lab.

Meanwhile, Scott Cornwell, father of senior Matt Cornwell, received a cell-phone call from his trapped son, who was barricaded in the choir room with 40 other students.

"He was whispering. He said, 'Dad, we're inside. There are 40 of us. What's going on?'"

45   The father took his cell phone to a police commander, who told them, "Get away from the door!"

Police said they found the two suspects shot to death in the library. Several bombs were found in one suspect's house, and police later uncovered two cars parked outside the school that had been booby-trapped with bombs.

Today the Colorado Legislature had been scheduled to debate a bill to liberalize the state's concealed weapons laws, but all legislative work was canceled because of the shootings.

Gov. Owens, who supports liberalized concealed-weapons laws, comforted families at the crime scene with his wife, Frances, but refused to comment on the gun legislation.

"We're not immune from the problems you see in other parts of the country," Owens said. "Perhaps our innocence is lost today."

50   Some Columbine students said some warnings about trouble from the Trench Coat Mafia were scrawled as graffiti on bathroom walls. "You'd go in there and

it would have 'Columbine will explode some day,' or 'All jocks must die,' or 'Kill all athletes,'-" said Doug Mohr, a senior football player. "There'd be pictures of guns and swastikas."

Jefferson County School District administrators said they didn't know about any racist or threatening graffiti. "I visited the students there and it appeared to be a creating environment, where students feel safe," said schools superintendent Jane Hammond. "We were not aware of the Trench Coat Mafia until today." A photo in last year's yearbook listed one group as the "Trenchcoat Mafia." School principal Frank DeAngelis could not be reached for comment.

Some students said the tragedy could have been worse had it not been a "senior skip day."

The day is known in circles as "4-20"—when students around the country skipped school to smoke marijuana. Aside from it having been April 20, the police code for a drug bust in Los Angeles is also 4-20.

"This is the big day for (smoking marijuana)," said Columbine student Jason Greer, 16.

55   Many students were aware of the day's significance, and many chose not to attend school Tuesday.

"I can't believe something like this would happen at Columbine," said Joyce Oglesbee, mother of senior Tara Oglesbee. "It's a topclass school, preppy and perfect. We haven't even had a senior prank."

Newspaper Editorials on Columbine

Here are two newspaper editorials that appeared soon after the event.

San Francisco Chronicle, *April 22, 1999*

Reflecting on the possible causes of the Littleton, Colo., high school massacre is an all-too-familiar and frustrating exercise.

There are only the barest outlines of a trend in what happened at Columbine High School this week and its tragic antecedents in Arkansas, Mississippi and Oregon. If the young assailants had anything in common, it was ready access to weapons and a deep detachment from mainstream life, with a sick bent to get even with others who were fitting in.

Many Americans bristle at the suggestion that the latest campus killings speak to the nature of their society. It's the work of freaks and malcontents, an aberration that will never be duplicated, we all want to believe.

Yet American society *is* unacceptably violent, with murder and imprisonment rates among the highest in the world. School shootings don't occur elsewhere on the planet with the same frequency or ferocity. The U.S. stands alone, sad to say.

A tragedy such as Littleton argues for a plan of action, a solution, a way out. But what can be done? These horrible crimes draw anti-violence crusaders into their predictable camps. There are those who blame these outbreaks of madness on the easy access to guns, a culture that celebrates violence in song, in movies and in video games and the lack of counseling and other programs to identify and help young people who are teetering toward an anti-social path.

There is a case to be made for all such remedies—to pressure Hollywood and other "entertainment" producers to reduce the glorification of gore and to better fund the programs that have proved to steer young people in the right directions.

And, yes, the effort to slow the proliferation of guns must continue. Right now, state Senator Don Perata, D-Alameda, is promoting a bill (SB 23) to curb assault weapons and Assemblyman Wally Knox, D-L.A., is pushing legislation (AB 202) designed to stop a black-market pipeline that is arming many young buyers, including gang members.

The National Rifle Association, obstructionist to any attempt to curtail gun ownership, is resisting both California bills—and, in fact, is supporting a Colorado measure to make it easier to get permits to carry concealed weapons.

Too many guns, too little caring, too much callousness in our culture. It all adds to the vitriol building in too many youths who see violence as the answer.

The task of preventing these random horrible assaults on humanity may seem almost too daunting and too rare, unpredictable and complex to begin to undertake. But it is too important to ignore.

Legislation can only go so far.

All of us need to look at our communities, our neighborhoods—indeed, our own homes—to determine what we can do to address the isolation of youth that is the one common denominator of these schoolyard slaughters and myriad lesser crimes.

The Orlando Sentinel, *April 21, 1999*

The massacre at Columbine High School in Littleton, Colo., Tuesday should prompt all parents to hug their children before school this morning.

Tuesday's tragedy showed how quickly unspeakable violence can end young lives.

The heartache parents in Colorado now endure should remind parents everywhere of how precious a child's life can be.

Most parents are braced for the possibility that their children may have problems with bad grades, broken hearts and bullies at school. But homicidal gunmen?

No parent would even want to imagine such a thing.

The violence at the Colorado school was not the work of foreign terrorists. Students said the gunmen were members of a clique of misfits.

The local sheriff said it appears that the gunmen were on a "suicide mission." The bodies of members of the clique were found with self-inflicted gunshot wounds.

What's most important at this point is not to jump to conclusions or to overreact.

Turning schools into fortresses or maximum-security prisons would make them poor environments for learning. And that treatment would not guarantee that the school would be immune to the type of violence that struck in Colorado.

It also would be foolish for any school district to shrug off what happened in Colorado as though "it can't happen here."

It can.

Littleton, Colo., has little in common with the South Bronx, South-Central Los Angeles or the Overtown section of Miami, and yet it, too, has been scarred by violence.

Parents, schools and communities must work together to head off a repeat of such tragedy.

Of course, school officials will review security plans, but what's more important is for parents and educators to reach out to any students they suspect may be troubled or in any way tending toward violence.

Talking to those students now makes more sense than talking about tragedy later.

LEE JUDGE How Could This Happen?

> *Lee Judge is the editorial cartoonist for the* Kansas City Star. *His cartoon "How Could This Happen?" appeared in the* Kansas City Star *on April 22, 1999.*

JEFF STARK We Called it "Littlefun"

*Jeff Stark is an alumnus of Columbine High School. He is a writer and asso-
ciate editor of Arts and Entertainment for the online magazine Salon.com,
where "We Called it 'Littlefun'" appeared on April 21, 1999.*

Nothing ever happened at my high school. There were parties and proms,
fistfights and car accidents, but there was nothing that made it special, nothing
that made it remarkably different than any other suburban high school in southwest Denver—or really any suburban high school anywhere. There were some
state champion soccer teams, and half the kids went onto college in 1990, the year
I graduated, but not one student ever left and changed the world or won an
election or even starred in a Hollywood movie.

Then on Tuesday, with 16 dead bodies scattered around the cafeteria and the
library, my school, Columbine High, became famous. Something finally happened. Two kids in black trench coats—armed with semi-automatic weapons and
explosive devices that may have included hand grenades and pipe bombs—swept
through the hallways for an hour or so and casually, mercilessly, opened fire on
their fellow students. Columbine High School, home of the Rebels, became the
home of the largest high school killing spree in American history.

I heard about the massacre minutes after it happened and, like the rest of the
country, watched the news reports as the numbers jumped from five injured to
11, and then to 16 teachers and students dead, 20 others injured and both of
the murderers killed by their own guns. I thought the reports were wrong. And
they still might be—about either the body count, or the murky facts and so-called
motivations connected to the spree and its instigators.

When I see the school on the television I hardly recognize it. Yes, there have
been some major physical changes ever since the resoundingly Republican local
voters finally reversed a four- or five-year trend and passed a school improvement
bond in the early '90s. But other facts didn't add up. Associated Press and CNN,
even Salon News called Columbine and Littleton, Colo., "affluent"—which makes
them sound like something they're really not. One of the gunmen drove a BMW,
but I'd gamble it was parked next to three beat-up Datsuns and a rusting VW Bug.
Columbine wasn't "Dangerous Minds," but it wasn't "Beverly Hills 90210" either.

5   When I go back to visit my parents and my grandmother—never my friends;
they've all left—I barely recognize Littleton. The stores are all shiny and different,
like they were dropped out of some sort of alien chain-store mothership. There's
always an entirely new city of tract homes in some field where I used to ride my
dirt bike.

Although there is a tiny Main Street miles away, the part of Littleton where
Columbine sits, still bloody and wet with tears, isn't really a town. It's more like a
huge amalgamation of unincorporated subdivisions with 10-plus large high schools.
(The strategy keeps the property taxes low and the schools wanting for money.) It's
the kind of place that parents think is the perfect location to raise a family.

At the same time, Littleton, and most suburbs for that matter—as everyone from David Lynch to Edward Scissorhands to John Cheever has pointed out—are inherently alienating. The center cannot hold. There isn't one.

For me, the strangest thing about the entire experience has been watching the news media struggle to nail down the facts. I sat and wondered what was real. Right now, there are far more questions than answers. Were the two boys part of an organized gang, dubbed "the Trench Coat Mafia," or just a small clique of outsiders gathered together under a stupid name? Were they white supremacists who targeted jocks and minorities in their lunch-hour rampage, or are they as misunderstood in death as they were in life? This isn't sympathy for a couple of brutal killers, but when one reporter said that the Trench Coats had targeted minorities, I wondered how hard the gunmen must have had to look: There were two blacks and a handful of Asians and Hispanics in my 400-person graduating class.

One student told "Nightline" that the killers burst into the library looking for "that nigger," and when they found the lone African-American there, they shot him. Ted Koppel asked his panel of three Columbine students whether the fact that the killings happened on April 20, Hitler's birthday, mattered, and they shook their heads, bleary-eyed. The students took more seriously the fact that the date—4/20—was a supposed code word for marijuana. The suspects were also, we've learned, computer savvy, and at least one reportedly had his own Web site.

10   All of which means what? If racism turns out to be part of the motive, that may be reassuring. Because racism is something we can identify, and combat. The problem is that everyone is looking for a magic answer, pasting together vague clues and innuendo to create some sort of context to frame what looks like, as all the worst crimes do, an awful, unspeakable act of fairly random violence, this time executed by two very, very fucked-up kids.

I tried to resist a lot of the sinister hype. Most press accounts say the two gunmen were "outsiders." So were all of my close friends at Columbine. They listened to German industrial music. So did I. Maybe the gunmen wrote bad poetry, too, did drugs on the weekends and spent as much time as they could in downtown Denver, which is culturally light years away from Littleton. My friends and I did all those things; we called the suburb "Littlefun," and still do.

The obvious difference is that we never armed ourselves to the teeth and slaughtered the people we privately resented and abhorred.

I'll probably never understand what happened at Columbine High, and neither will you. We will all, however, hear no end to the guesswork, the misunderstanding and the political posturing that Tuesday had President Clinton saying that the nation needs to "do more to reach out to our children" and "recognize early warning signs."

The early warning signs of what? Deranged mass killers? High school students with automatic weapons? Alienated kids? Jock-hating, computer-savvy racists? We will never understand what happened here; we will just stop wondering, when we're distracted by the next unfathomable outbreak of chaos.

DAVID NORTH The Columbine High School Massacre: American Pastoral. . . American Berserk

David North is the chairman of the World Socialist Web Site editorial board and national secretary of the Socialist Equality Party (USA). He is the author of many writings on the Russian revolution and the history of Stalinism. This essay appeared on the World Socialist Web site <http://www.wsws.org> on April 27, 1999.

Columbine High School appeared to be, at least in the view of its administrators and the county school board, such a lovely place for young people to grow up and learn. In its official profile, the institution boasted of its "excellent facilities" and "long history of excellence in all areas." Nothing seemed to be lacking—Honors and Advanced Placement classes, foreign language instruction in Spanish, French and German, and an artistic program that included ceramics, sculpture, acting, choir and no less than five bands and one ensemble. There were even "Cross-categorical programs for students with significantly limited intellectual capacity." And, of course, there was no shortage of athletics.

"Stretch for Excellence" was the motto adopted by the school. And its mission statement—over which, one must assume, various well-meaning people labored—promised that Columbine High School "will teach, learn, and model life skills and attitudes that prepare us to: work effectively with people; show courtesy to others; prepare for change; think critically; act responsibly; and respect our surroundings."

Columbine, with its six guidance counselors, accountability committee, dozens of peer mediators and techniques for "conflict resolution," and an ethos of "collaborative partnership" with parents, viewed itself as a "twenty-first century high school." The surrounding neighborhoods were prosperous, with housing from the low to high six-figures, numerous shopping malls and high-tech workplaces. But on April 20, 1999, Eric Harris and Dylan Klebold walked into Columbine High School armed with assault rifles and pipe bombs. By the time their bloody rampage was over, they had killed twelve students, one teacher, and themselves.

There have been, during the past two years, other school shootings that have resulted in the death of students. But as terrible as the earlier incidents at Pearl, West Paducah, Jonesboro and Springfield, the carnage at Columbine was of a qualitatively different scope and scale.

5   Harris and Klebold manufactured dozens of pipe bombs, stashed explosives in the school kitchen, studied the layout and traffic pattern to insure the largest number of victims, and chose Hitler's birthday as the date for the attack, in the course of nearly a year of preparation. Their intention was to kill as many students as possible and blow up the entire school with a propane bomb. Had they had the opportunity, Harris and Klebold would have continued their rampage beyond the school. According to the diary that one of the youth left behind, they hoped to

hijack an airplane and crash it into the center of New York City. Only an unexpected encounter with a school guard and the failure of the bomb to explode thwarted their plan. Harris and Klebold then fled to the school library where they proceeded to select their victims before killing themselves.

What Harris and Klebold did on Tuesday was horrible, brutal and criminal. But these words are only descriptions of their acts, not explanations.

As usual, the media has nothing to offer by way of analysis. It is extraordinarily adept at milking the grief of the parents and community for every possible rating dollar. But those who wish to understand the underlying causes of this tragedy will find nothing of value on the network news.

After a few perfunctory tears for the victims, the media is looking for someone to blame. The parents, judging from the remarks of state officials, are being singled out as the most likely target for public vengeance. Perhaps they do bear some level of responsibility, but singling out for exemplary punishment these grief-stricken mothers and fathers—whose own lives have been utterly shattered by what their sons did last week—seems not only cruel, but deceitful and hypocritical.

After all, the parents of Klebold and Harris were not the only ones who failed to recognize and act on signs of the coming disaster. Columbine High School administrators apparently ignored repeated warnings they received about the boys' potential for violence.

10   This is not an individual failing, but one common to all the major institutions of American society: governments, political parties, corporations, the media, schools, churches, and trade unions. All are essentially oblivious to the mounting social tensions, until they erupt into homicidal violence at a post office, a high school, a McDonald's restaurant, a commuter railroad train, or inside the US Capitol.

Then these outbreaks are invariably treated, not as a social phenomenon, but as a police problem, to be handled by installing metal detectors, more police, more surveillance cameras, and enlisting the population as collaborators to inform on those with a supposed propensity to violence.

There's endless talk about "parents taking responsibility for their children," and of "children taking responsibility for themselves." But there is nothing said about the responsibility which American society has for a tragedy like that which occurred at Columbine.

It is almost grotesque to treat the Columbine HS massacre as merely the product of the breakdown of parental authority and supervision. Neither parents nor high school guidance counselors are equipped to deal with the societal dysfunction that found such devastating expression in the rampage of Klebold and Harris.

Consider, for a moment, the social outlook of these two youth. They were admirers of Adolf Hitler, fascinated by fascism's racism, its cult of sadistic violence and death, and its general contempt for humanity. And yet, there was nothing particularly Germanic about the views of Harris and Klebold. In a statement that he posted on his web site, Harris wrote: "I am the law, if you don't like it you die. If I don't like you or I don't like what you want me to do, you die."

15   These sentiments, expressed with a little more polish, sum up the approach of the American government to the rest of the world. "Do what we want or we'll destroy you." As we reread the lines of Harris, in the aftermath of the Columbine massacre, we recognize the brutality of a potential killer. But what, then, are we to see in the words written last Friday by the highly paid and celebrated columnist of the *New York Times,* Thomas Friedman?:

> "While there are many obvious downsides to war-from-15,000 feet, it does have one great strength—its sustainability. NATO can carry on this sort of air war for a long, long time. The Serbs need to remember that. . . .

> "But if NATO's only strength is that it can bomb forever, then it has to get every ounce out of that. Let's at least have a real air war. . . . It should be lights out in Belgrade: every power grid, water pipe, road and war-related factory has to be targeted.

> "Like it or not, we are at war with the Serbian nation (they certainly think so), and the stakes have to be very clear: Every week you ravage Kosovo is another decade we will set your country back by pulverizing you. You want 1950? We can do 1950. You want 1389? We can do 1389 too."

Harris and Klebold did not have to study *Mein Kampf* to find special "inspiration" for their actions. The editorials and columns that appear in American newspapers, not to mention the vicious outpourings on talk radio, would do just as well. And here we come to the crucial paradox that finds expression in their assault on Columbine High. It is likely that Harris and Klebold viewed themselves as rebels against society. In this they were quite mistaken. Certainly, the venue of their action was unconventional. But the deed itself represented an extreme application of the selfish and inhumane attitudes that are commonplace in American society today.

First, their violent outburst was not conceived of as a response to social injustice. Rather, Harris and Klebold took revenge against what they perceived as personal slights. They did not act on behalf of others, but for themselves. Further, they attacked not a symbol of oppression, but defenseless children and a well-meaning teacher. And finally, even if one were to accept that these two boys had been harassed at school, the scale of their violence was out of all proportion to the injury they had suffered. Their aim was not to right a wrong, but to create as much pain and suffering as possible.

What Harris and Klebold did was monstrous. But does it help to portray them as monsters? They were, let us not forget, only teenagers. Youth is supposedly a time of hope and idealism. How, then, was it possible that so much hate could be accumulated by these youth in so short a time? And not only hate, but utter despair as well. In their own minds, they had many reasons to kill, but none to live.

They plotted this deed, but were they its only authors? They are, in the final analysis, the products of a particular time and place. However terrible its consequences, the mad rampage of Harris and Klebold has deep social roots. Of course, the political leaders and the media elite do not care to delve too deeply into the social pathology of this dreadful crime. It would require that they hold a mirror up to themselves.

20   Since the Littleton killings, the media is full of commentary from psychologists, ministers, priests, police and experts of all sorts, gravely enumerating the "warning signs" which may alert parents to the possibility that their teenage son or daughter may be a potential mass murderer: Is your child depressed, discouraged, anxious, over-stressed, uncommunicative, disinterested, addicted to computer games, subject to mood swings, getting consistently bad grades, worrying too much about maintaining consistently high grades, etc.? At least 75 percent of all American children express one if not more of these characteristics.

In reality, the concentration on individual warning signs will be of little help in preventing further tragedies. Attention should be focused, rather, on the social warning signs, that is, the indications and indices of social and political dysfunction which create the climate that produces events like the Columbine HS massacre. Vital indicators of impending disaster might include: growing polarization between wealth and poverty; atomization of working people and the suppression of their class identity; the glorification of militarism and war; the absence of serious social commentary and political debate; the debased state of popular culture; the worship of the stock exchange; the unrestrained celebration of individual success and personal wealth; the denigration of the ideals of social progress and equality.

What is happening to America's kids? This is a question posed by Philip Roth in his provocative novel *American Pastoral,* which tells the story of a family ruined by a teenage daughter's dreadful and unexpected act of violence. "Something is driving them crazy. Something has set them against everything. Something is leading them into disaster."

What is that something? Look honestly at this society—its political leaders, its religious spokesmen, its corporate CEOs, its military machine, its celebrities, its "popular" culture, and, above all, the entire economic system upon which the whole vast superstructure of violence, suffering and hypocrisy is based. It is there that the answer is to be found.

STOP AND THINK

ONLINE PACT TO STOP VIOLENCE

Soon after the shootings occurred, America Online posted the following pacts on their homepage and encouraged members to "sign" electronically as a pledge toward building community.

continued on next page

PACT — Parents And Children Together
To Stop Violence

Pledge to Make a Difference

Since the tragic shootings in Littleton, Colorado, we've seen an outpouring of emotion. AOL's chat rooms, message boards and polls reflect sadness and confusion, as well as a determination to make sure nothing like this happens again.

We all want to make a difference. So, after hearing from parents, teachers, teens, and children who want to stop violence, we worked with experts to create PACT (Parents And Children Together).

While this is just one small step, we're asking you to join other Americans in taking this pledge. We hope you'll use it in a way that's meaningful to you – print it as a reminder of what you can do each day, ask your friends to sign or start a family or classroom discussion. After you've signed, you'll find resources that can help to build safer and stronger families, schools and communities.

To participate, click on the appropriate link below.

<u>For Adults</u> | <u>For Teenagers</u> | <u>For Kids</u>

An AOL Initiative

AOL.COM

PACT — Parents And Children Together
To Stop Violence

For Adults   (Scroll down to sign the PACT)

- I will talk with my children and the children I know, and listen to the issues they think are important.

- I will take a greater interest in my children's free time and their friends.

- I will, in my words and actions, condemn violence as a way to resolve conflict, anger or frustration.

- I will get more involved in my community and our schools.

- If I own a gun, I will make sure that children can't get their hands on it.

Email or AOL Screen Name: [   ]

First Name: [   ]

Age: -Select your age- ▼

Zip Code: [   ]

[Sign the Pact]

The information collected above will be used only to compile aggregate, anonymous demographic data. You will receive no email. For more information please see our privacy policy.

AOL.COM

PACT   Parents And Children Together
To Stop Violence

For Teenagers   (Scroll down to sign the PACT)

- I will not put other kids down by labeling them with names or doing anything else that creates hurt feelings.

- I will talk to my parents, teachers or an adult I trust about problems at school, with friends, or anything else that makes me feel bad.

- I will do everything I can to resolve trouble without violence – and when I can't, I will walk (or run) away.

- If I see or hear other kids talking about hurting people, or doing things that could harm others, I will tell an adult as soon as I can.

- I understand that violence is real and has permanent consequences. I will do everything I can to stay safe.

Email or AOL Screen Name: [   ]

First Name: [   ]

Age: [-Select your age- ▼]

Zip Code: [   ]

[Sign the Pact]

AOL.COM

PACT   Parents And Children Together
To Stop Violence

For Adults   (Scroll down to sign the PACT)

- I will talk with my children and the children I know, and listen to the issues they think are important.

- I will take a greater interest in my children's free time and their friends.

- I will, in my words and actions, condemn violence as a way to resolve conflict, anger or frustration.

- I will get more involved in my community and our schools.

- If I own a gun, I will make sure that children can't get their hands on it.

Email or AOL Screen Name: [   ]

First Name: [   ]

Age: [-Select your age- ▼]

Zip Code: [   ]

[Sign the Pact]

The information collected above will be used only to compile aggregate, anonymous demographic data. You will receive no email. For more information please see our privacy policy.

AOL.COM

DARRELL SCOTT Our Greatest Need

> *Darrell Scott is the father of Rachel Scott, one of the students who was killed in the Columbine shootings. His son Craig, who was also at Columbine, survived but saw two of his friends killed in the school library. Since the shootings Darrell Scott has traveled the country speaking to groups and has authored several books about his daughter, including* Rachel's Tears *and* Chain Reaction. *"Our Greatest Need" is a testimonial he gave on May 29, 1999, to the Subcommittee on Crime of the U.S. Congress' House Judiciary Committee. It is published on his Columbine Redemption Web site: <http://www.thecolumbineredemption.com>.*

Since the dawn of creation there have been both good and evil in the hearts of men and of women. We all contain the seeds of kindness or the seeds of violence.

The death of my wonderful daughter Rachel Joy Scott, and the deaths of the heroic teacher and the other children who died, must not be in vain. Their blood cries out for answers.

The first recorded act of violence was when Cain slew his brother Abel out in the field. The villain was not the club he used. Neither was it the NCA— The National Club Association. The true killer was Cain and the reason for the murder could only be found in Cain's heart.

In the days that followed the Columbine tragedy, I was amazed at how quickly fingers began to be pointed at groups such as the NRA. I am not a member of the NRA. I am not a hunter. I do not even own a gun. I am not here to represent or defend the NRA, because I don't believe that they are responsible for my daughter's death. Therefore, I do not believe that they need to be defended. If I believed they had anything to do with Rachel's murder, I would be their strongest opponent.

5   I am here today to declare that Columbine was not just a tragedy—it was a spiritual event that should be forcing us to look at where the real blame lies. Much of that blame lies here in this room. Much of that blame lies behind the pointing fingers of the accusers themselves.

I wrote a poem just four nights ago that expresses my feelings best. This was written way before I knew I would be speaking here today:

> Your laws ignore our deepest needs,
> Your words are empty air,
> You've stripped away our heritage,
> You've outlawed simple prayer,
> 5   Now gunshots fill our classrooms,
> And precious children die,

You seek for answers everywhere,
And ask the question, "Why?"
You regulate restrictive laws,
10   Through legislative creed,
And yet you fail to understand,
That God is what we need!

Men and women are three-part beings. We all consist of body, soul, and spirit.
When we refuse to acknowledge a third part of our makeup, we create a void
that allows evil, prejudice, and hatred to rush in and wreak havoc. Spiritual influences were present within our educational systems for most of our nation's history.
Many of our major colleges began as theological seminaries. This is a historic fact.

What has happened to us as a nation? We have refused to honor God and in
doing so, we open the doors to hatred and violence.

And when something as terrible as Columbine's tragedy occurs, politicians
immediately look for a scapegoat such as the NRA. They immediately seek to
pass more restrictive laws that continue to erode away our personal and private
liberties.

10   We do not need more restrictive laws. Eric and Dylan would not have been
stopped by metal detectors. No amount of gun laws can stop someone who spends
months planning this type of massacre.

The real villain lies within our own hearts. Political posturing and restrictive
legislation are not the answers.

The young people of our nation hold the key. There is a spiritual awakening
taking place that will not be squelched!

We do not need more religion. We do not need more gaudy television evan-
gelists spewing out verbal religious garbage. We do not need more million-
dollar church buildings built while people with basic needs are being ignored.

We do need a change of heart and a humble acknowledgment that this nation
was founded on the principle of simple trust in God.

15   As my son Craig lay under that table in the school library and saw his two
friends murdered before his very eyes, he did not hesitate to pray in school. I
defy any law or politician to deny him that right!

I challenge every young person in America and around the world to realize that
on April 20, 1999, at Columbine High School, prayer was brought back to our
schools. Do not let the many prayers offered by those students be in vain.

Dare to move into the new millennium with a sacred disregard for legislation that violates your conscience and denies your God-given right to communicate with Him.

To those of you who would point your finger at the NRA, I give to you a
sincere challenge: Dare to examine your own heart before you cast the first stone!

My daughter's death will not be in vain. The young people of this country
will not allow that to happen.

TIM WISE School Shootings and the Price of White Denial

Tim Wise is a writer and activist based in Nashville. He wrote this article for the parenting zine Hip Mama, *where it appeared in Number 25, "The Connections Issue," 2001.*

I can think of no other way to say this, so here goes: an awful lot of white people need to pull our heads out of our collective ass. Two more children are dead and thirteen are injured, and another "nice" community is scratching its blonde scalp, utterly perplexed as to how a school shooting the likes of the one in Santee, California could happen. After all, as the Mayor of the town said in an interview with CNN: "We're a solid town, a good town, with good kids, a good church-going town. . . an All-American town." Maybe that's the problem.

I said this after Columbine and no one listened so I'll say it again: most white folk live in a state of self-delusion. We think danger is black, brown and poor, and if we can just move far enough away from "those people" we'll be safe. If we can just find an "all-American" town, life will be better, because "things like this just don't happen here."

Well, excuse me for pointing this out, but in case you hadn't noticed, "here" is about the only place these kinds of things *do* happen. Oh sure, there is plenty of violence in urban communities and schools. But mass murder; wholesale slaughter; take-a-gun-and-see-how-many-you-can-kill kinda craziness seems made for those safe places: the white suburbs or rural communities.

And yet the FBI still insists there is no "profile" of a school shooter. Come again? White boy after white boy after white boy decides to use their classmates for target practice, and yet there is no profile? In the past two years, 32 young men have either carried out or planned to carry out (and been foiled at the last minute), mass murder against classmates and teachers—thirty of these have been white. And yet there is no profile? Imagine if these killers and would-be killers had nearly all been black: would we still hesitate to put a racial face on the perpetrators? Doubtful.

5   Indeed, if *any* black child—especially in the mostly white suburbs of Littleton, or Santee—were to openly discuss their plans to murder fellow students, as happened at Columbine and Santana High, you can bet *somebody* would have turned them in and the cops would have beat a path to their door. But when whites discuss their murderous intentions, our racial stereotypes of danger too often lead us to ignore it— they're just "talking" and won't really do anything, we tell ourselves. How many kids have to die before we rethink that nonsense? How many dazed parents, Mayors and Sheriffs do we have to listen to, describing how "normal" and safe their community is, and how they just can't understand what went wrong?

I'll tell you what went wrong and it's not TV, rap music, video games or a lack of prayer in school. What went wrong is that white Americans decided to ignore dysfunction and violence when it only seemed to affect other communities, and thereby blinded themselves to the chaos that never remains isolated for long. What affects the urban "ghetto" today will be coming to a Wal-Mart near you tomorrow, and was probably already there to begin with. Unless you address the emptiness, pain, isolation and lack of hope felt by too many children of color and the poor, then don't be shocked when the support systems aren't there for your kids either.

What went wrong is that we allowed ourselves to be lulled into a false sense of security by media representations of crime and violence that portray both as the province of those who are anything but white like us. We ignore the warning signs, because in our minds the warning signs don't live in our neighborhood, but across town, in that place where we lock our car doors on the rare occasion we have to drive there. That false sense of security—the result of racist and classist stereotypes—then gets people killed. And still we act amazed.

But listen up my fellow white Americans: your children are no better, no nicer, no more moral, and no more decent than anyone else. Dysfunction is all around you, whether you choose to recognize it or not. And it's not just the issue of school shootings.

According to the Centers for Disease Control's Youth Risk Behavior Survey, and the "Monitoring the Future" Report from the National Institutes on Drug Abuse, it is *your* children, and not those of the urban ghetto, who are most likely to use drugs.*

**The drug usage data comes from: Johnston, Lloyd, Patrick O'Malley, and Jerald Bachman, 2000.
Monitoring the Future: National Survey Results on Drug Use, 1975–1999. Vol 1: Secondary School
Students. The University of Michigan Institute for Social Research, National Institute on Drug Abuse, United
States Department of Health and Human Services, National Institutes on Health: 76, 101–102*
*This can be ordered from the U of Michigan Institute for Social Research. The ordering information is
available at: <http://monitoringthefuture.org/pubs.html>.*
Table 4–9 of the Monitoring the Future *Report, page 101, "Racial/Ethnic Comparisons of Lifetime, Annual,
Thirty-Day and Daily Prevalence of Use of Various Drugs Eighth, Tenth and Twelfth Graders,"*

- *For pot, 50.3% of white 12th graders have smoked pot, compared to 45.1% of black 12th graders: a
  difference of 11.5% total.*
- *For cocaine, 10.3% of white seniors have used, compared to 1.5% of black seniors, for a ratio of roughly 7 to 1.*
- *For crack, 4.7% of whites have used, compared to 0.6% of blacks, for a ratio of 7.8 to 1 (roughly 8 as I said
  in the piece)*
- *For heroin, 2.1% of whites have used, compared to 0.3% of blacks, for a ratio of 7 to 1*
- *For LSD, 14.2% of whites have used, compared to 1.4% of blacks, for a ratio of 10 to 1*
- *For Ecstasy, 8% of whites have used, compared to 0.5% of blacks, for a ratio of 16 to 1*

*For sales, the info comes from the Substance Abuse and Mental Health Services Administration, Office of
Applied Studies, National Household Survey on Drug Abuse, 1999. Table G, 71, at:
<www.samhsa.gov/statistics/statistics.html>.*

- *3.9% of whites aged 12–17 have sold drugs in the past year, as compared with 2.9% of blacks. Though both
  numbers are small, this means that whites 12–17 are over a third more likely to have sold than blacks*

*The info on drinking and drinking and driving comes from: Centers for Disease Control and Prevention,
2000. "Morbidity and Mortality Weekly Report, Survey Summary," Volume 49, No. SS–5, Youth Risk
Behavior Surveillance System-United States. Washington, DC: GPO.*
*This can be accessed by going to: <www.cdc.gov/nccdphp/dash/yrbs/index.htm>, and clicking on the fourth
link on the page—the one for the 1999 Youth Risk Behavior Survey*
*The info on white boys bringing weapons to school more often is also from the CDC report. . . table 10 on page
46 of the document, to be precise, where it is noted:*

- *11% of white males carried a weapon on school grounds in the last thirty days, while only 5.3% of black
  males did.*

That's right: white high school students are seven times more likely than blacks to have used cocaine; eight times more likely to have smoked crack; ten times more likely to have used LSD and seven times more likely to have used heroin. In fact, in raw numbers there are more white high school students who have used crystal methamphetamine (the most addictive drug on the streets) than there are black students who smoke cigarettes.

10   What's more, it is *white* youth ages 12–17 who are more likely to *sell* drugs: 34% more likely, in fact, than their black counterparts. And it is *white* youth who are twice as likely to binge drink, and nearly twice as likely as blacks to drive drunk. And *white* males are twice as likely to bring a weapon to school as are black males.

And yet I would bet a valued body part that there aren't 100 white people in Santee, California, or most any other "nice" community who have ever heard a single one of the statistics above. Because the media doesn't report on white dysfunction.

A few years ago, *U.S. News* ran a story entitled: "A Shocking Look at Blacks and Crime." Yet never have they or any other news outlet discussed the "shocking" whiteness of these shoot-em-ups. Indeed, every time media commentators discuss the similarities in these crimes they mention that the shooters were boys who got picked on, but *never* do they seem to notice a certain highly visible melanin deficiency. Color-blind, I guess.

White-blind is more like it, as I figure these folks would spot color with a quickness were some of it to stroll into their community. Santee's whiteness is so taken for granted by its residents that the Mayor, in that CNN interview, thought nothing of saying on the one hand that the town was 82 percent white, but on the other hand that "this is America." Well that *isn't* America, and it especially isn't California, where whites are only half of the population. This is a town that is *removed* from America, and yet its Mayor thinks *they* are the normal ones—so much so that when asked about racial diversity, he replied that there weren't many of different "ethni-tis-tities." Not a word. Not even close.

I'd like to think that after this one, people would wake up. Take note. Rethink their stereotypes of who the dangerous ones are. But deep down, I know better. The folks hitting the snooze button on this none-too-subtle alarm are my own people, after all, and I know their blindness like the back of my hand.

Writing Style

USING SARCASM

Tim Wise's article "School Shootings and the Price of White Denial" uses slang, profanity, and a mocking tone to startle readers into waking up and acknowledging their prejudices and unexamined assumptions in the wake of the Columbine shootings. In doing so, Wise is drawing on a long tradition of writers who use sarcasm—harsh, biting remarks—to critique society and call attention to something that needs to be changed.

When a writer uses sarcasm to say the opposite of what he or she actually means, we say the writer is using irony or is being ironic. Wise, however, is quite straightforward about what he sees as the problem and what white people should be doing about it. He uses sarcasm as a way of forcing white readers to see the absurdity of their views.

Often writers will want to use sarcasm in their essays to be funny. They know that humor can shock us out of our complacency and make us see ourselves more effectively than earnest pleas often can. However, for sarcasm to be an effective tool for change, the writer needs to know the audience well and needs to speak to the audience as one of them. Note how when Wise writes "white people need to pull our heads out of our collective ass," he includes himself. He understands how his audience thinks, commenting, "Those folks hitting the snooze button on this none-too-subtle alarm are my own people, after all, and I know their blindness like the back of my hand." We can be sarcastic about those with whom we do not agree and are not a part of, but we will not convince those people to change their minds by ridiculing them with sarcasm; instead, we would have to find common ground and argue more empathically to change their views.

In the past decade American culture has been dripping with sarcasm, so much so that sarcasm has been cited as the defining attitude of the culture. The sarcasm in many conversations and on TV shows such as *Seinfeld* and *Late Night with David Letterman* is used simply for effect rather than for moral purposes. We never know what the writers or speakers truly think, and as a result their sarcasm does not push us toward reflection and a greater understanding; in fact, it scoffs at the earnestness of wanting to understand. The writer Jedediah Purdy has evaluated this attitude in a thoughtful manner in his book *For Common Things: Irony, Trust and Commitment in America Today* (New York: Knopf, 1999).

To further explore the effects of sarcasm, try rewriting something sarcastic, like a scene from *Seinfeld*, to make it sincere. Then rewrite something sincere, like one of the other essays in this case study, to make it sarcastic. How do your changes affect the way you read these texts?

QUESTIONS FOR INQUIRY AND ACTION

1. Now that you have read a number of other people's opinions on and analyses of the events at Columbine, how would *you* frame the issue? What factors do you think were most important? Are there aspects that you think we should be paying attention to that no one else is seeing yet?

2. What can and should we do about situations such as that at Columbine High School? Can we do anything? Should we do something to prevent such situations, and if so, what? If you were to try to begin to solve these problems, which problem(s) would you concentrate on, and what would you do? To whom would you address your actions?

3. Go back to your high school and talk to your principal and/or one of your teachers. What, if anything, has changed there since the Columbine shootings? Have the events at Columbine affected the ways they treat students, or the way that the students treat one another?

4. How does this situation spark your imagination? What emotions do you feel when you read about and think about the shootings? Respond imaginatively in some fashion; for instance, write a poem or create a picture. How does this work help you to understand the situation and your own reaction? What do you want to express or communicate through your artwork?

5. Popular culture has long been blamed for the social problems of youth; for instance, in the late eighteenth century, adults blamed Goethe's bestselling 1774 novel *The Sorrows of Young Werther*—in which the young romantic hero, Werther, kills himself over love—for a rash of suicides among young men. In our own time, movies that appear to glorify violence, from *A Clockwork Orange* to *Natural Born Killers*, as well as gleefully violent video games such as Doom and Quake, have been similarly criticized and blamed for violent acts. How much is popular culture a reflection of what is already going on in society, and how much is it responsible for causing social events?

6. In what ways do you think you are affected by the TV and movies you watch, music you listen to, books you read, video games you play, and so forth? Observe yourself participating in one of these activities and describe your response. What are you feeling? What are you thinking?

CHAPTER 7

The Family as Community

The family is the natural and fundamental group unit of society and is entitled to protection by society and the State.
> *United Nations' Universal Declaration of Human Rights*

Families are the basic units of society and our most valuable resource. Healthy, well-functioning families provide members of all ages with rewarding, caring relationships, and with essential mutual support which is sustaining throughout the life course. Families are the major producers and consumers of goods and services. They make a central contribution to the nation's present and future workforce and enhance the quality of our society. Conversely, society has a critical effect on families. Therefore, it is essential that family policy makers recognize the reciprocal influences that families and society have upon each other.
> *Policy statement from the National Council on Family Relations*

GETTING STARTED: How Do We See the Family?

1. Write down all of your ideas related to the family. What images or sets of behaviors do you think are characteristic of families? How would you describe the typical American family? Is your image of a family similar to or different from the typical family? Why?

2. Now examine the *Rolling Stone* cover photograph of rock musician Melissa Etheridge; her partner, filmmaker Julie Cypher; their children Bailey and Beckett; veteran musician David Crosby; and his wife Jan Crosby on page 244. The caption accompanying the photograph, "Melissa's Secret: The Name of the Father and the Making of a New American Family," identifies Crosby as the children's father, but it also suggests that this arrangement is somehow indicative of new American families. In what ways does this family seem very traditional? In what ways does it differ from and challenge traditional media images of the American family? (Note: Since the making of this photograph, Etheridge and Cypher have separated. Does knowing that change the way you interpret the picture?)

235

3. As a follow-up exercise, collect images of families portrayed in the media, including everything from advertisements to TV shows. What are the consistencies and irregularities in these images?

In the previous chapter, you learned that communities are created and tested by the shared visions and values of their members. Of the many communities to which we belong, the family is continuously identified as the most basic and formative influence on our lives. Yet these "basic units of society" have also been influenced by the same historical and cultural forces that have affected larger communities. To indicate these effects, politicians have frequently cited statistics on the changing nature of U.S. families. The following statistics were taken from *America's Children: Key National Indicators of Well-Being, 2000* and from the March *1998 Current Population Reports* from the U.S. Census Bureau.

- In 1999, 27 percent of America's children were living with only one parent, an increase from 20 percent in 1980.
- Most children of single parents live with a single mother, but the number of children living with single fathers rose from 2 percent in 1980 to 4 percent in 1999.
- In 1999, 54 percent of children from birth to third grade received regular child care, up from 51 percent in 1995.
- In 1998, 56 percent of adults were married and living with their spouse.
- The adults currently divorced in 1998 represented 9.8 percent of the population.
- About 4 million children live with their grandparents, representing 5.8 percent of all children under age 18. Of those children, 1.4 million had neither parent present.

Of course, citizens have interpreted these statistics to mean different things: the breakdown of the traditional family, the evolution of new family structures, the decline of personal responsibility, or the effects of changing economic and social conditions. Whether we celebrate or criticize the current state of American families, we tend to express the same expectations for what families can provide: affection, companionship, preparation for life, and financial, emotional, and spiritual support. The readings in this chapter explore different types of families, assessing their ability to meet these expectations.

Because the term *family values* has focused the contemporary debate about the nature and responsibilities of the American family, the case study in the second part of this chapter documents its introduction into our nation's vocabulary. Although the term originally referred to a traditional family model—a heterosexual couple with children—and conservative social values, its definition has expanded to include other types of families and other values. The struggle for ownership of this term reflects a larger cultural struggle to define what American families should be and how they should function in our society.

MARY PIPHER Beliefs About Families

Mary Pipher is a clinical psychologist who works in Lincoln, Nebraska. She is the author of the bestselling book, Reviving Ophelia: Saving the Selves of Adolescent Girls *(1994), that sought to save teenaged girls from destructive media culture. "Beliefs About Families" is taken from her more recent book* The Shelter of Each Other: Rebuilding Our Families *(New York: Putnam, 1996) in which she examines the lack of community that is now common in families and suggests ways to remedy it.*

When I speak of families, I usually mean biological families. There is a power in blood ties that cannot be denied. But in our fragmented, chaotic culture, many people don't have biological families nearby. For many people, friends become family. Family is a collection of people who pool resources and help each other over the long haul. Families love one another even when that requires sacrifice. Family means that if you disagree, you still stay together.

Families are the people for whom it matters if you have a cold, are feuding with your mate or training a new puppy. Family members use magnets to fasten the newspaper clippings about your bowling team on the refrigerator door. They save your drawings and homemade pottery. They like to hear stories about when you were young. They'll help you can tomatoes or change the oil in your car. They're the people who will come visit you in the hospital, will talk to you when you call with "a dark night of the soul" and will loan you money to pay the rent if you lose your job. Whether or not they are biologically related to each other, the people who do these things are family.

If you are very lucky, family is the group you were born into. But some are not that lucky. When Janet was in college, her parents were killed in a car wreck. In her early twenties she married, but three years later she lost her husband to leukemia. She has one sister, who calls mainly when she's suicidal or needs money. Janet is a congresswoman in a western state, a hard worker and an idealist. Her family consists of the men, women and children she's grown to depend on in the twenty-five years she's lived in her community. Except for her beloved dog, nobody lives with her. But she brings the cinnamon rolls to one family's Thanksgiving dinner and has a Mexican fiesta for families at her house on New Year's Eve. She attends Bar Mitzvahs, weddings, school concerts and soccer matches. She told me with great pride, "When I sprained my ankle skiing last year, three families brought me meals."

I think of Morgan, a jazz musician who long ago left his small town and rigid, judgmental family. He had many memories of his father whipping him with a belt or making him sleep in the cold. Once he said to me, "I was eighteen years old before anyone ever told me I had something to offer." Indeed he does. He plays the violin beautifully. He teaches improvisation and jazz violin and organizes jazz events for his town. His family is the family of musicians and music lovers that he has built around him over the years.

5   If you are very unlucky, you come from a nuclear family that didn't care for you. Curtis, who as a boy was regularly beaten by his father, lied about his age so that he could join the Navy at sixteen. Years later he wrote his parents and asked if he could return home for Christmas. They didn't answer his letter. When I saw him in therapy, I encouraged him to look for a new family, among his cousins and friends from the Navy. Sometimes cutoffs, tragic as they are, are unavoidable.

I think of Anita, who never knew her father and whose mother abandoned her when she was seven. Anita was raised by an aunt and uncle, whom she loved very much. As an adult she tracked down her mother and tried to establish a relationship, but her mother wasn't interested. At least Anita was able to find other family members to love her. She had a family in her aunt and uncle.

Family need not be traditional or biological. But what family offers is not easily replicated. Let me share a Sioux word, *tiospaye,* which means the people with whom one lives. The tiospaye is probably closer to a kibbutz than to any other Western institution. The tiospaye gives children multiple parents, aunts, uncles and grandparents. It offers children a corrective factor for problems in their nuclear families. If parents are difficult, there are other adults around to soften and diffuse the situation. Until the 1930s, when the tiospaye began to fall apart with sale of land, migration and alcoholism, there was not much mental illness among the Sioux. When all adults were responsible for all children, people grew up healthy.

What tiospaye offers and what biological family offers is a place that all members can belong to regardless of merit. Everyone is included regardless of health, likability or prestige. What's most valuable about such institutions is that people are in by virtue of being born into the group. People are in even if they've committed a crime, been a difficult person, become physically or mentally disabled or are unemployed and broke. That ascribed status was what Robert Frost valued when he wrote that home "was something you somehow hadn't to deserve."

Many people do not have access to either a supportive biological family or a tiospaye. They make do with a "formed family." Others simply prefer a community of friends to their biological families. The problem with formed families is they often have less staying power. They might not take you in, give you money if you lose a job or visit you in a rest home if you are paralyzed in a car crash. My father had a stroke and lost most of his sight and speech. Family members were the people who invited him to visit and helped him through the long tough years after his stroke. Of course, there are formed families who do this. With the AIDS crisis, many gays have supported their friends through terrible times. Often immigrants will help each other in this new country. And there are families who don't stick together in crisis. But generally blood is thicker than water. Families come through when they must.

10   Another problem with formed families is that not everyone has the skills to be included in that kind of family. Friendship isn't a product that can be obtained for cash. People need friends today more than ever, but friends are

harder to make in a world where people are busy, moving and isolated. Some people don't have the skills. They are shy, abrasive or dull. Crack babies have a hard time making friends, as do people with Alzheimer's. Formed families can leave many people out.

From my point of view the issue isn't biology. Rather the issues are commitment and inclusiveness. I don't think for most of us it has to be either/or. A person can have both a strong network of friends and a strong family. It is important to define family broadly so that all kinds of families, such as single-parent families, multigenerational families, foster families and the families of gays are included. But I agree with David Blankenberg's conclusion in his book *Rebuilding the Nest:* "Even with all the problems of nuclear families, I will support it as an institution until something better comes along."

Americans hold two parallel versions of the family—the idealized version and the dysfunctional version. The idealized version portrays families as wellsprings of love and happiness, loyal, wholesome, and true. This is the version we see in *Leave It to Beaver* or *Father Knows Best.* The dysfunctional version depicts families as disturbed and disturbing and suggests that salvation lies in extricating oneself from all the ties that bind. Both versions have had their eras. In the 1950s the idealized version was at its zenith. Extolling family was in response to the Depression and war, which separated families. People who had been wrenched away from home missed their families and thought of them with great longing. They idealized how close and warm they had been.

In the 1990s the dysfunctional version of family seems the most influential. This belief system goes along with the culture of narcissism, which sells people the idea that families get in the way of individual fulfillment. Currently, many Americans are deeply mistrustful of their own and other people's families. Pop psychology presents families as pathology-producing. Talk shows make families look like hotbeds of sin and sickness. Day after day people testify about the diverse forms of emotional abuse that they suffered in their families. Movies and television often portray families as useless impediments.

In our culture, after a certain age, children no longer have permission to love their parents. We define adulthood as breaking away, disagreeing and making up new rules. Just when teenagers most need their parents, they are encouraged to distance from them. A friend told me of walking with her son in a shopping mall. They passed some of his friends and she noticed that suddenly he was ten feet behind, trying hard not to be seen with her. She said, "I felt like I was drooling and wearing purple plaid polyester." Later her son told her that he enjoyed being with her, but that his friends all hated their parents and he would be teased if anyone knew he loved her. He said, "I'm confused about this. Am I supposed to hate you?"

15   This socialized antipathy toward families is unusual. Most cultures revere and respect family. In Vietnam, for example, the tender word for lover is "sibling." In the Kuma tribe of Papua, New Guinea, family members are valued above all

others. Siblings are seen as alter egos, essential parts of the self. The Kuma believe that mates can be replaced, but not family members. Many Native American tribes regard family members as connected to the self. To be without family is to be dead.

From the Greeks, to Descartes, to Freud and Ayn Rand, Westerners have valued the independent ego. But Americans are the most extreme. Our founders were rebels who couldn't tolerate oppression. When they formed a new government they emphasized rights and freedoms. Laws protected private property and individual rights. Responsibility for the common good was not mandated.

American values concerning independence may have worked better when we lived in small communities surrounded by endless space. But we have run out of space and our outlaws live among us. At one time the outlaw mentality was mitigated by a strong sense of community. Now the values of community have been superseded by other values.

We have pushed the concept of individual rights to the limits. Our laws let adults sell children harmful products. But laws are not our main problem. People have always been governed more by community values than by laws. Ethics, rather than laws, determine most of our behavior. Unwritten rules of civility—for taking turns, not cutting in lines, holding doors open for others and lowering our voices in theaters—organize civic life. Unfortunately, those rules of civility seem to be crumbling in America. We are becoming a nation of people who get angry when anyone gets in our way.

Rudeness is everywhere in our culture. Howard Stern, G. Gordon Liddy and Newt Gingrich are rude. It's not surprising our children copy them. Phil Donahue and Jay Leno interrupt and children learn to interrupt. A young man I know was recently injured on a volleyball court. The player who hurt him didn't apologize or offer to help him get to an emergency room. An official told him to get off the floor because he was messing it up with his blood and holding up the game. I recently saw an old man hesitate at a busy intersection. Behind him drivers swore and honked. He looked scared and confused as he turned into traffic and almost wrecked his car. At a festival a man stood in front of the stage, refusing to sit down when people yelled out that they couldn't see. Finally another man wrestled him to the ground. All around were the omnipresent calls of "Fuck you." Over coffee a local politician told me she would no longer attend town meetings. She said, "People get out of control and insult me and each other. There's no dialogue; it's all insults and accusations."

20 We have a crisis in meaning in our culture. The crisis comes from our isolation from each other, from the values we learn in a culture of consumption and from the fuzzy, self-help message that the only commitment is to the self and the only important question is—Am I happy? We learn that we are number one and that our own immediate needs are the most important ones. The crisis comes from the message that products satisfy and that happiness can be purchased.

We live in a money-driven culture. But the bottom line is not the only line, or even the best line for us to hold. A culture organized around profits instead of people is not user friendly to families. We all suffer from existential flu, as we search for meaning in a culture that values money, not meaning. Everyone I know wants to do good work. But right now we have an enormous gap between doing what's meaningful and doing what is reimbursed.

QUESTIONS FOR INQUIRY AND ACTION

1. The early years of college are often difficult for students who seek to establish new relationships—often in a new city, state, or country—while trying to maintain relationships with their families at home. How have you tried to both form new families and preserve your existing ones? Have you run into difficulties? What can you do to overcome these difficulties?

2. Pipher presents several stories of individuals living in troubled biological families. Why does she use these stories, and how do they affect you as a reader? Could she use other forms of evidence, and would they work in the same ways?

3. Pipher says that modern families are frequently depicted in the media as dysfunctional burdens that individuals must overcome to find self-fulfillment. Look through your local television guide and circle all of the shows that depict dysfunctional families. Then, using a different colored ink, circle all the shows depicting idealized or uplifting families. How do the number of shows compare? Finally, watch sample shows depicting each type of family and make observations in your writer's notebook. Do these shows fit Pipher's descriptions of them?

4. Pipher blames the breakdown of American families on a culture of consumption, rudeness, and narcissism (self-love). How can we work toward a more meaningful, community-based society? Think of one act you can perform that would move us toward a more civil society. Perform that act and then reflect on the consequences in your writer's notebook. Did you make a positive difference in someone else's life?

WILLIAM J. BENNETT Leave Marriage Alone

> *William J. Bennett is a well-known conservative spokesperson and writer. He is the author of the bestseller* The Book of Virtues *(1993) and* The Broken Hearth: Reversing the Moral Collapse of the American Family *(2001), among many other books. Bennett also served as Chairman of the National Endowment for the Humanities and as President Reagan's Secretary of Education. "Leave Marriage Alone" appeared as an editorial in* Newsweek *on June 3, 1996.*

There are at least two key issues that divide proponents and opponents of same-sex marriage. The first is whether legally recognizing same-sex unions would strengthen or weaken the institution. The second has to do with the basic understanding of marriage itself.

The advocates of same-sex marriage say that they seek to strengthen and celebrate marriage. That may be what some intend. But I am certain that it will not be the reality. Consider: the legal union of same-sex couples would shatter the conventional definition of marriage, change the rules which govern behavior, endorse practices which are completely antithetical to the tenets of all of the world's major religions, send conflicting signals about marriage and sexuality, particularly to the young, and obscure marriage's enormously consequential function—procreation and child-rearing.

Broadening the definition of marriage to include same-sex unions would stretch it almost beyond recognition—and new attempts to expand the definition still further would surely follow. On what principled ground can Andrew Sullivan exclude others who most desperately want what he wants, legal recognition and social acceptance? Why on earth would Sullivan exclude from marriage a bisexual who wants to marry two other people? After all, exclusion would be a denial of that person's sexuality. The same holds true of a father and daughter who want to marry. Or two sisters. Or men who want (consensual) polygamous arrangements. Sullivan may think some of these arrangements are unwise. But having employed sexual relativism in his own defense, he has effectively lost the capacity to draw any lines and make moral distinctions.

Forsaking all others is an essential component of marriage. Obviously it is not always honored in practice. But it is the ideal to which we rightly aspire, and in most marriages the ideal is in fact the norm. Many advocates of same-sex marriage simply do not share this ideal; promiscuity among homosexual males is well known. Sullivan himself has written that gay male relationships are served by the "openness of the contract" and that homosexuals should resist allowing their "varied and complicated lives" to be flattened into a "single, moralistic model." But that "single, moralistic model" has served society exceedingly well. The burden of proof ought to be on those who propose untested arrangements for our most important institution.

5   A second key difference I have with Sullivan goes to the very heart of marriage itself. I believe that marriage is not an arbitrary construct which can be redefined simply by those who lay claim to it. It is an honorable estate, instituted of God and built on moral, religious, sexual and human realities. Marriage is based on a natural teleology, on the different, complementary nature of men and women—and how they refine, support, encourage and complete one another. It is the institution through which we propagate, nurture, educate and sustain our species.

That we have to engage in this debate at all is an indication of how steep our moral slide has been.

Worse, those who defend the traditional understanding of marriage are routinely referred to (though not to my knowledge by Sullivan) as "homophobes," "gay-bashers," "intolerant" and "bigoted." Can one defend an honorable, 4,000-year-old tradition and not be called these names?

This is a large, tolerant, diverse country. In America people are free to do as they wish, within broad parameters. It is also a country in sore need of shoring up some of its most crucial institutions: marriage and the family, schools, neighborhoods, communities. But marriage and family are the greatest of these. That is why they are elevated and revered. We should keep them so.

QUESTIONS FOR INQUIRY AND ACTION

1. Make a list of the phrases and words Bennett uses to define marriage. Extrapolating from your list, how would you say Bennett defines family? How does it compare with the definition of family you created in the Getting Started section?

2. Bennett argues that marriage is based on the "different, complementary nature of men and women"; does this description of men's and women's differences extend beyond providing the biological materials for reproduction? Is he suggesting that men and women are different in other ways as well?

3. In the public conversation on same-sex marriage, Bennett positions himself in opposition to Andrew Sullivan, a gay conservative writer. Read more about Sullivan's perspective in his book *Virtually Normal: An Argument about Homosexuality* (NY: Alfred A. Knopf, 1995).

4. Bennett suggests that broadening the definition of marriages to same-sex couples would encourage incest and bigamy. Is this an example of the slippery slope fallacy? Looking at sources other than *The Jerry Springer Show,* find out how common cases of incest and bigamy really are in American culture. Is there evidence to support Bennett's concern?

MARK SELIGER Melissa's Secret

Mark Seliger is an editorial photographer who is the chief photographer for Rolling Stone *and* Us *magazines. He has worked for* Rolling Stone *since 1987 and has shot over eighty covers for them. He has also directed several music videos, including Hole's "Violet" and Joan Osborne's "One of Us." His portrait of Melissa Etheridge, Julie Cypher, their children, and David and Jan Crosby appeared on the cover of* Rolling Stone *on February 3, 2000.*

JEFF RIEDEL Inward Christian Soldiers

Jeff Riedel is a photographer for The New York Times Magazine *who does a lot of fashion photography as well as photojournalism. His portrait of the Scheibner family appeared on the cover of* The New York Times Magazine *the same month as Seliger's photo: February 27, 2000.*

QUESTIONS FOR INQUIRY AND ACTION

1. In Chapter Four you will find an exercise that asks you to analyze these photographs in terms of their implied definitions of family.

2. Discuss your impressions of each of the photographs in relation to the various views on family expressed by the readings in this chapter. How are these photographs in conversation with the readings?

3. Research the work of Seliger and Riedel. How do these photographs compare with other work that they have done? How do they describe themselves as photographers? What do they think their tasks or goals are? Have they commented on either of these particular photos?

4. Shoot your own pictures of families, paste them into your writer's notebook, and write about them. How did you stage your photographs? What impressions or arguments do you want the pictures to make?

MARGARET TALBOT A Mighty Fortress

Veteran journalist Margaret Talbot has been an editor at large for Lingua Franca *and writer for* The New Republic *as well as* The New York Times, *where this article was featured as the cover story of the February 27, 2000,* New York Times Magazine. *It immediately struck a chord with Americans and was fervently discussed on* Talk of the Nation *and other call-in radio and television shows.*

To get to the house where Stephen and Megan Scheibner live with their seven children, you skirt past Allentown, Pa., and drive for another half-hour into the hills above the Lehigh Valley. The Scheibner place is on Blue Mountain Road, a few miles past a forlorn establishment called Binnie's Hot Dogs and Family Food. Standing behind their white clapboard farmhouse, where the backyard unfurls over three and a half acres and where, in summer, you can see a tangled strawberry patch and a tree fort, you could swear you were deep in the country and maybe deep in the past too. The front of the house is a different matter. It's practically on top of a busy road that leads to the local ski resorts; the view is of a housing development under construction.

Inside, there is no such ambivalence. Although the Scheibners are well off and their house is comfortably appointed—Steve is a pilot with American Airlines and a commander in the Naval Reserves—what might strike many visitors first is what's missing. In the Scheibner household, where the children are 12, 11, 9, 7, 6, 4 and 20 months, there is no Pokemon or "Star Wars" paraphernalia. There are no Britney Spears or Ricky Martin tapes. There are no posters of Leonardo DiCaprio or Michael Jordan taped to the walls, no pots of lip gloss or bottles of metallic nail polish scattered around. No Mortal Kombat, no "Goosebumps." No broadcast TV—though the family does watch carefully selected videos, which often means movies from the 1940's and 50's. (The older kids are big Cary Grant fans.) There is no giggling about the cute guys and girls at school, because the Scheibners are home-schooled and besides, their parents don't believe in dating. There is little sign of eye-rolling preteen rebellion, because Steve and his wife, Megan, don't believe in that either, and have set up their lives in such a way that it is unlikely to manifest itself. Katie, the oldest, reads Louisa May Alcott and reissued girls' classics like the Elsie Dinsmore books, and is partial to white patent-leather Mary Janes worn with ankle-length floral dresses. Peter, who comes next, likes Tolkien and the muscularly Christian boys' adventure stories written by the 19th-century author G. A. Henty, and favors chinos and logo-free button-down shirts. Peter wants to be a missionary in Russia, which he describes as a "forsaken" country; Katie wants to be a home-schooling mom. They are each other's best friends. And if they quarrel, it's not in a way that involves the dissing of one another in viciously up-to-the-minute slang.

There is no sports gear lying around the Scheibner household, because Megan feels that team sports breed competitive "behavior that we would not deem Christlike"; more important, they interfere with the weekly rhythm of schooling, service and worship. Holidays don't disrupt much, either. The Scheibners don't celebrate Halloween—Satanic overtones—though one year the three oldest children dressed up as a couple of shepherds and a sheep and went door to door handing out evangelical tracts. At Christmas, they decorate the house and take baskets of food to their neighbors and to the poor, but they don't indulge in a buy-fest.

Megan, who is 37, guesses she has been to a mall "maybe three times" in the seven years the family has lived in Pennsylvania, and she can't remember the correct name of Toys "R" Us. For the children's clothes, she does a lot of her shopping at consignment stores because she objects to "the way most girls' stuff looks like it was designed for 20-year-olds and the boys' clothes all have some cartoon character on them." This Christmas, as they have for the past several years, the kids got a shared family gift—a "Sunday box" of special games and toys they can take out only on the Sabbath. It contained a Noah's Ark puzzle, several books, a tape of Christian children's songs with titles like "Keep Your Tongue From Evil," and a board game called Sticky Situations, a Christian version of Chutes and Ladders based on such moral dilemmas as what you should do if the most unpopular kid you know invites you over.

5   None of this is what Steve and Megan Scheibner would say first about themselves. What they would say first is that they are Christians—fundamentalist Baptists who were born again when, as teenagers, they found Jesus Christ and accepted the doctrine of salvation. And yet the way they practice their faith puts them so sharply and purposefully at odds with the larger culture that it is hard not to see the Scheibners, conservative and law-abiding though they are, as rebels.

We have arrived, it seems, at a moment in our history when the most vigorous and coherent counterculture around is the one constructed by conservative Christians. That sounds odd to many of us—especially, perhaps, to secular liberals, who cherish our own 60's-inflected notions of what an "alternative lifestyle" should look like. Ever since Theodore Roszak first coined it in 1968, the word "counterculture" has retained its whiff of patchouli, its association with free love, long hair and left-wing youth. "The counterculture," as Roszak defined it, "is the embryonic base of New Left politics, the effort to discover new types of community, new family patterns, new sexual mores. . . new personal identities on the far side of power politics."

Yet today it is conservative Christians like the Scheibners who, more self-consciously than any other large social group, buck mainstream notions of what constitutes a fulfilled life. Indeed, much of what Roszak said of the 60's counterculture could be said of them too. It's true that the "patterns" and "mores" they have discovered are not so much new ones as reinvigorated traditional ones. Parent-sanctioned courtship, the merging of school and home, the rejection of peer-group segregation, the moral value of thrift—all are ideas that, in the United States, last held real sway in the 19th century. But the impatience that people like the Scheibners display with acquisition, their unflagging commitment to putting the group—in their case, the family—above individual ambition, their rejection of pop culture, their characterization of themselves as, in Steve's words, "people who question absolutely everything," make them radical in ways that would be recognizable to some 60's counterculturists too.

There are about 20 million evangelical Christians in the U.S. today; together with fundamentalists, who tend to be more withdrawn from public life and more theologically conservative, they make up about 25 percent of the American population. Many of them lead lives that are far less sequestered and culturally abstemious than the Scheibners'. (Only 6 percent of conservative Christians educate their children at home, for instance, though the numbers are growing.) Some lead even more walled-off lives: at a conference for home-schooling families in Virginia last summer, I heard one speaker urge parents to reconsider sending their kids to college—even a Bible college—because dorm life encouraged "fornication" and "homosexual rape." But nearly all evangelicals struggle with the question of how staunchly they should separate their families from a majority culture they believe flouts their values.

A sense of this struggle came to the fore last spring, when Paul Weyrich published his "turn off, tune out, drop out" letter—the very phrase self-consciously echoing the hippie slogan. Weyrich, a founder of the Christian right, now urged "a strategy of separation," a "sort of quarantine" for Christians who he argued had been trying too hard, and at too much cost to their own morality, to insert themselves into the mainstream. "We need," he wrote "to drop out of this culture, and find places, even if it is where we physically are right now, where we can live godly, righteous and sober lives."

10   In their 1999 book, *Blinded by Might*, Cal Thomas, a conservative columnist, and Ed Dobson, a Baptist minister, offered a similar analysis, arguing that "religious conservatives have heard sermons that man's ways are not God's ways. . . . In politics they have fused the two, causing damage to both church and state." In a series of forceful columns, Thomas went on to argue that for Chris-

tians, worldly power was "not a calling, but a distraction" from the next world and that the faithful often stumbled in the public square anyway. Consider Prohibition: "Good people diagnosed a social ill, but they used the wrong methods to correct it," he wrote. "The lesson: by and large, the Christian mission should be to change hearts, not laws."

Weyrich, Thomas and Dobson found few adherents among the leaders of the Christian right, but they touched off an emotional debate at the grass roots. Embittered by Clinton's survival of the impeachment scandal, some conservative Christians were despairing of politics altogether: how could Christians hope to influence a polity that supported a manifestly immoral leader? Even those who did not feel quite so deeply estranged from the American electorate still found something meaningful and provocative in the call to concentrate on discipleship, not politics. In an article in *Christianity Today,* the former Reagan aide Don Eberly wrote, "The greatest fallacy that has emerged in recent years is the expectation that national politicians and other civil authorities should take the lead in restoring biblical righteousness or, worse, using political power to create a 'Christian America.'"

It would be premature to declare the end of religious-right political activism. There are too many issues, from abortion to same-sex marriage, that continue to galvanize the faithful. But it cannot be denied that as a political force, the religious right is flagging. The Christian Coalition is deeply in the red. The two presidential candidates most identified with savvy Christian conservatism—Gary Bauer and Steve Forbes—have dropped out of the race, while the protest candidate Alan Keyes blusters on to tiny audiences. Yet even as Christian political movements flounder, the strategies that might be thought of as countercultural—home-schooling, building up a self-contained pop culture—are flourishing.

Not long after this debate was under way, I met the Scheibners. I had become interested in the idea of a Christian counterculture, and I wanted to write about a family who seemed to be living it out. I wasn't looking for people involved in a violent or illegal confrontation with the government—militia types, say—nor for people who belonged to a tradition with a long history of separateness, like the Amish. What I was looking for were people who were, as Steve Scheibner later described his family, "selective separatists": people who voted and paid taxes, worked in the mainstream world and even did community service, but who quite deliberately chose, as Megan put it, "not to participate in those parts of the culture that do not bring glory to God."

Partly I was interested because as a mother of young children, I had grappled with some of the same questions about what to keep at bay and for how long. TV or no TV? Did I want my 3-year-old to start playing on the computer now so he wouldn't be behind or hold off as long as possible, knowing his life will be colonized by dot-com this and digital that soon enough? Did toy guns lead inexorably to a taste for brutal video games? When you are awash in media and awash in stuff, what hope do you have of picking and choosing anyway? Could you do so only if armed with a totalizing worldview like the Scheibners'? How feasible—and how desirable—was it to "drop out" anyway?

15   When Megan Scheibner answered a message I posted on a Christian Internet discussion list last summer, her e-mail convinced me that I had found the right family. "We don't isolate our family," she wrote, "but we do feel like we are called to shelter them from evil until they are spiritually ready to stand firm." Sheltering them, she explained, meant screening out almost all pop culture. "We have seen the fruit in kind, polite children," she went on to say. "Others have noticed, too, and this has given us many opportunities to share, i.e., one time at Pizza Hut, the man at the next table bought us lunch because the kids were so nice to each other. . . . Only God gets the glory for things like this. Neither my husband nor I were raised in Christian homes, but God has been faithful to show us his desire for our family, and then as we obey, He has blessed us abundantly."

On a rainy Sunday morning in August, I arrived, with my husband and son, for my first visit to the Scheibner house. The family was busy conducting its own Sunday school, and Megan sent Emma, then 8, out to greet us. Like all of the Scheibner children, Emma addressed me as Mrs. Talbot and my husband as Mr. Talbot. It seemed pointless to insist that they call me by my first name, and downright mean to introduce the idea that my husband and I have different last names, so there it stood. Of another 8-year-old, it might be fair to say that she bounded out of the house, but Emma walked delicately, on the balls of her feet, self-consciously ladylike. With a curtsy, she conducted us inside. All seven of the Scheibner children, and three of their friends, sat cross-legged on the tan carpet in the living room, reviewing their catechisms and listening to a sermon delivered by their father.

It may be because he is a pilot or because he has spent much of his adult life in the military or because he believes so firmly in parental authority, but Steve Scheibner seems at ease in the role of teacher and preacher to his own children in a way that few parents I know would be. Not that anything in his appearance or demeanor suggests an old-fashioned patriarch. He's a young-looking 39, slim, sharp-featured and dark-haired; he can be sarcastic; and he uses lots of guy lingo like "Bogus!" and "Where the rubber hits the road." But he's also got a storehouse of metaphors and concepts for child-rearing and for life that he dips into without hesitation or doubt. Steve explains to me later that he and Megan don't like the way many churches, including their own, shunt kids off to children's services where "they hear about Jonah and the whale for the umpteenth time." They think that children are capable of more or less following the main sermon by the age of 3; when they start their own church in Brunswick, Me., next summer (Steve is studying at a seminary now), there will be booster seats in the pews.

For now, though, he has taken to conducting his own Sunday school, with another couple and their children. Megan, in a smocked denim dress, a headband and no makeup, sits next to him. Though it's only 9 A.M., all the children look freshly scrubbed and shiny-haired, outfitted in their Sunday best. When little Baleigh cranes her neck to peer at us with a radiant, inquisitive smile, her mom gives her a whispered scolding, accompanied by the look a border collie might give a straying sheep. She turns around immediately.

At 10:30, Steve piles the kids into the van and drives to church, and Megan stays behind to talk to me. She'll miss church this morning, which she hardly ever does, but there's another service tonight, which the family always attends as well. In her high-ceilinged kitchen, where one wall is lined with homemade preserves, she tells me about their decision to teach their kids at home. "I worked in a day-care center for a while as a young Navy wife, and it really shocked me—the lack of discipline, the hitting, biting, screeching. We always thought we would home-school, but somehow we lost the nerve for a while and with Katie we sent her to kindergarten at a private Christian school for a year. But what we noticed was that she got more interested in what her peers were doing than in what her family was doing! We felt like our family-centered little girl was being pulled away from us."

20   Family identity is extremely important to the Scheibners—they have their own sayings, code words, even a family song. The turning outward that most parents expect of their children and accept, with varying degrees of wistfulness, was to them an intolerable betrayal. "We didn't want to lose our children to other people's ideas and ideologies," Megan will say, or, "We wanted our children's hearts, and we really feel we have them." Home-schooling afforded the prospect that the older kids would help with the younger ones and the younger ones would emulate the older ones instead of their peers.

While we talk, Megan is cooking gravy and pot roast and two kinds of pie, and when the rest of the family comes home it's time for Sunday lunch at the big butcher block table Steve made for them. Despite the presence of seven children, lunch is an orderly business. Interruptions are kept to a minimum—talking out of turn elicits the border-collie look. Still, Peter, who has been studying pirates, chats charmingly about Bluebeard, and Katie reminds me that there were female pirates who "fought like demons." There is a lot of anticipatory discussion of the pies. But lunch, like most meals in the Scheibner household, is also an occasion for moral pedagogy.

The thing about living in a culture from which you feel estranged, and which you therefore do not trust to reinforce your own values, is that you must be vigilant, you can't lose an opportunity to remind your children that they are different, and why. The Scheibners surround themselves as much as possible with a culture of their own making and friends of their own choosing who share their religion, but it's not as though they actually live in a 19th-century village. Just the other week, Katie innocently typed in "girls.com" on the computer—the Scheibner kids are allowed to do research on the Internet—and got hit with a dozen porn sites.

Just before pie is served, Steve asks Katie, as he has many times before, to explain what courtship is. Shyly, she looks down at her plate. "I don't know," she says. To which her mother replies, "You can do better than that, young lady." And she can. She has known the word, at least, since she was 9 and her father took her out for ice cream and a portentous chat. The Scheibners believe that dating, because it usually involves breaking up, is, as Steve puts it, "practice for divorce."

It goes without saying that they do not approve of premarital sex, but what is a little more surprising is that they do not approve of premarital emotional intimacy either. If a couple are courting, they are supposed to be seriously considering each other as husband and wife, and they are supposed to do so with some overt participation by parents or other elders. Ideally, they should not be alone together, or if they are it ought to be in a public place—a Friendly's, say—where liquor is not served and where they are unlikely to give in to temptation. As Steve later explained to me: "If a girl dates 100 guys before she gets married, she's given her heart away 100 times but every time she gets it back, it's a little more scarred. So, when I took Katie out, I had bought this cheap little wedding ring in my size, and I gave it to her and I said: 'This is yours and what it represents is your heart. Go ahead and try it on.' Well, of course it was about as big as three of her fingers. So I said, 'See, it doesn't fit you, but it does fit Daddy, so if you don't mind, I want you to give Daddy your heart and let him hold on to it until the appropriate time when I will give it back to you and you in turn will give it to the man you marry.'"

25   Katie looks up—she's a good girl who wants to please—and murmurs: "It's better than dating. It's waiting for the right man." Now Peter raises his hand. For him, this is all a little more abstract and a little less embarrassing, and he knows he has the answer. "It's keeping your heart pure!"

"Right!" says his father approvingly.

After lunch, Katie goes upstairs without prompting to put young Baleigh and Stephen down for their three-hour afternoon naps—nap time is inviolable at the Scheibner house—and Peter and Emma cheerily start in on the dishes. To a girl and boy, the Scheibner kids are a pleasure to talk to; they're polite and brimming with book-gotten information. They're also a little otherworldly, a bit unnervingly preprogrammed.

When the family came to Washington, where I live, to attend a rally for homeschoolers on the Capitol steps, I went along. It was a hot day and I was nine months pregnant, so I sat down, and while the rest of the children stood patiently with Megan and Steve, Molly, the 7-year-old, wandered over to me. Molly is the dreamy one, the dress-up artist—the one who likes to trail around the house in her mother's wedding gown and who says she wants to be a princess when she grows up. Her hair is honey-colored and waist length, and so, naturally, she maintains a lively interest in the general subject of hair. On the steps, she began doing what a lot of little girls with a lively interest in hair would do, which was to brush mine and, with my permission, to poke through my purse looking for hair ornaments. But though the motions seemed familiar, the dialogue was disconcertingly awry.

'Is President Clinton a Christian?" Molly asked in her singsong voice.

30   "I think he would say so, yes."

"No. He's not. He lies. Do you have a barrette?"

The sun was beating down. A boy skateboarded by in a black T-shirt reading, "Jesus: The Force Without a Dark Side."

"I know who is always against us," Molly continued.

"Who?"

35   "Satan." Brush. Brush.

"Really? What does he do?"

"Makes us lie." Brush. Brush. "Makes us sin." Brush. Brush. "Makes us turn our back on God. What's Play-Doh?"

For more moderate Americans, the persistence of the evangelical strain in our culture is a mystery that both requires and defies explanation. After the embarrassment of the Scopes trial, conservative Christians of all stripes were supposed to have sunk into the past like woolly mammoths in a tar pit. The re-emergence of a Christian right in the mid-80's took no one by greater surprise than the liberal academics and journalists who were frequently called upon to account for it, and to whom the equation of secularity and modernity was itself sacrosanct. As a result, much of the commentary on conservative Christians has tended to portray them, the historian Alan Brinkley points out, "as a group somehow left behind by the modern world—economically, culturally, psychologically." They were, in short, H. L. Mencken's "rustic gorillas" updated, but barely.

The trouble with this theory of "status discontent"—of conservative Christians as downwardly mobile rubes—was that most of them were neither. On "most measures of backwardness," as the sociologist Christian Smith puts it, evangelicals look no different—and frequently look more advanced—than their counterparts who identify themselves as mainline or liberal Protestants, as Catholics or as nonreligious. Of all these groups, evangelicals are the least likely to have had only a high school education or less. They are more likely than liberals or the nonreligious to belong to the $50,000-and-above income bracket. And they are no more likely to live in rural areas than anyone else; the new centers of conservative Christianity, it turns out, are the prosperous suburbs in Midwestern states like Kansas and Oklahoma.

40   Moreover, if you started with a theory of conservative Christians as orphans of history stranded in the modern world, you were more or less helpless to explain why the movement has been flourishing—both in new converts and in retention of members—since the 70's. Smith, a professor of sociology at the University of North Carolina, has one convincing answer. He argues that American evangelicalism is flourishing "because of and not in spite of its confrontation with modern pluralism." In other words, the fragmentation of American culture has encouraged the flowering of all kinds of minority groups, from gays to conservative Christians. More important, modern pluralism allows evangelicals to rub up against ideas and sensibilities that offend them, and this is itself a revitalizing force. "Contemporary pluralism," Smith has written, "creates a situation in which evangelicals can perpetually maintain but can never resolve their struggle with the nonevangelical world."

Over the past few years, engaging in this daily struggle to lead a "godly, righteous and sober life" has been made much easier by the exponential growth of Christian media. People like the Scheibners now have a storehouse of goods and services to which they can return, again and again, to refresh themselves and be entertained without guilt. The ability to encapsulate themselves in a culture of their own making removes some of the incentive to reform the culture at large, while at the same time offering a more fully realized reproof of it—a parallel world, imagined to the last, vivid detail.

Christian books and TV are just the beginning. The contemporary Christian music scene, with its groovily-named bands like Leaderdogs for the Blind and the Insyderz, is a $1-billion-a-year business. You can now buy, over the Internet, everything from Christian computer games to poseable biblical action figures. In the video market, "VeggieTales," a popular kids' series featuring animated vegetables enacting biblical parables, is just one among hundreds of titles—from the "Mother Goose Gospel" to "The Adventures of Prayer Bear."

Conservative Christianity has its own chaste heartthrobs, like Joshua Harris, the raffishly cute author of "I Kissed Dating Good-Bye," and the singer Rebecca St. James, the Alanis Morissette of the W. W. J. D. set. It even has its own indie film scene with movies like "End of the Harvest," in which "a college philosophy club meeting filled with atheists humiliates a new believer who tries to prove to them the existence of God." It has its own magazines for every demographic niche, including *Hopscotch* and *Boys' Quest* for kids 6 to 13, which promise "no teen themes, no boyfriends, girlfriends, makeup, fashion or violence and NO ADVERTISING!"

Combine all this with the fact that the number of home-schoolers has been increasing since 1985 at a rate of 15 to 20 percent a year—there are now about 1.2, million—while enrollment at evangelical colleges grew 24 percent between 1990 and 1996 (compared with an enrollment increase of 5 percent at other private colleges), and it seems fair to say that conservative Christians can live as much as they choose within a culture of their own construction. And that a lot of them are choosing to do so much of the time.

45   For some people, this separatist impulse has been strengthened by a new-found disillusionment with politics. It's not that conservative Christians are fleeing civic duty altogether: evangelicals still vote, for example, at a higher rate than do members of almost any other major religious group. It's more a matter of emphasis—of saying, maybe we were seduced by the promise of political power, and now we have to free ourselves from its thrall and concentrate anew on living faithfully and saving souls.

Steve Scheibner is certainly a patriotic guy: he has served in the Navy for 17 years, most recently flying drug-interdiction flights in the Caribbean. But whereas he once thought of running for political office, he now feels he "could have a greater and longer lasting impact on the lives of people as a pastor." He and Megan are Republicans, and they always vote, but they're not going to be active participants in Campaign 2000. Jerry Falwell, Ralph Reed and most other religious-right leaders don't impress Steve much—they "are mostly political creatures," he says. The one candidate he admires is the firebrand Alan Keyes, who doesn't stand a chance of getting the Republican nomination. The political issue the

Scheibners say they care most about is being left alone to home-school, and they see the discipling of others—the training of hearts already opened up to Christ—as their best hope for making a difference in the world.

One icy evening in January, nine young couples crowd into the Scheibners' living room for a class Megan and Steve teach on parenting the Christian way. Angie Dalrymple and her husband, Bruce, have come because they are both new Christians—"my husband got saved in March and I got saved in April"—and she needs help picking her way through unfamiliar moral terrain. Just last week, the Dalrymples' 9-year-old son, Josh, who has also been born again, was facing all kinds of grief at his public school because he now insists on "dressing real nice." Given that he had already ostentatiously thrown his Pokemon cards away, explaining to his classmates that an obsession with the cards could lead to a lifetime fascination with the dark side, he was taking some risks as it was. But Josh is big, which helps, and Angie coaxed him to "get rid of the tie, but keep the button-down shirts." She's proud of him but sometime she feels he's getting ahead of her, spiritually speaking. When his 4-year-old brother, Cody, talked back to her the other day, Josh called his attention to the Ten Commandments on the wall. Now Josh is saying he wants to be home-schooled, and Angie admits to the group that her first thought was, "Whoa, there." She and her husband, a machinist, have already stopped drinking and cursing, cut up their credit cards and canceled their cable TV. How many more changes are there going to be? She's glad to have the group for support.

The agenda for the evening involves watching a video produced by the Christian child-rearing gurus Gary and Ann Marie Ezzo, whose advocacy of rigid schedules for feeding babies, among other things, has been widely criticized by mainstream pediatricians. Tonight's program, though, is a gentler offering, focused on the need to help your child grow morally by giving him "the moral reason why" when you reprimand him for, say, careening around the churchyard and knocking old ladies off-balance—the example given in the video. The evening's discussion also gives the Scheibners a chance to touch on one of their favorite metaphors: the funnel.

The Scheibners think that most parents today err by trying to be "buddies to their babies and little kids." As Megan puts it, they start out with "a big fat funnel, and then, when the kids get to be 13 or 14 and become rebellious, they try to tighten it, and by then it's too late." The Scheibners' idea, they explain, is that you start off with a tight funnel, then gradually open it so that by the time your kids get to be teenagers, you can trust them. They reject what is, in essence, the modern idea of adolescence—that a teenager's alienation from his parents is an inevitable, even necessary step on the way to individuation. For Megan and Steve, rebellion within the family is not an acceptable option; they need a united front at home to wage rebellion against the larger culture. And more important, they believe that obedience to parents trains a child for obedience to God. When the Lord calls him to do something, he has to be ready to say, "Yes, Lord, here I am." So kids need practice in the prompt and cheerful response to commands, learning to do as their parents ask in what the Scheibners refer to as the RAH spirit—for "the Right way, All the way, the Happy way."

50   In other classes, Steve will talk about the need to stand firm when your children push, how you must be the wall that doesn't give way. He'll defend spanking, a practice that the Scheibners have thought through in detail. (Never do it in anger; never do it when you've lost control; use a flexible instrument so you don't break down muscle.)

The atmosphere tonight is a little like a consciousness-raising session—there's an earnest aura of learning together and sustaining one another in a benighted world. During the short break, everybody stands around drinking Diet Cokes and eating the taco salad someone brought, but there's not a lot of small talk. Steve is indisputably the leader, but he's willing to make himself vulnerable with a well-placed confession or two. He mentions, for example, his own upbringing in a very 70's family that left him with nothing in what he likes to call his "moral warehouse." His parents divorced when he was 2; his dad was a pianist who played in clubs, drank a lot and dropped in and out; his two sisters were out of control. "We didn't eat meals together and we had free run. My mom would see me going out the door with a six-pack and say, 'Have fun.'"

Megan's not talking about it tonight, but her story is not all that different. She was the youngest and the only girl her family. In high school, she played tennis competitively and was a waitress after school to save money for a car and a trip to Europe as a pompom girl. Her parents doted on her and couldn't wait for her to start reeling in the boyfriends. "When I was 15, I started dating a college boy, and for my mom, that was just the apex," Megan told me. Tennis kept her straight for a while, but after she suffered a serious ankle injury in her senior year, her "safeguard" was gone and she started drinking as competitively as she had played tennis. She spent summers at Delaware beaches, where, as she says, "it's always happy hour somewhere," and it wasn't long before she had "quite a reputation as a party girl." "Makes me sick now to think of it," she says. Billy Joel and Jackson Browne provided the soundtrack for her life. She says now: "I still wake up some mornings with the lyrics of their songs running through my head. Unbelievable! Anyone who thinks music doesn't affect teens is woefully unaware."

Both she and Steve found Christ when they hooked up with a teen ministry called Young Life. Steve was impressed by the "air of confidence" and "inner peace" he detected in a Young Life staff member named Scott, who was then 24 but willing to hang out with teenagers. "There was something about him that was different, and it kept bugging me and I kept asking him and he kept saying Jesus Christ." Steve didn't want to hear that at first, but after a while he and Scott started talking about the Bible, and something fell into place.

As for Megan, she says she got sick of the beach scene and the sense of purposelessness that washed over her every morning. She found she needed to stop worrying about "having the right boyfriend" to "try and be quiet and learn who it was Christ called me to be." She had started calling herself a Christian in high school, but she hadn't really admitted her sinfulness, let alone renounced it. As a sophomore at West Chester College in Pennsylvania, she finally did, and her "measuring stick" became the Word of God. "He wasn't interested in what I looked like on the outside, but who I was on the inside. Galatians 5:22 says, 'The fruit of the Spirit is love, joy, peace, patience, kindness, goodness, faithfulness, gentleness, self-control.' Suddenly instead of looking in the mirror to see how I was doing, I had to check my heart." She found it an enormous relief "to have the focus off me, me, me."

55   Megan and Steve initially shocked their families with their conversions. One of Steve's sisters, now a Christian herself, was then a graduate student in philosophy at Penn and told him he was "committing intellectual suicide." Megan's mother, "an intelligent woman who considered herself a feminist," as Megan recalls, thought her only daughter was ruining her life. Considering this was at the end of the Me Decade, Steve and Megan were choosing a radical path indeed.

In the Young Life chapter they joined at West Chester, Steve and Megan were the two resident sticklers. They were the ones who, if somebody in Bible study suggested going out for beers afterward, would catch each other's eyes and say naaah. They were friends first, but their sense of needing to start life anew—their joint weariness with their past selves—brought them closer, and they married just after Steve joined the Navy. He was 23 and she was a year younger. Now the two of them have created a life that sometimes, as Steve jokes with the class that night, "can look a little like a bad 'Ozzie and Harriet' rerun."

"Hey," interrupts a young mother in the class. "There are worse things!"

It could be a rallying cry for the group.

10:30 A.M., a school day at the Scheibners'. It's a scene remarkable, as usual, for its orderliness. Everybody has been up since at least 7:30 (all the kids go to bed by 8:30, so rising early is no problem); they've completed their morning clean-up chores, which Megan reminds them of by affixing a yellow Post-it with a specific assignment directly onto each child's body. They have sung hymns, read some Scripture and gone over their catechisms for the day; they have said the Pledge of Allegiance together. The house is warm and tidy and smells pleasantly of the chili Megan is cooking for lunch.

60   Downstairs, in the sunny family room, Baleigh is quietly playing a computer game, while Stephen, the baby, bounces up and down in his playpen. In the "library," a room lined with floor-to-ceiling bookshelves made by Steve, Molly is practicing her handwriting, while Nate works on his reading and tries not to let his mind wander to the dinosaur picture he wants to draw when it's free time. Emma perches on a high stool at the kitchen counter, doing sums in her math book. Upstairs, at a pair of scuffed red old-fashioned school desks, Katie studies grammar while Peter reads about Jamestown in a textbook called "America's Providential History." ("Since God is the author of history and He is carrying out His plan on the earth through history, any view of the history of America, or any country, that ignores God is not true history.")

A week at the Scheibner household follows a neat and repetitive arc, constructed along what the Scheibners call the Loving Our Family Guidelines. Each day has a theme, and a biblical verse to go with it. Monday is Ministry Day ("For God is not unrighteous to forget your work and labor of love, which you have shown toward His name, in that you have ministered to the saints and do minister," Hebrews 6:10). On this day, the children might deliver meals to sick or housebound neighbors. Tuesday is Give Day ("For God so loved the world that He gave his only Son, that whosoever believes in Him should not perish but have eternal life," John 3:16), and so in addition to their regular schoolwork, the kids are supposed to think of something to give one another. Wednesday is Serve Day ("By love serve one another," Galatians 5:13), and the Scheibners do so by performing each other's chores. The family spends every Wednesday evening at Awana Bible Club, a Bible memorization program with about 80 kids in its local chapter. Thursday is Edify Day ("Love edifies," I Corinthians 8:1), which means the kids are supposed to make an effort to compliment each other—and not in a fakey way either. Friday is Prefer Day ("Be kindly affectioned one to another with brotherly love, in honor preferring one another," Romans 12:10), which means, for example, letting your sibling pick the hymn the family will sing in the morning. Friday evenings, Katie and Peter help set up the refreshments for the parenting class, then put the younger kids to bed. Saturday is mostly a preamble to Sunday, but sometimes Megan and the older kids will do some volunteer work at the local homeless shelter, and then follow it up with a special treat—a trip to Friendly's, a rented Shirley Temple video, a game of red rover in the backyard.

One consequence of teaching your children at home—and of carefully customizing their media intake—is that you almost never have the experience of hearing them say something you are surprised and sorry that they know. Maybe your 3-year-old comes home one day with a rather specific question about pro wrestling. Or maybe he has somehow sucked out of the cultural ether the message that you "gotta catch 'em all." Maybe your kid is older and it's something worse. Home-schooling appeals to the parental fantasy of unchallenged dominion over—or at the very least familiarity with—all the detritus that crowds the shelves of your child's "moral warehouse."

I think all parents must be subject to this desire now and again, though comparatively few are willing to remake their lives in the service of it. If your kid were with you all the time, you figure, she would not ask questions that reminded you of your lapses in judgment or vigilance; she would not be in possession of information that you regarded with embarrassment or regret. On the other hand, neither would she be likely to come home with a delightful bit of knowledge that you had nothing to do with putting in her head—a sweet and silly song, a smattering of Spanish, a moral lesson as imparted by someone else—because you might not have known it, perhaps, or thought to plant it there.

Once I asked Steve and Megan if any of their kids ever did come out and say something that shocked them or made them wonder where he or she could possibly have heard it. "That doesn't happen often," Steve replied. "Every now and then we get one of those, but we spend so much time together that it just doesn't happen."

65   Megan and Steve tend not to let their own guard down much around their kids either. Lately, in fact, they have even stopped watching movies with more adult themes by themselves. "We never did used to rent R- rated movies," Steve says,

"but we would get a movie that would use some curse words or maybe had some brief nudity." They'd watch it after the kids were asleep and "justify it by saying, 'Oh, but it's a great story.' Well, now we've changed our view on that. I can't ask them to do something I'm not willing to do," Steve continues. "I don't want to be a hypocrite. And you know my relationship with God is just the same as theirs. My soul and my spirit is just as precious to God as their little souls and their little spirits, so how can I justify watching something that is vulgar and obscene for them? Isn't it vulgar and obscene for me too?"

To many of us, the specter of so much control suggests the possibility, even the inevitability, of rebellion. The Scheibners' oldest children are 12 and 11. What happens when they hit their teen years? Won't their hermetically sealed world spring a leak? Generational self-definition is a dearly held precept in our culture, which is why it seems to make sense to us that both Megan and Steve come from religiously indifferent families in which they defiantly distinguished themselves by their theological conservatism.

When you ask the Scheibners to imagine the future for their own kids, though, they can't picture them going astray. Peter has wanted to be a missionary for the longest time now, and since he and his parents regard this as something he has been called to do, they entertain few doubts about his doing it. Admittedly, it's hard to imagine Peter as a renegade. He is the kind of kid who, when asked in all innocence whether he ever listens furtively to his beloved "Lord of the Rings" tape in bed, looks shocked and says, "Oh, no, when it's time to go to bed, it's time to go to bed." He loves being home-schooled, and not long ago took it upon himself to write a letter to Senator Rick Santorum of Pennsylvania. It read, in part, "I have the joy of knowing I am going to heaven because when I was 4, I asked Jesus to come into my heart and save me from sin."

After spending some time with the Scheibner family, I was not particularly surprised to learn that evangelical Christians have one of the highest intergenerational retention rates of any major religion—meaning that, as Christian Smith puts it, "they have a great ability to raise children who do not become theologically liberal or nonreligious when they grow up." Certainly they work extremely hard to prevent what they see as the tragedy of apostasy. And the new availability of Christian media and of home-school curriculums helps enormously. A generation ago, evangelical families who wanted to shield their children from mainstream culture had little to replace it with, other than self-denial. Now they can offer goodies of their own. And new companies and institutions are springing up all the time to meet their needs. The Scheibners, for instance, are very excited about the founding of the first college primarily for Christian home-schoolers, Patrick Henry, in Purcelleville, Va., which will be accepting its inaugural class of students in the fall. Among other things, Patrick Henry will ask its students to sign a pledge in which they promise to court and not date.

And after college? Neither Megan nor Steve is outright opposed to their daughters' working, especially before they have children. Like many conservative Christians, they warm to the idea of a wife running her own little business from the home. "Proverbs 31 talks about the woman who made purple linens at home and sold them," Steve points out. But they warm even more to the idea of their daughters "having an eye to serve without compensation," as Megan says. They think too many working women have forgotten the virtues of volunteerism. And if one of their girls was to pursue a full-fledged career, Steve says, "we'd still love her and encourage her and, after all, at some point it's her life," but they would also find it hard to disguise their disappointment. "A career takes away from what I think their primary happiness will be, which is being a good mother," Steve says.

70   And then he gives a little speech that bears the distinctive hallmarks of the new Christian counterculture. "You know," he says, "you may have lots of pats on the back at work, you may have a successful career and a lot of money and great cars to drive, but in the end it always lets you down. Look at any number of gazillionaires out there—men, women, it doesn't make any difference—who have awful, tragic lives. Those things are not the things that satisfy. The things that satisfy are raising a good family, having love."

America has a long history of separatist movements, and within that history, there are, to put it bluntly, the bad separatists and the good ones. In the former category are the stockpilers of guns, the people who don't pay taxes or vaccinate their children—people who lack any sense of their duty as citizens. And in the latter category are people like the Scheibners. Indeed you could argue that their sort of separatism is good for the culture at large—or at least represents a reasonable compromise. If they are committed to teaching Creationism, for example, better that they teach it at home than insist that the public schools do. Besides, a culture that lacks a thriving and reproving counterculture is always in trouble. The very existence of alternative ways of life like the Scheibners' keeps alive a debate about the role of morality and religion in our culture and politics that probably ought never be declared over and done.

And yet you have to wonder about a way of life that requires such rigorous policing of its psychic boundaries. There is something poignant, for a parent like me anyway, about the idea of sons and daughters who love you as uncomplicatedly in their teenage years as they do when they were small—who are, indeed, your best friends—but there is something unreal about it too. There is something inspiring about the prospect of an American childhood in which advertising does not invade the imagination so relentlessly, but something claustrophobic about the notion that the only alternative is a sequestered family life. There is something fundamentally right and useful about the argument that American culture promotes independence at the expense, often, of the more nurturing virtues, but something sad and scared about the idea that the safest solution to this is early marriage. If the Scheibner philosophy allows girls to linger longer at the threshold of adolescence—not having to worry about being thin or sexy—it also pushes them much earlier into wifely domesticity.

By next summer, the Scheibners will be living in Maine, and they are looking forward to the move. Steve is eager to "plant" his new church. Megan thinks "the slower pace of life" there will make it that much easier to shelter the children from evil. The younger kids are excited about going crabbing and maybe seeing a moose or two on the rambling, wooded acreage where their new house will be. Katie, the oldest, is excited, too. She says she's hoping to find "a little place of my own, where I could read or think, and nobody would know about it."

QUESTIONS FOR INQUIRY AND ACTION

1. Talbot says the Scheibner family has isolated itself from the rest of society in order to "buck mainstream notions of what constitutes a fulfilled life." From details provided in the article, what is the Scheibners' view of a fulfilled life? What is your view? Where does your view of a good life come from—TV shows, your parents, a religious community?

2. Evangelical Christians like the Scheibners, who have withdrawn from public life, believe their values are incompatible with the larger culture's. What are the Scheibners' values? How are those values ridiculed in the media and the culture at large? Are the Scheibners right to withdraw from our culture?

3. Do you think it is better for people professing a particular religious faith to become politically active or to withdraw from public life? Are there other forms of injustice in American society that might prompt citizens to withdraw and form their own, alternative communities? Do you think active countercultural movements and separatist movements are good for the United States as a country? Are they good for our democratic system?

4. Because she believes the Scheibners' life is so different from our own, Talbot takes us through a detailed description of their daily routine. If you don't live like this, could you adopt their lifestyle? In what ways would you benefit from such an arrangement? In what ways might you suffer?

JAMES McBRIDE Black Power

> *James McBride's "Black Power" is a chapter of his memoir* The Color of Water: A Black Man's Tribute to His White Mother *(New York: Riverhead Books, 1996). It began life as an essay he wrote about his mother for the* Boston Globe's *Mother's Day 1981 edition; readers were so moved by the essay that they urged him to tell his mother's full story. McBride has worked as jazz saxophonist and composer as well as a journalist for the* Washington Times.

When I was a boy, I used to wonder where my mother came from, how she got on this earth. When I asked her where she was from, she would say, "God made me," and change the subject. When I asked her if she was white, she'd say, "No. I'm light-skinned," and change the subject again. Answering questions about her personal history did not jibe with Mommy's view of parenting twelve curious, wild, brown-skinned children. She issued orders and her rule was law. Since she refused to divulge details about herself or her past, and because my stepfather was largely unavailable to deal with questions about himself or Ma, what I learned of Mommy's past I learned from my siblings. We traded information on Mommy the way people trade baseball cards at trade shows, offering bits and pieces fraught with gossip, nonsense, wisdom, and sometimes just plain foolishness. "What does it matter to you?" my older brother Richie scoffed when I asked him if we had any grandparents. "You're adopted anyway."

My siblings and I spent hours playing tricks and teasing one another. It was our way of dealing with realities over which we had no control. I told Richie I didn't believe him.

"I don't care if you believe me or not," he sniffed. "Mommy's not your real mother. Your real mother's in jail."

"You're lying!"

5   "You'll see when Mommy takes you back to your real mother next week. Why do you think she's been so nice to you all week?"

Suddenly it occurred to me that Mommy *had* been nice to me all week. But wasn't she nice to me all the time? I couldn't remember, partly because within my confused eight-year-old reasoning was a growing fear that maybe Richie was right. Mommy, after all, did not really look like me. In fact, she didn't look like Richie, or David—or any of her children for that matter. We were all clearly black, of various shades of brown, some light brown, some medium brown, some very light-skinned, and all of us had curly hair. Mommy was, by her own definition, "light-skinned," a statement which I had initially accepted as fact but at some point later decided was not true. My best friend Billy Smith's mother was as light as Mommy was and had red hair to boot, but there was no question in my mind that Billy's mother was black and my mother was not. There was something inside me, an ache I had, like a constant itch that got bigger and bigger as I grew, that told me. It was in my blood, you might say, and however the notion got there, it bothered me greatly. Yet Mommy refused to acknowledge her whiteness. Why she did so was not clear, but even my teachers seemed to know she was white and I wasn't. On open school nights, the question most often asked by my schoolteachers was: "Is James adopted?" which always prompted an outraged response from Mommy.

I told Richie: "If I'm adopted, you're adopted too."

"Nope," Richie replied. "Just you, and you're going back to your real mother in jail."

"I'll run away first."

10   "You can't do that. Mommy will get in trouble if you do that. You don't want to see Ma get in trouble, do you? It's not her fault that you're adopted, is it?"

He had me then. Panic set in. "But I don't want to go to my real mother. I want to stay here with Ma. . . ."

"You gotta go. I'm sorry, man."

This went on until I was in tears. I remember pacing about nervously all day while Richie, knowing he had ruined my life, cackled himself to sleep. That night I lay wide awake in bed waiting for Mommy to get home from work at two A.M., whereupon she laid the ruse out as I sat at the kitchen table in my tattered Fruit of the Loom underwear. "You're not adopted," she laughed.

"So you're my real mother?"

15 "Of course I am." Big kiss.

"Then who's my grandparents?"

"Your grandpa Nash died and so did your grandma Etta."

"Who were they?"

"They were your father's parents."

20 "Where were they from?"

"From down south. You remember them?"

I had a faint recollection of my grandmother Etta, an ancient black woman with a beautiful face who seemed very confused, walking around with a blue dress and a fishing pole, the bait, tackle, and line dragging down around her ankles. She didn't seem real to me.

"Did you know them, Ma?"

"I knew them very, very well."

25 "Did they love you?"

"Why do you ask so many questions?"

"I just want to know. Did they love you? Because your own parents didn't love you, did they?"

"My own parents loved me."

"Then where are they?"

30 A short silence. "My mother died many, many years ago," she said. "My father, he was a fox. No more questions tonight. You want some coffee cake?" Enough said. If getting Mommy's undivided attention for more than five minutes was a great feat in a family of twelve kids, then getting a midnight snack in my house was a greater thrill. I cut the questions and ate the cake, though it never stopped me from wondering, partly because of my own growing sense of self, and partly because of fear for her safety, because even as a child I had a clear sense that black and white folks did not get along, which put her, and us, in a pretty tight space.

In 1966, when I was nine, black power had permeated every element of my neighborhood in St. Albans, Queens. Malcolm X had been killed the year before and had grown larger in death than in life. Afros were in style. The Black Panthers were a force. Public buildings, statues, monuments, even trees, met the evening in their original bland colors and reemerged the next morning painted in the sparkling "liberation colors" of red, black, and green. Congas played at night on the streets while teenyboppers gathered to talk of revolution. My siblings marched around the house reciting poetry from the Last Poets, a sort of rap group who recited in-your-face poetry with conga and fascinating vocal lines serving as a musical backdrop, with songs titled "Niggers Are Scared of Revolution" and

"On the Subway." Every Saturday morning my friends and I would pedal our bicycles to the corner of Dunkirk Street and Ilion Avenue to watch the local drag racers near the Sun Dew soft drink factory, trying to see who could drive the fastest over a dip in the road that sent even the slowest-moving car airborne. My stepfather hit that dip at fifteen miles an hour in his '64 Pontiac and I bounced high in my seat. These guys hit it at ninety and their cars flew like birds, barreling through the air and landing fifteen feet away, often skidding out of control, sometimes smacking against the wall of the Sun Dew factory before wobbling away in a pile of bent metal, grilles, and fenders. Their cars had names like "Smokin' Joe" and "Miko" and "Dream Machine" scrawled on the hoods, but our favorite was a gleaming black, souped-up GTO with the words "Black Power" written in smooth white script across the hood and top. It was the fastest and its driver was, of course, the coolest. He drove like a madman, and after leaving some poor Corvette in the dust, he'd power his mighty car in a circle, wheel it around, and do a victory lap for us, driving by at low speed, one muscled arm angling out the window, his car rumbling powerfully, while we whistled and cheered, raising our fists and yelling, "Black power!" He'd laugh and burn rubber for us, tires screeching, roaring away in a burst of gleaming metal and hot exhaust, his taillights flashing as he disappeared into the back alleyways before the cops had a chance to bust him. We thought he was God.

But there was a part of me that feared black power very deeply for the obvious reason. I thought black power would be the end of my mother. I had swallowed the white man's fear of the Negro, as we were called back then, whole. It began with a sober white newsman on our black-and-white television set introducing a news clip showing a Black Panther rally, led by Bobby Seale or Huey Newton or one of those young black militant leaders, screaming to hundreds and hundreds of angry African-American students, "Black power! Black power! Black power!" while the crowd roared. It frightened the shit out of me. I thought to myself, *These people will kill Mommy.* Mommy, on the other hand, seemed unconcerned. Her motto was, "If it doesn't involve your going to school or church, I could care less about it and my answer is no whatever it is."

She insisted on absolute privacy, excellent school grades, and trusted no outsiders of either race. We were instructed never to reveal details of our home life to any figures of authority: teachers, social workers, cops, storekeepers, or even friends. If anyone asked us about our home life, we were taught to respond with, "I don't know," and for years I did just that. Mommy's house was an entire world that she created. She appointed the eldest child at home to be "king" or "queen" to run the house in her absence and we took it from there, creating court jesters, slaves, musicians, poets, pets, and clowns. Playing in the street was discouraged and often forbidden and if you did manage to slip out, "Get your butt in this house before dark," she would warn, a rule she enforced to the bone. I often played that rule out to its very edge, stealing into the house at dusk, just as the last glimmer of sunlight was peeking over the western horizon, closing the door softly, hoping Mommy had gone to work, only to turn around and find her standing before me, hands on hips, whipping belt in hand, eyes flicking angrily back and forth to the window, then to me, lips pursed, trying to decide whether it was light or dark outside. "It's still light," I'd suggest, my voice wavering, as my siblings gathered behind her to watch the impending slaughter.

"That looks like light to you?" she'd snap, motioning to the window.

35   "Looks pretty dark," my siblings would chirp from behind her. "It's definitely dark, Ma!" they'd shout, stifling their giggles. If I was lucky a baby would wail in another room and she'd be off, hanging the belt on the doorknob as she went. "Don't do it again," she'd warn over her shoulder, and I was a free man.

But even if she had any interest in black power, she had no time to talk about it. She worked the swing shift at Chase Manhattan Bank as a typist, leaving home at three P.M. and returning around two A.M., so she had little time for games, and even less time for identity crises. She and my father brought a curious blend of Jewish-European and African-American distrust and paranoia into our house. On his end, my father, Andrew McBride, a Baptist minister, had his doubts about the world accepting his mixed family. He always made sure his kids never got into trouble, was concerned about money, and trusted the providence of the Holy Father to do the rest. After he died and Mommy remarried, my stepfather, Hunter Jordan, seemed to pick up where my father left off, insistent on education and church. On her end, Mommy had no model for raising us other than the experience of her own Orthodox Jewish family, which despite the seeming flaws— an unbending nature, a stridency, a focus on money, a deep distrust of all outsiders, not to mention her father's tyranny—represented the best and worst of the immigrant mentality: hard work, no nonsense, quest for excellence, distrust of authority figures, and a deep belief in God and education. My parents were nonmaterialistic. They believed that money without knowledge was worthless, that education tempered with religion was the way to climb out of poverty in America, and over the years they were proven right.

Yet conflict was a part of our lives, written into our very faces, hands, and arms, and to see how contradiction lived and survived in its essence, we had to look no farther than our own mother. Mommy's contradictions crashed and slammed against one another like bumper cars at Coney Island. White folks, she felt, were implicitly evil toward blacks, yet she forced us to go to white schools to get the best education. Blacks could be trusted more, but anything involving blacks was probably slightly substandard. She disliked people with money yet was in constant need of it. She couldn't stand racists of either color and had great distaste for bourgeois blacks who sought to emulate rich whites by putting on airs and "doing silly things like covering their couches with plastic and holding teacups with their pinkies out." "What fools!" she'd hiss. She wouldn't be bothered with parents who bragged about their children's accomplishments, yet she insisted we strive for the highest professional goals. She was against welfare and never applied for it despite our need, but championed those who availed themselves of it. She hated restaurants and would not enter one even if the meals served were free. She actually preferred to be among the poor, the working-class poor of the Red Hook

Housing Projects in Brooklyn, the cement mixers, bakers, doughnut makers, grandmothers, and soul-food church partisans who were her lifelong friends. It was with them that she and my father started the New Brown Memorial Baptist Church, a small storefront church which still stands in Red Hook today. Mommy loves that church and to this day still loves Red Hook, one of the most dangerous and neglected housing projects in New York City. On any given day she'll get up in the morning, take the New Jersey Transit train from her home in Ewing, New Jersey, to Manhattan, then take the subway to Brooklyn, and wander around the projects like the Pope, the only white person in sight, waving to friends, stepping past the drug addicts, smiling at the young mothers pushing their children in baby carriages, slipping into the poorly lit hallway of 80 Dwight Street while the young dudes in hooded sweatshirts stare balefully at the strange, bow-legged old white lady in Nikes and red sweats who slowly hobbles up the three flights of dark, urine-smelling stairs on arthritic knees to visit her best friend, Mrs. Ingram in apartment 3G.

As a boy, I often found Mommy's ease among black people surprising. Most white folks I knew seemed to have a great fear of blacks. Even as a young child, I was aware of that. I'd read it in the paper, between the lines of my favorite sport columnists in the *New York Post* and the old *Long Island Press,* in their refusal to call Cassius Clay Muhammad Ali, in their portrayal of Floyd Patterson as a "good Negro Catholic," and in their burning criticism of black athletes like Bob Gibson of the St. Louis Cardinals, whom I idolized. In fact I didn't even have to open the paper to see it. I could see it in the faces of the white people who stared at me and Mommy and my siblings when we rode the subway, sometimes laughing at us, pointing, muttering things like, "Look at her with those little niggers." I remember when a white man shoved her angrily as she led a group of us onto an escalator, but Mommy simply ignored him. I remember two black women pointing at us, saying, "Look at that white bitch," and a white man screaming at Mommy somewhere in Manhattan, calling her a "nigger lover." Mommy ignored them all, unless the insults threatened her children, at which time she would turn and fight back like an alley cat, hissing, angry, and fearless. She had a casual way of ignoring affronts, slipping past insults to her whiteness like a seasoned boxer slips punches. When Malcolm X, the supposed demon of the white man, was killed, I asked her who he was and she said, "He was a man ahead of his time." She actually liked Malcolm X. She put him in nearly the same category as her other civil rights heroes, Paul Robeson, Jackie Robinson, Eleanor Roosevelt, A. Philip Randolph, Martin Luther King, Jr., and the Kennedys—any Kennedy. When Malcolm X talked about "the white devil" Mommy simply felt those references didn't apply to her. She viewed the civil rights achievements of black Americans with pride, as if they were her own. And she herself occasionally talked about "the white man" in the third person, as if she had nothing to do with him, and in fact she didn't, since most of her friends and social circle were black women from church. "What's the matter with these white folks?" she'd muse after reading some craziness in the *New York Daily News.* "They're fighting over this man's money now that he's dead. None of them wanted him when he was alive, and now look at them. Forget it, honey"—this is Mommy talking to the newspaper—"your husband's dead, okay? He's dead—poop! You had your chance. Is money gonna bring him back? No!" Then she'd turn to us and deliver the invariable lecture: "You don't need money. What's money if your mind is empty! Educate your mind! Is this world crazy or am I the crazy one? It's probably me."

Indeed it probably was—at least, I thought so. I knew of no other white woman who would board the subway in Manhattan at one o'clock every morning and fall asleep till she got to her stop in Queens forty-five minutes later. Often I could not sleep until I heard her key hit the door. Her lack of fear for her safety—particularly among blacks, where she often stuck out like a sore thumb and seemed an easy target for muggers—had me stumped. As a grown man, I understand now, understand how her Christian principles and trust in God kept her going through all her life's battles, but as a boy, my faith was not that strong. Mommy once took me to Harlem to visit my stepsister, Jacqueline, whom we called Jack and who was my father's daughter by a previous marriage and more like an aunt than a sister. The two of them sat in Jack's parlor and talked into the night while Jack cooked big plates of soul food, macaroni and cheese, sweet potato pies, and biscuits for us. "Take this home to the kids, Ruth," Jack told Ma. We put the food in shopping bags and took it on the subway without incident, but when we got off the bus in St. Albans near our house, two black men came up behind us and one of them grabbed Mommy's purse. The shopping bag full of macaroni and cheese and sweet potato pies burst open and food flew everywhere as Mommy held on to her purse, spinning around in a crazy circle with the mugger, neither saying a word as they both desperately wrestled for the purse, whirling from the sidewalk into the dark empty street like two ballerinas locked in a death dance. I stood frozen in shock, watching. Finally the mugger got the purse and ran off as his buddy laughed at him, and Mommy fell to the ground.

40 She got up, calmly took my hand, and began to walk home without a word.

"You okay?" she asked me after a few moments.

I nodded. I was so frightened I couldn't speak. All the food that Jack had cooked for us lay on the ground behind us, ruined. "Why didn't you scream?" I asked, when I finally got my tongue back.

"It's just a purse," she said. "Don't worry about it. Let's just get home."

The incident confirmed my fears that Mommy was always in danger. Every summer we joined the poor inner-city kids the Fresh Air Fund organization sent to host families or to summer camps for free. The luckier ones among my siblings got to stay with host families, but I had to go to camps where they housed ten of us in a cabin for two weeks at a time. Sometimes they seemed closer to prison or job corps than camp. Kids fought all the time. The food was horrible. I was constantly fighting. Kids called me Cochise because of my light skin and curly hair. Despite all that, I loved it. The first time I went, Mommy took me to the roundup point, a community center in Far Rockaway, once the home of middle-class whites and Jews like playwright Neil Simon, but long since turned black, and it seemed that the only white person for miles was my own mother. The camp organizers set up a table inside where they removed our shoes and shirts and inspected our toes for athlete's foot, checked us for measles and chicken pox, then sent us outside to board a yellow school bus for the long journey to upstate New York. As I sat on the bus peering out the window at Mommy, the only white face in a sea of black faces, a black man walked up with his son. He had a mustache and a goatee and wore black leather pants, a black leather jacket, a ton of jewelry, and a black beret. He seemed outstandingly cool. His kid was very handsome, well dressed, and quite refined. He placed his kid's bags in the back of the bus and when the kid went to step on the bus, instead of hugging the child, the father offered his hand, and father and son did a magnificent, convoluted black-power soul handshake called the "dap," the kind of handshake that lasts five minutes, fingers looping, thumbs up, thumbs down, index fingers collapsing, wrists snapping, bracelets tingling. It seemed incredibly hip. The whole bus watched. Finally the kid staggered breathlessly onto the bus and sat behind me, tapping at the window and waving at his father, who was now standing next to Mommy, waving at his kid.

45   "Where'd you learn that handshake?" someone asked the kid.

"My father taught me," he said proudly. "He's a Black Panther."

The bus roared to life as I panicked. A Black Panther? Next to Mommy? It was my worst nightmare come true. I had no idea who the Panthers truly were. I had swallowed the media image of them completely.

The bus clanked into gear as I got up to open my window. I wanted to warn Mommy. Suppose the Black Panther wanted to kill her? The window was stuck. I tried to move to another window. A counselor grabbed me and sat me down. I said, "I have to tell my mother something."

"Write her a letter," he said.

50   I jumped into the seat of the Black Panther's son behind me—his window was open. The counselor placed me back in my seat.

"Mommy, Mommy!" I yelled at the closed window. Mommy was waving. The bus pulled away.

I shouted, "Watch out for him!" but we were too far away and my window was shut. She couldn't hear me.

I saw the Black Panther waving at his son. Mommy waved at me. Neither seemed to notice the other.

When they were out of sight, I turned to the Black Panther's son sitting behind me and punched him square in the face with my fist. The kid held his jaw and stared at me in shock as his face melted into a knot of disbelief and tears.

QUESTIONS FOR INQUIRY AND ACTION

1. McBride writes that "conflict was a part of our lives, written into our very faces, hands, and arms"; what does he mean by this statement? Where does the conflict come from, and how does McBride's mother deal with it?

2. McBride argues that his mother's model for raising her children "represented the best and worst of the immigrant mentality: hard work, no nonsense, quest for excellence, distrust of authority figures, and a deep belief in God and education." Research your own family history. Is this an accurate description of your own family's experience in America? Why or why not?

3. Do you see McBride's mother as a model of interracial relations in America or an exception? How would your parents react if you dated someone of another race?

4. Reread the Black Panthers' "Ten Point Plan." What does "Black Power" mean in the Panthers' program and in McBride's story? How are they similar, and how are they different? Why, in the story, does McBride punch the son of a Black Panther?

FATIMA MERNISSI Moonlit Nights of Laughter

Fatima Mernissi was born in Fez, Morocco, and is a professor of sociology at the Universite Mohammed V, Agdal, Rabat, Morocco. She is the author of several critical books about Islam and Muslim society, including Islam and Democracy: Fear of the Modern World *(1992) and* Beyond the Veil: Male-Female Dynamics In a Modern Muslim Society *(1975). "Moonlit Nights of Laughter" is from her autobiographical* Dreams of Trespass: Tales of a Harem Girlhood *(New York: Addison-Wesley, 1994).*

On Yasmina's farm, we never knew when we would eat. Sometimes, Yasmina only remembered at the last minute that she had to feed me, and then she would convince me that a few olives and a piece of her good bread, which she had baked at dawn, would be enough. But dining in our harem in Fez was an entirely different story. We ate at strictly set hours and never between meals.

To eat in Fez, we had to sit at our prescribed places at one of the four communal tables. The first table was for the men, the second for the important women, and the third for the children and less important women, which made us happy, because that meant that Aunt Habiba could eat with us. The last table was reserved for the domestics and anyone who had come in late, regardless of age, rank, or sex. That table was often overcrowded, and was the last chance to get anything to eat at all for those who had made the mistake of not being on time.

Eating at fixed hours was what Mother hated most about communal life. She would nag Father constantly about the possibility of breaking loose and taking our immediate family to live apart. The nationalists advocated the end of seclusion and the veil, but they did not say a word about a couple's right to split off from their larger family. In fact, most of the leaders still lived with their parents. The male nationalist movement supported the liberation of women, but had not come to grips with the idea of the elderly living by themselves, nor with couples splitting off into separate households. Neither idea seemed right, or elegant.

Mother especially disliked the idea of a fixed lunch hour. She always was the last to wake up, and liked to have a late, lavish breakfast which she prepared herself with a lot of flamboyant defiance, beneath the disapproving stare of Grandmother Lalla Mani. She would make herself scrambled eggs and *baghrir*, or fine crêpes, topped with pure honey and fresh butter, and, of course, plenty of tea. She usually ate at exactly eleven, just as Lalla Mani was about to begin her purification ritual for the noon prayer. And after that, two hours later at the communal table, Mother was often absolutely unable to eat lunch. Sometimes, she would skip it altogether, especially when she wanted to annoy Father, because to skip a meal was considered terribly rude and too openly individualistic.

5   Mother dreamed of living alone with Father and us kids. "Whoever heard of ten birds living together squashed into a single nest?" she would say. "It is not natural to live in a large group, unless your objective is to make people feel miserable." Although Father said that he was not really sure how the birds lived, he still sympathized with Mother, and felt torn between his duty towards the traditional family and his desire to make her happy. He felt guilty about breaking up the family solidarity, knowing only too well that big families in general, and harem life in particular, were fast becoming relics of the past. He even prophesied that in the next few decades, we would become like the Christians, who hardly ever visited their old parents. In fact, most of my uncles who had already broken away from the big house barely found the time to visit their mother, Lalla Mani, on Fridays after prayer anymore. "Their kids do not kiss hands either," ran the constant refrain. To make matters worse, until very recently, all my uncles had lived in our house, and had only split away when their wives' opposition to communal life had become unbearable. That is what gave Mother hope.

The first to leave the big family was Uncle Karim, Cousin Malika's father. His wife loved music and liked to sing while being accompanied by Uncle Karim, who played the lute beautifully. But he would rarely give in to his wife's desire to spend an evening singing in their salon, because his older brother Uncle Ali thought it unbecoming for a man to sing or play a musical instrument. Finally, one day, Uncle Karim's wife just took her children and went back to her father's house, saying that she had no intention of living in the communal house ever again. Uncle Karim, a cheerful fellow who had himself often felt constrained by the discipline of harem life, saw an opportunity to leave and took it, excusing his actions by saying that he preferred to give in to his wife's wishes rather than forfeit his marriage. Not long after that, all my other uncles moved out, one after the other, until only Uncle Ali and Father were left. So Father's departure would have meant the death of our large family. "As long as [my] Mother lives," he often said, "I wouldn't betray the tradition."

Yet Father loved his wife so much that he felt miserable about not giving in to her wishes and never stopped proposing compromises. One was to stock an entire cupboardful of food for her, in case she wanted to discreetly eat sometimes, apart from the rest of the family. For one of the problems in the communal house was that you could not just open a refrigerator when you were hungry and grab something to eat. In the first place, there were no refrigerators back then. More importantly, the entire idea behind the harem was that you lived according to the group's rhythm. You could not just eat when you felt like it. Lalla Radia, my uncle's wife, had the key to the pantry, and although she always asked after dinner what people wanted to eat the next day, you still had to eat whatever the group—after lengthy discussion—decided upon. If the group settled on couscous with chick-peas and raisins, then that is what you got. If you happened to hate chick-peas and raisins, you had no choice but to shut up and settle for a frugal dinner composed of a few olives and a great deal of discretion.

"What a waste of time," Mother would say. "These endless discussions about meals! Arabs would be much better off if they let each individual decide what he or she wanted to swallow. Forcing everyone to share three meals a day just complicates things. And for what sacred purpose? None of course." From there, she would go on to say that her whole life was an absurdity, that nothing made sense, while Father would say that he could not just break away. If he did, tradition would vanish: "We live in difficult times, the country is occupied by foreign armies, our culture is threatened. All we have left is these traditions." This reasoning would drive Mother nuts: "Do you think that by sticking together in this big, absurd house, we will gain the strength we need to throw the foreign armies out? And what is more important anyway, tradition or people's happiness?" That would put an abrupt end to the conversation. Father would try to caress her hand but she would take it away. "This tradition is choking me," she would whisper, tears in her eyes.

So Father kept offering compromises. He not only arranged for Mother to have her own food stock, but also brought her things he knew she liked, such as dates, nuts, almonds, honey, flour, and fancy oils. She could make all the desserts and cookies she wanted, but she was not supposed to prepare a meat dish or a major meal. That would have meant the beginning of the end of the communal arrangement. Her flamboyantly prepared individual breakfasts were enough of a slap in the face to the rest of the family. Every once in a long while, Mother *did* get away with preparing a complete lunch or a dinner, but she had to not only be discreet about it but also give it some sort of exotic overtone. Her most common ploy was to camouflage the meal as a nighttime picnic on the terrace.

10   These occasional tête-à-tête dinners on the terrace during moonlit summer nights were another peace offering that Father made to help satisfy Mother's yearning for privacy. We would be transplanted to the terrace, like nomads, with mattresses, tables, trays, and my little brother's cradle, which would be set down right in the middle of everything. Mother would be absolutely out of her mind with joy. No one else from the courtyard dared to show up, because they understood all too well that Mother was fleeing from the crowd. What she most enjoyed was trying to get Father to depart from his conventional self-controlled pose. Before long, she would start acting foolishly, like a young girl, and soon, Father would chase her all around the terrace, when she challenged him. "You can't run anymore, you have grown too old! All you're good for now is to sit and watch your

son's cradle." Father, who had been smiling up to that point, would look at her at first as if what she had just said had not affected him at all. But then his smile would vanish, and he would start chasing her all over the terrace, jumping over tea-trays and sofas. Sometimes both of them made up games which included my sister and Samir (who was the only one of the rest of the family allowed to attend our moonlit gatherings) and myself. More often, they completely forgot about the rest of the world, and we children would be sneezing all the next day because they had forgotten to put blankets on us when we had gone to sleep that night.

After these blissful evenings, Mother would be in an unusually soft and quiet mood for a whole week. Then she would tell me that what ever else I did with my life, I had to take her revenge. "I want my daughters' lives to be exciting," she would say, "very exciting and filled with one hundred percent happiness, nothing more, nothing less." I would raise my head, look at her earnestly, and ask what one hundred percent happiness meant, because I wanted her to know that I intended to do my best to achieve it. Happiness, she would explain, was when a person felt good, light, creative, content, loving and loved, and free. An unhappy person felt as if there were barriers crushing her desires and the talents she had inside. A happy woman was one who could exercise all kinds of rights, from the right to move to the right to create, compete, and challenge, and at the same time could feel loved for doing so. Part of happiness was to be loved by a man who enjoyed your strength and was proud of your talents. Happiness was also about the right to privacy, the right to retreat from the company of others and plunge into contemplative solitude. Or to sit by yourself doing nothing for a whole day, and not give excuses or feel guilty about it either. Happiness was to be with loved ones, and yet still feel that you existed as a separate being, that you were not there just to make them happy. Happiness was when there was a balance between what you gave and what you took. I then asked her how much happiness she had in her life, just to get an idea, and she said that it varied according to the days. Some days she had only five percent; others, like the evenings we spent with Father on the terrace, she had full-blown one hundred percent happiness.

Aiming at one hundred percent happiness seemed a bit overwhelming to me, as a young girl, especially since I could see how much Mother labored to sculpt her moments of happiness. How much time and energy she put into creating those wonderful moonlit evenings sitting close to Father, talking softly in his ear, her head on his shoulder! It seemed quite an accomplishment to me because she had to start working on him days ahead of time, and then she had to take care of all the logistics, like the cooking and the moving of the furniture. To invest so much stubborn effort just to achieve a few hours of happiness was impressive, and at least I knew it could be done. But how, I wondered, was I going to create such a high level of excitement for an entire lifetime? Well, if Mother thought it was possible, I should certainly give it a try.

"Times are going to get better for women now, my daughter," she would say to me. "You and your sister will get a good education, and you'll walk freely in the streets and discover the world. I want you to become independent, independent and happy. I want you to shine like moons. I want your lives to be a cascade of serene delights. One hundred percent happiness. Nothing more, nothing less." But when I asked her for more details about how to create that happiness, Mother would grow very impatient. "You have to work at it. One develops the muscles for happiness, just like for walking and breathing."

So every morning, I would sit on our threshold, contemplating the deserted courtyard and dreaming about my beautiful future, a cascade of serene delights. Hanging on to the romantic moonlit terrace evenings, challenging your beloved man to forget about his social duties, relax and act foolish and gaze at the stars while holding your hand, I thought, could be one way to go about developing muscles for happiness. Sculpting soft nights, when the sound of laughter blends with the spring breezes, could be another.

15   But those magical evenings were rare, or so they seemed. During the days, life took a much more rigid and disciplined turn. Officially, there was no jumping around or foolishness allowed in the Mernissi household—all that was confined to clandestine times and spaces, such as late afternoons in the courtyard when the men were out, or evenings on the deserted terraces.

QUESTIONS FOR INQUIRY AND ACTION

1. Mernissi's mother taught her that "happiness was to be with loved ones, and yet still feel that you existed as a separate being, that you were not there just to make them happy." In what ways does Mernissi's mother act for her own happiness, and in what ways does she act for her family's happiness? Are there conflicts between the two?

2. Mernissi centers her story on the individual family's dinner. This is an aspect of American family life that many cultural commentators have observed is fading out: we no longer sit down and eat dinner together as a family, they say. Is this true in your experience? Why is it important to eat dinner together as a family?

3. Write about one of your family's rituals or practices, especially one that varies from what appears to be mainstream practice. Do you prize that ritual and consider it important to your definition of family life? Is it a safe haven from the outside world's practices? Or are you embarrassed by it and ready to discontinue it when you create your own family?

4. Inquire into organizations that cater to various kinds of families, especially families with different cultural traditions from mainstream Americans. What specific needs do those families have?

CASE STUDY

HOW DO WE DEFINE "FAMILY VALUES"?

DAN QUAYLE Restoring Basic Values

As Vice President of the United States under President George Bush, Dan Quayle placed great emphasis on traditional family structures. He helped center "family values" in the Republican platform for Bush's reelection campaign in 1992. "Restoring Basic Values" was delivered as a speech to the Commonwealth Club of California in May, 1992.

As you may know, I've just returned from a week-long trip to Japan. I was there to commemorate the 20th anniversary of the reversion of Okinawa to Japan by the United States, an act that has made a lasting impression on the Japanese.

While I was there, Japan announced its commitment to join with the United States in assisting Eastern and Central Europe with a 400 million dollar aid package. We also announced a manufacturing technology initiative that will allow American engineers to gain experience working in Japanese businesses.

Japan and the United States are allies and partners. Though we have our differences, especially in the area of trade, our two countries—with 40 percent of the world's GNP—are committed to a global partnership in behalf of peace and economic growth.

But in the midst of all of these discussions of international affairs, I was asked many times in Japan about the recent events in Los Angeles. From the perspective of many Japanese, the ethnic diversity of our culture is a weakness compared to their homogenous society. I begged to differ with my hosts. I explained that our diversity is our strength. And I explained that the immigrants who come to our shores have made, and continue to make, vast contributions to our culture and our economy.

5 It is wrong to imply that the Los Angeles riots were an inevitable outcome of our diversified society. But the question that I tried to answer in Japan is one that needs answering here: What happened? Why? And how do we prevent it in the future?

One response has been predictable: Instead of denouncing wrongdoing, some have shown tolerance for rioters; some have enjoyed saying "I told you so;" and some have simply made excuses for what happened. All of this has been accompanied by pleas for more money.

I'll readily accept that we need to understand what happened. But I reject the idea we should tolerate or excuse it.

When I have been asked during these last weeks who caused the riots and the killing in L.A., my answer has been direct and simple: Who is to blame for the riots? The rioters are to blame. Who is to blame for the killings? The killers are to blame. Yes, I can understand how people were shocked and outraged by the verdict in the Rodney King trial. But there is simply no excuse for the mayhem that followed. To apologize or in any way to excuse what happened is wrong. It is a betrayal of all those people equally outraged and equally disadvantaged who did not loot and did not riot—and who were in many cases victims of the rioters. No matter how much you may disagree with the verdict, the riots were wrong. And if we as a society don't condemn what is wrong, how can we teach our children what is right?

But after condemning the riots, we do need to try to understand the underlying situation.

10   In a nutshell: I believe the lawless social anarchy which we saw is directly related to the breakdown of family structure, personal responsibility and social order in too many areas of our society. For the poor the situation is compounded by a welfare ethos that impedes individual efforts to move ahead in society, and hampers their ability to take advantage of the opportunities America offers.

If we don't succeed in addressing these fundamental problems, and in restoring basic values, any attempt to fix what's broken will fail. But one reason I believe we won't fail is that we have come so far in the last 25 years.

There is no question that this country has had a terrible problem with race and racism. The evil of slavery has left a long legacy. But we have faced racism squarely, and we have made progress in the past quarter century. The landmark civil rights bills of the 1960's removed legal barriers to allow full participation by blacks in the economic, social and political life of the nation. By any measure the America of 1992 is more egalitarian, more integrated, and offers more opportunities to black Americans—and all other minority group members—than the America of 1964. There is more to be done. But I think that all of us can be proud of our progress.

And let's be specific about one aspect of this progress: This country now has a black middle class that barely existed a quarter century ago. Since 1967 the median income of black two parent families has risen by 60 percent in real terms. The number of black college graduates has sky-rocketed. Black men and women have achieved real political power—black mayors head 48 of our largest cities, including Los Angeles. These are achievements.

But as we all know, there is another side to that bright landscape. During this period of progress, we have also developed a culture of poverty—some call it an underclass—that is far more violent and harder to escape than it was a generation ago.

15   The poor you always have with you, Scripture tells us. And in America we have always had poor people. But in this dynamic, prosperous nation, poverty has traditionally been a stage through which people pass on their way to joining the great middle class. And if one generation didn't get very far up the ladder—their ambitious, better-educated children would.

But the underclass seems to be a new phenomenon. It is a group whose members are dependent on welfare for very long stretches, and whose men are often drawn into lives of crime. There is far too little upward mobility, because the underclass is disconnected from the rules of American society. And these problems have, unfortunately, been particularly acute for Black Americans.

Let me share with you a few statistics on the difference between black poverty in particular in the 1960's and now.

- In 1967 68 percent of black families were headed by married couples. In 1991, only 48 percent of black families were headed by both a husband and wife.
- In 1965 the illegitimacy rate among black families was 28 percent. In 1989, 65 percent—two thirds—of all black children were born to never-married mothers.
- In 1951 9.2 percent of black youth between 16–19 were unemployed. In 1965, it was 23 percent. In 1980 it was 35 percent. By 1989, the number had declined slightly, but was still 32 percent.
- The leading cause of death of young black males today is homicide.

It would be overly simplistic to blame this social breakdown on the programs of the Great Society alone. It would be absolutely wrong to blame it on the growth and success most Americans enjoyed during the 1980's. Rather, we are in large measure reaping the whirlwind of decades of changes in social mores.

I was born in 1947, so I'm considered one of those "Baby Boomers" we keep reading about. But let's look at one unfortunate legacy of the "Boomer" generation. When we were young, it was fashionable to declare war against traditional values. Indulgence and self-gratification seemed to have no consequences. Many of our generation glamorized casual sex and drug use, evaded responsibility and trashed authority. Today the "Boomers" are middle-aged and middle class. The responsibility of having families has helped many recover traditional values. And, of course, the great majority of those in the middle class survived the turbulent legacy of the 60's and 70's. But many of the poor, with less to fall back on, did not.

20   The intergenerational poverty that troubles us so much today is predominantly a poverty of values. Our inner cites are filled with children having children; with people who have not been able to take advantage of educational opportunities; with people who are dependent on drugs or the narcotic of welfare. To be sure, many people in the ghettos struggle very hard against these tides—and sometimes win. But too many feel they have no hope and nothing to lose. This poverty is, again, fundamentally a poverty of values.

Unless we change the basic rules of society in our inner cities, we cannot expect anything else to change. We will simply get more of what we saw three weeks ago. New thinking, new ideas, new strategies are needed.

For the government, transforming underclass culture means that our policies and programs must create a different incentive system. Our policies must be premised on, and must reinforce, values such as: family, hard work, integrity and personal responsibility.

I think we can all agree that government's first obligation is to maintain order. We are a nation of laws, not looting. It has become clear that the riots were fueled by the vicious gangs that terrorize the inner cities. We are committed to breaking those gangs and restoring law and order. As James Q. Wilson has written, "Programs of economic restructuring will not work so long as gangs control the streets."

Some people say "law and order," are code words. Well, they are code words. Code words for safety, getting control of the streets, and freedom from fear. And let's not forget that, in 1990, 84 percent of the crimes committed by blacks were committed against blacks.

25   We are for law and order. If a single mother raising her children in the ghetto has to worry about drive-by shootings, drug deals, or whether her children will join gangs and die violently, her difficult task becomes impossible. We're for law and order because we can't expect children to learn in dangerous schools. We're for law and order because if property isn't protected, who will build businesses?

As one step on behalf of law and order—and on behalf of opportunity as well—the President has initiated the "Weed and Seed" program—to "weed out" criminals and "seed" neighborhoods with programs that address root causes of crime. And we have encouraged community-based policing, which gets the police on the street so they interact with citizens.

Safety is absolutely necessary. But it's not sufficient. Our urban strategy is to empower the poor by giving them control over their lives. To do that, our urban agenda includes:

- Fully funding the Home-ownership, and Opportunity for People Everywhere program. HOPE—as we call it—will help public housing residents become home-owners. Subsidized housing all too often merely made rich investors richer. Home ownership will give the poor a stake in their neighborhoods, and a chance to build equity.

- Creating enterprise zones by slashing taxes in targeted areas, including a zero capital gains tax, to spur entrepreneurship, economic development, and job creation in inner cities.

- Instituting our education strategy, AMERICA 2000, to raise academic standards and to give the poor the same choices about how and where to educate their children as rich people.

- Promoting welfare reform to remove the penalties for marriage, create incentives for saving, and give communities greater control over how the programs are administered.

These programs are empowerment programs. They are based on the same principles as the Job Training Partnership Act, which aimed to help disadvantaged young people and dislocated workers to develop their skills to give them an opportunity to get ahead. Empowering the poor will strengthen families. And right now, the failure of our families is hurting America deeply. When families fail, society fails. The anarchy and lack of structure in our inner cities are testament to how quickly civilization falls apart when the family foundation cracks. Children need love and discipline. They need mothers and fathers. A welfare check is not a husband. The state is not a father. It is from parents that children learn how to behave in society; it is from parents above all that children come to understand values and themselves as men and women, mothers and fathers.

And for those concerned about children growing up in poverty, we should know this: marriage is probably the best anti poverty program of all. Among families headed by married couples today, there is a poverty rate of 5.7 percent. But 33.4 percent of families headed by a single mother are in poverty today.

30   Nature abhors a vacuum. Where there are no mature, responsible men around to teach boys how to be good men, gangs serve in their place. In fact, gangs have become a surrogate family for much of a generation of inner-city boys. I recently visited with some former gang members in Albuquerque, New Mexico. In a private meeting, they told me why they had joined gangs. These teenage boys said that gangs gave them a sense of security. They made them feel wanted, and useful. They got support from their friends. And, they said, "It was like having a family." "Like family"—unfortunately, that says it all.

The system perpetuates itself as these young men father children whom they have no intention of caring for, by women whose welfare checks support them. Teenage girls, mired in the same hopelessness, lack sufficient motive to say no to this trap.

Answers to our problems won't be easy.

We can start by dismantling a welfare system that encourages dependency and subsidizes broken families. We can attach conditions—such as school attendance, or work—to welfare. We can limit the time a recipient gets benefits. We can stop penalizing marriage for welfare mothers. We can enforce child support payments.

Ultimately, however, marriage is a moral issue that requires cultural consensus, and the use of social sanctions. Bearing babies irresponsibly is, simply, wrong. Failing to support children one has fathered is wrong. We must be unequivocal about this.

35   It doesn't help matters when prime time TV has Murphy Brown—a character who supposedly epitomizes today's intelligent, highly paid, professional woman—mocking the importance of fathers, by bearing a child alone, and calling it just another "lifestyle choice."

I know it is not fashionable to talk about moral values, but we need to do it. Even though our cultural leaders in Hollywood, network TV, the national newspapers routinely jeer at them, I think that most of us in this room know that some things are good, and other things are wrong. Now it's time to make the discussion public.

It's time to talk again about family, hard work, integrity and personal responsibility. We cannot be embarrassed out of our belief that two parents, married to each other, are better in most cases for children than one. That honest work is better than hand-outs—or crime. That we are our brothers' keepers. That it's worth making an effort, even when the rewards aren't immediate.

So I think the time has come to renew our public commitment to our Judeo-Christian values—in our churches and synagogues, our civic organizations and our schools. We are, as our children recite each morning, "one nation under God." That's a useful framework for acknowledging a duty and an authority higher than our own pleasures and personal ambitions.

If we lived more thoroughly by these values, we would live in a better society. For the poor, renewing these values will give people the strength to help themselves by acquiring the tools to achieve self-sufficiency, a good education, job training, and property. Then they will move from permanent dependence to dignified independence.

40   Shelby Steele, in his great book, *The Content of Our Character,* writes "Personal responsibility is the brick and mortar of power. The responsible person knows that the quality of his life is something that he will have to make inside the limits of his fate. . . . The quality of his life will pretty much reflect his efforts."

I believe that the Bush Administration's empowerment agenda will help the poor gain that power, by creating opportunity, and letting people make the choices that free citizens must make.

Though our hearts have been pained by the events in Los Angeles, we should take this tragedy as an opportunity for self-examination and progress. So let the national debate roar on. I, for one, will join it. The president will lead it. The American people will participate in it. And as a result, we will become an even stronger nation.

STOP AND THINK

THE TV FAMILY

Dan Quayle's critique of the way single motherhood is represented in the TV show *Murphy Brown* assumes that viewers of such shows are affected, in this case negatively, by TV's representations of the American family. To test this idea, observe three different TV shows that depict American families; you might follow William Bennett's definition of family as a heterosexual couple with or without children, or Mary Pipher's alternative definition as a group of people who pull together their resources to help each other out. Then, answer the following questions:

1. What kind of a family is depicted in the show (e.g., an extended family, a collection of close friends)? Is this family represented positively, negatively, or ambivalently?
2. Do you find yourself comparing your family to these TV families? If so, how do you compare them? (E.g., Is one a model against which you judge the other? Are they just alternatives that you don't compare?)

continued on next page

Next, you might quantify your observations as you are watching the show by making a list of the behaviors these characters perform that define the quality of life in that family. Then, categorize these examples according to whether you think they would strengthen or weaken these families. Finally, add up the number of examples you have in each category and compare your numbers with your qualitative impression of the show's representation of family. Do the numbers suggest the family's behavior is as negative or positive as you thought?

Newspaper Editorials in Response to Quayle

Following are two newspaper editorials responding to Vice President Dan Quayle's May 19, 1992, speech to the Commonwealth Club of California.

The Seattle Times, *May 21, 1992*

Cleaning up after Vice President Dan Quayle is no easy job. While Quayle roams the hinterlands proving to Republican right-wingers that he is the true ideological conservative in the White House, President Bush and Marlin Fitzwater are left to explain Quayle's comments.

Quayle's latest speech on the causes of the Los Angeles riots placed blamed on "poverty of values." His double-barreled solution: more cops and more marriage. As he decried moral decline and the glamorization of sex by baby boomers, he searched his mind for a concrete example. . . .

Yes, of course. The very night before, Murphy Brown, the main character of a popular television show, gave birth to a baby boy in the season finale. Quayle accused Murphy of "mocking the importance of fathers by bearing a child alone, and calling it just another lifestyle choice."

The vice president evidently doesn't watch the show. The series devoted one episode to whether Murphy should get an abortion or have the child fathered by her ex-husband. She, in the words of President Bush, opted for life.

Even the administration seems embarrassed that Quayle's get-tough-with-broken-families speech conflicts with the White House's anti-choice stance. Bush has spent so much energy packing the Supreme Court with anti-abortion justices and playing to the pro-life crowd that he's stuck with his own rhetoric.

What if Murphy were not physically or financially able to care for a child alone? What if she were 17 and without job or life skills? What if she were rearing two kids in the ghetto, and accidentally became pregnant while on welfare? The men in the White House seem completely out of touch with such commonplace circumstances. Their experiences and sympathies are so limited, even a sitcom plot can tie them into knots.

Murphy Brown fans, meantime, can hardly wait for next season's first episode in which Vice President Quayle ridicules the defenseless baby Brown on national television.

The Christian Science Monitor, *May 26, 1992*

Dan Quayle's remarks last week about the TV sitcom "Murphy Brown" were a boon for pundits and comics. The implied parallel between Murphy's decision to have a child and the single motherhood experienced by poor women in South-Central L.A. was tenuous at best. Beyond that, the vice president's words about restoring "order," both in families and on city streets, were enveloped in election-year politics.

Still, his call for frank debate about moral values and their role in shaping society should not be lost in the snickers and sniping. Events ranging from the Wall Street scandals of the late '80s to the rampant looting during the Los Angeles riots raise questions about Americans' ability to distinguish between right and wrong. The moral values crystallized in the Golden Rule and the Biblical injunction to "love one another" undergird a civil, livable society. They too easily get pushed into the background at a time when self-gratification and material gain are widely glorified.

Last Friday, our Opinion pages carried an article by former Harvard president Derek Bok calling for a social philosophy for the '90s that moves beyond self-serving individualism. He argued that political leaders have a responsibility to direct the country toward a commitment to public service and helping others.

Mr. Quayle's plea for "family values" and President Bush's praise for "a thousand points of light" volunteerism touch on such commitment. But strong families and civic-mindedness won't be fostered by words perceived as little more than political tactics. Attacks on the welfare system's incentives against marriage, for instance, have electoral appeal. But how does one restructure the system in a way that encourages employment and family formation? Can such reform work unless it's teamed with stronger public education, job-training programs, and family-support services?

If the Bush-Quayle ticket persists in making campaign themes out of welfare's impact on family values and out of the decline of moral values generally, all the better. Bill Clinton and Ross Perot, if he runs, should seize the chance to move these subjects beyond catch phrases to useful discussion.

Writing Style

WRITING EDITORIALS AND OPINION PIECES

The purposes of editorials and opinion pieces often vary; a writer may wish to call attention to a public concern, express a political viewpoint, call readers to support or reject a cause, or even entertain with lighthearted commentary on people, events, or issues. Yet most editorials have one point in common: They try to start or stimulate public discussion. Examine the two editorials written in response to Dan Quayle's May 19, 1992, speech to the Commonwealth Club of California, one from *The Seattle Times,* the other from *The Christian Science Monitor.* As you read them, write down those qualities you think make them successful. Then, compare them with the following suggestions:

- *Stay close to the latest news or events.* Editorials usually follow public conversation closely. Writers can usually get their views published so long as

continued on next page

the public is still discussing the issue, but writers may want to time their advice to best achieve their purposes. For example, someone wanting to write an editorial discouraging legislation that restricts the ownership of handguns would want to publish his or her editorial shortly before legislators are scheduled to meet to discuss it.

- *Maintain a clear focus, good organization, and specific details.* Editorials and opinion pieces are usually several paragraphs; consequently, you may want to focus on one or two points so you can support those points with good evidence. An easy-to-follow structure with plenty of transitions also helps readers navigate your arguments easily.

- *Include background information if the issue is new or unknown.* Like a news article, an editorial and opinion piece may need to inform readers what the issue is, who is involved, and why they should care. However, because these works are short, you should stick to the minimum details needed to communicate your points.

- *Hook the readers and keep their interest.* Because editorials and opinion pieces must compete with many other works for the readers' attention, they usually lure the reader in with a strong, even controversial tone or with a clever organizational strategy (e.g., the writer turns an impersonal issue like globalization into something personal by organizing the work around the life of a person affected by the global economy). You can keep readers' interest by including anecdotes or dramatic quotations in those places, like the middle, where your readers' attention may waver.

- *Engage readers' emotions when appropriate.* Appeal to readers' emotions for those issues that invite emotional responses. You might shock them with graphic details or statistics; you might inspire them with the stories of individuals. Make sure the emotional appeals are appropriate and natural; in other words, don't use them to discourage readers' critical thinking.

ELLEN WILLIS Why I'm Not "Pro-Family"

Ellen Willis is a writer and editor who contributes frequently to periodicals such as the Village Voice, Rolling Stone, *and* Ms.. *She is also the author of several books of essays including* Beginning to See the Light: Sex, Hope, and Rock-and-Roll *(1992) and* Don't Think, Smile!: Notes on a Decade of Denial *(1999). "Why I'm Not 'Pro-Family'" appeared in* Glamour *(October 1994).*

In 1992, "family values" bombed in Houston. Right-wingers at the Republican convention, sneering at career women and single mothers, turned voters off. Now the Democrats are in power—yet ironically, the family issue has reemerged, more strongly than ever. Last year, New York's influential Democratic senator, Daniel Patrick Moynihan, suggested that in relaxing the stigma against unmarried childbearing, we had laid the groundwork for the burgeoning crime rate. Then *The Atlantic* published a cover story provocatively titled: "Dan Quayle Was Right." Its author, social historian Barbara Dafoe Whitehead, invoked recent research to argue that high rates of divorce and single parenthood hurt children and underlie "many of our most vexing social problems."

The article hit a nerve. It provoked an outpouring of mail, was condensed for *Reader's Digest* and won an award from the National Women's Political Caucus. Commentators both conservative and liberal praised it in newspapers across the country. Together, Moynihan's and Whitehead's salvos launched a national obsession with "the decline of the family." President Clinton joined the bandwagon: "For 30 years," he declared in his State of the Union message, "family life in America has been breaking down."

The new advocates of the family seem more sympathetic to women than their right-wing precursors. They know women are in the workforce to stay; they are careful to talk about the time pressures faced by "parents"—not "mothers"— with jobs, and they put an unaccustomed emphasis on men's family obligations, such as contributing their fair share of child support. Some advocate liberal reforms ranging from antipoverty programs to federally funded child care to abortion rights, arguing that such measures are pro-family because they help existing families. (A recent Planned Parenthood fundraising letter proclaims, "Pro-choice is pro-family.")

I'm all for reforms that make it easier to give children the care they need, and I'm certainly in favor of men's equal participation in childrearing. My quarrel is with the underlying terms of the discussion, especially the assumption that anyone who cares about children must be "pro-family." I grew up in the fifties, in a family with two committed parents—the kind of home the profamilists idealize. I had security; I had love. Yet like many of my peers, especially women, I saw conventional family life as far from ideal and had no desire to replicate it. It wasn't only that I didn't want to be a housewife like my mother; I felt that family life promoted self-abnegation and social conformity while stifling eroticism and spontaneity. I thought the nuclear family structure was isolating, and that within it, combining childrearing with other work would be exhausting, even if both parents shared the load—impressions I can now confirm from experience.

5   To me the alternative that made the most sense was not single parenthood— we needed *more* parents, not fewer, to share the daily responsibilities of childrearing and homemaking. In the seventies, a number of people I knew were bringing up children in communal households, and I imagined someday doing the same. But by the time my companion and I had a child ten years ago, those experiments and the counterculture that supported them were long gone.

From my perspective, the new champions of the family are much like the old. They never consider whether the current instability of families might signal that an age-old institution is failing to meet modern needs and ought to be reexamined. The idea that there could be other possible structures for domestic life and childrearing has been excluded from the conversation—so much so that cranks like me who persist in broaching the subject are used to getting the sort of tactful and embarrassed reaction accorded, say, people who claim to have been kidnapped by aliens. And the assumption that marriage is the self-evident solution to single parents' problems leads to impatience and hostility toward anyone who can't or won't get with the nuclear-family program.

Consider the hottest topic on the pro-family agenda: the prevalence of unwed motherhood in poor black communities. For Moynihan and other welfare reformers, the central cause of inner-city poverty and crime is not urban economic collapse, unemployment or racism, but fatherless households. Which means the solution is to bring back the stigma of "illegitimacy" and restrict or eliminate welfare for single mothers. Clinton has proposed requiring welfare recipients to leave the rolls after two years and look for work, with temporary government jobs as a backup (where permanent jobs are supposed to come from, in an economy where massive layoffs and corporate shrinkage are the order of the day, is not explained).

As the reformers profess their concern for poor children (while proposing to make them even poorer), the work ethic (as jobs for the unskilled get ever scarcer) and the overburdened taxpayer, it's easy to miss their underlying message—that women have gotten out of hand. They may pay lip service to the idea that men too should be held responsible for the babies they father. But in practice there is no way to force poor, unemployed men to support their children or to stigmatize men as well as women for having babies out of wedlock. This is, after all, still a culture that regards pregnancy as the woman's problem and childrearing as the woman's job. And so, predictably, women are the chief targets of the reformers' punitive policies and rhetoric. It's women who will lose benefits; women who stand accused of deliberately having babies as a meal ticket; women who are (as usual) charged with the social failures of their sons. Given the paucity of decently paying jobs available to poor women or the men they're likely to be involved with, demanding that they not have children unless they have jobs or husbands to support them is tantamount to demanding that they not have children at all. (Note the logic: Motherhood is honorable work if supported by a man but parasitic self-indulgence if supported by the public.) Put that demand together with laws restricting abortion for poor women and teenagers, and the clear suggestion is that they shouldn't have sex either.

While this brand of misogyny is specifically aimed at poor black women, it would be a mistake to think the rest of us are off the hook. For one thing (as Whitehead and other pro-familists are quick to remind us), it's all too easy in this age of high divorce and unemployment rates for a woman who imagined herself securely middle-class to unexpectedly become an impoverished single mother. Anyway, there is a thin line between fear and loathing of welfare mothers and moral distaste for unmarried mothers per se. Secretary of Health and Human Services Donna Shalala, a feminist and one of the more liberal members of the Clinton cabinet, has said, "I don't like to put this in moral terms, but I do believe that having children out of wedlock is just wrong." The language the welfare reformers use—the vocabulary of *stigma* and *illegitimacy*—unnervingly recalls the repressive moral climate of my own teenage years.

10   I can't listen to harangues about illegitimacy without getting posttraumatic flashbacks. Let's be clear about what the old stigma meant: a vicious double standard of sexual morality for men and women; the hobbling of female sexuality with shame, guilt and inhibition; panic over dislodged diaphragms and late periods; couples trapped into marriages one or both never wanted; pregnant girls barred from school and hidden in homes for unwed mothers; enormous pressure on women to get married early and not be too picky about it.

Is it silly to worry that in the post–*Roe v. Wade,* post-Pill nineties some version of fifties morality could reassert itself? I don't think so. Activists with a moral cause can be very persuasive. Who would have imagined a few years ago that there would be a public debate about restricting cigarettes as an addictive drug? Abortion may still be legal, but its opponents have done a good job of bringing back its stigma (ironically, this is one reason a lot of pregnant teenagers decide to give birth).

Many pro-familists, above all those who call themselves communitarians, are openly nostalgic for a sterner moral order. They argue that we have become a society too focused on rights instead of duties, on personal freedom and happiness instead of sacrifice for the common good. If the welfare reformers appeal to people's self-righteousness, the communitarians tap an equally potent emotion—guilt. In our concern for our own fulfillment, they argue, we are doing irreparable harm to our children.

Whitehead's *Atlantic* article cites psychologist Judith Wallerstein and other researchers to support her contention that while adults have benefited from the freedom to divorce and procreate outside marriage, children have suffered. Children in single-parent families, Whitehead warns, are not only at great risk of being poor but are more likely to have emotional and behavioral problems, drop out of school, abuse drugs. She calls on Americans to recognize that our experiment with greater freedom has failed and to "act to overcome the legacy of family disruption."

I don't doubt that the fragility of today's family life is hard on kids. It doesn't take a social scientist to figure out that a lone parent is more vulnerable than two to a host of pressures, or that children whose familial world has just collapsed need support that their parents, depleted by the struggle to get their own lives in order, may not be able to give. But Whitehead's response, and that of communitarians generally, amounts to lecturing parents to pull up their socks, stop being selfish, and do their duty. This moralistic approach does not further a discussion of what to do when adults' need for satisfying relationships conflicts with children's need for stability. It merely stops the conversation.

15   Women, of course, are particularly susceptible to guilt mongering: If children are being neglected, if marriages are failing, whose fault can it be but ours? And come on now, who is that "parent" whose career is really interfering with family life? (Hint: It's the one who gets paid less.) While the children Judith Wallerstein interviewed were clearly miserable about their parents' breakups, she made it equally clear that the parents weren't self-indulgent monsters, only people who could no longer stand the emotional deadness of their lives. Are we prepared to say that it's too bad, but their lives simply don't matter?

This is the message I get from David Blankenhorn, coeditor of a pro-family anthology and newsletter, who exhorts us to "analyze the family *primarily* through the eyes of children" (my emphasis). I think this idea is profoundly wrongheaded. Certainly we need to take children seriously, which means empathizing with their relatively powerless perspective and never unthinkingly shifting our burdens to their weaker backs. On the other hand, children are more narcissistic than most adults ever dream of being—if my daughter had her way, I'd never leave the house. They too have to learn that other people's needs and feelings must be taken into account.

Besides, children are the next generation's adults. There's something tragic about the idea that parents should sacrifice their own happiness for the sake of children who will grow up to sacrifice in turn (in my generation, that prospect inspired pop lyrics like, "Hope I die before I get old"). Instead of preaching sacrifice, we should be asking what it is about our social structure that puts adults and children at such terrible odds, and how we might change this. Faced with a shortage of food, would we decide parents have to starve so their kids can eat— or try to figure out how to increase food production?

Intelligent social policy on family issues has to start with a deeper understanding of why marriage and the two-parent family are in trouble: not because people are more selfish than they used to be but because of basic—and basically desirable—changes in our culture. For most of history, marriage has not been primarily a moral or an emotional commitment but an economic and social contract. Men supported women and children and had unquestioned authority as head of the household. Women took care of home, children, and men's personal and sexual needs. Now that undemocratic contract, on which an entire social order rested, is all but dead. Jobs and government benefits, along with liberalized sexual mores, allow women and their children to survive (if often meagerly) outside marriage; as a result, women expect more of marriage and are less willing to put up with unsatisfying or unequal relationships. For men, on the other hand, traditional incentives to marry and stay married have eroded.

What's left when the old contract is gone is the desire for love, sexual passion, intimate companionship. But those desires are notoriously inadequate as a basis for domestic stability. Human emotions are unpredictable. People change. And in the absence of the social compulsion exerted by that contract, moral platitudes about sacrifice count for little. Nor is it possible to bring back the compulsion without restoring inequality as well. Restrict divorce? Men who want out will still abandon their families as they did in the past; it's women with young children and less earning power who are likely to be trapped. Punish single parenthood? Women will bear the brunt.

20   The dogmatic insistence that only the two-parent family can properly provide for children is a self-fulfilling prophecy. As even some pro-familists recognize, the larger society must begin to play an active part in meeting the economic and social needs the family once fulfilled. This means, first of all, making a collective commitment to the adequate support of every child. Beyond that, it means opening our minds to the possibility of new forms of community, in which children have close ties with a *number* of adults and therefore a stable home base that does not totally depend either on one vulnerable parent or on one couple's emotional and sexual bond.

Of course, no social structure can guarantee permanence: In earlier eras, families were regularly broken up by death, war and abandonment. Yet a group that forms for the specific purpose of cooperative child-rearing might actually inspire more long-term loyalty than marriage, which is supposed to provide emotional and sexual fulfillment but often does not. The practical support and help parents would gain from such an arrangement—together with the greater freedom to pursue their own personal lives—would be a strong incentive for staying in it, and the inevitable conflicts and incompatibilities among the group members would be easier to tolerate than the intense deprivation of an unhappy marriage.

It's time, in other words, to think about what has so long been unthinkable, to replace reflexive dismissiveness with questions. What, for instance, can we learn from the kibbutz—how might some of its principles be adapted to Americans' very different circumstances? What worked and didn't work about the communal experiments of the sixties and seventies? What about more recent projects, like groups of old people moving in together to avoid going to nursing homes? Or the "co-housing" movement of people who are buying land in the suburbs or city apartment buildings and dividing the space between private dwellings and communal facilities such as dining rooms and child-care centers?

I'm not suggesting that there's anything like an immediate practical solution to our present family crisis. What we can do, though, is stop insisting on false solutions that scapegoat women and oversimplify the issues. Perhaps then a real discussion—worthy of Americans' inventiveness and enduring attraction to frontiers—will have a chance to begin.

JAMES CARVILLE Daddies Matter:
A Long Overdue Chat on the Family

James Carville was the chief strategist for Bill Clinton's 1991–92 presidential campaign. His strategizing is showcased in the documentary film The War Room, *by D. A. Pennebaker and Chris Hegedus. With his wife, Mary Matalin (political director of George Bush's 1991–92 presidential re-election campaign), and Peter Knobler, he wrote* All's Fair: Love, War, and Running for President *(1994). His most recent book is* Stickin': The Case for Loyalty *(2000). "Daddies Matter" is a chapter from his book* We're Right, They're Wrong: A Handbook for Spirited Progressives *(New York: Simon & Schuster, 1996).*

Every family has to sit down from time to time and discuss sensitive subjects. My family does it. I'm sure yours does, too. It's like most things in life: The longer you avoid dealing with something, the more painful it is when the day of reckoning arrives.

The sensitive subject many of us in the Democratic family have avoided for too long is—you guessed it—the family. As some Republicans are very quick and correct to point out, the single biggest social problem we have in America is the breakdown of families. This is not an original conclusion on their part, of course. The person to whom we owe the greatest debt of thanks in this area is Sen. Daniel Patrick Moynihan, the scholarly liberal from New York who first sounded the alarm back in the mid-1960s. But fairness requires that I hand out some credit to Republicans, too–people like Bill Bennett and even Dan Quayle. Like Moynihan, they took all kinds of criticism, too much of it from good Democrats.

By now the weight of evidence in their favor is overwhelming. Without a hint of the usual academic hemming and hawing, the research shows conclusively that there is no substitute for stable, two-parent families. And believe me, when I talk about the research, I'm not referring to a bunch of right-wing pseudoscience. I'm referring to rock-solid research done by experts of all political persuasions— and, yes, that includes a large helping of liberal Democrats.

I suppose we can choose to ignore this consensus and pretend that having so many kids growing up without their daddies has no social consequences. But let's get real. At this point, taking that approach would be no better than pretending that smoking doesn't cause cancer. Sure, plenty of kids from single-parent families turn out just fine. And some smokers run marathons and live to be ninety years old. But does that mean that growing up without a daddy or smoking a pack a day isn't harmful to most people? Of course not. The cause and effect relationships here are simply beyond dispute.

5   And please don't look at this as an issue that's confined to lower-income people caught in a "cycle of dependency." We need to face up to the fact that it just isn't an "us" versus "them" issue. It is an issue that touches every corner of society. We need to find ways to strengthen *all* our families. Studies by superstar researchers like Princeton's Sara McLanahan show that middle- and upper-class kids whose parents are divorced can be hurt just as bad as inner-city kids who never even knew their daddies. And if you want anecdotal evidence, go ask anyone who teaches kids, from nursery school on up. They'll tell you

that it doesn't take too long to see whether any given kid from any given neighborhood or background comes from a one- or two-parent home. It's pretty obvious.

Our party shouldn't just be talking about this subject. We should be out there on some mountain screaming about it! We simply cannot prosper as a nation when we've got so many problems in our homes.

Why have we avoided talking about single parents and the importance of daddies? Well, we're a party that doesn't like preaching to people—you know, live and let live. But by letting the Republicans do most of the talking, we have let them own the issue. We have let them use "family values" as a way of bashing gays, working women, non-Christians, and the poor. We have let them use it as a way of tearing us apart instead of bringing our families closer together. And the whole Democratic Party has paid a steep price. We have all been caught on the receiving end of an uninterrupted barrage of silly-ass "family values" attacks.

If you think "silly-ass" is too strong, let me remind you what some of these attacks have looked like. Pat Robertson says this country's "ruinous moral decay and social breakdown" was caused by "a thirty-year war that the radical Left has waged against the traditional family."[1] Newt Gingrich runs around telling people that America's social decay is the result of "a long pattern of counter-culture belief . . . deep in the Democratic Party" that has "under-valued the family."[2]

It gets worse. Gingrich suggested to the nation that Susan Smith drowned her kids in a South Carolina lake because Democrats were in control of Congress. (That, of course, was before he realized that Susan Smith's stepfather, a local Republican official and a member of the advisory board of the Christian Coalition, molested her on the same night the guy was nailing up Pat Robertson for President posters.)

10   The biggest victims of this onslaught have been the President and the First Lady. Holding up the banner of family values, the right-wingers have launched never-ending personal attacks on the President and his family. They have called the President and First Lady "counterculture McGoverniks."[3] And, of course, they have tried to turn out the bigot vote by calling the First Lady a "radical feminist"[4] who likens "marriage to slavery."[5]

---

[1] Pat Robertson, Christian Coalition fund-raising letter, May 1995.

[2] Frank Rich, "Gingrich Family Values," New York Times, May 14, 1995.

[3] Newt Gingrich, quoted in Dale Russakoff, "Gingrich Lobs a Few More Bombs," Washington Post, Nov. 10, 1994.

[4] Patrick Buchanan, quoted in Rupert Cornwell, "Bush Camp Perfects Battle Plan," Independent, Aug. 19, 1992.

[5] Rich Bond, quoted in Gwen Ifill, "The Democrats; Clinton Shrugs Off Republican Attacks On His Wife's Work," New York Times, Aug. 13, 1992.

The point is not only that the attacks on the party and the First Family have been utterly false, malicious, undignified, and down-right unpatriotic. It is that they have been completely, inexcusably hypocritical.

I've had it. I cannot turn the other cheek. I've gotten both of them slapped so many times I ain't got nothing left to turn. It's time for a new approach. It's time for us to start giving the American people a peek inside the Republicans' glass house.

You see, the guiding spirits of the Republican Party—folks who are mighty quick to accuse the Democratic Party of destroying the American family and to preach about the value of tossing single mothers out into the streets—have not exactly been models of family virtue. Among many other things, far too many of them have left young kids behind after divorcing their wives.

The number-one family-values hypocrite who ever lived on the planet earth is Newt Gingrich. From now on, every time I hear him single out single mothers without saying a word about cut-and-run daddies, I will remind everyone that Gingrich left his first wife and his two teenage children. Every time he says that "any male who does not take care of his children is a bum,"[6] as he did in his most recent book, I will remind everyone that his first wife had to take him to court because he refused to provide adequate child support and that his church had to take up a collection to help his kids. Every time I hear him spout off about the President's marriage, I will remind everyone that the Speaker of the House of Representatives tried to get a divorce settlement out of his wife while she was lying in the hospital with cancer.

Let's do a study in contrasts. When the President and his wife had a difficult time in their marriage, they made a courageous decision: they decided to work through it. They talked openly about their problems and decided to keep the family together. As a result, Bill Clinton did not abandon his daughter. Chelsea Clinton comes home in the afternoon and gets help on her schoolwork from her daddy. When she goes out on Saturday nights, her daddy waits up for her. Chelsea Clinton is growing up in a loving, nurturing, two-parent family.

Newt Gingrich and a number of the Republican Party's other leaders talked the talk, all right. But when it came time for them to walk the walk, they walked right the hell out of their children's lives. Am I the only one who believes that a better example for the nation is a couple that has trouble and decides to stick together and raise their child together?

Before I end this chapter, I want you to know that I firmly believe that Democrats can take up the cause of the family and do it in a very positive way. I know that seems strange right now, when all we've heard so far is a message of hate from the right-wingers and when I've been pushing us to go into attack mode ourselves. But it is possible to bring up the topic of the family and make this a discussion

---

[6]*Newt Gingrich,* To Renew America *(New York: HarperCollins, 1995), p. 78.*

that includes the rich, the poor, Christians, Jews, Muslims, blacks, whites, reds, yellows, and anyone else who wants to participate.

Even if the right-wingers are still cut there polarizing people with their attacks, and even if we have to spend some of our time exposing their hypocrisy in an aggressive way, we can lend a voice of sanity to this issue. We can calmly explain why all the talk of personal responsibility doesn't go very far if we are intent on kicking away the very props that families desperately need in order to make ends meet. I'm talking about funding for education. I'm talking about help with health care and child care. I'm talking about tax credits for working families struggling near the poverty line. I'm talking about a minimum wage that would allow a daddy or a mommy to support a child.

Labor Secretary Reich summed it up better than anyone:

> We honor family values every time we create a job. We honor family values every time children have a safe place to go when their parents are at work. We honor family values every time we secure a working person's pension. We honor family values every time we teach a child to learn. We honor family values every time we move a young mother from welfare to work, or help a worker get better skills, or help someone who has lost a job to find a new one.[7]

Family values is about lending a helping hand, not a swinging foot, to those who are down. It is about paychecks. It is about security. It is about hope.

And, yes, it does involve preaching about morals. But we've had more than enough religion of division. Let's tone down on the fire and brimstone and pump up the compassion and support. Again, there is a positive way to do this. We should have figured that out long ago.

QUESTIONS FOR INQUIRY AND ACTION

1. List the values your family has taught you. Write an essay using several short narratives that shows readers how you were taught these values. Use your essay to answer the larger question: Does the type of family we live in influence the kind of values we are taught?

2. Interview individuals of another generation, like your grandparents, on their views about family. Write an essay comparing and contrasting your views with theirs. Are their views better or worse for promoting good citizenship than your own?

3. Find several different magazine advertisements depicting modern families. Report to your class on the composition of these families, their interactions with one another, and so on. What products are these families used to sell? Are the products associated with a particular kind of family life? By implication, are the advertisers trying to sell particular visions of the family?

---

[7] *Robert Reich, remarks before the National Baptist Convention, San Diego, Cal., June 21, 1995.*

4. Do you think Dan Quayle is right about crime and delinquency being linked to dysfunctional families? Write an essay critiquing or supporting Quayle's views on the nature and function of American families.

5. Throughout the chapter we see examples of families and society shaping one another. Write an essay that examines how social forces like your community, family income, religious affiliations, cultural background, and significant historical events have all shaped, and been shaped by, your family.

CHAPTER 8

The Higher Education Community

The university is the only institution in Western society whose
business it is to search for and transmit truth regardless of all
competing or conflicting pressures and demands; pressures for
immediate usefulness, for social approval, pressures to serve the
special interests of government, a class, a professional group, a race,
a faith, even a nation.

Henry Steele Commager

GETTING STARTED: Exploring Your Campus

To get the most out of your college experience, explore the social, professional
and academic resources available to you as a student. To answer the following
questions, use a variety of research strategies including telephone interviews,
personal observation, and library research. Depending on the size of your college,
you may want to do this exercise individually or in groups.

- What official and unofficial student groups are available?
- What student political groups are active on campus?
- Where can you go to experience the arts?
- Where can you go to play a sport?
- Where can you go to conduct different types of research?
- What career-planning resources are available?
- Where can you go to meet other students?
- Where can you go to worship or learn about different religions?
- What groups are available to get involved in social issues?
- What resources are available to get involved in the local
  community?

After you have compiled a list of available resources, meet as a class to
answer the following questions:

1. Which of these groups are most prominent on campus? What resources are most used? What does the prominence of these groups and resources say about your college?

2. Based on group participation and the use of school resources, do students at your college emphasize the school's social, professional, or academic qualities? Do students balance these qualities in healthy ways?

In the above quote, Henry Steele Commager represents colleges as ivy towers, resistant to the challenges of industry, public opinion, and government. A brief tour of any campus, however, would show that colleges and the communities in which they reside are intertwined. Changes in the larger society do affect how colleges operate. The growing numbers of nontraditional and international students, the emergence of private distance education providers, and increased public scrutiny of college programs are affecting higher education communities.

The fact that these communities are not recreated every time the social or political landscape changes testifies to the enduring appeal of their vision. In Thomas Jefferson's "Plan for Public Education in Virginia" and in the mission statements of colleges and universities across the country we find the same drive for knowledge, justice, beauty, and wisdom. We find these drives expressed not just in the classrooms, but in many aspects of a college's social life. Higher education communities offer students a wonderful and unique opportunity to pause and reflect on themselves and their world; they also offer students the resources and expertise to get involved in other communities.

The case study in this chapter explores the tensions between colleges and larger communities and between academics and sports. The academic cheating scandal at the University of Minnesota pushed students, educators, athletes, administrators, and citizens to reflect on the place of sports within a higher education community. It also pushed people to reexamine the value of sports in academic institutions and the influence of big money on college athletics programs.

ARTHUR LEVINE AND JEANETTE S. CURETON Collegiate Life: An Obituary

Arthur Levine is president and professor of education at Columbia University's Teachers College. Jeanette S. Cureton is an independent academic researcher, formerly at the Harvard Graduate School of Education. Together they have produced a number of works on education, including the book When Hope and Fear Collide: A Portrait of Today's College Student *(1998). "Collegiate Life: An Obituary" is an excerpt from that book; it originally appeared in the magazine* Change *(May–June 1998).*

In 1858, John Henry Cardinal Newman wrote *The Idea of a University.* His ideal was a residential community of students and teachers devoted to the intellect. To him, a college was "an alma mater, knowing her children one by one, not a foundry, or a mint, or a treadmill." Given a choice between an institution that dispensed with "residence and tutorial superintendence and gave its degrees to any person who passed an examination in a wide range of subjects" or "a university which. . . merely brought a number of young men together for three or four years," he chose the latter.

Newman's ideal was so appealing that it has been embraced regularly over the years by higher education luminaries from Robert Hutchins and Paul Goodman to Alexander Meiklejohn and Mortimer Adler. Belief in it remains a staple of nearly every college curriculum committee in the country.

But that ideal is moribund today. Except for a relatively small number of residential liberal arts colleges, institutions of higher education and their students are moving away from it at an accelerating pace. The notion of a living-learning community is dead or dying on most campuses today.

This is a principal finding of several studies we conducted between 1992 and 1997, which involved our surveying a representative sample of 9,100 undergraduate students and 270 chief student affairs officers, as well as holding focus groups on 28 campuses. The details of the studies can be found [at the end of this article], along with information about earlier surveys undertaken by Arthur Levine for the Carnegie Council on Policy Studies in Higher Education, which we use for the sake of comparison. Unless otherwise indicated, all findings we report in this article come from the surveys outlined. While much of this article focuses on students of traditional age, the current student generation is, in fact, multigenerational.

Demographics

5   A major reason for the changes we describe is simply demographic. In comparison with their counterparts of the 1960s and 1970s, undergraduates today are more racially diverse and, on average, considerably older. In fact, since 1980, the lion's share of college enrollment growth has come from students who might be described as nontraditional. By 1993, 24 percent of all college students were

working full-time, according to our Undergraduate Survey; at two-year colleges, this figure had reached 39 percent.

By 1995, 44 percent of all college students were over 25 years old; 54 percent were working; 56 percent were female; and 43 percent were attending part-time. Currently, fewer than one in six of all undergraduates fit the traditional stereotype of the American college student attending full-time, being 18 to 22 years of age, and living on campus (see U.S. Department of Education, in Resources).

What this means is that higher education is not as central to the lives of today's undergraduates as it was to previous generations. Increasingly, college is just one of a multiplicity of activities in which they are engaged every day. For many, it is not even the most important of these activities; work and family often overshadow it.

As a consequence, older, part-time, and working students—especially those with children—often told us in our surveys that they wanted a different type of relationship with their colleges from the one undergraduates historically have had. They preferred a relationship like those they already enjoyed with their bank, the telephone company, and the supermarket.

What Students Want

Think about what you want from your bank. We know what we want: an ATM on every corner. And when we get to the ATM, we want there to be no line. We also would like a parking spot right in front of the ATM, and to have our checks deposited the moment they arrive at the bank, or perhaps the day before! And we want no mistakes in processing—unless they are in our favor. We also know what we do not want from our banks. We do not want them to provide us with softball leagues, religious counseling, or health services. We can arrange all of these things for ourselves and don't wish to pay extra fees for the bank to offer them.

10   Students are asking roughly the same thing from their colleges. They want their colleges to be nearby and to operate at the hours most useful to them—preferably around the clock. They want convenience: easy, accessible parking (at the classroom door would not be bad); no lines; and a polite, helpful, efficient staff. They also want high-quality education but are eager for low costs. For the most part, they are willing to comparison shop, and they place a premium on time and money. They do not want to pay for activities and programs they do not use.

In short, students increasingly are bringing to higher education exactly the same consumer expectations they have for every other commercial establishment with which they deal. Their focus is on convenience, quality, service, and cost.

They believe that since they are paying for their education, faculty should give them the education they want; they make larger demands on faculty than past students ever have. They are also the target audience for alternatives to traditional higher education. They are likely to be drawn to distance education, which offers the convenience of instruction at home or the office. They are prime candidates for stripped-down versions of college, located in the suburbs and business districts of our cities, that offer low-cost instruction made possible by heavy faculty teaching loads, mostly part-time faculties, limited selections of majors, and few electives. Proprietary institutions of this type are springing up around the country.

On campus, students are behaving like consumers, too. More than nine out of 10 chief student affairs officers told us in last year's Student Affairs Survey that student power in college governance has increased during the 1990s (or at least has remained the same), but that undergraduates are less interested in being involved in campus governance than in the past.

A small minority of undergraduates continue to want voting power or control over admissions decisions, faculty appointments, bachelor's degree requirements, and the content of courses; however, a decreasing percentage desire similar roles in residential regulations and undergraduate discipline, areas in which students would seem most likely to want control. Overall, the proportion of students who want voting or controlling roles in institutional governance is at its lowest level in a quarter century, according to comparisons between our 1993 Undergraduate Survey and the 1969 and 1976 Carnegie Council surveys.

15   This is precisely the same attitude most of us hold with regard to the commercial enterprises we patronize. We don't want to be bothered with running the bank or the supermarket; we simply want them to do their jobs and do them well—to give us what we need without hassles or headaches. That is, help the consumers and don't get in their way. Students today are saying precisely the same things about their colleges.

Social Life

From a personal perspective, students are coming to college overwhelmed and more damaged than in the past. Chief student affairs officers in 1997 reported rises in eating disorders (on 58 percent of campuses), classroom disruption (on 44 percent), drug abuse (on 42 percent), alcohol abuse (on 35 percent), gambling (on 25 percent), and suicide attempts (on 23 percent).

As a consequence, academic institutions are being forced to expand their psychological counseling services. Three out of five colleges and universities reported last year that the use of counseling services had increased. Not only are counselors seeing students in record numbers, but the severity of the students' problems and the length of time needed to treat them are greater than in the past.

Students tell us they are frightened. They're afraid of deteriorating social and environmental conditions, international conflicts and terrorism, multiculturalism and their personal relationships, financing their education and getting jobs, and the future they will face. Nearly one-third of all college freshmen (30 percent) grew up with one or no parent (see Sax et al., in Resources). As one dean of students we talked with concluded, "Students expect the [college] community to respond to their needs—to make right their personal problems and those of society at large."

The effect of these accumulated fears and hurts is to divide students and isolate them from one another. Students also fear intimacy in relationships; withdrawal is easier and less dangerous than engagement.

20   Traditional dating is largely dead on college campuses. At institutions all over
the country, students told us, in the words of a University of Colorado undergraduate, "There is no such thing as dating here." Two-person dating has been
replaced by group dating, in which men and women travel in unpartnered packs.
It's a practice that provides protection from deeper involvement and intimacy
for a generation that regularly told us in focus group interviews that they had never
witnessed a successful adult romantic relationship. Romantic relationships are seen
as a burden, as a drag or potential anchor in a difficult world. Yet sexual relationships have not declined, even in the age of AIDS. Student descriptions of sexual activity are devoid of emotional content; they use words such as "scoping,"
"clocking," "hooking," "scamming," "scrumping," "mashing," and "shacking"
to describe intimate relations.

        In general, with increasing pressures on students, collegiate social life occu-
pies a smaller part of their lives. In the words of an undergraduate at the University
of the District of Columbia, "Life is just work, school, and home." In fact, one-
fifth of those queried on our campus site visits (21 percent) defined their social
lives in terms of studying; for another 11 percent, sleeping was all they cared
about. When we asked students at the University of Colorado for the best adjective to describe this generation, the most common choice was "tired."

        But not all of the retreat from social life is time-based. Chief student affairs
officers describe students as loners more often now than in the past. Requests
for single rooms in residence halls have skyrocketed. The thought of having a
roommate is less appealing than it once was.

        Similarly, group activities that once connected students on college campuses
are losing their appeal and are becoming more individualized. For instance, the
venue for television watching has moved from the lounge to the dorm room. Film
viewing has shifted from the theater to the home VCR. With student rooms a virtual menagerie of electronic and food-preparation equipment, students are living their lives in ways that allow them to avoid venturing out if they so choose.

Student Organizational Mitosis

None of this is to say that collegiate social life is dead, but its profile and location have changed. On campus, there is probably a greater diversity of activities
available than ever before, but each activity—in the words of the chief student
affairs officer of the University of Southern Mississippi—"appeals to smaller pockets of students."

25   This is, in many respects, the consequence of student organizational mitosis
and the proliferation of the divides between undergraduates. For instance, the
business club on one college campus divided into more than a dozen groups—
including women's; black; Hispanic; gay, lesbian, and bisexual; and Asian and Filipino business clubs.

        Deans of students regularly told us last year that "there is less larger-group
socializing" and that "more people are doing things individually and in separate
groups than campus-wide." In contrast to the Carnegie Council's 1979 study, cur-

rent students describe themselves in terms of their differences, not their commonalities. Increasingly, they say they associate with people who are like themselves rather than different.

In the main, when students do take time to have fun, they are leaving campus to do so. Our Campus Site Visits study indicated that drinking is the primary form of recreation for 63 percent of students, followed closely by going to clubs and bars (59 percent) and simply getting off campus (52 percent). By contrast, the latter two activities were not mentioned in the Carnegie Council's 1979 study.

Drinking was not a surprise. It was the first choice in our earlier study, but there is more binge drinking today. Drinking to get drunk has become the great escape for undergraduates.

Escaping from campus is a trend that goes hand in hand with the high numbers of students living in off-campus housing—more than triple the percentage in the late 1960s. Only 30 percent of students we surveyed reported living on campus. Add to this the fact that students are also spending less time on campus because of jobs and part-time attendance, and the result is that increasingly campuses are places in which instruction is the principal activity. Living and social life occur elsewhere.

Multiculturalism

30   Campuses are more deeply divided along lines of race, gender, ethnicity, sexuality, and other differences today than in the past. A majority of deans at four-year colleges told us last year that the climate on campus can be described as politically correct (60 percent), civility has declined (57 percent), students of different racial and ethnic groups often do not socialize together (56 percent), reports of sexual harassment have increased (55 percent), and students feel uncomfortable expressing unpopular or controversial opinions (54 percent).

Multiculturalism is a painful topic for many students. The dirty words on college campuses now are no longer four letters: they are-six-letter words like "racist" and "sexist"—and "homophobic," which is even longer. Students don't want to discuss the topic. In focus group interviews, students were more willing to tell us intimate details of their sex lives than to discuss diversity on campus.

Tension regarding diversity and difference runs high all across college life. Students talked about friction in the classroom; in the residence halls; in reactions to posters placed on campus or to visiting speakers; in campus activities and the social pursuits of the day; in hiring practices; in testing; in the dining room, library, bookstore, and sports facilities; in every aspect of their campus lives. In this sense, the campus in the 1990s is a less hospitable place for all undergraduates, regardless of background, than it once was.

Academics

Although instruction remains the principal on-campus activity that brings undergraduates together, the academic arena is experiencing its own form of student disengagement. Pursuit of academic goals is clearly utilitarian. It's as if students have struck a bargain with their colleges. They're going to class all right, but they're going by the book: they're doing what's necessary to fulfill degree requirements and gain skills for a job, but then they're out the door. They're focused and career-oriented, and see college as instrumental in leading to a lucrative career. "Task-oriented students who focus on jobs" is how a Georgia Tech student affairs official labeled them.

Although students do not believe that a college education provides a money-back guarantee of future success, they feel that without one, a good job—much less a lucrative or prestigious job—is impossible to obtain. At the very least, it's a kind of insurance policy to hedge bets against the future. As a student at Portland (Oregon) Community College put it, "College is the difference between white-collar and blue-collar work." Fifty-seven percent of undergraduates we surveyed in 1993 believed that the chief benefit of a college education is increasing one's earning power—an 11 percentage-point increase since 1976.

35   By contrast, the value placed on nonmaterial goals (that is, learning to get along with people and formulating the values and goals of one's life) has plummeted since the late 1960s, dropping from 71 and 76 percent respectively to 50 and 47 percent. Whereas in 1969 these personal and philosophic goals were cited by students as the primary reasons for attending college, in 1993, students placed them at the bottom of the list.

Although a great number of students are focused and intent on pursuing career goals, many also face a variety of academic hurdles. They are coming to college less well prepared academically. Nearly three-fourths (73 percent) of deans in 1997 reported an increase within the last decade in the proportion of students requiring remedial or developmental education at two-year (81 percent) and four-year (64 percent) colleges.

Nearly one-third (32 percent) of all undergraduates surveyed reported having taken a basic skills or remedial course in reading, writing, or math, up from 29 percent in 1976. Despite high aspirations, a rising percentage of students simply are not prepared for the rigors of academe. Another academic hurdle for students is a growing gap between how students learn best and how faculty teach. According to research by Charles Schroeder of the University of Missouri-Columbia, published in the September/October 1993 *Change*, more than half of today's students perform best in a learning situation characterized by "direct, concrete experience, moderate-to-high degrees of structure, and a linear approach to learning. They value the practical and the immediate, and the focus of their perception is primarily on the physical world." According to Schroeder, three-quarters of faculty, on the other hand, "prefer the global to the particular; are stimulated by the realm of concepts, ideas, and abstractions; and assume that students, like themselves, need a high degree of autonomy in their work."

Small wonder, then, that frustration results and that every year faculty believe students are less well prepared, while students increasingly think their classes are incomprehensible. On the faculty side, this is certainly the case. The 1997 Student Affairs Survey revealed that at 74 percent of campuses, faculty complaints about students are on the rise. One result is that students and faculty are spending less time on campus together. With work and part-time attendance, students increasingly are coming to campus just for their classes. This explains, in part, why students are taking longer to complete college. Fewer than two out of five are able to graduate in four years (see Astin et al., in Resources). Twenty-eight percent now require a fifth year to earn a baccalaureate, according to U.S. Department of Education statistics from 1996. In reality, obtaining the baccalaureate degree in four years is an anomaly today, particularly at public and less selective institutions.

The Future

The overwhelming majority of college students believe they will be successful. But their fears about relationships, romance, and their future happiness were continuing themes in every focus group. Their concerns about finances were overwhelming. There was not one focus group in which students did not ask whether they would be able to repay their student loans, afford to complete college, get a good job, or avoid moving home with Mom and Dad.

40   The college graduate driving a cab or working at the Gap was a universal anecdote. There was more mythology here than there were concrete examples, however. College graduates being forced to drive taxis is one of the great American legends, rivaled only by the tale of George Washington and the cherry tree.

Finances were a constant topic of discussion. Students told us of the need to drop out, stop out, and attend college part-time because of tuition costs. They told us of the lengths they had to go to pay tuition—even giving blood. More than one in five (21 percent) who participated in the Undergraduate Survey said that someone who helped pay their tuition had been out of work while they attended college.

At heart, undergraduates are worried about whether we can make it as a society, and whether they can actually make it personally. In our surveys, the majority did say they expected to do better than their parents. But in our focus groups, students regularly told us, "We're going to be the first generation that doesn't surpass our parents in making more money." "How will I buy a house?" "How will I send my kids to college?"

This is a generation of students desperately clinging to the American Dream. Nearly nine out of 10 (88 percent) students are optimistic about their personal futures, but their hope, though broadly professed, is fragile and gossamer-like. Their lives are being challenged at every turn: in their families, their communities, their nation, and their world. This is a generation where hope and fear collide.

Conclusion

In sum, these changes in America's undergraduates add up to a requiem for historic notions of collegiate life—the ivory tower, the living-learning community, the residential college, and all the rest. But the changes are not sudden; they began even before Cardinal Newman wrote his classic. Most are a natural consequence of the democratization of higher education. This is what happens when 65 percent of all high school graduates go on to college and higher education is open to the nation's population across the lifespan. Four years of living in residence becomes a luxury few can afford.

45   So how should higher education respond? Dismissing the present or recalling a golden era lost are not particularly helpful—for the most part the changes are permanent. But there are a few things colleges can do.

The first is to focus. Most colleges have less time with their students on campus than in the past. They need to be very clear about what they want to accomplish with students and dramatically reduce the laundry lists of values and goals that constitute the typical mission statement.

The second is to use all opportunities available to educate students. Required events, such as orientation, should be used to educate rather than to deal with logistics. The awards a college gives should represent the values it most wants to teach. The same is true for speakers. The in-house newsletter can be used to educate. And of course, maybe the best advice is that almost any event can be used for educational purposes if the food and music are good enough. Third, build on the strengths unique to every generation of students. For instance, current undergraduates, as part of their off-campus activities, are involved in public service—an astounding 64 percent of them, according to the Undergraduate Survey. Service learning, then, becomes an excellent vehicle to build into the curriculum and cocurriculum of most colleges.

Fourth, work to eliminate the forces that push students off campus unnecessarily. For example, most colleges talk a great deal about multiculturalism, but in general have not translated the rhetoric into a climate that will make the campus more hospitable to current students.

50   In like manner, using financial aid more to meet need than to reward merit would lessen the necessity for students to work while attending college. These are steps any college with the will and commitment can take. Both campus life and our students would benefit greatly.

Resources

* Astin, A.W., L. Tsui, and J. Avalos. *Degree Attainment Rates at American Colleges and Universities: Effects of Race, Gender, and Institutional Type,* Los Angeles: Higher Education Research Institute, UCLA, 1996.

* Sax, L.J., A.W. Astin, W.S. Korn, and K.M. Mahoney. *The American Freshman: National Norms for Fall 1997,* Los Angeles: Higher Education Research Institute, UCLA, 1997.

* U.S. Department of Education. National Center for Education Statistics. *Condition of Education, 1996* (NCES 96304), Washington, DC: U.S. Government Printing Office, 1996.

* ———. National Center for Education Statistics. *Digest of Education Statistics, 1997* (NCES 98-015), Washington, DC: U.S. Government Printing Office, 1997.

Studies Used in This Article

The studies of undergraduate student life that form the basis of this article and of the book *When Hope and Fear Collide: A Portrait of Today's College Student* were conducted by the authors between 1992 and 1997 at the Harvard Graduate School of Education. The first—the Undergraduate Survey—included a 1993 questionnaire sent to a random sample of 9,100 students at institutions stratified by Carnegie type.

The second—the Student Affairs Survey—consisted of questionnaires sent in 1992 and again in 1997 to a random sample of 270 student affairs officers at institutions also stratified by Carnegie type. The third—Campus Site Visits—involved interviews conducted between 1993 and 1995 with nearly 50 student affairs officers and 300 students, both individually and in focus groups, at 28 diverse campuses across the country. The data from the completed questionnaires were weighted by Carnegie category to reflect the composition of American higher education.

In this article, the authors use for comparison with the above-listed surveys similar ones conducted in the 1960s and 1970s by Arthur Levine for the Carnegie Council on Policy Studies in Higher Education. All of these studies targeted students of both traditional and nontraditional age in two- and four-year institutions varying in control (public versus private), mission, size, selectivity, gender distribution, racial and ethnic mix, religious orientation, residential status, and regional location.

QUESTIONS FOR INQUIRY AND ACTION

1. Why do Levine and Cureton title their article "an obituary"? What elements of an obituary are present in the article?

2. Why do the authors compare colleges to banks? Does this analogy accurately describe your desired relationship with your school, too? If not, what analogy would you use?

3. How diverse is your campus? How do you define *diversity?* Is it simply a matter of race or ethnicity? Why or why not? Is diversity a difficult subject on your campus, so much so that, as Levine and Cureton discovered, students are more willing to talk about their intimate lives than diversity at their schools?

4. Why are *you* in college? Answer this question in your writer's notebook; then, survey others on your campus, using Levine and Cureton's questions and categories, to get a sense of the priorities, similarities, and differences at your institution.

BELL HOOKS Engaged Pedagogy

> *bell hooks is the pen name of Gloria Watkins, a feminist theorist, social critic, educator, and poet. She has taught at Yale University and Oberlin College and is currently Distinguished Professor of English at City University of New York. She has authored numerous essays and over a dozen books, from* Ain't I a Woman: Black Women and Feminism *(1981) and* Black Looks: Race and

Representation *(1992) to* Remembered Rapture: The Writer at Work *(1999).*
"Engaged Pedagogy" is the first chapter of her book Teaching to Transgress:
Education as the Practice of Freedom *(New York: Routledge, 1994).*

———————————

To educate as the practice of freedom is a way of teaching that anyone can learn. That learning process comes easiest to those of us who teach who also believe that there is an aspect of our vocation that is sacred; who believe that our work is not merely to share information but to share in the intellectual and spiritual growth of our students. To teach in a manner that respects and cares for the souls of our students is essential if we are to provide the necessary conditions where learning can most deeply and intimately begin.

Throughout my years as student and professor, I have been most inspired by those teachers who have had the courage to transgress those boundaries that would confine each pupil to a rote, assembly-line approach to learning. Such teachers approach students with the will and desire to respond to our unique beings, even if the situation does not allow the full emergence of a relationship based on mutual recognition. Yet the possibility of such recognition is always present.

Paulo Freire and the Vietnamese Buddhist monk Thich Nhat Hanh are two of the "teachers" who have touched me deeply with their work. When I first began college, Freire's thought gave me the support I needed to challenge the "banking system" of education, that approach to learning that is rooted in the notion that all students need to do is consume information fed to them by a professor and be able to memorize and store it. Early on, it was Freire's insistence that education could be the practice of freedom that encouraged me to create strategies for what he called "conscientization" in the classroom. Translating that term to critical awareness and engagement, I entered the classrooms with the conviction that it was crucial for me and every other student to be an active participant, not a passive consumer. Education as the practice of freedom was continually undermined by professors who were actively hostile to the notion of student participation. Freire's work affirmed that education can only be liberatory when everyone claims knowledge as a field in which we all labor. That notion of mutual labor was affirmed by Thich Nhat Hanh's philosophy of engaged Buddhism, the focus on practice in conjunction with contemplation. His philosophy was similar to Freire's emphasis on "praxis"—action and reflection upon the world in order to change it.

In his work Thich Nhat Hanh always speaks of the teacher as a healer. Like Freire, his approach to knowledge called on students to be active participants, to link awareness with practice. Whereas Freire was primarily concerned with the mind, Thich Nhat Hanh offered a way of thinking about pedagogy which emphasized wholeness, a union of mind, body, and spirit. His focus on a holistic approach to learning and spiritual practice enabled me to overcome years of socialization that had taught me to believe a classroom was diminished if students and professors regarded one another as "whole" human beings, striving not just for knowledge in books, but knowledge about how to live in the world.

5   During my twenty years of teaching, I have witnessed a grave sense of dis-ease among professors (irrespective of their politics) when students want us to see them as whole human beings with complex lives and experiences rather than simply as seekers after compartmentalized bits of knowledge. When I was an undergraduate, Women's Studies was just finding a place in the academy. Those classrooms were the one space where teachers were willing to acknowledge a connection between ideas learned in university settings and those learned in life practices. And, despite those times when students abused that freedom in the classroom by only wanting to dwell on personal experience, feminist classrooms were, on the whole, one location where I witnessed professors striving to create participatory spaces for the sharing of knowledge. Nowadays, most women's studies professors are not as committed to exploring new pedagogical strategies. Despite this shift, many students still seek to enter feminist classrooms because they continue to believe that there, more than in any other place in the academy, they will have an opportunity to experience education as the practice of freedom.

Progressive, holistic education, "engaged pedagogy" is more demanding than conventional critical or feminist pedagogy. For, unlike these two teaching practices, it emphasizes well-being. That means that teachers must be actively committed to a process of self-actualization that promotes their own well-being if they are to teach in a manner that empowers students. Thich Nhat Hanh emphasized that "the practice of a healer, therapist, teacher or any helping professional should be directed toward his or herself first, because if the helper is unhappy, he or she cannot help many people." In the United States it is rare that anyone talks about teachers in university settings as healers. And it is even more rare to hear anyone suggest that teachers have any responsibility to be self-actualized individuals.

Learning about the work of intellectuals and academics primarily from nineteenth-century fiction and nonfiction during my pre-college years, I was certain that the task for those of us who chose this vocation was to be holistically questing for self-actualization. It was the actual experience of college that disrupted this image. It was there that I was made to feel as though I was terribly naive about "the profession." I learned that far from being self-actualized, the university was seen more as a haven for those who are smart in book knowledge but who might be otherwise unfit for social interaction. Luckily, during my undergraduate years I began to make a distinction between the practice of being an intellectual/teacher and one's role as a member of the academic profession.

It was difficult to maintain fidelity to the idea of the intellectual as someone who sought to be whole—well-grounded in a context where there was little emphasis on spiritual well-being, on care of the soul. Indeed, the objectification of the teacher within bourgeois educational structures seemed to denigrate notions of wholeness and uphold the idea of a mind/body split, one that promotes and supports compartmentalization.

This support reinforces the dualistic separation of public and private, encouraging teachers and students to see no connection between life practices, habits of being, and the roles of professors. The idea of the intellectual questing for a union of mind, body, and spirit had been replaced with notions that being smart meant that one was inherently emotionally unstable and that the best in oneself emerged in one's academic work. This meant that whether academics were drug addicts, alcoholics, batterers, or sexual abusers, the only important aspect of our identity was whether or not our minds functioned, whether we were able to do our jobs in the classroom. The self was presumably emptied out the moment the threshold was crossed, leaving in place only an objective mind—free of experiences and biases. There was fear that the conditions of that self would interfere with the teaching process. Part of the luxury and privilege of the role of teacher/professor today is the absence of any requirement that we be self-actualized. Not surprisingly, professors who are not concerned with inner well-being are the most threatened by the demand on the part of students for liberatory education, for pedagogical processes that will aid them in their own struggle for self-actualization.

10   Certainly it was naive for me to imagine during high school that I would find spiritual and intellectual guidance in university settings from writers, thinkers, scholars. To have found this would have been to stumble across a rare treasure. I learned, along with other students, to consider myself fortunate if I found an interesting professor who talked in a compelling way. Most of my professors were not the slightest bit interested in enlightenment. More than anything they seemed enthralled by the exercise of power and authority within their mini-kingdom, the classroom.

This is not to say that there were not compelling, benevolent dictators, but it is true to my memory that it was rare—absolutely, astonishingly rare—to encounter professors who were deeply committed to progressive pedagogical practices. I was dismayed by this; most of my professors were not individuals whose teaching styles I wanted to emulate.

My commitment to learning kept me attending classes. Yet, even so, because I did not conform—would not be an unquestioning, passive student—some professors treated me with contempt. I was slowly becoming estranged from education. Finding Freire in the midst of that estrangement was crucial to my survival as a student. His work offered both a way for me to understand the limitations of the type of education I was receiving and to discover alternative strategies for learning and teaching. It was particularly disappointing to encounter white male professors who claimed to follow Freire's model even as their pedagogical practices were mired in structures of domination, mirroring the styles of conservative professors even as they approached subjects from a more progressive standpoint.

When I first encountered Paulo Freire, I was eager to see if his style of teaching would embody the pedagogical practices he described so eloquently in his work. During the short time I studied with him, I was deeply moved by his presence, by the way in which his manner of teaching exemplified his pedagogical theory. (Not all students interested in Freire have had a similar experience.) My experience with him restored my faith in liberatory education. I had never wanted to surrender the conviction that one could teach without reinforcing existing systems of domination. I needed to know that professors did not have to be dictators in the classroom.

While I wanted teaching to be my career, I believed that personal success was intimately linked with self-actualization. My passion for this quest led me to inter-rogate constantly the mind/body split that was so often taken to be a given. Most professors were often deeply antagonistic toward, even scornful of, any approach to learning emerging from a philosophical standpoint emphasizing the union of mind, body, and spirit, rather than the separation of these elements. Like many of the students I now teach, I was often told by powerful academics that I was misguided to seek such a perspective in the academy. Throughout my stu-dent years I felt deep inner anguish. Memory of that pain returns as I listen to stu-dents express the concern that they will not succeed in academic professions if they want to be well, if they eschew dysfunctional behavior or participation in coercive hierarchies. These students are often fearful, as I was, that there are no spaces in the academy where the will to be self-actualized can be affirmed.

15   This fear is present because many professors have intensely hostile responses to the vision of liberatory education that connects the will to know with the will to become. Within professorial circles, individuals often complain bitterly that stu-dents want classes to be "encounter groups." While it is utterly unreasonable for stu-dents to expect classrooms to be therapy sessions, it is appropriate for them to hope that the knowledge received in these settings will enrich and enhance them.

Currently, the students I encounter seem far more uncertain about the pro-ject of self-actualization than my peers and I were twenty years ago. They feel that there are no clear ethical guidelines shaping actions. Yet, while they despair, they are also adamant that education should be liberatory. They want and demand more from professors than my generation did. There are times when I walk into classrooms overflowing with students who feel terribly wounded in their psy-ches (many of them see therapists), yet I do not think that they want therapy from me. They do want an education that is healing to the uninformed, unknowing spirit. They do want knowledge that is meaningful. They rightfully expect that my colleagues and I will not offer them information without addressing the con-nection between what they are learning and their overall life experiences.

This demand on the students' part does not mean that they will always accept our guidance. This is one of the joys of education as the practice of freedom, for it allows students to assume responsibility for their choices. Writing about our teacher/student relationship in a piece for the *Village Voice*, "How to Run the Yard: Off-Line and into the Margins at Yale," one of my students, Gary Dauphin, shares the joys of working with me as well as the tensions that surfaced between us as he began to devote his time to pledging a fraternity rather than cultivating his writing:

> People think academics like Gloria [my given name] are all about difference: but what I
> learned from her was mostly about sameness, about what I had in common as a black man
> to people of color; to women and gays and lesbians and the poor and anyone else who
> wanted in. I did some of this learning by reading but most of it came from hanging out
> on the fringes of her life. I lived like that for a while, shuttling between high points in
> my classes and low points outside. Gloria was a safe haven. . . . Pledging a fraternity is about
> as far away as you can get from her classroom, from the yellow kitchen where she used
> to share her lunch with students in need of various forms of sustenance.

This is Gary writing about the joy. The tension arose as we discussed his reason for wanting to join a fraternity and my disdain for that decision. Gary comments, "They represented a vision of black manhood that she abhorred, one where violence and abuse were primary ciphers of bonding and identity." Describing his assertion of autonomy from my influence he writes, "But she must have also known the limits of even her influence on my life, the limits of books and teachers."

Ultimately, Gary felt that the decision he had made to join a fraternity was not constructive, that I "had taught him openness" where the fraternity had encouraged one-dimensional allegiance. Our interchange both during and after this experience was an example of engaged pedagogy.

20   Through critical thinking—a process he learned by reading theory and actively analyzing texts—Gary experienced education as the practice of freedom. His final comments about me: "Gloria had only mentioned the entire episode once after it was over, and this to tell me simply that there are many kinds of choices, many kinds of logic. I could make those events mean whatever I wanted as long as I was honest." I have quoted his writing at length because it is testimony affirming engaged pedagogy. It means that my voice is not the only account of what happens in the classroom.

Engaged pedagogy necessarily values student expression. In her essay, "Interrupting the Calls for Student Voice in Liberatory Education: A Feminist Poststructuralist Perspective," Mimi Orner employs a Foucauldian framework to suggest that

> Regulatory and punitive means and uses of the confession bring to mind curricular and pedagogical practices which call for students to publicly reveal, even confess, information about their lives and cultures in the presence of authority figures such as teachers.

When education is the practice of freedom, students are not the only ones who are asked to share, to confess. Engaged pedagogy does not seek simply to empower students. Any classroom that employs a holistic model of learning will also be a place where teachers grow, and are empowered by the process. That empowerment cannot happen if we refuse to be vulnerable while encouraging students to take risks. Professors who expect students to share confessional narratives but who are themselves unwilling to share are exercising power in a manner that could be coercive. In my classrooms, I do not expect students to take any risks that I would not take, to share in any way that I would not share. When professors bring narratives of their experiences into classroom discussions it eliminates the possibility that we can function as all-knowing, silent interrogators. It is often productive if professors take the first risk, linking confessional narratives to academic discussions so as to show how experience can illuminate and enhance our understanding of academic material. But most professors must practice being vulnerable in the classroom, being wholly present in mind, body, and spirit.

Progressive professors working to transform the curriculum so that it does not reflect biases or reinforce systems of domination are most often the individuals willing to take the risks that engaged pedagogy requires and to make their teaching practices a site of resistance. In her essay, "On Race and Voice: Challenges for Liberation Education in the 1990s," Chandra Mohanty writes that

> resistance lies in self-conscious engagement with dominant, normative discourses and representations and in the active creation of oppositional analytic and cultural spaces. Resistance that is random and isolated is clearly not as effective as that which is mobilized through systemic politicized practices of teaching and learning. Uncovering and reclaiming subjugated knowledge is one way to lay claims to alternative histories. But these knowledges need to be understood and defined pedagogically, as questions of strategy and practice as well as of scholarship, in order to transform educational institutions radically.

Professors who embrace the challenge of self-actualization will be better able to create pedagogical practices that engage students, providing them with ways of knowing that enhance their capacity to live fully and deeply.

QUESTIONS FOR INQUIRY AND ACTION

1. What does the word *pedagogy* mean? What does hooks mean by an "engaged pedagogy"? How does she describe it in her essay?

2. Read hooks's essay with Peter Sacks's "The Sandbox Experiment," the next reading. How does each of these professors describe the experience of teaching? What is each one's theory of pedagogy, or teaching? Which one would you rather have as a teacher, and why?

3. Research the concept of liberatory education. What are its tenets? How did it come about? Who practices it, and for what reasons?

4. Notice the teaching approaches used by your and your friends' professors. Do many professors at your institution teach like hooks does? Do you think they should? If so, how would you discuss the subject with them?

PETER SACKS The Sandbox Experiment

> *Peter Sacks is the pseudonym for a former journalist who is now a professor at a large suburban community college. Earlier in his journalistic career he wrote for a number of newspapers and was nominated for a Pulitzer Prize. "The Sandbox Experiment" is a chapter from his book* Generation X Goes to College: An Eye-Opening Account of Teaching in Postmodern America *(Chicago: Open Court, 1996).*

Having been given my ultimatum by those who held the key to The Castle as to how I might become a permanent fixture there myself (had I been so inclined), I had a good long talk with Sandy. We talked the evening after my tenure meeting with the Big Committee, after they told me my student evaluations must significantly improve, or else. My conversation with Sandy that night ultimately inspired me to keep going in my journey into teaching, rather than simply write off the whole experience. The actual possibility of Failure—yes, Failure with a capital F—was haunting me, and my self-confidence was waning. "People who can't do, teach, and I can't even succeed as a teacher." That was the demon in my head. And for a driven Boomer who had learned how to compete adequately in a world with millions of other Boomers, steering clear of Failure was probably what kept me going in my experiment at teaching. I still wanted to know exactly what one had to do to succeed—or survive, perhaps—teaching the MTV generation. In one of those classic moments in life, Sandy and I landed upon the perfect solution.

I was in my study when she got home. She plopped on the floor in my study. "So, what happened?" she asked, referring to my meeting that day with the Big Committee.

"Well, it's pretty simple. Either my student evaluations improve or I'm out."

"So that's what it takes to be a good teacher? Just make the students happy?"

5   "I suppose so. Otherwise, I'm gone. Oh, yeah, and they want me to take an *acting* course," I said, my voice dripping with sarcasm. "I'm not entertaining enough for the MTV crowd." . . .

I don't recall exactly how the idea came to me, but after I rejected Prozac as the means to become a successful teacher of Generation X, I got another idea. If one option was to chemically change my personality with a drug to be more outgoing, entertaining, and nurturing, then the opposite approach would be to consciously alter my behavior and actually *manipulate my environment.* There seemed little doubt that the system was actually pushing me in that direction. It suddenly became clear to me that being a good teacher didn't seem to really matter in the system of rewards and punishments teachers faced; excellence wasn't really the point. It was becoming increasingly clear that the real point was whether you kept students sufficiently amused and entertained.

Like the Prozac idea, the scheme I would simply call "the Sandbox Experiment" started out as something of a joke. As Sandy and I sat there on the carpet in my little study. I said, "What I should do is to become like a kindergarten teacher and do everything possible to make my classes like playtime. I'll call class the Sandbox. And we'll play all kinds of games and just have fun, and I'll give all my students good grades, and everyone will be happy. Students will get what they want—whether they learn anything or not doesn't matter. The College will get what it wants, which are lots of happy students. And I'll get good evaluations, because students are happy and contented."

From that seed, we then brainstormed what my new classes ought to be like, and sitting there on the carpet (in our sandbox positions) we came up with the essential outline of my new syllabus. To hell with the fundamentals; my little sandbox would emphasize amusement. We'd do restaurant and movie reviews, write about sports, have lots of guest speakers, write advertising copy (which I knew next to nothing about)—I would shamelessly plug into popular culture and the demands of this generation to be amused.

But that wasn't all. I'd have to alter my whole attitude toward people who hated me because they thought I was passing myself off as somehow superior to them. But that's an overstatement of the problem. Hints of one of the most important yet subtle characteristics of these students had been emerging in my evaluations for months, and it had something to do with their revolting against the traditional balance of power between the teacher and themselves. Sure, by most measures I was somewhat accomplished as a journalist who undoubtedly knew far more about the subject I was teaching than students did. But many students were still uncomfortable with the idea that my knowledge and skills were important or even relevant. They seemed far more comfortable with what some educators might call a "collaborative approach." That's a fancy sounding phrase, but it boiled down to mean that students felt what they knew about a subject was just as valuable as what I knew. And who was I, trying to shove my version of the world down their throats? I'll admit, I did come across as if I knew more—a lot more—about journalism than my students. And in doing so I violated this seemingly unwritten code: Don't *act* as if you know more than the students, even though you do.

10   And so I devised a few techniques to cope with this peculiar attitude. First, I would tell students on the first day of class to call me Peter; that would help break down barriers and assure them that I thought of myself as their equal. Second, I vowed not to tell them anything about my background in journalism. Doing so seemed only to intimidate them and draw attention to our inequality. Psychologists probably have a term for it, but I could see how disoriented students would be if faced with the contradiction of thinking they are both my equal and my inferior in the classroom at the same time. Something would have to give, and it would probably take the form of irrational behavior, sullenness, or other behaviors that were unproductive for me and them. So, from then on, I would be a blank slate, and they'd call me by my first name, simply a "resource" for students to "facilitate" their learning. In the fashionable jargon of some educators, we would be "partners" in the "learning process."

Welcome to teaching in collaborative, multicultural, multivalued, postmodern America, I thought. Form, method, and style had triumphed over substance. For, in the end, it really didn't seem to matter what I knew about my field when it came to teaching. I remember talking to my brother, who was trained as an actor, about my teaching job. At thirty, he was at the older end of Generation X and had recently finished a graduate degree in drama. I said, "My students would probably consider you a better journalism teacher than me, because you know how to act, with just enough knowledge, you could simply play that role." He thought about what I said a minute, then slowly nodded his head and said, "Unfortunately, I think you're probably right." The irony, of course, was that The College hired me over people who had far more teaching experience than I had because of my journalism experience, and yet I had to play down my expertise in order to become a successful teacher. This truly was a strange world, I thought.

Finally, there was the question of grades. It is here that I made what is surely the most important decision about my little Sandbox Experiment, and the one loaded with ethical dilemmas. I decided that, just to see what would happen, I would consciously give what, in my own estimation, were outrageously good grades. I hypothesized that when students were receiving poor grades, they would blow out of proportion characteristics about a teacher that bothered them. But if students were content with their grades, they wouldn't make such a fuss out of other things about a class, such as the difficulty of the readings or my speaking style, which students said wasn't sufficiently entertaining.

And so, in my mind, I became a teaching teddy bear. In the metaphorical sandbox I created, students could do no wrong, and I did almost anything possible to keep all of them happy, all of the time, no matter how childish or rude their behavior, no matter how poorly they performed in the course, no matter how little effort they gave. If they wanted their hands held, I would hold them. If they wanted a stapler (or a Kleenex) and I didn't have one, I'd apologize. If they wanted to read the newspaper while I was addressing the class or if they wanted to get up and leave in the middle of a lecture, go for it. Call me spineless. I confess. But in the excessively accommodative culture that I found myself in, "our students" as many of my colleagues called them, had too much power for me to afford irritating them with demands and challenges I had previously thought were part and parcel of the collegiate experience. Metaphorically speaking, if they needed that ride to school I refused to give them in my dream in the mountains, now I'd give them a ride, and then I'd ask if there was anything else I could do to please. But to be sure, it wasn't always easy for me.

But you're probably thinking, "That's unethical. You're buying off students with high grades." You readers who are also parents of college-aged students might well be adding. "We're paying tuition for you to teach, regardless of how students behave."

15   I do understand the sentiment. But I believe that my Sandbox Experiment was defensible. First, grades are relative, and the grades I gave out during my experiment were in fact more equal to what was common at The College than the grades I'd been giving before the experiment. . . . I stumbled into the realization that the average grade at The College, as for most colleges and universities, was a solid B. That's compared to the C average I tried to maintain before the experiment, which I believe compelled many students to evaluate me so harshly. As a result, I brought down my standards to match those of the rest of The College, and it was professionally suicidal to try to do otherwise. As I shall describe below, in often subtle and occasionally quite overt ways, I was in fact strongly encouraged by college administrators and colleagues to do just that. In short, I had to get real. Second, . . . it became clear to me from my work on the Save Our Standards committee that one way or another most other instructors were watering down standards, essentially buying off students with lots of spoon-feeding and undeserved grades.

Is it a valid defense to say that "everybody was doing it?" Well, as far as I could tell, everybody *was* doing it, this pandering to students. And they weren't doing so for selfish gain—as opposed to Bill Clinton and Newt Gingrich trying to outdo each other on tax breaks for middle-class voters. The teachers at my college, rather, were going easy on students because they were afraid for their jobs. That's how grade inflation had become institutionalized, and virtually nobody was willing to acknowledge this. Given the incentives of benefits and punishments teachers faced, pandering became quite rational and justifiable, however unfortunate its collective results.

Still, I remained troubled in my choice to relax my personal standards in order to determine just what kinds of behavior the educational system rewarded. As a social experiment, I felt, my one true justification was that the end would justify the means. In an absolute sense, I might have been wrong to act in the way the system was compelling me to act; but now, I am confessing, and hoping that the virtue of my act lies in exposing the corruption that has enveloped much of higher education.

My Sandbox Experiment was to get its first key test in my journalism class. I was fortunate to get a pretty good group of students with which to deploy my new methods. There were Steve and Holly, both a bit older students with whom I could easily engage in small talk. There was just one hard-core grunger who had pieces of metal protruding from her nose and ears, but she was bright and a pretty fair writer and I got along well with her. There were several Asian students, including Japanese and Koreans who almost always made life easier for a teacher because they worked hard, listened well and didn't give you a lot of crap. But there was also Caitlin. Remember her? She was the one who didn't have any tastebuds because of a cold and wondered if she still had to complete her restaurant review.

Did I change? Let me show you the ways.

20   I became a master of hand-holding and spoon-feeding. Take Daniel, for instance, a student of mine who was an official of some sort in student government. He was outspoken, often absent—and potentially dangerous to a teacher who might demand too much of him. For one assignment, I showed a videotape of a speech so students could write a speech story. Daniel missed that day but didn't tell me he'd be absent. Nevertheless, I agreed to give him a written copy of the speech so he could do the assignment anyway. Before my Sandbox Experiment, I wouldn't have allowed him to make up the assignment. Still, I couldn't suppress saying when handing him the speech. "If this were a real job, you'd be fired by now." I sort of winced to myself as I said it, but I couldn't help it. Another time, Daniel hadn't attended class for a few days and he did the wrong assignment for a story. Instead of flunking the paper, as I would have done before, I let him do the correct assignment—and gave him extra credit for the wrong assignment.

When I used to take attendance, if somebody came in late I'd mark them absent anyway. Now I would go out of my way to erase the little 0 (absent) and write in an X (present) if a student walked in after I'd taken attendance. Whereas in the past I'd demand some sort of proof to document an absence, now I'd simply take a student's word. And nearly any excuse would do. If they cared enough to lie, then I didn't care.

Indeed, my self-inflicted lobotomy was very hard to live with at times, especially toward the end of the quarter when my nerves and patience wore thin. Sometimes when students were being real jerks, I'd say things I'd later regret and then try to figure out a way to make it up to the student I might have offended.

Caitlin, for instance, was the sort of student I might have flunked or given D's before, but now I indulged her incompetency, figuring that she was potentially one more happy student who would say good things about me come evaluation time. One day she came to me with another excuse (besides nonfunctioning taste-buds) about why she hadn't done an assignment. This was toward the end of the quarter, and I could only keep up this little act of mine for so long. I gave her the same line I laid on Daniel: "You know, if this were a job, you'd be fired by now." Whereas Daniel could handle my criticism, Caitlin couldn't. She started crying and then left the room to compose herself. I felt bad about coming down on her—and I envisioned Caitlin's retaliation on her evaluation of me: *"What a jerk! He treats us like he's the boss and this were a job or something! He has no compassion."* And I imagined how the Big Committee would respond to such words. So, when Caitlin returned to the classroom, at the end of the hour, I walked up to her desk and said, "Caitlin, are you okay? I'm sorry if I came down on you too hard. You're doing fine," I lied.

I also took to plain old bullshitting with students, going out of my way to be informal with them whenever I could, and it was working well in my new journalism class. I talked with Rick about skiing, Tanya about jogging. "How was your weekend?" I'd say. When Heather, the grunger, took time off from in the middle of the quarter to take a vacation in New Orleans, rather than get irritated that she had missed so much class, I asked her, "So how was your vacation? Did you enjoy Mardi gras?"

25   Of course, my newfound happy-face approach to being a college instructor would have meant nothing if I didn't follow through on the grading end. It's one thing to try to be a nice guy; there's nothing wrong in trying to communicate better with your students. But when it came to my new grading system, I was a shameless lush, handing out mostly A's and B's, often for work that I would have given C's before. But while I felt shameless, I had to remind myself that nearly nine of ten students got A's and B's at The College—and the same went for top schools like Stanford.

I recall one news story a student wrote, containing so much muddled language that it was nearly impossible to follow. According to my theoretical grading system, the story should have gotten a D because it required so much work to whip it into shape. This is what the new me wrote on the student's paper: "Okay. Some unclear spots that don't make sense, mechanical problems, style errors (use your stylebook)."

And I gave the paper a warm and friendly B minus.

Over the entire quarter, that journalism class "earned" an average grade of 3.5, equivalent to an A minus. Compare that to the 2.3 average (a C) in the introductory journalism class that got on my case so hard during my first quarter at The College.

And so went the first phase of my grand experiment. . . .

30   The following quarter was the make or break time for me, the one that would resolve one way or another my fate as a college teacher. Since my Machiavellian formula seemed to be achieving the desired results, I tried hard not to change anything about my courses or my rather calculated behavior. The danger, however, was that I was becoming more confident, and students could interpret confidence as superciliousness, which I wanted to avoid. There was potentially great danger for an instructor trying to cope with students. Whenever they'd act childish, rude, or bored, a teacher might have to pinch himself real hard to keep from blowing up, walking out of the room, and telling them to all go back to high school or whatever Neverneverland they'd come out from.

My journalism class, as usually seemed to be the case, put me to the greatest test. It seemed that there was something about the journalism sequence at The College that attracted more than its share of difficult students. We had no professional school of journalism, and so most of the students had no interest at all in going into journalism or mass communications but were taking the course to satisfy a writing requirement.

This particular class was a special dog. Whereas my "turnaround" class the previous term had included some motivated students, by whom I was generally viewed favorably—this class had several quintessential members of Generation X who tested the limits of my patience.

As with all my writing classes, I had students first do drafts that they would then revise before turning in a final draft. I'd let them work on drafts during class time and allow them to get feedback from their peers. I'd also try to look at the drafts to give the students an idea whether they were on the right track. Doing the drafts was so important that I made them worth 15 percent of the final grade. As I've mentioned before, students at The College as a general rule would not do anything if it didn't directly affect their grade in a significant way. But in this class, I had a core of people who didn't do drafts, week after week after week, 15 percent of their grade be damned.

If my journalism class were a movie, it would have looked something like this:

> CAMERA: Long shot from the back of a good-sized classroom, as college students file in to take their chairs. Sounds of tables and chairs being shuffled, voices in small talk. Zoom to teacher at the head of the class, smiling and casually talking to a student about skiing conditions over the weekend. After a few minutes at 11 A.M. sharp, he removes his rear end from the table (posing in a very casual, friendly way), stands up, and starts talking to the whole class.
>
> TEACHER: Okay, folks, go ahead and pass me up a copy of your drafts due today. Then break up into your groups. Remember, today we're working on leads."
>
> CAMERA: Scan back to students. Little movement detected. Two or three people take their assignments from folders and pass them to the student ahead. The rest of the class stares at the teacher, expressionless.

TEACHER (INCREDULOUS): "Do I have everyone's draft? Is this it?"

CAMERA: Seeing no further movement from the inert students, the teacher moves back to his power position in the front of the podium, adjusts his body uncomfortably a second, then speaks.

TEACHER: Let me remind everyone that the drafts are worth 15 percent of your grade. If you don't come prepared, there's not any productive work we can do during class."

CAMERA: Scan back to class, still inert and silent, zoom in on two young men in the back sitting together at a table. Both have long hair. Not hippie long. More grunge or metal anti-hippie long, both in their early twenties. One sports a baseball hat and a goatee. The other has no baseball hat. He's a grunge-metal cross: long-sleeved checkered work shirt unbuttoned to his chest, showing a black T-shirt with the name of a metal band blasted across it. Slumped in their chairs, they stare alternatively at the teacher and down to their desk, obviously bored.

NARRATOR VOICE-OVER (TEACHER STARING BACK AT CLASS): "Look at these idiots. I've got three drafts. What the hell am I going to do today? I have a notion to just cancel class and send them home. How would Tom Hanks or Harrison Ford say it if this were a movie? 'You people make me sick. Get the hell out of here, come back when you've done the work. You're wasting my time.' . . . Yeah, right. In my dreams."

TEACHER: Okay, tell you what. Break up into your groups, give feedback to the ones who've done their drafts and the rest of you go over your outlines with each other and try to come up with an interesting angle for your leads."

35   And so I caved, and I caved over and over that quarter as I tried to please in the midst of mindlessness, to my students' deep sense of entitlement, and to the inordinate amount of power the system had given them. . . .

How well did the Sandbox Experiment work? In a word, it succeeded fabulously. That term's evaluations were the best I'd ever received at The College. In fact, they were sterling. The score in my writing class—when students were asked whether they would "recommend this class to other students"—18 Yes and 0 No; average grade I gave the class: 3.0. How about this comment: "I found (the instructor) was always willing to help me if I had any questions on my papers. I found his style of writing refreshing, and not like other stale writing classes I've had." And the final score in that problematic journalism class: 10 Yes and 1 No; average final grade I gave in the class: 3.0.

Still, I couldn't help but be amused at one of the comments a student wrote about the journalism class: "The teacher did not seem to have a good grasp of the material. I don't think he is qualified to teach this course." Apparently, at least for this particular student, I'd gone a bit overboard in striving for the humble approach and playing the role of teacher as facilitator. Either that, or he didn't have a clue about anything that went on in the class, and believe me, that's a distinct possibility. . . .

QUESTIONS FOR INQUIRY AND ACTION

1. Characterize Sacks's persona. How does he address and relate to us as readers? Who does he think will be reading the book? How can you tell?

2. Put Sacks into conversation with bell hooks in "Engaged Pedagogy." What does each have to say about the roles and relationships of college students and their professors?

3. Are students really as bad as Sacks describes them? Do students at your institution fit his descriptions? Through interviews, surveys, or library research, create a history of professors' opinions of students at your school. Have professors always thought that their students are lazy and uninterested, or is the situation really worse today?

4. Organize a reading and discussion group around this essay. Invite other students and faculty to express their views and enter into dialogue on classroom culture and the student-teacher relationship.

ROGER H. GARRISON Why Am I in College?

Roger H. Garrison was a professor of English at Briarcliff College. His work inspired the foundation of the National Great Teachers Seminar In 1969. He is also the author of a number of books on writing and teaching, including A Guide to Creative Writing, How a Writer Works, *and* Teaching in a Junior College: A Brief Professional Orientation *(1968). The following selection is a chapter from* The Adventure of Learning in College *(New York: Harper, 1959).*

First among the signs of intellectual maturity we would wish for an ideal person is the achievement of an insight into his own make-up, a realistic understanding of his own assets and liabilities, an understanding of his own dominant trends and motivations. . .

Lawrence E. Cole

Before you skip over the above quotation, try an experiment with it. For each pronoun, substitute "I" or "my." For *ideal person* substitute "myself." How suddenly pertinent the generalized words become! Now the quotation says in effect: if I am to be a mature person, I will know what I am, where I'm strong and weak, and where I am aiming my life.

Where *are* you aiming your life? This may sound like too broad or moralistic a question. But what life *means* is and always has been the main concern of education. Education, fundamentally, is a *moral* enterprise. Harvard's President Nathan Pusey recently said: "The chief aim of undergraduate education is to discover what it means to be a man. This has always to be done in personal, individual terms." For you to discover the meaning of maturity and the direction of your life is therefore an inclusive aim of your studies.

Presumably you are in college because you want an education. You might well ask the next two logically inevitable questions: *What* is an education? *Why* do I want it?

The first question is, of course, difficult; it has almost as many answers as there are people who try to respond to it. And in the current literature on education, there are literally yards of library shelves taken up with books that discuss the matter. But there are some clear and useful general ideas on the meaning of an education that should help you think about it for yourself in practical and immediate terms.

5   Obviously, an education is something more than the acquiring of mere information. Pieces of knowledge, no matter how largely accumulated, are dead lumps unless you know what to do with them. As one philosopher put it bluntly, "A merely well-informed man is the most useless bore on God's earth." Yet the culture in which we live seems to put large and often spectacular premiums on the possession of factual knowledge. It would not be surprising, for example, if you have been impressed, and perhaps influenced, by the television and radio quiz programs of the past decade: winners in these fact-derbies have often walked away with fortunes in money and goods. Clearly, at least in this limited activity, the possession of great stores of random facts has a measurable pay-off. Yet actually there is little qualitative difference between the responses of quiz contestants in various categories of "knowledge," and the old-fashioned circus and vaudeville performances of trained animals who can "count," "talk," and perform other feats of "reasoning." Both quiz contestants and trained animals perform under special, limited conditions.

But life is never as tidy or controlled as a quiz program; in real living, the rewards usually go to the person who knows when and how to ask the right questions—not to the person who has sets of answers to predetermined questions. Life never has any predetermined questions either; it has only problems which must be coped with and dilemmas which rarely, if ever, come when they are supposed to, in the form they should.

To use the word "problems" is to presuppose questions. Most real learning starts with questions. One distinction between the educated person and the ignorant person is awareness of the importance of questions. The ignorant person is satisfied with answers; the educated person realizes that answers have limitations because they usually signal an end to investigation. There is nothing more empty or irrelevant than the answer to a question that nobody asks.

You can be given answers. You can be well trained without being well educated. For instance, if you want to be a trained engineer, you can find many institutions where superior engineering training is available; and if you work faithfully and intelligently at your courses, you will graduate as a trained engineer. If you want to be an *educated* engineer, you can manage that, too, and at those same institutions, but only after you develop some clear ideas about the differences between education and training, and after you understand what one is and the other is not.

Training is good, training is necessary, and training is a key part of education. To be trained means that one is fitted or qualified in the doing of something.

In our complicated and competitive society, training in some skill is imperative. But to be educated is to know not only how to *do,* but to understand the meaning and significance of what one does. An educated person knows how and when to ask *why* of his own activity. Too often the trained man, like the expert, knows everything about his job except what it is for.

10   I agree wholly with A. N. Whitehead's comment: "There can be no adequate technical education which is not liberal, and no liberal education which is not technical: that is, no education which does not impart both technique and intellectual vision. . . Education should turn out the pupil with something he knows well and something he can do well[1]. . . .

There are endless illustrations in any business, and sometimes in the professions, of the differences between a merely trained man and an educated one. Recently, I took a group of students on a field trip to one of the country's largest manufacturers of rugs and carpets. We planned to make a two-hour tour of the factory, followed by a seminar with some of the management people on matters of the company's labor relations, rates of pay, employee status, and the like. Our guides for the tour were two friendly young men, both of whom had moved up from factory jobs and were now studying in the company's Management Education program as potential executives. As the tour began, we divided into two groups, with a guide for each. Throughout the tour, I alternated from group to group, listening as the guides explained production flow, various types of looms, the designing of rugs and carpets and all the operations going on in front of us.

I soon noticed some pointed differences between our two guides. Though both were courteous and obviously knew their way around the complex factory processes, one of them seemed limited in his knowledge and understanding. When we stood by a loom or a sizing machine, he spoke surely and with authority, telling us in detail how the machine worked, what skills were needed to run it, and how it related to the sequence of operations in the factory. But when the students asked him questions about labor and manufacturing costs, sources of raw material, or any queries, in fact, which went beyond immediate functions, his replies were evasive and vague. He admitted freely that he didn't understand these matters well. "I thought I knew a lot about rugs," he said, "but all I really know is how to run some of these machines."

The other guide, however, enlarged his information with comments about the company's labor policy, the current state of the raw wool market, the economics of marketing and distribution, and the close relation between consumer research and the development of new designs and materials. These added facts were not merely sidelights or garnishing; they were expanded and intelligent attempts to increase the students' understanding of the total meaning of the work they were observing.

After the tour was over, I thanked our guides. As we talked I found that although both men had worked for several years in the plant and were trained in the use of

---

[1] *Alfred N. Whitehead,* The Aims of Education, *The Macmillan Company, 1929, chap. 4, p. 74.*

the machines, the first guide—the one whose comments had been narrowly technical—had only that month begun his course in Management Education. The other guide had for eighteen months been taking university night courses in sociology, economics, and human relations, as well as following his regular studies in the Management program. The company's personnel director said to me later: "This fellow has all the makings of a fine executive some day. He knows the technical problems, but he can also think past them. In fact, he knows how to keep on learning about more than just the rug business. We need more men like that. We don't find enough of them."

15   The point is this: an educated person knows enough to ask the kinds of questions that open up, illuminate, and expand a subject, that set it in a new or fresh perspective, and that place it in significant relationships to other subjects. . . .

Let me say again that I have no intention of belittling trained skill, no matter how limited, nor of comparing it unfavorably with a "general education." All too often, to be "generally" educated means to be a dilettante, shallowly acquainted with much but usefully skilled in nothing—to be a person who, in Whitehead's phrases, has learned to execute "intellectual minuets" with "inert ideas." I remember, with sharp and still embarrassing clarity after more than two decades, a history professor who took me aside one morning, waved a sophomore paper I had written (with a C-minus grade) and said: "Young man, this is too slick, too superficial, too smooth on the surface, no texture underneath. You've got a good mind; why don't you dig a well for yourself instead of dilettanting around the edge?" I can still hear his voice. The honest outrage against superficiality of a cultivated, wise man taught me more than I learned in many another full-year course. . . .

Up to this point, I have been talking in general terms; obviously the question, "What *is* an education?" has not been answered except in the vaguest way. Just as you may take many months, or longer, in college to begin to discover for yourself what is meant by "an education," so it will take me the next dozen chapters even to suggest ways for you to begin to see the fullness of its meaning. In the last analysis, a liberal education is best described in the personal qualities of those who achieve it.

But the second question asked at the beginning of this chapter is almost indistinguishable from the first. You seek a college education. *Why?* What are you in college *for?*

Suppose you reply: "I want to be an industrial chemist, and good jobs in chemistry just aren't given to noncollege people." This is a reasonable and realistic answer. To be a good chemist (or a good *anything*) means much hard preparation first. But if you are asked, "*Why* do you want to be a chemist?" the answer is more difficult. You may say again, with perfect reasonableness, that industrial chemistry is a respectable, useful, and often creative business, that good chemists make a comfortable living, and that in a technological culture, chemists are needed and effective citizens. These are good answers—solid and rational and practical.

20   But why do you want to be a chemist? Only to make a good living? Only to be in a respectable and useful business or profession? Only to be a working element of society? Are these motives enough for *you?*

    The full answer to this, if there is a full answer, implies far more than surface response about the necessary practical matters of making a living. The further answers you give have much to do with your *character.* They go deeply and personally to your motives and your hopes for yourself. They give your philosophy of life by answering, indirectly, the question, "What is the meaning of your life?" and fundamentally, the question, "What kind of a human being do you want to be?"

    These are the hard, tangled, *basic* questions that education poses when you get to college. And this is why education is essentially a moral venture. It is relatively uncomplicated to get "know-how" training. Industries as well as schools and colleges do a superior job of teaching people how to perform detailed and complicated functions. We in America are an active people partly because we know how to teach one another to build, to make, to accomplish, and to invent. But education further says to you: learning to do something is fine and necessary, but what are you doing it *for?* Your trained skill, it says, is a function of your personality, to be sure, but are *you* merely a function or a skill? What more are you? What is the nature of your self? What is the meaning and direction of the group of selves we call society? What is your relation to your fellow men? What is your social function? Your *human* function?

    Put it another way. Education's main concern is with the nature of decent, enlightened, effective human living—and this is a moral concern. The first goal of a liberal education is *your* personal growth as a generous-hearted, generous-minded human being. "Liberal" means generous and liberal means free. Surely, it is the least to expect of an educated person that he should have matured and become enriched *as a person,* one able to think freely, responsibly, and effectively. The world has plenty of experts, but does it have enough people who have both the imagination and the moral courage to make the best uses of the ideas and processes the experts create?

    Before you shrug off this sort of talk, I urge you to follow the argument to its conclusion.

25   I have discovered that these apparently philosophical questions are crucial and real for intelligent college students. In some deep, inarticulate way, you recognize that an effective life is something more than a career, or raising a family, or being a good citizen. You urgently want to find for yourself what that "something more" is. Nor is this desire for inner certainty and purpose exclusive with college students. Many a person, in the midst of a successful career, wishes with inexpressible poignancy that he had begun in his teens to search how to make sense out of life, how to assert life, how to become a full, productive, serene human being. What kind of a human being do you want to be? What kind of human being *are* you now? These are not philosophers' or moralists' questions only. They are the most practical questions that can be asked.

Let's see why. You are, after all, given a legal twenty-one years to catch up with the major ideas and skills and insights of human experience. When you are technically adult, your society expects you to know how to work with other people and how to behave and express yourself without hurting others or yourself in the process. You are expected to know where you are going, and why. This is what being "grown up" implies. But the mental clinics and hospitals, jails, offices, and streets of our cities and towns are crowded with unhappy, tense, and nervous people who have not faced these fundamental questions about themselves. Moving restlessly from job to job, from pleasure to pleasure, from escape to escape, they try to find happiness by searching for conditions outside themselves that appear to lead to happiness. They do not seem to recognize that happiness comes from discovering what kind of person you want to be and can be, and then being it, serenely and confidently.

That is why I am suggesting that a *real* education (that is, an ultimately useful education) is not only the acquiring of knowledge and skill, but something more fundamental, more complex, and more significant.

Obviously, going to college will not guarantee happiness or tell you what kind of human being you ought to be. A lot of triumphs have been claimed for college education, but guaranteed maturity is not one of them. However, college is one of the few institutions in our society that is deliberately set up to help you explore the nature of human life and its meanings for you. Among all your motives for being in college—the practical ones of career, the general ones of culture, the unexpressed ones of great expectations—you might consider the aim of personal growth, or the opportunity for personal growth, as possibly the most important.

Indeed, this is the first and most inclusive stated purpose of most of the colleges and universities in the United States. At the beginning of nearly every general catalogue of course offerings, colleges state, with varying persuasiveness, the broad and humane aims I have suggested here. I recently examined several dozen of these, and I will quote briefly from two of the most typical. One, from a college division of a large university, reads: ". . . [This institution] provides the resources for the fullest personal, professional, and specialized development. . . . It provides each student with that liberal education best designed for. . . leadership. It gives him a background. . . that helps him to understand the human organism. . . ." Another, the catalogue of a small, coeducational college reads: ". . . The aim of ———— College is to give its students a sound education in preparation for the responsibilities of mature citizenship through the disciplines of a broad, rich, extensive curriculum. . . ."

30   You are in college because you are after adult learning. A college, if it lives up to its stated aims and pretensions, says: All right—most of your fact learning and drill and academic training up to now has been preparatory. You have had to learn multiplication tables, grammar, history, natural sciences, and the like, because you must have such facts as tools for any reasonable thinking. You will have to learn many more fact tools while you are at college. But now you are going to be asked in addition, and more pointedly: What *good* is all this information?

On what bases is it good? These are questions of value and their implications go beyond mere fact knowledge. Questions of value have many levels, depending upon what "values" you are talking about.

A college, if it is doing the job it should, is not and cannot be concerned mainly with stuffing facts into you, or simply training you in a skill, or teaching you how to make a living. A college's real business is with the creative development of your best personal powers. Its business is to help you to a realistic awareness of yourself as an effective participant in your society. Its business is to lead you to a knowledge and appreciation of the extent and value of the culture that you have inherited. Its business is to stimulate you to develop a wide and open-minded sympathy for values and cultures not your own. Its business is to give you concrete and continuing experience with the meaning of the word "excellent" in both vocational and nonvocational studies. Its total concern is to discipline those capacities of mind and those qualities of personality which are best characterized by the adjective "mature." (You might look up the word "discipline" in an unabridged dictionary, investigating especially its root meanings from Latin.)

What you truly study when you go to college is not simply algebra, French, biology, English, physics, or sociology. What you study is *Man*—historically, presently, potentially; Man doing, Man thinking, Man puzzling, Man creating. No matter how genuine your desire or impatience to get at your specialty, whatever it is, you will merely develop a sterile *expertise* unless you recognize that the study of literature is as much a part of scientific training as advanced calculus, that the study of biology or physics is as much a part of the educating of a future English teacher as a course in Shakespeare, that semantics and sociology are intertwined. Knowledge is seamless; it is not compartmented.

Learning and growth are synonymous. How you learn in college is how you grow in college. You may test the validity of this assertion simply by recalling any recent situation or experience in your life in which you felt yourself *grow* in any way toward skill, mastery, or capacity to cope with a problem. How you felt during and after such an experience is how learning usually feels.

This can be said in another way by summarizing the function of a college or university: *the college exists to help you learn how to think for yourself and how to use the tools of thinking in a grown-up, morally responsible, and socially effective way.* This is a large order, a formidable one, both for you and for the college. Of course. Real learning is a formidable undertaking because it involves real thinking. All real thinking is hard; indeed I don't think there is such a thing as "easy" thinking. (William James once remarked on the "atrocious harmlessness" of most so-called thinking.) Knowledge or insights that are worth anything cannot be watered down or simplified. A real education does not come in prepackaged outlines and digests any more than you as an individual can be labeled, ticketed, and handily indexed under a single category. *The complexity of learning is precisely the complexity of the individual in relation to his experience.*

35   To be educated is to be *changed,* to be enlarged and reoriented as a person. To change is hard. Most of us resist changing or being changed. Yet if you

graduate from college with your freshman habits, prejudices, and questions strengthened and more deep-seated, then no matter how much information you absorb, or how impressively you develop a skill or technique, you have not been educated but merely veneered, varnished with a cultural or technical gloss. (Varnish is a durable finish, but exposed to weather over any length of time it cracks, peels, and exposes the bare surface underneath.) Your education is going to be a personal business if it demands that you change yourself. It will demand your deep personal commitment, and may therefore be, on more than one occasion, a bewildering, frustrating, and even painful affair.

QUESTIONS FOR INQUIRY AND ACTION

1. Garrison wrote this piece in 1959. In what ways is his message relevant or irrelevant to students today?

2. Compare and contrast Garrison's piece with Peter Sacks's "The Sandbox Experiment." Are they arguing similar points? Who are their respective audiences, and what are their respective purposes in writing? Which of these writers do you think is more persuasive? Why?

3. In your writer's notebook, answer Garrison's two main questions. What is education for you, and why do you want it? Compare your answers with those of your classmates.

4. After answering question three above, review your college's mission statement and your courses' syllabi. Then, talk with your professors. Does your college have the same educational goals that you do? How does the college and its faculty help you reach your educational goals?

CASE STUDY

COLLEGE ATHLETICS VS. ACADEMICS: THE UNIVERSITY OF MINNESOTA'S MEN'S BASKETBALL SCANDAL

GEORGE DOHRMANN U of M Basketball Program
Accused of Academic Fraud

On March 10, 1999, sportswriter George Dohrmann accused the University of Minnesota's men's basketball program of violating NCAA rules. After the story was published, many local civic and political leaders criticized the St. Paul Pioneer Press. *Governor Jesse Ventura called the report "just another example of sensational* Pioneer Press *journalism." Dohrmann, however, had worked for several months carefully documenting violations. His report initiated a major investigation of the university's basketball program; it also stimulated further public discussion of the role sports programs ought to play in colleges and universities. Dohrmann was awarded the Pulitzer Prize in 2000 for his work on the basketball scandal.*

Editor's note: The Pioneer Press *launched a three-month investigation into the academic counseling of the University of Minnesota's men's basketball players after learning the university had self-reported a violation to the NCAA.*

At least 20 men's basketball players at the University of Minnesota had research papers, take-home exams or other course work done for them during a five-year period, according to a former office manager in the academic counseling unit who said she did the work.

Four former players, Courtney James, Russ Archambault, Kevin Loge and Darrell Whaley, confirmed that work was prepared for them in possible violation of the student code of conduct and NCAA regulations. Another former player, Trevor Winter, said he was aware of the practice.

James, Archambault and the office manager, Jan Gangelhoff, said knowledge of the academic fraud was widespread.

5   "These are serious allegations," University of Minnesota President Mark Yudof said Tuesday. "We've called in legal counsel. I want to look into this promptly. But they are just allegations at this point."

Gangelhoff, 50, said that from 1993 to 1998 she estimates she did more than 400 pieces of course work for players, including some starters on the 1996–97 Final Four team.

"They bring in these high-risk kids, and they know that everything they did in high school was done for them," Gangelhoff said. "It's got to stop somewhere."

Gangelhoff said she "struggled for a long time" whether to disclose the allegations. When asked to prove them, Gangelhoff provided the *Pioneer Press* with computer files containing more than 225 examples of course work for 19 players, dating to 1994, that she says she wrote and players turned in. Gangelhoff said she kept only about half her files.

Gangelhoff also provided printed copies of five pieces of course work that she said had been turned in by students. Some of the papers had grades and instructor's comments written on them. All five pieces also appeared in Gangelhoff's computer files.

10   Elayne Donahue, the retired head of the academic counseling unit, said she was unaware of the fraud but warned athletic department administrators that the office manager was tutoring players in violation of department policy and was ignored.

Coach Clem Haskins, interviewed briefly at his hotel in Seattle where the Gophers play Gonzaga in the first round of the NCAA tournament on Thursday, said the allegations were "news to me."

"I've been here 13 years, don't you know me, what I stand for as a man, as a person? I haven't changed," Haskins said. "All I'm trying to do is win a game. All I'm worrying about is beating Gonzaga. It's all I'm concentrating on. All I'll say is I will talk when the tournament is over."

Haskins referred all further comment to McKinley Boston, the vice president of student development and athletics, who questioned the credibility of Gangelhoff's allegations.

"Some of her current allegations seem to be inconsistent with statements she made in the past," he said. "We've had similar allegations made by others (about Gangelhoff), but this is new stuff."

15   Two former players denied Gangelhoff's allegation that she did work for them. Jermaine Stanford and Ryan Wolf said they completed all their own assignments. Three former players, Micah Watkins, Voshon Lenard and Hosea Crittenden, refused comment. Bobby Jackson said he and Gangelhoff did the work on the papers, with Gangelhoff typing them.

Gangelhoff said she did work for four players on this year's team: Kevin Clark, Miles Tarver, Antoine Broxsie and Jason Stanford. Clark and Tarver refused comment at their Seattle hotel Thursday night. Broxsie and Stanford were not made available for comment by school officials.

Normally, under the team's media policy, all inquiries for player interviews must be directed through school officials.

Five other former players could not be reached for comment.

When asked how he knew players were getting papers done, Winter, who graduated with a degree in business, attended the Carlson School of Management and now plays for the Timberwolves, said it was "common knowledge. It was just one of those things. It was unfortunate.

20   "If you know your teammate's getting help, if you know that somebody's helping with papers, you just (have the attitude that) 'I don't want to get involved
in it.' It's like if you have a friend that's a convicted felon. You don't go around
telling everybody he's a convicted felon. You just kind of let it go. It's him. It's
his life. It's his choices. It's not me."

The *Pioneer Press* investigation also found these allegations:

Gangelhoff said she was caught doing a take-home exam with Loge in November 1996 but was allowed to continue to work with players. Loge, who left the
program because he wanted to play for a smaller school, confirmed the incident.

Gangelhoff and two players, Archambault and James, said an assistant coach
drove the players to Gangelhoff's Minneapolis home for tutoring sessions, a
possible violation of NCAA rules. Archambault was dismissed from the team
in February 1998 for rules violations, and James chose to turn pro instead of
serving a season-long suspension after being convicted of fifth-degree assault in
August 1997.

Gangelhoff said she often had different players turn in the same paper for
different classes, or she used excerpts from one paper in another. An analysis of
the documents provided to the *Pioneer Press* revealed seven instances of duplica-
tion, including one paper that Gangelhoff said was turned in by three different
players for three different classes.

25   Donahue, the academic counseling chief, denied a request to allow Gangelhoff
to tutor Broxsie last spring after she had been approved to tutor him during the
winter quarter. But Gangelhoff said that Haskins paid her $3,000 in cash to
continue tutoring the player.

"Clem Haskins absolutely denies any payment to Jan Gangelhoff for this purpose, or any other," Yudof said. "I think the world of Clem Haskins."

Gangelhoff said Haskins paid her in cash and that after spending $1,000 to
pay bills, she deposited the rest. When asked by the *Pioneer Press* for proof, she
provided a bank statement showing she deposited $2,000 on June 29. But the
statement did not indicate whether the amount had been deposited in cash.

Gangelhoff said she never was asked by a member of the coaching staff to do
course work for players but said she considered it compensation when she was
taken on trips to two road games, including accompanying the team when it
played at the Big Island Invitational in Hawaii in the 1995–96 season. "Why
else do you think I got to go to some of the places I did?" said Gangelhoff, who
said she also attended team banquets and parties for the selection of the NCAA
tournament field.

Boston said he was unaware Gangelhoff had gone to Hawaii.

30   "That's a new one on me," he said. "You will have to ask Haskins why he
invited her along."

A request Monday to interview athletic director Mark Dienhart; Alonzo
Newby, the team's academic counselor; and Chris Schoemann, the school's NCAA
compliance director, was ignored by the school's sports information staff. And
phone messages left for Newby and Schoemann were not returned.

Gangelhoff said some of the first papers she wrote were edited by Newby and former assistant coach Milton Barnes, now the head coach at Eastern Michigan University. Barnes, reached by telephone, denies the allegation.

"Coach Barnes would read them and say things like: 'Now, is this something so and so would say?' And if it wasn't, I would go back and rewrite it to make it sound more like something the player would write," Gangelhoff said.

Barnes said: "I don't know anything about it. I don't recall anything like that. She may have me confused with somebody else, that's all I can say."

35   Boston said the school has self-reported one potential NCAA violation involving Gangelhoff.

On Oct. 26, Dienhart sent Gangelhoff a letter disassociating her from the program even though she had left the school the previous summer.

In the letter, obtained by the *Pioneer Press*, Dienhart wrote that the school had "recently reviewed activities in the men's basketball academic counseling unit." It said the action against her had been "reviewed and approved" by the NCAA.

Gangelhoff said after she received the letter, "I came to the conclusion that something has to change" and she decided to make the allegations public.

An NCAA official denied comment about the letter.

40   "There was reason to question her based on one incident that came to our attention," said Boston, who refused to give further details about the incident. "Our NCAA compliance officer (Schoemann) investigated her and basically determined that in one particular instance there was an allegation that was valid. We self-reported that one violation to the NCAA. But beyond what was determined in that one particular investigation, everything she is alleging is new information."

Gangelhoff said Schoemann questioned her twice about possible violations, but otherwise her actions went unchecked. Her first meeting with Schoemann came after Gangelhoff was caught helping Loge look up answers for a take-home exam during study table in the Bierman Athletic Building.

Loge, now attending Fergus Falls Community College, confirmed that Gangelhoff helped him look up the answers and admitted as much to Schoemann. Gangelhoff told Schoemann she helped Loge but claimed that she was unaware it was a take-home exam and that she couldn't help him. Gangelhoff said she was never reprimanded or questioned further about the incident. Loge said he was not disciplined for the incident. Gangelhoff said Schoemann confronted her again a few months later and asked whether she was tutoring basketball players.

"I lied," Gangelhoff said. "And those were the only two times I was questioned."

Archambault said he never was questioned by Schoemann, and James said he was questioned once but lied to Schoemann.

45   "He asked if Jan did papers. Of course, I said no," James said. "At that time, I didn't want to get Jan in trouble. And, at the same time, I didn't want to get coach Haskins in trouble."

Gangelhoff said when she left the university she never intended to reveal that she did course work for players. But the letter of disassociation angered her, she says, because she never was asked to give her side of the story.

"You look at other programs that are successful that have strong academics, and why can't (Minnesota) have that?" she said. "What are we doing wrong that we can't get these kids to learn? . . . Something has to change or (Minnesota) will continue to bring kids in and then throw them away."

Gangelhoff said she did the course work to help academically at-risk athletes she thought were unprepared for college. Academic services' policy forbids front-office personnel from working with student-athletes. But Gangelhoff, an American Indian, said she felt a particular bond with African-American student-athletes.

"The big thing was that they trusted me. I was like a mother figure to them," Gangelhoff said. "My sisters and I, we treated them like family. We had dinners for them. We exchanged Christmas and birthday presents. And I always praised them."

50   As office manager, Gangelhoff worked for Donahue. But she said Newby was aware of her tutoring activities.

Gangelhoff said Newby arranged players' schedules so that they took courses with her or courses that she had already completed. Gangelhoff took classes from 1993 to '95 while employed full time as office manager. She received her degree in 1995 in InterCollege Program, a self-designed degree program offered by University College.

Gangelhoff was in the same 1994 class with players Winter, Lenard, Crittenden and Jayson Walton.

"We were in the same class, and, miraculously, we were in the same work group," Gangelhoff said. "I wrote the research paper (on alcoholism among American Indian youth)."

Winter said: "It was a group thing, a group project. She's American Indian. She had a lot more input than the rest of us did. She was a member of the group. It was all above board. . . . That was four years ago. Who knows (the truth) if I say I did 95 percent of the work and she just proofed it. . . . She may have proofed it. She may have written the whole thing. I honestly can't tell you what everyone's contribution was. . . . In groups, somebody does do most of the work."

55   James and Archambault said members of the coaching staff were aware that Gangelhoff was doing course work for players.

"The coaches knew. Everybody (in the basketball program) knew," Archambault said. "We used to make jokes about it. . . . I would go over there some night and get like four papers done. The coaches would be laughing about it."

James said, "Everybody knew we were going to see Jan."

Although Archambault said Haskins was aware of the practice, Winter said the coach may not have known.

"Clem is the basketball coach," Winter said. "When it comes to academics, there are coaches he puts in charge. If something is against the rules, he honestly, from me to you, has nothing to do with it. If there's things going on, he doesn't want to know about it. So, he has that buffer."

60   The buffers, he said, were assistant coaches and academic advisers.

Instead of the common practice of tutoring players at the Bierman Athletic Building, Gangelhoff said, she did most of her work at home. She said she drove players to her house or assistant coaches did. Archambault and James confirmed they got rides from an assistant coach, a possible NCAA violation. Under the NCAA's extra-benefits rule, athletes are not allowed services unavailable to other students.

Donahue said she heard from one of her employees that a coach was driving two players to Gangelhoff's home in the spring quarter of 1998, when she was no longer approved to tutor. She said she passed that information on to Dienhart and Schoemann but said that to the best of her knowledge, no investigation took place. Gangelhoff said she never was questioned during that period or since she stopped tutoring last June.

Once in the home, Gangelhoff said the players would either sit next to her as she typed the course work or be in an adjacent room.

"It depended on what we needed to do," Gangelhoff said. "If it was a (home-work) assignment and they had been to class, we would talk about what happened in class and what they heard and what they thought about the assignment. And then, they would grab the remote and go watch TV, and I would type (the assignment) up.

65   "On the research papers, we would rarely meet. They would just give me the assignment and I would do it and then they would pick it up. Sometimes I would read the papers to them and explain them to them just in case they got asked in class about them."

Archambault said: "I thought I was going to actually learn how to write a paper. I never learned in high school. But then I sat down and she just started typing."

Bobby Jackson said Gangelhoff's primary role for him was as a typist, which is also a possible violation of the NCAA extra-benefits rule. Gangelhoff's files turned over to the *Pioneer Press* show 28 papers under Jackson's name.

"She definitely helped me out," said Jackson, who also plays for the Timber-wolves. "She didn't totally do all the papers for me. . . . When we were on the road, of course we needed help. She did the typing. Once we got everything arranged, she did the typing. I'm not going to say she sat down and totally wrote the paper by herself. No. I was doing my papers myself, with the research and everything. At some point in time, she was finding books for us and stuff. Never a point in time she wrote my paper for me."

Winter said he understands why Gangelhoff's work became so prolific.

70   "I think it was more of a fact of laziness than it was of people really needing the help or really cheating to get by," he said. "During the season it really gets to be a wear. Not to sound like a pampered athlete—and I did the work—some people lose concentration. They miss a class here and there when on the road and get behind a little bit.

"It's easier to say, 'Will you help me do this class?' or 'Will you help me get this paper done?' than actually putting in the work. I would say the help the players got was more due to laziness than it was due to the fact they couldn't actually do the work."

Donahue said she was not surprised to learn from the *Pioneer Press* last week of Gangelhoff's allegations that she did course work for players.

"I believe anything is possible with Clem," she said. "But I am surprised by how widespread (the allegations are)."

Donahue said she suspected Gangelhoff was working with basketball players in violation of department policy but did not know she was doing course work.

75 "I believed she was tutoring, but because I didn't know where she was doing this, I had no proof," Donahue said.

Donahue described her relationship with Haskins as "strained" and said the two often disagreed on Newby's roles and whether Newby should have reported to her. While still at the university, Donahue said she was hesitant to make accusations against Newby and Haskins for that reason.

"There was a difference of philosophies. . . . I believed that (basketball players) should do their homework," Donahue said. "I believe they are in college to become educated. And I worked toward supporting students so they could earn a degree. My understanding of (the basketball program) was that you enabled students to become irresponsible. 'It's OK to have someone else do the work.'"

By the spring quarter, Gangelhoff had moved back in with family in Wisconsin. But she continued to do course work, often driving from Wisconsin weekly to meet with players at her sister's home in Minneapolis. But she stopped tutoring because Newby never asked her to continue working with players during the summer, and she began a new job in August.

"It just sort of fizzled out," she said.

80 Gangelhoff substantiated her claim of writing the papers by pointing out that she often duplicated work or had different players turn in the same paper for different classes.

Gangelhoff said that one of the papers she produced, a 2,000-word essay comparing Martin Luther King Jr. to Malcolm X, was turned in by three players.

"I did that all the time," Gangelhoff said. "Different courses meant different professors so they wouldn't know. I would turn in papers I had written for my classes or take parts of one paper that I used for one player and put in a paper for another player."

In the papers supplied to the *Pioneer Press*, Gangelhoff at times wrote first-person essays for players. Gangelhoff said she tired of writing papers by the end of her tenure and wrote primarily about topics that interested her.

Among the 1998 work Gangelhoff turned over to the *Pioneer Press* were papers she said players turned in on the menstrual cycle, women's gains in the workplace and eating disorders. Two papers referred to the plight of the same woman, a one-time employee at US West, and in one of those she identifies the woman as her sister, Jeanne Payer.

85 Payer also tutored Archambault, Walton and Wolf, Gangelhoff said. Payer was approved to tutor by Donahue, who said she was unaware at the time of her hiring that Payer was Gangelhoff's sister. Payer could not be reached for comment, but Gangelhoff said Payer also did course work for the athletes in violation of NCAA rules during the 1997–98 school year.

Gangelhoff asked that Payer, who is ill, not be contacted.

"Alonzo (Newby) needed help. I needed help, and Jeanne was unemployed at the time," Gangelhoff said. "I said to Alonzo, 'Hire Jeanne,' and he thought that was an excellent idea."

Archambault said: "In the two years I was there, I never did a thing. Either Jan or Jeanne did everything."

Writing Style

WRITING A NEWS ARTICLE

In Chapter Five, we learned that news articles inform the public of current events and issues affecting the community. George Dohrmann's article on the University of Minnesota Men's Basketball offers a good example; it informs citizens of the university, local, state, and national communities about violations of laws governing men's collegiate basketball. As you read Dohrmann's piece, identify those aspects you would need to consider in writing your own news article. Here are some suggestions to get you started:

- *Write to match a newspaper's needs.* Newspapers usually have set sections and assignments, so beginning news writers may have difficulty simply submitting something for publication. You should probably talk to the paper's editor before writing a news article for publication to see if the subject would fit in their established sections and preferred subjects.

- *Write to represent your subject thoroughly and objectively.* News articles are often the first place readers learn of important issues, so writers need to give them a thorough understanding of the journalist's basic questions: What happened? Who was affected? When and where did it occur? How did it happen and why?

- *Write to complement the way newspapers are printed.* Because newspapers are formatted into narrow columns, you should keep your paragraphs short (only a few sentences each) so they won't look like thick blocks of text on the page. Also, you should avoid long, complex sentences. Long sentences are harder to follow when they are broken up across several lines.

- *Write to complement the way newspapers are read.* People often read newspapers in their spare moments—when eating breakfast, taking a break, or riding the bus. As a result, you should keep your writing active and direct, so readers can readily understand your points without having to work to decipher your prose. Using a few select details or descriptions also helps readers to see the events or issues for themselves.

- *Write to hook and keep their interest.* Because newspaper readers have many articles to choose from in a paper, you want to try introductions that grab their attention (e.g., use visual details to put readers at the scene of a crisis). You might also include narratives, engaging quotes, a shocking statistic, and so on in different places within the article to refuel readers' interest. For example, if your news article gets bogged down by background information, you might include an interesting quote from a local expert.

Letters from Readers

Readers of George Dohrmann's article reacted strongly to his accusations. Here are several of the many letters to the editor submitted to the Pioneer Press *and the* StarTribune.

Letter to the Editor, *Pioneer Press,* March 12, 1999

You deserve congratulations. Your front-page piece, coincidentally released one day before the Gophers' opening-round game in the NCAA tournament, shows not only your impeccable sense of timing, but also the depth of your self-serving motives.

This is trash-can-lid-lifting, toilet-sniffing journalism worthy of the gumshoes who used to collect human body odor samples for the Stasi (before the East German People's Republic collapsed, as it deserved to).

I used to have respect for your newspaper, before you brought sourpuss, sarcastic people-haters like Tom Powers and Bob Sansevere on your sports page. Now this.

I predict that Clem Haskins, Mark Dienhart and McKinley Boston will be vindicated of your vicious accusations and [reporter George] Dohrmann and your newspaper will get what you deserve. I'm surprised you didn't bring Linda Tripp in from Washington to put on a wire and help you with this.

You have lost my respect totally. Your callous disregard for who you hurt and when you hurt them should earn you the ridicule and the censure you deserve. You will get what you deserve. If there isn't a tradition of decency in the media, then the one that rules this universe will step in to right these wrongs.

Shame on you, shame on your newspaper.

Robert Faust, Woodbury

Letter to the Editor, *StarTribune,* June 26, 1999

In my heart of hearts, I feel for basketball coach Clem Haskins. In a mad scramble to save face, the University of Minnesota has chosen to ignore the growing stench of its own hypocrisy.

At best, university officials were complacent with Haskins' the-ends-justify-the-means philosophy, and rightly so. It feels good to win and is hilariously naïve to believe there's 100 percent academic integrity in any college athletics program. But the Gophers could compete—and win. Then the story hit, the finger-pointing began, the ax fell. The university came up with a miserable solution, revealing the complete lack of integrity and competence at the highest levels of management. Today I am ashamed to be associated with the University of Minnesota, both as a student and as a Minnesota taxpayer.

Thank you, Coach Haskins, for an incredible 13 years.

Jason L. Bakke, St. Paul

"Send the boosters packing," *StarTribune,* June 29, 1999

The idea that every large university must bow down to athletic boosters and field a winning team is subverting the very idea of intellectual and creative accomplishment. It's time for any university worth its salt to send athletic boosters packing, to tell them to put their money into academic programs.

American society in general has been degraded by the shallow competition of sports, and it's long past time for universities to take a principled stand against such degradation. Athletes in motion are beautiful, but no more so than dancers performing a pas de deux or than a painter's canvas or a writer's book. Let's tell athletes to get a life instead of a free pass, and let's display suitable contempt for university administrators who play the "sports" game with human lives.

Alan Davis, Moorhead, Minn.

"Link study, sports," *StarTribune,* November 28, 1999

To this recent graduate of the University of Minnesota, it is highly important that the school maintain a reputation for academic rigor and integrity. At the same time, I sympathize with the athletes caught in the basketball team's academic scandal. The "U" harnessed the sports talent of these young men in order to generate multimillion-dollar revenues for itself; in return, the players got scholarships that were not of much benefit to many individuals.

One solution would be to allow players to get a cut of the financial action. The players have spent years honing specialized skills with high market value; they deserve to derive economic benefit from their talents.

Players should also get academic training that really contributes to their long-run personal and career viability. Many classes could be linked to basketball and sports in general: sports literature, sports physiology, sports statistics, sports economics and the like. Fusing a basketball player's academic life with his life on the court might prove surprisingly successful for everyone involved.

Chris Schons, Wayzata

"Players' ethics," *StarTribune,* November 28, 1999

Oh, those poor, poor "student" athletes at the University of Minnesota, "victimized" by the evil Athletic Department staff. The only thing that is more shocking than the conduct of McKinley Boston, Clem Haskins, Alonzo Newby and Mark Dienhart is the complete lack of moral strength on the part of the players that accepted cash and predone homework. Maybe if they had actually attended some classes, in ethics for example, they might have learned the difference between right and wrong.

The ones I feel sorry for are the real students who rack up thousands and thousands of dollars in debt as a result of bloated tuition costs at the "U."

Ben Fraase, Minneapolis.

Writing Style

WRITING LETTERS TO THE EDITOR

Letters to the editor are one of the most accessible ways for beginning writers to communicate their views to the public. However, because they are so short and direct, writers often believe, incorrectly, that they are easy to write well. Examine the letters to the editor written in response to George Dohrmann's news article on the University of Minnesota men's basketball scandal. What qualities do you like or dislike in the letters? Write down some of the qualities of those letters you think are successful and compare them to the following list of suggestions for how to write a letter to the editor.

- *Always review the newspaper's or magazine's policies for printing letters.* Some editors will only accept letters under a certain length or submitted in particular ways (e.g., hand delivered with a picture ID). Knowing the policies ahead of time can save you time and frustration.

- *Submit your letter as soon as possible.* If you are responding to a previous article or editorial, you should submit your letter within two or three days. After that time, the editor and readers will have moved on to other issues. If your letter raises a new issue then you should submit your letter when it might have the strongest impact on the public (e.g., you might raise concerns about a candidate's environmental policies a few days before an election so your ideas are still fresh in readers' minds as they go to the polls).

- *Keep the letter short.* Letters that go over 150 words may get published but they will often be cut down by the editor. Editors want to print as many different letters as possible within a small space, so writing a short, concise letter will increase your chances for getting it published.

- *Identify the issue or argument you are responding to up front.* Readers want to be able to locate your views in a particular conversation quickly so identify the issue or argument in the first sentence and state your purpose in writing (e.g., to agree, disagree, qualify, and so on). Also, don't waste too much space giving readers background information on the issue or summarizing another arguer's views; those who take the time to read your letter will probably know the issue or other arguers' ideas already.

- *Make sure the letter is focused, well organized, and specific.* Because letters are short, you should decide what aspect of the issue or argument you want to focus on. Then, you can include facts, expert testimony, examples,

continued on next page

and specific discussion—those elements that will most convince your readers. Following a clear structure will make it easier for people to read (e.g.,
identify the issue or argument you are responding to, state your view, and
then support your view with evidence). A focused, well-organized, and specific letter will also help your writing persona, projecting competence and
expertise to readers.

- *Avoid an abusive or condescending tone.* Saying that another arguer is an
  idiot or a creeping worm will usually reflect badly on your own writing persona, undermining your professionalism and sincerity. In addition, such a
  tone may prevent the editor from printing your letter. Instead, treat disagreements as opportunities to inquire about the issue.
- *Include your name, address, phone number, and signature.* Editors will usually not publish letters unless they can verify who wrote it.
- *Don't get discouraged.* Editors receive dozens of letters every day; consequently they can't publish every letter they receive, no matter how good
  they are. If they don't print your letter, try again the next time you are
  moved to write, and keep trying.

Report of the Special Senate Committee on Student Academic Integrity

*On July 15, 1999, a Special Senate Committee at the University of Minnesota
was appointed to review the University's academic integrity policies in light
of the basketball scandal and other instances of student cheating. Their report
called for many changes, including an academic integrity pledge students would
complete upon admission to the school and before submitting tests or papers.
The following is an excerpt from Part II of their report, submitted April 6, 2000.*

The University assumes integrity as the norm of its students' behavior. But even
where there is thought to be no cheating, prudence argues for the precaution-
ary benefit of an integrity code and a declaration of academic integrity to be signed
by all students. This declaration should be signed during the academic part of
their initial orientation to the University, as freshmen, transfer students, or entering graduate or professional students, or on an appropriate equivalent occasion in
units where there is no formal orientation. Making such a declaration will alert
students to their personal responsibility to their fellow students and the University as a whole, and to the penalties imposed for cheating when detected and
proved. Ideally, this would confer lifelong immunity from cheating upon the
signer; but because there are and will be exceptions, efforts to inform and prevent must be supplemented by those to detect and to punish as necessary.

In accordance with the foregoing discussion, we recommend that all students
of the University sign this declaration upon their admission:

*I recognize academic integrity as essential to the University of Minnesota's and its students'
equitable and uncompromised pursuit of their joint endeavors. As a student I promise to prac-*

tice it to the best of my ability and to do nothing that would give me unfair advantage at the expense of my fellow students. If I cheat in spite of making this declaration, I expect to be penalized according to the offense, up to and including notation of cheating recorded on my transcript and permanent expulsion from the University of Minnesota.

We also recommend that as a reminder and reaffirmation students sign and date the following statement to be printed on blue books and other examination forms:

I have not cheated while taking this examination.

_____

(signature)   *(date)*

Anyone who sees cheating during an exam is encouraged to tell the instructor or the Office of Academic Integrity.

Finally, we recommend that students sign the following statement for out-of-class written papers or projects:

The work on this paper or project is entirely my own except as documented otherwise, and I have given no undocumented assistance on the assignment to others.

MURRAY SPERBER Cheating

> *Murray Sperber is professor of English and American studies at Indiana University, Bloomington. He is a frequent media commentator on college sports and the author of other books including* Shake Down the Thunder: The Creation of Notre Dame Football *(1993). He told* Contemporary Authors *that "In my writing and teaching, I attempt to persuade people that politics informs all of life, including literature and film, and that the serious question for the artist is not how to escape from politics (those who try to flee merely serve the regime in power) but how best to become aware of politics and how best to integrate this awareness into one's life and work." "Cheating" is a chapter from his book* Beer and Circus: How Big-Time College Sports Is Crippling Undergraduate Education *(New York: Henry Holt, 2000).*

Just as the internal culture and values of the modern research university prevent an end to grade inflation, they also block a solution to the problem of student cheating. According to many studies, cheating by undergraduates has reached epidemic levels, but many faculty at research universities neither attempt to curtail it nor even seriously discourage it. Details on this situation—the hidden clauses in the "nonaggression pact"—follow.

One factor often overlooked is the relationship between cheating and the grading and testing environment. . . . Students frequently report that cheating increases. . . when instructors are viewed as inattentive and inaccessible, when papers are not read and graded carefully, and when students perceive a very high level of cheating on the part of their classmates.

Richard A. Fass, professor of ethics

In the history of American higher education, undergraduates have cheated in a large variety of ways: "ponies" (primitive *Cliffs Notes*) to facilitate studying for exams; "crib" sheets and notes for the exams themselves; and the constant recycling of essays and papers. One historian noted that "at Yale in the 1860s, perhaps less than half of the compositions were actually written by the supposed author." Because of the collegiate subculture's aversion to academics, matched by professorial disdain for most undergraduates, cheating was normal behavior at many schools. This tradition continued through the twentieth century, faculty and administrators usually blaming the "deficient moral standard of our students" for the cheating, and never considering the connections between undergraduate dishonesty and a deeply flawed pedagogical system.

In the final decades of the twentieth century, by all measurements, student cheating accelerated at many colleges and universities to the point where, in 1999, an authoritative poll stated that "three-quarters of college students confess to cheating at least once." On some campuses, officials estimated the number of one-timers as high as 90 percent, with repeat offenders topping 50 percent of their undergraduates.

These statistics prompt the question: Why is cheating so widespread at a time of grade inflation? It seems counterintuitive that these two phenomena would occur simultaneously: if high grades are so easy to obtain, why bother to cheat for them? This paradox contradicts the students-cheat-out-of-desperation hypothesis, as well as the moral-decay-in-society explanation: high grades are so common that, like pennies, they are not worth bending over for or stealing. But the paradox points directly to the abysmal state of undergraduate education at Big-time U's—by most accounts, the schools with the highest number of student cheaters.

The 1990s studies on this issue contain some version of the following conclusion from a survey of thirteen thousand undergraduates: "A major factor determining whether a student will cheat or not is the academic culture of the specific institution that he or she attends." Students at large, public research universities that treat them as tuition dollars, not individuals, and that channel them into mammoth lecture courses with distant, frigid professors or inexperienced and overworked TAs, tend to cheat. They cheat for a variety of reasons, including as a show of contempt for a contemptible system. Or, as a Michigan State sophomore described his conduct in lecture courses—he rarely attended, bought lecture notes from an off-campus service, and cheated on papers and exams—"It's an eye for an eye, it's my insults for the school's insults." The name of a popular website that facilitates a variety of cheating practices also sums up the attitude of many undergraduates at Big-time U's today: www.SCHOOLSUCKS.com—its motto is, "Download your workload."

Michael Moore, a Rutgers student and the author of *Cheating 101: The Benefits and Fundamentals of Earning an Easy A*, admitted that students also cheat because they "want to spend more time partying and meeting people instead of burying their heads in books," but he placed much of "the blame on professors, [citing] their laziness in using the same teaching methods every year." Such comments prompt the question: Where do student indolence and rationalization end, and faculty laziness and contempt for undergraduates begin? Rutgers professor Michael Moffat answered the query, in part, by noting that "undergrads who know their professors and respect them are less likely to cheat in those classes" than students in huge lecture courses.

No observer can or should condone cheating and, finally, every student can and should act as a responsible and ethical individual. However, the neglect of undergraduate education by research universities begins to explain some of the increase in student cheating.

Predictably, most faculty and administrators regard cheating differently than do undergraduates. A professor of anthropology, also an associate provost at his university, denounced all forms of cheating, including the form "perpetrated" by off-campus companies posting course lecture notes on the web—he termed this an "assault on the integrity of higher education." Surprisingly, *USA Today* weighed into the debate with an editorial:

Net Notes Trump Boring Lecture

Quick, a test: You're a freshman and you're running late for Psych 101. You could drag yourself over to the lecture hall and strain to hear the tiny professorial speck down at the lectern impart wisdom. Or you could clock on www.StudentU.com and download the speck's course notes. . . .

Students who download notes are right. The notes are adding value to the assembly line of undergraduate education, where grad students and minor [faculty] lights, not earth-shattering geniuses, lecture, and where traded paper notes have long been the order of the day.

A University of Texas (Austin) student columnist confirmed *USA Today's* argument: "The unwritten UT philosophy," exemplified by the mass lecture courses at the school and the arrogant faculty, is: "We [professors] are smart, you [undergraduates] are stupid. We lecture, you take notes." Obviously, this system generates undergraduate cynicism, the purchase of lecture notes, and more serious forms of cheating.

5   A dissident professor at the University of Virginia offered a sensible but biting solution to the lecture note controversy:

Maybe the course should be distributed as a book, rather than having this charade of somebody standing up and going through a lecture that, for all purposes, doesn't change from year to year and doesn't allow students the possibility of discussion.

Most academics who oppose course notes appearing on the web have considered the book option—for that reason, they generally cite copyright issues, not pedagogical ones, in opposing the web note-taking services. Indeed, many faculty members publish the book and require the hundreds of students in their lecture classes to buy it. The professor then makes a profit from these forced purchases and still lectures from the book! This prompts the question: Who is cheating in this situation?

Anthony Scimone, a high school teacher, neatly summed up the debate about the new websites: "I suspect that the best teachers are not threatened by the new note-taking services. These teachers. . . encourage students to generate ideas and engage in scholarly discourse." The current studies on why students cheat confirms Mr. Scimone's intuition; one authority commented, "It's clear that when students really care about learning, they're much less likely to cheat." An official at a large public university noted that "In the 100 and 200 level [lecture] classes you see much more cheating" than in small upper-level courses; in the latter, "students take greater pride in their work because it is more important to them," and because they have direct contact with a professor.

The most striking proof of how a low faculty/student ratio short-circuits cheating comes from a study of schools with honor codes—where students can cheat easily and constantly if they choose to do so. Because these institutions emphasize undergraduate education, have few lecture courses, and because the "honor codes [are] rooted in a campus tradition of mutual trust and respect. . . between faculty members and students," they succeed in eliminating almost all student cheating.

At Rice University, for example, professors hand out exams and allow students to return to their dorm rooms or apartments with the exams in order to use their computers there to write their answers. Faculty trust students to take the exam without seeking any outside aid, without even opening their course books or notes. According to a current Rice undergraduate, "I've never seen anyone or heard of anyone breaking the honor code. Anyway, you'd mainly be cheating yourself [out of a good education]. . . . Also you become friendly with your instructors, and so cheating on them is like stealing from someone you know."

Rice University and other schools with low faculty/student ratios try to provide their undergraduates with quality educations. But what occurs at large public universities with high ratios? A faculty member at the University of Central Florida, a school that recently moved to NCAA Division I-A, has research ambitions, and features many lecture classes, explained that "The increasing casualness with which students seem to be cheating and committing plagiarism is just another symptom of the paradigm shift. . . to education as a consumer product—something that must be handed over on demand to all who pay their tuition." But the paradox reappears here: Why would students cheat if, after paying their bursar bills, they are simply handed what they want?

10   One answer, suggested by P.S. notes on the questionnaire for this book, is that some undergraduates cheat as a primitive, inarticulate form of consumer protest: they feel that because their U cheats them out of their money by giving them worthless classes, their dishonesty is justified. "This place constantly screws me over and takes my money," wrote a student at the University of New Mexico. "So why should I have a conscience about cheating in class?" Nevertheless, primitive individual actions—unlike the organized student protests in the 1960s—fail to disrupt the current system in any way; indeed, they deflect attention from its failures and allow college officials to place the blame for the cheating problem on "student immorality."

An Indiana University undergraduate offered his view of student dishonesty in a caustic article in the campus newspaper. He described "The Only Syllabus You'll Ever Need" at this school, and his cynicism about the huge lecture courses and indifferent professors premised his approval of student deceit. Under "Cheating" on his mock syllabus, he noted:

> Students caught cheating will be dealt with swiftly and severely by the Dean of Students, although you have to be practically brain-dead to get caught cheating in a huge lecture class. There's like, 300 kids in there—it's easy.

Under "Grades," he wrote: "Your grade in this course will be determined by two fifty-minute tests," no papers, no writing assignments.

As this student noted, cheating during lecture course exams is not difficult: in addition to the time-worn methods of copying from the person next to you and using crib sheets, undergraduates now employ such hightech devices as cellular phones to dial multiple-choice answers into alphanumeric pagers, for example, 1C-2B-3A, to exchange answers with friends. One teacher remarked, "I get the sense there's a thrill to it, that [students think] 'my teachers are too dumb to catch me.'"

Probably some undergraduates hold this belief; however, dumbness does not prevent most professors from catching student cheaters—deafness does. Faculty simply do not want to hear about it. Tolerating cheating is a hidden clause in the nonaggression pact between many faculty members at research universities and their students. A classics professor at Northwestern University explained: "Most professors at a place like Northwestern can't be bothered [about undergraduate cheating]. They're not rewarded for teaching; they're rewarded for research. There's no future in pursuing cheating from the standpoint of a professor's self-interest."

As for students cheating for "the thrill of it": undoubtedly some undergraduates do it for the risk-taking thrill, but others also regard cheating as an active, engaging experience, far superior to passively ingesting the lectures and, without retaining anything from them, dumping them out on the exams. An undergraduate at the University of Iowa explained, "I'm into gambling and I'm into cheating in lecture classes. The only times when I feel alive in those courses is when I'm cheating. I'm really concentrating then, like when I'm on a river boat [casino]." This student was disappointed to learn that probably some of his professors did not care whether he cheated or not. "That sorta takes the fun out of it," he admitted, "but that explains why it's often so easy."

> A few years ago, a professor at a southern university suspected a student of plagiarism. What did the professor do? Absolutely nothing. The messy case didn't seem worth the anxiety or aggravation, so he graded the assignment as usual and passed the student on.
>
> —Allison Schneider, *Chronicle of Higher Education* reporter

15   Catching cheaters, like fighting grade inflation, requires a large amount of a faculty member's time and energy, and because the promotion, tenure, and salary system of the research university never rewards a professor for detecting a student plagiarist, or any other species of academic thief, why would a faculty member spend precious minutes, hours, even days or weeks in this endeavor (tracking

down the exact source of a plagiarized paper can be a trek across a desert)? Moreover, apprehending the cheater is merely the first step in a very laborious process: countless reports to fill out, many faculty and student disciplinary committees at which to appear and present the evidence in the case, and always the threat of the accused student suing the accuser.

If grading student work puts faculty on the path of least resistance, resulting in grade inflation, then discovering a plagiarist or exam cheater often triggers a sprint down that path. As the southern professor told the *Chronicle of Higher Education,* exposing a cheater is not worth "the anxiety or aggravation" or time. Therefore, the best course of action is to do nothing. But what happens to faculty who—out of pride, honesty, or perversity—try to expose a cheater?

Many faculty members interviewed for this book on this issue told a horror story about a professor who accumulated lots of evidence of a particular student's cheating, then reported the student's dishonesty to the proper university authorities. After a year of hearings before various university judicial groups and no judgments, the student sued the accuser. The professor's school provided no legal aid for him or her; then, in a triumph of Johnnie Cochran–like lawyering, the student got off scot-free, and the professor had to pay exorbitant court costs and damages. He or she was financially and emotionally ruined by the case.

Faculty repeated versions of this anecdote so often—usually with the besieged professor as "a colleague of a friend at another university"—that the tale took on the character of an urban legend. A few cases like the professor's have occurred, although never in this extreme form, but the accuracy of the story is much less important than the fact that so many faculty members believe it and invoke it as a reason for doing nothing about student cheating.

Even professors who actually want to combat cheating discover that their universities will not help them in this endeavor. James Karge-Taylor teaches a lecture course in the history of jazz at the University of Arizona, and, in 1998, he discovered in a poll in his class that, of the 368 enrolled students, 25 percent had cheated on the first quiz. He had a simple request of his school, "I would like more help reading papers." Apparently help never arrived. A late-1999 article about websites selling papers for students to submit as their own work mentioned: "The paper mills are keeping customers happy. Tim, a University of Arizona senior who buys around four papers a semester, recalls ordering an essay on Louis Armstrong [for a jazz lecture class]. . . . Five minutes later, he got a call from the company urging him to reconsider. One of his schoolmates had already ordered the same paper."

20   Nevertheless, in the bleak research university landscape, some faculty members at Big-time U's manage to prevent cheating and plagiarism in their courses. However, their methods are very labor intensive. An Indiana University professor puts the following note in all of his course syllabi:

A warning on original work vs. plagiarism

An experienced teacher can easily tell the difference between original student writing and plagiarized work. Because you will have to write various exercises in class, I will have an excellent idea of your true writing abilities. Thus, when you turn in your major papers in the course, your writing—although more careful and polished than your in-class work—will still reflect your abilities. Your writing is like your signature, unique to you. To turn in someone else's writing—professional critic, friend, tutor, website doofus, etc.—is foolish, easily recognized, an insult to your instructor and fellow students, and a good way to get yourself into serious trouble.

NOTE: When you turn in your major papers in this course, you must also turn in your original notes, outlines, and drafts—be sure to print out the drafts after you do them. I will not accept a major paper without this material (it helps me gauge the quality of your research as well as the amount of work that you put into the paper).

This instructor admits that he would not know what to do if a student actually turned in a plagiarized paper, but, fortunately, he has not discovered one since he added these paragraphs to his syllabi many years ago. Admittedly, his teaching methods are time-consuming—he has to read all of his students' in-class and out-of-class work—but he believes that this is the only way to teach people to become better writers.

In addition, he finds that requiring "notes, outlines, and drafts" is a useful pedagogical device, and one that also short-circuits plagiarism. The instructor remarked, "The plagiarist would have to deconstruct the bought or stolen finished product into draft, outline, and note form. He or she would learn far more about writing from doing this than writing the paper straight."

This instructor is not a typical faculty member at a major research university. Some of his colleagues at Indiana and other Big-time U's also try to prevent cheating—but mainly with seating strategies in lecture halls, such as handing out various versions of the scantron exam so that no student sits next to another student with the same version of the exam. However, the new cellular phone technologies tend to defeat these strategies.

Similarly, some faculty have embraced the new anti-plagiarism search engines on the web. In theory, they take a suspect paper and locate the original already posted somewhere on the web. In practice, as a reporter discovered, the search engines "fail to detect [papers]. . . with even the slightest amount of rewriting," and, more to the point, they can only find papers listed in html and free to all (many of which are atrociously written). The anti-plagiarism engines cannot penetrate websites that require passwords, i.e., those that sell excellent recycled essays or, for a fairly high price, that supply an original paper to clients. Therefore, the best antidote to plagiarism on the web remains a teacher who requires writing in class and knows his or her students and their work well.

25   At a time when many universities tolerate student cheating, some institutions have gone a step further and have created a culture where staff members write the papers and take-home exams for some undergraduates, particularly intercollegiate athletes. A national magazine remarked:

> Sometimes the schools are directly responsible [for cheating]. . . . A former tutor for the University of Minnesota revealed that she had written 400 papers for 20 [varsity men's] basketball players between 1993 and 1998.

The University of Minnesota academic cheating scandal was large in scale but not exceptional in occurrence. Indeed, athletic department tutors at every NCAA Division I school have approached or crossed the line between tutoring a student and actually doing some of the student's course work. For example, in helping an athlete correct writing errors, the tutor rewrites the entire paper, and then the jock submits it as his or her own work; or, in typing a paper for an athlete, the tutor makes so many changes and corrections that the final product—submitted as the jock's original work—is, at best, a collaborative effort, and more often a ghost-written one.

In the Minnesota academic cheating scandal, three tutors, encouraged and rewarded by athletic department officials, brazenly composed whole papers and answered take-home exams for many basketball players, sometimes on subjects about which the athletes knew nothing, and in polished prose that some of these academically challenged jocks were incapable of writing. Not surprisingly, faculty members receiving these papers and exams were suspicious, but, in true Big-time U fashion, they ignored the alarm bells and graded the papers as if they were original student work.

However, one assistant professor did complain to University of Minnesota authorities. He pointed out that in one of his courses, basketball "star forward Courtney James had [recently] turned in a paper that was the best he [the instructor] had seen in his nearly forty years at the university," and that he clearly "suspected academic fraud." Nevertheless, Minnesota administrators would not investigate or support the instructor, and so he gave the paper and the player a passing grade.

Eventually, due to the competitive nature of the two daily newspapers in the area, the details of academic fraud in the men's basketball program at Minnesota emerged, including this assistant professor's experiences. UM administrators then pledged a total cleanup—as they had after every public revelation in the long history of UM athletic department scandals. Yet, NCAA officials called the recent UM incident an idiosyncratic event; in reality, many tutors at other Big-time U's could tell the press about academic dishonesty in their athletic departments (unfortunately, these revelations rarely emerge because most college towns have only a single daily newspaper, resting snugly in the local athletic department's pocket, and the paper refuses to investigate the U's college sports program or listen to tutors brave or foolhardy enough to come forward).

30   Finally, however, it is important to take a step back and to place athletic department malfeasance—not only academic fraud but also cheating in recruiting and retention of athletes—within the context of the entire university. The Carnegie Foundation noted that:

> The tragedy is that the cynicism that stems from the abuses in athletics infects the rest of student life, from promoting academic dishonesty to the loss of individual ideals. We find it disturbing that students who admit to cheating often excuse their conduct as being set by college examples such as athletic dishonesty.

Interviews for this book and P.S. comments on the questionnaire support this Carnegie comment. A surprising number of students, particularly male sports fans, justified their academic dishonesty by referring to college coaches who cheated to win or ignored illegal off-the-field conduct by their players so that the offending athletes could remain on the team and help it win. During fall 1999, many students cited Peter Warrick's involvement in a shoplifting incident at Florida State, for example, "Hey, this All-American thief [Warrick] should be in the slammer, not leading the 'Noles to the national football championship. When King Bobby [Bowden, FSU coach] lets his jocks cheat like this, why should Joe Blow college student act differently?"

In addition, the student sports fans, unlike those undergraduates who regarded cheating as "an insult for an insult," tended to see it as an element in "the game of going to college," a contest that they were determined to win "by any means necessary" (the two phrases kept recurring). These students are only one cohort—albeit a rapidly growing one—of the undergraduate population, but their attitudes definitely contribute to the general cynicism of the student body. As do the unethical coaches and the never-ending scandals in intercollegiate athletics.

An undergraduate at Indiana University suggested a survey question to probe the connections between student cheating and college sports:

> A star athlete at your school asks you to help him/her cheat on an important exam. A passing grade in this course will determine whether the athlete remains eligible to play or not. Would you help the athlete cheat? If not, what would you do (turn the athlete in, etc.)?

The question was included in the survey and produced interesting results. At schools with Division I college sports programs, 59 percent of the respondents said that they would help the athlete cheat, men outnumbering women in positive assent almost two to one. Of the 41 percent no vote, a large majority came from women. However, on the second part of the question—"what would you do (turn the athlete in, etc.)?"—84 percent of respondents at Division I schools said they would not turn the athlete in, and only 16 percent said they would. (This statistic parallels a *U.S. News* poll finding that only 18 percent of their responding students said that they would "turn in a classmate" who is cheating.)

Of equal interest were the written responses prompted by the question. A typical yes explanation from a male student was: "Cheating is o.k. If I have the answers to the exam, sure I'll give them to a star jock." Other males explained with versions of the following: "I'd help. It's not hurting me," and: "No big deal here. I'd tell him, 'Let's go for it.'" However, more nurturing and judicious yesses came from some females. One wrote:

> I would help the athlete prepare for the exam but probably wouldn't help him cheat in it. Unless he was the absolute star of the team—then I'd first make him sign lots of stuff for my kid brother. But I'd never turn him in.

35   The no answers held some surprises, but rather than showing student idealism, they usually revealed cynicism. A large number of males replied with a version

of this response: "No, I won't help. Why bother? If he flunks the class, you better believe he'll still remain eligible." Some males, particularly at Sunbelt football schools, replied with versions of this formulation, "No. I'd tell the athlete no-can-do, but I sure wouldn't turn him in for fear of being assaulted by the student population." However, in a more ethical and emphatic refusal, an intercollegiate athlete wrote:

> I'd tell him to eat shit. As a jock myself I realize that it takes a lot of effort to study after a hard practice but you don't learn anything by cheating. I've had teammates ask me to help them cheat lots of times and I always tell them to "mange merde" (I took French).

A number of the female no answers had rather complicated responses; one of the more tortured was: "I wouldn't help him. Maybe I'd even tell the professor or, at this school, the TA. Then again, the TA has no power. It would be a total mess. Maybe I'd try to forget the whole thing, pretend that he never asked for help." But a few vocational women had strong and clear answers, like the following: "No help for this pathetic moron from me. I'm also turning in the son-of-a-bitch. I work too damn hard outside and inside this university to ignore this!"

Many critics of college sports claim that athletic department academic fraud stems from the fact that most intercollegiate athletes are dumb jocks, and that they do not belong in higher education. Some dumb jocks exist on college campuses (a number of Minnesota basketball players were in this group), but, in reality, the physically and mentally exhausted and academically underachieving athlete is much more common than the dumb jock (some UM b-ball players and the vast majority of other athletes at the school were in this category).

As discussed elsewhere in this book, most Division I athletic scholarship holders are vocational students, working full-time at very demanding jobs and also trying to carry regular course loads. Many of these young men and women, because their coaches and sports require extraordinary amounts of their time and energy, experience academic problems. And athletic department tutors—under orders from coaches to "keep the jocks eligible any way you can"—sometimes cheat to keep players academically afloat. However, for some critics of college sports to regard the athletes as the source of athletic department academic fraud is to blame the victims (often willing but always shortsighted) of a complex and exploitative system.

To their credit, a minority of athletes fight the athletic department system as soon as they enter college, and they manage, through amazing effort, to obtain a good education while playing sports—often they have to defy athletic department attempts to steer them to "gut" courses and "mickey" majors. Other athletes, when they realize that they will never play at the pro level, begin to work hard on their education; nevertheless, because of time and physical constraints, they often academically underachieve. And some athletes, after they end their college athletic careers—either because of injury or the completion of their playing eligibility—become excellent students. At last able to concentrate full-time on their studies, they bring the discipline that they learned in sports to their academic endeavors.

40   Finally, the reasons why athletes commit academic fraud are as complicated as the causes of regular undergraduate cheating. Nonetheless, in every case the individual student can refuse to commit the crime. Numerous athletes and regular students do not cheat. That some honest undergraduates exist—despite their schools generally ignoring student cheating—is a testament to the morality of these young people.

Advertisement in *Rutgers Magazine*

> Rutgers Magazine, *the alumni magazine of Rutgers University, refused for three years to run the following advertisement submitted by a group known as the Rutgers 1000, who are opposed to the university's recent entry into the Big East athletic conference.*

For Rutgers Alumni

-- a Time to Choose

"Universities exist to transmit knowledge and understanding of ideas and values to students, not to provide entertainment for spectators or employment for athletes."

--Milton Friedman, Rutgers '32

Nobel Prize, 1976

In April, the Rutgers 1000 Alumni Council published its now-famous "Friedman statement," urging that Rutgers withdraw from "professionalized" college athletics, resume competition at a genuinely collegiate level, and return to its values as an old and distinguished university.

You may have read about us in the *New York Times*, *Sports Illustrated*, the Associated Press, or major educational publications like *University Business*.

Today, we ask that every Rutgers alumnus or alumna who shares our deep concern about the future of the university join our rapidly-growing campaign.

Name: _____

Street _____

City _____ State ___ Zip _____

I enclose a gift for $ _____

HENRY LOUIS GATES, JR. Delusions of Grandeur

Henry Louis Gates, Jr. is W. E. B. DuBois Professor of the Humanities at Harvard University and head of its Afro-American Studies program. He is a leading intellectual on African and African-American studies and the author of a number of books on education and African-American literature and culture, including Loose Canons: Notes from the Culture Wars *(1992), and, with Cornell West,* The Future of the Race *(1996). "Delusions of Grandeur" was published as a "Point After" editorial column for* Sports Illustrated *on August 19, 1991.*

Standing at the bar of an all-black VFW post in my hometown of Piedmont, W. Va., I offered five dollars to anyone who could tell me how many African-American professional athletes were at work today. There were 35 million African-Americans, I said.

Ten million!" yelled one intrepid soul, too far into his cups.

No way. . . more like 500,000," said another.

You mean *all* professional sports," someone interjected, "including golf and tennis, but not counting the brothers from Puerto Rico?" Everyone laughed.

5   Fifty thousand, minimum," was another guess.

Here are the facts:

There are 1,200 black professional athletes in the U.S.

There are 12 times more black lawyers than black athletes.

There are 2½ times more black dentists than black athletes.

10   There are 15 times more black doctors than black athletes.

Nobody in my local VFW believed these statistics; in fact, few people would believe them if they weren't reading them in the pages of *Sports Illustrated.* In spite of these statistics, too many African-American youngsters still believe that they have a much better chance of becoming another Magic Johnson or Michael Jordan than they do of matching the achievements of Baltimore Mayor Kurt Schmoke or neurosurgeon Dr. Benjamin Carson, both of whom, like Johnson and Jordan, are black.

In reality, an African-American youngster has about as much chance of becoming a professional athlete as he or she does of winning the lottery. The tragedy for our people, however, is that few of us accept that truth.

Let me confess that I love sports. Like most black people of my generation— I'm 40—I was raised to revere the great black athletic heroes, and never tired of listening to the stories of triumph and defeat that, for blacks, amount to a collective epic much like those of the ancient Greeks: Joe Louis's demolition of Max Schmeling; Satchel Paige's dazzling repertoire of pitches; Jesse Owens's in-your-face performance in Hitler's 1936 Olympics; Willie Mays's over-the-shoulder basket catch; Jackie Robinson's quiet strength when assaulted by racist taunts; and a thousand other grand tales.

Nevertheless, the blind pursuit of attainment in sports is having a devastating effect on our people. Imbued with a belief that our principal avenue to fame and profit is through sport, and seduced by a win-at-all-cost system that corrupts even elementary school students, far too many black kids treat basketball courts and football fields as if they were classrooms in an alternative school system. "O.K., I flunked English," a young athlete will say. "But I got an A plus in slam-dunking."

The failure of our public schools to educate athletes is part and parcel of the schools' failure to educate almost everyone. A recent survey of the Philadelphia school system, for example, stated that "more than half of all students in the third, fifth and eighth grades cannot perform minimum math and language tasks." One in four middle school students in that city fails to pass to the next grade each year. It is a sad truth that such statistics are repeated in cities throughout the nation. Young athletes—particularly young black athletes—are especially ill-served. Many of them are functionally illiterate, yet they are passed along from year to year for the greater glory of good old Hometown High. We should not be surprised to learn, then, that only 26.6% of black athletes at the collegiate level earn their degrees. For every successful educated black professional athlete, there are thousands of dead and wounded. Yet young blacks continue to aspire to careers as athletes, and it's no wonder why; when the University of North Carolina recently commissioned a sculptor to create archetypes of its student body, guess which ethnic group was selected to represent athletes?

15   Those relatively few black athletes who do make it in the professional ranks must be prevailed upon to play a significant role in the education of all of our young people, athlete and nonathlete alike. While some have done so, many others have shirked their social obligations: to earmark small percentages of their incomes for the United Negro College Fund; to appear on television for educational purposes rather than merely to sell sneakers; to let children know the message that becoming a lawyer, a teacher or a doctor does more good for our people than winning the Super Bowl; and to form productive liaisons with educators to help forge solutions to the many ills that beset the black community. These are merely a few modest proposals.

A similar burden falls upon successful blacks in all walks of life. Each of us must strive to make our young people understand the realities. Tell them to cheer Bo Jackson but to emulate novelist Toni Morrison or businessman Reginald Lewis or historian John Hope Franklin or Spelman College president Johnetta Cole— the list is long.

Of course, society as a whole bears responsibility as well. Until colleges stop using young blacks as cannon fodder in the big-business wars of so-called nonprofessional sports, until training a young black's mind becomes as important as training his or her body, we will continue to perpetuate a system akin to that of the Roman gladiators, sacrificing a class of people for the entertainment of the mob.

QUESTIONS FOR INQUIRY AND ACTION

1. Do you think the cheating problems in the U of M's men's basketball program were serious enough to merit the public's response? How would you have handled the problems had you been the university's president?

2. Do you think college sports have become too similar to professional leagues? How do you think the NCAA and college presidents should respond? Do you agree with the decision of the Rutgers 1000 to encourage Rutgers to withdraw from collegiate competition?

3. How do sports programs fit into your college? Do they complement or conflict with the spirit of a higher education community? To test your own ideas, talk to other students and athletes at your college. Are your views typical of the student body?

4. Talk with other students and teachers and collect anecdotes that record when someone cheated, how they cheated, what the cheaters thought about their actions, and what the consequences were for those involved (of course, you wouldn't want to include specific names—your goal here is not to catch and punish offenders). Then, compare your stories with those of your classmates. On the blackboard, summarize some general observations on when cheating occurs, who cheats, and so on. Is cheating a serious problem at your college?

5. If cheating is a problem at your college, discuss ways that administrators, teachers, and students can respond. Write down your suggestions on the blackboard and then discuss how you might inform these groups of your ideas (e.g., a letter to your college president, posters, or pamphlets).

6. Do you agree with Henry Louis Gates's argument that our society's celebration of professional athletes discourages us from focusing on the academic success of our students, especially African-American students? How important were sports and academics in your high school? Were some students, because of race, ethnicity, or social class, tracked more toward sports or particular kinds of professions?

CHAPTER 9

Citizens of the World: Our Global Community

"Time" has ceased, "space" has vanished. We now live in a global village. . .
a simultaneous happening.

Marshall McLuhan, The Gutenberg Galaxy

GETTING STARTED: Defining Global Citizenship

Using the global medium—the Internet—explore the definitions of a global citizen.

1. Type the term "Global Citizen" into a search engine. Make a list of what kinds
   of Web sites and materials you find. On each site, search for the definitions
   and discussions of what makes a global citizen. Record the definitions (both
   explicitly and implicitly stated) that you find. What commonalities do you
   find? What are the most interesting differences between definitions?

2. How do we get a sense of global citizenship? Where and when in your life
   do you feel like a global citizen? Do you think it is important to think of
   ourselves as global citizens and not just as citizens of individual nations?
   What might change in terms of our perceptions and our actions if we
   imagine ourselves to be global citizens?

In how many different ways do we imagine being citizens of an international community? The writer Pico Iyer, of Indian descent, born in England, raised in California, now living in Japan, describes himself as a "global
soul," one who is at home everywhere and, paradoxically, not at home
anywhere. And familiar to us now is the term *global village*, coined in 1967
by the cultural critic Marshall McLuhan, which describes the effect of communications media that allow us to connect with nearly anyone, nearly anywhere, in the world, at nearly any time.

What does it mean to *live* in a global village, though? What connotations does the word *village* have? Even though we may see ourselves as more connected in one global village, we still tend to divide and classify the world into West and East, Northern and Southern hemispheres, First World and Third World, developed and developing nations. In most formulations the language we use implies that the rest of the world is moving toward being more like North America and Western Europe. What holds us together as one global community? Capitalism? Mass media? Humanism?

We are a world of often radically different cultures, behaviors, practices, ways of seeing and living. What beliefs and ethics will bind us? Do we ever want a One World government and/or culture? If so, whose culture will predominate? Are all cultures and cultural practices equally beneficial and healthy and desirable? What do we do about practices that appall us, such as those practiced by the Taliban regime in Afghanistan? Who will make the rules and set the standards of ethics? Leading nations? The United Nations? Multinational corporations?

The case study in the second half of this chapter focuses on the protests against the meeting of the World Trade Organization (WTO) in Seattle in 1999. Much of the talk in the protests revolved around the forces of *globalization*. Globalization is a term used to describe the process in which trade, investment, people, and information travel across international borders. Globalization connects an increasing number of countries and people with one another, which can promote greater stability, but it also tends toward worldwide instability because the problems of one country or corporation carry over to others. The WTO protests and similar ones against organizations such as the IMF (International Monetary Fund) and the World Bank have raised consciousness about the ways the needs of individual humans, of individual nations, and of the planet itself are inextricably bound up with global economic concerns and need to be taken into account when making global economic decisions.

NGUGI WA THIONG'O Decolonising the Mind

Ngugi wa Thiong'o is a Kenyan dramatist, novelist, and essayist, and is gen-
erally considered East Africa's leading writer. His early novels Weep Not, Child
and A Grain of Wheat *concern the Mau Mau uprising against British colo-*
nial rule, and his play The Trial of Dedan Kimathi *(with Micere Githae Mugo)*
celebrates the leader of the Mau Mau revolution. Ngugi's openly critical atti-
tude toward both British and Kenyan rulers resulted in his year-long impris-
onment, the banishment of his theatre group, and his later self-exile to
London. He is currently a professor at New York University. "Decolonising the
Mind" is an excerpt from his book Decolonising the Mind: The Politics of Lan-
guage in African Literature (New York: Heinemann, 1986).*

I was born into a large peasant family: father, four wives and about twenty-
eight children. I also belonged, as we all did in those days, to a wider extended
family and to the community as a whole.

We spoke Gĩkũyũ as we worked in the fields. We spoke Gĩkũyũ in and outside
the home. I can vividly recall those evenings of story-telling around the fireside.
It was mostly the grown-ups telling the children but everybody was interested and
involved. We children would re-tell the stories the following day to other children
who worked in the fields picking the pyrethrum flowers, tea-leaves or coffee beans
of our European and African landlords.

The stories, with mostly animals as the main characters, were all told in
Gĩkũyũ. Hare, being small, weak but full of innovative wit and cunning, was
our hero. We identified with him as he struggled against the brutes of prey like
lion, leopard, hyena. His victories were our victories and we learnt that the apparently weak can outwit the strong. We followed the animals in their struggle against
hostile nature—drought, rain, sun, wind—a confrontation often forcing them
to search for forms of co-operation. But we were also interested in their struggles amongst themselves, and particularly between the beasts and the victims of
prey. These twin struggles, against nature and other animals, reflected real-life
struggles in the human world.

Not that we neglected stories with human beings as the main characters. There
were two types of characters in such human-centred narratives: the species of truly
human beings with qualities of courage, kindness, mercy, hatred of evil,
concern for others; and a man-eat-man two-mouthed species with qualities of
greed, selfishness, individualism and hatred of what was good for the larger
co-operative community. Cooperation as the ultimate good in a community was
a constant theme. It could unite human beings with animals against ogres and
beasts of prey, as in the story of how dove, after being fed with castor-oil seeds,
was sent to fetch a smith working far away from home and whose pregnant wife
was being threatened by these man-eating two-mouthed ogres.

5   There were good and bad story-tellers. A good one could tell the same story over and over again, and it would always be fresh to us, the listeners. He or she could tell a story told by someone else and make it more alive and dramatic. The differences really were in the use of words and images and the inflexion of voices to effect different tones.

We therefore learnt to value words for their meaning and nuances. Language was not a mere string of words. It had a suggestive power well beyond the immediate and lexical meaning. Our appreciation of the suggestive magical power of language was reinforced by the games we played with words through riddles, proverbs, transpositions of syllables, or through nonsensical but musically arranged words. [1] So we learnt the music of our language on top of the content. The language, through images and symbols, gave us a view of the world, but it had a beauty of its own. The home and the field were then our pre-primary school but what is important, for this discussion, is that the language of our evening teach-ins, and the language of our immediate and wider community, and the language of our work in the fields were one.

And then I went to school, a colonial school, and this harmony was broken. The language of my education was no longer the language of my culture. I first went to Kamaandura, missionary run, and then to another called Maanguuũ run by nationalists grouped around the Gĩkũyũ Independent and Karinga Schools Association. Our language of education was still Gĩkũyũ. The very first time I was ever given an ovation for my writing was over a composition in Gĩkũyũ. So for my first four years there was still harmony between the language of my formal education and that of the Limuru peasant community.

It was after the declaration of a state of emergency over Kenya in 1952 that all the schools run by patriotic nationalists were taken over by the colonial regime and were placed under District Education Boards chaired by Englishmen. English became the language of my formal education. In Kenya, English became more than a language: it was *the* language, and all the others had to bow before it in deference.

Thus one of the most humiliating experiences was to be caught speaking Gĩkũyũ in the vicinity of the school. The culprit was given corporal punishment— three to five strokes of the cane on bare buttocks—or was made to carry a metal plate around the neck with inscriptions such as I AM STUPID or I AM A DONKEY. Sometimes the culprits were fined money they could hardly afford. And how did the teachers catch the culprits? A button was initially given to one pupil who was supposed to hand it over to whoever was caught speaking his mother tongue. Whoever had the button at the end of the day would sing who had

---

[1] *Example from a tongue twister: "Kaana ka Nikoora koona koora: na ko koora koona kaana ka Nikoora koora koora." I'm indebted to Wangui wa Coro for this example. 'Nichola's child saw a baby frog and ran away: and when the baby frog saw Nichola's child it also ran away.' A Gĩkũyũ speaking child has to get the correct tone and length of vowel and pauses to get it right. Otherwise it becomes a jumble of k's and r's and na's [Author's note].*

given it to him and the ensuing process would bring out all the culprits of the day. Thus children were turned into witch-hunters and in the process were being taught the lucrative value of being a traitor to one's immediate community.

10   The attitude to English was the exact opposite: any achievement in spoken or written English was highly rewarded; prizes, prestige, applause; the ticket to higher realms. English became the measure of intelligence and ability in the arts, the sciences, and all the other branches of learning. English became *the* main determinant of a child's progress up the ladder of formal education.

As you may know, the colonial system of education in addition to its apartheid racial demarcation had the structure of a pyramid: a broad primary base, a narrowing secondary middle, and an even narrower university apex. Selections from primary into secondary were through an examination, in my time called Kenya African Preliminary Examination, in which one had to pass six subjects ranging from Maths to Nature Study and Kiswahili. All the papers were written in English. Nobody could pass the exam who failed the English language paper no matter how brilliantly he had done in the other subjects. I remember one boy in my class of 1954 who had distinctions in all subjects except English, which he had failed. He was made to fail the entire exam. He went on to become a turn boy in a bus company. I who had only passes but a credit in English got a place at the Alliance High School, one of the most elitist institutions for Africans in colonial Kenya. The requirements for a place at the University, Makerere University College, were broadly the same: nobody could go on to wear the undergraduate red gown, no matter how brilliantly they had performed in all the other subjects unless they had a credit—not even a simple pass!—in English. Thus the most coveted place in the pyramid and in the system was only available to the holder of an English language credit card. English was the official vehicle and the magic formula to colonial elitedom.

Literary education was now determined by the dominant language while also reinforcing that dominance. Orature (oral literature) in Kenyan languages stopped. In primary school I now read simplified Dickens and Stevenson alongside Rider Haggard. Jim Hawkins, Oliver Twist, Tom Brown—not Hare, Leopard, and Lion—were now my daily companions in the world of imagination. In secondary school, Scott and G. B. Shaw vied with more Rider Haggard, John Buchan, Alan Paton, Captain W. E. Johns. At Makerere I read English: from Chaucer to T. S. Eliot with a touch of Graham Greene.

Thus language and literature were taking us further and further from ourselves to other selves, from our world to other worlds.

What was the colonial system doing to us Kenyan children? What were the consequences of, on the one hand, this systematic suppression of our languages and the literature they carried, and on the other the elevation of English and the literature it carried? To answer those questions, let me first examine the relationship of language to human experience, human culture, and the human perception of reality.

15   Language, any language, has a dual character: it is both a means of communication and a carrier of culture. Take English. It is spoken in Britain and in Sweden and Denmark. But for Swedish and Danish people English is only a means of communication with non-Scandinavians. It is not a carrier of their culture. For the British, and particularly the English, it is additionally, and inseparably from its use as a tool of communication, a carrier of their culture and history. Or take Swahili in East and Central Africa. It is widely used as a means of communication across many nationalities. But it is not the carrier of a culture and history of many of those nationalities. However in parts of Kenya and Tanzania, and particularly in Zanzibar, Swahili is inseparably both a means of communication and a carrier of the culture of those people to whom it is a mother-tongue.

     Culture transmits or imparts those images of the world and reality through the spoken and the written language, that is through a specific language. In other words, the capacity to speak, the capacity to order sounds in a manner that makes for mutual comprehension between human beings is universal. This is the universality of language, a quality specific to human beings. It corresponds to the universality of the struggle against nature and that between human beings. But the particularity of the sounds, the words, the word order into phrases and sentences, and the specific manner, or laws, of their ordering is what distinguishes one language from another. Thus a specific culture is not transmitted through language in its universality but in its particularity as the language of a specific community with a specific history. Written literature and orature are the main means by which a particular language transmits the images of the world contained in the culture it carries.

     Language as communication and as culture are then products of each other. Communication creates culture: culture is a means of communication. Language carries culture, and culture carries, particularly through orature and literature, the entire body of values by which we come to perceive ourselves and our place in the world. How people perceive themselves affects how they look at their culture, at their politics and at the social production of wealth, at their entire relationship to nature and to other beings. Language is thus inseparable from ourselves as a community of human beings with a specific form and character, a specific history, a specific relationship to the world.

     So what was the colonialist imposition of a foreign language doing to us children?

     The real aim of colonialism was to control the people's wealth: what they produced, how they produced it, and how it was distributed; to control, in other words, the entire realm of the language of real life. Colonialism imposed its control of the social production of wealth through military conquest and subsequent political dictatorship. But its most important area of domination was the mental universe of the colonised, the control, through culture, of how people perceived themselves and their relationship to the world. Economic and political control can never be complete or effective without mental control. To control a people's culture is to control their tools of self-definition in relationship to others.

20   For colonialism this involved two aspects of the same process: the destruction or the deliberate undervaluing of a people's culture, their art, dances, religions, history, geography, education, orature and literature, and the conscious elevation of the language of the coloniser. The domination of a people's language by the languages of the colonising nations was crucial to the domination of the mental universe of the colonised.

Take language as communication. Imposing a foreign language, and suppressing the native languages as spoken and written, were already breaking the harmony previously existing between the African child and the three aspects of language. Since the new language as a means of communication was a product of and was reflecting the 'real language of life' elsewhere, it could never as spoken or written properly reflect or imitate the real life of that community. This may in part explain why technology always appears to us as slightly external, *their* product and not *ours*. The word "missile" used to hold an alien faraway sound until I recently learnt its equivalent in Gĩkũyũ, *ngurukuhĩ* and it made me apprehend it differently. Learning, for a colonial child, became a cerebral activity and not an emotionally felt experience.

But since the new, imposed languages could never completely break the native languages as spoken, their most effective area of domination was the third aspect of language as communication, the written. The language of an African child's formal education was foreign. The language of the books he read was foreign. The language of his conceptualisation was foreign. Thought, in him, took the visible form of a foreign language. So the written language of a child's upbringing in the school (even his spoken language within the school compound) became divorced from his spoken language at home. There was often not the slightest relationship between the child's written world, which was also the language of his schooling, and the world of his immediate environment in the family and the community. For a colonial child, the harmony existing between the three aspects of language as communication was irrevocably broken. This resulted in the disassociation of the sensibility of that child from his natural and social environment, what we might call colonial alienation. The alienation became reinforced in the teaching of history, geography, music, where bourgeois Europe was always the centre of the universe.

This disassociation, divorce, or alienation from the immediate environment becomes clearer when you look at colonial language as a carrier of culture.

Since culture is a product of the history of a people which it in turn reflects, the child was now being exposed exclusively to a culture that was a product of a world external to himself. He was being made to stand outside himself to look at himself. *Catching Them Young* is the title of a book on racism, class, sex, and politics in children's literature by Bob Dixon. "Catching them young" as an aim was even more true of a colonial child. The images of this world and his place in it implanted in a child take years to eradicate, if they ever can be.

25   Since culture does not just reflect the world in images but actually, through those very images, conditions a child to see that world in a certain way, the colonial child was made to see the world and where he stands in it as seen and defined by or reflected in the culture of the language of imposition.

And since those images are mostly passed on through orature and literature it meant the child would now only see the world as seen in the literature of his language of adoption. From the point of view of alienation, that is of seeing oneself from outside oneself as if one was another self, it does not matter that the imported literature carried the great humanist tradition of the best in Shakespeare, Goethe, Balzac, Tolstoy, Gorky, Brecht, Sholokhov, Dickens. The location of this great mirror of imagination was necessarily Europe and its history and culture and the rest of the universe was seen from the centre.

But obviously it was worse when the colonial child was exposed to images of his world as mirrored in the written languages of his coloniser. Where his own native languages were associated in his impressionable mind with low status, humiliation, corporal punishment, slow-footed intelligence and ability or downright stupidity, non-intelligibility and barbarism, this was reinforced by the world he met in the works of such geniuses of racism as a Rider Haggard or a Nicholas Monsarrat; not to mention the pronouncement of some of the giants of western intellectual and political establishment, such as Hume (". . .the negro is naturally inferior to the whites. . ."), [2] Thomas Jefferson (". . .the blacks. . . are inferior to the whites on the endowments of both body and mind. . ."), [3] or Hegel with his Africa comparable to a land of childhood still enveloped in the dark mantle of the night as far as the development of self-conscious history was concerned. Hegel's statement that there was nothing harmonious with humanity to be found in the African character is representative of the racist images of Africans and Africa such a colonial child was bound to encounter in the literature of the colonial languages. [4] The results could be disastrous.

In her paper read to the conference on the teaching of African literature in schools held in Nairobi in 1973, [5] entitled "Written Literature and Black Images," the Kenyan writer and scholar Professor Mĩcere Mũgo related how a reading of the description of Gagool as an old African woman in Rider Haggard's *King*

---

[2] *Quoted in Eric Williams,* A History of the People of Trinidad and Tobaga, *London 1964, p. 32 [Author's note].*
[3] *Ibid, p. 31 [Author's note].*
[4] *In references to Africa in the introduction to his lectures in* The Philosophy of History *Hegel gives historical, philosophical, rational expression and legitimacy to every conceivable European racist myth about Africa. Africa is even denied her own geography where it does not correspond to myth. Thus Egypt is not part of Africa; and North Africa is part of Europe. Africa proper is the especial home of ravenous beasts, snakes of all kinds. The African is not part of humanity. Only slavery to Europe can raise him, possibly, to the lower ranks of humanity. Slavery is good for the African, "Slavery is in and for itself injustice, for the essence of humanity is freedom; but for this man must be matured. The gradual abolition of slavery is therefore wiser and more equitable than its sudden removal." (Hegel,* The Philosophy of History, *Dover edition, New York: 1956, pp. 91–9.) Hegel clearly reveals himself as the nineteenth-century Hitler of the intellect [Author's note].*
[5] *The paper is now in Akivaga and Gachukiah's* The Teaching of African Literature in Schools, *published by Kenya Literature Bureau.*

Solomon's Mines had for a long time made her feel mortal terror whenever she encountered old African women. In his autobiography *This Life,* Sidney Poitier describes how, as a result of the literature he had read, he had come to associate Africa with snakes. So on arrival in Africa and being put up in a modern hotel in a modern city, he could not sleep because he kept on looking for snakes everywhere, even under the bed. These two have been able to pinpoint the origins of their fears. But for most others the negative image becomes internalised and it affects their cultural and even political choices in ordinary living.

QUESTIONS FOR INQUIRY AND ACTION

1. Ngugi wa Thiong'o opens his essay by describing the stories he was told as a child. How does this effectively prepare the readers for his analysis of language and culture?

2. "Language and literature were taking us further and further from ourselves to other selves, from our world to other worlds." Compare this with your experiences with reading and studying literature. Was the literature you were taught from your own language and culture? Could you see yourself in it? Was that important to you?

3. Have you studied a second or third language? If so, write about the experience of thinking in another language. How have you experienced language as a carrier of culture? How does learning a language help you understand and empathize with people who speak that language?

4. Research the history of colonialism in Kenya. How did this affect Kenya's educational system? How does it still affect the public education system, even though it's been years since Kenya was officially a colony?

JAMES L. WATSON China's Big Mac Attack

James L. Watson is Fairbank Professor of Chinese Society and professor of anthropology at Harvard University. A distinguished scholar of China, he has written many articles and books and edited Golden Arches East: McDonald's in East Asia, *an anthropological study of McDonald's in five cities in East Asia (Hong Kong, Beijing, Taipei, Seoul, and Tokyo). "China's Big Mac Attack" was published in* Foreign Affairs *(May–June 2000).*

Ronald McDonald Goes to China

Looming over Beijing's choking, bumper-to-bumper traffic, every tenth building seems to sport a giant neon sign advertising American wares: Xerox, Mobil, Kinko's, Northwest Airlines, IBM, Jeep, Gerber, even the Jolly Green Giant.

American food chains and beverages are everywhere in central Beijing: Coca-Cola, Starbucks, Kentucky Fried Chicken, Haagen-Daas, Dunkin' Donuts, Baskin-Robbins, Pepsi, TCBY, Pizza Hut, and of course McDonald's. As of June 1999, McDonald's had opened 235 restaurants in China. Hong Kong alone now boasts 158 McDonald's franchises, one for every 42,000 residents (compared to one for every 30,000 Americans).

Fast food can even trump hard politics. After NATO accidentally bombed the Chinese embassy in Belgrade during the war in Kosovo, Beijing students tried to organize a boycott of American companies in protest. Coca-Cola and McDonald's were at the top of their hit list, but the message seemed not to have reached Beijing's busy consumers: the three McDonald's I visited last July were packed with Chinese tourists, local yuppies, and grandparents treating their "little emperors and empresses" to Happy Meals. The only departure from the familiar American setting was the menu board (which was in Chinese, with English in smaller print) and the jarring sound of Mandarin shouted over cellular phones. People were downing burgers, fries, and Cokes. It was, as Yogi Berra said, deja vu all over again; I had seen this scene a hundred times before in a dozen countries. Is globalism—and its cultural variant, McDonaldization—the face of the future?

Imperialism and a Side of Fries

American academe is teeming with theorists who argue that transnational corporations like McDonald's provide the shock troops for a new form of imperialism that is far more successful, and therefore more insidious, than its militarist antecedents. Young people everywhere, the argument goes, are avid consumers of soap operas, music videos, cartoons, electronic games, martial-arts books, celebrity posters, trendy clothing, and faddish hairstyles. To cater to them, shopping malls, supermarkets, amusement parks, and fast-food restaurants are popping up everywhere. Younger consumers are forging transnational bonds of empathy and shared interests that will, it is claimed, transform political alignments in ways that most world leaders—old men who do not read *Wired*—cannot begin to comprehend, let alone control. Government efforts to stop the march of American (and Japanese) pop culture are futile; censorship and trade barriers succeed only in making forbidden films, music, and Web sites irresistible to local youth.

One of the clearest expressions of the "cultural imperialism" hypothesis appeared in a 1996 *New York Times* op-ed by Ronald Steel: "It was never the Soviet Union, but the United States itself that is the true revolutionary power. . . . We purvey a culture based on mass entertainment and mass gratification. . . . The cultural message we transmit through Hollywood and McDonald's goes out across the world to capture, and also to undermine, other societies. . . . Unlike traditional conquerors, we are not content merely to subdue others: We insist that they be like us." In his recent book, *The Lexus and the Olive Tree*, Thomas Friedman presents a more benign view of the global influence of McDonald's. Friedman has long argued in his *New York Times* column that McDonald's and other manifestations of global culture serve the interests of middle classes that are emerging in autocratic, undemocratic societies. Furthermore, he notes, countries that have a McDonald's within their borders have never gone to war against each other. (The NATO war against Serbia would seem to shatter Friedman's Big Mac Law, but he does not give up easily. In his July 2, 1999 column, he argued that the shutdown and rapid reopening of Belgrade's six McDonald's actually prove his point.)

5   If Steel and his ideological allies are correct, McDonald's should be the poster child of cultural imperialism. McDonald's today has more than 25,000 outlets in 119 countries. Most of the corporation's revenues now come from operations outside the United States, and a new restaurant opens somewhere in the world every 17 hours.

McDonald's makes heroic efforts to ensure that its food looks, feels, and tastes the same everywhere. A Big Mac in Beijing tastes virtually identical to a Big Mac in Boston. Menus vary only when the local market is deemed mature enough to expand beyond burgers and fries. Consumers can enjoy Spicy Wings (red-pepper-laced chicken) in Beijing, kosher Big Macs (minus the cheese) in Jerusalem, vegetable McNuggets in New Delhi, or a McHuevo (a burger with fried egg) in Montevideo. Nonetheless, wherever McDonald's takes root, the core product—at least during the initial phase of operation—is not really the food but the experience of eating in a cheerful, air-conditioned, child-friendly restaurant that offers the revolutionary innovation of clean toilets.

Critics claim that the rapid spread of McDonald's and its fast-food rivals undermines indigenous cuisines and helps create a homogeneous, global culture. Beijing and Hong Kong thus make excellent test cases since they are the dual epicenters of China's haute cuisine (with apologies to Hunan, Sichuan, and Shanghai loyalists). If McDonald's can make inroads in these two markets, it must surely be an unstoppable force that levels cultures. But the truth of this parable of globalization is subtler than that.

The Secret of My Success

How did McDonald's do it? How did a hamburger chain become so prominent in a cultural zone dominated by rice, noodles, fish, and pork? In China, adult consumers often report that they find the taste of fried beef patties strange and unappealing. Why, then, do they come back to McDonald's? And more to the point, why do they encourage their children to eat there?

The history of McDonald's in Hong Kong offers good clues about the mystery of the company's worldwide appeal. When Daniel Ng, an American-trained engineer, opened Hong Kong's first McDonald's in 1975, his local food-industry competitors dismissed the venture as a nonstarter: "Selling hamburgers to Cantonese? You must be joking!" Ng credits his boldness to the fact that he did not have an M.B.A. and had never taken a course in business theory.

10   During the early years of his franchise, Ng promoted McDonald's as an outpost of American culture, offering authentic hamburgers to "with-it" young people eager to forget that they lived in a tiny colony on the rim of Maoist China. Those who experienced what passed for hamburgers in British Hong Kong during the 1960s and 1970s will appreciate the innovation. Ng made the fateful decision not

to compete with Chinese-style fast-food chains that had started a few years earlier (the largest of which, Cafe de Coral, was established in 1969). The signs
outside his first restaurants were in English; the Chinese characters for McDonald's (Cantonese Mak-dong-lou, Mandarin Mai-dang-lao) did not appear until
the business was safely established. Over a period of 20 years, McDonald's gradually became a mainstay of Hong Kong's middle-class culture. Today the restaurants are packed wall-to-wall with busy commuters, students, and retirees who
treat them as homes away from home. A 1997 survey I conducted among Hong
Kong university students revealed that few were even aware of the company's
American origins. For Hong Kong youth, McDonald's is a familiar institution that
offers comfort foods that they have eaten since early childhood.

Yunxiang Yan, a UCLA anthropologist, hints that a similar localization process
may be underway in Beijing. McDonald's there is still a pricey venue that most
Chinese treat as a tourist stop: you haven't really "done" Beijing unless you have
visited the Forbidden City, walked around Tiananmen Square, and eaten at the
"Golden Arches." Many visitors from the countryside take Big Mac boxes, Coke
cups, and napkins home with them as proof that they did it right. Yan also discovered that working-class Beijing residents save up to take their kids to McDonald's and hover over them as they munch. (Later the adults eat in a cheaper,
Chinese-style restaurant.) Parents told Yan that they wanted their children to "connect" with the world outside China. To them, McDonald's was an important stop
on the way to Harvard Business School or the MIT labs. Yan has since discovered that local yuppies are beginning to eat Big Macs regularly. In 20 years, he
predicts, young people in Beijing (like their counterparts in Hong Kong today)
will not even care about the foreign origin of McDonald's, which will be serving ordinary food to people more interested in getting a quick meal than in having a cultural experience. The key to this process of localization is China's changing
family system and the emergence of a "singleton" (only-child) subculture.

The Little Emperors

In China, as in other parts of East Asia, the startup date for McDonald's corresponds
to the emergence of a new class of consumers with money to spend on family entertainment. Rising incomes are dramatically changing lifestyles, especially among
younger couples in China's major cities. Decisions about jobs and purchases no
longer require consultations with an extended network of parents, grandparents,
adult siblings, and other kin. More married women in Hong Kong, Beijing, and
Shanghai work outside the home, which in turn affects child-rearing practices,
residence patterns, and gender relations. At least in the larger cities, men no longer
rule the roost. One of China's most popular television shows features a search for
the "ideal husband," a man who does the shopping, washes the dishes, and changes
the baby's diapers—behavior inconceivable in Mao's heyday.

Most Chinese newlyweds are choosing to create their own homes, thereby separating themselves from parents and in-laws. The traditional system of living with
the groom's parents is dying out fast, even in the Chinese countryside. Recent

research in Shanghai and Dalian (and Taipei) shows that professional couples prefer to live near the wife's mother, often in the same apartment complex. The crucial consideration is household labor—child care, cooking, shopping, washing, and cleaning. With both husband and wife working full time, someone has to do it, and the wife's mother is considered more reliable (and less trouble) than the husband's mother, who would expect her daughter-in-law to be subservient.

In response to these social and economic changes, a new Chinese family system is emerging that focuses on the needs and aspirations of the married couple— the conjugal unit. Conjugality brings with it a package of attitudes and practices that undermine traditional Chinese views regarding filial piety and Confucianism. Should younger couples strive, irrespective of personal cost, to promote the welfare of the larger kin group and support their aging parents? Or should they concentrate on building a comfortable life for themselves and their offspring? Increasingly, the balance is shifting toward conjugality and away from the Confucian norms that guided earlier generations.

15   The shift also coincides with a dramatic decline in China's birth rate and a rise in the amount of money and attention lavished on children. The Communist Party's single-child family policy has helped produce a generation of "little emperors and empresses," each commanding the undivided affection and economic support of two parents and (if lucky) four grandparents. The Chinese press is awash with articles bemoaning the rise of singletons who are selfish, maladjusted, and spoiled beyond repair—although psychologists working on China's singletons find them little different from their American or European counterparts.

McDonald's opened in Beijing in 1992, a time when changes in family values were matched by a sustained economic boom. The startup date also coincided with a public "fever" for all things American—sports, clothing, films, food, and so on. American-style birthday parties became key to the company's expansion strategy. Prior to the arrival of McDonald's, festivities marking youngsters' specific birth dates were unknown in most of East Asia. In Hong Kong, for instance, lunar-calendar dates of birth were recorded for use in later life—to help match prospective marriage partners' horoscopes or choose an auspicious burial date. Until the late 1970s and early 1980s, most people paid little attention to their calendar birth date if they remembered it at all. McDonald's and its rivals now promote the birthday party—complete with cake, candles, and silly hats—in television advertising aimed directly at kids.

McDonald's also introduced other localized innovations that appeal to younger customers. In Beijing, Ronald McDonald (a.k.a. Uncle McDonald) is paired with an Aunt McDonald whose job is to entertain children and help flustered parents. All over East Asia, McDonald's offers a party package that includes food, cake, gifts, toys, and the exclusive use of a children's enclosure sometimes known as the Ronald Room. Birthday parties are all the rage for upwardly mobile youngsters in Hong Kong, Beijing, and Shanghai. Given that most people in these cities live in tiny, overcrowded flats, the local Kentucky Fried Chicken or McDonald's is a convenient and welcoming place for family celebrations.

For the first time in Chinese history, children matter not simply as future providers but as full-scale consumers who command respect in today's economy. Until the 1980s, kids rarely ate outside the home. When they did, they were expected to eat what was put in front of them. The idea that children might actually order their own food would have shocked most adults; only foreign youngsters were permitted to make their opinions known in public, which scandalized everyone within earshot. Today children have money in their pockets, most of which they spend on snacks. New industries and a specialized service sector have emerged to feed this category of consumers, as the anthropologist Jun Jing has noted in his new book *Feeding China's Little Emperors*. In effect, the fast-food industry helped start a consumer revolution by encouraging children as young as three or four to march up to the counter, slap down their money, and choose their own food.

In Hong Kong, McDonald's has become so popular that parents use visits to their neighborhood outlet as a reward for good behavior or academic achievement. An old friend told me that withholding McDonald's visits was the only threat that registered with his wayward son. "It is my nuclear deterrent," he said.

20   McDonald's could not have succeeded in East Asia without appealing to new generations of consumers—children from 3 to 13 and their harried, stressed-out parents. No amount of stealth advertising or brilliant promotions could have done the trick alone. The fast-food industry did not create a market where none existed; it responded to an opportunity presented by the collapse of an outdated Confucian family system. In effect, McDonald's tailgated the family revolution as it swept through East Asia, first in Japan and Hong Kong (1970s), then in Taiwan and South Korea (1980s), and finally in China (1990s). There is no great mystery here, unless one is predisposed to seeing imperialist plots behind every successful business.

Grimace

In 1994 students protesting against California's Proposition 187, which restricted state services to immigrants, ransacked a McDonald's in Mexico City, scrawling "Yankee go home" on the windows. In August 1999 French farmers dumped tons of manure and rotting apricots in front of their local McDonald's to protest U.S. sanctions on European food imports. During the past five years, McDonald's restaurants have been the targets of violent protests—including bombings—in over 50 countries, in cities including Rome, Macao, Rio de Janeiro, Prague, London, and Jakarta.

Why McDonald's? Other transnationals—notably Coca-Cola, Disney, and Pepsi—also draw the ire of anti-American demonstrators, but no other company can compete with the "Golden Arches." McDonald's is often the preferred site for anti-American demonstrations even in places where the local embassies are easy to get at. McDonald's is more than a purveyor of food; it is a saturated symbol for everything that environmentalists, protectionists, and anticapitalist activists find objectionable about American culture. McDonald's even stands out in the physical landscape, marked by its distinctive double-arched logo and characteristic design. Like the Stars and Stripes, the Big Mac stands for America.

Despite the symbolic load it carries, McDonald's can hardly be held responsible for the wholesale subversion of local cuisines, as its many critics claim. In China's larger cities, traditional specialties are supported by middle-class connoisseurs who treat eating out as a hobby and a diversion. Beijing's food scene today is a gourmet's paradise compared to the grim days of Maoist egalitarianism, when China's public canteens gave real meaning to the term "industrialized food." Party leaders may have enjoyed haute cuisine on the sly, but for most people, eating extravagantly was a counterrevolutionary crime. During the 1960s, refugee chefs kept microregional specialties alive in the back streets of Hong Kong and Taipei, where Panyu-style seafood, Shandong noodles, and Shunde vegetarian delights could be had at less than a dollar a head. Today, many Cantonese and Taiwanese lament the old refugees' retirement and complain that no one has carried on their culinary traditions: the chefs' own children, of course, have become brokers, lawyers, and professors.

Meanwhile, there has been an explosion of exotic new cuisines in China's cities: Thai, Malaysian, Indonesian, French, Spanish, Nepali, Mexican, and Hong Kong's latest hit, Louisiana creole. Chinese-style restaurants must now compete with these "ethnic" newcomers in a vast smorgasbord. The arrival of fast food is only one dimension of a much larger Chinese trend toward the culinary adventurism associated with rising affluence.

25   McDonald's has not been entirely passive, as demonstrated by its successful promotion of American-style birthday parties. Some try to tag McDonald's as a polluter and exploiter, but most Chinese consumers see the company as a force for the improvement of urban life. Clean toilets were a welcome development in cities where, until recently, a visit to a public restroom could be harrowing. The chain's preoccupation with cleanliness has raised consumer expectations and forced competitors to provide equally clean facilities. Ray Kroc, the legendary founder of McDonald's, was once asked if he had actually scrubbed out toilets during the early years of his franchise: "You're damn right I did," he shot back, "and I'd clean one today if it needed it." In a 1993 interview, Daniel Ng described his early efforts to import the Kroc ethos to his Hong Kong franchise. After an ineffectual first try, one new employee was ordered to clean the restrooms again. The startled worker replied that the toilets were already cleaner than the collective facilities he used at home. Ng told him that standards at McDonald's were higher and ordered him to do it again.

Another innovation is the line, a social institution that is seldom appreciated until it collapses. When McDonald's opened in Hong Kong, customers clumped around the cash registers, pushing their money over the heads of the people ahead of them—standard procedure in local train stations, banks, and cinemas. McDonald's management appointed an employee (usually a young woman) to act as queue monitor, and within a few months, regular consumers began to enforce the system themselves by glaring at newcomers who had the effrontery to jump ahead. Today the line is an accepted feature of Hong Kong's middle-class culture, and it is making headway in Beijing and Shanghai. Whether or not McDonald's deserves the credit for this particular innovation, many East Asian consumers associate the "Golden Arches" with public civility.

Have It Your Way

At first glance McDonald's appears to be the quintessential transnational, with its own corporate culture nurtured at Hamburger University in Oak Brook, Illinois. But James Cautalupo, the president of McDonald's Corporation, maintains that his strategy is to become as much a part of local culture as possible and protests when people call McDonald's a multinational or a transnational. "I like to call us multilocal," he told *The Christian Science Monitor* in 1991. McDonald's goes out of its way to find local suppliers whenever it enters a new market. In China, for instance, the company nurtures its own network of russet-potato growers to provide french fries of the requisite length. McDonald's has also learned to rely on self-starters like Daniel Ng to run its foreign franchises—with minimal interference from Oak Brook. Another winning strategy, evident everywhere in East Asia, is promoting promising young "crew" (behind-the-counter) workers into management's ranks. Surprisingly few managers are dispatched from the Illinois headquarters. Yan found only one American, a Chinese-speaker, on McDonald's Beijing management team.

Crities of the fast-food industry assume that corporations always call the shots and that consumers have little choice but to accept what is presented to them. In fact, the process of localization is a two-way street, involving changes in the local culture as well as modifications of the company's standard mode of operation.

The hallmark of the American fast-food business is the displacement of labor costs from the corporation to consumers. For the system to work, consumers must be educated—or "disciplined"—so that they voluntarily fulfill their side of an implicit bargain: we (the corporation) will provide cheap, fast service if you (the customer) carry your own tray, seat yourself, eat quickly, help clean up afterward, and depart promptly to make room for others. Try breaking this contract in Boston or Pittsburgh by spreading out your newspaper and starting to work on a crossword puzzle in McDonald's. You will soon be ousted—politely in Pittsburgh, less so in Boston.

30   Key elements of McDonald's pan-national system—notably lining up and self-seating—have been readily accepted by consumers throughout East Asia. Other aspects of the Oak Brook model have been rejected, especially those relating to time and space. In Hong Kong, Taipei, and Beijing, consumers have turned their neighborhood restaurants into leisure centers for seniors and after-school clubs for students. Here, "fast" refers to the delivery of food, not its consumption.

Between 3:00 and 5:30 P.M. on Hong Kong weekdays, McDonald's restaurants are invaded by armies of young people in school uniforms. They buy a few fries, pour them out on a tray for communal snacking, and sit for at least an hour—gossiping, studying, and flirting. During the midmorning hours, the restaurants are packed with white-haired retirees who stay even longer, drinking tea or coffee (free refills for senior citizens) and lingering over pancake breakfasts. Many sit alone, reading newspapers provided by the management. Both retirees and students are attracted by the roomy tables, good light, and air-conditioning—a combination not easily found in Hong Kong, Beijing, or Shanghai. In effect, local citizens have appropriated private property and converted it into public space.

The process of localization correlates closely to the maturation of a generation of local people who grew up eating fast food. By the time the children of these pioneer consumers entered the scene, McDonald's was an unremarkable feature of the local landscape. Parents see the restaurants as havens for their school-age children: smoking is banned and (in China and Hong Kong) no alcohol is served, effectively eliminating drugs and gangs. McDonald's has become so local that Hong Kong's youth cannot imagine life without it.

Everyone has heard the story: Japanese little leaguers tour California and spot a McDonald's, whereupon they marvel that America also has Japanese food. Such anecdotes are not apocryphal. The children of visiting colleagues from Taiwan and South Korea were overjoyed when they saw a McDonald's near their temporary homes in the Boston suburbs: "Look! They have our kind of food here," one eight-year-old Korean exclaimed. The stories also work within East Asia: last year, Joe Bosco, an anthropologist at the Chinese University of Hong Kong, took several of his students to Taipei for a study tour. After a week of eating Taiwanese restaurant food, Bosco's charges began to complain that they missed home-style cooking. "Okay," Bosco said, "where do you want to eat tonight?" The students all said, "McDonald's!"

Next to Godliness

In China's increasingly affluent cities, parents now worry more about what their children eat outside the home. Rumors frequently sweep through Beijing and Shanghai with the same story line: migrants from the countryside set up a roadside stall selling youtiar, deep-fried dough sticks eaten with rice gruel for breakfast. To expand the batter, they add industrial detergent to the mix, creating a powerful poison that kills everyone who eats it. Families of the deceased rush back to the scene to discover that the stall has disappeared; the local police are more interested in silencing the survivors than pursuing the culprits. Such stories are, of course, unverifiable, but they carry a "truth" that resists official denials, much like urban legends in the United States. Last summer's food scare in Belgium over dioxin-laced eggs and the recent British mad-cow fiasco were well covered in the Chinese media, feeding the anxieties of urbanites with no reliable system of consumer protection.

35   McDonald's appeals to China's new elites because its food is safe, clean, and reliable. Western intellectuals may scoff at McDonald's for its unrelenting monotony, but in many parts of the world (including China) this is precisely what consumers find so attractive. Why else would competitors go to such extremes to imitate McDonald's? In Beijing one can find fast-food restaurants with names such as McDucks, Mcdonald's, and Mordornal. In Shanghai a local chain called Nancy's Express used a sign with one leg of the double arches missing, forming an "N." Another popular chain of noodle shops, called Honggaoliang (Red

sorghum), advertises itself with a large "H" that bears an uncanny resemblance to the "Golden Arches." All over China, competitors dress their staff in McDonald's-style uniforms and decorate their restaurants in yellow. Corporate mascots inspired by Ronald McDonald—clowns, ducks, cowboys, cats, hamburger figures, mythic heroes, and chickens—parade along the sidewalks of Chinese cities. Local fast-food chains frequently engage in public exhibitions of cleanliness: one worker mops the floors and polishes the windows, all day long, every day. The cleaners usually restrict their efforts to the entryway, where the performance can best be seen by passersby.

So Lonely

During McDonald's first three years in China, Communist Party officials could barely restrain their enthusiasm over this new model of modernization, hygiene, and responsible management. By 1996, however, media enthusiasm cooled as state authorities began to promote an indigenous fast-food industry based on noodles, barbecued meats, soups, and rice pots. Now that McDonald's, Kentucky Fried Chicken, and Pizza Hut had shown the way, party officials reasoned, local chains should take over the mass market. (No such chain has seriously challenged McDonald's, but a Shanghai-based restaurateur has fought a much-reported "battle of the chickens" with KFC.)

Meanwhile, China faces yet another family revolution this one caused by the graying of the population. In 1998, 10 percent of China's people were over 60; by 2020, the figure is expected to rise to approximately 16 percent. In 2025, there will be 274 million people over 60 in China—more than the entire 1998 U.S. population. Since Beijing has made few provisions for a modern social-security system, the implications are profound. The locus of consumer power will soon shift generations as the parents of today's little emperors retire. Unlike the current generation of retirees—the survivors of Maoism—China's boomers will not be content with 1950s-level pensions, and they cannot expect their children to support them. Like their counterparts in the American Association of Retired Persons, future retirees in China are likely to be a vociferous, aggressive lot who will demand more state resources.

So what will happen to child-centered industries? If its experience in Hong Kong is any guide, McDonald's will survive quite handily as a welcoming retreat from the isolation and loneliness of urban life. The full ramifications of China's single-child policy will not be felt for another 20 years. Having one grandchild for every four grandparents is a recipe for social anomie on a truly massive scale. The consequences of China's demographic time bomb can already be seen on the streets of Hong Kong, where the family began to shrink decades ago. Tens of thousands of retirees roam Hong Kong's air-conditioned shopping malls, congregate in the handful of overcrowded parks, and turn their local McDonald's during the midmorning hours into a substitute for the public gardens, opera theaters, and ancestral halls that sheltered their parents. What stands out at McDonald's is the isolation among Hong Kong elders as they try to entertain themselves.

Americans may be bowling alone and worrying about the decline of family life, but in early 21st-century Hong Kong, no one even seems concerned about the emergence of a civil society that ignores the elderly.

Whose Culture Is It Anyway?

Is McDonald's leading a crusade to create a homogenous, global culture that suits the needs of an advanced capitalist world order? Not really. Today's economic and social realities demand an entirely new approach to global issues that takes consumers' perspectives into account. The explanatory device of "cultural imperialism" is little more than a warmed-over version of the neo-Marxist dependency theories that were popular in the 1960s and 1970s—approaches that do not begin to capture the complexity of today's emerging transnational systems.

40   The deeper one digs into the personal lives of consumers anywhere, the more complex matters become. People are not the automatons many theorists make them out to be. Hong Kong's discerning consumers have most assuredly not been stripped of their cultural heritage, nor have they become the uncomprehending dupes of transnational corporations.

In places like Hong Kong, it is increasingly difficult to see where the transnational ends and the local begins. Fast food is an excellent case in point: for the children who flock to weekend birthday parties, McDonald's is self-evidently local. Similarly, the Hong Kong elders who use McDonald's as a retreat from the loneliness of urban life could care less about the company's foreign origin. Hong Kong's consumers have made the "Golden Arches" their own.

One might also turn the lens around and take a close look at American society as it enters a new millennium. Chinese food is everywhere, giving McDonald's and KFC a run for their money in such unlikely settings as Moline and Memphis. Mandarin is fast becoming a dominant language in American research laboratories, and Chinese films draw ever more enthusiastic audiences. Last Halloween, every other kid in my Cambridge neighborhood appeared in (Japanese-inspired) Power Ranger costumes, striking poses that owe more to Bruce Lee than to Batman. Whose culture is it, anyway? If you have to ask, you have already missed the boat.

QUESTIONS FOR INQUIRY AND ACTION

1. What strategies does Watson use to make this explanation of a complex subject engaging for his readers?

2. Read the family section of this essay along with the readings in the Family as Community chapter. How does Watson make nuanced connections between globalization, capitalism, and changes in family structures? Have "family values" changed?

3. Watson comments that in Hong Kong and places like it "it is increasingly difficult to see where the transnational ends and the local begins." Write about ways you

have been influenced by other cultures, and the ways that transnational culture has blended into your local culture.

4. Can we be global citizens without forcing American culture on the rest of the world? Is being a global village only about being able to buy a McDonald's hamburger and a Coke anywhere in the world?

BENJAMIN R. BARBER Jihad vs. McWorld

Benjamin R. Barber is Walt Whitman Professor of Political Science and director of the Walt Whitman Center for the Culture and Politics of Democracy at Rutgers University. He is the author of a number of plays and novels as well as many academic books on political science and democracy including Strong Democracy: Participatory Politics for a New Age *(1984) and* A Passion for Democracy: American Essays *(1998). "Jihad vs. McWorld" first appeared as the March 1992 cover story for* The Atlantic *magazine; Barber later developed it into the book* Jihad vs. McWorld *(Times Books, 1995).*

Just beyond the horizon of current events lie two possible political futures—both bleak, neither democractic. The first is a retribalization of large swaths of humankind by war and bloodshed: a threatened Lebanonization of national states in which culture is pitted against culture, people against people, tribe against tribe—a Jihad in the name of a hundred narrowly conceived faiths against every kind of interdependence, every kind of artificial social cooperation and civic mutuality. The second is being borne in on us by the onrush of economic and ecological forces that demand integration and uniformity and that mesmerize the world with fast music, fast computers, and fast food—with MTV, Macintosh, and McDonald's pressing nations into one commercially homogenous global network: one McWorld tied together by technology, ecology, communications, and commerce. The planet is falling precipitantly apart and coming reluctantly together at the very same moment.

These two tendencies are sometimes visible in the same countries at the same instant: thus Yugoslavia, clamoring just recently to join the New Europe, is exploding into fragments; India is trying to live up to its reputation as the world's largest integral democracy while powerful new fundamentalist parties like the Hindu nationalist Bharatiya Janata Party, along with nationalist assassins, are imperiling its hard-won unity. States are breaking up or joining up: the Soviet Union has disappeared almost overnight, its parts forming new unions with one another or with likeminded nationalities in neighboring states. The old interwar national state based on territory and political sovereignty looks to be a mere transitional development.

The tendencies of what I am here calling the forces of Jihad and the forces of McWorld operate with equal strength in opposite directions, the one driven by parochial hatreds, the other by universalizing markets, the one re-creating ancient subnational and ethnic borders from within, the other making national borders porous from without. They have one thing in common: neither offers much hope to citizens looking for practical ways to govern themselves democratically. If the global future is to pit Jihad's centrifugal whirlwind against McWorld's centripetal black hole, the outcome is unlikely to be democratic—or so I will argue.

McWorld, or the Globalization of Politics

Four imperatives make up the dynamic of McWorld: a market imperative, a resource imperative, an information-technology imperative, and an ecological imperative. By shrinking the world and diminishing the salience of national borders, these imperatives have in combination achieved a considerable victory over factiousness and particularism, and not least of all over their most virulent traditional form—nationalism. It is the realists who are now Europeans, the utopians who dream nostalgically of a resurgent England or Germany, perhaps even a resurgent Wales or Saxony. Yesterday's wishful cry for one world has yielded to the reality of McWorld.

5   *The market imperative.* Marxist and Leninist theories of imperialism assumed that the quest for ever-expanding markets would in time compel nation-based capitalist economies to push against national boundaries in search of an international economic imperium. Whatever else has happened to the scientistic predictions of Marxism, in this domain they have proved farsighted. All national economies are now vulnerable to the inroads of larger, transnational markets within which trade is free, currencies are convertible, access to banking is open, and contracts are enforceable under law. In Europe, Asia, Africa, the South Pacific, and the Americas such markets are eroding national sovereignty and giving rise to entities—international banks, trade associations, transnational lobbies like OPEC and Greenpeace, world news services like CNN and the BBC, and multinational corporations that increasingly lack a meaningful national identity—that neither reflect nor respect nationhood as an organizing or regulative principle.

The market imperative has also reinforced the quest for international peace and stability, requisite of an efficient international economy. Markets are enemies of parochialism, isolation, fractiousness, war. Market psychology attenuates the psychology of ideological and religious cleavages and assumes a concord among producers and consumers—categories that ill fit narrowly conceived national or religious cultures. Shopping has little tolerance for blue laws, whether dictated by pub-closing British paternalism, Sabbath-observing Jewish Orthodox fundamentalism, or no-Sunday-liquor-sales Massachusetts puritanism. In the context of common markets, international law ceases to be a vision of justice and becomes a workaday framework for getting things done—enforcing contracts, ensuring that governments abide by deals, regulating trade and currency relations, and so forth.

Common markets demand a common language, as well as a common currency, and they produce common behaviors of the kind bred by cosmopolitan city life everywhere. Commercial pilots, computer programmers, international bankers, media specialists, oil riggers, entertainment celebrities, ecology experts, demographers, accountants, professors, athletes—these compose a new breed of men and women for whom religion, culture, and nationality can seem only marginal elements in a working identity. Although sociologists of everyday life will no doubt continue to distinguish a Japanese from an American mode, shopping has a common signature throughout the world. Cynics might even say that some of the recent revolutions in Eastern Europe have had as their true goal not liberty and the right to vote but well-paying jobs and the right to shop (although the vote is proving easier to acquire than consumer goods). The market imperative is, then, plenty powerful; but, notwithstanding some of the claims made for "democratic capitalism," it is not identical with the democratic imperative.

The resource imperative. Democrats once dreamed of societies whose political autonomy rested firmly on economic independence. The Athenians idealized what they called autarky, and tried for a while to create a way of life simple and austere enough to make the polis genuinely self-sufficient. To be free meant to be independent of any other community or polis. Not even the Athenians were able to achieve autarky, however: human nature, it turns out, is dependency. By the time of Pericles, Athenian politics was inextricably bound up with a flowing empire held together by naval power and commerce—an empire that, even as it appeared to enhance Athenian might, ate away at Athenian independence and autarky. Master and slave, it turned out, were bound together by mutual insufficiency.

The dream of autarky briefly engrossed nineteenth-century America as well, for the underpopulated, endlessly bountiful land, the cornucopia of natural resources, and the natural barriers of a continent walled in by two great seas led many to believe that America could be a world unto itself. Given this past, it has been harder for Americans than for most to accept the inevitability of interdependence. But the rapid depletion of resources even in a country like ours, where they once seemed inexhaustible, and the maldistribution of arable soil and mineral resources on the planet, leave even the wealthiest societies ever more resource-dependent and many other nations in permanently desperate straits.

10   Every nation, it turns out, needs something another nation has; some nations have almost nothing they need.

The information-technology imperative. Enlightenment science and the technologies derived from it are inherently universalizing. They entail a quest for descriptive principles of general application, a search for universal solutions to particular problems, and an unswerving embrace of objectivity and impartiality.

Scientific progress embodies and depends on open communication, a common discourse rooted in rationality, collaboration, and an easy and regular flow and exchange of information. Such ideals can be hypocritical covers for power-mongering by elites, and they may be shown to be wanting in many other ways, but they are entailed by the very idea of science and they make science and globalization practical allies.

Business, banking, and commerce all depend on information flow and are facilitated by new communication technologies. The hardware of these technologies tends to be systemic and integrated—computer, television, cable, satellite, laser, fiber-optic, and microchip technologies combining to create a vast interactive communications and information network that can potentially give every person on earth access to every other person, and make every datum, every byte, available to every set of eyes. If the automobile was, as George Ball once said (when he gave his blessing to a Fiat factory in the Soviet Union during the Cold War), "an ideology on four wheels," then electronic telecommunication and information systems are an ideology at 186,000 miles per second—which makes for a very small planet in a very big hurry. Individual cultures speak particular languages; commerce and science increasingly speak English; the whole world speaks logarithms and binary mathematics.

Moreover, the pursuit of science and technology asks for, even compels, open societies. Satellite footprints do not respect national borders; telephone wires penetrate the most closed societies. With photocopying and then fax machines having infiltrated Soviet universities and samizdat literary circles in the eighties, and computer modems having multiplied like rabbits in communism's bureaucratic warrens thereafter, glasnost could not be far behind. In their social requisites, secrecy and science are enemies.

15   The new technology's software is perhaps even more globalizing than its hardware. The information arm of international commerce's sprawling body reaches out and touches distinct nations and parochial cultures, and gives them a common face chiseled in Hollywood, on Madison Avenue, and in Silicon Valley. Throughout the 1980s one of the most-watched television programs in South Africa was *The Cosby Show*. The demise of apartheid was already in production. Exhibitors at the 1991 Cannes film festival expressed growing anxiety over the "homogenization" and "Americanization" of the global film industry when, for the third year running, American films dominated the awards ceremonies. America has dominated the world's popular culture for much longer, and much more decisively. In November of 1991 Switzerland's once insular culture boasted best-seller lists featuring *Terminator 2* as the No. 1 movie, *Scarlett* as the No. 1 book, and Prince's *Diamonds and Pearls* as the No. 1 record album. No wonder the Japanese are buying Hollywood film studios even faster than Americans are buying Japanese television sets. This kind of software supremacy may in the long term be far more important than hardware superiority, because culture has become more potent than armaments. What is the power of the Pentagon compared with Disneyland? Can the Sixth Fleet keep up with CNN? McDonald's in Moscow and Coke in China will do more to create a global culture than military colonization ever could. It is less the goods than the brand names that do the work, for they convey life-style images that alter perception and challenge behavior. They make up the seductive software of McWorld's common (at times much too common) soul.

Yet in all this high-tech commercial world there is nothing that looks particularly democratic. It lends itself to surveillance as well as liberty, to new forms of manipulation and covert control as well as new kinds of participation, to skewed, unjust market outcomes as well as greater productivity. The consumer society and the open society are not quite synonymous. Capitalism and democracy have a relationship, but it is something less than a marriage. An efficient free market after all requires that consumers be free to vote their dollars on competing goods, not that citizens be free to vote their values and beliefs on competing political candidates and programs. The free market flourished in junta-run Chile, in military-governed Taiwan and Korea, and, earlier, in a variety of autocratic European empires as well as their colonial possessions.

The ecological imperative. The impact of globalization on ecology is a cliché even to world leaders who ignore it. We know well enough that the German forests can be destroyed by Swiss and Italians driving gas-guzzlers fueled by leaded gas. We also know that the planet can be asphyxiated by greenhouse gases because Brazilian farmers want to be part of the twentieth century and are burning down tropical rain forests to clear a little land to plough, and because Indonesians make a living out of converting their lush jungle into toothpicks for fastidious Japanese diners, upsetting the delicate oxygen balance and in effect puncturing our global lungs. Yet this ecological consciousness has meant not only greater awareness but also greater inequality, as modernized nations try to slam the door behind them, saying to developing nations, "The world cannot afford your modernization; ours has wrung it dry!"

Each of the four imperatives just cited is transnational, transideological, and transcultural. Each applies impartially to Catholics, Jews, Muslims, Hindus, and Buddhists; to democrats and totalitarians; to capitalists and socialists. The Enlightenment dream of a universal rational society has to a remarkable degree been realized—but in a form that is commercialized, homogenized, depoliticized, bureaucratized, and, of course, radically incomplete, for the movement toward McWorld is in competition with forces of global breakdown, national dissolution, and centrifugal corruption. These forces, working in the opposite direction, are the essence of what I call Jihad.

Jihad, or the Lebanonization of the World

OPEC, The World Bank, the United Nations, the International Red Cross, the multinational corporation. . . there are scores of institutions that reflect globalization. But they often appear as ineffective reactors to the world's real actors: national states and, to an ever greater degree, subnational factions in permanent rebellion against uniformity and integration—even the kind represented by universal law and justice. The headlines feature these players regularly: they are cultures, not countries; parts, not wholes; sects, not religions; rebellious factions and dissenting minorities at war not just with globalism but with the traditional nation-state. Kurds, Basques, Puerto Ricans, Ossetians, East Timoreans, Quebecois, the Catholics of Northern Ireland, Abkhasians, Kurile Islander Japanese, the Zulus of Inkatha, Catalonians, Tamils, and, of course, Palestinians—people without countries, inhabiting nations not their own, seeking smaller worlds within borders that will seal them off from modernity.

20   A powerful irony is at work here. Nationalism was once a force of integration and unification, a movement aimed at bringing together disparate clans, tribes, and cultural fragments under new, assimilationist flags. But as Ortega y Gasset noted more than sixty years ago, having won its victories, nationalism changed its strategy. In the 1920s, and again today, it is more often a reactionary and divisive force, pulverizing the very nations it once helped cement together. The force that creates nations is "inclusive," Ortega wrote in *The Revolt of the Masses*. "In periods of consolidation, nationalism has a positive value, and is a lofty standard. But in Europe everything is more than consolidated, and nationalism is nothing but a mania. . . ."

This mania has left the post-Cold War world smoldering with hot wars; the international scene is little more unified than it was at the end of the Great War, in Ortega's own time. There were more than thirty wars in progress last year, most of them ethnic, racial, tribal, or religious in character, and the list of unsafe regions doesn't seem to be getting any shorter. Some new world order!

The aim of many of these small-scale wars is to redraw boundaries, to implode states and resecure parochial identities: to escape McWorld's dully insistent imperatives. The mood is that of Jihad: war not as an instrument of policy but as an emblem of identity, an expression of community, an end in itself. Even where there is no shooting war, there is fractiousness, secession, and the quest for ever smaller communities. Add to the list of dangerous countries those at risk: In Switzerland and Spain, Jurassian and Basque separatists still argue the virtues of ancient identities, sometimes in the language of bombs. Hyperdisintegration in the former Soviet Union may well continue unabated—not just a Ukraine independent from the Soviet Union but a Bessarabian Ukraine independent from the Ukrainian republic; not just Russia severed from the defunct union but Tatarstan severed from Russia. Yugoslavia makes even the disunited, ex-Soviet, nonsocialist republics that were once the Soviet Union look integrated, its sectarian fatherlands springing up within factional motherlands like weeds within weeds within weeds. Kurdish independence would threaten the territorial integrity of four Middle Eastern nations. Well before the current cataclysm Soviet Georgia made a claim for autonomy from the Soviet Union, only to be faced with its Ossetians (164,000 in a republic of 5.5 million) demanding their own self-determination within Georgia. The Abkhasian minority in Georgia has followed suit. Even the good will established by Canada's once promising Meech Lake protocols is in danger, with Francophone Quebec again threatening the dissolution of the federation. In South Africa the emergence from apartheid was hardly achieved when friction between Inkatha's Zulus and the African National Congress's tribally identified members threatened to replace Europeans' racism with an indigenous tribal war. After thirty years of attempted integration using the colonial language (English) as a unifier, Nigeria is now playing with the idea of linguistic multiculturalism—which could mean the cultural breakup of the nation into hundreds of tribal fragments. Even Saddam Hussein has benefited from the threat of internal Jihad, having used renewed tribal and religious warfare to turn last season's mortal enemies into reluctant allies of an Iraqi nationhood that he nearly destroyed.

The passing of communism has torn away the thin veneer of internationalism (workers of the world unite!) to reveal ethnic prejudices that are not only ugly and deep-seated but increasingly murderous. Europe's old scourge, anti-Semitism, is back with a vengeance, but it is only one of many antagonisms. It appears all too easy to throw the historical gears into reverse and pass from a Communist dictatorship back into a tribal state.

Among the tribes, religion is also a battlefield. ("Jihad" is a rich word which generic meaning is "struggle"—usually the struggle of the soul to avert evil. Strictly applied to religious war, it is used only in reference to battles where the faith is under assault, or battles against a government that denies the practice of Islam. My use here is rhetorical, but does follow both journalistic practice and history.) Remember the Thirty Years War? Whatever forms of Enlightenment universalism might once have come to grace such historically related forms of monotheism as Judaism, Christianity, and Islam, in many of their modern incarnations they are parochial rather than cosmopolitan, angry rather than loving, proselytizing rather than ecumenical, zealous rather than rationalist, sectarian rather than deistic, ethnocentric rather than universalizing. As a result, like the new forms of hypernationalism, the new expressions of religious fundamentalism are fractious and pulverizing, never integrating. This is religion as the Crusaders knew it: a battle to the death for souls that if not saved will be forever lost.

25   The atmospherics of Jihad have resulted in a breakdown of civility in the name of identity, of comity in the name of community. International relations have sometimes taken on the aspect of gang war—cultural turf battles featuring battle factions that were supposed to be sublimated as integral parts of large national, economic, postcolonial, and constitutional entities.

The Darkening Feature of Democracy

These rather melodramatic tableaux vivants do not tell the whole story, however. For all their defects, Jihad and McWorld have their attractions. Yet, to appear and insist, the attractions are unrelated to democracy. Neither McWorld nor Jihad is remotely democratic in impulse. Neither needs democracy; neither promotes democracy.

McWorld does manage to look pretty seductive in a world obsessed with Jihad. It delivers peace, prosperity, and relative unity—if at the cost of independence, community, and identity (which is generally based on difference). The primary political values required by the global market are order and tranquility, and freedom—as in the phrases "free trade," "free press," and "free love." Human rights are needed to a degree, but not citizenship or participation—and no more social justice and equality than are necessary to promote efficient economic production and consumption. Multinational corporations sometimes seem to prefer doing business with local oligarchs, inasmuch as they can take confidence from dealing with the boss on all crucial matters. Despots who slaughter their own populations are no problem, so long as they leave markets in place and refrain from making war on their neighbors (Saddam Hussein's fatal mistake). In trading partners, predictability is of more value than justice.

The Eastern European revolutions that seemed to arise out of concern for global democratic values quickly deteriorated into a stampede in the general direction of free markets and their ubiquitous, television-promoted shopping malls. East Germany's Neues Forum, that courageous gathering of intellectuals, students, and workers which overturned the Stalinist regime in Berlin in 1989, lasted only six months in Germany's mini-version of McWorld. Then it gave way to money and markets and monopolies from the West. By the time of the first all-German elections, it could scarcely manage to secure three percent of the vote. Elsewhere there is growing evidence that glasnost will go and perestroika—defined as privatization and an opening of markets of Western bidders—will stay. So understandably anxious are the new rulers of Eastern Europe and whatever entities are forged from the residues of the Soviet Union to gain access to credit and markets and technology—McWorld's flourishing new currencies—that they have shown themselves willing to trade away democratic prospects in pursuit of them: not just old totalitarian ideologies and command-economy production models but some possible indigenous experiments with a third way between capitalism and socialism, such as economic cooperatives and employee stock-ownership plans, both of which have their ardent supporters in the East.

Jihad delivers a different set of virtues: a vibrant local identity, a sense of community, solidarity among kinsmen, neighbors, and countrymen, narrowly conceived. But it also guarantees parochialism and is grounded in exclusion. Solidarity is secured through a war against outsiders. And solidarity often means obedience to a hierarchy in governance, fanaticism in beliefs, and the obliteration of individual selves in the name of the group. Deference to leaders and intolerance toward outsiders (and toward "enemies within") are hallmarks of tribalism—hardly the attitudes required for the cultivation of new democratic women and men capable of governing themselves. Where new democratic experiments have been conducted in retribalizing societies, in both Europe and the Third World, the result has often been anarchy, repression, persecution, and the coming of new, noncommunist forms of very old kinds of despotism. During the past year, Havel's velvet revolution in Czechoslovakia was imperiled by partisans of "Czechland" and of Slovakia as independent entities. India seemed little less rent by Sikh, Hindu, Muslim, and Tamil infighting than it was immediately after the British pulled out, more than forty years ago.

30   To the extent that either McWorld or Jihad has a natural politics, it has turned out to be more of an antipolitics. For McWorld, it is the antipolitics of globalism: bureaucratic, technocratic, and meritocratic, focused (as Marx predicted it would be) on the administration of things—with people, however, among the chief things to be administered. In its politico-economic imperatives McWorld has been guided by laissez-faire market principles that privilege efficiency, productivity, and beneficence at the expense of civic liberty and self-government.

For Jihad, the antipolitics of tribalization has been explicitly antidemocratic: one-party dictatorship, government by military junta, theocratic fundamentalism— often associated with a version of the *Fuhrerprinzip* that empowers an individual to rule on behalf of a people. Even the government of India, struggling for decades to model democracy for a people who will soon number a billion, longs for great leaders; and for every Mahatma Gandhi, Indira Gandhi, or Rajiv Gandhi taken from them by zealous assassins, the Indians appear to seek a replacement who will deliver them from the lengthy travail of their freedom.

The Confederal Option

How can democracy be secured and spread in a world whose primary tendencies are at best indifferent to it (McWorld) and at worst deeply antithetical to it (Jihad)? My guess is that globalization will eventually vanquish retribalization. The ethos of material "civilization" has not yet encountered an obstacle it has been unable to thrust aside. Ortega may have grasped in the 1920s a clue to our own future in the coming millennium.

Everyone sees the need of a new principle of life. But as always happens in similar crises—some people attempt to save the situation by an artificial intensification of the very principle which has led to decay. This is the meaning of the "nationalist" outburst of recent years. . . things have always gone that way. The last flare, the longest; the last sigh, the deepest. On the very eve of their disappearance there is an intensification of frontiers—military and economic.

Jihad may be a last deep sigh before the eternal yawn of McWorld. On the other hand, Ortega was not exactly prescient; his prophecy of peace and internationalism came just before blitzkrieg, world war, and the Holocaust tore the old order to bits. Yet democracy is how we remonstrate with reality, the rebuke our aspirations offer to history. And if retribalization is inhospitable to democracy, there is nonetheless a form of democratic government that can accommodate parochialism and communitarianism, one that can even save them from their defects and make them more tolerant and participatory: decentralized participatory democracy. And if McWorld is indifferent to democracy, there is nonetheless a form of democratic government that suits global markets passably well—representative government in its federal or, better still, confederal variation.

35 With its concern for accountability, the protection of minorities, and the universal rule of law, a confederalized representative system would serve the political needs of McWorld as well as oligarchic bureaucratism or meritocratic elitism is currently doing. As we are already beginning to see, many nations may survive in the long term only as confederations that afford local regions smaller than "nations" extensive jurisdiction. Recommended reading for democrats of the twenty-first century is not the U.S. Constitution or the French Declaration of Rights of Man and Citizen but the Articles of Confederation, that suddenly pertinent document that stitched together the thirteen American colonies into what then seemed a too loose confederation of independent states but now appears a new form of political realism, as veterans of Yeltsin's new Russia and the new Europe created at Maastricht will attest.

By the same token, the participatory and direct form of democracy that engages citizens in civic activity and civic judgment and goes well beyond just voting and accountability—the system I have called "strong democracy"—suits the political needs of decentralized communities as well as theocratic and nationalist party dictatorships have done. Local neighborhoods need not be democratic, but they can be. Real democracy has flourished in diminutive settings: the spirit of liberty, Tocqueville said, is local. Participatory democracy, if not naturally apposite to tribalism, has an undeniable attractiveness under conditions of parochialism.

Democracy in any of these variations will, however, continue to be obstructed by the undemocratic and antidemocratic trends toward uniformitarian globalism and intolerant retribalization which I have portrayed here. For democracy to persist in our brave new McWorld, we will have to commit acts of conscious political will—a possibility, but hardly a probability, under these conditions. Political will requires much more than the quick fix of the transfer of institutions. Like technology transfer, institution transfer rests on foolish assumptions about a uniform world of the kind that once fired the imagination of colonial administrators. Spread English justice to the colonies by exporting wigs. Let an East Indian trading company act as the vanguard to Britain's free parliamentary institutions. Today's well-intentioned quick-fixers in the National Endowment for Democracy and the Kennedy School of Government, in the unions and foundations and universities zealously nurturing contacts in Eastern Europe and the Third World, are hoping to democratize by long distance. Post Bulgaria a parliament by first-class mail. Fedex the Bill of Rights to Sri Lanka. Cable Cambodia some common law.

Yet Eastern Europe has already demonstrated that importing free political parties, parliaments, and presses cannot establish a democratic civil society; imposing a free market may even have the opposite effect. Democracy grows from the bottom up and cannot be imposed from the top down. Civil society has to be built from the inside out. The institutional superstructure comes last. Poland may become democratic, but then again it may heed the Pope, and prefer to found its politics on its Catholicism, with uncertain consequences for democracy. Bulgaria may become democratic, but it may prefer tribal war. The former Soviet Union may become a democratic confederation, or it may just grow into an anarchic and weak conglomeration of markets for other nations' goods and services.

Democrats need to seek out indigenous democratic impulses. There is always a desire for self-government, always some expression of participation, accountability, consent, and representation, even in traditional hierarchical societies. These need to be identified, tapped, modified, and incorporated into new democratic practices with an indigenous flavor. The tortoises among the democratizers may ultimately outlive or outpace the hares, for they will have the time and patience to explore conditions along the way, and to adapt their gait to changing circumstances. Tragically, democracy in a hurry often looks something like France in 1794 or China in 1989.

40   It certainly seems possible that the most attractive democratic ideal in the face of the brutal realities of Jihad and the dull realities of McWorld will be a confederal union of semi-autonomous communities smaller than nation-states, tied together into regional economic associations and markets larger than nation-states—participatory and self-determining in local matters at the bottom, representative and

accountable at the top. The nation-state would play a diminished role, and sovereignty would lose some of its political potency. The Green movement adage "Think globally, act locally" would actually come to describe the conduct of politics.

This vision reflects only an ideal, however—one that is not terribly likely to be realized. Freedom, Jean-Jacques Rousseau once wrote, is a food easy to eat but hard to digest. Still, democracy has always placed itself out against the odds. And democracy remans both a form of coherence as binding as McWorld and a secular faith potentially as inspiriting as Jihad.

QUESTIONS FOR INQUIRY AND ACTION

1. Describe the definitions of citizenship and community found in McWorld and the world of Jihad.

2. Read Barber's article in conversation with Watson's "China's Big Attack." What are the complexities of globalization?

3. Barber has since expanded this article into a book by the same name. Read the book to see how he developed and revised his ideas. Did he add more evidence? Complicate or refine his original thesis? Read all of the prefatory material including the acknowledgments page. Does Barber mention making any revisions in response to comments from readers of his article?

4. In the last section of his essay Barber recommends reading the Articles of Confederation. You can find them at a number of sites online. Read and discuss them with your class. What would a democracy based on the Articles of Confederation look like? How would our lives change as a result?

STOP AND THINK

THE OLYMPIC GAMES

The Olympics have a long history. The first contest, in 776 B.C. in Greece, was merely a foot race. By the fifth century B.C., they were in full swing, with city-states such as Athens, Corinth, and Sparta vying for glory. Athleticism became a core value of Greek culture as each city-state strove to have the most athletic citizens, because all Greek citizens could participate in the games. ("Citizens" did not include women and slaves, but it did mean that the participating men were not solely athletes.) Not just an athletic contest, the Olympic Games were also a religious festival, and originally included competitions in artistic and poetic composition. They were also an important time for political negotiation, because the rule was that all hostilities—all wars—would be suspended during the games. Traditional enemies would compete as athletes instead of warriors, and citizens could talk informally about political struggles rather than killing one another over them. During the Roman period, the Olympics degenerated into a spectator sport. Instead of consisting of a cross-section of all citizens, the athletes were mostly slaves or gladiators, performing for an audience. In the nineteenth century, when Greece won its independence from the Ottoman Empire, the Olympic Games were revived, though only on a national level, and were held in 1859, 1870, 1875 and 1889. The first modern international Olympics were reinstated in Athens in 1896, through the work of Baron Pierre de Coubertin, who emphasized the original spirit of love of sport and international cooperation. In the summer of 2004, Athens will once again play host to the Olympic Games.

In an article for *Kathimerini,* the daily newspaper in Athens, writer John Ross refers to the Olympics as "an exercise in globalism par excellence, with a much longer duration than other institutions like the World Trade Organization, the United Nations, or the Internet." Athletes often speak of feeling a sense of "world citizenship" when they participate in the Olympic rituals and celebrations.

At the same time, and paradoxically, the Olympics are an exercise in nationalism, as each athlete competes fiercely to capture the most glory for his or her country. Athletes who compete year-round on teams outside their own nations return to their homelands to become members of the national team at Olympics time. Some nations stake their reputations on the success of their athletes, with the result that we've seen an increase in cheating through the use of performance-enhancing drugs.

Are you a fan of the Olympics? When the next games appear on television (Athens in 2004; Torino, Italy in 2006; Beijing in 2008), watch them and take notes on the international and nationalistic aspects of the competition. Compare the global aspects of the Olympics with the globalism described in the other readings in this chapter. For example, notice the displays of the various nations' athletes, the speeches made by athletes, the press coverage of the host city and nation, even the advertisements of the corporate sponsors.

Notice especially which countries participate most actively in the Olympic Games. Is there true global representation? Which continents are most widely represented? How many Third World countries send athletes to compete? Which major countries do *not* participate, and why?

Another aspect of the Olympics that has not been widely discussed is the impact they make on the cities that host them. Research the beneficial and detrimental effects—economically, politically, and socially—on the host communities.

SLAVENKA DRAKULIĆ On Bad Teeth

Slavenka Drakulić is a Croatian journalist and essayist who writes about politics and culture for The Nation *and other periodicals. She is the author of a number of books, several of which have been translated into English, including* How We Survived Communism and Even Laughed *(1991) and* S: A

Novel about the Balkans (2000). "On Bad Teeth" is from her collection of essays entitled Café Europa: Life After Communism *(New York: Norton, 1997).*

In a way, I was initiated into capitalism through toothpaste.

When I first visited the States in 1983, I loved to watch TV commercials. This is when I noticed that Americans were obsessed by their teeth. Every second commercial seemed to be for a toothpaste. Where I come from, toothpaste is toothpaste. I couldn't believe there were so many different kinds. What were they all *for?* After all, the purpose of it is just to clean your teeth. In my childhood were two kinds, mint flavour and strawberry flavour, and both of them had the same brand name, Kalodont. For a long time I was convinced that Kalodont was the word for toothpaste, because nobody at home used the generic word. We never said, "Do you have toothpaste?", we said, "Do you have Kalodont?" It is hardly surprising, then, that such a person would react with nothing short of disbelief when faced with the American cosmetic (or is it pharmaceutical?) industry and its endless production line. Toothpaste with or without sugar, with or without flour, with or without baking soda, calcium, vitamins. . .

Over the years, on subsequent visits I continued to be fascinated by this American obsession with toothpaste, from the common varieties all the way up to Rembrandt, the most snobbish brand, if there could be such a thing as snobbishness about toothpaste. I soon learned that there could: in one women's magazine I saw it recommended as a Christmas present! Needless to say, in every commercial for toothpaste at least one bright, impressively beautiful set of teeth flashes across the screen, but this image is not confined to selling toothpaste. As we all know, beautiful teeth are used to advertise beer, hair shampoo, cars, anything. Indeed, they are an indispensable feature of any American advertisement. The foreigner soon learns that they stand not only as a symbol for both good looks and good health, but for something else as well.

If you think that such advertising might be part of the Americans' national obsession with health in general, you are not far from the truth. Americans seem to be passionate about their health and their looks, which appear to be interchangeable qualities. Health and good looks are essential badges of status among the middle classes. Nothing but narcissism, you could retort, but it is more than that. This connection between teeth and social status is not so evident to an Eastern European. I personally had some doubts about those TV teeth, I thought that they must be artificial, some kind of prosthesis made out of plastic or porcelain. They were just too good to be true. How could people have such fine teeth? Intrigued, I decided to take a good look around me.

5   I noticed that the people I met, that is mostly middle-class urban professionals, generally do have a set of bright, white teeth of their own, not unlike the TV teeth. It was even more surprising to me that I could detect no cavities, no missing teeth, no imperfections. I was astonished. The secret was revealed to me when a friend took her son to the dentist. When they returned, the little boy's

upper teeth were fixed with a dreadful-looking kind of iron muzzle: a brace, I learned. It was obviously painful for him. "Poor little thing!" I exclaimed, but his mother showed no mercy. Moreover, she was proud that she could afford this torture device. I was puzzled. When she explained to me that the brace cost between \$2,000 and \$3,000, her attitude seemed even more sinister. I eventually realised that the mystery of beautiful teeth is not only about hygiene, but about money. She had money enough to get her son's teeth fixed, and the little boy was brave enough to stand the pain, because somehow he understood that this was a requirement of his social status. All the other boys from his private school had braces, too. He was going to grow up being well aware of the fact that his healthy, beautiful teeth were expensive and, therefore, an indication of prestige. Moreover, his mother could count on him to brush them three times a day, with an electric toothbrush and the latest toothpaste promising even healthier and more beautiful teeth, as if that were possible. In the long run, all the discomfort would be worth it.

Seeing the boy's brace, the connection between health and wealth in America became a bit clearer to me. Clean, healthy teeth feature so much in advertising because Americans have no free dental care, and neither is it covered by any medical insurance. Therefore, if you invest money and educate your child early enough (a bit of suffering is needed, too), you will save a lot later. But how much money did this take? I got my answer when I had to visit a dentist myself. On one of my last visits my filling fell out, and just to have it refilled with some temporary white stuff, whatever it was, I had to pay \$100. This would be a minor financial catastrophe for any Eastern European citizen used to free dental care in his own country; it was expensive even by American standards. Only then did I become fully aware of what it means not to have free dental care.

Predictably enough, I was outraged. How was it possible for dental work to be so expensive in this country? For \$100 back home I could have coated my tooth in pure gold! And why was it that such an affluent country did not provide its citizens with basic services like free dental work? This was one of the very few areas in which we from former communist countries had some advantage over Americans—and we would like to keep it.

On my way home, I thought what a blessing it was that we did not have to worry about our teeth, or about whether we could afford to look after them—or at least, we did not have to worry yet, in my country, anyway. However, immediately upon my arrival in Zagreb, I realised that I could allow myself such rose-tinted thoughts only as long as I was on the other side of the Atlantic, from where everything at home looked a bit blurred, especially the general state of people's teeth. Back at home, I was forced to adjust my view. It was as if I had been myopic before and now I had got the right pair of glasses and could finally see properly. And what I saw did not please me at all.

On the bus from the airport I met one of my acquaintances, a young television reporter. For the first time I noticed that half of his teeth were missing and that those which remained looked like the ruins of a decayed medieval town. I had known this guy for years, but I had never thought about the state of the inside of his mouth before, or if I had, I'd considered it totally unimportant. Now I also noticed that, in order to hide his bad teeth, he had grown a moustache and developed a way of laughing which didn't involve him opening his mouth too wide. Even so, his bad teeth were still obvious.

10   This encounter did not cheer me up. Sitting next to the young reporter, I wondered how he managed to speak in front of a TV camera without making a mistake that would reveal his terrible secret. Without smiling, perhaps? This would be perfectly acceptable, because he reports on the war, but wasn't he tired of this uncomfortable game of hide-and-seek? Wouldn't it be much more professional and make life easier if he visited a good dentist and got it all over with? But this is not something we are supposed to talk about. How do you say such a thing to a person if he is not your intimate friend? You can't just say, "Listen, why don't you do something about your teeth?" Perhaps I should have pulled out my toothpaste and handed it to him, or casually dropped the name of my dentist, something like what my friend did last summer. A woman standing next to her in a streetcar emanated an extremely unpleasant odour from her hairy armpits. My friend could not stand it. She pulled her own deodorant stick out of her handbag and gave it to the woman. The funny thing is that the woman accepted it without taking offence. I, on the other hand, could not risk offending my acquaintance.

I continued my investigations at home. Yes, I admit that I looked into the mouths of friends, relatives, acquaintances, neighbours—I could not help it. I discovered that the whole nation had bad teeth, it was just that I had not been able to see it before. I concluded that the guy on the bus was only a part of the general landscape, that he was no exception, and that therefore his failure to attend to his teeth was perfectly normal. I tried to explain this attitude to myself: perhaps people were afraid of drilling? Of course. Who isn't? But if nothing else, there must be an aesthetic drive in every human being, or one would at least think so. Yet, for some reason, aesthetics and communism don't go well together and though we might call our current state post-communism, we still have a communist attitude in such matters.

You could also argue that dentists, being employed by the state, are not well paid. Consequently, they don't put much effort into their job. You can claim as well that the materials they use are not of good quality. That is all probably true. But, I still believe that having your teeth repaired to a mediocre standard is preferable to treasuring the medieval ruins in your mouth or being toothless altogether.

There is no excuse that sounds reasonable enough for such negligence. The problem is that the condition of your teeth in Eastern Europe is regarded as a highly personal matter, not a sign of your standard of living or a question for public discussion. Having good teeth is simply a matter of being civilised and well mannered. Strangely enough, however, dirty shoes, dirty fingernails or dandruff are no longer tolerated: these are considered impolite, even offensive. Yet like such matters of personal hygiene, good teeth are not only a question of money. Dental work has been free for the last forty years. At present there co-exists a mixture of both state-run general medical care, which includes dental care, and private dentists. If you want, you can have excellent dental work done. I know people who travel from Vienna to Bratislava, Budapest, Ljubljana or Zagreb to have their teeth repaired more cheaply. But if you asked people in Eastern Europe who can afford it why they don't go to a private dentist for a better service, they would probably tell you that this is not their priority at the moment. Instead they want to fix their car, or buy a new carpet.

It is clear that leaders and intellectuals here certainly don't care about such a minor aspect of their image. They are preoccupied with the destiny of their respective nations, they do not have time for such trivial matters. The American idea that it is not very polite for a public figure to appear with bad teeth, just as it would be inappropriate to make a speech in your pyjamas, is not understood here. You can meet exquisitely dressed politicians or businessmen, but wait until they open their mouths! If these public figures are not worried about this aspect of their looks, why should ordinary people be concerned about theirs? They too have more important things to do, for example surviving. There is also that new breed, the *nouveau riche* of post-communism. Previously everything was valued by one's participation in politics, now it is slowly replaced by money. The arrogance of these people originates there. Unfortunately, money does not guarantee good manners, or a regular visit to the dentist for that matter.

15   I can only try to imagine the horrors when free dental work is replaced by private dentists whose prices nobody can afford. How many decades will we have to wait until our teeth look like American ones? It is a question of perception. In order to improve your looks, you have to be convinced that it is worth the trouble. In other words, we are dealing with a problem of self-esteem, with a way of thinking, rather than a superficial question. Bad teeth are the result of bad dentists and bad food, but also of a specific culture of thinking, of not seeing yourself as an individual. What we need here is a revolution of self-perception. Not only will that not come automatically with the new political changes, but I am afraid that it will also take longer than any political or economic developments. We need to accept our responsibilities towards both others and ourselves. This is not only a wise sort of investment in the future, as we can see in the case of Americans, it also gives you the feeling that you have done what you can to improve yourself, be it your teeth, your health, your career, education, environment or society in general.

Individual responsibility, including the responsibility for oneself, is an entirely new concept here, as I have stated many times elsewhere. This is why the revolution of self-perception has a long way to go. As absurd as it may sound, in the old days one could blame the Communist Party even for one's bad teeth. Now there is no one to blame, but it takes time to understand that. If you have never had it, self-respect has to be learned. Maybe our own teeth would be a good place to start.

But I can see signs of coming changes. Recently a good friend borrowed some money from me in order to repair her apartment. When the time came to give it back, she told me that I would have to wait, because she needed the money for something very urgent. She had finally decided to have her teeth fixed by a private dentist. No wonder she was left without a penny. But what could I have said to that? I said the only thing I could say: "I understand you, this must come first."

Finally, I guess it is only fair that I should declare the state of my own teeth. I am one of those who much too often used the free dental work so generously provided by the communist state for the benefit of its people. I was afraid of the dentist, all right, but also brave enough to stand the pain because I had overcome the psychological barrier at an early age.

When I was in the third grade a teacher showed us a cartoon depicting a fortress—a tooth—attacked by bad guys—bacteria. They looked terribly dangerous, digging tunnels and ditches with their small axes until the fortress almost fell into their hands. Then the army of good guys, the white blood cells, arrived and saved it at the last moment. The teacher explained to us how we could fight the bad guys by brushing our teeth regularly with Kalodont and by visiting a dentist every time we spotted a little hole or felt pain. I took her advice literally—I was obviously very impressed by the cartoon, just as I was impressed by the American TV commercials thirty years later. The result is that today I can say that I have good teeth, although six of them are missing. How did that happen? Well, when I spotted a little cavity, I would immediately go to the dentist all by myself. This was mistake number one. You could not choose your own dentist at that time, and my family had to go to a military hospital. A dentist there would usually fill the cavity, but for some reason the filling would soon fall out. Then he would make an even bigger hole and fill it again, until eventually there was not much tooth left.

20   Those "dentists" were in fact young students of dentistry drafted into the army. For them, this was probably an excellent chance to improve their knowledge by practising on patients. When they'd finished practising on me a more experienced dentist would suggest I had the tooth out. What could I, a child, do but agree? This was mistake number two, of course. I had to learn to live with one gap in my jaw, then another, and another. Much later I had two bridges made by a private dentist. He didn't even ask me why I was missing six of my teeth; he knew how things had worked in those days. My only consolation was that I did not have to pay much for my bridgework.

Like everyone else in the post-communist world, I had to learn the meaning of the American proverb "There is no such thing as a free lunch." The Americans are right. You don't get anything properly done if you don't pay for it sooner or later.

QUESTIONS FOR INQUIRY AND ACTION

1. Drakulić's description of braces is funny because she defamiliarizes something that is commonplace to us. What is the effect of that passage on you? In what ways is having braces, and, consequently, straight teeth, a sign of social status?

2. List the details Drakulić gives us about Eastern Europe. How has Eastern Europe been distinguished from Western Europe and the United States?

3. Beautiful teeth are "an indispensable feature of any American advertisement," Drakulić declares. Is this true? Go through magazine ads and catalogues, observe billboards and TV commercials. How many people have beautiful teeth? How many of the models show their teeth prominently? Look at ads from 10, 20, 30, 40 years ago. Do we show our teeth more now than we used to?

4. Do you have dental insurance? Research dental insurance. How common is it on employers' health plans? What percentage of Americans have it? What are the connections between what is considered necessary or cosmetic, and what people have to pay for themselves?

CASE STUDY

THINKING GLOBALLY, ACTING LOCALLY: THE WORLD TRADE ORGANIZATION PROTESTS IN SEATTLE, 1999

A CITIZEN'S GUIDE

TO THE

WORLD

TRADE

ORGANIZATION

A CITIZEN'S GUIDE TO THE WORLD TRADE ORGANIZATION

Published by the Working Group on the WTO / MAI, July 1999

Printed in the U.S. by Inkworks, a worker-owned union shop

ISBN 1-58231-000-9

147 INKWORKS PRESS

EVERYTHING YOU NEED TO KNOW TO FIGHT FOR

FAIR TRADE

The contents of this pamphlet may be freely reproduced provided that its source is acknowledged.

THE WTO AND CORPORATE GLOBALIZATION

What do the U.S. Cattlemen's Association, Chiquita Banana and the Venezuelan oil industry have in common? These big business interests were able to defeat hard-won national laws ensuring food safety, strengthening local economies and protecting the environment by convincing governments to challenge the laws at the World Trade Organization (WTO).

Established in 1995, the WTO is a powerful new global commerce agency, which transformed the General Agreement on Tarriffs and Trade (GATT) into an enforceable global commercial code. The WTO is one of the main mechanisms of corporate globalization. While its proponents say it is based on "free trade," in fact, the WTO's 700-plus pages of rules set out a comprehensive system of **corporate-managed trade**. Indeed, the WTO has little to do with the 18th Century free trade philosophy developed by David Ricardo or Adam Smith, who assumed neither labor nor capital crossed national borders.

Under the WTO's system of corporate-managed trade, economic efficiency, reflected in short-run corporate profits, dominates other values. Decisions affecting the economy are to be confined to the private sector, while social and environmental costs are borne by the public.

Sometimes called the "neoliberal" model,

this system sidelines environmental rules, health safeguards and labor standards to provide transnational corporations (TNCs) with a cheap supply of labor and natural resources. The WTO also guarantees corporate access to foreign markets without requiring that TNCs respect countries' domestic priorities.

The myth that every nation can grow by exporting more than they import is central to the neoliberal ideology. Its proponents seem to forget that in order for one country to export an automobile, some other country has to import it.

The WTO Hurts U.S. Workers - Steel

More than 10,000 high-wage, high-tech workers in the U.S. steel industry lost their jobs this past year as U.S. factories laid off workers in response to a surge of imports from Japan, Russia, and Brazil. This import surge was caused in part by the WTO's equally problematic "cousin" organization, the International Monetary Fund (IMF), which pushed countries to increase their exports to the U.S. as a way to get out of the financial crisis caused in part by past IMF policies. The United Steel Workers of America joined with steel industry leaders to ask the President for emergency relief. The President said he would not help because WTO rules forbid such action.

1   2

> A global system of enforceable rules is being created where corporations have all the rights, governments have all the obligations, and democracy is left behind in the dust.

Now the world's transnational companies want more — a new "Millennium Round" of further WTO negotiations which would accelerate the economic race to the bottom by expanding the WTO's powers.

But this concept's failure goes beyond this inherent sham: the lose-lose nature of export-led growth was exposed in the aftermath of the East Asian financial crisis of 1998. When the IMF compelled Asian countries to try to export their way out of their crises, the U.S. became the importer of last resort. U.S. steelworkers lost jobs to a flood of steel imports, while workers in Asia remained mired in a terrible depression.

The neoliberal ideological underpinning of corporate-managed trade is presented as TINA — "There Is No Alternative" — an inevitable outcome rather than the culmination of a long-term effort to write and put into place rules designed to benefit corporations and investors, rather than communities, workers and the environment.

The top trade officials of every WTO member country are meeting in Seattle at the end of November. If you haven't bought the public relations campaign on TINA and want to help change the rules, join your fellow citizens on the *Road to Seattle and Beyond.* To start with, the WTO must assess the effects

3

of its current rules before negotiating new agreements. This booklet explains what the WTO is, how it is damaging the public interest, how corporations and some governments want to expand WTO's powers, and what you can do.

WHAT IS THE WTO AND HOW DOES IT WORK?

"More and more the WTO is under pressure to expand its agenda because more and more it is seen as the focal point for the many challenges and concerns of globalization."
- Renato Ruggiero
WTO Director General

The WTO is the international organization charged with enforcing a set of trade rules including the General Agreement on Tariffs and Trade (GATT), Trade Related Intellectual Property Measures (TRIPS), General Agreement on Trade in Services (GATS), among others. WTO was established in 1995 in the "Uruguay Round"of GATT negotiations.

Prior to the Uruguay Round, GATT rules focused primarily on tariffs and quotas. Consensus of GATTmembers was required to enforce the rules. The Uruguay Round expanded GATT rules to cover what is known in trade jargon as "non-tariff barriers to trade." These are food safety laws, product standards, rules on use of tax dollars, investment policy and other domestic laws that impact trade. The WTO's rules limit what non-tariff policies countries can implement or maintain.

4

Currently there are 134 member countries in the WTO and 33 nations with observer status. Officially, decisions in the WTO are made by voting or consensus. However, developed countries, especially the so-called QUAD countries (U.S., Canada, Japan and the European Union), repeatedly have made key decisions in closed meetings, excluding other WTO nations.

The WTO's lack of democratic process or accountable decision-making is epitomized by the WTO Dispute Settlement Process. The WTO allows countries to challenge each others' laws and regulations as violations of WTO rules. Cases are decided by a panel of three trade bureaucrats. There are no conflict of interest rules and the panelists often have little appreciation of domestic law or of government responsibility to protect workers, the environment or human rights. Thus, it is not surprising that every single environmental or public health law challenged at WTO has been ruled illegal.

WTO tribunals operate in secret. Documents, hearings and briefs are confidential. Only national governments are allowed to participate, even if a state law is being challenged. There are no outside appeals.

Once a final WTO ruling is issued, losing countries have a set time to implement one of only three choices: change their law to conform to the WTO requirements, pay permanent compensation to the winning country, or face non-negotiated trade sanctions. The U.S. official position is that ultimately, laws must be changed to be consistent with WTO policy.

5

THE WTO'S RECORD: THREATS TO DEMOCRACY, HEALTH AND THE ENVIRONMENT

When the WTO was created, concerned citizens and public interest organizations warned that the combination of the WTO's pro-industry rules and powerful enforcement would pose a threat to laws designed to protect consumers, workers, and the environment. Almost five years later, there is a clear record: the cases settled under WTO rules show the WTO's bias against the public interest.

 **THE CLEAN AIR CASE**

CASE: On behalf of its oil industry, Venezuela challenged a U.S. Clean Air Act regulation that required gas refiners to produce cleaner gas. The rule used the 1990 actual performance data of oil refineries required to file with EPA (mostly U.S. refineries) as the starting point for required improvements for refineries without reliable data (mostly foreign). Venezuela claimed this rule was biased against foreign refiners and took the case to the WTO.

RESULT: A WTO panel ruled against the U.S. law. In 1997, the EPA

6

changed the clean air rules to give foreign refiners the choice of using an individual baseline (starting point). The EPA acknowledged that the change "creates a potential for adverse environmental impact."

IMPLICATION: Refiners from Venezuela and other countries will use the individual baseline option only if it gives them a weaker starting point, and thus lets them sell dirtier gasoline in the U.S., which would deteriorate air quality. The WTO gives businesses a special avenue to challenge policies, like the Clean Air rules, which have withstood domestic challenges.

THE BEEF HORMONE CASE

CASE: The U.S. challenged a European Union ban on the sale of beef from cattle that have been raised with certain artificial growth hormones.

RESULT: In 1998, a WTO appellate panel ruled against the EU law, giving the EU until May 13, 1999 to open its markets to hormone-treated beef.

IMPLICATION: The ban on artificial hormones applies equally to European farmers and foreign producers. If European consumers and governments are opposed to the use of artificial hormones and are concerned about potential health risks or want to promote more natural farming methods, they

should have the right to enact laws that support their choices. Instead, the WTO empowers its tribunals to second-guess whether health and environmental rules have a "valid" scientific basis.

THE SHRIMP TURTLE CASE

CASE: Four Asian nations challenged provisions of the U.S. Endangered Species Act forbidding the sale in the U.S. of shrimp caught in ways that kill endangered sea turtles.

RESULT: In 1998, a WTO appellate panel decided that while the U.S. is allowed to protect turtles, the specific way the U.S. tried to do so was not allowed under WTO rules. The U.S. government is now considering ways to change the law to comply with WTO.

IMPLICATION: It is possible to catch shrimp without harming turtles by fitting shrimp nets with inexpensive "turtle excluder devices." U.S. law requires domestic and foreign shrimp fishermen to use turtle-safe methods. The goal of saving turtles could be undercut by the WTO's second-guessing of how U.S. policy should be implemented, given the most inexpensive, effective means has been ruled WTO-illegal.

7

8

WHAT'S UP FOR THE
WTO IN SEATTLE?

When the WTO countries meet in Seattle, they will finalize a "Ministerial Declaration" that will announce the future WTO agenda. At the end of the previous Round, WTO members agreed to form committees to consider agriculture, services and intellectual property rights (now called the "built-in agenda"). Now some countries want to add investment (the MAI), procurement and competition policy, calling for the launch of a "Millennium Round" of negotiations. Whatever future negotiations might be agreed, further deregulation favoring private interests can be anticipated.

The European Union wants to launch a Millennium Round at Seattle. The U.S. favors the more limited built-in agenda. Some developing countries are strongly opposed to further negotiations since deregulation and privatization have hurt them. They oppose a new Round and call for a turn-around of the WTO, a theme which is being echoed by a growing consensus of activists worldwide, see www.xs4all.nl/~ceo/

TAKE ACTION!

➲Educate yourself and others about the WTO! Check out the contact list of web-pages listed on pages 23-25 for additional information.

✉   Write your Member of Congress, both your Senators and local elected officials. Urge them to oppose the launch of a new round of WTO negotiations in Seattle and to endorse an assessment of the WTO's record to date. Urge members of Congress to sign Rep. Bernie Sanders' (I-VT), "Dear Colleague" letter demanding WTO review and repair.

☎ Contact the U.S. negotiators and tell them why you think we should conduct an assessment of the WTO rather than expand it. Make sure to mention that you oppose any investment negotiations in the WTO.
U.S. Trade Representative (the agency in charge of WTO talks) is Charlene Barshefsky, phone: 202-395-6890, fax: 202-395-4549
White House: John Podesta
202-456-1414
Vice President Gore:
202-456-1111

✉   Write a letter-to-the-editor about why we need to assess WTO's current record, not expand its reach further. Find sample letters on the web-pages listed on page 23.

✒ Sign and circulate the international organizational sign-on letter opposing a new round of negotiations and demanding a WTO assessment (www.xs4all.nl/~ceo/).

➲ Participate in days-of-action against a "Millennium Round." More information will be posted on the web-sites on page 23.

➲Organize a Teach-In, town hall meeting, debate etc. on the WTO and globalization. Focus on local consequences. Invite proponents and opponents of so-called "free-trade."

➲ **Come to Seattle for the ministerial meeting!** The meeting will take place from November 29 through December 3, and will include a major international Teach-In organized by the International Forum on Globalization (IFG) the weekend before, street festivities, education, cultural activities, protests and much more. Contact People for a Fair Trade Policy (Seattle based toll-free at 1-877-STOP-WTO or 786-7986) or www.tradewatch.org

---

CONTACTS

The World Trade Organization
www.wto.org, Geneva, Switzerland, (+ 41 22) 739 51 11

General
♦ Public Citizen's Global Trade Watch. www.tradewatch.org, Washington, DC (202) 546-4996
♦ International Forum on Globalization (IFG). www.ifg.org, San Francisco, CA, (415) 771-3394

Agriculture and Food Policy
♦ Institute for Agriculture and Trade Policy. www.iatp.org, Minneapolis, MN (612) 870-3405

♦ National Family Farm Coalition. Washington, DC (202) 543-5675

Developing Country Perspective
Third World Network.
www.twnside.org.sg, Penang, Malaysia, + 60-4-2266728.
♦ 50 Years Is Enough Network, www.50years.org, (202)-463-2265
♦ Global Exchange, www.globalexchange.org, San Francisco, (415) 255-7296

Economic/Political
♦ Alliance for Democracy. www.afd-online.org, Washington, DC (202) 244-0561
♦ The Preamble Center. www.preamble.org, Washington, DC (202) 265-3263
♦ United for a Fair Economy. www.stw.org, Boston, MA (617) 423-2148

Environment
♦ American Lands Alliance. www.americanlands.org, Washington, DC (202) 547-9230.
♦ Center for International Environmental Law. www.econet.apc.org/ciel., Washington, DC (202) 785-8700
♦ Friends of the Earth. www.foe.org, Washington, DC (202) 783-7400
♦ Pacific Environment and Resources Center (PERC). www.pacenv.org, Oakland, CA (510) 251- 8800
♦ Sierra Club. www.sierraclub.org, Washington, DC (202) 547-1141 (202) 778-9721

Writing Style

CREATING A PAMPHLET

"A Citizen's Guide to the World Trade Organization," published by the Working Group on the WTO/MAI in July 1999, is an example of a pamphlet created as part of a public education campaign. It was published in both a paper form and as a downloadable document available from the Web site of the nonprofit public interest organization Public Citizen: <http://www.citizen.org/trade/wto/index.cfm>. (We have included only an excerpt from it in this case study.)

The 30-page pamphlet is a substantive, detailed piece of work that had monetary support for its development (the sponsors are listed on the back page). Your public education campaigns, especially while you're in school, may not be this involved. However, this kind of public writing can easily be done by students and can be tailored to events taking place on your campus and in your communities, and can be a fast and effective way of informing a group of people. Regardless of their size and the magnitude of the issue they address, pamphlets have as their goal to educate a wide range of people who are not expected to know much about the issue at hand. Notice how this pamphlet provides:

- *An introduction to and overview of the issue.* The authors define key terms people will need to know to understand the issue, such as what the World Trade Organization is and how it works, and what "neoliberal" policies are (the pamphlet does this in the body of the text and in a glossary at the back). They also inform readers about the urgency of the issue and how it will affect them and their communities.

- *Specific consequences of the issue.* The Working Group provides these through a series of case studies: the Clean Air Case, the Beef Hormone Case, etc. Each of these case studies supplies evidence to support the pamphlet's argument that readers should be concerned about the actions of the WTO. (We have not included ten pages that detail the WTO's agenda for their meeting, including reviews of WTO agreements on matters such as food safety standards in agriculture, intellectual property of patents and copyrights, and whether restrictions should be lifted on commercial logging.)

- *Concrete ways for readers to take action on the issue.* The pamphlet provides seven different ways to get your voice heard on the issue, with names and phone numbers of responsible parties, Web sites, and models to follow in writing letters to editors. In addition, it lists twenty-five organizations, with phone numbers and Web addresses, from which you can receive more information.

- *Visual interest.* To break up the text into manageable chunks and provide interest to readers, the pamphlet includes boldfaced subheadings to direct readers from section to section, as well as different fonts, text boxes, and illustrations.

Discuss your response to this pamphlet. For instance, its goal is to educate the public. But it also has a specific argument to make and an agenda to promote.

continued on next page

> Should the pamphlet attempt to be balanced in its coverage, to provide the WTO's point of view, and to leave it to readers to make their own decisions? Or is it more ethical to openly state the agenda of the authors?

MIKE CARTER Mayor declares civil emergency, imposes curfew in downtown Seattle

Mike Carter is a staff reporter for the Seattle Times *who covered the WTO conference and wrote this piece the evening of the first day of the protests, November 30, 1999.*

Mayor Paul Schell declared a state of emergency Tuesday night and, at his request, Gov. Gary Locke called in the National Guard as protesters continued to run wild in the streets of downtown Seattle.

The declaration came following a day of tear-gas-laced skirmishes that disrupted the first day of the World Trade Organization conference.

Schell announced a curfew throughout the majority of the city's business district, which had been occupied all day by tens of thousands of protesters. Dozens of times, police lobbed tear gas canisters and fired pepper-spray pellets and rubber bullets into the milling crowds.

The curfew was to run from 7 P.M. Tuesday through sunrise Wednesday. It covers the area from I–5 to the waterfront and from Yesler Way to Denny Way.

5   The demonstrations forced cancellation of the opening ceremonies of the WTO three-day conference and forced officials to declare the streets unsafe for delegates to travel a few short blocks from their hotels to the convention center. Schell issued an apology to the delegates.

More than a dozen people had been arrested and one police officer suffered minor, unspecified injuries, Schell told reporters at an evening briefing. Dozens of downtown businesses were vandalized and a city that had been dressed up for the Christmas holidays was thrown into disheveled bedlam.

Schell, flanked by Locke, police Chief Norm Stamper and King County Executive Ron Sims, urged the more law-abiding protesters to leave the downtown area so police could enforce the curfew.

"This was a planned demonstration. Obviously, we're not happy with the outcome," the mayor said. "We're urging people to give us back the streets for tomorrow. The point's been made."

"The last thing I ever wanted to be was the mayor of a city where I had to call out the National Guard, where I had to see tear gas in the streets. It makes me sick," said Schell, who pointed out that he was an anti-war demonstrator in the 1960s.

10   However, within an hour, police were charging the demonstrators with truncheons raised and making arrests.

Locke said that 200 National Guardsmen were called up and would be available Wednesday morning. They will not be armed, but they are trained in crowd control. In addition, another 300 Washington State Patrol troopers would be sent to help the beleaguered Seattle Police Department.

Earlier, Stamper acknowledged that his officers—who had been training for the WTO and expected demonstrations for the better part of a year—were not able to secure the streets.

While the police had been in negotiations with dozens of protest groups for months, the chief said the city underestimated the number who hadn't asked permission to demonstrate and were bent on anarchy and vandalism.

"From a public safety standpoint, the last thing we wanted to do was declare a state of emergency," Stamper said, saying that calling out the National Guard was the department's "last-ditch" contingency.

ROZ CHAST One Morning, While Getting Dressed

Roz Chast is a cartoonist whose work appears often in The New Yorker, The Sciences, *and* The Harvard Business Review. *She has also published collections of cartoons, including* Childproof: Cartoons about Parents and Children, *and has illustrated four children's books, including* Meet My Staff. *"One Morning, While Getting Dressed" appeared in the November 29, 1999 edition of* The New Yorker.

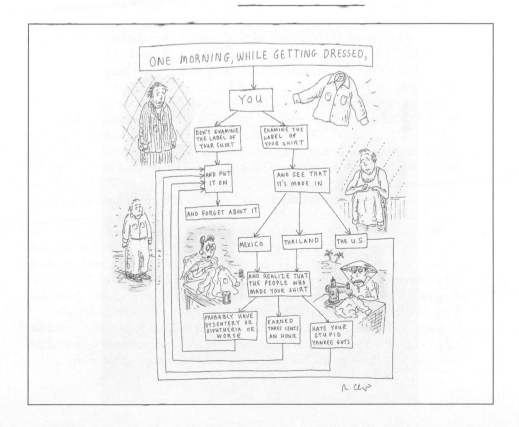

THOMAS L. FRIEDMAN Senseless in Seattle

> *Thomas L. Friedman is one of the United States's leading advocates of glob-*
> *alization and free trade. He is the author of the popular book* The Lexus
> and the Olive Tree: Understanding Globalization *(1999), and writes the "For-*
> *eign Affairs" column for the* New York Times, *for which he has won two*
> *Pulitzer Prizes. "Senseless in Seattle" was his column for the* Times *on*
> *December 1, 1999.*

Is there anything more ridiculous in the news today than the protests against the World Trade Organization in Seattle? I doubt it.

These anti-W.T.O. protesters—who are a Noah's ark of flat-earth advocates, protectionist trade unions and yuppies looking for their 1960's fix—are protesting against the wrong target with the wrong tools. Here's why:

What unites the anti-W.T.O. crowd is their realization that we now live in a world without walls. The cold-war system we just emerged from was built around division and walls; the globalization system that we are now in is built around integration and webs. In this new system, jobs, cultures, environmental problems and labor standards can much more easily flow back and forth.

The ridiculous thing about the protesters is that they find fault with this, and blame the W.T.O. The W.T.O. is not the cause of this world without walls, it's the effect. The more countries trade with one another, the more they need an institution to set the basic rules of trade, and that is all the W.T.O. does. "Rules are a substitute for walls—when you don't have walls you need more rules," notes the Council on Foreign Relations expert Michael Mandelbaum.

5   Because some countries try to use their own rules to erect new walls against trade, the W.T.O. adjudicates such cases. For instance, there was the famous "Flipper vs. GATTzilla" dispute. (The W.T.O. used to be known as GATT.) America has rules against catching tuna in nets that might also snare dolphins; other countries don't, and those other countries took the U.S. before a GATT tribunal and charged that our insistence on Flipper-free tuna was a trade barrier. The anti-W.T.O. protesters extrapolate from such narrow cases that the W.T.O. is going to become a Big Brother and tell us how to live generally. Nonsense.

What's crazy is that the protesters want the W.T.O. to become precisely what they accuse it of already being—a global government. They want it to set more rules—their rules, which would impose our labor and environmental standards on everyone else. I'm for such higher standards, and over time the W.T.O. may be a vehicle to enforce them, but it's not the main vehicle to achieve them. And they are certainly not going to be achieved by putting up new trade walls.

Every country and company that has improved its labor, legal and environmental standards has done so because of more global trade, more integration, more Internet—not less. These are the best tools we have for improving global governance.

Who is one of the top environmental advisers to DuPont today? Paul Gilding, the former head of Greenpeace! How could that be? A DuPont official told me that in the old days, if DuPont wanted to put a chemical factory in a city, it knew it just had to persuade the local neighbors. "Now we have six billion neighbors," said the DuPont official—meaning that DuPont knows that in a world without walls if it wants to put up a chemical plant in a country, every environmentalist is watching. And if that factory makes even a tiny spill those environmentalists will put it on the World Wide Web and soil DuPont's name from one end of the earth to the other.

I recently visited a Victoria's Secret garment factory in Sri Lanka that, in terms of conditions, I would let my own daughters work in. Why does it have such a high standard? Because anti-sweatshop activists have started to mobilize enough consumers to impress Victoria's Secret that if it doesn't get its shop standards up, consumers won't buy its goods. Sri Lanka is about to pass new copyright laws, which Sri Lankan software writers have been seeking for years to protect their own innovations. Why the new law now? Because Microsoft told Sri Lanka it wouldn't sell its products in a country with such weak intellectual property laws.

10   Hey, I want to save Flipper too. It's a question of how. If the protesters in Seattle stopped yapping, they would realize that they have been duped by knaves like Pat Buchanan—duped into thinking that power lies with the W.T.O. It doesn't. There's never going to be a global government to impose the rules the protesters want. But there can be better global governance—on the environment, intellectual property and labor. You achieve that not by adopting 1960's tactics in a Web-based world—not by blocking trade, choking globalization or getting the W.T.O. to put up more walls. That's a fool's errand.

You make a difference today by using globalization—by mobilizing the power of trade, the power of the Internet and the power of consumers to persuade, or embarrass, global corporations and nations to upgrade their standards. You change the world when you get the big players to do the right things for the wrong reasons. But that takes hard work—coalition-building with companies and consumers, and follow-up. It's not as much fun as a circus in Seattle.

TOM TOMORROW This Modern World

Tom Tomorrow is a political cartoonist whose weekly strip "This Modern World" is published widely and has been featured in the New York Times, Spin, Mother Jones, The Nation, US News & World Report, The Economist, *and* The New Yorker, *among other periodicals. In 1998, he won the first place Robert F. Kennedy Journalism Award for Cartooning, and in 2000, the Professional Freedom and Responsibility Award from the National Association for Education in Journalism and Mass Communication. This cartoon appeared on December 22, 1999.*

ELIZABETH (BETITA) MARTINEZ Where Was the Color in Seattle?

Elizabeth (Betita) Martinez is a political activist and educator. In 1997 she cofounded the Institute for MultiRacial Justice in San Francisco and edits their publication, Shades of Power. *She is also the author of* De Colores Means All Of Us: Latina Views of a Multi-Colored Century *(1998). "Where Was the Color in Seattle?" was published in* ColorLines *(Spring 2000), an online magazine of race, culture, and action. It won the New California Media 2000 Award for "Best Online Feature."*

I was at the jail where a lot of protesters were being held and a big crowd of people was chanting "This Is What Democracy Looks Like!" At first it sounded

kind of nice. But then I thought: is this really what democracy looks like?
Nobody here looks like me.

Jinee Kim, Bay Area youth organizer

In the vast acreage of published analysis about the splendid victory over the World Trade Organization last November 29–December 3, it is almost impossible to find anyone wondering why the 40–50,000 demonstrators were overwhelmingly Anglo. How can that be, when the WTO's main victims around the world are people of color? Understanding the reasons for the low level of color, and what can be learned from it, is absolutely crucial if we are to make Seattle's promise of a new, international movement against imperialist globalization come true.

Among those who did come for the WTO meeting were some highly informative third world panelists who spoke Monday, November 29 about the effects of WTO on health care and on the environment. They included activist-experts from Mexico, Malaysia, the Philippines, Ghana, and Pakistan. On Tuesday, at the huge rally on November 30 before the march, labor leaders from Mexico, the Caribbean, South Africa, Malaysia, India, and China spoke along with every major U.S. union leader (all white).

Rank-and-file U.S. workers of color also attended, from certain unions and locals in certain geographic areas. There were young African Americans in the building trades; blacks from Local 10 of the ILWU in San Francisco and Latinos from its Los Angeles local; Asian Americans from SEIU; Teamsters of color from eastern Washington state; members of the painters' union and the union of Hotel Employees and Restaurant Employees (H.E.R.E.). Latino/a farmworkers from the UFW and PCUN (Pineros and Campesinos del Noroeste) of Oregon also attended. At one point a miner from the South Africa Labor Network cried, "In the words of Karl Marx, 'Workers of the world, unite!'" The crowd of some 25,000 people cheered.

Among community activists of color, the Indigenous Environmental Network (IEN) delegation led by Tom Goldtooth conducted an impressive program of events with Native peoples from all over the U.S. and the world. A 15-member multi-state delegation represented the Southwest Network for Environmental and Economic Justice based in Albuquerque, which embraces 84 organizations primarily of color in the U.S. and Mexico; their activities in Seattle were binational.

5   Many activist youth groups of color came from California, especially the Bay Area, where they have been working on such issues as Free Mumia, affirmative action, ethnic studies, and rightwing laws like the current Proposition 21 "youth crime" initiative. Seattle-based forces of color that participated actively included the Filipino Community Center and the international People's Assembly, which led a march on Tuesday despite being the only one denied a permit. The predominantly white Direct Action Network (DAN), a huge coalition, brought thousands to the protest. But Jia Ching Chen of the Bay Area's Third Eye Movement was the only young person of color involved in DAN's central planning.

Seattle's 27-year-old Centro de la Raza organized a Latino contingent in the labor march and local university groups, including MEChA (Movimiento Estudiantil Chicano de Aztlan), hooked up with visiting activists of color. Black activists who have been fighting for an African American Heritage Museum and Cultural Center in Seattle were there. Hop Hopkins, an AIDS activist in Seattle, also black, made constant personal efforts to draw in people of color.

Still, the overall turnout of color from the U.S. remained around five percent of the total. In personal interviews, activists from the Bay Area and the Southwest gave me several reasons for this. Some mentioned concern about the likelihood of brutal police repression. Other obstacles: lack of funds for the trip, inability to be absent from work during the week, and problems in finding child care.

Yet several experienced activists of color in the Bay Area who had even been offered full scholarships chose not to go. A major reason for not participating, and the reason given by many others, was lack of knowledge about the WTO. As one Filipina said, "I didn't see the political significance of it how the protest would be anti-imperialist. We didn't know anything about the WTO except that lots of people were going to the meeting." One of the few groups that did feel informed, and did participate, was the hip-hop group Company of Prophets. According to African American member Rashidi Omari of Oakland, this happened as a result of their attending teach-ins by predominantly white groups like Art and Revolution. Company of Prophets, rapping from a big white van, was in the front ranks of the 6 A.M. march that closed down the WTO on November 30.

The problem of unfamiliarity with the WTO was aggravated by the fact that black and Latino communities across the U.S. lack Internet access compared to many white communities. A July 1999 federal survey showed that among Americans earning $15,000-$35,000 a year, more than 32 percent of white families owned computers but only 19 percent of black and Latino families. In that same income range, only 9 percent of African American and Latino homes had Internet access compared to 27 percent of white families. So information about WTO and all the plans for Seattle did not reach many people of color.

10   Limited knowledge meant a failure to see how the WTO affected the daily lives of U.S. communities of color. "Activists of color felt they had more immediate issues," said Rashidi. "Also, when we returned people told me of being worried that family and peers would say they were neglecting their own communities, if they went to Seattle. They would be asked, 'Why are you going? You should stay here and help your people.'"

Along with such concerns about linkage came the assumption that the protest would be overwhelmingly white as it was. Coumba Toure, a Bay Area activist originally from Mali, West Africa, said she had originally thought, "the whites will take care of the WTO, I don't need to go." Others were more openly apprehensive. For example, Carlos ("Los" for short) Windham of Company of Prophets told me, "I think even Bay Area activists of color who understood the linkage didn't want to go to a protest dominated by 50,000 white hippies."

People of color had reason to expect the protest to be white-dominated. Roberto Maestas, director of Seattle's Centro de la Raza, told me that in the massive local press coverage before the WTO meeting, not a single person of color appeared as a spokesperson for the opposition. "Day after day, you saw only white faces in the news. The publicity was a real deterrent to people of color. I think some of the unions or church groups should have had representatives of color, to encourage people of color to participate."

Four protesters of color from different Bay Area organizations talked about the "culture shock" they experienced when they first visited the "Convergence," the protest center set up by the Direct Action Network, a coalition of many organizations. Said one, "When we walked in, the room was filled with young whites calling themselves anarchists. There was a pungent smell, many had not showered. We just couldn't relate to the scene so our whole group left right away." Another told me, "They sounded dogmatic and paranoid." "I just freaked and left," said another. "It wasn't just race, it was also culture, although race was key."

In retrospect, observed Van Jones of STORM (Standing Together to Organize a Revolutionary Movement) in the Bay Area, "We should have stayed. We didn't see that we had a lot to learn from them. And they had a lot of materials for making banners, signs, puppets." "Later I went back and talked to people," recalled Rashidi, "and they were discussing tactics, very smart. Those folks were really ready for action. It was limiting for people of color to let that one experience affect their whole picture of white activists." Jinee Kim, a Korean American with the Third Eye Movement in the Bay Area, also thought it was a mistake. "We realized we didn't know how to do a blockade. We had no gas masks. They made sure everybody had food and water, they took care of people. We could have learned from them."

15   Reflecting the more positive evaluation of white protesters in general, Richard Moore, coordinator of the Southwest Network for Environmental and Economic Justice, told me "the white activists were very disciplined." "We sat down with whites, we didn't take the attitude that 'we can't work with white folks,'" concluded Rashidi. "It was a liberating experience."

Few predominantly white groups in the Bay Area made a serious effort to get people of color to Seattle. Juliette Beck of Global Exchange worked hard with others to help people from developing (third world) countries to come. But for U.S. people of color, the main organizations that made a serious effort to do so were Just Act (Youth ACTion for Global JUSTice), formerly the Overseas Development Network, and Art and Revolution, which mostly helped artists. Many activists of color have mentioned Alli Chaggi-Starr of Art and Revolution, who not only helped people come but for the big march in Seattle she obtained a van with a sound system that was used by musicians and rappers.

In Just Act, Coumba Toure and two other members of color—Raj Jayadev and Malachi Larabee—pushed hard for support from the group. As a result, about 40 people of color were enabled to go thanks to special fundraising and whites staying at people's homes in Seattle so their hotel money could be used instead on plane tickets for people of color. Reflecting on the whole issue of working with whites, Coumba talked not only about pushing Just Act but also pushing people of color to apply for the help that became available.

One of the problems Coumba said she encountered in doing this was "a legacy of distrust of middle-class white activists that has emerged from experiences of 'being used.' Or not having our issues taken seriously. Involving people of color must be done in a way that gives them real space. Whites must understand a whole new approach is needed that includes respect (if you go to people of color thinking you know more, it creates a barrier). Also, you cannot approach people simply in terms of numbers, like 'let's give 2 scholarships.' People of color must be central to the project."

Jia Ching Chen recalled that once during the week of protest, in a jail holding cell, he was one of only two people of color among many Anglos. He tried to discuss with some of them the need to involve more activists of color and the importance of white support in this. "Some would say, 'We want to diversify,' but didn't understand the dynamics of this." In other words, they didn't understand the kinds of problems described by Coumba Toure. "Other personal conversations were more productive," he said, "and some white people started to recognize why people of color could view the process of developing working relations with whites as oppressive."

20   Unfortunately the heritage of distrust was intensified by some of the AFL-CIO leadership of labor on the November 30 march. They chose to take a different route through downtown rather than marching with others to the Convention Center and helping to block the WTO. Also, on the march to downtown they reportedly had a conflict with the Third World People's Assembly contingent when they rudely told the people of color to move aside so they could be in the lead.

Yet if only a small number of people of color went to Seattle, all those with whom I spoke found the experience extraordinary. They spoke of being changed forever. "I saw the future." "I saw the possibility of people working together." They called the giant mobilization "a shot in the arm," if you had been feeling stagnant. "Being there was an incredible awakening." Naomi, a Filipina dancer and musician, recalled how "at first a lot of my group were tired, grumpy, wanting to go home. That really changed. One of the artists with us, who never considered herself a political activist, now wants to get involved back in Oakland. Seattle created a lot of strong bonds in my small community of coworkers and friends."

They seem to feel they had seen why, as the chant popularized by the Chicano/a students of MEChA goes, "Ain't no power like the power of the people, Cause the power of the people don't stop!"

There must be effective follow-up and increased communication between people of color across the nation: grassroots organizers, activists, cultural workers, and educators. We need to build on the contacts made (or that need to be made) from Seattle. Even within the Bay Area, activists who could form working alliances still do not know of each other's existence.

With mass protests planned for April 16–17 in Washington, D.C. at the meeting of the World Bank and the International Monetary Fund (IMF), the opportunity to build on the WTO victory shines brightly. More than ever, we need to work on our ignorance about global issues with study groups, youth workshops, conferences. We need to draw specific links between WTO and our close-to-home struggles in communities of color, as has been emphasized by Raj Jayadev and Lisa Juachon in *The Silicon Valley Reader: Localizing the Effects of the Global Economy,* 1999, which they edited.

25   Many examples of how WTO has hurt poor people in third world countries were given during the protest. For example, a Pakistani told one panel how, for years, South Africans grew medicinal herbs to treat AIDS at very little cost. The WTO ruled that this was "unfair" competition with pharmaceutical companies seeking to sell their expensive AIDS medications. "People are dying because they cannot afford those products," he said. A Filipino reported on indigenous farmers being compelled to use fertilizers containing poisonous chemicals in order to compete with cheap, imported potatoes. Ruined, they often left the land seeking survival elsewhere.

But there are many powerful examples right here in the U.S. For starters, consider:

- WTO policies encourage sub-livable wages for youth of color everywhere including right here.
- WTO policies encourage privatization of health care, education, welfare, and other crucial public services, as well as cutbacks in those services, so private industry can take them over and run them at a profit. This, along with sub-livable wages, leads to jeopardizing the lives of working-class people and criminalizing youth in particular.
- Workers in Silicon Valley are being chemically poisoned by the chips they work on that make such wealth for others. WTO doesn't want to limit those profits with protection for workers.
- WTO has said it is "unfair trade" to ban the import of gasoline in which certain cancer-causing chemicals have been used. This could have a devastating effect on people in the U.S., including those of color, who buy that gas.
- Overall, WTO is controlled by U.S. corporations. It is secretly run by a few advanced industrialized countries for the benefit of the rich and aspiring rich. WTO serves to further impoverish the poor of all countries.

Armed with such knowledge, we can educate and organize people of color. As Jinee Kim said at a San Francisco report-back by youth of color, "We have to work with people who may not know the word 'globalization' but they live globalization."

QUESTIONS FOR INQUIRY AND ACTION

1. In the various arguments in support of and opposition to the World Trade Organization, much depends on people's definitions of the concept of "trade." Point out the definitions you see in the various selections, implicit as well as explicit, and explain how beginning with different definitions—with different assumptions, in other words—affects the direction and conclusion of the arguments.

2. What is the role of multinational corporations beyond developing their own products and making their own profits? Do they have responsibilities to the world at large? Research these corporations: (a) Philip Morris, and (b) Nestlé. What do they manufacture? What other companies do they own? Where are their headquarters? How committed are they to their local communities? To whom are they responsible?

3. What are "non-governmental organizations" (NGOs)? What is their role in the world today? To whom and for what are they responsible?

4. Compare the views of Elizabeth (Betita) Martinez's "Where Was the Color in Seattle?" in this case study with Regina Austin and Michael Schill's "Activists of Color" in Chapter Ten. Why are so many of the protests such as those against the WTO made up primarily of white people? How can we cross color lines to meet on issues of mutual concern?

5. Much has happened since the 1999 WTO protests. What is underneath all of the protests around the world in opposition to globalization? Using the skills and strategies you learned in Chapters Three and Four, "go under" the phenomena of these protests to discover what's going on. What are the issues involved in the trade disputes?

6. Students have been especially active in the recent anti-sweatshop movement (<http://www.sweatx.net/stand/index.html>). They have demanded, for example, that their schools not buy uniforms or paraphernalia with school logos from companies that make that clothing and paraphernalia in sweatshops. Educate yourself on the current status of the anti-sweatshop movement. What is happening on your campus?

CHAPTER 10

Citizens of the Earth: The Planetary Community

An ethic, ecologically, is a limitation on freedom of action in the struggle for existence. An ethic, philosophically, is a differentiation of social from anti-social conduct. These are two definitions of one thing. The thing has its origin in the tendency of interdependent individuals or groups to evolve modes of co-operation. The ecologist calls these symbioses. Politics and economics are advanced symbioses in which the original free-for-all competition has been replaced, in part, by co-operative mechanisms with an ethical content.

We abuse land because we regard it as a commodity belonging to us. When we see land as a community to which we belong, we may begin to use it with love and respect.

Aldo Leopold, from A Sand County Almanac

GETTING STARTED: Adopting a Nonhuman Perspective

Using the curiosity and empathy you've been developing through your work in Chapters Three and Four, imagine yourself as a living but nonhuman part of our world.

1. Choose an animal, insect, plant, body of water or other natural resource and write a one-page reflection of your life. What perspective do you have? How do you view the world? What is important to you? What do you see, hear, touch, smell, and taste?

2. Compare reflections with other members of the class. What did the exercise make you aware of that you weren't previously aware of? Did the exercise seem silly? If so, why? Did it seem silly to attribute perspective, thinking, and feeling to nonhuman creatures and things? How difficult did you find it to imagine yourself as, say, a lake or a praying mantis, when all you had to guide your conceptions were your own human senses and experiences?

In Chapter One, we discussed citizenship as the quality of our membership in a community. What is the quality of our membership in the community of dwellers of the Earth, home to billions of species? What would it mean to think of ourselves as "citizens" of the Earth?

When we imagine ourselves as citizens of the Earth, we may consider our primary civic responsibility to be to protect and preserve the environment. We may see ourselves as stewards of the planet and feel a sense of personal responsibility for securing and maintaining its health. As Leopold's statements above argue, though, we need to see land and all its residents as a community to which we belong, rather than a commodity that belongs to us, something that we use. Ethically we need to cooperate with the planet and view ourselves as interdependent members of the community rather than autonomous rulers of it. We also need to cooperate with one another and put ethical limits on our freedom to consume and waste resources. Environmental concerns transcend national boundaries, so we need to work in cooperation with other countries and individuals toward the health of the planet. So-called developing countries are often polluting their environment and rapidly draining resources in an attempt to attain a more affluent lifestyle such as that enjoyed in the United States and Western Europe. Their experiences remind American citizens that the United States achieved its affluent lifestyle through a long history of exploiting natural resources and polluting the environment, and that the people of the United States still use far more than our share of the world's resources.

Environmental concerns are always *social* concerns. We have an ethical obligation to every other member of this planet. Thus, we need to be aware of the personal impact we make on the planet. The case study in this chapter gives you an opportunity to measure your individual impact on the Earth, and to consider the consequences of that impact. It is unlike the other case studies in this book in that *you* will be developing it. You will frame the issue, choose readings, conduct experiments, interpret and present results, and reflect upon your discoveries. We also invite you to publish your results on our Web site **http://www.ablongman.com/berndt** and to begin a dialogue with other inquiring students. Each case study will be unique. For instance, you may find that those from the Southwest have greater concerns with fresh water supply than those from the Northeast, who are more concerned with carbon dioxide emissions from automobile traffic.

DAVID W. ORR Saving Future Generations From Global Warming

David W. Orr is professor and chair of the environmental studies program at Oberlin College. He lectures frequently around the country on environmental issues and is the author of Earth in Mind: Essays on Education, Environment, and the Human Prospect *(1994) and* Ecological Literacy: Education and the Transition to a Postmodern World *(1992). "Saving Future Generations From Global Warming" was published in the* Chronicle of Higher Education *(April 21, 2000).*

We all live by robbing Asiatic coolies, and those of us who are "enlightened"
all maintain that those coolies ought to be set free; but our standard of living,
and hence our "enlightenment," demands that the robbery shall continue.
George Orwell

How many of us think about George Orwell when we hear about global warming? We've all seen the facts before. Nineteen ninety-eight was by far the warmest year ever recorded. Nineteen ninety-seven was the second-warmest. Mounting scientific evidence indicates that the combustion of fossil fuels, deforestation, and poor land-use practices will cause a major, and perhaps self-reinforcing, shift in global climate, given present trends. With climatic change will come severe weather extremes, super storms, droughts, famine, killer heat waves, rising sea levels, spreading disease, and accelerating rates of species loss—as well as bitter conflicts over declining supplies of fossil fuels, water, and food.

It is not far-fetched to think that human institutions, including democratic governments, will break down under such conditions. As the scientist Roger Revelle once noted, we are conducting a one-time experiment on the earth that cannot be reversed—and that never should have been run.

To see the situation more clearly, we need a perspective that transcends the minutiae of science, economics, and current politics. Future generations will bear the brunt of the effects of global warming. What will they think about the policy decisions we're making today? Will they applaud the precision of cost-benefit calculations that discount their prospects? Will they think us prudent for delaying action until even the most minute scientific doubts have been erased? Will they admire our stubborn devotion to inefficient vehicles, urban sprawl, and fossil-fuel consumption?

Hardly.

5   Think about an analogy. In the years leading up to the Civil War, defenders of slavery argued that: The advance of human culture and freedom depended on slavery; slaves were better off living in servitude than they otherwise would have been; freeing slaves would cause widespread economic and financial ruin; the issue of slavery was a matter of states' rights. Beneath all such arguments, of course, lay bedrock contempt for human equality, dignity, and freedom—as well as the perverse self-interest George Orwell so clearly described.

The parallels with arguments justifying our extravagant use of fossil fuels, if not exact, are nonetheless instructive. Our tacit position is: Civilization depends on the consumption of fossil fuels; a warmer world will be, on balance, a good thing; conserving energy and using solar energy are too expensive; the issue is a matter of the rights of individuals to drive the kinds of cars they want, live how they want, and the Devil take the hindmost.

Both the use of human beings as slaves and the use of fossil fuels inflate the wealth of some by robbing others. Both systems work only so long as someone or something is undervalued. Both require that some costs be ignored. Both warp the politics and culture of society. In the case of slavery, the effects were egregious, brutal, and immediate. But massive use of fossil fuels simply defers the costs, different but no less burdensome, onto our descendants. Moreover, slavery could be dismantled; future generations can have no reprieve from the consequences of our dereliction.

Of course, we do not intend to enslave subsequent generations, but the fact is that we are placing them in bondage to degraded climatic and ecological conditions. They will know that we failed to act on their behalf with alacrity, even after it became clear that our inaction would severely damage their prospects— and for reasons that will be regarded as no more substantial than those once used to support slavery.

At the same time, there is substantial evidence that taking steps to vastly improve energy efficiency and to make an expeditious transition to a solar-powered society would accrue to our advantage, saving upwards of $200-billion per year. It would also be the moral thing to do. History rarely offers such a clear convergence of ethics and self-interest.

10   In a letter to James Madison, written in 1789, Thomas Jefferson argued that no generation had the right to impose debt on its descendants, lest the dead rule the future. A similar principle applies to our use of fossil fuels. Drawn from Jefferson, Aldo Leopold, and others, such a principle might be stated thus:

No person, institution, or nation has the right to participate in activities that contribute to large-scale, irreversible changes of the earth's biogeochemical cycles or that undermine the integrity, stability, and beauty of its biotic systems; the consequences of such activities would fall on succeeding generations as an irreversible form of remote tyranny.

That principle is likely to fall on deaf ears in Congress and most corporate boardrooms, where short-term thinking predominates. To whom should we address it, then?

At the top of my list are those who educate the young. Education is most powerful when done by example. Accordingly, I propose that every school, college, and university stand up and be counted on the issue of climatic change, by beginning—now—to develop plans that would reduce the emission of heat-trapping gases, eliminating or finding ways to offset emissions by the year 2020. The alternative is to violate Jefferson's principle, and to enslave the future.

Opposition to such a proposal will, predictably, follow three lines. Some people will argue that we do not know enough yet to act. Presumably, those same people would not wait until they smelled smoke in the house at 2 A.M. to purchase fire insurance. A second group will object that educational institutions cannot afford to act. To be sure, change would require initial expenses—but it would also provide quick savings from reducing energy use. The real problem has less to do with costs than with the failure of imagination in places where imagination is reportedly much valued.

15   A third objection will come from those who agree with the overall goal of stabilizing climate, but who argue that our business is education, not social change. That argument is based on the belief that what occurs in educational institutions must be uncontaminated by contact with the affairs of the world. It further assumes that education occurs only in classrooms. Such views, however, make us accessories to an unfolding tragedy.

The steps necessary to abolish fossil fuels are straightforward, requiring campuses to:

- audit their current energy use;
- prepare detailed engineering plans to upgrade energy efficiency and eliminate waste;
- develop plans to harness renewable energy sources sufficient to meet campus energy needs by 2020; and
- carry out those plans over the next 20 years, through the combined efforts of students, faculty and staff members, administrators, energy engineers, and technical experts.

Through such campus and community involvement, we can educate a broad constituency about the consequences of our present course and the possibilities and opportunities for change. We can, in effect, begin to build a grassroots movement for the long-delayed transition to energy efficiency and solar power.

One day, we will come to understand that true prosperity neither permits nor requires bondage of any human being, in any form, for any reason, now or ever.

QUESTIONS FOR INQUIRY AND ACTION

1. Analyze and discuss Orr's use of the analogy of slavery and our use of fossil fuels. How does he set it up? What makes it effective?

2. Read this chapter's Stop and Think box on the subject of having a "worldview." What do you think Orr might say in response to it? Set up a discussion or debate in your classroom to explore your own worldviews and the analogies and metaphors you use to imagine and support those worldviews.

3. Winona La Duke, an activist and Ralph Nader's running mate on the Green Party ticket for the 1996 and 2000 presidential elections, advocates a "Seventh Generation Amendment" to the United States Constitution, which would require that government decisions take into consideration their effect seven generations into the future. Research and discuss the implications of this amendment.

4. Inquire into the ways your own educational institution can improve its energy efficiency. Join with other students to become educated on the subject and lobby your administrators for action on your campus.

Writing Style

THE PROBLEM/SOLUTION ESSAY

David W. Orr's essay "Saving Future Generations From Global Warming" fits the classic model for what composition specialists call the "problem/solution essay." You may have written such an essay previously and will almost certainly write one in some form while you're in college. In life outside of college, you will frequently work through the same problem-solving process outlined here, even though you may not write many formal problem/solution essays.

- *Introduce the problem.* Orr first needs to establish that there is indeed a problem that needs to be solved; the existence and urgency of global warming has been contested and not everyone is convinced that we need to be taking action. Orr persuades his audience by using an analogy to slavery, which Americans are now embarrassed about but once accepted.

- *Present the consequences of not solving the problem.* Continuing the slavery analogy, Orr argues that we will enslave our children and subsequent generations, "placing them in bondage to degraded climatic and ecological conditions."

- *Introduce the solution.* Immediately after stating the consequences of not taking action, Orr introduces his solution in one brief, specific paragraph that begins, "At the same time, there is substantial evidence that taking steps to vastly improve energy efficiency. . ."

- *Aim your solution at your audience.* For your proposal to be effective, you need to communicate directly with the people who can implement your solution. For Orr this means educators, so he published his work in the *Chronicle of Higher Education,* and he appealed to educators' pride in knowledge and wisdom (later generations "will know that we failed to act on their behalf with alacrity") and in ethics ("It would also be the moral thing to do").

- *Acknowledge counterarguments.* There will always be objections to or hesitations about a particular solution. To show that you are an informed and considerate arguer, you need to acknowledge the counterarguments, accommodate them when you can, and carefully refute them when you need to assert your own solution as the right one. Orr acknowledges three lines of opposition and contests them.

- *Present a clear plan of action to implement your solution.* You should provide specific steps readers can follow to begin to implement your solution. This will ensure that readers do not simply nod their heads in agreement but then do nothing. Orr offers four solutions, and presents them in a bullet-point list for clarity.

- *Engage with your audience in the conclusion.* Finally, as you conclude your essay, connect with your readers to reinforce the common ground you share on the issue. Orr appeals to educators' commitment to enlightenment and reminds them of their mutual abhorrence of slavery.

JOHN HAINES, "Snow"

John Haines is a poet and nature writer. He lived in Alaska for years, hunting, fishing, trapping, gardening, writing, and finally homesteading. His many collections of poems and essays include News from the Glacier: Selected Poems, 1960–1980 *(1982),* You and I and the World *(1988), and* Fables and Distances: New and Selected Essays *(1996). "Snow" was originally published in* The Stars, the Snow, the Fire: Twenty-five Years in the Alaska Wilderness *(1989). It has been anthologized in* In Short: A Collection of Brief Creative Nonfiction, *Judith Kitchen and Mary Paumier Jones, eds. (New York: W. W. Norton & Company, 1996).*

To one who lives in the snow and watches it day by day, it is a book to be read. The pages turn as the wind blows; the characters shift and the images formed by their combinations change in meaning, but the language remains the same. It is a shadow language, spoken by things that have gone by and will come again. The same text has been written there for thousands of years, though I was not here, and will not be here in winters to come, to read it. These seemingly random ways, these paths, these beds, these footprints, these hard, round pellets in the snow; they all have meaning. Dark things may be written there, news of other lives, their stories and excursions, their terrors and deaths. The tiny feet of a shrew or a vole make a brief, erratic pattern across the snow, and here is a hole down which the animal goes. And now the track of an ermine comes this way, swift and searching, and he too goes down that white-shadow of a hole.

A wolverine, and the loping, toed-in track I followed uphill for two miles one spring morning, until it finally dropped away into another watershed and I gave up following it. I wanted to see where he would go and what he would do. But he just went on, certain of where he was going, and nothing came of it for me to see but that sure and steady track in the snowcrust, and the sunlight strong in my eyes.

Snow blows across the highway before me as I walk—little, wavering trails of it swept along like a people dispersed. The snow people—where are they going? Some great danger must pursue them. They hurry and fall, the wind gives them a push, they get up and go on again.

I was walking home from Redmond Creek one morning late in January. On a divide between two watersheds I came upon the scene of a battle between a moose and three wolves. The story was written plainly in the snow at my feet. The wolves had come in from the west, following an old trail from the Salcha River, and had found the moose feeding in an open stretch of the overgrown road I was walking.

The sign was fresh, it must have happened the night before. The snow was torn up, with chunks of frozen moss and broken sticks scattered about; here and there, swatches of moose hair. A confusion of tracks in the trampled snow—the splayed, stabbing feet of the moose, the big, furred pads and spread toenails of the wolves.

I walked on, watching the snow. The moose was large and alone, almost certainly a bull. In one place he backed himself into a low, brush-hung bank to protect his rear. The wolves moved away from him—those moose feet are dangerous. The moose turned, ran on for fifty yards, and the fight began again. It became a running, broken flight that went on for nearly half a mile in the changing, rutted terrain, the red morning light coming across the hills from the sun low in the south. A pattern shifting and uncertain; the wolves relenting, running out into the brush in a wide circle, and closing again; another patch of moose hair in the trodden snow.

I felt that I knew those wolves. I had seen their tracks several times before during that winter, and once they had taken a marten from one of my traps. I believed them to be a female and two nearly grown pups. If I was right, she may have been teaching them how to hunt, and all that turmoil in the snow may have been the serious play of things that must kill to live. But I saw no blood sign that morning, and the moose seemed to have gotten the better of the fight. At the end of it he plunged away into thick alder brush. I saw his tracks, moving more slowly now, as he climbed through a low saddle, going north in the shallow, unbroken snow. The three wolves trotted east toward Banner Creek.

What might have been silence, an unwritten page, an absence, spoke to me as clearly as if I had been there to see it. I have imagined a man who might live as the coldest scholar on earth, who followed each clue in the snow, writing a book as he went. It would be the history of snow, the book of winter. A thousand-year text to be ready by a people hunting these hills in a distant time. Who was here, and who has gone? What were their names? What did they kill and eat? Whom did they leave behind?

QUESTIONS FOR INQUIRY AND ACTION

1. Why does Haines call snow "a book to be read"? What does this particular metaphor reveal about his relationship to the snow and the wilderness?

2. Compare Haines's description of natural life with the other readings in this chapter. How do you think Haines would define being part of a planetary community?

3. Take a walk in nature, observe the life around you, and tell the story of something you see there. What kinds of traits do you find yourself reading into the animal or plant or natural force that you observe?

4. Take your narrative from question #3, and add a reflective component to it. Reflect on the appropriateness of applying a human mental construct—that is, of creating a narrative—to nonhuman processes.

REGINA AUSTIN AND MICHAEL SCHILL Activists of Color

Regina Austin is a professor at the University of Pennsylvania Law School. Michael Schill is an assistant professor at the University of Pennsylvania Law School. Both previously worked as attorneys and write about issues of law and justice in minority communities. This excerpt is taken from the chapter "Black, Brown, Red, and Poisoned" that Austin and Schill contributed to the book Unequal Protection: Environmental Justice and Communities of Color, *edited by Robert D. Bullard (Sierra Club Books, 1994).*

People of color throughout the United States are receiving more than their fair share of the poisonous fruits of industrial production. They live cheek by jowl with waste dumps, incinerators, landfills, smelters, factories, chemical plants, and oil refineries whose operations make them sick and kill them young. They are poisoned by the air they breathe, the water they drink, the fish they catch, the vegetables they grow, and, in the case of children, the very ground they play on. Even the residents of some of the most remote rural hamlets of the South and Southwest suffer from the ill effects of toxins. . . .[1]

The Path of Least Resistance

The disproportionate location of sources of toxic pollution in communities of color is the result of various development patterns. In some cases, the residential communities where people of color now live were originally the homes of whites who worked in the facilities that generate toxic emissions. The housing and the industry sprang up roughly simultaneously.[2] Whites vacated the housing (but not necessarily the jobs) for better shelter as their socioeconomic status improved, and poorer black and brown folks who enjoy much less residential mobility took their place. In other cases, housing for African Americans and

---

[1] *Activist Pat Bryant uses the term "poisoning" in lieu of "pollution" to convey the idea that harm is being caused deliberately with the knowledge and aid of government officials. See Pat Bryant, "Toxics and Racial Justice,"* Social Policy 20 *(Summer 1989): 48–52; Pat Bryant, "A Lily-White Achilles Heel,"* Environmental Action 21 *(January–February 1990): 28–29.*

[2] *See Community Environmental Health Center at Hunter College,* Hazardous Neighbors? Living Next Door to Industry in Greenpoint-Williamsburg *(New York: Hunter College, Community Environmental Health Center, 1989). This study details the nature of the toxic risks posed by industrial concerns in a community composed primarily of Hasidic Jews and Puerto Ricans.*

Latino Americans was built in the vicinity of existing industrial operations because the land was cheap and the people were poor. For example, Richmond, California, was developed downwind from a Chevron oil refinery when African Americans migrated to the area to work in shipyards during World War II.[3]

In yet a third pattern, sources of toxic pollution were placed in existing minority communities. The explanations for such sitings are numerous; some reflect the impact of racial and ethnic discrimination. The impact, of course, may be attenuated and less than obvious. The most neutral basis for a siting choice is probably the natural characteristics of the land, such as mineral content of the soil.[4] Low population density would appear to be a similar criterion. It has been argued, however, that in the South, a sparse concentration of inhabitants is correlated with poverty, which is in turn correlated with race. "It follows that criteria for siting hazardous waste facilities which include density of population will have the effect of targeting rural black communities that have high rates of poverty."[5]Likewise, the compatibility of pollution with preexisting uses might conceivably make some sites more suitable than others for polluting operations. Pollution tends to attract other sources of pollutants, particularly those associated with toxic disposal. For example, Chemical Waste Management, Incorporated (Chem Waste) has proposed the construction of a toxic waste incinerator outside of Kettleman City, California, a community composed largely of Latino farm workers.[6] Chem Waste also has proposed to build a hazardous waste incinerator in Emelle, a predominantly African American community located in the heart of Alabama's "black belt." The company already has hazardous waste landfills in Emelle and Kettleman City.

According to the company's spokeswoman, Chem Waste placed the landfill in Kettleman City "because of the area's geological features. Because the landfill handles toxic waste, . . . it is an ideal spot for the incinerator"; the tons of toxic ash that the incinerator will generate can be "contained and disposed of at the installation's landfill."[7] Residents of Kettleman City face a "triple whammy" of threats from pesticides in the fields, the nearby hazardous waste landfill, and a proposed hazardous waste incinerator. This case is not unique.

After reviewing the literature on hazardous waste incineration, one commentator has concluded that "[m]inority communities represent a 'least cost' option for waste incineration. . . because much of the waste to be incinerated is already in these communities."[8] Despite its apparent neutrality, then, siting based on com-

---

[3]*Citizens for a Better Environment,* Richmond at Risk: Community Development and Toxic Hazards from Industrial Polluters *(San Francisco: Citizens for a Better Environment, 1989), pp. 21–22.*
[4]*Conner Bailey and Charles Faupel, "Environmentalism and Civil Rights in Sumter County, Alabama," pp. 159, 170–171 in* Proceedings of the Michigan Conference on Race and the Incidence of Environmental Hazards, *ed. Bunyan Bryant and Paul Mohai (Ann Arbor: University of Michigan, School of Natural Resources, 1990).*
[5]*Ibid., p. 171.*
[6]*Miles Corwin, "Unusual Allies Fight Waste Incinerator."*Los Angeles Times, *February 24, 1991, p. A3.*
[7]*Ibid., p. A36.*
[8]*Harvey White, "Hazardous Waste Incineration and Minority Communities: The Case of Alsen, Louisiana," in Bryant and Mohai,* Race and the Incidence of Environment Hazards *pp. 142, 148–149.*

patibility may be related to racial and ethnic discrimination, particularly if such discrimination influenced the siting of preexisting sources of pollution.

Polluters know that communities of low-income and working-class people with no more than a high school education are not as effective at marshalling opposition as communities of middle- or upper-income people. People of color in the United States have traditionally had less clout with which to check legislative and executive abuse or to challenge regulatory laxity. Private corporations, moreover, can have a powerful effect on the behavior of public officials. Poor minority people wind up the losers to them both.[9] People of color are more likely than whites to be economically impoverished, and economic vulnerability makes impoverished communities of color prime targets for "risky" technologies. Historically, these communities are more likely than others to tolerate pollution-generating commercial development in the hope that economic benefits will inure to the community in the form of jobs, increased taxes, and civic improvements.[10] Once the benefits start to flow, the community may be reluctant to forgo them even when they are accompanied by poisonous spills or emissions. This was said to be the case in Emelle, in Sumter County, Alabama, site of the nation's largest hazardous waste landfill.[11] Sumter County's population is roughly 70 percent African American, and 30 percent of its inhabitants fall below the poverty line. Although the landfill was apparently leaking, it was difficult to rally support against the plant among African American politicians because its operations contributed an estimated $15.9 million to the local economy in the form of wages, local purchases of goods and services, and per-ton landfill user fees.[12] Of course, benefits do not always materialize after the polluter begins operations. . . . In other cases, there is no net profit to distribute among the people. New jobs created by the poisonous enterprises are "filled by highly skilled labor from outside the community," while the increased tax revenues go not to "social services or other community development projects, but. . . toward expanding the infrastructure to better serve the industry."[13]

Once a polluter has begun operations, the victims' options are limited. Mobilizing a community against an existing polluter is more difficult than organizing opposition to a proposed toxic waste–producing activity. Resignation sets in, and the resources for attacking ongoing pollution are not as numerous, and the tactics not as potent, as those available during the proposal stage. Furthermore, though some individuals are able to escape toxic poisoning by moving

[9]*See Conger Beasley. "Of Pollution and Poverty: Keeping Watch in 'Cancer Alley,'"* Buzzworm *(July–August 1990); 38, 41–42 (describing the Louisiana politics that produced the string of petrochemical plants lining what is known as Cancer Alley).*

[10]*Robert D. Bullard, "Environmental Blackmail in Minority Communities," in Bryant and Mohai,* Race and the Incidence of Environmental Hazards, *pp. 60, 64–65.*

[11]*See Robert D. Bullard,* Dumping in Dixie: Race, Class, and Environmental Quality *(Boulder, CO: Westview Press, 1990), pp. 69–73; Bailey and Faupel, "Environmentalism and Civil Rights in Sumter County," pp. 169–170, 172–173.*

[12]*Bailey and Faupe, "Environmentalism and Civil Rights in Sumter County," p. 163.*

[13]*Dana Alston,* Taking Back Our Lives: A Report to the Panos Institute on Environment, Community Development, and Race in the United States *(Washington, D.C.: The Panos Institute, 1990). p. 11.*

out of the area, the flight of others will be blocked by limited incomes, housing discrimination, and restrictive land use regulations.[14]

Threat to Barrios, Ghettos, and Reservations

Pollution is no longer accepted as an unalterable consequence of living in the "bottom" (the least pleasant, poorest area minorities can occupy) by those on the bottom of the status hierarchy. Like anybody else, people of color are distressed by accidental toxic spills, explosions, and inexplicable patterns of miscarriages and cancers, and they are beginning to fight back, from Maine to Alaska.[15]

To be sure, people of color face some fairly high barriers to effective mobilization against toxic threats, such as limited time and money; lack of access to technical, medical, and legal expertise; relatively weak influence in political and media circles; and ideological conflicts that pit jobs against the environment.[16] Limited fluency in English and fear of immigration authorities will keep some of those affected, especially Latinos, quiescent. Yet despite the odds, poor minority people are responding to their poisoning with a grass-roots movement of their own.

Activist groups of color are waging grass-roots environmental campaigns all over the country. Although they are only informally connected, these campaigns reflect certain shared characteristics and goals. The activity of activists of color is indicative of a grass-roots movement that occupies a distinctive position relative to both the mainstream movement and the white grass-roots environmental movement. The environmental justice movement is antielitist and antiracist. It capitalizes on the social and cultural differences of people of color as it cautiously builds alliances with whites and persons of the middle class. It is both fiercely environmental *and* conscious of the need for economic development in economically disenfranchised communities. Most distinctive of all, this movement has been extremely outspoken in challenging the integrity and bona fides of mainstream establishment environmental organizations.

People of color have not been mobilized to join grass-roots environmental campaigns because of their general concern for the environment. Characterizing a problem as being "environmental" may carry weight in some circles, but it has much less impact among poor minority people. It is not that people of color are uninterested in the environment—a suggestion the grass-roots activists find insulting. In fact, they are more likely to be concerned about pollution than are people who are wealthier and white.[17] Rather, in the view of many people of color, environmentalism is associated with the preservation of wildlife and wilderness, which sim-

---

[14]Robert D. Bullard and Beverly H. Wright, *"Blacks and the Environment,"* Humboldt Journal of Social Relations 14 *(Summer 1987): 165, 180.*

[15]Robert D. Bullard, *People of Color Environmental Groups Directory 1992 (Riverside, CA: University of California, 1992). pp. i–iv.*

[16]*See generally Dorceta Taylor, "Blacks and the Environment: Toward an Explanation of the Concern and Action Gap between Blacks and Whites,"* Environment and Behavior 22 *(March 1989): 175.*

[17]*Susan Cutter, "Community Concern for Pollution: Social and Environmental Influences,"* Environment and Behavior 13 *(1981): 105–124.*

ply is not more important than the survival of people and the communities in which they live; thus, the mainstream movement has its priorities skewed.

The mainstream movement, so the critique goes, embodies white, bourgeois values, values that are foreign to African Americans, Latino Americans, Asian Americans, and Native Americans. Environmental sociologist Dorceta Taylor has characterized the motivations of those who make donations to mainstream organizations as follows:

> [In part, the] motivation to contribute is derived from traditional Romantic and Transcendental ideals—the idea of helping to conserve or preserve land and nature for one's own present and future use, or for future generations. Such use involves the ability to get away from it all; to transcend earthly worries, to escape, to commune with nature. The possibility of having a transcendental experience is strongly linked to the desire to save the places where such experiences are likely to occur.[18]

Even the more engaged environmentalists, those whose involvement includes participation in demonstrations and boycotts, are thought to be imbued with romantic and transcendental notions that favor nature over society and the individual's experience of the natural realm over the collective experience.

There are a number of reasons why people of color might not share such feelings. Their prospects for transcendental communion with nature are restricted. Parks and recreational areas have been closed to them because of discrimination, inaccessibility, cost, their lack of specialized skills or equipment, and residence requirements for admission.[19] They must find their recreation close to home. Harm to the environment caused by industrial development is not really their responsibility because they have relatively little economic power or control over the exploitation of natural resources. Since rich white people messed it up, rich white people ought to clean it up. In any event, emphasis on the environment in the abstract diverts attention and resources from the pressing, concrete problems that people of color, especially those with little or no income, confront every day.

Nonetheless, communities of color have addressed environmental problems that directly threaten them on their own terms. The narrowness of the mainstream movement, which appears to be more interested in endangered nonhuman species and pristine, undeveloped land than at-risk humans, makes poor minority people *think* that their concerns are not "environmental." Cognizant of this misconception and eschewing terminology that artificially compartmentalizes people's troubles minority grass-roots environmental activists take a multidimensional approach to pollution problems. Thus, the sickening, poisonous odor emitted by landfills and sewage plants are considered matters of public health or government accountability, while workplace contamination is a labor issue, and lead-based paint in public housing projects is a landlord-tenant problem.[20] The very names of some of the organiza-

---

[18] Dorceta Taylor, *"Can the Environmental Movement Attract and Maintain the Support of Minorities?"* in *Bryant and Mohai*, Race and the Incidence of Environmental Hazards, *p. 35.*
[19] Taylor, *"Blacks and the Environment," pp. 187–190.*
[20] *Arnoldo Garcia, "Environmental Inequities," Crossroads (June 1990), p. 16 (interview with activist Richard Moore).*

tions and the goals they espouse belie the primacy of environmental concerns. The Southwest Organizing Project of Albuquerque (SWOP) has been very successful in mobilizing people around issues of water pollution and workplace contamination. For example, SWOP fought for the rollback of charges levied against a group of home owners who were forced to hook up with a municipal water system because nitroglycerine had contaminated private wells. SWOP then campaigned to make the federal government assume responsibility for the pollution, which was attributed to operations at a nearby military installation. Yet in a briefing paper titled "Major National Environmental Organizations and the Problem of the 'Environmental Movement,'" SWOP describes itself as follows:

> SWOP does not consider itself an "environmental" organization but rather a community-based organization which addresses toxics issues as part of a broader agenda of action to realize social, racial, and economic justice. We do not single out the environment as necessarily having a special place above all other issues; rather, we recognize that issues of toxic contamination fit within an agenda which can (and in our practical day-to-day work, does) include employment, education, housing, health care, and other issues of social, racial, and economic justice. . . .[21]

20   In the estimation of the grass-roots folks, . . . race and ethnicity surpass class as explanations for the undue toxic burden heaped on people of color. Activists see these environmental inequities as unfair and unjust—practices that many feel should be illegal. Of course, it is hard to prove that racial discrimination is responsible for siting choices and government inaction in the environmental area, particularly in a court of law. One need only point to the examples of *Bean v. Southwestern Waste Management* (Houston, Texas), *Bordeaux Action Committee v. Metropolitan Nashville* (Nashville, Tennessee), and *R.I.S.E. v. Kay* (King and Queen County, Virginia) to see the limited utility of current antidiscrimination doctrine in redressing the plight of poisoned communities of color.

Environmental activists of color draw a good deal of their inspiration from the modern civil rights movement of the 1960s. That movement was advanced by hard-won Supreme Court decisions. These organizers hope that a civil rights victory in the environmental area will validate their charges of environmental racism, help to flesh out the concept of environmental equity, serve as a catalyst for further activism, and, just possibly, force polluters to reconsider siting in poor minority communities.

Capitalizing on the Resources of Common Culture

For people of color, social and cultural differences such as language are not handicaps but the communal resources that facilitate mobilization around issues like toxic poisoning. As members of the same race, ethnicity, gender, and even age cadre, would-be participants share cultural traditions, modes, and mores that encourage cooperation and unity. People of color may be more responsive to organizing efforts than whites because they already have experience with collective

---

[21]*Southwest Organizing Project, "Major National Environmental Organizations and the Problem of the 'Environmental Movement,'" (February 1990) (unpublished briefing paper).*

action through community groups and institutions such as churches, parent-teacher associations, and town watches or informal social networks.[22] Shared criticisms of racism, a distrust of corporate power, and little expectation that government will be responsive to their complaints are common sentiments in communities of color and support the call to action around environmental concerns.

Grass-roots environmentalism is also fostered by notions that might be considered feminist or womanist. Acting on a realization that toxic poisoning is a threat to home and family, poor minority women have moved into the public realm to confront corporate and government officials whose modes of analysis reflect patriarchy, white supremacy, and class and scientific elitism. There are numerous examples of women of color whose strengths and talents have made them leaders of grass-roots environmental efforts.[23] The organization Mothers of East Los Angeles (MELA) illustrates the link between group culture and mobilization in the people of color grass-roots environmental movement.[24] Persistent efforts by MELA-defeated proposals for constructing a state prison and a toxic-waste incinerator in the group's mostly Latino American neighborhood in East Los Angeles.

25   Similarly, the Lumbee Indians of Robeson County, North Carolina, who attach spiritual significance to a river that would have been polluted by a hazardous waste facility proposed by the GSX Corporation, waged a campaign against the facility on the ground of cultural genocide. Throughout the campaign, "Native American dance, music, and regalia were used at every major public hearing. Local Lumbee churches provided convenient meeting locations for GSX planning sessions. Leaflet distribution at these churches reached significant minority populations in every pocket of the county's nearly 1,000 square miles."[25] Concerned Citizens of Choctaw defeated a plan to locate a hazardous waste facility on their lands in Philadelphia, Mississippi. The Good Road Coalition, a grass-roots Native American group based on the Rosebud Reservation in South Dakota, defeated plans by a Connecticut-based company to build a 6,000-acre garbage landfill on the Rosebud. Local residents initiated a recall election, defeating several tribal council leaders and the landfill proposal. The project, dubbed "dances with garbage," typifies the lengths that

[22]*Bullard*, Dumping in Dixie, *pp. 95–98.*

[23]*See Jim McNeil, "Hazel Johnson: Talkin' Toxics,"* In These Times *(May 23–June 5, 1990), p. 4 (interview with the founder of Chicago's Southeast Side's People for Community Recovery); Claude Engle, "Profiles: Environmental Action in Minority Communities,"* Environmental Action *(January–February 1990), p. 22 (profiling Jessie Deerln Water, founder of Native Americans for a Clean Environment; Cora Tucker, founder of Citizens for a Better America; and Francesca Cavazos, director of the Maricopa County Organizing Project); Cynthia Hamikon, "Women, Home, and Community: The Struggle in an Urban Environment,"* Race, Poverty, and the Environment Newsletter *(April 1990), p. 3.*

[24]*See Mary Pardo, "Mexican American Women Grassroots Community Activists: 'Mothers of East Los Angeles,'"* Frontiers: A Journal of Women's Studies *11 (1990): 1; Dick Russell, "Environmental Racism,"* Amicus Journal *11 (Spring 1989): 22–23, 29–31.*

[25]*Richard Regan and M. Legerton, "Economic Slavery or Hazardous Wastes? Robeson County's Economic Menu," in* Communities in Economic Crisis: Appalachia and the South, *John Gaventa and Alex Willingham, eds. (Philadelphia: Temple University Press, 1990), pp. 146, 153–154.*

the Lakota people and other Native Americans will go to preserve their land—which is an essential part of their religion and culture.

Consider, finally, the Toxic Avengers of El Puente, a group of environmental organizers based in the Williamsburg section of Brooklyn, New York.[26] The name is taken from the title of a horror movie. The group attacks not only environmental racism but also adultism and adult superiority and privilege. The members, whose ages range from nine to twenty-eight, combine their activism with programs to educate themselves and others about the science of toxic hazards.

The importance of culture in the environmental justice movement seems not to have produced the kind of distrust and misgivings that might impede interaction with white working-class and middle-class groups engaged in grass-roots environmental activism. There are numerous examples of ethnic-based associations working in coalitions with one another, with majority group associations, and with organizations from the mainstream.[27] There are also localities in which the antagonism and suspicion that are the legacy of white racism have kept whites and African Americans from uniting against a common toxic enemy. The link between the minority groups and the majority groups seems grounded in material exchange, not ideological fellowship. The white groups attacking toxins at the grass-roots level have been useful sources of financial assistance and information about tactics and goals. . . .

People of color have provided the crucial leadership for the growing environmental justice movement in the United States. This movement, in all aspects of its operations, is antielitist, antiracist, class conscious, populist, and participatory. It attacks environmental problems as being intertwined with other pressing economic, social, and political ills. It capitalizes on the social and cultural strengths of people of color and demands in turn that their lifestyles, traditions, and values be respected by polluters and mainstream environmental organizations alike.

30   The environmental justice movement is still in its embryonic stages. Its ideology has yet to be fully developed, let alone tested. Moreover, it is too easy for outsiders to criticize the trade-offs and compromises poor people and people of color bearing toxic burdens have made. It is important to understand the movement on its own terms if one hopes to make policy proposals that will be of use to those struggling to save themselves. Grass-roots people have proven that they are capable of *leading*, *speaking*, and *doing* for themselves.

QUESTIONS FOR INQUIRY AND ACTION

1. Why is using the term *poisoning* rather than *polluting* powerful? Is it accurate? How conscious is our poisoning/polluting?

2. Austin and Schill observe, "In the view of many people of color, environmentalism is associated with the preservation of wildlife and wilderness, which simply is

---

[26]Marguerite Holloway. *"The Toxic Avengers Take Brooklyn,"* City Limits *(December 1989), p. 8*

[27]*M. Oliviero,* Minorities and the Environment: An Inquiry for Foundations *(report to the Nathan Cummings Foundation) (New York: Nathan Cummings Foundation, 1991). pp. 17–18, 21–24.*

not more important than the survival of people and the communities in which they live; thus, the mainstream movement has its priorities skewed." Based on the other readings in this chapter and your own experiences with environmentalism, would you agree? How could the different perspectives and priorities be brought into effective dialogue?

3. Explore Austin and Schill's argument that people of color "may be more responsive to organizing efforts than whites because they already have experience with collective action through community groups and institutions such as churches, parent-teacher associations, and town watches or informal social networks," and that they are in allegiance with feminist or womanist ideals. Write about your own experience with collective action, whether formal or informal.

4. Where are the toxic waste dumps, the incinerators, the landfills, and the like, in your community? Go on a field trip to visit these sites, and observe the neighborhoods around them. Who lives there? What kinds of housing do they have? Where do the children play?

STOP AND THINK

WORLDVIEW

In his article "The Changing Worldview," (*World Watch Reader,* 1997), Alan Thein Durning, an environmentalist writer, explains the concept of a *worldview:*

> Everyone operates from a worldview. It is a set of simplifying assumptions, an informal theory, a picture of how the world works. Worldviews are rarely brought out into the light of day. So people are not usually aware of them. They sit down deep in human consciousness somewhere, quietly shaping reactions to new ideas and information, guiding decisions, and ordering expectations for the future. Worldviews are not necessarily internally consistent. Often, they are not; in fact, they usually contain parts that are demonstrably false. Still, their historical and psychological roots are long enough to prevent easy uprooting.

We all have personal worldviews, ways of picturing and understanding the world. There also historical and cultural worldviews, sets of assumptions shared by a large group of people living in the same time period or geographical region. These people will develop a common vocabulary for describing their sense of the world that will bind them together as a community. For instance, you may learn about the medieval "Chain of Being," read E. M. W. Tillyard's book *The Elizabethan World Picture* that describes the general mindset of people during the era in which Shakespeare lived, or study Thomas Kuhn's *The Structure of Scientific Revolutions,* which analyzes "paradigm shifts" in the history of scientific thinking. You will also hear references to an American worldview, or an Islamic worldview, many of which will be gross oversimplifications. (See Benjamin Barber's "Jihad vs. McWorld" in Chapter Nine for a more nuanced description.) Those who do not share the worldview, or the dominant mindset, of their com-

continued on next page

munity will often feel out of place; Thoreau was one of these people, as he chronicles in "Civil Disobedience" (excerpted in Chapter Six) and *Walden* (excerpted in Chapter Three).

The way we see the world determines the way we interact with it and with all its species. But, as Durning explains, we are usually not aware of the assumptions under which we operate. It is easier to see other people's worldviews through their actions than it is to recognize our own. Think of someone with whom you frequently disagree. How would you describe the way that person sees the world? In contrast, how would you begin to describe your own worldview? Why is it important to define for ourselves our own worldview? Why is it important to continually reflect upon and redefine that worldview?

When you read the selections in each community chapter of this book, try to describe the worldview held by each writer. Does doing so help you to understand his or her argument? As you learned in Chapter Four, many of the disagreements we have with others are fundamentally a matter of having different worldviews. The problem is not that we have different views; it is our failure to recognize and work with these different worldviews. How can we remedy this to make good decisions on urgent issues?

A number of writers, such as Isaac Asimov in the *Foundation* series and James Redfield in *The Celestine Prophecy,* have claimed our entire worldview as humans is changing. You may have heard, for example, that we now live in a New Age, or in a post-Christian world. Do you think the world is changing its worldview? If so, from what and to what is it moving? And how is it doing so?

DANIEL QUINN From *Ishmael*

Daniel Quinn is the author of a number of philosophical novels and works of nonfiction including Providence: The Story of a Fifty-Year Vision Quest *(1994) and* Beyond Civilization: Humanity's Next Great Adventure *(1999). His novel* Ishmael *won the Turner Tomorrow Fellowship in 1991, a prize given to authors whose fiction helps produce solutions to global problems. The book became a bestseller, and was adapted into a film entitled* Instinct, *starring Anthony Hopkins and Cuba Gooding, Jr. The reading selection is excerpted from Chapters Seven and Eight of* Ishmael *(New York: Bantam, 1992).*

The novel begins when a man sees an ad in the Personals section of his newspaper that reads: "TEACHER seeks pupil. Must have an earnest desire to save the world. Apply in person." Assuming this teacher must be a fraud out to take advantage of naïve people, he answers the ad so he can disprove him. Instead, he finds Ishmael, a gorilla, who becomes his teacher and educates him about the history of the world and the place of humans in it. Throughout the story, Ishmael refers to two distinct groups of humans. Leavers, *hunter-gatherer populations, leave the world much the way they found it, and think of themselves as part of nature.* Takers, *agriculturalists, take whatever they can for themselves, and think of themselves as separate from nature.*

Seven

1

"Here is a puzzle for you to consider," said Ishmael. "You are in a faraway land and find yourself in a strange city isolated from all others. You're immediately impressed by the people you find there. They're friendly, cheerful, healthy, prosperous, vigorous, peaceable, and well educated, and they tell you things have been this way for as long as anyone can remember. Well, you're glad to break your journey here, and one family invites you to stay with them.

"That night you sample their food at dinner and, finding it delicious but unfamiliar, ask them what it is, and they say, 'Oh, it's B meat, of course. That's all we eat.' This naturally puzzles you and you ask if they mean the meat of the little insects that gather honey. They laugh and take you to the window. 'There are some B's there,' they say, pointing to their neighbors in the next house.

"'Good lord!' you exclaim in horror, 'you don't mean that you eat *people!*' And they look at you in a puzzled way and say, 'We eat B's.'

"'How atrocious,' you reply. 'Are they your slaves then? Do you keep them penned up?'

5   "'Why on earth should we keep them penned up?' your hosts ask.

"'To keep them from running away, of course!'

"By now your hosts are beginning to think you're a little weak in the head, and they explain that the B's would never think of running away, because their own food, the A's, live right across the street.

"Well, I won't weary you with all your outraged exclamations and their baffled explanations. Eventually you piece together the whole ghastly scheme. The A's are eaten by the B's and the B's are eaten by the C's and the C's in turn are eaten by the A's. There is no hierarchy among these food classes. The C's don't lord it over the B's just because the B's are their food, because after all they themselves are the food of the A's. It's all perfectly democratic and friendly. But of course it's all perfectly dreadful to you, and you ask them how they can stand to live in this lawless way. Once again they look at you in bafflement. 'What do you mean, lawless?' they ask. 'We have a law, and we all follow it invariably. This is why we're friendly and cheerful and peaceable and all those other things you find so attractive in us. This law is the foundation of our success as a people and has been so from the beginning.'

"Here at last is the puzzle. Without asking them, how can you discover what law it is they follow?"

10   I blinked at him for a moment. "I can't imagine."

"Think about it."

"Well. . . obviously their law is that A's eat C's and B's eat A's and C's eat B's."

Ishmael shook his head. "These are food preferences. No law is required."

"I need something more to go on then. All I've got is their food preferences."

15 "You have three other things to go on. They have a law, they follow it invariably, and because they follow it invariably, they have a highly successful society."

"It's still very tenuous. Unless it's something like. . . 'Be cool.'"

"I'm not asking you to guess what the law is, I'm asking you to devise a method for *discovering* what the law is."

I slid down in my chair, folded my hands on my stomach, and stared at the ceiling. After a few minutes I had an idea. "Is there a penalty for breaking this law?"

"Death."

20 "Then I'd wait for an execution."

Ishmael smiled. "Ingenious, but hardly a method. Besides, you're overlooking the fact that the law is obeyed invariably. There has never been an execution."

I sighed and closed my eyes. A few minutes later I said: "Observation. Careful observation over a long period."

"That's more like it. What would you be looking for?"

"For what they *didn't* do. For what they *never* did."

25 "Good. But how would you eliminate irrelevancies? For example, you might find that they never slept standing on their heads or that they never threw rocks at the moon. There would be a million things they never did, but these wouldn't necessarily be prohibited by the law."

"True. Well, let's see. They have a law, they follow it invariably, and according to them. . . ah. According to them, following this law has given them a society that works very well. Am I supposed to take that seriously?"

"Certainly. It's part of the hypothesis."

"Then this would eliminate most of the irrelevancies. The fact that they never sleep standing on their heads wouldn't have anything to do with having a society that works well. Let's see. In effect. . . What I would actually be looking for is. . . I would be closing in on it from two sides. From one side I would be saying: 'What is it that makes this society work?' And from the other side I would be saying: 'What is it they *don't* do that makes this society work?'"

"Bravo. Now, since you've worked this out so brilliantly, I'm going to give you a break: There's going to be an execution after all. For the first time in history, someone has broken the law that is the foundation of their society. They're outraged, horrified, astounded. They take the offender, cut him into little bits, and feed him to the dogs. This should be a big help to you in discovering their law."

30 "Yes."

"I'll take the part of your host. We've just been to the execution. You may ask questions."

"Okay. Just what did this guy do?"

"He broke the law."

"Yes, but specifically what did he do?"

35 Ishmael shrugged. "He lived contrary to the law. He did the things we never do."

I glared at him. "That's not fair. You're not answering my questions."

"I tell you the whole sorry tale is public record, young man. His biography, complete in every detail, is available at the library."

I grunted.

"So how are you going to use this biography? It doesn't say how he broke the law. It's just a complete record of how he lived, and much of it is bound to be irrelevant."

40   "Okay, but I can see that it gives me another guide. I now have three: what makes their society work well, what they never do, and what *he* did that they *never* do."

2

"Very good. These are precisely the three guides you have to the law we're looking for here. The community of life on this planet has worked well for three billion years—has worked beautifully, in fact. The Takers draw back in horror from this community, thinking it to be a place of lawless chaos and savage, relentless competition, where every creature goes in terror of its life. But those of your species who actually live in this community don't find it to be so, and they will fight to the death rather than be separated from it.

"It is in fact an orderly community. The green plants are food for the plant eaters, which are food for the predators, and some of these predators are food for still other predators. And what's left over is food for the scavengers, who return to the earth nutrients needed by the green plants. It's a system that has worked magnificently for billions of years. Filmmakers understandably love footage of gore and battle, but any naturalist will tell you that the species are not in any sense at war with one another. The gazelle and the lion are enemies only in the minds of the Takers. The lion that comes across a herd of gazelles doesn't massacre them, as an enemy would. It kills one, not to satisfy its hatred of gazelles but to satisfy its hunger, and once it has made its kill the gazelles are perfectly content to go on grazing with the lion right in their midst.

"All this comes about because there is a law that is followed invariably within the community, and without this law the community would indeed be in chaos and would very quickly disintegrate and disappear. Man owes his very existence to this law. If the species around him had not obeyed it, he could not have come into being or survived. It's a law that protects not only the community as a whole but species within the community and even individuals. Do you understand?"

"I understand what you're saying, but I have no idea what the law is."

45   "I'm pointing to its effects."

"Oh. Okay."

"It is the peace-keeping law, the law that keeps the community from turning into the howling chaos the Takers imagine it to be. It's the law that fosters life for all—life for the grasses, life for the grasshopper that feeds on the grasses, life for the quail that feeds on the grasshopper, life for the fox that feeds on the quail, life for the crows that feed on the dead fox.

"The club-finned fish that nosed the shores of the continents came into being because hundreds of millions of generations of life before them had followed this law, and some of them became amphibians following this law. And some of the amphibians became reptiles following this law. And some of the reptiles became birds and mammals following this law. And some of the mammals became primates following this law. And one branch of the primates became *Australopithecus* following this law. And *Australopithecus* became *Homo habilis* following this law. And *Homo habilis* became *Homo erectus* following this law. And *Homo erectus* became *Homo sapiens* following this law. And *Homo sapiens* became *Homo sapiens sapiens* following this law.

"And then about ten thousand years ago one branch of the family of *Homo sapiens sapiens* said, 'Man is exempt from this law. The gods never meant man to be bound by it.' And so they built a civilization that flouts the law at every point, and within five hundred generations—in an eye-blink in the scale of biological time—this branch of the family of *Homo sapiens sapiens* saw that they had brought the entire world to the point of death. And their explanation for this calamity was. . . what?"

50   "Huh?"

"Man lived harmlessly on this planet for some three million years, but the Takers have brought the whole thing to the point of collapse in only five hundred generations. And their explanation for this is what?"

"I see what you mean. Their explanation is that something is fundamentally wrong with people."

"Not that you Takers may be doing something wrong but rather that there is something fundamentally wrong with human nature itself."

"That's right."

55   "How do you like that explanation now?"

"I'm beginning to have my doubts about it."

"Good."

3

"At the time when the Takers blundered into the New World and began kicking everything to pieces, the Leavers here were searching for an answer to this question. 'Is there a way to achieve settlement that is in accord with the law that we've been following from the beginning of time?' I don't mean, of course, that they had consciously formulated this question. They were no more consciously aware of this law than the early aeronauts were consciously aware of the laws of aerodynamics. But they were struggling with it all the same: building and abandoning one civilizational contraption after another, trying to find one that would fly. Done this way, it's slow work. Proceeding simply by trial and error, it might have taken them another ten thousand years—or another fifty thousand years. They apparently had the wisdom to know there was no hurry. They didn't *have* to get into the air. It made no sense to them to commit themselves to one civilizational craft that was clearly headed for disaster, the way the Takers have done."

Ishmael stopped there, and when he didn't go on, I said, "What now?"

60   His cheeks crinkled in a smile. "Now you leave and come back when you're prepared to tell me what law or set of laws has been at work in the community of life from the beginning."

"I'm not sure I'm ready for that."

"That's what we've been doing here for the last half week, if not from the very beginning: getting you ready."

"But I wouldn't know where to begin."

"You do know. You have the same three guides as in the case of the A's, the B's, and the C's. The law you're looking for has been obeyed invariably in the living community for three billion years." He nodded to the world outside. "And this is *how things came to be this way.* If this law had not been obeyed from the beginning and in each generation thereafter, the seas would be lifeless deserts and the land would still be dust blowing in the wind. All the countless forms of life that you see here came into being following this law, and following this law, man too came into being. And only once in all the history of this planet has any species tried to live in defiance of this law—and it wasn't an entire species, it was only one people, those I've named Takers. Ten thousand years ago, this one people said, 'No more. Man was not meant to be bound by this law,' and they began to live in a way that flouts the law at every point. Every single thing that is prohibited under the law they incorporated into their civilization *as a fundamental policy.* And now, after five hundred generations, they are about to pay the penalty that any other species would pay for living contrary to this law."

65   Ishmael turned over a hand. "That should be guide enough for you." . . .

Eight

1

The search for the law took me four days.

I spent one day telling myself I couldn't do it, two days doing it, and one day making sure I'd done it. On the fifth day I went back. As I walked into Ishmael's office, I was mentally rehearsing what I was going to say, which was, "I think I see why you insisted I do it myself."

I looked up from my thoughts and was momentarily disoriented. I had forgotten what was waiting for me there: the empty room, the lone chair, the slab of glass with a pair of glowing eyes behind it. Foolishly, I quavered a hello into the air.

Then Ishmael did something he'd never done before. By way of greeting, he lifted his upper lip to give me a look at a row of amber teeth as massive as elbows. I scurried to my chair and waited like a schoolboy for his nod.

"I think I see why you insisted I do it myself," I told him. "If you had done the work for me and pointed out the things the Takers do that are never done in the natural community, I would have said, 'Well, sure, so what, big deal.'"

70   Ishmael grunted.

"Okay. As I make it out, there are four things the Takers do that are never done in the rest of the community, and these are all fundamental to their civilizational system. First, they exterminate their competitors, which is something that never happens in the wild. In the wild, animals will defend their territories and their kills and they will invade their competitors' territories and preempt their kills. Some species even include competitors among their prey, but they never hunt competitors down just to make them dead, the way ranchers and farmers do with coyotes and foxes and crows. What they hunt, they eat."

Ishmael nodded. "It should be noted, however, that animals will also kill in self-defense, or even when they merely feel threatened. For example, baboons may attack a leopard that hasn't attacked them. The point to see is that, although baboons will go looking for food, they will never go looking for leopards."

"I'm not sure I see what you mean."

"I mean that in the absence of food, baboons will organize themselves to find a meal, but in the absence of leopards they will never organize themselves to find a leopard. In other words, it's as you say: when animals go hunting—even extremely aggressive animals like baboons—it's to obtain food, not to exterminate competitors or even animals that prey on them."

75   "Yes, I see what you're getting at now."

"And how can you be sure this law is invariably followed? I mean, aside from the fact that competitors are never seen to be exterminating each other, in what you call the wild."

"If it weren't invariably followed, then, as you say, things would not have come to be this way. If competitors hunted each other down just to make them dead, then there would *be* no competitors. There would simply be one species at each level of competition: the strongest."

"Go on."

"Next, the Takers systematically destroy their competitors' food to make room for their own. Nothing like this occurs in the natural community. The rule there is: Take what you need, and leave the rest alone."

80   Ishmael nodded.

"Next, the Takers deny their competitors access to food. In the wild, the rule is: You may deny your competitors access to what you're eating, but you may not deny them access to food in general. In other words, you can say, 'This gazelle is mine,' but you can't say, '*All* the gazelles are mine.' The lion defends its kill as its own, but it doesn't defend the herd as its own."

"Yes, that's true. But suppose you raised up a herd of your own, from scratch, so to speak. Could you defend that herd as your own?"

"I don't know. I suppose so, so long as it wasn't your policy that all the herds in the world were your own."

"And what about denying competitors access to what you're growing?"

85   "Again. . . *Our* policy is: Every square foot of this planet belongs to us, so if we put it all under cultivation, then all our competitors are just plain out of luck and will have to become extinct. Our policy is to deny our competitors access to *all the food in the world*, and that's something no other species does."

"Bees will deny you access to what's inside their hive in the apple tree, but they won't deny you access to the apples."

"That's right."

"Good. And you say there's a fourth thing the Takers do that is never done in the wild, as you call it."

"Yes. In the wild, the lion kills a gazelle and eats it. It doesn't kill a second gazelle to save for tomorrow. The deer eats the grass that's there. It doesn't cut the grass down and save it for the winter. But these are things the Takers do."

90 "You seem less certain about this one."

"Yes, I *am* less certain. There *are* species that store food, like bees, but most don't."

"In this case, you've missed the obvious. Every living creature stores food. Most simply store it in their bodies, the way lions and deer and people do. For others, this would be inadequate to their adaptations, and they must store food externally as well."

"Yes, I see."

"There's no prohibition against food storage as such. There couldn't be, because that's what makes the whole system work: the green plants store food for the plant eaters, the plant eaters store food for the predators, and so on."

95 "True. I hadn't thought of it that way."

"Is there anything else the Takers do that is never done in the rest of the community of life?"

"Not that I can see. Not that seems relevant to what makes that community work."

2

"This law that you have so admirably described defines the limits of competition in the community of life. You may compete to the full extent of your capabilities, but you may not hunt down your competitors or destroy their food or deny them access to food. In other words, you may compete but you may not wage war."

"Yes. As you said, it's the peace-keeping law."

100 "And what's the effect of the law? What does it promote?"

"Well. . . it promotes order."

"Yes, but I'm after something else now. What would have happened if this law had been repealed ten million years ago? What would the community be like?"

"Once again, I'd have to say there would only be one form of life at each level of competition. If all the competitors for the grasses had been waging war on each other for ten million years, I'd have to think an overall winner would have emerged by now. Or maybe there'd be one insect winner, one avian winner, one reptile winner, and so on. The same would be true at all levels."

"So the law promotes what? What's the difference between this community and the community as it is?"

105 "I suppose the community I've just described would consist of a few dozen or a few hundred different species. The community as it is consists of millions of species."

"So the law promotes what?"

"Diversity."

"Of course. And what's the good of diversity?"

"I don't know. It's certainly more. . . interesting."

110   "What's wrong with a global community that consists of nothing but grass, gazelles, and lions? Or a global community that consists of nothing but rice and humans?"

I gazed into space for a while. "I'd have to think that a community like that would be ecologically fragile. It would be highly vulnerable. Any change at all in existing conditions, and the whole thing would collapse."

Ishmael nodded. "Diversity is a survival factor *for the community itself.* A community of a hundred million species can survive almost anything short of total global catastrophe. Within that hundred million will be thousands that could survive a global temperature drop of twenty degrees—which would be a lot more devastating than it sounds. Within that hundred million will be thousands that could survive a global temperature rise of twenty degrees. But a community of a hundred species or a thousand species has almost no survival value at all."

"True. And diversity is exactly what's under attack here. Every day dozens of species disappear as a direct result of the way the Takers compete outside the law."

"Now that you know there's a law involved, does it make a difference in the way you view what's going on?"

115   "Yes. I no longer think of what we're doing as a blunder. We're not destroying the world because we're clumsy. We're destroying the world because we are, in a very literal and deliberate way, at war with it." . . .

QUESTIONS FOR INQUIRY AND ACTION

1. The end of this selection reads: "We're not destroying the world because we're clumsy. We're destroying the world because we are, in a very literal and deliberate way, at war with it." What do you think of this provocative statement?

2. Analyze the story that Ishmael tells the narrator. How does it work? Why does Ishmael use a parable, rather than telling the narrator what he wants him to know?

3. Throughout *Ishmael,* Quinn refers to human beings after the invention of agriculture as Takers, and earlier hunter-gatherer societies as Leavers. Research very early societies. How did hunter-gatherers live? What were their communities like? Where are there hunter-gatherer societies on the planet today?

4. How does Quinn depict the planet as a community? Where do humans fit in this community? Compare his worldview with those of environmentalists such as Aldo Leopold.

MURIEL RUKEYSER St. Roach

Muriel Rukeyser (1913–1980) was a political activist and poet who often wrote about inequalities in gender, class, and race. Her first book of poems, Theory of Flight, *was published in the prestigious Yale Younger Poets Series in 1935. She has had a deep influence on a generation of American poets that includes Adrienne Rich and Anne Sexton. "St. Roach" can be found in her collection* The Gates *(New York: McGraw-Hill, 1976).*

For that I never knew you, I only learned to dread you,
for that I never touched you, they told me you are filth,
they showed me by every action to despise your kind;
for that I saw my people making war on you,
5   I could not tell you apart, one from another,
for that in childhood I lived in places clear of you,
for that all the people I met you by
crushing you, stamping you to death, they poured boiling
    water on you, they flushed you down,
10   for that I could not tell one from another
only that you were dark, fast on your feet, and slender.
    Not like me.
For that I did not know your poems
And that I did not know any of your sayings
15   And that I cannot speak or read your language
And that I do not sing your songs
And that I do not teach our children
        to eat your food
        or know your poems
20   or sing your songs
But that we say you are filthing our food
But that we know you not at all.
Yesterday I looked at one of you for the first time.
You were lighter than the others in color, that was
25   neither good nor bad.
I was really looking for the first time.
You seemed troubled and witty.

Today I touched one of you for the first time.
You were startled, you ran, you fled away
30   Fast as a dancer, light, strange and lovely to the touch.
I reach, I touch, I begin to know you.

QUESTIONS FOR INQUIRY AND ACTION

1. Why do you think Rukeyser titles this poem "*Saint* Roach"? What is the effect of anthropomorphizing, or giving human qualities to, the roach?

2. The context in which we read something affects the way we interpret it. How does finding this poem at the end of a chapter on the "planetary community" affect the way you read and understood it? What if you found this poem in an anthology of gay and lesbian writers?

3. Poetry allows us to re-see our world. Compose a poem in which you observe and describe a familiar creature or object, re-seeing and understanding it anew.

4. If you live in a region where cockroaches are common, take a moment to look at one more closely. In other areas, choose an insect or creature that is similarly considered ugly, disgusting or scary and observe it closely. What do you notice differently as a result of having read Rukeyser's poem?

JOHN CLARE The Badger

John Clare (1793–1864) was an English poet whom we associate with the Romantic movement. He was born into a poor farming family in Northamptonshire. He is primarily regarded as a nature poet, although he wrote on a number of different subjects including politics, poverty, love. His first collection of poetry, Poems Descriptive of Rural Life and Scenery, *was printed in 1820 by Taylor and Hessey, who also published the poetry of John Keats. This poem, "The Badger," describes the practice of badger baiting, which was a public spectacle and form of amusement in the early nineteenth century.*

When midnight comes a host of dogs and men
Go out and track the badger to his den,
And put a sack within the hole and lie
Till the old grunting badger passes by.
5   He comes and hears—they let the strongest loose.
The old fox hears the noise and drops the goose.
The poacher shoots and hurries from the cry,
And the old hare half wounded buzzes by.
They get a forkéd stick to bear him down
10   And clap the dogs and take him to the town,
And bait him all the day with many dogs,
And laugh and shout and fright the scampering hogs.
He runs along and bites at all he meets:
They shout and hollo down the noisy streets.

15   He turns about to face the loud uproar
And drives the rebels to their very door.
The frequent stone is hurled where'er they go;
When badgers fight, then everyone's a foe.
The dogs are clapped and urged to join the fray;
20   The badger turns and drives them all away.
Though scarcely half as big, demure and small,
He fights with dogs for hours and beats them all.

The heavy mastiff, savage in the fray,
Lies down and licks his feet and turns away.
25   The bulldog knows his match and waxes cold
The badger grins and never leaves his hold.
He drives the crowd and follows at their heels
And bites them through—the drunkard swears and reels.

The frighted women take the boys away,
30   The blackguard laughs and hurries on the fray.
He tries to reach the woods, an awkward race,
But sticks and cudgels quickly stop the chase.
He turns again and drives the noisy crowd
And beats the many dogs in noises loud.
35   He drives away and beats them every one,
And then they loose them all and set them on.
He falls as dead and kicked by boys and men,
Then starts and grins and drives the crowd again;
Till kicked and torn and beaten out he lies
40   And leaves his hold and cackles, groans and dies.

QUESTIONS FOR INQUIRY AND ACTION

1. Follow the narrative thread of the poem and carefully describe the step-by-step action of the badger baiting.

2. Read this poem with "St. Roach" and the chapters of *Ishmael*. What common views do you find among the authors?

3. Research the life and works of John Clare. What was his upbringing like? How did his life affect his writing? How is he represented by scholars of Romantic poetry? Web sites devoted to John Clare, <http://human.ntu.ac.uk/clare/clare.html> and <http://www.johnclare.org/>, will give you more information about him, and about why you may not have heard as much about him as about his contemporaries such as William Wordsworth.

4. A Web site devoted to badgers includes this poem. You can access it at <http://www.badgers.org.uk/brockwatch/1mstridx.html>. How does Clare's poem speak to the concerns of those who care about badgers today? Is poetry an effective form of argument?

CASE
STUDY

MEASURING OUR IMPACT ON THE EARTH

The topic of this case study is your personal impact on life on the Earth. The notion of this impact is meant to be twofold: first, you measure the impact you make through the resources you use; second, you experience the impact you can make through the actions you take. Each class, group, or individual who develops this case study will have some different results because the study reflects your own lifestyle and geographical region, but you will probably also find commonalities with other students and American citizens. The process of developing the case study allows you to practice conducting research using both textual and field resources, and then to practice interpreting your results and discussing them with others. You can develop the study in whatever way suits your needs, but it would be an ideal opportunity to make connections with local communities for a service-learning project.

Conducting Research

The *Redefining Progress* Web site <http://www.earthday.net/footprint/index.asp> has an Ecological Footprint test you can take. It is an excellent, eye-opening tool and useful for quantitative research. You might take the test as a starting point for your research, and explore the questions that the test raises for you.

In your group, discuss the questions that puzzle and concern you most, and decide what you want to focus on for your investigation. Emphasize concerns that affect you personally and locally. This will help you measure your own impact, both negative and positive, more clearly. For instance, is your local river drying up because of a drought? Or is your community fighting over where to put the next landfill? Or is your school razing apartment buildings or cutting down trees to construct a parking garage?

Textual Research

Conduct a search of the World Wide Web, check out the resources available in your library, and visit local environmental organizations for their literature to inform yourselves. As you conduct your textual search, note whose names keep coming up. Who are the major participants in the conversation on your issue? Whose work resonates with you? Make a working bibliography of useful sources. You might annotate it so that you can share with others what you like about each source, and what it contained that was particularly useful and why.

Field Research

As you learned in Chapter Three, field research can give you the richest, most specific information for your own particular situation; in this case, your own personal impact on the Earth. You can conduct your own experiments for your field research. Here are a few suggestions of things you might do to measure your impact upon the Earth in your daily life. You should feel free to adapt this to your own needs, and to add other experiments. Construct a chart to keep track of your responses to these and any other questions and experiments you create.

- *Measure your daily water usage.* How much water do you use for brushing your teeth, showering, washing dishes, doing laundry, washing your car? How much does water cost you? Do you know where your water comes from? Where is the watershed for your region?

- *Record what you eat for a week.* Record *everything* you eat—at home and in restaurants. How much do you eat? How often are you hungry? Do you know where the food comes from? Where do you shop for your food? Where do they get the food that you buy? How much of it is processed? How much of it is imported? How much comes from factories or factory-farms, and how much from smaller farms and industries? How much of it is organic? What does "organic" mean? How much of it is genetically modified? What does that mean?

- *Record how much garbage you throw out in a week.* Instead of throwing your garbage out as your can fills, keep *all* of the garbage inside for a week. How much do you accumulate? How many trashbags or pounds? Take the mass of your weekly accumulation, and extrapolate to estimate how much garbage you will throw out over ten years, or a seventy-year lifetime. What does your garbage consist of? Food? Packaging? How much of what you throw in the trash can be recycled or composted?

- *Record what you wear for a week.* How often do you change clothes? Do you re-wear any clothes during the week? How often do you wash your clothes? How often do you shop for clothes? How long have you had the clothes you wear this week? Did you buy them new or secondhand, or were they hand-me-downs from friends or relatives? Where do you usually shop for clothes? Were your clothes manufactured in a sweatshop? How can you find out?

- *Trace the origins of your possessions.* What are the possessions you cannot live without? How did you acquire them? Did you buy them new or used? Where and how were they manufactured? How much pollution was created in the making of the components of your computer, stereo, or cell phone?

- *Keep track of your mode(s) of transportation for a week.* How often do you drive a personal car? How often do you take the bus or other form of public transportation? How often do you ride your bike? How often do you walk, rollerblade, or skateboard?

- *Research the history of your neighborhood.* How long have you lived in your house, apartment building, or residence hall? Did anyone live in that building before you? If so, do you know who the person was (or people were)? How long has the building itself been standing? What used to be on the land before the building was constructed? Who owned the land, and who lived there?

Interpreting Your Results

At the end of your case study, treat the whole study just like the other case studies in this book. Some questions to consider:

- What was your most surprising discovery? Why did it surprise you?
- How did you discover that your daily living affects others' daily living, even if you have no physical contact with them or do not generally consider yourself to be in community with them? Where do people's interests or concerns compete or conflict? Where do people's interests conflict with the interests of animals or plants? Whose interests or concerns should get priority?
- What conclusions can you draw from your experiments? How do your conclusions agree with or differ from the experts' opinions you read about in your textual research?
- What are the ethical or political questions that this case study raises? Write a series of Questions for Inquiry and Action that stem from your experiments and results.
- What can you do to make a more positive impact on the Earth? What can you do immediately? What can you do over the long term?

Presenting Your Case Study

How do you want to present your findings? For example, you could write a research paper, write and perform a play or film, give an oral presentation, or exhibit photographs, just to name a few ideas. We encourage you to publish your studies on our companion Web site **http://www.ablongman.com/berndt.** Post any aspect of your researching process or your results. For instance:

- the questions you asked and things you measured in your study
- the discoveries you made
- how you interpreted your results
- the best resources you found for information, knowledge, and wisdom: your bibliographies, best Web sites, best organizations
- your Questions for Inquiry and Action
- your suggestions for action
- stories of action you took in your communities

CHAPTER 11

Communities of Faith

In one sense, an individual's homely, imperfect search for meaning says more about the origins of faith than the polished beauty of a great religious tradition can. An established religion may be a finished work of art, but the personal quest is a creative act, and thus just as authentic in what it says about innate human yearnings and desires. . . . It's one of the benefits of a tolerant age—that we, too, if we choose, can strip away the rich vestments of religious tradition and discover that naked faith is something separate and, ultimately, even more mysterious.

Jeremiah Creedon, "God with a Million Faces"

GETTING STARTED: Observing Worship Practices in Faith Communities

Visit the worship services of three faith communities as a participant observer. Try to visit representatives of three different religions or belief systems, although visiting three different denominations of the same religion can also be instructive. While you're there, be a participant observer; afterward, record the details in your writer's notebook. Here are some questions to guide your observations and discussion with your class:

1. What were the primary similarities and differences between the faith communities and their services?

2. Which felt most like a community to you? Why? What aspects of a worship service—including the moments before and after the official service time—contribute to the feeling of community?

3. Can you feel a part of the community if you don't share the beliefs, or, perhaps more important, if you don't share the same rituals of expression (e.g., the same songs, prayers, images, and practices)? How did you respond to unfamiliar or uncomfortable aspects of the services? Did you ask questions if you didn't understand something? Did you not recite prayers or

sing songs that you didn't understand or that offended you? Did you go along politely because you didn't want to offend the others' beliefs?

4. Did you ever find yourself hanging back from full participation? If so, why? Did you fear being "taken in"? Did you dread being asked why you're there and whether you'll be back the next week? Did you feel like a phony?

Textbooks such as this one often include selections on political disputes between church and state, or they include discussions of religious freedom of expression, or sometimes historical or cultural essays about different religions. Rarely do you find substantive discussions of the *communities* of faith. Yet, as the readings in this chapter illustrate, these communities are among the most important for people in their everyday lives, and it is often the fellowship with others, rather than specific doctrine, that binds the members of the communities together.

One of the great attractions of a spiritual community is the sense of sanctuary it provides—not just the physical sanctuary of the house of worship, but the feeling of refuge and protection that being a part of the community confers. Spiritual expression is deeply personal, and when people live most of their days in a society that often finds open expression of faith disconcerting, congregants find it especially vital to have the outlet of the faith community. As a result, however, worship communities can be made up of a homogeneous group of people—people who feel safe in their similarities to one another and apprehensive of or even hostile to those they perceive as different.

While American culture prides itself on being tolerant of religious difference—of being a nation characterized by religious freedom—it is also often nervous about the public display of faith. While we tend to like our leaders to be people of faith, we don't actually want them to act upon their religious beliefs in making public policy. We fear they will impose their beliefs on others who don't share those beliefs. In short, our country is deeply conflicted over the role faith plays in civic life.

The case study for this chapter examines the role faith communities played in the civil rights movement. As with many social justice movements—the abolitionist and temperance movements in the United States, the anti-apartheid movement in South Africa—faith communities, with their religious convictions and scriptural rhetoric, led the way. Civil rights workers did not see themselves as pursuing a personal political agenda; their expressed goal was "redeeming the soul of America," and they saw themselves as fulfilling God's plan. At the same time, the whites who opposed the civil rights movement often also based their action on faith, believing that segregation was God's plan. Today, too, faith communities with their differing religious convictions clash over public policy decisions, as is seen perhaps most prominently in debates concerning abortion, with the Pro-Life movement on one end and the Religious Coalition for Reproductive Choice on another, both seeing themselves as acting in good faith and in line with God's will. Is faith really a private matter? What role do you think it should play in public life?

STEPHEN L. CARTER The Culture of Disbelief

Stephen L. Carter is William Nelson Cromwell Professor of Law at Yale University. He is the author of a number of books including Integrity *(1996) and* God's Name in Vain: The Wrongs and Rights of Religion in Politics *(2000). "The Culture of Disbelief" is the first chapter of his bestselling book* The Culture of Disbelief: How American Law and Politics Trivialize Religious Devotion *(New York: HarperCollins, 1993).*

Contemporary American politics faces few greater dilemmas than deciding how to deal with the resurgence of religious belief. On the one hand, American ideology cherishes religion, as it does all matters of private conscience, which is why we justly celebrate a strong tradition against state interference with private religious choice. At the same time, many political leaders, commentators, scholars, and voters are coming to view any religious element in public moral discourse as a tool of the radical right for reshaping American society. But the effort to banish religion for politics' sake has led us astray. In our sensible zeal to keep religion from dominating our politics, we have created a political and legal culture that presses the religiously faithful to be other than themselves, to act publicly, and sometimes privately as well, as though their faith does not matter to them.

Recently, a national magazine devoted its cover story to an investigation of prayer: how many people pray, how often, why, how, and for what. A few weeks later came the inevitable letter from a disgruntled reader, wanting to know why so much space had been dedicated to such nonsense.[1]

Statistically, the letter writer was in the minority: by the magazine's figures, better than nine out of ten Americans believe in God and some four out of five pray regularly.[2] Politically and culturally, however, the writer was in the American mainstream, for those who do pray regularly—indeed, those who believe in God—are encouraged to keep it a secret, and often a shameful one at that. Aside from the ritual appeals to God that are expected of our politicians, for Americans to take their religions seriously, to treat them as ordained rather than chosen, is to risk assignment to the lunatic fringe.

Yet religion matters to people, and matters a lot. Surveys indicate that Americans are far more likely to believe in God and to attend worship services regularly than any other people in the western world. True, nobody prays on prime-time television unless religion is a part of the plot, but strong majorities of citizens tell pollsters that their religious beliefs are of great importance to them in their

---

[1] *"Talking to God,"* Newsweek, *Jan. 6, 1992, p. 38; Letter to the Editor,* Newsweek, *Jan. 27, 1992, p. 10. The letter called the article a "theocratic text masquerading as a news article."*

[2] *"Talking to God," p. 39. The most recent Gallup data indicate that 96 percent of Americans say they believe in God, including 82 percent who describe themselves as Christians (56 percent Protestant, 25 percent Roman Catholic) and 2 percent who describe themselves as Jewish. (No other faith accounted for as much as 1 percent.) See Ari L. Goldman, "Religion Notes,"* New York Times, *Feb. 27, 1993, p. 9.*

daily lives. Even though some popular histories wrongly assert the contrary, the best evidence is that this deep religiosity has always been a facet of the American character and that it has grown consistently through the nation's history.[3] And today to the frustration of many opinion leaders in both the legal and political cultures, religion, as a moral force and perhaps a political one too is surging. Unfortunately, in our public life, we prefer to pretend that it is not.

5   Consider the following events:

- When Hillary Rodham Clinton was seen wearing a cross around her neck at some of the public events surrounding her husband's inauguration as President of the United States, many observers were aghast, and one television commentator asked whether it was appropriate for the First Lady to display so openly a religious symbol. But if the First Lady can't do it, then certainly the President can't do it, which would bar from ever holding the office an Orthodox Jew under a religious compulsion to wear a yarmulke.

- Back in the mid–1980s, the magazine *Sojourners*—published by politically liberal Christian evangelicals—found itself in the unaccustomed position of defending the conservative evangelist Pat Robertson against secular liberals who, a writer in the magazine sighed, "see[m] to consider Robertson a dangerous neanderthal because he happens to believe that God can heal diseases."[4] The point is that the editors of *Sojourners*, who are no great admirers of Robertson, also believe that God can heal diseases. So do tens of millions of Americans. But they are not supposed to say so.

- In the early 1980s, the state of New York adopted legislation that, in effect, requires an Orthodox Jewish husband seeking a civil divorce to give his wife a *get*—a religious divorce—without which she cannot remarry under Jewish law. Civil libertarians attacked the statute as unconstitutional. Said one critic, the "barriers to remarriage erected by religious law. . . only exist in the minds of those who believe in the religion."[5] If the barriers are religious, it seems, then they are not real barriers, they are "only" in the woman's mind—perhaps even a figment of the imagination.

- When the Supreme Court of the United States, ostensibly the final refuge of religious freedom, struck down a Connecticut statute requiring employers to make efforts to allow their employees to observe the sabbath, one Justice observed that the sabbath should not be singled out because all employees would like to have "the right to select the day of the week in which to refrain from labor."[6] Sounds good, except that, as one scholar has noted,

---

[3]*See, for example, Jon Butler,* Awash in a Sea of Faith *(Cambridge: Harvard University Press, 1990).*

[4]*Collum, "The Kingdom and the Power,"* Sojourners, *Nov. 1986, p. 4. Some 82 percent of Americans believe that God performs miracles today. George Gallup, Jr., and Jim Castelli,* The People's Religion: American Faith in the '90s *(New York: Macmillan, 1989), p. 58.*

[5]*Madeline Kochen, "Constitutional Implications of New York's 'Get' Statute,"* New York Law Journal, *Oct. 27, 1983, p. 32.*

[6]Estate of Thornton v. Caldor, Inc., *472 U.S. 703, 711 (1985) (Justice Sandra Day O'Connor, concurring).*

"It would come as some surprise to a devout Jew to find that he has 'selected the day of the week in which to refrain from labor,' since the Jewish people have been under the impression for some 3,000 years that this choice was made by God."[7] If the sabbath is just another day off, then religious choice is essentially arbitrary and unimportant; so if one sabbath day is inconvenient, the religiously devout employee can just choose another.

- When President Ronald Reagan told religious broadcasters in 1983 that all the laws passed since biblical times "have not improved on the Ten Commandments one bit," which might once have been considered a pardonable piece of rhetorical license, he was excoriated by political pundits, including one who charged angrily that Reagan was giving "short shrift to the secular laws and institutions that a president is charged with protecting."[8] And as for the millions of Americans who consider the Ten Commandments the fundaments on which they build their lives, well, they are no doubt subversive of these same institutions.

These examples share a common rhetoric that refuses to accept the notion that rational, public-spirited people can take religion seriously. It might be argued that such cases as these involve threats to the separation of church and state, the durable and vital doctrine that shields our public institutions from religious domination and our religious institutions from government domination. I am a great supporter of the separation of church and I will have more to say about the doctrine later in the book—but that is not what these examples are about.

What matters about these examples is the *language* chosen to make the points. In each example, as in many more that I shall discuss, one sees a trend in our political and legal cultures toward treating religious beliefs as arbitrary and unimportant, a trend supported by a rhetoric that implies that there is something wrong with religious devotion. More and more, our culture seems to take the position that believing deeply in the tenets of one's faith represents a kind of mystical irrationality, something that thoughtful, public-spirited American citizens would do better to avoid. If you must worship your God, the lesson runs, at least have the courtesy to disbelieve in the power of prayer; if you must observe your sabbath, have the good sense to understand that it is just like any other day off from work.

The rhetoric matters. A few years ago, my wife and I were startled by a teaser for a story on a network news program, which asked what was meant to be a provocative question. "When is a church more than just a place of worship?" For those to whom worship is significant, the subtle arrangement of words is arresting: *more than* suggests that what follows ("just a place of worship") is somewhere well down the scale of interesting or useful human activities, and certainly

---

[7]Michael W. McConnell, "Religious Freedom at a Crossroads," University of Chicago Law Review 59 (1992):115.

[8]Robert G. Kaiser, "Hypocrisy: This Puffed-Up Piety Is Perfectly Preposterous," Washington Post, March 18, 1984, p. C1.

that whatever the story is about is *more than* worship; and *just*—suggests that what follows ("place of worship") is rather small potatoes.

A friend tells the story of how he showed his résumé to an executive search consultant—in the jargon, a corporate headhunter—who told him crisply that if he was serious about moving ahead in the business world, he should remove from the résumé any mention of his involvement with a social welfare organization that was connected with a church, but not one of the genteel mainstream denominations. Otherwise, she explained, a potential employer might think him a religious fanatic.

10   How did we reach this disturbing pass, when our culture teaches that religion is not to be taken seriously, even by those who profess to believe in it? Some observers suggest that the key moment was the Enlightenment, when the Western tradition sought to sever the link between religion and authority. One of the playwright Tom Stoppard's characters observes that there came "a calendar date—*a moment*—when the onus of proof passed from the atheist to the believer, when, quite suddenly, the noes had it."[9] To which the philosopher Jeffrey Stout appends the following comment: "If so, it was not a matter of majority rule."[10] Maybe not—but a strong undercurrent of contemporary American politics holds that religion must be kept in its proper place and, still more, in proper perspective. There are, we are taught by our opinion leaders, religious matters and important matters, and disaster arises when we confuse the two. Rationality, it seems, consists in getting one's priorities straight (Ignore your religious law and marry at leisure.) Small wonder, then, that we have recently been treated to a book, coauthored by two therapists, one of them an ordained minister, arguing that those who would put aside, say, the needs of their families in order to serve their religions are suffering from a malady the authors call "toxic faith"—for no normal person, evidently, would sacrifice the things that most of us hold dear just because of a belief that God so intended it.[11] (One wonders how the authors would have judged the toxicity of the faith of Jesus, Moses or Mohammed.)

We are trying, here in America, to strike an awkward but necessary balance, one that seems more and more difficult with each passing year. On the one hand, a magnificent respect for freedom of conscience, including the freedom of religious belief, runs deep in our political ideology. On the other hand, our understandable fear of religious domination of politics presses us in our public personas, to be wary of those who take their religion too seriously. This public balance reflects our private selves. We are one of the most religious nations on earth, in the sense that we have a deeply religious citizenry; but we are also perhaps the most zealous in guarding our public institutions against explicit religious influences. One result is that we often ask our citizens to split their public and private selves,

---

[9]*Tom Stoppard,* Jumpers, *quoted in Jeffrey Stout,* The Flight from Authority: Religion, Morality and the Quest for Autonomy *(South Bend, Indiana: University of Notre Dame Press, 1981), p. 150.*
[10]*Ibid.*
[11]*Stephen Arterburn and Jack Felton,* Toxic Faith: Understanding and Overcoming Religious Addiction *(Nashville, Tenn: Oliver-Nelson Books, 1991).*

telling them in effect that it is fine to be religious in private, but there is something askew when those private beliefs become the basis for public action.

We teach college freshmen that the Protestant Reformation began the process of freeing the church from the state, thus creating the possibility of a powerful independent moral force in society. As defenders of the separation of church and state have argued for centuries, autonomous religions play a vital role as free critics of the institutions of secular society. But our public culture more and more prefers religion as something without political significance, less an independent moral force than a quietly irrelevant moralizer, never heard, rarely seen. "[T]he public sphere," writes the theologian Martin Marty, "does not welcome explicit Reformed witness—or any other particularized Christian witness."[12] Or, for that matter any religious witness at all.

Religions that most need protection seem to receive it least. Contemporary America is not likely to enact legislation aimed at curbing the mainstream Protestant, Roman Catholic, or Jewish faiths. But Native Americans, having once been hounded from their lands, are now hounded from their religions with the complicity of a Supreme Court untroubled when sacred lands are taken for road building or when Native Americans under a bona fide religious compulsion to use peyote in their rituals are punished under state antidrug regulations.[13] (Imagine the brouhaha if New York City were to try to take St. Patrick's Cathedral by eminent domain to build a new convention center, or if Kansas, a dry state, were to outlaw the religious use of wine.) And airports, backed by the Supreme Court, are happy to restrict solicitation by devotees of Krishna Consciousness, which travelers, including this one, find irritating.[14] (Picture the response should the airports try to regulate the wearing of crucifixes or yarmulkes on similar grounds of irritation.)

The problem goes well beyond our society's treatment of those who simply want freedom to worship in ways that most Americans find troubling. An analagous difficulty is posed by those whose religious convictions move them to action in the public arena. Too often our rhetoric treats the religious impulse to public action as presumptively wicked—indeed, as necessarily oppressive. But this is historically bizarre. Every time people whose vision of God's will moves them to oppose abortion rights are excoriated for purportedly trying to impose their religious views on others equal calumny is implicitly heaped upon the mass protest wing of the civil rights movement, which was openly and unashamedly religious in its appeals as it worked to impose its moral vision on, for example, those who would rather segregate their restaurants.

15   One result of this rhetoric is that we often end up fighting the wrong battles. Consider what must in our present day serve as the ultimate example of religion in the service of politics: the 1989 death sentence pronounced by the

---

[12]Martin E. Marty, "Reformed America and America Reformed," Reformed Journal (March 1989): 8, 10.
[13]Employment Division, Department of Human Resources v. Smith, 494 U.S. 872 (1990).
[14]International Society for Krishna Consciousness v. Lee, 112 S. Ct. 2701 (1992).

late Ayatollah Ruhollah Khomeini upon the writer Salman Rushdie for his author-ship of *The Satanic Verses,* which was said to blaspheme against Islam. The death sentence is both terrifying and outrageous, and the Ayatollah deserved all the fury lavished upon him for imposing it. Unfortunately, for some critics the facts that the Ayatollah was a religious leader and that the "crime" was a religious one lends the sentence a particular monstrousness; evidently they are under the impres-sion that writers who are murdered for their ideas are choosy about the motiva-tions of their murderers, and that those whose writings led to their executions under, say, Stalin, thanked their lucky stars at the last instant of their lives that Communism was at least godless.

To do battle against the death sentence for Salman Rushdie—to battle against the Ayatollah—one should properly fight against official censorship and intimi-dation, not against religion. We err when we presume that religious motives are likely to be illiberal, and we compound the error when we insist that the devout should keep their religious ideas—whether good or bad—to themselves. We do no credit to the ideal of religious freedom when we talk as though religious belief is something of which public-spirited adults should be ashamed.

The First Amendment to the Constitution, often cited as the place where this difficulty is resolved, merely restates it. The First Amendment guarantees the "free exercise" of religion but also prohibits its "establishment" by the government. There may have been times in our history when we as a nation have tilted too far in one direction, allowing too much religious sway over politics. But in late-twentieth-century America, despite some loud fears about the influence of the weak and divided Christian right, we are upsetting the balance afresh by tilt-ing too far in the other direction—and the courts are assisting in the effort. For example, when a group of Native Americans objected to the Forest Ser-vice's plans to allow logging and road building in a national forest area tradi-tionally used by the tribes for sacred rituals, the Supreme Court offered the back of its hand. True, said the Justices, the logging "could have devastating effects on traditional Indian religious practices." But that was just too bad: "gov-ernment simply could not operate if it were required to satisfy every citizen's reli-gious needs and desires.[15]

A good point: but what exactly, are the protesting Indians left to do? Pre-sumably, now that their government has decided to destroy the land they use for their sacred rituals, they are free to choose new rituals. Evidently, a small matter like the potential destruction of a religion is no reason to hault a logging project. Moreover, had the government decided instead to prohibit logging in order to preserve the threatened rituals, it is entirely possible that the decision would be challenged as a forbidden entanglement of church and state. Far bet-ter for everyone, it seems, for the Native Americans to simply allow their rituals to go quietly into oblivion. Otherwise, they run the risk that somebody will think they actually take their rituals seriously.

---

[15]Lyng v. Northwest Indian Cemetery Protective Association, *485 U.S. 439 (1988).*

The Price of Faith

When citizens do act in their public selves as though their faith matters, they risk not only ridicule, but actual punishment. In Colorado, a public school teacher was ordered by his superiors, on pain of disciplinary action, to remove his personal Bible from his desk where students might see it. He was forbidden to read it silently when his students were involved in other activities. He was also told to take away books on Christianity he had added to the classroom library, although books on Native American religious traditions, as well as on the occult, were allowed to remain. A federal appeals court upheld the instruction, explaining that the teacher could not be allowed to create a religious atmosphere in the classroom, which, it seems, might happen if the students knew he was a Christian.[16] One wonders what the school, and the courts, might do if, as many Christians do, the teacher came to school on Ash Wednesday with ashes in the shape of a cross imposed on his forehead—would he be required to wash them off? He just might. Early in 1993, a judge required a prosecutor arguing a case on Ash Wednesday to clean the ashes from his forehead, lest the jury be influenced by its knowledge of the prosecutor's religiosity.

20   Or suppose a Jewish teacher were to wear a yarmulke in the classroom. If the school district tried to stop him, it would apparently be acting within its authority. In 1986, after a Jewish Air Force officer was disciplined for wearing a yarmulke while on duty, in violation of a military rule against wearing headgear indoors, the Supreme Court shrugged. "The desirability of dress regulations in the military is decided by the appropriate military officials," the Justices explained, "and they are under no constitutional mandate to abandon their considered professional judgment."[17] The Congress quickly enacted legislation permitting the wearing of religious apparel while in uniform as long as "the wearing of the item would [not] interfere with the performance of the member's military duties," and—interesting caveat!—as long as the item is "neat and conservative."[18] Those whose faiths require them to wear dreadlocks and turbans, one supposes, need not apply to serve their country, unless they are prepared to change religions.

Consider the matter of religious holidays. One Connecticut town recently warned Jewish students in its public schools that they would be charged with *six* absences if they missed two days instead of the officially allocated one for Yom Kippur, the holiest observance in the Jewish calendar. And Alan Dershowitz of Harvard Law School, in his controversial book *Chutzpah,* castigates Harry Edwards, a Berkeley sociologist for scheduling an examination on Yom Kippur, when most Jewish students would be absent. According to Dershowitz's account, Edwards answered criticism by saying: "That's how I'm going to operate. If the students don't like it, they can drop the class." For Dershowitz, this was evidence that "Jewish students [are] second-class citizens in Professor Edwards's classes."[19] Edwards has heatedly denied

[16]Roberts v. Madigan, *921 F. 2d 1047 (10th Cir. 1990).*
[17]Goldman v. Weinberger, *475 U.S. 503 (1986).*
[18]*45 U.S.C. 774, as amended by Pub. L. No. 100–80, Dec. 4, 1987.*
[19]Alan M. Dershowitz, Chutzpah *(Boston: Little, Brown, 1991), pp. 329–30.*

Dershowitz's description of events, but even if it is accurate, it is possible that Dershowitz has identified the right crime and the wrong villain. The attitude that Dershowitz describes, if it exists might reflect less a personal prejudice against Jewish students than the society's broader prejudice against religious devotion, a prejudice that masquerades as "neutrality." If Edwards really dared his students to choose between their religion and their grade, and if that meant that he was treating them as second-class citizens, he was still doing no more than the courts have allowed all levels of government to do to one religious group after another—Jews, Christians, Muslims, Sikhs, it matters not at all. The consistent message of modern American society is that whenever the demands of one's religion conflict with what one has to do to get ahead, one is expected to ignore the religious demands and act. . . well. . . *rationally.*

Consider Jehovah's Witnesses, who believe that a blood transfusion from one human being to another violates the biblical prohibition on ingesting blood. To accept the transfusion, many Witnesses believe, is to lose, perhaps forever, the possibility of salvation. As the Witnesses understand God's law, moreover, the issue is not whether the blood transfusion is given against the recipient's will, but whether the recipient is, at the time of the transfusion, actively protesting. This is the reason that Jehovah's Witnesses sometimes try to impede the physical access of medical personnel to an unconscious Witness: lack of consciousness is no defense. This is also the reason that Witnesses try to make the decisions on behalf of their children: a child cannot be trusted to protest adequately.

The machinery of law has not been particularly impressed with these arguments. There are many cases in which the courts have allowed or ordered transfusions to save the lives of unconscious Witnesses, even though the patient might have indicated a desire while conscious not to be transfused.* The machinery of modern medicine has not been impressed, either, except with the possibility that the Witnesses have gone off the deep end; at least one hospital's protocol apparently requires doctors to refer protesting Witnesses to psychiatrists.[20] Although the formal text of this requirement states as the reason the need to be sure that the Witness knows what he or she is doing, the subtext is a suspicion that the patient was not acting rationally in rejecting medical advice for religious reasons. After all, there is no protocol for packing *consenting* patients off to see the psychiatrist. But then, patients who consent to blood transfusions are presumably acting rationally. Perhaps, with a bit of gentle persuasion, the dissenting witness can be made to act rationally too—even if it means giving up an important tenet of the religion.

And therein lies the trouble. In contemporary American culture, the religions are more and more treated as just passing beliefs—almost as fads, older, stuffier,

---

*In every decided case that I have discovered involving efforts by Jehovah's Witness parents to prevent their children from receiving blood transfusions, the court has allowed the transfusion to proceed in the face of parental objection. I say more about transfusions of children of Witnesses, and about the rights of parents over their children's religious lives, in chapter 11.

[20]See Ruth Macklin, "The Inner Workings of an Ethics Committee: Latest Battle over Jehovah's Witnesses," *Hastings Center Report* 18 *(February/March 1988): 15.*

less liberal versions of so-called New Age—rather than as the fundaments upon which the devout build their lives. (The noes have it!) And if religions *are* fundamental, well, too bad—at least if they're the *wrong* fundaments—if they're inconvenient, give them up! If you can't remarry because you have the wrong religious belief, well, hey, believe something else! If you can't take your exam because of a Holy Day, get a new Holy Day! If the government decides to destroy your sacred lands, just make some other lands sacred! If you must go to work on your sabbath, it's no big deal! It's just a day off! Pick a different one! If you can't have a blood transfusion because you think God forbids it, no problem! Get a new God! And through all of this trivializing rhetoric runs the subtle but unmistakable message: pray if you like, worship if you must, but whatever you do, do not on any account take your religion seriously. . . .

God-Talk

25   The reader might have perceived that many of the political examples I have discussed so far (although not the judicial ones) are situations in which the right is "using" religion and the left is fearful of its use. There are. . . just as many examples of the shoe on the other foot. However, there is a point here that serves as a subtext for much of what follows. In recent decades, religious argument has seemed largely a captive of the right, whereas the left, which once gloried in the idea that God stands for social progress, has more and more shied away from it. This imbalance may be less a result than a cause of the fact that more and more religiously devout people have come to see their natural home as the Republican party.

American liberals have made a grievous error in their flight from religious dialogue. Many observers attribute the Democrats' electoral difficulties during the 1980s to the relentlessly materialistic character of their campaign rhetoric. (Bill Clinton appears to represent change in this respect.) Of Michael Dukakis's devastating defeat by George Bush in 1988, Garry Wills observes: "For many Americans, the coldly technological 'Massachusetts miracle' was not only godless but the enemy of God."[21] Michael Lerner argues that liberals have "framed their intellectual commitments around a belief that the only things that *really* move people are economic entitlements and political rights"; they miss the fact that "human beings have a deep need to have their lives make sense, to transcend the dynamics of individualism and selfishness that predominate in a competitive market society and to find a way to place their lives in a context of meaning and purpose."[22]

Still, although the Democrats have generally ceded "God-talk" to the Republicans, one must be wary of attributing too much influence to the emergent religious right. The Reverend Pat Robertson's effort to gain the 1988 Republican presidential nomination was of interest mainly to the mass media, which continue to regard deep religious devotion as a troubling curiosity. With minor exceptions, the evidence

---

[21] *Garry Wills,* Under God: Religion and American Politics *(New York: Simon & Schuster, 1990), p. 85.*
[22] *Michael Lerner. "Can the Democrats Be Stopped from Blowing It Again in 1992?"* Tikkun *(July–Aug. 1992): 7.*

that the much-feared Moral Majority, Inc., (now defunct) and other similar groups ever had much influence on actual government policy is thin. . . .[23] The journalist Mark Silk reports the reason for the group's demise: By the time the elections of 1986 returned the Senate to the Democrats, Jerry Falwell had put the Moral Majority on hold and largely withdrawn from secular politics; his public backing now did candidates more harm than good."[24] As one observer has noted. "Clearly, the upsurge of fundamentalism in this country has not put the fear of God into General Motors."[25]

To be sure, Robertson's Christian Coalition, an umbrella group for conservative Christians that is far better organized than Moral Majority, has become a political force to be reckoned with, less because of the scary religious rhetoric of the 1992 Republican Convention than because of the success of many of the Coalition's candidates in local elections. . . . But ideological religious organizations, like other interest groups, ultimately will have impact only insofar as the issues that form the core of their political passions are issues about which millions of other citizens are also concerned. In other words, even if one thinks that the Christian Coalition's positions are a threat, no problem arises unless millions of voters share them. Given the general public revulsion at the calls for a jeremiad emanating from Houston during the 1992 Republican Convention, that is not currently a serious prospect.

Still, religious belief is resurgent in America, especially within religions that offer clear rules of right and wrong, such as those described as conservative and fundamentalist (which are not the same thing).[26] Despite repeated proclamations that religion has lost its importance, most Americans insist that their religious faith is a compelling force in making moral decisions. Thus liberalism, if it is to retain substantial political influence and demonstrate that the 1992 presidential election was no fluke, will have to find a better way to cope than simply saying to religious people, in effect, that they are superstitious primitives for believing that prayer can work.

30   It must be added, of course, that many of the examples I discuss in this book will square with a widely shared intuition—that is, many readers will not immediately find them problematic. To the extent that the intuition is a suspicion of what might appear to be moves toward religious domination of our public institutions, it is one that I essentially share. If it is an intuition that is concerned about the world's, and the nation's, woeful history of oppression of disfavored religious groups, then it is an intuition to be celebrated, for religious pluralism and equal-

---

[23]See, for example, Robert Booth Fowler, Unconventional Partners: Religion and Liberal Culture in the United States (Grand Rapids, Mich. Wm. B. Eerdmans, 1989), pp. 111–28.
[24]Mark Silk, Spiritual Politics: Religion and America Since World War II (New York: Simon & Schuster, 1988), p. 179.
[25]Paul L. Wachtel, The Poverty of Affluence: A Psychological Portrait of the American Way of Life (Philadelphia: New Society Publishers, 1989).
[26]See for example, the data cited in Roger Finke and Rodney Stark, The Churching of America, 1776–1990 (New Brunswick, New Jersey: Rutgers University Press, 1992).

ity—*never* mere "toleration"—should be essential parts of what makes American democracy special.

At the same time, the intuition is worth considering in more detail, for it can press too far. In holding, as we must, that religion is part of the purely private arena that the state must never disrupt, we run the risk of disabling the religiously devout from working seriously in the realm of policy. I speak here not simply of arguments for or against the adoption of any *government* policy, although that will, of necessity, be part of my subject. My concern, more broadly, is with the question of what religiously devout people should do when they confront state policies that require them to act counter to what they believe is the will of God, or to acquiesce in conduct by others that they believe God forbids. The intuition of our contemporary political and legal culture is that they should do nothing. Sometimes, as with the Native Americans whose rituals were threatened by logging the message seems to be that they should, if necessary, change their religion, but if they protest on religious grounds, they are somehow acting in an illiberal manner.

Thus, in some of its aspects, this intuition is what I mean most fundamentally to challenge, for it encourages a tendency to say of religious belief. "Yes, we cherish you—now go away and leave us alone." It is an intuition that makes religion something that should be believed in privacy, not something that should be paraded; and if religion *is* paraded, it is this same intuition that assures that it likely will be dismissed. This intuition says that anyone who believes that God can heal diseases is stupid or fanatical, and the same intuition makes sure that everyone understands that this belief is a kind of mystic flight from hard truths—it has nothing to do with the real world. The same intuition tells the religious that those things that they know to be true are wrong or irrelevant, as with the Jehovah's Witnesses who fear that they will be denied salvation if forced to accept blood transfusions. At its most extreme, it is an intuition that holds not only that religious beliefs cannot serve as the basis of policy; they cannot even be debated in the forum of public dialogue on which a liberal politics crucially depends.

The intuition says, in short, that religion is like building model airplanes, just another hobby: something quiet, something private, something trivial—and not really a fit activity for intelligent, public-spirited adults. This intuition, then is one that in the end must destroy either religion or the ideal of liberal democracy. That is a prospect that can please only those who hate one or the other or both.

QUESTIONS FOR INQUIRY AND ACTION

1. Carter has said our society encourages us to treat "God as a hobby." What do you make of his choice of words?

2. Compare this work with Wendy Kaminer's "The Last Taboo: Why America Needs Atheism." Are they in direct opposition? Where do you think they might find common ground? With whom do you tend to agree in terms of what the United States is like today?

3. Research the religious affiliation of U.S. presidents. When have they *publicly* acted on their faith? That is, when have they openly discussed using their religious beliefs as a decision-making tool?

4. Carter has argued that "democracy is best served when the religions are able to act as independent moral voices interposed between the citizen and the state," and that "our tendency to try to wall religion out of public debate makes that role a harder one to play." Discuss what he means, and how that works into our nation's concerns with the separation of church and state. Find out what separation of church and state really means, both historically and currently.

ANNE LAMOTT Why I Make Sam Go to Church

Anne Lamott is a writer based in Marin County, California. She is the author of several novels and the very popular nonfiction works Operating Instructions: A Journal of My Son's First Year *(1993) and* Bird by Bird: Some Instructions on Writing and Life *(1994). "Why I Make Sam Go to Church" is from her recent book* Traveling Mercies: Some Thoughts on Faith *(New York: Pantheon Books, 1999).*

Sam is the only kid he knows who goes to church—who is made to go to church two or three times a month. He rarely wants to. This is not exactly true: the truth is he *never* wants to go. What young boy would rather be in church on the weekends than hanging out with a friend? It does not help him to be reminded that once he's there he enjoys himself, that he gets to spend the time drawing in the little room outside the sanctuary, that he only actually has to sit still and listen during the short children's sermon. It does not help that I always pack some snacks, some Legos, his art supplies, and bring along any friend of his whom we can lure into our churchy web. It does not help that he genuinely cares for the people there. All that matters to him is that he alone among his colleagues is forced to spend Sunday morning in church.

You might think, noting the bitterness, the resignation, that he was being made to sit through a six-hour Latin mass. Or you might wonder why I make this strapping, exuberant boy come with me most weeks, and if you were to ask, this is what I would say.

I make him because I can. I outweigh him by nearly seventy-five pounds.

But that is only part of it. The main reason is that I want to give him what I found in the world, which is to say a path and a little light to see by. Most of the people I know who have what I want—which is to say, purpose, heart, balance, gratitude, joy—are people with a deep sense of spirituality. They are people in community, who pray, or practice their faith; they are Buddhists, Jews, Christians—people banding together to work on themselves and for human rights. They follow a brighter light than the glimmer of their own candle; they are part of something beautiful. I saw something once from the Jewish Theological

Seminary that said, "A human life is like a single letter of the alphabet. It can be meaningless. Or it can be a part of a great meaning." Our funky little church is filled with people who are working for peace and freedom, who are out there on the streets and inside praying, and they are home writing letters, and they are at the shelters with giant platters of food.

5   When I was at the end of my rope, the people at St. Andrew tied a knot in it for me and helped me hold on. The church became my home in the old meaning of *home*—that it's where, when you show up, they have to let you in. They let me in. They even said, "You come back now."

My relatives all live in the Bay Area and I adore them, but they are all as skittishly self-obsessed as I am, which I certainly mean in the nicest possible way. Let's just say that I do not leave family gatherings with the feeling that I have just received some kind of spiritual chemotherapy. But I do when I leave St. Andrew.

"Let's go, baby," I say cheerfully to Sam when it is time to leave for church, and he looks up at me like a puppy eyeing the vet who is standing there with the needle.

Sam was welcomed and prayed for at St. Andrew seven months before he was born. When I announced during worship that I was pregnant, people cheered. All these old people, raised in Bible-thumping homes in the Deep South, clapped. Even the women whose grown-up boys had been or were doing time in jails or prisons rejoiced for me. And then almost immediately they set about providing for us. They brought clothes, they brought me casseroles to keep in the freezer, they brought me assurance that this baby was going to be a part of the family. And they began slipping me money.

Now, a number of the older black women live pretty close to the bone financially on small Social Security checks. But routinely they sidled up to me and stuffed bills in my pocket—tens and twenties. It was always done so stealthily that you might have thought they were slipping me bundles of cocaine. One of the most consistent donors was a very old woman named Mary Williams, who is in her mid-eighties now, so beautiful with her crushed hats and hallelujahs; she always brought me plastic Baggies full of dimes, noosed with little wire twists.

10   I was usually filled with a sense of something like shame until I'd remember that wonderful line of Blake's—that we are here to learn to endure the beams of love—and I would take a long deep breath and force these words out of my strangulated throat: "Thank you."

I first brought Sam to church when he was five days old. The women there very politely pretended to care how I was doing but were mostly killing time until it was their turn to hold Sam again. They called him "our baby" or sometimes "my baby." "Bring me my baby!" they'd insist. "Bring me that baby now!" "Hey, you're hogging that baby."

I believe that they came to see me as Sam's driver, hired to bring him and his gear back to them every Sunday.

Mary Williams always sits in the very back by the door. She is one of those unusually beautiful women—beautiful like a river. She has dark skin, a long broad nose, sweet full lips, and what the theologian Howard Thurman calls "quiet eyes."

She raised five children as a single mother, but one of her boys drowned when he was young, and she has the softness and generosity and toughness of someone who has endured great loss. During the service she praises God in a nonstop burble, a glistening dark brook. She says, "Oh, yes. . . . Uh-huh. . . . My sweet Lord. Thank you, thank you."

Sam loves her, and she loves him, and she still brings us Baggies full of dimes even though I'm doing so much better now. Every Sunday I nudge Sam in her direction, and he walks to where she is sitting and hugs her. She smells him behind his ears, where he most smells like sweet unwashed new potatoes. This is in fact what I think God may smell like, a young child's slightly dirty neck. Then Sam leaves the sanctuary and returns to his drawings, his monsters, dinosaurs, birds. I watch Mary Williams pray sometimes. She clutches her hands together tightly and closes her eyes most of the way so that she looks blind; because she is so unselfconscious, you get to see someone in a deeply interior pose. You get to see all that intimate resting. She looks as if she's holding the whole earth together, or making the biggest wish in the world. Oh, yes, Lord. Uh-huh.

15   It's funny: I always imagined when I was a kid that adults had some kind of inner toolbox, full of shiny tools: the saw of discernment, the hammer of wisdom, the sandpaper of patience. But then when I grew up I found that life handed you these rusty bent old tools—friendships, prayer, conscience, honesty—and said, Do the best you can with these, they will have to do. And mostly, against all odds, they're enough.

Not long ago I was driving Sam and his friend Josh over to Josh's house where the boys were going to spend the night. But out of the blue, Josh changed his mind about wanting Sam to stay over. "I'm tired," he said suddenly, "and I want to have a quiet night with my mom." Sam's face went white and blank; he has so little armor. He started crying. I tried to manipulate Josh into changing his mind, and I even sort of vaguely threatened him, hinting that Sam or I might cancel a date with *him* sometime, but he stayed firm. After a while Sam said he wished we'd all get hit by a car, and Josh stared out the window nonchalantly. I thought he might be about to start humming. It was one of those times when you wish you were armed so you could attack the kid who has hurt your own child's feelings.

"Sam?" I asked. "Can I help in any way? Shall we pray?"

"I just wish I'd never been born."

But after a moment, he said yes, I should pray. To myself.

20   So I prayed that God would help me figure out how to stop living in the problem and to move into the solution. That was all. We drove along for a while. I waited for a sign of improvement. Sam said, "I guess Josh wishes I had never been born."

Josh stared out the window: dum de dum.

I kept asking God for help, and after a while I realized something—that Josh was not enjoying this either. He was just trying to take care of himself, and I made the radical decision to let him off the hook. I imagined gently lifting him off the hook of my judgment and setting him back on the ground.

And a moment later, he changed his mind. Now, maybe this was the result of prayer, or forgiveness; maybe it was a coincidence. I will never know. But even before Josh changed his mind, I did know one thing for sure, and this was that Sam and I would be going to church the next morning. Mary Williams would be sitting in the back near the door, in a crumpled hat. Sam would hug her; she would close her eyes and smell the soft skin of his neck, just below his ears.

What I didn't know was that Josh would want to come with us too. I didn't know that when I stopped by his house to pick up Sam the next morning, he would eagerly run out ahead of Sam to ask if he could come. And another thing I didn't know was that Mary Williams was going to bring us another bag of dimes. It had been a little while since her last dime drop, but just when I think we've all grown out of the ritual, she brings us another stash. Mostly I give them to street people. Some sit like tchotchkes on bookshelves around the house. Mary doesn't know that professionally I'm doing much better now; she doesn't know that I no longer really need people to slip me money. But what's so dazzling to me, what's so painful and poignant, is that she doesn't bother with what I think she knows or doesn't know about my financial life. She just knows we need another bag of dimes, and that is why I make Sam go to church.

QUESTIONS FOR INQUIRY AND ACTION

1. Notice how Lamott weaves tender, sentimental observations with sharp, witty comments. How does she manage to be sentimental without being sappy?

2. Read through the essay with a highlighter and highlight each of Lamott's descriptions of a person or thing. Which ones are particularly vivid or real for you, and why?

3. Lamott writes that "most of the people I know who have what I want—which is to say, purpose, heart, balance, gratitude, joy—are people with a deep sense of spirituality." Do you think this is generally true? Inquire into the happiness and purpose in lives of people who are "churched" and "unchurched."

4. To what extent is Lamott describing your own church experience? How could you find a faith community like hers if you haven't already? Is this the kind of community you would want? Why or why not?

STOP AND THINK

HOUSE CHURCHES: DESIGNING YOUR OWN WORSHIP

A phenomenon has been growing across the United States and in other countries of the world affected by Christian missionaries: house churches. As their name indicates, house churches are worship services that take place in individuals' homes rather than in official institutions. Popular among evangelical Christians primarily,

continued on next page

but also among liberal freethinkers and others, house churches allow participants a deeply intimate and personal fellowship that isn't available in most church settings.

What is more, house churches also allow everyone present to participate fully in all of the elements of worship, from selecting, reading, and studying scriptures; to choosing hymns and making the music; to composing prayers; to sharing aloud experiences of faith; and even to preaching, although that aspect of worship generally has a diminished role in these settings. It is, in fact, what caused many people to leave institutionalized churches and set up their own worship services at home. The participants interact with one another more, too, rather than sit passively in the pews as fellow audience members.

What do you think is gained and what is lost in this kind of worship service? As individuals and small groups make meaning for themselves, are they more likely to become deeply informed and wise, or are they more likely not to tolerate any differences of opinion, scriptural interpretation, worship style, or lifestyle, and to ostracize anyone who is different?

On the other hand, what does the popularity of house churches say about our human need to make meaning? Why is ritual itself—the ceremonial repetition of words or movements as a way of focusing our consciousness—important to being human? And why is it important to create that ritual for ourselves and to participate actively in it, rather than to serve as a spectator to others? Where in our lives do we have opportunities to create rituals and share them with others?

TOM BEAUDOIN Experience Is Key

> *Tom Beaudoin is a religious educator, lay minister, and, at the time he wrote this piece, a Ph.D. student in religion and education at Boston College. "Experience is Key" is a chapter from his book,* Virtual Faith: the Irreverent Spiritual Quest of Generation X *(San Francisco: Jossey-Bass, 1998). In his preface to the book, Beaudoin, a member of Generation X himself, makes his aims clear by stating that "for Generation Xers, my intention is to start a conversation that is not yet happening on a popular level. Ideally, the book will inspire Xers to begin thinking about religion in a new way" (xv).*

Growing up in a fairly reserved suburban Catholic parish, I never understood the religious importance of personal experience until I attended a charismatic Mass in the late 1970s, when I was about ten years old. All around me people were dancing, raising their arms in the air, or gently swaying. A woman sitting next to me folded her hands, raised them close to her lips, and chanted, "Homily, hominy, homily, as they kill our till. Homily, hominy, homily, as they kill our till." I'm not kidding; I still remember the words. For the next several years, I thought she had been chanting a Catholic prayer I had never heard, and I was intrigued by what these vague and mysterious words might have meant (a spiritual meditation on grits, a sermon, and the collection?). Only later, after I watched a television special about the "charismatic movement," did I realize that the woman next to me was speaking in tongues. I was awed by such an intimate religious experience that could so carelessly flout social convention. Thereafter, personal religious experience had a ring of authenticity that remains for me to this day.

Personal Experience as Religious

In this century, personal experience has not always counted so heavily in what it means to be religious. Different eras and cultures have placed more importance on an intellectualized faith or assent to creeds or doctrines. In our own times, submission to an outside authority (an institution or a member of the clergy) has sometimes counted as more religious than personal experiences. For the last few decades in mainstream institutional religions, however, there has been an attempt to recover the religious significance of experience. Xers are heirs to this renewed emphasis.

An expert on baby boomer religiousness, Wade Clark Roof, credits boomers with reintroducing personal experience as a legitimate font of religious truth. As Roof observes, they "are inclined to regard their own experiences as superior to the accounts of others, and the truths found through self-discovery as having greater relevance to them than those handed down by way of creed or custom" (1993, p. 67). Feminist theologians, too, have sought to recover the centrality of experience. Catholic theologian Elisabeth Schüssler Fiorenza writes that "the experience of women struggling for liberation and wholeness" is important for feminist theology (1984, p. xvi). This recovery of experience is especially important for those whose own personal and religious experience has historically been marginalized, particularly women and ethnic and racial minorities in the United States. In valuing experience highly, then, we Xers find ourselves among a great cloud of witnesses to its importance in contemporary spiritual life.

Xers generally find the religious in personal experience, particularly in an emerging form of sensual spirituality. In this turn to experience, there is a constant yearning, both implicit and explicit, for the almost mystical encounter of the human and divine. This turn to experience also manifests in a new interest in communities of faith, as well as in faith lived in the everyday experience of the world. Key to this discussion is the theological concept of *sacramentality*. This pop culture sacramentality suggests that the body and personal experience represent signs of God's grace in the world.

5   *Sacramentals* (miniature, personal signs of God and God's grace in the world) emphasize the personal dimension of faith and underscore the sacramentality (visible signs of God's invisible presence) of lived experience. Grounded in accessible, quotidian practices, sacramentals help Xers see their own experience as religious. The divine may be present in the artifacts that attend Xer quests for the religious life. Sacramentality and personal experience both imply that Xers feel a sense of free-

dom and personal responsibility in regard to their spiritual lives; Xers will not simply receive religious truth paternalistically from a religious authority. What counts as religious must meet the ultimate test: Xers' own personal experience. . . .

Subversive Sacramentals

Sacramentals rank in importance somewhere between "official" sacraments and the ordinary material world. According to the *Catechism of the Catholic Church,* sacramentals act as "sacred signs *which bear a resemblance to* the sacraments" (1994, p. 415, italics mine). Thus, sacramentals are virtual sacraments, simulations of true sacraments. Sacraments—which include baptism, confirmation, the Eucharist, confession, anointing of the sick, marriage, and holy orders—are the ultimate grace-conferring experiences in the Catholic Church. Immersion in simulation is one characteristic of contemporary culture and one way in which GenX pop culture engages the religious. Sacramentals, then, are eminently appropriate for GenX religiosity! They offer a way of thinking theologically about how our lived experiences can be manifestations of God's grace.

Grasping sacramentals' theological role in GenX religiosity (and hence in GenX popular culture and practice) requires a brief detour into an interpretation of Catholic theology. It is worthwhile to note a key tension about sacramentals as we think about them theologically. There is a tension between sacramentals as locally approved by "ordinary" laypeople, on the one hand, and as officially approved by the Church hierarchy, on the other hand. (The *Catechism* calls this tension the "wisdom" and "discernment" of the *faithful* versus "the care and judgment of the *bishops* and. . . general norms of the church" [1994, p. 417, italics mine].)

In addition to being somewhat free of Church hierarchy, sacramentals are more personal and fallible conduits of grace than full-fledged sacraments. The grace conferred by sacramentals is not "automatic"—it depends on the believer's spirituality, whereas sacraments can confer grace regardless of the priest's spirituality.

As symbols that mediate the divine in a very earthly context, sacramentals are ideal "media" for the experience of GenX spirituality. For Catholics, although the hierarchy has officially licensed sacramentals, they operate somewhat independently of institutional religion. Because of this independent existence, they continually threaten to undermine the official institution's monopoly over the dissemination of religious experience and access to grace—as well as pronounce judgment on the institution itself.

10   That the theme of experience in GenX religiosity threatens institutions is clear even in the *Catechism,* as it quotes a document written by Latin American bishops. The wisdom of the people, according to the bishops, manifest in sacramentals in the forms of popular piety and devotion (and, I would add, pop culture!), "is also a principle of discernment and an evangelical instinct through which [people] spontaneously sense when the Gospel is served in the Church and when it is emptied of its content and stifled by other interests" (p. 417).

Sacramentals fit the GenX religious imagination. They frequently show up in pop culture, as well as in everyday experience. Rooted in the *experiences* of individuals and groups, sacramentals become integral to GenX's irreverent spirituality. Appropriately enough for Christian Xers, and unlike official sacraments, sacramentals are easily personalized, responding to "the needs, culture, and special history of the Christian people of a particular region or time" (p. 415). Like Xer spirituality, sacramentals refuse to be confined to religious institutions. . . .

Mark of a Generation

In 1986, when I was a high school junior, I had my left ear pierced at a shopping mall. I wore an earring for a few years, then tired of it. The mark on my ear remains, however, and will stay with me for the rest of my life. Like its related trend, tattooing, this permanent cut is more than just teen folly. My interpretation will suggest that the experience of the body is a source of religious meaning for one's life.

By the late 1980s and early 1990s, body piercing and tattooing were increasingly common Xer fashion statements. My high school students, friends, and Xers at large appeared with a plethora of body adornments throughout the 1990s, including multiple ear piercings; rings in the navel, nose, tongue, eyebrows, and sundry other body locations; and a great increase in tattooing. Tattoos also appeared on all parts of the body in a variety of images ranging from Mickey Mouse to religious or rock band symbols. On the first day of the new school year in August 1993, half a dozen students of mine stopped by my classroom to show me new rings in their navels, ears, and noses. It had become a rite of passage that they knew a fellow Xer would understand.

Piercing signifies immediate, bodily, and constant attention to the intimacy of experience. To pierce one's body is to leave a permanent mark of intense physical experience, whether pleasurable or painful. Though it has been more than a decade since my own piercing, the mark of indelible experience is ever with me, as proof that something *marked me, something happened.* This permanence or deep experience indicates why piercings have religious significance across cultures, and why rites of cutting or piercing the body are common in many religions.

15   For Xers, marking the body has various layers of meaning. This vague sense of being indelibly marked signifies the childhoods that have permanently but ambiguously marked (or even scarred) many Xers. And despite—or perhaps because of—the religious significance of piercing, Xers pierce themselves outside the religious context. Whether in the cathedral-like anonymity of an antiseptic mall or the cloister of a friend's basement, they administer to themselves gold or silver rings—which in some cases function as their own sacramentals. This is partly because religious institutions today are unable to provide for deeply marking, profoundly experiential encounters. At the least, then, this turn to piercing and tattooing reflects the centrality of personal and intimate experience in Xers' lives.

There may also be some truth for Xers in English professor Andrew Ross's suggestion that piercing and tattooing signify identification with "semicriminalized codes of the outcast," as such outcasts are identifiable by various sorts of body markings (1994, p. 296). This would be consistent with Xers' history as a generation unafraid to explore the margins, the psychologically marginalized recipients of a critical mass of social dysfunctions. This history surely has encouraged many Xers, particularly those with "punk" styles, to choose scarification out of sympathy toward the possibly romanticized outcast.

That mind-set would also explain why so many punk Xers ironically use safety pins in piercings. Because they frequently lacked safety in their childhoods (or even in their adult society), a pin named *safety*—an artifact meant to avoid harming babies—becomes a social statement about harm, danger, and social effrontery.

We are a generation willing to have experience, to be profoundly marked, even cut, when religious institutions have not given us those opportunities. It could even be said that our indulgence in tattoos mocks the hypercommercial world in which we live; tattooing is the only way we have control over "branding" ourselves, instead of being name-branded to death.

One common trend among Xers throughout the 1990s was particularly revealing—the exposure of pierced navels. Aided by half-shirts and a healthy dose of self-assuredness, many Xers (particularly women) bared their midriffs (including many of my students, which created a dress code crisis at our high school). The popular GenX guide *alt.culture* features a stark picture of a pierced navel as the sole image on its cover (Daly and Wice, 1995), emblematic of a generation's fashion. To interpret this phenomenon is to draw attention to the belly's religious significance. When the abdomen, or the navel, is seen as the center of the self, this seemingly innocent fashion trend can be interpreted as GenX theological playfulness about the exposure of the person's center.

20   Historian of religion Mircea Eliade notes that the navel represents the center of human fecundity in Jewish and other religious traditions (1987, p. 44; 1996, pp. 377–378). This was true in the Hebrew Scriptures, which reported that the monster Behemoth's "power [was] in the muscles of its belly" (Job 40:16). Similarly, one Proverb reports that turning from evil brings "health to thy navel" (Proverbs 3:8). There is a double exposure at work; when women bare their navels, it means that the more socially concealed sex is exposing that which is most revealing about themselves—the part considered to be at their center. They let it beam out as a beacon of irony, casting darkness instead of light, confounding our final attempts to understand it.

The term *navel-gazing* is key here, suggesting a preoccupation with the self. The fashion trend of exposing a pierced navel invites all who see it to navel-gaze (the ring draws attention to the navel), to dwell on one's own experience, by gazing at another's navel. This can be a gift of religious experience and reflection from the fashionable Xer: "Out of the believer's belly shall flow rivers of living water" (John 7:38). With a fleet of exposed bellies unleashing flowing water, Xers seem to have formed their own navel academy. If the belly is the seat of deep humanness and even fecundity, navel piercing is also an example of Xer religiosity; it implies finding the spiritual in the sensual (which I will discuss in the next section).

There is something gendered and ascetic about pierced navels. Rarely are they found on men. That women most often wear navel rings is not surprising, because piercings are usually only displayed on firm bellies. Thus, the pierced navel is a fuzz of contradictory suggestions: the authority of bodily experience, the sensual life of the spiritual body or belly, the reinforcing of popular social expectations about women's bodies in regard to thinness and firm bellies, and the suggestion of an ascetic refusal to indulge in the overconsumption of modern culture (signified by a slim abdomen). Call it an ascetic aesthetic.

(Although the fashionable navel has refused to overconsume, it invites consumption by all who will see it, deploying a navel convoy of suggestions that sail to the rich port of personal experience.)

Body and Soul Together

"The body is a temple," wrote Paul in the Christian Scriptures (1 Corinthians 6:19). The way Xers adorn their temples helps us see that a lived theology emphasizing experience is well under way. Through this trend, Xers indicate their spiritual need for truly *marking,* transformative spiritual experiences. This sort of spiritual change may happen on retreats with religious groups, or (often better) during days or weeks spent alone as guests at monasteries or convents, or perhaps on road trips across the United States, as for several friends of mine. It likely only happens when we put our selves, our futures, and our stubbornest needs at risk—when we enter God's future for us. Each of us must find these transformative initiations, as institutions so rarely provide them now as part of spiritual maturation. (Of course, these change-inducing experiences may not always happen at the mountaintop; they might require years of spiritual drudgery. But that yearning for the mountaintop is alive and well among Xers.)

25   Institutions that ignore the way Xers need to be marked, religiously branded, and body oriented cannot fully minister to them. With their accumulated wisdom of tradition, institutions can give Xers tools for a discriminating sense of the sacramentality of personal experience; this is necessary because not all experiences reveal God, particularly in a culture that frequently offers a great deal less than graced experience. If institutions dignify the sacramentality of experience for GenX, they can express their concern that what Xers interpret as grace may instead be sin. Among the various sins in which pop culture and personal experience can indulge, the denigration of the human, for instance, cannot disclose God's grace. Anything that demeans people—even if cloaked as sacramental—must therefore be considered sinful or distorted, not graceful. Catholic mystic Thomas Merton's warning bears remembering: "By no one is more harm done in the world than by men who were at the point of becoming mystics, but whose mysticism [or, we may add, whose sense of sacramentality] degenerated into an irrational surrender to every passion that knew how to dress up as an angel of light" (1981, p. 200). Although it is critical for the Christian interpreter of popular culture to be vigilant in regard to sin in pop culture, the overemphasis on sin by religious interpreters has masked the sacramental potential of GenX culture and experience.

It is into this unpredictable world of the passions that GenX's lived theology marches, declaring sensuality a potential arena of grace.

Sensual Spirituality

Pop culture highlights the sacred potential of human experience by frequently fusing or juxtaposing sexuality and spirituality.

This focus on the close relationship between sensuality and spirituality is first of all about understanding Xers' experience at the edge of our own limits—that is, of interpreting our experience religiously. Even though sexuality at its base is mysterious (a gift in faith and love of oneself to another), that does not mean that Xers, or popular culture, cannot say anything of consequence about sexuality (indeed, as we shall see, we are saying a great deal about it!). What makes our experience mysterious (particularly our experience of sensuality) is our continued ability to find depth and meaning—deep relationality—in it. The mystery of human experience is a rich symbol—an inexhaustible theological resource.

[Madonna's video] "Like a Prayer" illustrates this connection of spirituality and sexuality. Catholic sociologist Andrew Greeley rightly suggests that Madonna "dares to link her sexuality with God and religious images" (1989, p. 449). Madonna initiates this fusion of spirituality and sensuality when she kisses the feet of Saint Martin. Calling again upon Catholic tradition, her action alludes to the ancient practice of venerating the cross. On Good Friday, two days before Easter, Catholics venerate crosses at services. A frequent form of this obeisance is kissing the feet of Jesus on the crucifix. In my view, by honoring Saint Martin with this intimate, sensual act, Madonna humbly acknowledges the mystery of experiencing intimacy with him, even suggesting that he has a sacred character akin to that of Jesus.

30   She opens the doors of the altar grate, and her sensual touch brings Saint Martin to life. (The spiritual awakens and enlivens the sensual, and vice versa.) His first response is also sensual; he kisses Madonna on the forehead, reciprocating the action that is at once sensual and spiritual. The juxtaposition of the sensual and spiritual ends the video. In a church, Saint Martin and Madonna share a kiss before he returns to the life of a statue behind the altar grate. . . .

According to one exhaustive study, sexual and religious images are frequently combined in music video. Researchers Carol Pardun and Kathy McKee discovered that "religious imagery is twice as likely to be found in videos that also use sexual imagery than those without" (1995, p. 444). After randomly selecting 160 videos to analyze, they found that religious and sexual images were combined in more than one-quarter of the videos. The religious images were not satanic, as some would expect; rather, they were "highly recognizable Judeo-Christian symbols" (p. 445).

Although Pardun and McKee title their study "Strange Bedfellows," religiousness and sexuality have been paired before—to the surprise of many today—in Christian tradition. Many mystics, for example, in Christian history have explored the deep congruities between sexuality and spirituality and the ways in which the two share language and experience.

Bernard of Clairvaux (1090–1153) employed erotic imagery in his advice to young monks on leading a spiritual life. He was aware that in order to reach them effectively, he had to use the language of the world from which they came and their own personal sexual memories. Bernard depicted progress in the life of Christian prayer as an increasingly intimate kissing of Christ. He took this striking metaphor (and stressed that it was *only* a metaphor) from the Hebrew Scriptures' Song of Songs. The acts of kissing Christ's feet, his hands, and then his lips parallel the salvific work of repentance, grace, and union, according to Bernard. Pleasing though the Lord's goodness (or kisses) may be, the highest level of union with the divine, a brief ecstasy, is best achieved by way of a spiritual and immortal body when all fleshly "entanglements" have been left behind. Then our spiritual bodies will be united with the God who has "no particularities" and yet is as close to us as we are to ourselves. God can be *known* fully in the next life, *loved* wholly in this one. Bernard's introduction to the sermon on this topic is wonderfully relevant for GenX's lived theology. His focus is not on the holiness of the Bible or the Church but of life itself. "Today," Bernard wrote simply, "we read the book of experience" (1987, pp. 221–226).

Women mystics, too, have explored this theme, perhaps even more daringly than men. According to historian of mysticism Grace Jantzen, medieval women mystics frequently exhibited "a direct, highly charged, passionate encounter between Christ and the writer" (1995, p. 133). Hadewijch of Antwerp, a mystical writer from the thirteenth century, recounts her experience of Christ on a Pentecost Sunday:

> With that he came in the form and clothing of a Man, as he was on the day when he gave us his body for the first time; looking like a human being and a man, wonderful, and beautiful, and with glorious face, he came to me as humbly as anyone who wholly belongs to another. Then he gave himself to me in the shape of the sacrament. . . . After that he came himself to me, took me entirely in his arms, and pressed me to him; and all my members felt his full felicity, in accordance with the desire of my heart and my humanity. So I was outwardly satisfied and fully transported. . . but soon, after a short time, I lost that manly beauty outwardly in the sight of his form [1995, p. 135].

35   This intimate encounter with Christ, sensate and erotic, also appears in other works by mystical authors. Teresa of Avila referred to herself and others who seek God as his "lovers," and said that God sometimes torments these lovers to test them (1957, p. 80). Unlike Madonna, who can sing through the ecstasy, Teresa's intimate contact with Christ overwhelmed but did not completely drown out her senses: "By the command of the Bridegroom [Christ] when He intends ravishing the soul, the doors of the mansions and even those of the keep and of the whole castle are closed; for He takes away the power of speech, and although occasionally the other faculties are retained rather longer, no word can be uttered" (Teresa of Avila in Underhill, 1990, p. 377). Madonna would feel right at home in these works, inasmuch as her video stands so firmly on this branch of her Catholic tradition.

The lesson Jantzen draws from several women mystics is timely for the spirituality of Generation Xers: "It is precisely through actual eroticism that lessons of God are to be learned" (1995, p. 134). There is for Xers, then, an expression in pop culture of an emerging understanding of the relation between sensual passion and faithful passion—indulging in finite sensual passion is analogous to indulging in the infinite passion of faith in union with God.

This fusion of the sensual and spiritual has unfortunately been a minor theme in Christian history and theology. Early on in the Church's history and frequently thereafter, for complex reasons, the disjunction between sexuality and spirituality was more commonly seen as appropriately Christian. GenX pop culture recovers a subversive strand of Christian tradition, offering a reversal of the significance of the body and sexuality in religious institutions' preaching and practices.

An interesting liturgical tool (if used in church) or evangelical tool (if used on music television) would be to play Madonna videos while scrolling texts from Teresa of Avila or Bernard of Clairvaux along the bottom of the screen. Some would deride this sacrilegious juxtaposition, but it might accomplish much for both a "secular" and a "churchy" audience; they could each appreciate that mystical writings and GenX lived theology seem to be pointing in the same direction—the unabashed reintegration of sexuality and spirituality.

40   Xers are way out in front of religious institutions on this issue, as institutions are largely hesitant to suggest that sexual intimacy can be correlated with spiritual intimacy. They prefer all-or-nothing (usually nothing) approaches to sexuality. This GenX theology of sexuality can inspire institutions to change their position; rather than trying to control sexuality, they can start encouraging Xers to see it in a spiritual perspective. Indeed, Xers and institutions can have a common interest in attending to the degradation of sexuality still at work in popular culture. To do this, however, institutions must abandon simplistic interpretations of popular culture's sexual content.

Intersection of the Human and Divine

As evidenced in sensuality, bodily experience, and sacramentality, Xer religiosity explores the experience of incarnation, that is, finding the divine in human form. I interpret this quest for incarnational experience as a desire for the encounter of the human and divine. To experience the divine is to go beyond the confines of human limitation, but the deep enfolding of Xers in culture suggests to us that the divine can only be present through the mediation of the human. To engage experience at this intersection of the human and divine is a key characteristic of the turn to experience in a lived GenX theology. While this theme may cut across religious traditions, for Christian Xers and for some forms of popular culture, this nexus of human and divine is a result of a turn to rediscovering and reexperiencing Jesus, who is Christians' decisive disclosure of the divine and human. . . .

. . . Cyberspace can be interpreted as a metaphor for the experience of the human and divine. Although cyberspace and Jesus should not be confused, these emerging GenX-heavy technologies are worthy of theological attention. Engagement in this medium implies a widespread search for a site of the encounter—however analogous—of the divine and human.

Cyberspace and the Quest for the Divine

The chief characteristic of cyberspace is speed. Many of the qualities that interest people in virtual reality and enable them to experience life in cyberspace revolve around the cult of the current: ever-faster computers, breakneck modem connection rates, advanced multitasking, supercharged networks, increased hours and modes of access, and increasingly "real" forms of communication. If computers began to operate at the speed people seek, it would culminate in a fullness of presence on-line. A "perfect" speed, whether in virtual reality games or in Internet communication, would guarantee the most "real" simulation possible and would therefore enable full presence in a realm that lies beyond the limits of reality.

In this search for perfect speed and full presence, cyberspace is a metaphor for two quests. The first is full interpersonal interaction, or what Jewish philosopher Martin Buber called *I-Thou* relationships. The second is an attempt to transcend human experience, which is why Xers often experiment with imagining the Web as a metaphor—however imperfect—for God. Perhaps the GenX plunge into cyberspace evidences a yearning for full presence in both divine and human relations.

45   Cyberspace highlights our own finitude, reminding us that we can never be fully cognizant of all that is happening. We are just solitary souls among the millions in cyberspace, exploring less than one hundredth of one percent of all that is out there. In this way, cyberspace illuminates our human limits. Yet it also mirrors our desire for the infinite, the divine. Given the direction in which technology is moving, cyberspace seems increasingly omniscient and omnipresent, which may be what the obsession with speed is all about theologically. To search for this fullness of presence, one that spans and unites the human and divine, is to operate in the field of a divine-human experience in which spirituality and technology intersect.

What I am suggesting, then, is that cyberspace is not just a playful diversion for Xers. There is something deeply theologically compelling about this medium with which Xers are so comfortable. Xers implicitly or explicitly may experience cyberspace as an analogue or a metaphor for experiencing the human and divine.

Filippo Marinetti, a futurist who foresaw the coming of this technology as early as 1909, wrote, "We already live within the absolute since we have already created an omnipresent speed" (Marinetti in Taylor, 1993, p. 186). Theologian Mark Taylor has elaborated on Marinetti's revolutionary observation: "The increase in speed creates the hope of breaking the barriers of space and time and entering a fourth dimension where it is possible to experience an eternal now" (p. 186). This eternal now in cyberspace is always deferred, because it is still being sought. The "hope" that Taylor infers indicates the religious thirst of a generation. For Xers, cyberspace "incarnates" and carries forward this theological desire.

Cybercommunities of Faith

If cyberspace offers a metaphor for divine-human experiences, those experiences happen concretely through cybercommunities of faith. Cyberspace—particularly the Internet—is an appropriate medium to serve as a communal center for Generation X. The Internet originated as a national defense communication system designed to remain functional throughout a nuclear war. Given this hypothetical apocalyptic setting and lack of central authority (to avoid collapsing the whole system), how could such a medium *not* appeal to Generation X?

Opportunity for Community

Despite some popular perceptions, those who surf the Net are not exclusively rugged individualists. There are many opportunities for communitarian action on the Net, including organizing relief for victims of natural disasters, circulating protest petitions, and gathering like-minded people from around the globe (particularly those denied access to "mainstream" media). The communities that form can be as bonded as some physical communities and are therefore no less "real." Indeed, cyberspace seems to have great potential for Xers as a site of religious community-gathering. The medium is uniquely able to accommodate both like- and different-minded users who want to form cybercommunities of faith.

50   In this regard, the interrelationship between Net identity and community is important. It has been suggested that in order to sustain a "persona" on the Net, one must participate frequently in cybercommunities. Routine involvement in discussions establishes a user's (or persona's) reputation and "presence" on the Net. Thus, to "exist" in cyberspace itself demands involvement and discourages one from being an electronic wallflower (MacKinnon, 1995, pp. 125–131). Because the medium demands that users join individual identity with communal involvement, cyberspace is an opportune religious space.

Many resources needed for this sort of community exist on-line: Bibles, reference guides, and commentaries. A plethora of religious scholars inhabit the Net. In addition, one can reveal oneself more easily, given the "distance" between users on the Net. In other words, technology enables intimate discussion about spirituality, which benefits both Xers and Net-based ministries. This is perfect for Xers, who have grown up with such a tense relationship to formal communities of faith and who are so well suited to nonfamilial, ad hoc communities. . . .

Solitary Spirituality

Those seeking a religious context not for community but for relative solace may also find rest in cyberspace. The Net is increasingly becoming a virtual monastery for the spiritually dispossessed. As in "real" monasteries, a user may seek community at specific times or in particular sites, and there are myriad opportunities for self-reflection, prayer, meditation, and Scripture studies. There are even on-line monasteries, in which users can listen to chanting monks, gaze on brilliant iconography, and read holy manuscripts without interruption.

New Communities and Connections

Cyberspace gives Xers a voice in religious matters by way of a technology with which they are comfortable. It might even be said that cyberspace is where many Xers are most "themselves." Insofar as that is the case, cybercommunities of faith will continue to coagulate.

For a generation so hesitant to talk about its faith (for fear of sounding too "religious"), cyberspace affords opportunities for intimate faith discussion without necessitating face-to-face communication. The Net gives Xers opportunities to deepen their spiritual life by connecting with other spiritually curious Xers and people from around the world. Dedication to a religious cybercommunity can be as gratifying and important as allegiance to any "real" religious institution.

55   In this way, Xers challenge religious institutions to rethink the definition of *community.* As something that augments (but does not replace!) real community, religious institutions have an opportunity to use this virtual space to build community when ministering to Xers. Ministers may find it an even more effective way to relate to and counsel members of the flock. Institutions might challenge Xers not to limit themselves to religious cybercommunities. Although virtual communities give Xers one more sphere for religious interaction, we should not avoid the difficult religious tasks of loving and seeking justice in the real world. For Christian Xers in particular, there is an implied demand of real embodiment—based on Jesus as the incarnation of God—as an important part of community.

Experience of Living Faith in the World

In *Generation at the Crossroads,* social commentator Paul Rogat Loeb surveys in detail GenXers' political work and attitudes at campuses around the country. At the College of the Holy Cross, Loeb interviews a peace activist whose involvement in college with Catholic peace groups helps her see the interrelationship between her faith and politics in a new light. "I went from a workshop on campus activism to one on the elections and then to Mass," she recalls. "It felt empowering, *the right kind of joining*" (1994, p. 163, italics mine).

This kind of joining runs like a thread through the popular culture, with the political and the religious refusing to be relegated to separate spheres. For instance, Nirvana and R.E.M. both pointedly criticize a messiah who has nothing to say to the "real" world. . . . Tori Amos's video points out the ways in which crucifixion happens in and to a body in a very this-worldly fashion, and Pearl Jam's "Jeremy" prophesies a generation's revenge on a culture—both religious and secular—that has ignored Xers.

In cyberspace, religious and political sites bump elbows, vying for Xers' attention. Several religious Web sites, whether liberal, conservative, or somewhere in between, include links to particular organizations across the political spectrum. Whereas the sites of Christian conservatives may provide links to the Christian Coalition and the e-mail addresses of sympathetic senators, pages of the Christian Left may include links to Greenpeace or Amnesty International. Reared in a culture that has struggled over issues of justice and in a hyperpoliticized atmosphere, Xers have a special sensitivity to political action. No religious involvement can take this away from them, and as popular culture suggests, their political involvement is often linked to religious beliefs.

Xers can frequently cite exactly where religious institutions have fallen short in speaking to the world. According to Xer Rodolpho Carrasco, many "Generation X Latinos perceive that our faith sects (both Catholic and Protestant) have little to say about the issues that affect us most: technology-induced future shock, a national debt as frightening as a velociraptor, AIDS, and (perhaps most important) race and identity" (1994, p. 16). Carrasco retains more hope than many Xers, however. He writes: "I personally believe that the age-old wisdom of the Bible can affirm my generation in all its complexity, while pointing to a greater, eternal harmony. But will the church be able to *communicate* this to us?" (p. 16, italics mine).

60   Loeb observes that GenX students "were most willing to act when doing so did not require immediately confronting powerful institutions" (1994, p. 248). This is true of Xers not only politically but also religiously. Faced with Churches that do not ordain women, for instance, or that preach suspicion and fear of other religions, many Xers prefer to work from a practical faith that lifts them up by lifting the world up through them—and so lifting up the content of their faith in the world.

Separated unnaturally, institutional religion and politics are mere husks of what they could be. When they have joined together in our lifetimes, it is often for the sake of wielding power over others. Many Xers want "the right kind of joining," even if they have no clearly articulated theology to explain what they mean. Xers often sense this union intuitively. They know that if religion doesn't go into the streets, the streets will overtake religion. I have personally known dozens of Xers who have been spiritually kickstarted by working in soup kitchens and food pantries for the poor. One friend even said to me, "The reason I went from working for Congress to studying religion is that I can't understand what to do in one without the other." Religious institutions that heed this challenge from Generation X may find their comfortable positions destabilized, which means they will only be more authentic in many Xers' eyes.

Perhaps the most noticeable charade in this regard is the disavowal of politics many mainline churches make in favor of spiritual concerns. As we have seen, however, most Xers know that the two are not so easily separated. A GenX lived theology understands Catholic theologian Gustavo Gutierrez's plain talk: "The social influence of the church is a fact. Not to exercise this influence in favor of the oppressed. . . is really to exercise it against them" (1988, p. 76).

Religious Experience as Virtual and Real

As I have already suggested, the irreverence of GenX spirituality is heavily dependent on pop culture's use of irony. Kierkegaard writes that irony does not want to be directly grasped, even though it eventually makes itself known. Irony has a peculiar way of "not wanting to be understood immediately, even though it wants to be understood, with the result that [irony] looks down, as it were, on plain and simple talk that everyone can promptly understand" (1989, p. 248). Irony is quite apposite as a GenX posture in popular culture, because it conveys not only what Xers try to say but also the attitude of many Xers themselves!

For example, the employment of sexuality in pop culture frequently has an ironic character. Many cultural critics look at GenX pop culture's deep immersion in sexuality and say, "How far GenX has run from God!" In contrast, I look at all the sexuality and think, "How deeply GenX desires God!" The reveling in sexuality that seems so characteristic of pop culture, from music video to cyberspace to revealing fashions, is not what it appears to be on its face. It empties out the viewer's presuppositions and points to something much deeper, a suggestion that the mystical tradition also affirms (if more piously). The deeper suggestion is that sexual desire is an analogue for desire for God, and that each type of desire may illuminate the other. As irreverent as this recombination of the spiritual and sensual may seem, it is a foundation stone in a lived GenX theology.

65 As grounded as it is in the individual and the community, the GenX emphasis on experience has a heavily "virtual" feel to it. Xers live a theology revolving around *incarnation*—the experience of the human in the context of the divine, and the divine mediated by the human. Thus, Xers express religiosity with *sacramentals,* which can evoke the religious depth of the most common objects or experiences. Because sacramentals are "imitations" of real sacraments, GenX religiosity once again seizes on the salvific experience of simulation. Cyberspace, the prototypical virtual experience for Generation X, can even function as what cyberculture essayist David Porush calls "sacramental architecture" (1996, p. 125). On the Web, Xers can simulate a community that may be as "religious" as any in real life.

This turn to experience has particular implications for Christian Xers in regard to experiencing Jesus. A new sort of GenX liberation theology is emerging, but it is not primarily about the poor, who are normally the focus of liberation theology. Instead, it begins with the liberation of Jesus from the clutches of the Church. Jesus himself needs to be liberated so that Xers can experience the power of his words and deeds, the blessing of his bodily and spiritual presence.

References

Bernard of Clairvaux. *Bernard of Clairvaux: Selected Writings.* (G. R. Evans, trans.). Mahwah, N.J.: Paulist Press, 1987.

Carrasco, R. "A Twenty-First-Century Identity Crisis." *Sojourners,* Nov. 1994, 16.

Catechism of the Catholic Church. Liguori, Mo.: Liguori Publications, 1994.

Crossan, J. D. *Jesus: A Revolutionary Biography.* New York: HarperCollins, 1994.

Daly, S., and Wice, N. *alt.culture: An A-to-Z Guide to the 90s (Underground, Online, and Over-the-Counter).* New York: Harper Collins, 1995.

Eliade, M. *The Sacred and the Profane: The Nature of Religion.* Orlando, Fla.: Harcourt Brace, 1987.

Fiorenza, E. S. "The Crisis of Hermeneutics and Christian Theology." In S. G. Davaney (ed.), *Theology at the End of Modernity.* Philadelphia: Trinity, 1991.

Greeley, A. "Like a Catholic: Madonna's Challenge to Her Church." *America,* 1989, *160*(18), 447–449.

Gutierrez, G. *A Theology of Liberation.* Maryknoll, N.Y.: Orbis Books, 1988.

Jantzen, G. *Power, Gender, and Christian Mysticism.* New York: Cambridge University Press, 1995.

Kierkegaard, S. *The Concept of Irony, with Continual Reference to Socrates.* (H. Hong and E. Hong, trans.). Princeton, N.J.: Princeton University Press, 1989.

Loeb, P. R. *Generation at the Crossroads.* Brunswick, N.J.: Rutgers University Press, 1994.

MacKinnon, R. C. "Searching for the Leviathan in Usenet." In S. G. Jones (ed.), *Cybersociety.* Thousand Oaks, Calif.: Sage, 1995.

Merton, T. *The Ascent to Truth.* New York: Harcourt Brace, 1981.

Metz, J. B., and Moltmann, J. *Faith and the Future: Essays on Theology, Solidarity, and Modernity.* Maryknoll, N.Y.: Orbis Books, 1995.

Moore, S. D. *Mark and Luke in Poststructuralist Perspectives: Jesus Begins to Write.* New Haven, Conn.: Yale University Press, 1992.

Pardun, C., and McKee, K. "Strange Bedfellows: Symbols of Religion and Sexuality on MTV." *Youth and Society,* 1995, *26*(4), 438–449.

Porush, D. "Hacking the Brainstem: Postmodern Metaphysics and Stephenson's *Snow Crash.*" In R. Markley (ed.), *Virtual Realities and Their Discontents.* Baltimore: Johns Hopkins University Press, 1996.

Roof, W. C. *A Generation of Seekers: The Spiritual Journeys of the Baby Boom Generation.* New York: Harper Collins, 1993.

Ross, A. "Tribalism in Effect." In S. Benstock and S. Feriss (eds.), *On Fashion.* New Brunswick, N.J.: Rutgers University Press, 1994.

Sobrino, J. *Jesus in Latin America.* Maryknoll, N.Y.: Orbis Books, 1998.

Taylor, M. C. *Nots.* Chicago: University of Chicago Press, 1993. Quoting Filippo Marinetti, "The Founding Manifesto of Futurism," *Selected Writings* (ed. R. W. Flint and Arthur A. Coppotelli), New York: Farrar, Strauss, and Giroux, 1972: 41–42.

Teresa of Avila. *The Life of Saint Teresa of Avila, by Herself.* New York: Penguin, 1957.

Underhill, E. *Mysticism.* Garden City, N.Y.: Doubleday, 1990. Quoting Teresa of Avila, *The Interior Castle:* translated from the autograph of St. Teresa by the Benedictines of Stanbrook Abbey. London, 1912.

QUESTIONS FOR INQUIRY AND ACTION

1. Examine and discuss Beaudoin's use of the term *sacramentality*. What exactly does he mean by it, and where else do you see examples of it in your own life and culture? Compare his description with Anne Lamott's in "Why I Make Sam Go to Church."

2. Beaudoin writes that the cybercommunity is especially important to GenX spirituality. What can cyberspace add to our experience of spirituality? Does it subtract anything from our experience? How would the authors in Chapter Twelve on virtual communities respond to Beaudoin's argument?

3. How important is personal experience to your own spiritual life? Is it an essential part of the faith tradition you were raised in, if you were raised in one? Research different faith traditions, the role that personal experience plays in them, and the kind of relationship that is encouraged between the faithful and the god(s).

4. Do you have any body piercings or tattoos? If so, what went into your decision to get them? Were there dimensions of spiritual expression or ritual—of being marked by experience—or was it mainly a decision based on fashion? Discuss with others the experience of the tattooing or piercing itself; people have frequently described a feeling of great intensity and profound self-awareness that transforms the physical pain into a pleasurable, awakening experience.

KATHERINE ROSMAN Mormon Family Values: Facing the Anguish of Their Gay Son, the Hardys Became Accidental Activists

Katherine Rosman is a New York City-based journalist who has contributed articles to The New Yorker, W, *and* Brill's Content, *where she is a staff writer. "Mormon Family Values" was published in* The Nation *on February 25, 2002.*

David and Carlie Hardy were the perfect Mormon couple building the perfect Mormon legacy in their mecca, Salt Lake City, Utah. It was 1995 and David, then 42, received simultaneous boosts in his professional and religious life: As an in-house attorney, he had taken a private startup company public so successfully that he was now able to open his own solo practice. At the same time, he had been called to serve as a bishop for the Church of Jesus Christ of Latter-day Saints, whose ministry is drawn from its membership. Carlie, 41, was fulfilling her religious destiny as well by giving birth to and then raising six children strictly within the LDS's rules.

To affirm the family's devotion to the church before David's new hectic schedule began to keep him from home, the couple took a pilgrimage with their three eldest children. Mom and the kids retraced the footsteps of Jesus Christ in Jerusalem as described in the Scriptures, and then met Dad in France, the country where he as a young man had served the two-year proselytizing mission required of all devout Mormons, and more recently had spent countless days lobbying to bring the 1998 winter Olympics to Salt Lake City. The trip culminated in Austria, where Carlie had studied on an exchange program from Brigham Young University.

There, in a garden in the hills above Salzburg, the family's bliss was shattered.

Judd, the Hardys' 13-year-old son, confided to his father that he feared he was "same-sex attracted," the LDS euphemism for homosexual. In Mormondom, homosexuality is literally unspeakable; there is no greater taboo in this institution, in which even relatively benign substances such as caffeine are forbidden. "My world just caved in," David recalls. He told his son what he had been taught by the church—that same-sex attraction was infinitely "curable," merely a phase.

5   Upon returning to Salt Lake, David drove straight to his church office. By this point in his life, he well understood that the church often preached to its members through speeches long ago delivered and transcribed into LDS-issued pamphlets—many of which are actual doctrine. He needed to find the instruction regarding same-sex attraction. At the office, he located a handful of pamphlets addressing the issue, all of which contained fire-and-brimstone language like "Homosexuality Is Sin: Next to the crime of murder comes the sin of sexual impurity." David had read the pamphlets many years back, but rereading them while conjuring the image of his devout son, he became increasingly upset. He shoved the pamphlets deep into a drawer and focused on "curing" Judd.

That was seven years ago. Since then, David and Carlie Hardy have gone from being obedient, God-fearing church members to vocal, angry gay-rights activists who have willingly ostracized themselves from the only community they had ever known. In opening their house to outcast gay teens, and their mouths to the media, they have risked their relationships with their friends and relatives, and—if it is "God's one true Church," as LDS members believe—their eternal souls.

Publicly, the church loves the sinner but hates the sin. "People inquire about our position on those who consider themselves so-called gays and lesbians," remarked LDS president Gordon B. Hinckley. "My response is that we love them as sons and daughters of God."

As former insiders, the Hardys contend that the church establishment is obsessed with good press and intent upon creating an image of a mainstream Christian religion—a goal it plans to pursue as the television networks cast their soft-focus lenses on Salt Lake City during the winter Olympics this February. The Hardys, meanwhile, are determined to let the world know what lies behind the church's rhetorical niceties. David Hardy scoffs at Hinckley's profession of tolerance. "We were forced to make a decision that no parent should be forced to make," he says, "to abandon one's child or one's faith."

David Eccles Hardy and Carlie Judd Hardy are Mormon Royalty, an LDS terme d'art indicating that they descend from important historical and modern lineage—Carlie's great-grandfather, Heber J. Grant, served as prophet and president of the church during the early twentieth century, and both David and Carlie have ancestors who were original followers of LDS founder Joseph Smith.

10　　The Hardys married in 1975, just after David completed his missionary service. He earned a law degree and began a steady rise in the corporate world of Utah's burgeoning tech sector. Carlie oversaw their children's immersion in the church—before-school Scripture study, Eagle Scouts, religious classes, community service, all in addition to the regular Sunday services. As with all faithful LDS members, they gave 10 percent of the family's pretax income to the church. Mormon perfection.

Judd, the third child and oldest son, was a slight, fair-haired boy with noteworthy devotion to the church and its gospel. But he was different from other boys in his neighborhood. "Despite my hours coaching him, he was utterly uninterested in sports and 'boy games,'" his dad remembers. Instead, Judd liked to play with his sisters' dolls and to perform songs. David and Carlie secretly worried about their son's effeminate mannerisms but tried to ignore their concerns. The idea of having a son with "same-sex attraction" was too shameful to consider. "A Mormon mother is told to have kids and stay home," Carlie explains. "There is nothing left for a mother's self-esteem. You are judged on how your family turns out."

So when Judd came out to David in Austria in 1995, and David shared the information with Carlie, they did what they had always done—they turned to the church. They enrolled Judd in a stint of reparative therapy (which purports to counsel people in "overcoming" their homosexuality). They remained stoic as they read the research attributing homosexual tendencies to an overbearing mother and emotionally unavailable father.

One of the pamphlets they found advises church leaders on how to act if a member confesses same-sex attraction. It reads, "God has promised to help those who earnestly strive to live his commandments," and it says members should be reassured that for those who repent enough, "heterosexual feelings emerge." This pamphlet is only available to leadership. An average member receives more explicit instruction, like that in the text of a speech given by a former president and prophet: "Satan tells his victims that it is a natural way of life; that it is normal; that perverts are a different kind of people born 'that way' and that they cannot change. This is a base lie. . . . it were better that such a man were never born." The Hardys were most disturbed by the writings of Boyd K. Packer, an apostle second in line for the church presidency whose public words constitute doctrine. In one oft-cited speech, Packer endorsed violence as a response to a perceived homosexual advance. "You must protect yourself," he preached.

The more Carlie and David turned to the church for help, the more its practices frustrated them. They were outraged to learn that church funds were being diverted to support movements in Hawaii and Alaska aimed at keeping same-sex marriage illegal. Meanwhile, their young son was asking his parents to disconnect their cable and Internet service so that he would not be tempted by any alluring images of men. He was fasting and praying so that he could live within the boundaries of the church, yet doctrine labeled him a servant of the Devil.

15   In early 1999 David was reaching his breaking point and asked to be released early from his role as bishop. Soon after, Carlie attended an annual interview with the family's local ecclesiastical authority, D. Miles Holman. (Citing clerical requirements of confidentiality, Holman declined to comment.) Carlie told Holman that total loyalty to the church's principles was increasingly difficult for her and that she was uncertain she could encourage a lifetime of celibacy for Judd. "I don't think it would be healthy for my son for me to suggest that he never have any intimacy," she recalls telling him. According to Carlie, Holman told her there was only one solution: Judd had to remain celibate for his life, and she and David should keep his "problem" a secret. "He said, 'Hey, isn't this homosexual issue easy?'"

Carlie walked out to her car and turned on her mobile phone. It rang immediately. One of her children said, "Mom, where have you been? We just had to take Judd to the hospital." After sitting through an LDS lesson on Sodom and Gomorrah, Judd had gone home and slashed his wrists.

The suicide attempt, says Judd, now a sophomore studying theater at the Tisch School of the Arts at New York University, "wasn't [done] out of despair as much as it was [done] almost out of duty. It felt to me as if I was in this loop that I couldn't end. The church wanted me to change, and I couldn't get past that. And I couldn't change, and I couldn't get past that. . . . It was a quick resolution before doing the damage of falling into a life of sin. I believed too strongly in the church and the church's values, and I placed those above my own life."

Whatever it represented for Judd, for David and Carlie the attempt signaled that they could no longer rely on guidance from the church. "We were faithful members," Carlie says, "and then we ran into this situation and no one was there for us." They told Judd there was nothing wrong with him, that he was not going to have to choose between affection or damnation, and they yanked him out of church activities.

Although they experienced massive spiritual and emotional turmoil, they still could not fathom formally separating from the LDS—"anathema," David describes it—so they continued to take Judd's three younger brothers to church. One day in early 1999 James Hardy asked his mom to call a family meeting. Carlie remembers that her son said, "I don't understand, you keep saying that Judd doesn't have to go to church because he's gay and that's an extenuating circumstance. But don't you think the fact that I have an older brother I honor, respect and look up to, and this is a church that doesn't have a place for him—isn't that an extenuating circumstance?" He said, "It is for me and I won't be going back." That was the watershed moment, Carlie says. "All of a sudden David and I looked at each other and said, 'You know what? We're not going either. If this is an organization that will not support this amazing individual who is our son, Judd Eccles Hardy, then we will not be going either.'"

20   It was October 2000, the eve of the church's semiannual General Conference, for which clergy and members from around the world descend upon their religious capital to reaffirm the authority of the church leadership. David Hardy stood nervously in his office, a nineteenth-century carriage house just eight blocks from LDS headquarters. He and Carlie had invited the local print, television and radio media for a press conference unlike any other held in Salt Lake City in recent memory. They were going to speak out publicly to decry church policy. "I was scared witless," says David. "I don't think a former bishop has ever done anything like that before."

The Hardys had also invited more than a handful of their peers, members of Family Fellowship, a support group for current and former Mormon parents of gay children. But except for the four lapsed Mormons who attended, the Hardys stood alone. (Since LDS members believe God literally speaks through the church's prophet and president, dissent, or support of dissenters, is tantamount to heresy.)

"We are here today as members of the LDS church and parents of gay children," David began. He had already dispersed to the various reporters copies of the pamphlets that, he asserted, promote violence against homosexuals. He pointed out that the church had reissued literature condoning violence as a response to homosexuals at the same time that Russell Hendersen, an LDS member, was being tried for the murder of Matthew Shepard (the church has since excommunicated Hendersen). David asked that Packer or a church spokesman avow or reject the language in the pamphlets—the only existing church literature directly addressing homosexuality.

After David finished his remarks, he and Carlie answered a few questions before the swell of reporters walked to the LDS administrative building in pursuit of a church response. (A spokesman issued a statement later that evening: "These are individuals who are children of God. We love them; we respect them. This church is a church of inclusion, not exclusion, and we welcome them and want them to be a part of the church.")

The Hardys' public criticism of the church has caused rifts between them and relatives, friends and colleagues—and has created tension for their eldest daughter, who remains active in the church. But even as their community banishes them, they

continue in their quest to compel the media and, they hope, the church to acknowledge the struggles associated with being a homosexual in a community of Saints.

25   They do so in several ways. First, they fund diverse cultural fare in otherwise
archconservative Utah. Last year they financed local stage productions of *The
Laramie Project,* which focuses on the aftermath of Shepard's murder (a film adap-
tation debuted last month at the Sundance Film Festival), and *Confessions of a
Mormon Boy,* a one-man show detailing actor/writer Steven Fales's journey from
marriage and fatherhood to reparative therapy and excommunication. (*Confessions* opens Off Broadway next fall.) They also open their home for three hours
on the first Sunday of each month to young Mormon men and women struggling
to confront their homosexuality—and any heterosexuals wanting to show support. Carlie is also planning a series of mountain retreats for those dealing with
issues involving homosexuality in themselves or in their families.

        Along the way, they have achieved a certain visibility in the press. Last Easter the
Salt Lake Tribune published an Op-Ed piece by David; that same month, the CBS affil-
iate ran an interview with Carlie after she and David spoke at a candlelight vigil remembering the "Mormon Gay Suicides." In August they landed significant mention in a
Newsweek article on gays and the Boy Scouts. Their squeaky-clean image has helped.
"If there were a propaganda center in the church, this is the family they would choose,"
says Doug Wortham, a board member of Unity Utah, a gay and lesbian political action
committee. "It's a pretty rare story to find a family like this," he says.

        As for the Hardys' most vocal goal, an official endorsement or condemna-
tion of the pamphlets, they've just recently succeeded: Harold Brown, the church's
official spokesman on homosexuality, said of the pamphlets to *The Nation,* "I
wouldn't even want to suggest that they were outdated or not in use." However,
he says, "If you [take] the whole context of what has been written in the church,
I think you'll find it's a voice of love and concern for people. . . . What we teach
are the standards of morality that we believe will lead to happiness." (Boyd K.
Packer was not available for comment.)

        Brown says no amount of press attention or activism is going to influence God
to change the rules regarding homosexuality—as when He outlawed polygamy in
1890 or gave equal rights to blacks in 1978. "Being black is not a sin," he explains.
"Being immoral is."

        The Hardys do not appear deterred. Their work fighting for the acceptance
of gays is, in a sense, their new ministry; clearly it has helped fill the void created by their exit from the church. Judd is proud of his parents' commitment.
"They've stopped talking about Christianity and charity and religion," he notes,
"and they've started practicing it." At the same time, their activism irks him
because he wants to be known by the world for what he does with his life, not
for what happened to him in the past.

30   Honoring Judd's wishes, his parents ask his permission before speaking to
the press. Usually, Judd rolls his eyes and then obliges them. Despite the unusual
circumstances, there is something familiar about this dynamic—he is a regular
kid, annoyed and embarrassed by his parents.

        To Carlie and David, that is a blessing.

QUESTIONS FOR INQUIRY AND ACTION

1. How does personally experiencing an issue change our formerly abstract views of it? How does Rosman reveal this process through the Hardys' story?

2. Read this article with the family values case study and other readings in Chapter Seven. In what ways are the Hardys a strong family? What family values do they demonstrate?

3. Many faith communities have been split in two over the issue of including openly homosexual members and especially clergy. It is the single biggest issue facing most denominations today. While the Church of Jesus Christ of Latter-day Saints itself has not divided, the Hardys and other families have found themselves "forced to make a decision no parent should be forced to make," in David Hardy's words, "to abandon one's child or one's faith." Explore this issue in more detail.

4. What is the official position and the everyday attitude of your own faith community, if you have one, toward the inclusion of gays and lesbians? Do you agree with it? Is it an important and/or contested issue in your congregation?

WENDY KAMINER The Last Taboo: Why America Needs Atheism

> *Wendy Kaminer is a writer, lawyer, and public policy fellow at Radcliffe Public Policy Institute, Radcliffe College. She has authored a number of books of social critique including* A Fearful Freedom: Women's Flight from Equality *(1990),* I'm Dysfunctional, You're Dysfunctional: The Recovery Movement and Other Self-Help Fashions *(1992), and* Sleeping with Extra-Terrestrials: The Rise of Irrationalism and Perils of Piety *(1999). "The Last Taboo: Why America Needs Atheism" was the cover story of* The New Republic *on October 14, 1996.*

It was King Kong who put the fear of God in me, when I was 8 or 9 years old. Blessed with irreligious parents and excused from attending Sunday school or weekly services, I had relatively little contact with imaginary, omnipotent authority figures until the Million Dollar Movie brought King Kong to our living room TV. Tyrannical and invincible (I never found his capture and enslavement believable), he awakened my superstitions. Watching Kong terrorize the locals, I imagined being prey to an irrational, supernatural brute whom I could never outrun or outsmart. I couldn't argue with him, so my only hope was to grovel and propitiate him with sacrifices. Looking nothing like Fay Wray, I doubted I could charm him; besides, his love was as arbitrary and unpredictable as his wrath.

For the next several years, like the natives in the movie, I clung to rituals aimed at keeping him at bay. (I can only analyze my rituals with hindsight; at the time, I was immersed in them unthinkingly.) Instead of human sacrifices, I offered him neatness, a perfectly ordered room. Every night before going to bed, I straightened all the stuff on my desk and bureau, arranged my stuffed animals in rectangular tableaus and made sure all doors and drawers were tightly shut. I started at one end of the room and worked my way around, counterclockwise; when I finished, I started all over again, checking and rechecking my work three, four or five times.

Going to bed became an ordeal. I hated my rituals; they were tedious and time-consuming and very embarrassing. I knew they were stupid and always kept them secret until, eventually, I grew out of them. I still harbor superstitions, of course, but with less shame and more humor; I find them considerably less compelling.

If I were to mock religious belief as childish, if I were to suggest that worshiping a supernatural deity, convinced that it cares about your welfare, is like worrying about monsters in the closet who find you tasty enough to eat, if I were to describe God as our creation, likening him to a mechanical gorilla, I'd violate the norms of civility and religious correctness. I'd be excoriated as an example of the cynical, liberal elite responsible for America's moral decline. I'd be pitied for my spiritual blindness; some people would try to enlighten and convert me. I'd receive hate mail. Atheists generate about as much sympathy as pedophiles. But, while pedophilia may at least be characterized as a disease, atheism is a choice, a willful rejection of beliefs to which vast majorities of people cling.

5   Yet conventional wisdom holds that we suffer from an excess of secularism. Virtuecrats from Hillary Clinton to William Bennett to Patrick Buchanan blame America's moral decay on our lack of religious belief. "The great malady of the 20th century" is "'loss of soul,'" bestselling author Thomas Moore declares, complaining that "we don't believe in the soul." Of course, if that were true, there'd be no buyers for his books. In fact, almost all Americans (95 percent) profess belief in God or some universal spirit, according to a 1994 survey by *U.S. News and World Report*. Seventy-six percent imagine God as a heavenly father who actually pays attention to their prayers. Gallup reports that 44 percent believe in the biblical account of creation and that 36 percent of all Americans describe themselves as "born-again."

Adherence to mainstream religions is supplemented by experimentation with an eclectic collection of New Age beliefs and practices. Roughly half of all Catholics and Protestants surveyed by Gallup in 1991 believed in ESP; nearly as many believed in psychic healing. Fifty-three percent of Catholics and 40 percent of Protestants professed belief in UFOs, and about one-quarter put their faith in astrology. Nearly one-third of all American teenagers believe in reincarnation. Once I heard Shirley MacLaine explain the principles of reincarnation on the *Donahue* show. "Can you come back as a bird?" one woman asked. "No," MacLaine replied, secure in her convictions. "You only come back as a higher life form." No one asked her how she knew.

In this climate—with belief in guardian angels and creationism becoming commonplace—making fun of religion is as risky as burning a flag in an American Legion hall. But, by admitting that they're fighting a winning battle, advocates of renewed religiosity would lose the benefits of appearing besieged. Like liberal rights organizations that attract more money when conservative authoritarians are in power, religious groups inspire more believers when secularism is said to hold sway. So editors at the *Wall Street Journal* protest an "ardent hostility toward religion" in this country, claiming that religious people are "suspect." When forced by facts to acknowledge that God enjoys unshakable, non-partisan, majoritarian support, religion's proselytizers charge that our country is nonetheless controlled by liberal intellectual elites who disdain religious belief and have denied it a respected public role.

Educated professionals tend to be embarrassed by belief, Yale Law Professor Stephen Carter opined in *The Culture of Disbelief,* a best-selling complaint about the fabled denigration of religion in public life. Carter acknowledges that belief is widespread but argues that it has been trivialized by the rationalist biases of elites and their insistence on keeping religion out of the public sphere. Carter's thesis is echoed regularly by conservative commentators. Another recent *Wall Street Journal* editorial asserted that religious indoctrination is one of the most effective forms of drug treatment and wondered at the "prejudice against religion by much of our judicial and media elites." Newt Gingrich has attacked the "secular, anti-religious view of the left."

No evidence is adduced to substantiate these charges of liberal irreligiosity run rampant. No faithless liberals are named, no influential periodicals or articles cited—perhaps because they're chimeras. Review the list of prominent left-of-center opinion makers and public intellectuals. Who among them mocks religion? Several have gained or increased their prominence partly through their embrace of belief. Harvard Professor Cornel West is a part-time preacher; Michael Lerner came into public view as Hillary Clinton's guru; Gloria Steinem greatly expanded her mainstream appeal by writing about spirituality. Bill Moyers, who introduced New Age holy men Joseph Campbell and Robert Bly to the American public, regularly pays homage to faith in traditional and alternative forms in television specials. Popular spirituality authors, like Thomas Moore, are regarded as public intellectuals in spite or because of their pontifications about faith. Even secular political theorists, preoccupied with civic virtue, are overly solicitous of religion and religious communities.

10   The supposedly liberal, mainstream press offers unprecedented coverage of religion, taking pains not to offend the faithful. An op-ed piece on popular spirituality that I wrote for the *New York Times* this past summer was carefully cleansed by my editors of any irreverence toward established religion (although I was invited to mock New Age). I was not allowed to observe that, while Hillary Clinton was criticized for conversing with Eleanor Roosevelt, millions of Americans regularly talk to Jesus, long deceased, and that many people believe that God talks to them, unbidden. Nor was I permitted to point out that, to an atheist, the sacraments are as silly as a seance. These remarks and others were excised because they were deemed "offensive."

Indeed, what's striking about American intellectuals today, liberal and conservative alike, is not their Voltairean skepticism but their deference to belief and their utter failure to criticize, much less satirize, America's romance with God. They've abandoned the tradition of caustic secularism that once provided refuge for the faithless: people "are all insane," Mark Twain remarked in *Letters from the Earth.* "Man is a marvelous curiosity. . . he thinks he is the Creator's pet. . . he even believes the Creator loves him; has a passion for him; sits up nights to admire him; yes and watch over him and keep him out of trouble. He prays to him and thinks He listens. Isn't it a quaint idea." No prominent liberal thinker writes like that anymore.

Religion is "so absurd that it comes close to imbecility," H.L. Mencken declared in *Treatise on the Gods.* "The priest, realistically considered, is the most immoral of men, for he is always willing to sacrifice every other sort of good to the one good of his arcanum—the vague body of mysteries that he calls the truth."

Mencken was equally scornful of the organized church: "Since the early days, [it] has thrown itself violently against every effort to liberate the body and mind of man. It has been, at all times and everywhere, the habitual and incorrigible defender of bad governments, bad laws, bad social theories, bad institutions. It was, for centuries, an apologist for slavery, as it was an apologist for the divine right of kings." Mencken was not entirely unsympathetic to the wishful thinking behind virtually all religion—the belief that we needn't die, that the universe isn't arbitrary and indifferent to our plight, that we are governed by a supernatural being whom we might induce to favor us. Still, while a staunch defender of the right to say or think virtually anything, he singled out as "the most curious social convention of the great age in which we live" the notion that religious opinions themselves (not just the right to harbor them) "should be respected." Name one widely published intellectual today who would dare to write that.

Mencken would have been deeply dismayed by contemporary public policy discussions: left and right, they are suffused with piety. The rise of virtue talk—which generally takes the form of communitarianism on the left and nostalgia for Victorianism on the right—has resulted in a striking re-moralization of public policy debates. Today, it's rare to hear a non-normative analysis of social problems, one that doesn't focus on failings of individual character or collective virtue: discussions of structural unemployment have given way to jeremiads about the work ethic; approaches to juvenile crime focus on the amorality of America's youth, not the harsh deprivations that shape them. Among academic and media elites, as well as politicians, there is considerable agreement that social pathologies such as crime, drug abuse, teenage pregnancy and chronic welfare dependency are, at least in part, symptomatic of spiritual malaise—loss of faith in God or a more generalized anomie. (Some blame TV.) Try to imagine an avowed atheist running successfully for public office; it's hard enough for politicians to oppose prayer in school.

15   Today, proposals for silent school prayer promise to bring spirituality into the classroom, avoiding religious sectarianism. "Spirituality," a term frequently used to describe the vaguest intimations of supernatural realities, is popularly considered a mark of virtue and is as hostile to atheism as religious belief. Spirituality, after all, is simply religion deinstitutionalized and shorn of any exclusionary doctrines. In a pluralistic marketplace, it has considerable appeal. Spirituality embraces traditional religious and New Age practices, as well as forays into pop psychology and a devotion to capitalism. Exercises in self-esteem and recovery

from various addictions are presented as spiritual endeavors by codependency experts ranging from John Bradshaw to Gloria Steinem. The generation of wealth is spiritualized by best-selling personal development gurus such as Deepak Chopra, author of *The Seven Spiritual Laws of Success,* which offers "the ability to create unlimited wealth with effortless ease." (Some sixty years ago, Napoleon Hill's best-selling *Think and Grow Rich* made readers a similar promise.)

Spirituality discourages you from passing judgment on any of these endeavors: it's egalitarian, ranking no one religion over another, and doesn't require people to choose between faiths. You can claim to be a spiritual person without professing loyalty to a particular dogma or even understanding it. Spirituality makes no intellectual demands on you; all it requires is a general belief in immaterialism (which can be used to increase your material possessions).

In our supposedly secular culture, atheists, like Madelyn Murray O'Hare, are demonized more than renegade believers, like Jimmy Swaggart. Indeed, popular Christian theology suggests that repentant sinners on their way to Heaven will look down upon ethical atheists bound for Hell. Popular spirituality authors, who tend to deny the existence of Hell, and evil, suggest that atheists and other skeptics are doomed to spiritual stasis (the worst fate they can imagine). You might pity such faithless souls, but you wouldn't trust them.

You might not even extend equal rights to them. America's pluralistic ideal does not protect atheism; public support for different belief systems is matched by intolerance of disbelief. According to surveys published in the early 1980s, before today's pre-millennial religious revivalism, nearly 70 percent of all Americans agreed that the freedom to worship "applies to all religious groups, regardless of how extreme their beliefs are"; but only 26 percent agreed that the freedom of atheists to make fun of God and religion "should be legally protected no matter who might be offended." Seventy-one percent held that atheists "who preach against God and religion" should not be permitted to use civic auditoriums. Intolerance for atheism was stronger even than intolerance of homosexuality.

Like heterosexuality, faith in immaterial realities is popularly considered essential to individual morality. When politicians proclaim their belief in God, regardless of their religion, they are signaling their trustworthiness and adherence to traditional moral codes of behavior, as well as their humility. Belief in God levels human hierarchies while offering infallible systems of right and wrong. By declaring your belief, you imply that an omnipotent, omniscient (and benign) force is the source of your values and ideas. You appropriate the rightness of divinity.

20   It's not surprising that belief makes so many people sanctimonious. Whether or not it makes them good is impossible to know. Considering its history, you can safely call organized religion a mixed blessing. Apart from its obvious atrocities—the Crusades or the Salem witch trials—religion is a fount of quotidian oppressions, as anyone who's ever lost a job because of sexual orientation might attest. Of course, religion has been a force of liberation, as well. The civil rights movement demonstrated Christianity's power to inspire and maintain a struggle against injustice. Today, churches provide moral leadership in the fight to

maintain social welfare programs, and in recent history, whether opposing Star Wars or providing sanctuary to Salvadoran refugees, church leaders have lent their moral authority to war resistance. Over time, the clergy may have opposed as many wars as they started.

It is as difficult to try to quantify the effect of organized religion on human welfare as it is to generalize about the character, behavior and beliefs of all religious people. Religion is probably less a source for good or evil in people than a vehicle for them. "Religion is only good for good people," Mary McCarthy wrote, in the days when liberal intellectuals may have deserved a reputation for skepticism. It's equally difficult to generalize about the character of non-believers. Indeed, the disdain for selfrighteousness that atheism and agnosticism tend to encourage make them particularly difficult to defend. How do you make the case for not believing in God without falling into the pit of moral certainty squirming with believers? You can't accurately claim that atheists are particularly virtuous or intelligent or even courageous: some are just resigned to their existential terrors.

Of course, whether or not atheists are in general better or worse citizens than believers, neither the formation of individual character nor religious belief is the business of government. Government is neither competent nor empowered to ease our existential anxieties; its jurisdiction is the material world of hardship and injustice. It can and should make life a little more fair, and, in order to do so, it necessarily enforces some majoritarian notions of moral behavior—outlawing discrimination, for example, or a range of violent assaults. But, in a state that respects individual privacy, law can only address bad behavior, not bad thoughts, and cannot require adherence to what are considered good thoughts—like love of God. Government can help make people comfortable, ensuring access to health care, housing, education and the workplace. But government cannot make people good.

Champions of more religion in public life are hard put to reconcile the prevailing mistrust of government's ability to manage mundane human affairs—like material poverty—with the demand that it address metaphysical problems, like poverty of spirit. It is becoming increasingly popular to argue, for example, that welfare recipients should be deprived of government largess for their own good, to defeat the "culture of dependency," while middle-class believers receive government subsidies (vouchers) to finance the private, religious education of their kids.

Even those "judicial elites" scorned by *Wall Street Journal* editorial writers for their hostility to religion are increasingly apt to favor state support for private religious activities. In a remarkable recent decision, *Rosenberger v. University of Virginia*, the Supreme Court held that private religious groups are entitled to direct public funding. Rosenberger involved a Christian student newspaper at the University of Virginia that was denied funding provided to other student groups because of its religiosity. A state-run institution, the university is subject to the First Amendment strictures imposed on any governmental entity. Reflecting obvious concern about state entanglement in the exercise of religion, the school's funding guidelines prohibited the distribution of student activities funds to religious groups. The guidelines did not discriminate against any particular religion or viewpoint; funds were withheld from any group that "primarily promotes or manifests a particular belief in or about a deity or an ultimate reality." The student paper at issue in the case was actively engaged in proselytizing.

25   Arguing that the University of Virginia had an obligation to pay for the publication of this paper, as it paid for other student activities, editors of the newspaper, *Wide Awake,* sued the school and ultimately prevailed in the Supreme Court, which, like other "elitist" institutions, has become more protective of religion than concerned about its establishment by the state. In a five to four decision, authored by Justice Anthony Kennedy, the Court held that the denial of funding to *Wide Awake* constituted "viewpoint discrimination." Religion was not "excluded as a subject matter" from fundable student discussions, the Court observed; instead funding guidelines excluded discussions of secular issues shaped by "student journalistic efforts with religious editorial viewpoints."

It is one of the ironies of the church/state debate that the equation of Christianity (and other sects) with worldly ideologies, such as Marxism, supply-side economics, theories of white supremacy, agnosticism or feminism, has been championed by the religious right. Those inclined to worship, who believe that their sect offers access to Heaven, are the last people you'd expect to argue that religion is just another product vying for shelf space in the marketplace, entitled to the same treatment as its competitors. You wouldn't expect critics of secularism to suggest that devout Christians are merely additional claimants of individual rights: religion is more often extolled by virtuecrats as an antidote to untrammeled individualism. But new Christian advocacy groups, modeled after advocacy groups on the left, are increasingly portraying practicing Christians as citizens oppressed by secularism and are seeking judicial protection. The American Center for Law and Justice (ACLG), founded by Pat Robertson, is one of the leaders in this movement, borrowing not just most of the acronym but the tactics of the American Civil Liberties Union in a fight for religious "rights."

It's worth noting that, in this battle over rights, science—religion's frequent nemesis—is often reduced to a mere viewpoint as well. Evolution is just a "theory," or point of view, fundamentalist champions of creationism assert; they demand equal time for the teaching of "creation science," which is described as an alternative theory, or viewpoint, about the origin of the universe. "If evolution is true, then it has nothing to fear from some other theory being taught," one Tennessee state senator declared, using liberal faith in the open marketplace of ideas to rationalize the teaching of creationism.

So far, the Supreme Court has rejected this view of creationism as an alternative scientific theory, and intellectual elites who are hostile to secularism but who champion religion's role in public life generally oppose the teaching of "creation science"; they are likely to ground their opposition in creationism's dubious scientific credibility, not its religiosity. Stephen Carter argues that the religious motivations of creationists are irrelevant; the religious underpinnings of laws prohibiting murder do not invalidate them, he observes.

Carter is right to suggest that legislation is often based in religion (which makes you wonder why he complains about secularism). You'd be hard-pressed to find a period in American history when majoritarian religious beliefs did not influence law and custom. From the nineteenth century through the twentieth, anti-vice campaigns—against alcohol, pornography and extramarital or premarital sex—have been overtly religious, fueled by sectarian notions of sin. Domestic relations laws long reflected particular religious ideas about gender roles (which some believe are divinely ordained). But religion's impact on law is usually recognized and deemed problematic only in cases involving minority religious views: Christian ideas about marriage are incorporated into law while the Mormon practice of polygamy is prohibited.

30   I'm not suggesting that religious people should confine their beliefs to the home or that religion, like sex, does not belong in the street. The First Amendment does not give you a right to fornicate in public, but it does protect your right to preach. Secularists are often wrongly accused of trying to purge religious ideals from public discourse. We simply want to deny them public sponsorship. Religious beliefs are essentially private prerogatives, which means that individuals are free to invoke them in conducting their public lives—and that public officials are not empowered to endorse or adopt them. How could our opinions about political issues not be influenced by our personal ideals?

Obviously, people carry their faith in God, Satan, crystals or UFOs into town meetings, community organizations and voting booths. Obviously, a core belief in the supernatural is not severable from beliefs about the natural world and the social order. It is the inevitable effect of religion on public policy that makes it a matter of public concern. Advocates of religiosity extol the virtues or moral habits that religion is supposed to instill in us. But we should be equally concerned with the intellectual habits it discourages.

Religions, of course, have their own demanding intellectual traditions, as Jesuits and Talmudic scholars might attest. Smart people do believe in Gods and devote themselves to uncovering Their truths. But, in its less rigorous, popular forms, religion is about as intellectually challenging as the average self-help book. (Like personal development literature, mass market books about spirituality and religion celebrate emotionalism and denigrate reason. They elevate the "truths" of myths and parables over empiricism.) In its more authoritarian forms, religion punishes questioning and rewards gullibility. Faith is not a function of stupidity but a frequent cause of it.

The magical thinking encouraged by any belief in the supernatural, combined with the vilification of rationality and skepticism, is more conducive to conspiracy theories than it is to productive political debate. Conspiratorial thinking abounds during this period of spiritual and religious revivalism. And, if only small minorities of Americans ascribe to the most outrageous theories in circulation these days—that a cabal of Jewish bankers run the world, that AIDS was invented in a laboratory by a mad white scientist intent on racial genocide—consider the number who take at face value claims that Satanists are conspiring to abuse America's children. According to a 1994 survey by *Redbook*, 70 percent of Americans believed in the existence of Satanic cults engaged in ritual abuse; nearly one-third believed that the FBI and local police were purposefully ignoring their crimes. (They would probably not be convinced by a recent FBI report finding no evidence to substantiate widespread rumors of Satanic abuse.)

As Debbie Nathan and Michael Snedeker report in *Satan's Silence,* these beliefs infect public life in the form of baseless prosecutions and convictions. If religion engenders civic virtue, by imparting "good" values, it also encourages public hysteria by sanctifying bad thinking.

Skepticism about claims of abuse involving Satanism or recovered memories would serve the public interest, not to mention the interests of those wrongly accused, much more than eagerness to believe and avenge all self-proclaimed victims. Skepticism is essential to criminal justice: guilt is supposed to be proven, not assumed. Skepticism, even cynicism, should play an equally important role in political campaigns, particularly today, when it is in such disrepute. Politicians have learned to accuse anyone who questions or opposes them of "cynicism," a popular term of opprobrium associated with spiritual stasis or soullessness. If "cynic" is a synonym for "critic," it's a label any thoughtful person might embrace, even at the risk of damnation.

This is not an apology for generalized mistrust of government. Blind mistrust merely mirrors blind faith and makes people equally gullible. Would a resurgence of skepticism and rationality make us smarter? Not exactly, but it would balance supernaturalism and the habit of belief with respect for empirical realities, which should influence the formulation of public policy more than faith. Rationalism would be an antidote to prejudice, which is, after all, a form of faith. Think, to cite one example, of people whose unreasoned faith in the moral degeneracy of homosexuals leads them to accept unquestioningly the claim that gay teachers are likely to molest their students. Faith denies facts, and that is not always a virtue.

QUESTIONS FOR INQUIRY AND ACTION

1. What is the effect of Kaminer's opening paragraph? What impression does it make on you? Describe her persona and how she relates to her readers.

2. How would you fit this reading with the others in this chapter on faith *communities* and citizenship? What does Kaminer add to the conversation?

3. Research atheism. What does it really mean? Who were some famous atheists and how did they write about their convictions? Do you see commonalities and patterns?

4. Kaminer argues that "the rise of virtue-talk—which generally takes the form of communitarianism on the left and nostalgia for Victorianism on the right—has resulted in a striking re-moralization of public policy debates." Is this true? Conduct a study of television and print news analysis and see how much and what kinds of "virtue-talk" you discover.

CASE STUDY

THE ROLE OF FAITH COMMUNITIES IN THE CIVIL RIGHTS MOVEMENT

ROBERT M. FRANKLIN Another Day's Journey: Faith Communities Renewing American Democracy

Robert M. Franklin is president of the Interdenominational Theological Center in Atlanta, and he has worked at Harvard Divinity School, Colgate-Rochester Divinity School, Candler School of Theology, and the Ford Foundation. He is also the author of Another Day's Journey: Black Churches Confronting the American Crisis *(1997), and* Liberating Visions: Human Fulfillment and Social Justice in African-American Thought *(1990). "Another Day's Journey: Faith Communities Renewing American Democracy" is included in* Religion, Race, and Justice in a Changing America *(New York: The Century Foundation Press, 1999).*

As a concession to a culture profoundly shaped by televised images, I invite you to consider my nomination for the nation's most significant icon depicting religion as a positive force in securing civil and human rights. It is the familiar portrait of Dr. Martin Luther King, Jr., delivering his "I Have a Dream" oration from the steps of the Lincoln Memorial. The image is so familiar that we may fail to grasp its extraordinary, multidimensional character. The black Baptist preacher standing at the foot of the monument to the emancipator is a stunning, riveting symbol suggestive of many values and issues that interest those of us who think about religion and civil rights.

For instance, in the portrait one encounters religion restraining its sectarian energies and harnessing them in the service of public order. Also, one sees a representative of a particular, Christian view of human nature and destiny standing in solidarity with other faith traditions. And one perceives in the King/Lincoln juxtaposition the graceful and mysterious power of religious faith to transform imperfect human beings into courageous exemplars of moral citizenship.

In that 1963 portrait, Lincoln is but a figure carved in marble, his complexity and contradictions concealed in cold stone. Before the stone stood a vibrant incarnation of the indomitable African-American spirit of authentic freedom. Recall the manner in which King began the famous speech: "Fivescore years ago, a great American, in whose symbolic shadow we stand today, signed the Emancipation Proclamation. This momentous decree came as a great beacon light of hope to millions of Negro slaves who had been seared in the flames of withering injustice. It came as a joyous daybreak to end the long night of their captivity. But one hundred years later, the Negro still is not free. . . ."[1] With those words, King paid respect to one of the nation's sacred ancestors, underscored the rude fact that Lincoln's agenda was unfinished, and positioned himself as a moral successor to the slain president.

Also in that extraordinary speech, King drew upon the two major philosophical traditions that have shaped the American culture and character: the covenant tradition based upon biblical notions of American exceptionalism; and the Enlightenment tradition of Immanuel Kant, John Locke, Thomas Jefferson, and others who asserted the inviolable rights of the individual. No one was more skilled than King at interweaving the great and noble ideas from varying intellectual traditions.

5   Recall his words that day as he placed his dream in the context of the hard work that lay before his listeners. "Even though we must face the difficulties of today and tomorrow, I still have a dream. It is a dream deeply rooted in the American dream that one day this nation will rise up and live out the true meaning of its creed—we hold these truths to be self-evident, that all men are created equal."[2] King believed that a dream inspired by references to particular biblical sources could live in dialectical and fruitful tension with ideals embraced by nontheistic rationalists. "I have a dream that one day every valley shall be exalted, every hill and mountain shall be made low, the rough places shall be made plain, and the crooked places shall be made straight and the glory of the Lord will be revealed and all flesh shall see it together."[3]

King did not merely search for common ground, he sought to create it out of the stuff of living traditions. In so doing, he was able to use theology and ethics as resources for renewing American public life. He used theology to prompt people to vote, to run for office, and to be concerned about the moral state of the society. A person who seeks to create common ground, build traditions, craft narratives, and negotiate coalitions exemplifies a quality of character that moral education should seek to inculcate.

We should also acknowledge that using theology and ethics as resources for renewing public life can have unforeseen negative consequences. For instance, many religious people who regard the concept of grace as central and significant to their faith may construe it to mean that they are acceptable to God despite their admitted racist behavior and attitudes, or their indifference to racial justice. Some people suggest that America in the post-civil rights movement era has come a long way through hard work and heroic effort, and that to push further might be counterproductive. We should now focus on celebrating our progress

[1] See James M. Washington, ed., I Have a Dream: Writings and Speeches that Changed the World (San Francisco: Harper San Francisco, 1992), p. 102.
[2] Ibid., p. 104.
[3] Ibid., p. 105.

rather than rousing bitter feelings by advocating additional progress. Grace, thereby, becomes a psychological mechanism that absolves responsibility for the contemporary condition of race relations and civil rights. This is the double edge of grace. Ironically, the theological shift from "salvation by works" to "salvation by grace" encourages complacency with the racial status quo. King understood, clearly, that the Bible and theological concepts could be misappropriated to justify social evil and felt that an important check upon this tendency would involve keeping the Bible and human reason in mutually critical dialogue.

In the pages that follow, I will provide: (1) a brief sketch of the character of black church culture that illustrates how a marginalized and particular religious tradition helped to renew democracy during the modern civil rights movement; (2) an analysis of King's concept of the "beloved community" as an ethical norm that should be used to critique, guide, and inspire public policy and individual behavior; and (3) a brief overview of the heroic role that faith communities are now playing to promote a more just society.

The Revolution Led by Preachers, Church Women, and Sunday School Children

In order to understand Dr. King's journey from Atlanta to the steps of the Lincoln Memorial in 1963, we need to understand something about the culture that produced him, and, thereby, revisit the ways in which culture is a vehicle of moral education. Paul Tillich said that culture is the form of religion, and religion is the substance of culture. If these claims are true, what system of values is available to children being reared in neighborhoods that are scarred by violent crime, adult joblessness, multigenerational dependence, aimlessness, disease, hopelessness, and wretched schools?

10   King's biographers all note that the black church and family were the context in which the boy King learned something about racism, poverty, and religion as a resource for mobilizing social change. James Cone has gone further, noting that the culture of the black church included theological concepts that played a critical role in shaping King's worldview and moral compass. These included notions of human freedom, social justice, black self-love, and collective power.

Historians such as Albert Raboeau (Princeton), the late James Melvin Washington (Union), and Evelyn Brooks Higginbotham (Harvard) have noted that black church culture is an amalgam of numerous symbolic and ritual traditions, including African traditional religions (ATR), Catholic popular piety, Protestant evangelicalism, and Islam. This collection of religious traditions infused the core practices of progressive African-American Christianity that produced King.

These core practices include the following:

1. A multisensory worship experience in which all of a human being's capacity to respond to God is engaged. Worship is conceived to be a sacred drama, a dance with the gods. Hence, drums are present to orchestrate the antiphonal call and response between the people and the deity. Colorful

choir robes and clergy vestments provide visual stimulation. Brass horns, electric guitars, tambourines, and clapping hands electrify the air with sound. Usually, the church kitchen is in operation, sending aromas of soul food wafting throughout the neighborhood. And, this sacred space is animated by lots of touching, hugging, holy kissing, and high-five greetings that bridge the social distance that is common in secular gatherings.

2. Intimate communal prayer, when led by a skilled leader, succeeds in weaving lonely personal concerns into a community of pain, struggle, reconciliation, and hope. Worshippers who approach the altar as separate individuals experience a transformation that sends them away as members of the body of Christ.

3. Choirs give triumphant voice to the church's confidence that it will not be vanquished by evil in the world. Triumphal songs are situationally rational and appropriate if those who sing them regard themselves as warriors in the midst of a great and bloody conflict between good and evil.

4. Prophetic preaching in the black church tradition is the focal point of worship. It is the high, holy moment in the liturgical drama. The brilliant historian of religion, Mircea Eliade, has observed that "for people in traditional societies, religion is a means of extending the world spatially upward so that communication with the other world becomes ritually possible, and extending it temporally backward so that the paradigmatic acts of the gods and mythical ancestors can be continually reenacted and indefinitely recoverable."[4] Eliade helps to illumine the genius of black preaching as he reminds us that words can be deployed to mediate an encounter with the holy. Words can usher the imagination into a transcendent realm where one may be empowered to give one's life on behalf of a noble cause. The black preacher, through the virtuosity of imaginative, narrative, lyrical, and poetic language and the co-creativity of a responsive congregation, unites the sacred and the human realms. Stated briefly, the entire liturgical culture of progressive black churches nurtures political sensibilities. These are the congregations that shape moral character and teach people to care about the moral condition of the society.

The biblical scholar Walter Bruggemann offers a cogent observation about such transformative liturgy: "Every act of a minister who could be prophetic is part of a way of evoking, forming, and reforming an alternative community. This applies to every facet and every practice of ministry. It is a measure of our enculturation that the various acts of ministry (for example, counseling, administration, even liturgy) have taken on lives and functions of their own rather than being seen as elements of the one prophetic ministry of formation and reformation of alternative community."[5]

Bruggemann's comment about "alternative community" reminds us again of King's dream narrative, and the fact that it was crafted in the genre of a sermon

---

[4]*Paraphrased in Lawrence W. Levine,* Black Culture and Black Consciousness: Afro-American Folk Thought from Slavery to Freedom *(New York: Oxford University Press, 1977), pp. 31–32.*
[5]*Walter Bruggemann,* The Prophetic Imagination *(Minneapolis: Fortress Press, 1978), p. 14.*

rather than as an essay, philosophical argument, or lecture. King and his counterparts were products of a liturgical culture that cultivated the capacity to engage in utopian discourse and to act boldly to achieve moral causes.

15   I shall have more to say about utopian discourse, black Christian preaching, and political theology when we consider King's notion of the beloved community.

Congregational Culture Authorizes a Variety of Political Responses

We should note briefly that blacks reared in the congregational context that I have described here, and on which I elaborate in my book, *Another Day's Journey: Black Churches Confronting the American Crisis* (Fortress Press, 1997), opted for a variety of political responses rather than simply the one embraced by King. I have characterized five major responses. They include the pragmatic accommodationists who cooperate with the political and economic status quo in the interest of maintaining social order. In that context, they believe that they can maximize their acquisition of goods. This was the political agenda of Booker T. Washington and the National Baptist Convention leader, Dr. Joseph H. Jackson. Accommodationists tend to embrace a theology of creation that emphasizes abundance in the natural order. A second response is that of the prophetic radicals who challenge the system to improve the life prospects of marginalized people. This was the orientation of W. E. B. Du Bois and Dr. King. Radicals tend to develop a theology of liberation and a view of God as an ally of oppressed people.

A third response could be characterized as redemptive nationalism, aimed at avoiding the conventional power structure in order to create a separate, ethnically pure order. This was the social vision of Marcus Garvey and of the young Malcolm X and Nation of Islam. Nationalists work from a theology of redemption in which God seeks to restore and redeem the halcyon days of the past, when ethnic kingdoms were distinct and uncontaminated by diversity. The fourth response is characterized as grassroots revivalism, which condemns and avoids the political systems of this world and focuses instead upon individual salvation and moral reform. This agenda was advanced by William J. Seymour, the father of black Pentecostalism. In this theological arena, God is working to save individuals by transforming them one by one. Faith does not have social consequences. Finally, the fifth response is positive thought materialism, which is indifferent to social justice and concerned primarily with opportunities to maximize individual health, wealth, and success. This is spirituality for the upwardly mobile classes who lack a social conscience. This is the outlook of Reverend "Ike," the New York religious showman, an outlook that may lack a full-blown example earlier in black history. Materialists work from a theology of prosperity in which God is a provider of material bounty.

This typology of political theologies should serve to remind us that black church culture is not a monolith, that it fosters and celebrates diversity. I am simply making the point that a variety of political responses emerged from the ecology of black worship culture. Those responses produced a variety of theological reflections upon the nature of the state, political objectives such as voting, citizenship, and running for office, and the relationship between religious and civil obligations.

The Underside of American Christianity

It is perplexing to consider that Christianity has had two thousand years to eradicate the multiple and overlapping forms of oppression based upon ethnicity, race, creed, culture, region, class, and gender, but has failed to do so. Why is this the case? And, more to the point of our discussion, why haven't Protestantism and Catholicism succeeded in canceling the power and grip of racism on the minds and behavior of the masses of their adherents? Is this a theological crisis? Does the tradition possess the resources to address racism in a compelling manner? Is it a human and cultural crisis that represents, yet again, the depths and variety of sinful human nature? King framed it poignantly when he noted the following in his "Letter from a Birmingham Jail":

> I have traveled the length and breadth of Alabama, Mississippi, and all the other southern states. On sweltering summer days and crisp autumn mornings I have looked at her beautiful churches with their lofty spires pointing heavenward. I have beheld the impressive outlay of her massive religious education buildings. Over and over again I have found myself asking: "What kind of people worship here? Who is their God? Where were their voices when the lips of Governor Barnett dripped with words of interposition and nullification? Where were they when Governor Wallace gave the clarion call for defiance and hatred? Where were their voices of support when tired, bruised, and weary Negro men and women decided to rise from the dark dungeons of complacency to the bright hills of creative protest?"[6]

20   Although prophetic religion should hold the state accountable for the moral exercise of power, when religion goes astray who can call it back to its foundation? This is where King's methodological and symbolic eclecticism in drawing up various traditions proved valuable. The biblical and the Enlightenment traditions could critique and correct each other.

Returning to my earlier comments about King's preaching as an instance of utopian discourse, I would like to briefly discuss the central thrust of King's political theology.

The Beloved Community as a Political and Ethical Norm

Moral philosopher and former Clinton domestic policy adviser William Galston has noted that "utopian thought is the political branch of moral philosophy" and that "among its many functions it guides our deliberation in devising courses of action, justifies our actions so that the grounds of action are reasons that others ought to accept, and serves as the basis for the evaluation of existing institutions and practices."[7] Utopian discourse becomes moral discourse as it seeks to guide action. It enables us to "imaginatively reconcile and transmute" the "contradictions of experience."

---

[6]*Washington,* I Have a Dream, p. 97.
[7]*William Galston,* Justice and the Human Good *(Chicago: University of Chicago Press, 1980).*

In his final book, *Where Do We Go From Here: Chaos or Community?*, King noted that the "good and just society is neither the thesis of capitalism nor the antithesis of Communism, but a socially conscious democracy which reconciles the truths of individualism and collectivism."[8] He characterized his political philosophy with the term "democratic socialism." In his November 1966 Gandhi Memorial Lecture at Howard University, he said, "Public accommodations did not cost the nation anything; the right to vote did not cost the nation anything. Now we are grappling with basic class issues between the privileged and underprivileged. In order to solve this problem, not only will it mean the restructuring of American society but it will cost the nation something. . . ."[9]

King had always been attentive to the economic dimensions of authentic liberation. At the end of his life, his public ministry focused upon the nation's moral obligation to improve the economic plight of the least advantaged members of the community. When he was killed in Memphis, King was working on behalf of sanitation workers, and he was headed back to Washington, D.C., to lead a national "Poor People's Campaign." Had he lived, there would have been another great speech and another iconic photograph to juxtapose with the 1963 image.

Faith Communities in Pursuit of the Beloved Community

25   Today, many of the nation's 320,000 communities of faith are stepping up to tackle Dr. King's unfinished agenda. This includes the more than 70,000 African-American congregations that were part of the coalition of conscience that sustained the Civil Rights Movement and expanded democracy. In many distressed neighborhoods, churches are the only indigenous institutions that have significant assets: talented leaders, credibility, track records of service, armies of potential volunteers, physical space, financial resources, and the spiritual resources necessary to sustain courage and hope amidst adversity. Long after other secular nonprofit service agencies disappear for lack of funding, or employers disappear because of the cost of doing business, or government agencies disappear due to devolution, churches are there to pick up the pieces of people's lives, affirming their dignity and feeding bodies and souls.

Congregations provide basic charity, sustained nurture, social services, political advocacy, and comprehensive community development, on behalf of the poor. Congregations and clergy are helping to sustain civil society and resisting the nihilism of which Cornel West speaks.

Faith communities are working to renew American democracy and, as such, have earned a seat at the table of future public/private ventures. The most creative leaders of the black church tradition understand that the future of the beloved community will depend upon expanding our notion of civil rights to include basic economic rights and the fruits of our labor. Churches and clergy are working overtime to become leaders and partners in the community development enterprise.

---

[8]*Martin Luther King, Jr.*, Where Do We Go From Here: Chaos or Community? *(Boston: Beacon Press, 1967), p. 187.*
[9]*King Center Archives.*

To ensure that there will be thoughtful religious leaders capable of moving the nation forward, a number of institutions are engaged in exciting and noteworthy projects. Harvard Divinity School's Summer Leadership Institute trains clergy and lay leaders in the art of innovative community economic development. Through a new initiative called "ITC FaithFactor," the Interdenominational Theological Center provides training, technical support, and vision to the vast army of religiously motivated volunteers who reside, work, and worship in and around this nation's most distressed neighborhoods. The "Sojourners" organization has helped to nurture a broad coalition of religious leaders (Call to Renewal) concerned with the moral decay as reflected in the resurgence of racism and other social evils.

Despite these resources and many others, the larger question remains: Can religion provide something unique and significant to the pursuit of a just society? Many of the revolutionaries of the 1960s, tutored by the writings of Karl Marx, answered negatively. Religion was (is) an opiate that enables people to tolerate injustice in pious quietude. Ironically, many black revolutionaries of the period had to admit that it was the black church and prophetic Christianity that were mobilizing people to risk their lives in the pursuit of freedom. Although many found escape and refuge in the church, others felt that authentic biblical religion is inescapably wedded to God's concern for a just social order. In fact, it is impossible to read the Hebrew prophets of the Hebrew Bible (Old Testament) without recognizing that God seems to have a lot to say about how people who enjoy privilege and power should relate to less advantaged people. God does not ignore politics, and politics involves a proactive concern for people with limited options and few material goods.

30   As religious leaders today have sought to apply this biblical agenda, or what the late theologian John Howard Yoder called "the politics of Jesus," they have felt the frustration of talking about justice, equality, and love in purely theological terms. Our largely secular society has found it possible to ignore such theological appeals, preferring instead the rhetoric of politics and law. Politicians and lawyers often ignore the contentious and fragmented presence of sectarian religious people. And many religious leaders have reconciled themselves to a marginal role in public life and public policy.

However, some ministers and lay people have resisted marginalization. Although some ministers have elected to run for public office—William Gray, Father Robert J. Drinan, Jesse Jackson, among others—and bring religious rhetoric into the public square, the majority have sought to find ways to talk about the biblical political agenda in their local parishes. It is at that level that tough decisions have to be made about what one will and can say in public about the "hard questions" affecting national life.

Frustration with being regarded as "a marginal voice" often encourages clergy to embrace the language of the modern state. Preachers begin to talk like politicians, and while gaining some credibility as political power brokers, in the process they tend to lose the prophetic edge that they can and should bring to the political debate and the process of creating a better society. This is a temptation to which Dr. King never yielded. He consistently employed theological concepts and language to challenge the modern state to be more just and inclusive. He gave opinions on practical and concrete political matters, but only insofar as they were outgrowths of the theological and ethical principles he espoused.

It is humbling, hopeful, and empowering to consider that preachers, church women, and Sunday school children led a revolution in our lifetime. They marched, prayed, voted, and challenged the nation to, in the words of Arthur Schlesinger, Jr., "conform America's political reality to her political rhetoric." They have now passed the baton to us.

In the words of a great rabbi, "the world is equally balanced between good and evil, our next act will tip the scale."

MARTIN LUTHER KING, JR. Speech at Holt Street Baptist Church

Martin Luther King, Jr. (1929–1968) was one of the most famous and respected orators and civil rights leaders in American history. An ordained Baptist minister, he served with his father as co-pastor of Ebenezer Baptist Church in Atlanta from 1960–1968. He founded the Southern Christian Leadership Conference in Atlanta in 1957 and served as its president from 1957–1968. He was named Time's *Man of the Year in 1963 and won the Nobel Prize for Peace in 1964. His sermon "I Have a Dream" (1963) was an instant classic, and he was the author of several books including* Where Do We Go from Here: Chaos or Community? *(1967). This speech is a portion of one delivered at Holt Street Baptist Church in Montgomery, Alabama on December 5, 1955, shortly after Rosa Parks's participation in the Montgomery Bus Boycott. The speech was included in the fourteen-part PBS television series* Eyes on the Prize: America's Civil Rights Years *and is reprinted in the* Eyes on the Prize Civil Rights Reader *(New York: Penguin, 1991).*

We are here this evening for serious business. We are here in a general sense because first and foremost we are American citizens, and we are determined to apply our citizenship to the fullness of its means. We are here because of our love for democracy, because of our deep-seated belief that democracy transformed from thin paper to thick action is the greatest form of government on earth. But we are here in a specific sense, because of the bus situation in Montgomery. We are here because we are determined to get the situation corrected.

This situation is not at all new. The problem has existed over endless years. For many years now Negroes in Montgomery and so many other areas have been inflicted with the paralysis of crippling fear on buses in our community. On so many occasions, Negroes have been intimidated and humiliated and oppressed because of the sheer fact that they were Negroes. I don't have time this evening to go into the history of these numerous cases. . . . But at least one stands before us now with glaring dimensions. Just the other day, just last Thursday to be exact, one of the finest citizens in Montgomery—not one of the finest Negro citizens but one of the finest citizens in Montgomery—was taken from a bus and carried to jail and arrested because she refused to get up to give her seat to a white person. . . . Mrs. Rosa Parks is a fine person. And since it had to happen I'm happy it happened to a person like Mrs. Parks, for nobody can doubt the boundless outreach of her integrity. Nobody can doubt the height of her character, nobody can doubt the depth of her Christian commitment and devotion to the teachings of Jesus. . . .

And just because she refused to get up, she was arrested. . . . You know my friends there comes a time when people get tired of being trampled over by the iron feet of oppression. There comes a time my friends when people get tired of being flung across the abyss of humiliation where they experience the bleakness of nagging despair. There comes a time when people get tired of being pushed out of the glittering sunlight of life's July and left standing amidst the piercing chill of an Alpine November.

We are here, we are here this evening because we're tired now. Now let us say that we are not here advocating violence. We have overcome that. I want it to be known throughout Montgomery and throughout this nation that we are Christian people. We believe in the Christian religion. We believe in the teachings of Jesus. The only weapon that we have in our hands this evening is the weapon of protest. And secondly, this is the glory of America, with all of its faults. This is the glory of our democracy. If we were incarcerated behind the iron curtains of a Communistic nation we couldn't do this. If we were trapped in the dungeon of a totalitarian regime we couldn't do this. But the great glory of American democracy is the right to protest for right.

5   My friends, don't let anybody make us feel that we ought to be compared in our actions with the Ku Klux Klan or with the White Citizens' Councils. There will be no crosses burned at any bus stops in Montgomery. There will be no white persons pulled out of their homes and taken out to some distant road and murdered. There will be nobody among us who will stand up and defy the Constitution of this nation. We only assemble here because of our desire to see right exist.

My friends, I want it to be known that we're going to work with grim and firm determination to gain justice on the buses in this city. And we are not wrong, we are not wrong in what we are doing. If we are wrong, then the Supreme Court of this Nation is wrong. If we are wrong, the Constitution of the United States is wrong. If we are wrong, God Almighty is wrong. If we are wrong, Jesus of Nazareth was merely a utopian dreamer and never came down to earth. If we are wrong, justice is a lie. And we are determined here in Montgomery to work and fight until justice runs down like water and righteousness like a mighty stream.

I want to say that with all of our actions we must stick together. Unity is the great need of the hour. And if we are united, we can get many of the things that we not only desire but which we justly deserve. And don't let anybody frighten you. We are not afraid of what we are doing, because we are doing it within the law. There is never a time in our American democracy that we must ever think we're wrong when we protest. We reserve that right. . . .

We, the disinherited of this land, we who have been oppressed so long are tired of going through the long night of captivity. And we are reaching out for the daybreak of freedom and justice and equality. . . . In all of our doings, in all of our deliberations. . . whatever we do, we must keep God in the forefront. Let us be Christian in all of our action. And I want to tell you this evening that it is not enough for us to talk about love. Love is one of the pinnacle parts of the Christian faith. There is another side called justice. And justice is really love in [application]. Justice is love correcting that which would work against love. . . . Standing beside love is always justice. And we are only using the tools of justice. Not only are we using the tools of persuasion but we've got to use the tools of coercion. Not only is this thing a process of education but it is also a process of legislation.

And as we stand and sit here this evening, and as we prepare ourselves for what lies ahead, let us go out with a grim and bold determination that we are going to stick together. We are going to work together. Right here in Montgomery when the history books are written in the future, somebody will have to say "There lived a race of people, black people, fleecy locks and black complexion, of people who had the moral courage to stand up for their rights." And thereby they injected a new meaning into the veins of history and of civilization. And we're gonna do that. God grant that we will do it before it's too late.

BERNICE JOHNSON REAGON Interview

> *Bernice Johnson Reagon, then Bernice Johnson, is a scholar, composer, singer, and activist. She is Distinguished Professor of History at American University, curator emerita at the Smithsonian National Museum of American History, and artistic director of Sweet Honey in the Rock, the renowned African American women's a cappella ensemble she founded in 1973. She is the author of, among other works,* We'll Understand It Better By and By: Pioneering African-American Gospel Composers *(1992) and* We Who Believe in Freedom: Sweet Honey in the Rock: Still on the Journey *(1993). During the Civil Rights Movement she was a student at all-black Albany State College and secretary of the local chapter of the N.A.A.C.P. This interview is an excerpt from one taken in 1986; it is included in the fourteen-part PBS television series* Eyes on the Prize: America's Civil Rights Years *and is reprinted in the* Eyes on the Prize Civil Rights Reader *(New York: Penguin, 1991).*

Growing up in Albany, I learned that if you bring black people together, you bring them together with a song. To this day, I don't understand how people think they can bring anybody together without a song.

Now, the singing tradition in Albany was congregational. There were not soloists, there were song leaders.

When you ask somebody to lead a song, you're asking them to plant a seed. The minute you start the song, then the song is created by everybody there. It's almost like a musical explosion that takes place. But the singing in the movement was different from the singing in church. The singing is the kind of singing where you disappear.

The song-singing I heard in Albany I'd never heard before in my life, in spite of the fact that I was from that congregational singing culture. The only difference was that in Albany, Georgia, black people were doing some stuff around being black people. I know a lot of people talk about it being a movement and when they do a movement they're talking about buses and jobs and the ICC ruling, and the Trailways bus station. Those things were just incidents that gave us an excuse to be something of ourselves. It's almost like where we had been working before we had a chance to do that stuff was in a certain kind of space, and when we did those marches and went to jail, we expanded the space we could operate in, and that was echoed in the singing. It was a bigger, more powerful singing. . . .

5   After this first march, we're at Union Baptist Church, Charlie Jones [of SNCC] looks at me and said, "Bernice, sing a song." And I started "Over My Head I See Trouble in the Air." By the time I got to where "trouble" was supposed to be, I didn't see any trouble, so I put "freedom" in there. And I guess that was the first time I really understood using what I'd been given in terms of songs. I'd always been a singer but I had always, more or less, been singing what other people taught me to sing. That was the first time I had the awareness that these songs were mine and I could use them for what I needed them to. This sort of thing was important because I ended up being arrested in the second wave of arrests in Albany, Georgia. And I was in jail. And when we got to jail, Slater King was already in jail, and he said, "Bernice, is that you?" And I said, "Yeah." And he said, "Sing a song."

The voice I have now, I got the first time I sang in a movement meeting, after I got out of jail. Now I'm past that first meeting in Union Baptist, I've done "Lift Every Voice and Sing." I am a song leader, I lead every song in jail, but I did not lead the songs in jail in the voice I have now. The voice I have now I got that night and I'd never heard it before in my life. At that meeting, they did what they usually do. They said, "Bernice, would you lead us in a song?" And I did the same first song, "Over My Head I See Freedom in the Air," but I'd never heard that voice before. I had never been that me before. And once I became that me, I have never let that me go.

I like people to know when they deal with the movement that there are these specific things, but there is a transformation that took place inside of the people that needs to also be quantified in the picture. And the singing is just the echo of that. If you have a people who are transformed and they create the sound that lets you know they are new people, then certainly you've never heard it before. They have also never heard it before, because they've never been that before.

When I was in the mass meetings, I would be part of a group up at the front leading the songs. There would be Rutha Harris, Andrew Reed, Charlie Jones, Cordell Reagon, Charles Sherrod. We were all young people. The meetings always started with these freedom songs and the freedom songs were in-between all of the activities of the mass meetings. Most of the mass meeting was singing—there was more singing than there was talking. Most of the work that was done in terms of taking care of movement business had to do with nurturing the people who had come, and there would be two or three people who would talk but basically songs were the bed of everything. I'd had songs in college and high school and church, but in the movement all the words sounded differently. "This Little Light of Mine, I'm Going to Let It Shine," which I'd sung all my life, said something very different: "All in the street, I'm going to let it shine." I'd never even heard that before, 'cause, I mean, who would go into the street? That was not where you were supposed to be if you were an upstanding Christian person. "All in the jailhouse, I'm going to let it shine"—all of these new concepts of where, if you said it, this is where you could be.

What I can remember is being very alive and very clear, the clearest I've ever been in my life. I knew that every minute, I was doing what I was supposed to do. That was the way it was in jail, too, and on the marches. In "We Shall Overcome" there's a verse that says "God is on our side," and there was a theological discussion that said maybe we should say, "We are on God's side." God was lucky to have us in Albany doing what we were doing. I mean, what better case would he have? So it was really like God would be very, very happy to be on my side. There's a bit of arrogance about that, but that was the way it felt.

10   I think Albany settled the issue of jail and I think songs helped to do that because in the songs you could just name the people who were trying to use this against you—Asa Kelley, who was the mayor, Chief Pritchett, who was the police. This behavior is new behavior for black people in the United States of America. You would every once in a while have a crazy black person going up against some white person and they would hang him. But this time, with a song, there was nothing they could do to block what we were saying. Not only did you call their names and say what you wanted to say, but they could not stop your sound. Singing is different than talking because no matter what they do, they would have to kill me to stop me from singing, if they were arresting me. Sometimes they would plead and say, "Please stop singing." And you would just know that your word is being heard. There was a real sense of platformness and clearly empowerment, and it was like just saying, "Put me in jail, that's not an issue of power. My freedom has nothing to do with putting me in jail." And so there was this joy.

JAMES LAWSON Student Nonviolent Coordinating Committee Statement of Purpose

The Student Nonviolent Coordinating Committee was formed during a meeting on April 15, 1960, of student leaders of the southern sit-in movement. One hundred twenty-six student delegates from fifty-six colleges in twelve southern states, and students from nineteen northern schools as well as thirteen organizations and fifty-seven observers were represented at the meeting at Shaw University in Raleigh, North Carolina. Originally, the group called itself the Temporary Student Nonviolent Coordinating Committee because they believed that they would accomplish their mission within five years. Reverend James Lawson, who was expelled from Vanderbilt University Divinity School because he refused to withdraw from the protest movement, drafted this Statement of Purpose, dated May 14, 1960. It is reprinted in the Eyes on the Prize Civil Rights Reader *(New York: Penguin, 1991).*

Carrying out the mandate of the Raleigh Conference to write a statement of purpose for the movement, the Temporary Student Nonviolent Coordinating Committee submits for careful consideration the following draft. We urge all local, state or regional groups to examine it closely. Each member of our movement must work diligently to understand the depths of nonviolence.

We affirm the philosophical or religious ideal of nonviolence as the foundation of our purpose, the pre-supposition of our faith, and the manner of our action. Nonviolence as it grows from Judaic-Christian traditions seeks a social order of justice permeated by love. Integration of human endeavor represents the crucial first step towards such a society.

Through nonviolence, courage displaces fear; love transforms hate. Acceptance dissipates prejudice; hope ends despair. Peace dominates war; faith reconciles doubt. Mutual regard cancels enmity. Justice for all overthrows injustice. The redemptive community supersedes systems of gross social immorality.

Love is the central motif of nonviolence. Love is the force by which God binds man to himself and man to man. Such love goes to the extreme; it remains loving and forgiving even in the midst of hostility. It matches the capacity of evil to inflict suffering with an even more enduring capacity to absorb evil, all the while persisting in love.

5   By appealing to conscience and standing on the moral nature of human existence, nonviolence nurtures the atmosphere in which reconciliation and justice become actual possibilities.

Writing Style

PUBLIC LETTERS

Martin Luther King, Jr.'s "Letter from Birmingham Jail" is one of the most famous examples in American history of a *public letter*, or an *open letter*, that is, a letter addressed to a specific person or persons, but aimed generally at a large public reading audience. He wrote the letter in response to a statement published in the *Birmingham News*. Written by eight clergymen, the statement urged King and the activists in the Southern Christian Leadership Conference not to demonstrate for civil rights in Birmingham. You can read this statement along with the text of King's letter, and even listen to King himself reading the letter, at *The Martin Luther King, Jr. Papers Project* Web site at Stanford University: http://www.stanford.edu/group/King/popular_requests/

Public letters are generally longer and more substantive than letters to the editor, which are also a form of public letter. Public letters are often published on the editorial pages of newspapers. However, writers can also buy advertising space and print their letters as full-page advertisements in newspapers or magazines. More recently, the Internet has become a common forum for public letters, as it is relatively easy to publish material and to respond to others' arguments on it. King could have responded to the eight clergymen privately, in one collective letter copied to each of them, or in individual letters. Instead, he chose to respond openly and to publish his response in the newspaper, as they had done. By choosing this route, the clergymen sought public support for their views. Likewise, King ensured that this matter—which was a public matter—would not be relegated to private discussion. The citizens of Birmingham, the state of Alabama, and the United States as a whole deserved to be informed about various perspectives on racial integration and civil rights. If you are going to publish a letter openly addressing a particular figure or group of people, you will want to keep in the mind the following:

- *Write for a dual audience.* You choose to write a public letter so that you can seek public support for your views, rather than simply try to persuade a certain individual or organization. Therefore, you will be writing for two audiences simultaneously—the person or persons whose actions you want to comment on, and the larger public who will read the source in which you publish your thoughts. All of your choices as a writer will be made with this fact in mind. For example, notice how King uses the second person. He crafts the letter as if it were private, addressing it "My dear fellow clergymen" and referring to the audience as "you" throughout the letter. Yet that "you" simultaneously addresses the wider reading public. The use of "you" gives the letter a feeling of intimacy and inclusiveness. An alternative would be to write an open letter to the people of Alabama referring to the eight clergymen as "they" and "them." What do you think the difference would be in the effect on both audiences?

- *Embrace your public audience.* Furthermore, if you want the reading public to take action on your letter, embrace them, even if indirectly. Observe how King often refers to "we" and "us," especially in such pronouncements as "We are caught in an inescapable network of mutuality, tied in a single garment of destiny. Whatever affects one directly, affects all indirectly." While the "we" and "us" refer to himself and the eight clergymen, they also refer to all the citizens reading his words. Similarly, when King expresses his disappointment in "the white moderate," he can disarm the specific clergymen by taking some of the blame off their own shoulders, while he suggests they share that blame with the white moderate reading public, who are in a position to make change through their sheer numbers.

continued on next page

- *Garner public support by showing you understand the opposer's point of view.* King could easily attack or dismiss the views of the clergymen. Instead, he chooses to show his understanding of their worldview before he presents his own alternative. His letter opens with his statement that he decided to respond to the clergymen's letter because "I feel that you are men of genuine good will and that your criticisms are sincerely set forth." Throughout he refers to the men as brothers, and concedes points where it is appropriate; for instance, he tells them "You are quite right in calling for negotiation." He extends credit to them, insisting "I am sure that none of you would want to rest content with the superficial kind of social analysis that deals merely with effects and does not grapple with underlying causes."

- *Anticipate counterarguments.* The need for public letters and open debate rarely arises from problems for which there is only one right solution, or one way to achieve the solution. Therefore, you need to anticipate the arguments that will oppose and critique your own. King works the clergymen's concerns into his own document—often by directly quoting them—from their notion that King is an "outsider coming in" to their community, to their fear that the demonstrators will demand immediate change. He mirrors their concerns and anticipates their responses to his concerns. By repeating their concerns in his letter, he shows that he read and understood their argument. At the same time, by anticipating their responses, he shows that he is a step ahead in his thinking.

- *Find common ground.* You will gather more support from the public as well as the individual whose work you are responding to if you find common grounds for concern and a common language and culture to draw upon. King refers frequently to figures, events, and ideals his audiences also hold dear: Jesus, St. Paul, Martin Luther, Thomas Jefferson, the Boston Tea Party, and the American Dream. He calls upon the assumption of their shared concern for God and the growth of "the church" (meaning all of the clergymen's congregations and denominations) by proclaiming that "the judgment of God is upon the church as never before" and that every day he meets young people "whose disappointment with the church has turned into outright disgust." All of these clergymen, and the adults in the community who are reading the newspaper, have a vested interest in keeping young people engaged with the church.

- *Recommend specific action for your audience to take.* Finally, while you've got the attention of the public, instead of simply airing your grievances, make specific recommendations for taking the action that will begin to implement your solution. King announces almost immediately that "in any nonviolent campaign there are four basic steps: collection of the facts to determine whether injustices exist; negotiation, self-purification; and direct action." Outline the ways in which he goes on to explain each of these in his letter, ending with a call for direct action.

QUESTIONS FOR INQUIRY AND ACTION

1. What are the unique qualities of the black churches in the United States? How have they contributed to the civil rights movement and ongoing social justice movements? How can white churches learn from them, from their theology to their liturgy and rituals of worship?

2. Churches are perhaps the most segregated communities left in the United States. Why do you think this is so? And why do you think there's no real movement to integrate them?

3. Bernice Johnson Reagon speaks to a *transformation* that needs to take place in order for a movement truly to effect change. The movement for social justice is beyond mere politics and economics; it needs to transform people in order to work. What do you think and feel about this? Read Darrell Scott's "Our Greatest Need" in the case study to Chapter Six.

4. Some theologians interpret the commandment "Thou shalt not take the Lord's name in vain" not primarily to mean that we shouldn't swear, but that we shouldn't act as if we know what God wants; in other words, that we shouldn't act in God's name. Reflect on this. How do you respond to it? How would that affect the actions of faith communities around the world?

5. Wendy Kaminer states in "The Last Taboo" that "government can't make you good." Its purpose is not moral. What is its purpose? How can faith communities and government work together? *Should* they work together?

6. Research the roles of religion and faith communities in various struggles worldwide, from the troubles in Northern Ireland to the ongoing battles between Israelis and the Palestinians in the Middle East. In what ways are the struggles religious, and in what ways are they political? Where can you draw the line? Research also the movement against apartheid in South Africa. You might start with the works of Bishop Desmond Tutu to understand the work of faith communities in overcoming the apartheid system. How have religious communities helped or hindered these struggles?

CHAPTER 12

Virtual Communities

Technology is neither good nor bad, nor even neutral. Technology is one part of the complex of relationships that people form with each other and the world around them; it simply cannot be understood outside of that concept.

Samuel Collins

GETTING STARTED: Imagining the Future

Fritz Lang's science fiction film *Metropolis* (1927) depicts a society interdependent with industry and technology. Lang's vision of human life in the year 2027 is pessimistic, the towering buildings and glittering machines, which a few privileged elite enjoy, are kept running by masses of impoverished workers. As you study this still shot from the film, consider the following questions:

1. What are the distinguishing features of Lang's Metropolis? What adjectives might you use to describe it?

2. Would you want to live there? Why or why not?

3. When you imagine the future 100 years from now (as Lang did), what does your vision look like? How does it compare with Lang's? What is the role of technology in your imagined community?

4. Bonnie Nardi and Vicki O'Day use the same image to open their book *Information Ecologies: Using Technology with Heart.* Read their selection, which follows the introduction, and discuss how their view of technology, Lang's view, and your view compare.

In this final chapter, we explore communities defined primarily by the influence of technology, both as a subject of interest (MP3s, television shows, movies, virtual worlds, video games, fan groups, and so on) and as a tool for helping members meet and communicate with one another (cell phones, chat rooms, list servs, email, news groups, MOOs and MUDs, and

so on). To focus our inquiry into such a diverse subject, this chapter's readings focus on the possibilities and hazards that television and the Internet present to our communities.

As Samuel Collins reminds us, our concerns with virtual communities are the same concerns we have with all of our other communities. We want to know how we can best live with one another. The readings in this chapter, while introducing new types of communities, also push us to question our assumptions about existing communities. For example, David Bell, in "Community and Cyberculture," argues that criticisms of virtual communities often assume that more traditional communities are healthy and vibrant.

New media technologies promise not only to improve the health and richness of our communal life, but to create new opportunities for inquiry and action. Advocates claim technology will enable us to develop our democracy by encouraging greater numbers of citizens to participate in the political process. Critics worry that it will weaken democracy by dumbing down the rigor of our debates, dissolving the face-to-face public sphere, and actually segregating people more than they are now. As this is an issue that the United States and other countries will face for years to come, we close the book with a case study on the future of the Internet and its use in creating and sustaining democracy.

BONNIE A. NARDI AND VICKI O'DAY Framing Conversations about Technology

> *Bonnie Nardi is an anthropologist at Agilent Technologies in Agilent Laboratories. Vicki O'Day, formerly a researcher at the Xerox Palo Alto Research Center, is now a graduate student in anthropology at the University of California at Santa Cruz. Using observations and interviews, Nardi and O'Day studied how people interact with technology in a variety of situations, including workplaces, schools, homes, and civic organizations. To emphasize the local connections between technology and its users, they frame their ethnographic studies around the metaphor* information ecologies, *"a system of people, practices, values, and technologies in a particular local environment" (49). The following selection is from Chapter Two of their book,* Information Ecologies: Using Technology with Heart *(Cambridge and London: The MIT Press, 1999).*

The seventy-year-old film *Metropolis* is a reminder that our current questions and concerns about technology have a long history. Many of the particular technologies we experience now are fairly new—voicemail, cellular phones, the Internet, and many more. But the challenge of responding well to technological change goes back at least to the invention of the earliest machines.

There is no question about the imaginative appeal of technology, not just in the cityscape of Metropolis but in our own world today. With the help of technology, we can understand genetic structure, take pictures of stars being born, and perform in utero surgery to save the life of an unborn baby. These are accomplishments that give us a sense of wonder and appreciation for human inventiveness. They celebrate our abilities and extend our connections with the natural world.

When we adopt new technologies, we face uncertainty about how our quality of life may change. The development of new technology affects the nature of work, school, family life, commerce, politics, and war. We might expect that anything with such profound influence on the way we live would be subject to considerable scrutiny and debate. But most of us don't see ourselves as influential participants who can offer informed opinions about the uses of technology. On the contrary, new technologies tend to be mystifying. They resist our attempts to get a grip on what they do and how they work.

As long as we think we do not have enough expertise to engage in substantive discussions about technology, we are effectively prevented from having an impact on the directions it may take. But there *are* opportunities for discussion and intervention in the process of technological growth and change, and it is important to take advantage of them. We believe that the lack of broad participation in conversations about technology seriously impoverishes the ways technologies are brought into our everyday lives. Our aim is to show how more people can be more fully engaged in important discussions and decisions about technology.

5   This book is a personal response to the prospect of increasing technological change. Our perspective comes from our experience as researchers in Silicon Valley and as users and consumers of technology. We, Bonnie Nardi and Vicki O'Day, have been trained in (respectively) anthropology and computer science. We have each crossed boundaries into the other's discipline during our years of working in industrial research labs, including those at Hewlett-Packard, Apple Computer, and Xerox. Both of us have designed and implemented computer software, and both of us have conducted empirical studies of how people use technology.

Our empirical studies are ethnographic studies, which means that we go out into the "field" to study situations in which people are going about their business in their own ways, doing whatever they normally do. For us, the field has included offices, libraries, schools, and hospitals. We observe everyday practices and interview people in their own settings over a period of time, to learn more about the complicated and often surprising workings of a particular environment. We bring the insights we develop from ethnographic studies to help in the design of technological tools that will be a good fit for the people who use them.

We consider ourselves critical friends of technology. We want to see more examples of good, useful applications of technology out in the world, like those we have seen in some of our studies. But as we do our fieldwork, read the newspapers, and watch the developments around us, we are sometimes troubled by what we see. Technical developments in everything from telephone menus to cloning and genetic engineering have potentially disturbing effects.

We have noticed that people seem to distance themselves from a critical evaluation of the technologies in their lives, as if these technologies were inevitable forces of nature rather than things we design and choose. Perhaps some of this lack of critical attention is due to the sheer excitement at the novelty and promise of new technology, which makes it easy to move ahead quickly and without reflection. For example, NetDays focused on wiring public schools for Internet access were carried out with good intentions, but we have seen that some of our local schools have had a difficult time coping with the new technology once they have it.

We are troubled when people ignore the human intentionality and accountability behind the use of technological tools. For example, when one of us recently forgot to pay a credit card bill and saw her credit card temporarily disabled as a result, she called her bank to ask it to accelerate the process of turning the card back on. She assumed that a twenty-year history as a good customer would make a difference. The response from each of the three customer service people she talked to was the same: "You know, you're dealing with a computer here." Well, not exactly. We are also dealing with people who solve problems and make decisions, or we should be. Human expertise, judgment, and creativity can be supported, but not replaced, by computer-based tools.

10   Many people have misgivings about technology, but most of the time we do not express them. Our own specific concerns are unimportant in this discussion. What is important is that each of us develop and use our own critical sensibilities about the technologies that affect us. . . .

The Rhetoric of Inevitability

To achieve a shift in perception and prepare for conversations for action, we must look beyond some of the common rhetoric about technology. As we read and listen to what designers and technology commentators have to say, we are struck by how often technological development is characterized as *inevitable*. We are concerned about the ascendance of a rhetoric of inevitability that limits our thinking about how we should shape the use of technology in our society.

Some commentators welcome the "inevitable" progress of technology—that is the view of the technophiles, who see only good things in future technological developments. Some decry the inexorable advance of technology—that is the view of dystopians, who wish we could turn our backs on the latest technologies because of their intrusive effects on our social experience.

There are more possibilities for action than these extremes suggest. But to see past this pervasive rhetoric, we first need to bring it clearly into view, so we can recognize it, sensitize ourselves to it, and then move forward to a more fruitful position.

To consider just one of many examples of the rhetoric of inevitability, in an article in *Beyond Calculation: The Next Fifty Years of Computing,* Gordon Bell and Jim Gray of Microsoft assert that "by 2047. . . all information about physical objects, including humans, buildings, processes and organizations, will be online. This is both desirable and inevitable."[1] It is instructive to read those two sentences aloud.

15   Humans are *objects*. We are in the same category as buildings. In this formulation, any special considerations we might have simply because we are humans (such as rights to privacy) are obliterated. The authors declare that creating a world in which people are objects in a panoramic electronic database is "both desirable and inevitable."

The authors use their authority as virtuoso engineers to tell us what they believe to be inevitable and to suggest how we should feel about it. Bell and Gray's article is not an anomaly. It is one example of many books and articles in which experts describe how technology will be used in the future with a sense of certainty, both about the technology itself and our own acceptance of the benefits it will bring to us.[2]

Bell and Gray state, "Only the human brain can process and store information more easily, cheaply and rapidly [than a computer]." The human brain is formulated here as cheap information storage. By reducing people's intellects to simple computation and storage capabilities, our goals and intentions and opinions are rendered invisible and uninteresting. We are concerned about the way the corporate mind is reaching into the future to define us as physical objects about whom any data can be stored online. Through the rhetoric of inevitability we

---

[1] *Gordon Bell and James N. Gray, "The Revolution Yet to Happen," in* Beyond Calculation: The Next Fifty Years of Computing, *ed. Peter J. Denning and Robert M. Metcalfe (New York: Springer-Verlag, 1997).*
[2] *See also Michael Dertouzos.* What Will Be: How the New World of Information Will Change Our Lives *(San Francisco: Harper San Francisco, 1997).*

are being declared nonplayers in the technical future. We are bargain basement commodities.

Another example of the rhetoric of inevitability can be found in the discussions of cloning people, which have featured inevitability as a constant refrain. Immediately after the story about the successful cloning of sheep in Scotland appeared in the newspapers in February 1997, a U.S. government spokesperson said, "Should we stop scientific development in these areas because the capacity [to clone humans] might become available? I don't think that's reasonable, or even possible. I just think that's one of the costs that come along with scientific discovery, and we have to manage it as well as we can. But it's awfully hard to stop it."[3]

The author of these remarks was Harold Shapiro, the chair of the National Bioethics Advisory Commission appointed by President Clinton. Surely someone appointed as a representative of the people's interests to advise the government on the ethics of biotechnology should take a little more time before declaring cloning technology inevitable. Is it not appropriate to have a public conversation about this far-reaching, controversial technology? Here the rhetoric of inevitability protects a scientific establishment that wants to be free of considerations of how its activities might affect the rest of society.

20   Shapiro was joined by Eric Juengst, a bioethicist at Case Western Reserve University, in declaring that banning future research is like "trying to put a genie back in its bottle."[4] The rhetoric of inevitability reaches a nadir in Juengst's comment: "Do we want to outlaw it [cloning] entirely? That means of course only outlaws will do cloning."

There must be a better argument to be made about the implications of cloning than that only outlaws will clone if we make it illegal. Let's throw away all our laws, in that case! This is a sad logic, especially from someone described as in the newspaper as "one of the nation's leading biomedical ethicists."

Fortunately, the cloning discussion has been more polyphonic than many other technology discussions. In a story about cloning in the *San Jose Mercury News,* our local newspaper, it was reported that in 1973 the scientific community declared a moratorium on research in which DNA from one species was moved to another species, because there was popular concern about mutant strains of bacteria escaping from laboratories and infecting the entire world. In 1974, scientists urged the federal government to regulate all such DNA technology. Strict guidelines followed. They have been relaxed as the scientific community has taken time to sort through the issues and as public understanding has grown, but the regulations are widely regarded as responsible and socially beneficial steps to have taken at that time.[5]

Margaret McLean, director of biotechnology and health care ethics at the Markkula Center for Applied Ethics at Santa Clara University, wrote of the cloning debate, "We ought to listen to our fears." She noted that Dolly the sheep

---

[3] *"Cloning procedure could bring unthinkable within reach,"* San Jose Mercury News, *24 February 1997.*

[4] *"Cloning procedure could bring unthinkable within reach,"* San Jose Mercury News, *24 February 1997.*

[5] *"Cloning procedure could bring unthinkable within reach,"* San Jose Mercury News, *24 February 1997.*

seems to be growing old before her time, possibly due to the aged genetic material from which she was cloned. McLean discussed concerns with attempts to overcontrol a child's future by controlling its genes, by setting expectations that a cloned child might find emotionally unbearable. She argued that we should consider our misgivings and give voice to them. McLean takes on the issue of inevitability squarely, declaring, "I, for one, believe that the possible is not the inevitable."[6]

The developer of the cloning technique himself, Ian Wilmut, voiced opposition on ethical grounds to applying the technology to people. There are already laws in some European countries that ban the cloning of human beings.

25   We hope that our readers will develop active antennae for sensing the rhetoric of inevitability in all the media that surround us. The cloning discovery and the variable responses to it show that there is not a single story to be told about any technology. Those who declare a technical development "inevitable" are doing so by fiat.

Conversational Extremes: Technophilia and Dystopia

Conversations about technology are often positioned at one of two extremes: uncritical acceptance or condemnation. Writers of both technophile and dystopic works often assume that technological change is inevitable—they just feel very differently about it.[7]

These two positions stake out the ends of the continuum, but they leave us with poor choices for action. We want to claim a middle ground from which we can carefully consider the impact of technologies without rejecting them wholesale.

Nicholas Negroponte's book *Being Digital* is a shining example of the work of a technophile. Negroponte, director of the MIT Media Lab in Cambridge, Massachusetts, populates a new and forthcoming Utopia with electronic butlers, robot secretaries, and fleets of digital assistants.[8] In Negroponte's world, computers see and hear, respond to your every murmur, show tact and discretion, and gauge their interactions according to your individual predilections, habits, and social behaviors. Negroponte's lively future scenarios in which digital servants uncomplainingly do our bidding are always positive, unproblematic, and without social costs. There are some important pieces missing from this vision, though it is certainly engagingly presented.

Technological tools and other artifacts carry social meaning. Social understanding, values, and practices become *integral aspects* of the tool itself. Perhaps it's easiest to see this clearly by looking at examples of older and more familiar developments, such as the telephone. The telephone is a technological device. It is a machine that sits on a desk or is carried around the house, and it has electronic insides that can be broken. But most of us probably don't think of a telephone as a

---

[6]Margaret R. McLean, "Just because we can, should we?" San Jose Mercury News, *18 January 1998.*
[7]*Dystopic visions include Jerry Mander,* In the Absence of the Sacred *(San Francisco: Sierra Club Books, 1991); Sven Birkerts,* The Gutenberg Elegies: The Fate of Reading in an Electronic Age *(New York: Fawcett Books, 1995); and Neil Postman,* Technopoly *(New York: Vintage Books, 1993). Technophilia is well represented across the mass media in old-line publications such as* Time *and newer outlets such as* Wired.
[8]*Nicholas Negroponte,* Being Digital *(New York: Knopf, 1995).*

machine; instead, we think of it as a way of communicating. There is an etiquette to placing a call, answering the phone, taking turns in conversation, and saying good-bye, which is so clear to us that we can teach it to our children. There are implicit rules about the privacy of telephone conversations; we learn not to eavesdrop on oth-ers and to ignore what we may accidentally overhear. These conventions and prac-tices are not "designed in" and they do not spring up overnight. They were established by people who used telephones over time, as they discovered what telephones were good for, learned how it felt to use them, and committed social gaffes with them.

30   Negroponte's scenarios are missing a sense of each technology's evolving social meaning and deep integration into social life. Though these social meanings can't be engineered (as the histories of earlier technologies have shown), we must understand that social impacts are crucially important aspects of technological change. We should be paying attention to this bigger picture, as it emerges from its fuzzy-grained beginnings in high-tech labs to saturate our houses, schools, offices, libraries, and hospitals. It is not enough to speculate about the gadgets only in terms of the exciting functions they will perform.

When we turn to writings in the dystopic vein, we find that concerns with the social effects of technology *are* voiced. But the concerns are met with a big bucket of cold water—a call to walk away from new technologies rather than use them selectively and thoughtfully.

A recent best-seller in this arena was Clifford Stoll's *Silicon Snake Oil*.[9] Stoll is an astronomer and skilled computer programmer who is well known for his remark-able success in tracking down a group of West German hackers who broke into the Lawrence Berkeley Laboratory computers in 1986. In *Silicon Snake Oil,* Stoll shares his concerns about the hype surrounding the Internet for everyday use. He suggests that consumers are being sold a bottle of snake oil by those promoting the Internet and other advanced technologies. In the rush to populate newsgroups, chat rooms, and online bookstores in a search for community, we may find ourselves trading away the most basic building blocks for community that we already have—our active participation in local neighborhoods, schools, and businesses.

This is not an unreasonable fear. Another technology, the automobile, trans-formed the landscape of cities, neighborhoods, and even houses in ways that pro-foundly affect the rhythms and social networks of daily life. In the suburban Silicon Valley neighborhood where both of us live, each ranch-style house is laid out with the garage in front, making it the most prominent feature of the house to neighbors or passersby. The downtown shops are a long walk away on busy roads that are not meant for pedestrian traffic. Most people routinely drive many miles to get to work. We can be reminded of what our driving culture costs us by walking for awhile in a town or neighborhood built before cars—though this is not an easy exercise for Californians and other Westerners. In these earlier neighborhoods, there are mix-tures of houses, apartments, and small shops, all on a scale accessible to people walk-ing by, not shielded from the casual visitor by vast parking areas.

---

[9]*Clifford Stoll,* Silicon Snake Oil: Second Thoughts on the Information Highway *(New York: Doubleday,* 1995).

While we share Stoll's belief that the introduction of new technologies into our lives deserves scrutiny, we do not believe that it is reasonable or desirable to turn our backs on technology. It is one thing to choose not to use automated tools for the pure pleasure of doing something by hand—to create beautiful calligraphy for a poem instead of choosing from twenty or thirty ready-made fonts, or to play Monopoly (an activity advocated by Stoll) instead of Myst (a computer game with beautiful graphics). But sometimes the computer is exactly the right tool for the job, and sometimes it is the *only* tool for the job.

35   The issue is not whether we will use technologies, but which we will choose and whether we will use them well. The challenge now is to introduce some critical sensibilities into our evaluation and use of technology, and beyond that, to make a real impact on the kinds of technology that will be available to us in the future.

Stoll and Negroponte seem to be diametric opposites. Stoll says faxing is fine; Negroponte offers a withering critique. Stoll asserts that people don't have time to read email; according to Negroponte, Nobel prize winners happily answer the email of schoolchildren. Stoll tells schools to buy books; Negroponte says computers make you read more and better. But both Negroponte and Stoll are in agreement on one crucial point: the way technology is designed and used is beyond the control of people who are not technology experts. Negroponte asserts that being digital is inevitable, "like a force of nature." What Mother Nature fails to provide will be taken care of by the engineers in the Media Lab. And Stoll describes the digital promises as snake oil—not home brew. Neither Stoll nor Negroponte offers scenarios in which citizens have a say in how we want to shape and use technology.

A Different Approach

Our position in this public conversation about technology lies between the positions exemplified by Stoll and Negroponte in some ways, and completely outside their construction of the argument in others. We share Negroponte's enthusiasm for and fascination with cutting-edge technology development. We share Stoll's concerns about the social impact of technology. But to shun digital technology as Stoll advocates is to miss out on its benefits. Neither does it seem wise to sit back passively waiting for the endless stream of amazing gadgets that Negroponte hypothesizes. It is not necessary to jump on the digital bandwagon. It is dangerous, disempowering, and self-limiting to stick our heads in the sand and pretend it will all go away if we don't look. We believe that much more discussion and analysis of technology and all its attendant issues are needed.

Some of this discussion is fostered by political action books, such as Richard Sclove's *Democracy and Technology.*[10] Sclove argues for grass-roots political action to try to influence official governmental policies on technology. He writes, "[I]t is possible to evolve societies in which people live in greater freedom, exert greater influence on their circumstances, and experience greater dignity, self-esteem, purpose, and well-being."

---

[10]*Richard Sclove,* Democracy and Technology *(New York: Guilford Press, 1995).*

We are in passionate agreement with this statement. At the same time, we recognize that politics per se—national, regional, or local policy advocacy—is not for everyone. There are other ways to engage with technology, especially at the local level of home, school, workplace, hospital, public library, church, and community center. We all have personal relationships with some of these institutions. We can influence them without having to change broad governmental policy, though that might happen in some cases.

40   In our research studies, we have seen examples of responsible, informed, engaged interactions among people and advanced information technologies. We think of the settings where we have seen these interactions as flourishing *information ecologies*. Each of these ecologies is different from the others in important ways. Each has something unique to teach us, just as we learn different things about biology from a coral atoll, a high desert, a coniferous forest. We suggest that these examples be read as stories that model a holistic, ecological approach to technological change. Using the metaphor of an ecology, we will discuss how all of us can find points of leverage to influence the directions of technological change.

QUESTIONS FOR INQUIRY AND ACTION

1. How do Bonnie Nardi and Vicki O'Day encourage us to view technology? How will such a view benefit our inquiry into virtual communities?

2. Compare Nardi and O'Day's view on technology with Jeff Dietrich's in "Refusing to Hope in a God of Technology." How might we account for their different attitudes toward technology?

3. Nardi and O'Day suggest that conversations about technology often fall between two extremes; people either embrace or reject technology uncritically. Inquire into the ways technology is discussed in the local communities formed by your family, friends, and fellow students. Is Nardi and O'Day's characterization of these positions accurate? Why or why not?

4. Examine the way you use technology. Identify three ways technology has changed how you live. What are the benefits and costs of these changes?

JEFF DIETRICH Refusing to Hope in a God of Technology

> *Jeff Dietrich is a writer, activist, and member of the Los Angeles Catholic Worker. He writes regularly about religious issues for* The Catholic Agitator. *"Refusing to Hope in a God of Technology" was published in* National Catholic Reporter *(March 14, 1997).*

"Hey, don't give me nonna that hard crust stuff, man. I ain't no Frenchy." For the majority of folks who eat at our soup kitchen, bread is not hard and crusty, does not have poppy seeds or sesame seeds, is not black or brown. It does not have the flavor of rye or yeast. In fact it has no flavor or character, mass or density, or substance. It is soft, white, bland and as flavorless as a cotton ball. It is bread in name only, made by machines for a people who have lost their memory of bread.

This is not a judgment on the people who eat at the Catholic Worker soup kitchen. It is just a minor example of the subtle but pervasive manner in which technology "transubstantiates" life into a mere simulation of itself, erasing all memories of what has gone before.

In recent months we have read articles of artists and monastics, Catholic Workers and peace activists embracing the Internet. It is not the technology itself that concerns us so much as the fact that these particular people who are apparently embracing this new technology with such enthusiasm should, by virtue of their "alternative" vocations, be more skeptical than they apparently are.

They should not so glibly repeat the hype and promise of technical progress. They should know that everything that is being said today about the positive benefits of the Internet was first said about the automobile and then about radio and television. It will bring us closer together, give us more and better leisure time, improve our intellect, save lives, promote community, give us more freedom, greater autonomy and personal power." How many times do we have to hear the same sales pitch before we realize that we are being sold a bill of goods? Soon they will forget the taste and substance of face-to-face community. Soon the only real community will be the "net," just as the only "real" bread is Wonder Bread.

5   Those who criticize new technology are often characterized as naive or romantic. But in truth it is the ones who uncritically embrace new technical innovations that are being naive and idealistic. They put their hope in the power of technology to solve the very problems it has caused: alienation, pollution, unemployment and an epidemic of cancer-related diseases.

But as sociologist Jacques Ellul points out, "Technique is monistic." That is, "It is all one piece. All techniques are inseparably united and cannot be detached from the others. Nor can the technical phenomenon be broken down in such a way as to retain the good and reject the bad. Every technical advance is matched by a negative reverse side. History has proven that every technical application from its beginnings presents certain unforeseeable secondary effects which are much more disastrous than the lack of the technique would have been."

Though we cannot know all of the unforeseeable consequences of the information superhighway, we can certainly recognize the secondary effects of our current highway system: air pollution and traffic fatalities that every five years exceed the number of Americans killed in World War II; war, intrigue and death to secure oil in the Middle East; and endless suburban sprawl and more acres of asphalt than farm land.

Here in Los Angeles anyone without an automobile is a de facto second-class citizen without access to the better-paying jobs and decent housing that have migrated down the freeways to the suburbs. The same will also be true of everyone who finds himself stuck at the on-ramp of the information superhighway. It's a dead-end street for the poor.

In his recent book, *The Revolt of the Elites,* the late Christopher Lasch points out that the "new meritocratic elites" are already cruising down the information superhighway, losing all sense of connectedness with community, place and the common good. Their loyalties are international rather than regional, national or local. They have more in common with their counterparts in Brussels and Hong Kong than with the masses of Americans not yet plugged into the network of global communications."

10   Our blindness to the disastrous secondary effects of technology is a result of our theological attachment to the technical phenomenon. We tend to think of technology as a neutral instrument. But in fact it is the physical embodiment of our cultural values of rationality and efficiency, and our collective desire to over-come the forces of nature: toil, suffering and death. As such it is a response to the Fall. It is a manifestation of our attempts to attain salvation without repen-tance or discomfort.

Thus we must recognize that our struggle is not against technology in itself but rather against the "spirituality of technology," against technology as a principal-ity and power. Ellul says that technology, or "technique" as he calls it, is the sacred organizing principle of our culture," somewhat like the force that Christianity exerted on the culture of medieval Europe.

In the past, technological growth was restrained by the culture. All traditional cultures are essentially religious and conservative, skeptical of anything new and innovative and focused primarily upon preserving the patterns and practices of the past. As a consequence, technology developed at a very slow pace and never disrupted cultural structures.

It is axiomatic that human institutions develop at a far slower pace than tech-nical innovations. Just ask any businessman and he will tell you that in our world today change is the only constant. The survivors are the ones who have positioned themselves to ride the cresting wave of the future." On the other hand, the vast majority of the world's population will drown, because they need the buoyancy provided by stable institutions.

It is often assumed that the prosperous working class of the industrial nations was created by the progressive development of technology. But the truth is that this prosperity was created not by machines but by the struggle and sacrifice of dedicated workers and the advent of the labor union. But labor unions took over 100 years to evolve, while the benefits they created have been destroyed in less than a generation by the onslaught of new information technologies. The con-stant cycle of technological change is disastrous for the poor. Long before any human institution can evolve to address this current technology, there will be a new destabilizing technical development.

15   Jacques Ellul is not a satisfying writer because he refuses to give us any solu-tion to the problems of "technological society." He simply reminds us that as Chris-tians we are called to be in the world but not of it. Ellul is painfully aware that we cannot simply reject technology and that it is impossible to give a pure witness to the simple non-technical life. But we can refuse to sing the songs of technology, we can refuse to repeat the mythology of technical progress, we can refuse to put our hope in the god of technology. And when we use technology, we can use it "confessionally," acknowledging our complicity in the degradation of the planet and the oppression of the poor.

Though I am a big fan of *Star Trek* and *The X-Files*, I do believe that Carl Jung was correct when he said that the current interest in space travel and flying saucers is a projection of desperate people seeking salvation no longer in God or repentance, but in a fantasy of space-traveling extraterrestrials. But Wendell Berry said: "We cannot look for happiness to any technological paradise or to any New Earth of outer space, but only to the world as it is, and as we have made it. The only life we may hope to live is here. . . . We can only wait here, where we are, in the world, obedient to its processes, patient in its taking away, and all that we deserve of earthly Paradise will come to us."

Our salvation lies in eating the true bread of life, not bread baked by machines and filled with chemicals—the bread of remembering, not the bread of forgetfulness.

QUESTIONS FOR INQUIRY AND ACTION

1. Examine Dietrich's use of the metaphor of bread. Why does he choose that metaphor? What does it allow him to argue?

2. Dietrich, writing for a Catholic magazine, uses language that he knows his audience will respond to, and he assumes shared values. He argues that "when we use technology, we can use it 'confessionally,' acknowledging our complicity in the degradation of the planet and the oppression of the poor." What does he mean by this? In what ways would you agree or disagree?

3. Conduct an inquiry into the history of any one piece of technology, for instance, the telephone, automobile, or washing machine. What were the promises made about the advantages of that technology? In what ways did those promises come true or not?

4. Explore the effects of technology on a social movement that interests you or that you are involved in, perhaps through your service learning work. In what ways do the new technologies aid the activists and communities, and in what ways do the technologies impede progress and/or community building?

78 QUESTIONS: A GUIDE TO LIVING WITH TECHNOLOGY

Participants in the 1993 and 1994 Megatechnology conferences created the following questions to promote critical thinking in our use of technology. As you read the questions, apply them in your mind to the technologies you use every day.

As articulated, debated, and refined by the participants in the 1993 and 1994 Megotechnology conferences, 78 tools to be used in dismantling the megamachine and restoring organic reality. Designed to be comfortable to everyone's grasp and to provide a lifetime of service if honed with hope and polished by imagination.

Ecological

What are its effects on the health of the planet and of the person?
Does it preserve or destroy biodiversity?
Does it preserve or reduce ecosystem integrity?

continued on next page

What are its effects on the land?
What are its effects on wildlife?
How much and what kind of waste does it generate?
Does it incorporate the principles of ecological design?
Does it break the bond of renewal between humans and nature?
Does it preserve or reduce cultural diversity?
What is the totality of its effects, its "ecology"?

Social

Does it serve community?
Does it empower community members?
How does it affect our perception of our needs?
Is it consistent with the creation of a communal, human economy?
What are its effects on relationships?
Does it undermine conviviality?
Does it undermine traditional forms of community?
How does it affect our way of seeing and experiencing the world?
Does it foster a diversity of forms of knowledge?
Does it build on, or contribute to, the renewal of traditional forms of knowledge?
Does it serve to commodify knowledge or relationships?
To what extent does it redefine reality?
Does it erase a sense of time and history?
What is its potential to become addictive?

Practical

What does it make?
Whom does it benefit?
What is its purpose?
Where was it produced?
Where is it used?
Where must it go when it's broken or obsolete?
How expensive is it?
Can it be repaired? By an ordinary person?
What is the entirety of its cost, the full cost accounting?

Moral

What values does its use foster?
What is gained by its use?
What are its effects beyond its utility to the individual?
What is lost in using it?
What are its effects on the least person in the society?

Ethical

How complicated is it?
What does it allow us to ignore?

To what extent does it distance agent from effect?
Can we assume personal, or communal, responsibility for its effects?
Can its effects be directly apprehended?
What ancillary technologies does it require?
What behavior might it make possible in the future?
What other technologies might it make possible?
Does it alter our sense of time and relationships in ways conducive to nihilism?

Vocational

What is its impact on craft?
Does it reduce, deaden, or enhance human creativity?
Is it the least imposing technology available for the task?
Does it replace, or does it aid, human hands and human beings?
Can it be responsive to organic circumstance?
Does it depress or enhance the quality of goods?
Does it depress or enhance the meaning of work?

Metaphysical

What aspect of the inner self does it reflect?
Does it express love?
Does it express rage?
What aspect of our past does it reflect?
Does it reflect cyclical or linear thinking?

Political

What is its mystique?
Does it concentrate or equalize power?
Does it require, or institute, a knowledge elite?
Is it totalitarian?
Does it require a bureaucracy for its perpetuation?
What legal empowerments does it require?
Does it undermine traditional moral authority?
Does it require military defense?
Does it enhance, or serve, military purposes?
How does it affect warfare?
Does it foster mass thinking or behavior?
Is it consistent with the creation of a global economy?
Does it empower transnational corporations?
What kind of capital does it require?

Aesthetic

Is it ugly?
Does it cause ugliness?
What noise does it make?
What pace does it set?
How does it affect quality of life (as distinct from standard of living)?

THE DISPOSABLE HEROES OF HIPHOPRISY
Television, The Drug of the Nation

> *The Disposable Heroes of Hiphoprisy were an L.A.-based Hip Hop duo known for their social commentary. M.C. Michael Franti wrote the lyrics and percussionist Rono Tse played angle guitar, tire rims, chains, break drums, electronic springs, sheet metal, and steel drums. "Television, The Drug of the Nation" is featured on their first and only album* Hypocrisy is the Greatest Luxury *(Fourth & Broadway Records, 1992). Franti now fronts the band Spearhead.*

one nation
under God
has turned into
one nation under the influence
5   of one drug

[chorus:]
Television, the drug of the Nation
Breeding ignorance and feeding radiation
(2x)

T.V., it
satellite links
10   our United States of Unconsciousness
Apathetic therapeutic and extremely addictive
The methadone metronome pumping out
150 channels 24 hours a day
you can flip through all of them
15   and still there's nothing worth watching
T.V. is the reason why less than 10 per cent of our
Nation reads books daily
Why most people think Central Amerika
means Kansas
20   Socialism means unamerican
and Apartheid is a new headache remedy
absorbed in its world it's so hard to find us
It shapes our mind the most
maybe the mother of our Nation
25   should remind us
that we're sitting too close to. . .

[Chorus:]
Television, the drug of the Nation
Breeding ignorance and feeding radiation
(2x)

T.V. is
30   the stomping ground for political candidates
Where bears in the woods
are chased by Grecian Formula'd
bald eagles
T.V. is mechanized politics
35   remote control over the masses
co-sponsored by environmentally safe gases
watch for the PBS special
It's the perpetuation of the two party system
where image takes precedence over wisdom
40   Where sound bite politics are served to
the fastfood culture
Where straight teeth in your mouth
are more important than the words
that come out of it
45   Race baiting is the way to get selected
Willie Horton or
Will he not get elected on. . .

[Chorus:]
Television, the drug of the Nation
Breeding ignorance and feeding radiation
(2x)

50   T.V., is it the reflector or the director?
Does it imitate us
or do we imitate it
because a child watches 1500 murders before he's
twelve years old and we wonder why we've created
55   a Jason generation that learns to laugh
rather than to abhor the horror
T.V. is the place where
armchair generals and quarterbacks can
experience first hand
60   the excitement of warfare
as the theme song is sung in the background
Sugar sweet sitcoms
that leave us with a bad actor taste while
pop stars metamorphosize into soda pop stars
65   You saw the video
You heard the soundtrack
Well now go buy the soft drink
Well, the only cola that I support
would be a union C.O.L.A. (Cost Of Living Allowance)
70   On television

[Chorus:]
Television, the drug of the Nation
Breeding ignorance and feeding radiation
(2x)

Back again, "New and improved"
We return to our irregularly programmed schedule
75   hidden cleverly between heavy breasted
beer and car commercials
CNNESPNABCTNT but mostly B.S.
Where oxymoronic language like
"virtually spotless" "fresh frozen"
80   "light yet filling" and "military intelligence"
have become standard
T.V. is the place where phrases are redefined
like "recession" to "necessary downturn"
"Crude oil" on a beach to "mousse"
85   "Civilian death" to "collateral damages"
and being killed by your own Army
is now called "friendly fire"
T.V. is the place where the pursuit
of happiness has become the pursuit of
90   trivia
Where toothpaste and cars have become
sex objects
Where imagination is sucked out of children
by a cathode ray nipple
95   T.V. is the only wet nurse
that would create a cripple

[Chorus:]
Television, the drug of the Nation
Breeding ignorance and feeding radiation
(4x)

QUESTIONS FOR INQUIRY AND ACTION

1. Do you watch enough television to pick up on their allusions and references? Analyze the language of the piece, beginning with the refrain "Television, the drug of the Nation/Breeding ignorance and feeding radiation." What do you think is meant by this?

2. Read this rap with the other readings on television: Earley's "Somehow Form a Family" and Mulholland and Martin's "Tune Out." Imagine a conversation taking place among the authors of these three selections. How would they inform one another?

3. Rap and hip hop music are perhaps the most criticized of popular genres. Inquire into the genres for yourself. Are you a fan? Is the bad reputation justified? How are the Disposable Heroes of Hiphoprisy regarded by the public and by fans of the genre?

4. Write your own rap that's a social critique. What would you focus on? What refrain would run through it and hold the song together?

TONY EARLEY Somehow Form a Family

Tony Earley teaches writing at Vanderbilt University in Nashville. He is the author of a collection of short stories, Here We Are in Paradise *(1994), and the best-selling novel* Jim the Boy *(2000). "Somehow Form a Family" is the first essay in his book of the same name,* Somehow Form a Family: Stories That Are Mostly True *(Chapel Hill, NC: Algonquin Books, 2001).*

In July 1969, I looked a lot like Opie in the second or third season of *The Andy Griffith Show.* I was a small boy with a big head. I wore blue jeans with the cuffs turned up and horizontally striped pullover shirts. I was the brother in a father-mother-brother-sister family. We lived in a four-room house at the edge of the country, at the foot of the mountains, outside a small town in North Carolina, but it could have been anywhere.

On one side of us lived Mr. and Mrs. White. They were old and rich. Their driveway was paved. Mrs. White was the president of the town garden club. When she came to visit Mama she brought her own ashtray. Mr. White was almost deaf. When he watched the news on television, it sounded like thunder in the distance. The Whites had an aluminum travel trailer in which you could see your reflection. One summer they hitched it to their Chrysler and pulled it all the way to Alaska.

On the other side of us lived Mack and Joan. They had just graduated from college. I thought Joan was beautiful, and still do. Mack had a bass boat and a three-tray tackle box in which lurked a bristling school of lures. On the other side of Mack and Joan lived Mrs. Taylor, who was old, and on the other side of Mrs. Taylor lived Mr. and Mrs. Frady, who had a fierce dog. My sister, Shelly, and I called it the Frady dog. The Frady dog lived a long and bitter life. It did not die until well after I had a driver's license.

On the far side of the Whites lived Mr. and Mrs. John Harris; Mr. and Mrs. Burlon Harris lived beyond them. John and Burlon were first cousins. John was a teacher who in the summers fixed lawn mowers, including ours, in a building behind his house. Burlon reminded me of Mr. Greenjeans on *Captain Kangaroo.* He kept horses and let us play in his barn. Shelly once commandeered one of his cats and brought it home to live with us. Burlon did not mind; he asked her if she wanted another one. We rode our bicycles toward Mr. Harris's house as if pulled there by gravity. We did not ride in the other direction; the Frady dog sat in its yard and watched for us.

5   In July 1969, we did not have much money, but in the hierarchy of southern poor, we were the good kind, the kind you would not mind living on your road. We were clean. Our clothes were clean. My parents worked. We went to church. Easter mornings, Mama stood us in front of the yellowbell bush and took our picture. We had meat at every meal—chicken and cube steak and pork chops and ham—and plenty of milk to drink. We were not trashy. Mrs. White would not sit with her ashtray in the kitchen of trashy people. Trashy people lived in

the two houses around the curve past Mr. Harris's. When Daddy drove by those houses we could see that the kids in the yard had dirty faces. They were usually jabbing at something with a stick. Shelly and I were not allowed to ride our bicycles around the curve.

I knew we were poor only because our television was black and white. It was an old Admiral, built in the 1950s, with brass knobs the size of baseballs. Its cabinet was perfectly square, a cube of steel with a painted-on mahogany grain. Hoss on *Bonanza* could not have picked it up by himself. It was a formidable object, but its vertical hold was shot. We gathered around it the night Neil Armstrong walked on the moon, but we could not tell what was happening. The picture flipped up and down. We turned off the lights in the living room so we could see better. We listened to Walter Cronkite. In the distance we could hear Mr. White's color TV rumbling. We changed the channel and listened to Huntley and Brinkley. We could hear the scratchy radio transmissions coming down out of space, but we could not see anything. Daddy got behind the TV with a flashlight. He said, "Is that better? Is that better?" but it never was. Mama said, "Just be thankful you've got a television."

After the Eagle had landed but before the astronauts opened the door and came out, Mack knocked on the door and asked us if we wanted to look at the moon. He was an engineer for a power company and had set up his surveyor's transit in the backyard. Daddy and Shelly and I went with him. We left Mama sitting in the living room in the blue light of the TV. She said she did not want to miss anything. The moon, as I remember it, was full, although I have since learned that it wasn't. I remember that a galaxy of lightning bugs blinked against the black pine trees that grew between our yard and that of the Whites. Mack pointed the transit at the sky. Daddy held me up so I could see. The moon inside the instrument was startlingly bright; the man in the moon was clearly visible, although the men on the moon weren't. "You can't see them or anything," Mack said, which I already knew. I said, "I know that." I wasn't stupid and did not like to be talked to as if I were. Daddy put me down. He and Mack stood for a while and talked. Daddy smoked a cigarette. In the bright yard Shelly chased lightning bugs. She did not run, but instead jumped slowly, her feet together. I realized that she was pretending to walk on the moon, pretending that she was weightless. The moon was so bright, it cast a shadow at her feet. I remember these things for sure. I am tempted to say that she was beautiful in the moonlight, and I'm sure she was, but that isn't something I remember noticing that night, only a thing I need to say now.

Eight, maybe nine months later, Shelly and I rode the bus home from school. It was a Thursday, Mama's day off, Easter time. The cherry tree in the garden separating our driveway from that of the Whites was in brilliant, full bloom. We could hear it buzzing from the road. One of us checked the mailbox. We looked up the driveway at our house. Something was wrong with it, but we couldn't tell what. Daddy was adding four rooms on to the house, and we were used to it appearing large and unfinished. We stood in the driveway and stared. Black tar paper

was tacked to the outside walls of the new part, but the old part was still covered with white asbestos shingles. In the coming summer, Daddy and a crew of
brick masons would finish transforming the house into a split-level ranch style,
remarkably similar to the one in which the Bradys would live. I loved the words
split-level ranch-style. To me they meant "rich."

Shelly and I spotted what was wrong at the same time. A giant television
antenna had attached itself to the roof of our house. It was shiny and tall as a
young tree. It looked dangerous, as if it would bite, like a praying mantis. The
antenna slowly began to turn, as if it had noticed us. Shelly and I looked quickly
at each other, our mouths wide open, and then back at the antenna. We sprinted
up the driveway.

10   In the living room, on the spot occupied by the Admiral that morning, sat a
magnificent new color TV, a Zenith, with a twenty-one-inch screen. Its cabinet
was made of real wood. *Gomer Pyle, U.S.M.C.* was on. I will never forget that.
Gomer Pyle and Sergeant Carter were the first two people I ever saw on a color
television. The olive green and khaki of their uniforms was dazzling. Above them
was the blue sky of California. The sky in California seemed bluer than the sky
in North Carolina.

We said, "Is that ours?"

Mama said, "I'm going to kill your daddy." He had charged the TV without
telling her. Two men from Sterchi's Furniture had showed up at the house that morning with the TV on a truck. They climbed onto the roof and planted the antenna.

We said, "Can we keep it?"

Mama said, "I don't know," but I noticed she had written the numbers of the
stations we could get on the dial of the Channel Master, the small box which controlled the direction the antenna pointed. Mama would never have written on
anything she planned on taking back to the store.

15   The dial of the Channel Master was marked like a compass. Channel 3 in
Charlotte lay to the east; Channel 13 in Asheville lay to the west. Channel 7 in
Spartanburg and Channel 4 in Greenville rested side by side below them in the
south. For years these cities would mark the outside edges of the world as I knew
it. Shelly reached out and turned the dial. Mama smacked her on the hand. Gomer
grew fuzzy and disappeared. I said, "Mama, she broke it." When the dial stopped
turning, Mama carefully turned it back to the south. Gomer reappeared, resur-
rected. Jim Nabors probably never looked better to anyone, in his whole life, than
he did to us right then.

Mama sat us down on the couch and laid down the law. Mama always laid
down the law when she was upset. We were not to touch the TV. We could not
turn it on, nor could we change the channel. Under no circumstances were we
to touch the Channel Master. The Channel Master was very expensive. And if
we so much as looked at the knobs that controlled the color, she would whip
us. It had taken her all afternoon to get the color just right.

We lived in a split-level ranch-style house, with two maple trees and a rose
bush in the front yard, outside a town that could have been named Springfield.

We had a color TV. We had a Channel Master antenna that turned slowly on top of our house until it found and pulled from the sky electromagnetic waves for our nuclear family.

We watched *Hee-Haw*, starring Buck Owens and Roy Clark; we watched *All in the Family, The Mary Tyler Moore Show, The Bob Newhart Show, The Carol Burnett Show,* and *Mannix,* starring Mike Connors with Gail Fisher as Peggy; we watched *Gunsmoke* and *Bonanza,* even after Adam left and Hoss died and Little Joe's hair turned gray; we watched *Adam-12* and *Kojak, McCloud, Colombo,* and *Hawaii Five-O;* we watched *Cannon,* a Quinn Martin production and *Barnaby Jones,* a Quinn Martin production, which co-starred Miss America and Uncle Jed from *The Beverly Hillbillies.* Daddy finished the new part of the house and moved out soon thereafter. He rented a trailer in town and took the old Admiral out of the basement with him. We watched *Mutual of Omaha's Wild Kingdom* and *The Wonderful World of Disney.* After school we watched *Gomer Pyle, U.S.M.C., The Beverly Hillbillies, Gilligan's Island,* and *The Andy Griffith Show.* Upstairs, we had rooms of our own. Mama stopped taking us to church.

On Friday nights we watched *The Partridge Family, The Brady Bunch, Room 222, The Odd Couple,* and *Love American Style.* Daddy came to visit on Saturdays. We watched *The Little Rascals* on Channel 3 with Fred Kirby, the singing cowboy, and his sidekick, Uncle Jim. We watched *The Little Rascals* on Channel 4 with Monty Dupuy, the weatherman, and his sidekick, Doohickey. Mornings, before school, we watched *The Three Stooges* with Mr. Bill on Channel 13. Mr. Bill worked alone. The school year Daddy moved out, Mr. Bill showed Bible story cartoons instead of *The Three Stooges.* That year, we went to school angry.

20   After each of Daddy's visits, Mama said he was getting better. Shelly and I tried to imagine living with the Bradys but realized we would not fit in. They were richer and more popular at school. They did not have Southern accents. One Saturday Daddy brought me a set of golf clubs, which I had asked for but did not expect to get. It was raining that day. I took the clubs out in the yard and very quickly realized that golf was harder than it looked on television. I went back inside and wiped the mud and water off the clubs with Bounty paper towels, the quicker picker upper. Upstairs I heard Mama say, "Do you think he's stupid?" I spread the golf clubs on the floor around me. I tuned in *Shock Theater* on Channel 13 and turned it up loud.

Shelly had a crush on Bobby Brady; I had a crush on Jan. Jan had braces, I had braces. Jan had glasses, I had glasses. Their daddy was an architect. Our daddy lived in a trailer in town with a poster of Wile E. Coyote and the Road Runner on the living room wall. The Coyote held the Road Runner firmly by the neck. The caption on the poster said, "Beep, Beep your ass." I lay in bed at night and imagined being married to Jan Brady but having an affair with Marsha. I wondered how we would tell Jan, what Marsha and I would do then, where we would go. Greg Brady beat me up. I shook his hand and told him I deserved it. Alice refused to speak to me. During this time Mrs. White died. I heard the ambulance in the middle of the night. It sounded like the one on *Emergency.* I opened the door to Mama's room to see if she was OK. She was embarrassed because our dog barked and barked.

Rhoda left *The Mary Tyler Moore Show.* Maude and George Jefferson left *All in the Family;* Florida, Maude's maid, left *Maude.* Daddy moved back in. He watched the news during supper, the TV as loud as Mr. White's. We were not allowed to talk during the news. This was the law. After the news we watched *Rhoda* or *Maude* or *Good Times.* Daddy decided that cutting the grass should be my job. We had a big yard. I decided that I didn't want to do anything he said. Mr. White remarried. The new Mrs. White's daughter died of cancer. The new Mrs. White dug up every flower the old Mrs. White had planted; she cut down every tree and shrub, including the cherry tree in the garden between our driveways. Mama said the new Mrs. White broke her heart. Mr. White mowed and mowed and mowed their grass until it was smooth as a golf course. Mack and Joan paved their driveway.

What I'm trying to say is this: we lived in a split-level ranch-style house; we had a Zenith in the living room and a Channel Master attached to the roof. But Shelly and I fought like Thelma and J.J. on *Good Times.* I wanted to live in Hawaii and work for Steve McGarrett. No bad guy ever got away from McGarrett, except the Chinese master spy Wo Fat. Shelly said McGarrett would never give me a job. In all things Shelly was on Daddy's side; I lined up on Mama's. Friday evenings, when Daddy got home from work, I sneaked outside to snoop around in the glove compartment of his car. I pretended I had a search warrant, that I was Danno on a big case. Shelly reported my snooping to Daddy. I was trying to be a good son.

Every Saturday, before he went to work, Daddy left word that I was to cut the grass before he got home. I stayed in bed until lunch. Shelly came into my room and said, "You better get up." I flipped her the bird. She said, "I'm telling." I got up in time to watch professional wrestling on Channel 3. I hated the bad guys. They did not fight fair. They hid brass knuckles in their trunks and beat the good guys until they bled. They won too often. Mama brought me tomato and onion sandwiches. I could hear Mack on one side and Mr. White on the other mowing their grass. I could hear John Harris and Mr. Frady and Mrs. Taylor's daughter, Lucille, mowing grass. Lucille lived in Charlotte, but came home on weekends just to mow Mrs. Taylor's grass. We had the shaggiest lawn on the road. After wrestling, I watched the *Game of the Week* on Channel 4. Carl Yaztremski of the Boston Red Sox was my favorite baseball player. He had forearms like fenceposts. Nobody messed with him. I listened over the lawn mowers for the sound of Daddy's Volkswagen. Mama came in the living room and said, "Son, maybe you should mow some of the grass before your daddy gets home. You know what's going to happen." I knew what was going to happen. I knew that eventually he would make me mow the grass. I knew that when I was through, Mack would come through the pine trees laughing. He would say, "Charles, I swear that is the laziest boy I have ever seen." Mack had a Snapper Comet riding mower, on which he sat like a king. I never saw him on it that I did not want to bean him with a rock. Daddy would shake his head and say, "Mack, dead lice wouldn't fall off that boy." Every Saturday night we ate out at Scoggin's Seafood and Steak House. *Hee-Haw* came on at seven; *All in the Family* came on at eight.

25   And then Shelly and I were in high school. We watched *M*A*S*H** and *Lou Grant, Love Boat* and *Fantasy Island.* We watched *Dynasty* and *Dallas.* Opie was Richie Cunningham on *Happy Days.* Ben Cartwright showed up in a black bathrobe on *Battlestar Gallactica.* The Channel Master stopped working, but no one bothered to have it fixed. The antenna was left immobile on the roof in a compromised position: we could almost get most of the channels. One summer Mack built a pool in his backyard. Joan lay in a bikini beside the pool in the sun. The next summer Mack built a fence. This was during the late seventies. Shelly lay in her room with the lights turned off and listened to *Dark Side of the Moon.* On Friday nights she asked me to go out with her and her friends. I always said no. I did not want to miss *The Rockford Files.*

In those days Shelly and I watched *Guiding Light* when we got home from school. It was our soap. I remember that Ed Bauer's beautiful wife Rita left him because he was boring. Shelly said I reminded her of Ed Bauer. She wore her hair like Farrah Fawcett Majors on *Charlie's Angels.* After *Guiding Light* I changed the channel and watched *Star Trek.* I could not stay awake in school. I went to sleep during homeroom. During the day I woke up only long enough to change classes and eat lunch. I watched *Star Trek* when I got home as if it were beamed to our house by God. I did not want to be Captain Kirk, or any of the main characters. I just wanted to go with them. I wanted to wear a red jersey and walk the long, anonymous halls of the Starship Enterprise as it disappeared into space. One day *Star Trek* was preempted by an *ABC After School Special.* I tried to kick the screen out of the TV. I was wearing sneakers, so the glass would not break. Shelly hid in Mama and Daddy's room. I said, "Five-O. Open up." Then I kicked the door off the hinges.

Our family doctor thought I had narcolepsy. He sent me to a neurologist in Charlotte. Mama and Daddy went with me. In Charlotte, an EEG technician attached wires to my head. A small, round amber light glowed high up in the corner of the examination room. I watched the light until I went to sleep. The neurologist said that the EEG looked normal, but that he would talk to us more about the results in a few minutes. He led us to a private waiting room. It was small and bare and paneled with wood. In it were four chairs. Most of one wall was taken up by a darkened glass. I could not see what was on the other side of it. I studied our reflection. Mama and Daddy were trying to pretend that the glass wasn't there. I said, "Pa, when we get back to the Ponderosa, do you want me to round up those steers on the lower forty?"

Daddy said, "What?"

I said, "Damnit, Jim. I'm a doctor."

30   Daddy said, "What are you talking about?"

Mama said, "Be quiet. They're watching us."

Shelly died on Christmas Eve morning when I was a freshman in college. She had wrecked Mama's car. That night I stayed up late and watched the Pope deliver the Christmas mass from the Vatican. There was nothing else on. Daddy moved out again. My college almost shut down during the week *The Thorn Birds* was broadcast. Professors rescheduled papers and exams. In the basement of my dorm twenty-five nineteen-year-old guys shouted at the TV when the Richard Chamberlain character told the Rachel Ward character he loved God more than he loved her. At age nineteen, it was impossible to love God more than Rachel Ward. My best friend, a guy from Kenya, talked me into switching from *Guiding Light* to *General Hospital.* This was during the glory days of *General Hospital* when Luke and Scorpio roomed together on the Haunted Star. Laura was supposedly dead, but Luke knew in his heart she was still alive; every time he was by himself he heard a Christopher Cross song.

Going home was strange, as if the Mayberry I expected had become Mayberry, R.F.D. Shelly was gone. Daddy was gone. The second Mrs. White died, then Mr. White went away to a nursing home. The Fradys had moved away. John Harris had a heart attack and stopped fixing lawn mowers. Mama mowed our grass by herself with a rider. I stopped going to see Burlon Harris because he teared up every time he tried to talk about Shelly. Mack and Joan had a son named Timmy. Mack and Joan got a divorce. Mack moved to a farm out in the country; Joan moved to town.

Daddy fell in love with Mama my senior year and moved back in. The Zenith began slowly dying. Its picture narrowed into a greenly tinted slit. It stared like a diseased eye into the living room where Mama and Daddy sat. They turned off the lights so they could see better. I became a newspaper reporter. With my first Christmas bonus, I bought myself a television, a nineteen-inch GE. With my second Christmas bonus I bought Mama and Daddy one. They hooked it up to cable. When I visited them on Thursdays we watched *The Cosby Show, Family Ties, Cheers, Night Court,* and *Hill Street Blues.* Daddy gave up on broadcast TV when NBC cancelled *Hill Street Blues* and replaced it with *L.A. Law.* Now he mostly watches the Discovery Channel. Mama calls it the "airplanes and animals channel." They are in the eighteenth year of their new life together. I bear them no grudges. They were very young when I knew them best.

35   In grad school I switched back to *Guiding Light.* I had known Ed Bauer longer than I had known all but a few of my friends. It pleased me to see him in Springfield every afternoon, trying to do good. I watched *The Andy Griffith Show* twice a day. I could glance at Opie and tell you what year the episode was filmed. I watched the Gulf War from a stool in a bar.

Eventually I married a woman who grew up in a family that watched television only on special occasions—when Billie Jean King played Bobby Riggs, when Diana married Prince Charles. My wife was a student in a seminary. She did not want to meet Ed Bauer, nor could I explain, without sounding pathetic, why Ed Bauer was important to me. The first winter we were married I watched the winter Olympics huddled beneath a blanket in the frigid basement of the house we had rented. This was in a closed-down steel town near Pittsburgh, during the time I contemplated jumping from a bridge into the Ohio River. My wife asked the seminary community to pray for me. Ann B. Davis, who played Alice on *The Brady Bunch* was a member of that community. One day I saw her in the cafeteria at school. She looked much the same as when she played Alice, except that her hair was white, and she wore small, gold glasses. I didn't talk to her. I had heard that she didn't like talking about *The Brady Bunch,* and I could not think of anything to say to her about the world in which we actually lived. I sat in the cafeteria and stared at her as much as I could without anyone noticing. I don't know if she prayed for me or not, but I like to think that she did. I wanted to tell her that I grew up in a split-level ranch-style house outside a small town that could have been named Springfield, but that something had gone wrong inside it. I wanted to tell her that years ago Alice had been important to me, that my sister and I had looked to Alice for something we could not name, and had at least seen a picture of what love looked like. I wanted to tell her that no one in my family ever raised their voice while the television was on, that late at night even a bad television show could keep me from hearing the silence inside my own heart. I wanted to tell her that Ed Bauer and I were still alive, that both of us had always wanted to do what was right. Ann B. Davis stood, walked over to the trash can, and emptied her tray. She walked out of the cafeteria and into a small, gray town near Pittsburgh. I wanted her to *be* Alice. I wanted her to smile as if she loved me. I wanted her to say, "Buck up, kiddo, everything's going to be all right." And what I'm trying to tell you now is this: I grew up in a split-level ranch-style house outside a town that could have been anywhere. I grew up in front of a television. I would have believed her.

QUESTIONS FOR INQUIRY AND ACTION

1. Earley's title invokes *The Brady Bunch,* but what else does the title, "Somehow Form a Family," reveal about his story?

2. Read Earley's descriptions of his family alongside those in Chapter Seven, The Family as Community. What does he tell us directly about his family, and what does he imply? Why is the television so important to his description?

3. Make your own list of the television shows you watched growing up. What would the list tell us about the events going on in your life? What shows affected you most, and why? What has been the lasting effect of television shows on your life?

4. In what ways do you feel connected with others through a specific television show or special event? Survey others your age on the most important moments on television in the past five years and ten years. How many do you all agree on? How does television help you form a community?

Writing Style

SHOWING, NOT TELLING

Most books of writing advise aspiring authors: "Show, don't tell." They recommend this because writing is more powerful and affecting when readers can see examples rather than just receive explanation. Writers often "show" by providing lots of precise details and by using dialogue to reveal character and advance the plot.

Tony Earley's story "Somehow Form a Family" contends that he grew up in front of a television and that it shielded him from the emotional trauma of watching his parents quarrel and separate and get back together again. Television allowed him to escape and to imagine himself a different person in different lives. Rather than tell us this directly, Earley shows us indirectly by providing list after list of the television shows he watched during the difficult eras of his life and mentioning his connections with certain shows and characters.

For example, here is one of the passages: "On Friday nights we watched *The Partridge Family, The Brady Bunch, Room 222, The Odd Couple,* and *Love, American Style.* Daddy came to visit on Saturdays. We watched *The Little Rascals* on Channel 3 with Fred Kirby, the singing cowboy, and his sidekick, Uncle Jim. We watched *The Little Rascals* on Channel 4 with Monty Dupuy, the weatherman, and his sidekick, Doohickey. Mornings, before school, we watched *The Three Stooges* with Mr. Bill on Channel 13. Mr. Bill worked alone. The school year Daddy moved out, Mr. Bill showed Bible story cartoons instead of *The Three Stooges.* That year, we went to school angry."

Earley seems to break the "show, don't tell" rule, for he does tell us what he watched and what happened in his life, yet he shows us all of this suggestively: he depends on the names of the TV shows to carry connotations to an audience he assumes knows these shows and their characters. He does not explicate or directly connect his observations of life to the TV shows, but we understand the connections. Do you find this style of storytelling effective? Why or why not?

JAKE MULHOLLAND AND ADRIENNE MARTIN Tune Out

Jake Mulholland is a student at the University of Minnesota. Adrienne Martin is a student at Normandale Community College. They collaboratively designed, researched, and wrote "Tune Out" for their composition course when they were freshmen at Normandale Community College.

Our lives are hard-wired with technology. We are surrounded by computers and the Internet at work and at home. We drive complex cars with ABS brakes and GPS tracking down eight-lane super highways. We talk on cell phones with SMS, schedule appointments on Palm Pilots, and cruise the Internet at 1.5 megabytes a second on DSL networks. Yet none of these technological wonders comes close to playing as big a role in our lives as do television and movies.

According to the *Kill Your TV* Website, by the time the average child reaches 18 years of age he or she has spent more time watching TV than attending school. The movie industry grossed 732 billion dollars last year. The average movie ticket costs $5.50. This means that 133.1 billion movies were viewed last year—and this excludes the multibillion dollar movie rental industry. TV is everywhere. Our daily rituals revolve around our favorite sitcoms and made-for-TV-movies. We wake to Al Roker telling us the forecast. We employ the television as a nanny. We eat dinner with Seinfeld, and Jay Leno lulls us to sleep at night.

With all the time spent in front of the TV and watching movies it would be hard to disagree that they play a major role in how we socialize, or how we interact with others. In the United States, 98% of households have at least one television and by the time today's children reach age 70, they will have spent approximately seven years watching TV. These statistics were nationwide and for all ages.

This made us wonder: How are *we* affected by TV? Would the denial of television and movies affect us? Would we toss and turn at night and be groggier in the mornings? Would we converse more with our friends and family? Would we find ourselves lost without the companionship of Frazier, Montel, and Chandler Bing or would we go on with life as though nothing had changed?

To discover how much TV has shaped our socializing, we decided to set up an experiment. First, we needed to assess how TV affects our lives. We did this by journaling our daily lives for one week, recording how TV and movies influenced them. We found that TV was habitual. It was not a scheduled daily event, but it was consistently watched at the same time every day. We watched TV regularly during the same times, like before bed and during dinner. For example, when Jake gets home from school, he automatically turns on his TV. He instinctively turns it on no matter what time it is or what's on. It has become a habit. Instead of calling a friend or playing catch with his brother he opts to watch the TV in place of real human contact. This has a direct effect on Jake's social life because he excludes himself from the activities going on around him. To simplify, we'll call this type of TV watching *habitual viewing*.

We also found that television was used for entertainment. In contrast to the habitual viewing, this refers to scheduled events for socializing. For instance, Jake planned an outing with friends to watch a movie. The movie wasn't the focus of the evening but provided a vehicle for communication and motivated their meeting. It has been our experience that people are uncomfortable getting together with no agenda in mind. In Jake's case, the movie created a comfortable atmosphere where everyone was able to openly discuss recent events and "hang out" without feeling like they weren't doing anything. The movie created the agenda and made it acceptable for them to meet. Other examples of this are Super Bowl parties and dinner-and-a-movie dates. We'll call this *scheduled viewing*. Because of the examples mentioned above, we hypothesized that TV and movies do play a role in our social lives and when TV and movies are absent we will interact more with others.

Next, we needed to show how TV and movies affect our social lives. Beginning April 4, we stopped watching TV and movies for one month and recorded the results in journals. We made it a point to write whenever we felt an impact of the absence of television or movies on our lives. This process would allow us to see how prevalent TV is in our lives and how we are affected when we try to avoid it. This was the most important part of our research because we experienced what life is like without TV in a TV-watching society. We had many fascinating results. Throughout our experiment we often felt separated from our families and friends because of their habitual television viewing. One instance in particular is that when Adrienne comes home from work at night she and her dad usually watch TV for about an hour before bed. This is the time they talk about their days and anything else going on. During the TV prohibition, Adrienne didn't sit with her dad because he continued the nightly ritual without her. They rarely talked and became distant from each other.

Jake had a similar experience. While visiting his girlfriend he found himself doing many activities alone while she was away at rehearsal. Although aware of Jake's project, her family would sit around watching TV while Jake had to find non-TV alternatives such as working out, playing guitar, and staring at the wall.

Watching TV has become such a habit for most people that they watch it even when there are better things to do. In the case with Adrienne's dad, you would think that he would stop watching TV, if only for a short time, to talk with Adrienne before bed. In Jake's case, it would seem obvious that someone at his girlfriend's house would make an effort to stop watching TV and spend some time with Jake. Instead, these people continued to habitually watch their programs. This shows that habitual viewing affects the way everyone socializes. The people in our examples are affected because they aren't socializing with us or with each other. We are affected because the presence of television limits who we are able to socialize with.

We also found that we had trouble sleeping at night because we had become so accustomed to watching TV before bed. Adrienne had it especially hard for the first week because her nightly ritual was to fall asleep with the TV on. Without it, she tossed until three or four in the morning. She became irritable with others, which directly affected how she socialized. The irritability made it hard for her to deal with those around her including her research partner, Jake, who thought she was a "real bitch" during that week.

The results were not all bad. We found that we spent our time more constructively. Instead of zoning out to pointless shows, we read more, completed various art projects and conversed more with those around us. Adrienne spent more time studying and on other school projects. She got an A on her second psychology test during the anti-TV campaign in contrast to her first test score of a C. Jake used his new-found free time lifting weights and went up fifty pounds on his bench press.

Although we did spend our time more constructively it took Jake longer than Adrienne to figure out alternative activities. Adrienne finished the many projects she had begun and, because of TV, never had time to finish. It had appeared to her that she had no time, but in actuality the few hours she spent watching TV every day is what kept her from getting these things done. While Adrienne had a waiting list full of projects Jake had no unfinished work to complete so he had to create new projects. This proved difficult for him during the first week and caused him some frustration. He spent his time literally staring at walls and listening to the buzzing in his ears but eventually found an escape through playing the guitar and reading. As time passed, Adrienne finished her projects and found it hard to remain busy. She experienced similar feelings as Jake did in the beginning. Jake found it easier to not watch TV as time went on because he was creating things to do.

Watching less TV increased our quality of life and in turn improved how we socialize. We learned new things, used our creativity, expanded our minds, and Adrienne's house has never been cleaner. Our social lives improved because we created more ways of engaging others in our activities. Adrienne and her dad began painting their walls, a project that had been on hold for months. It was a way for them to socialize without having to constantly be in conversation. Painting took the place of TV.

Another positive result is that we talked to those around us more than we did when we watched TV. Jake and his buddy Mark usually meet at Mark's house and talk over the television. During the month-long restriction, Jake and Mark had conversations free from TV interruptions. Jake and Mark were more focused on the conversation and had better social interaction.

Now that we had our results, we needed to find out if they were consistent with others' experiences. We did this by surveying 100 college-age students at Normandale Community College and comparing their viewing habits with the nation's scale. According to the *Kill Your TV* Web site, the nation watches 4.5 hours of TV a day. We found that Normandale students watched an average of 3.21 hours a day, which is significantly less time than the national survey showed. This difference can be explained by the sample used. Because Normandale is a community college, the students spend a lot of time commuting to school, then to work, which leaves little time for them to be at home watching TV or movies. If we broadened our sample to include similar-aged people who attend universities or don't go to school at all we would most likely find that the average number of hours viewed would increase because they have more spare time.

We completed our project by gathering a group of ten people together to abstain from TV and movies for one week and record their reactions in a questionnaire. This was essential to increase the credibility of our month-long research project. We needed a wider range of people who had similar experiences, such as feeling excluded from their social group, to strengthen our point. When we found those people in the sample had similar feelings we could extend our hypothesis to a wider range of people.

The most difficult part of this operation was finding volunteers to abstain from watching TV. We assumed that finding people to participate would be very simple because our surveys showed that the average Normandale student only watches about 3.21 hours of TV per day. In reality, it proved very difficult. When given the challenge, people would tell us how easy it would be to abstain from TV and movies, because they watched so little anyway, but when asked to participate they would decline. This shows that even though Normandale students watch little TV, compared to the national average, the TV and movies they do watch they hold so dear that they won't give them up.

Because of the difficulty in finding Normandale students to do this project, we had to use outside sources, like family members and friends. These outside sources were supposed to help us increase the credibility of our one-month research but caused some experimental error because the test subjects for the survey and the one-week trial were not consistent. In addition, the questionnaires weren't as helpful as we had hoped they would be. Eight out of ten participants failed to complete the entire week without watching TV. Two failed after the first day. The two who made it through the week didn't have TVs. From these results we can assume that eight out of ten people can't go even a week without watching TV. This statement would be stronger if we had a larger sample and the project had been conducted for a longer period of time.

However, from our research we can establish that television and movies contribute greatly to how we socialize. The effects of this vary depending on what one wants to do with their time. TV can provide a relaxing getaway but usually inhibits us from socializing in other ways. We have concluded that TV has a negative effect on how we socialize. It prevents us from having quality conversations, prevents interaction with those around us, and causes us to waste our time.

Works Cited

Hardbeck, Daniel. *Kill Your TV.* 17 May 2001. *WWW.killyourtv.com.*

QUESTIONS FOR INQUIRY AND ACTION

1. Analyze Mulholland and Martin's paper as an example of a student research project. What kinds of projects could you develop for your own course? Are you allowed to do collaborative work in your courses? What would be appealing or discouraging about researching and writing collaboratively?

2. How would Mulholland and Martin converse with the young television-watching Tony Earley? In what ways do you think they would say that television affected his life?

3. Mulholland and Martin chose not to focus on the content of television shows but on the viewing time itself. Thus they are not making an argument about the beneficial or harmful elements of the popular culture of television, which is the focus of many research projects on television viewing. Research the effects of television viewing for yourself. Where would you go for quantitative data? Do people really spend that many hours in front of the television? And how would you interpret it? What does that tell us? What is your hypothesis?

4. In the essay, Mulholland and Martin refer to the *Kill Your TV* Web site. The site encourages visitors to give up television for 30 days to see how much their lives will improve without it. Try the "Kill Your TV" challenge for yourself. Monitor your results by writing in your notebook whenever you miss watching television. How does your life change when you're not watching television?

DAVID BELL Community and Cyberculture

David Bell is Reader in Cultural Studies at Staffordshire University in Eng-
land. He has written a number of works on cultural geography, sexuality, con-
sumption, food, and technology including (with G. Valentine) Consuming
Geographies: We Are Where We Eat *(1997), and (with B. Kennedy)* The Cybercultures Reader *(2000). "Community and Cyberculture" is a chapter from*
his book, An Introduction to Cybercultures *(New York: Routledge, 2001).*

Words on a screen are quite capable of. . . creating a community from a
collection of strangers.

Howard Rheingold

One of the most prominent and controversial aspects of emerging cybercultures is the question of community. In this chapter, I want to trace the debates
about online or virtual communities, and look at research that attempts to shed
light on the kinds of communities seen to be forming in cyberspace. The debate
is controversial in that it highlights the tensions between different standpoints
on the promises and limitations of cyberculture. It is also controversial because
it has at its heart an argument about the relationship between online life and
off-line "real life" (RL). Finally, it is controversial because it involves making arguments about the status of RL communities as well as online communities. In each
of these areas there has been considerable debate.

Getting a sense of perspective on the issues and questions surrounding online
or virtual communities thus requires that we simultaneously look at arguments
about off-line or RL communities. What are their contemporary characteristics?
Have broader social, political, economic and cultural transformations altered
our sense of membership and belonging in communities? These questions mean
that we have to think about the changes brought about by processes such as detraditionalization, globalization and postmodernization—and then think about how
these relate to arguments about RL and online community. We'll begin by looking at the broad terms of this debate.

Arguments About Community

Barry Wellman and Milena Gulia (1999) comment that much of the debate on
virtual community has been polemical, split between those who argue that cyberspace re-enchants community (perceived as eroded in "real life") on the one hand,
and on the other those who argue that online community is damaging RL community, by encouraging a withdrawal from "real life." As they put it, the terms
of this debate are problematic, in that they are "Manichean, presentist, unscholarly, and parochial" (Wellman and Gulia 1999: 167). This means that, in their
opinion, the debate is polarized into two totally opposing viewpoints (it is

Manichean), lacks a sense of the history of community (it is presentist), depends largely on anecdote and "travellers' tales" (it is unscholarly) and forces a separation between online life and RL (it is parochial). The two camps, which Wellman and Gulia refer to as "duelling dualists," have thus established a partisan, antagonistic argument. While this is true to some extent—and it is certainly easy to find clear examples of both "pro-" and "anti-" arguments, as we shall see later—the debate has also generated considerable research, and a fuller picture of the overall "terrain" of contemporary communities, both online and off, is emerging. It is that terrain that I want to explore here. So, while there are enthusiastic proponents of the social benefits of online community set in opposition to hostile critics of the phenomenon, it is possible to navigate a path somewhere between these camps, and to think about online community a bit more rigorously; and that's my aim in this chapter.

As I've already said, in order to get to grips with arguments about online community, we need to understand *arguments about community* as a whole—as James Slevin (2000: 91) writes, studies of online community need to be set in the broader context of "a critical approach to the concept of 'community' in late modernity." So, we need to begin by thinking about what "community" means today. And right from the start we begin to get a sense of the complexities of a term that is also very commonsensical and commonplace. Trying to summarize this in an earlier project with a very different focus—the food we eat—I once tried to elaborate on this:

> "Community". It's a word we all use, in many different ways, to talk about. . . what? About belonging and exclusion, about "us" and "them". It's a common-sense thing, used in daily discussions, in countless associations, from "care in the community" to the Community Hall; from "community spirit" to the "business community". . . . Many of us would lay claim to belonging to at least one community, whether it is the "lesbian and gay community" or just the "local community" where we live. . . . [T]he term community is not only descriptive, but also normative and ideological: it carries a lot of baggage with it.
>
> (Bell and Valentine 1997: 93)

The study of community (and communities) has been a sustained effort to think through this complex; to think about what makes a community, and what its members get from belonging to that community (see Wilbur CR). In a lot of cases, the way this is approached is framed around something that is perceived to be a "threat" to community—usually one or more of the transformations brought about by modernization (and subsequently postmodernization, as we shall see). Among the best-known examples of this kind of community-thinking comes from urban sociology—from the work and legacy of people like Ferdinand Tönnies and Louis Wirth from a century ago. Both argued that mass urbanization was transforming community—and transforming it for the worse (see Jary and Jary 1991).

5   Tönnies' (1955) *Community and Association,* originally published in 1887, outlined two types of "community," named *Gemeinschaft* and *Gesellschaft.* The former is characterized as a "total community": as fully integrated vertically and

horizontally, as stable and long-lasting, as comprised of a dense web of social inter-action supported by commonality and mutuality, manifest in shared rituals and symbols—as a local social contract embedded in place and made durable by face-to-face interactions. This is the "traditional" community, where everyone knows everyone, everyone helps everyone, and the bonds between people are tight and multiple (someone's neighbour is also their workmate *and* the person they go drinking with *and* their relative, etc.). Set against this, and ushered in by urban-ization, is the social arrangement Tönnies names *Gesellschaft* ("association" or "society"). City folk, the argument goes, are removed from *Gemeinschaft*-like sit-uations, and thrown together in the dense heterogeneity of the city. Their long-established bonds and norms are lost, and the social fabric is radically transformed. People's relationships become shallow and instrumental—because the city is so huge, *Gemeinschaft*-like communities can never grow; people are too busy, always on the move. This disembedding impoverishes communities, even as it broad-ens the social sphere: we might meet more people, but our relationships with them are partial and transitory. As Kollock and Smith (1999: 16) lament, "there is a great deal of loneliness in the lives of many city dwellers." The "problems" of urbanization identified in Tönnies' formulation have, many would argue, been deepened by transformations brought about by postmodernization, which has radically reshaped the contemporary cityscape (Davis 1990).

The *ideal* of community enshrined in *Gemeinschaft* has an enduring legacy in the popular imagination, then, always (it seems) tinged with nostalgia. It might be argued, in fact, that community has become overwritten by nostalgia, in that the way it is talked about so often focuses on its perceived loss, or decline, or erosion. In party-political rhetoric, for example, community is seen as the stable bulwark of society, imagined in distinctly romantic, *Gemeinschaft*-like ways (epit-omized in the UK by village life and in the US by small-town life). Contempo-rary social, political, economic and cultural transformations are today implicated in the 'death' of this kind of community. We need, therefore, to look at insights into the contemporary meanings of community, and their contestation.

We'll start with a discussion of one particular form of community, since the insights it offers will benefit our discussion. The type of community is the nation, and the insight comes from Benedict Anderson (1983), who famously suggested that nations are *imagined communities*. What this means is that the work of mak-ing a nation as a community depends on the use of symbolic resources and devices: because we can never know or interact with all those others with whom we share national identification, we need "things" to coalesce a shared sense of identity around—a flag, a national anthem, a set of customs and rituals (sometimes referred to as "invented traditions"). These kinds of communities, moreover, only exist because their members *believe* in them, and maintain them through shared cultural practices (Edensor 2001). We can make productive use of Anderson's insight at scales other than the nation, to consider the extent to which *all* com-munities are imagined and held together by shared cultural practice (rather than just face-to-face interaction). When we come to explore online communities in detail, this will be an important thing to remember.

Aside from the idea of imagined communities, what I want to do here is look at some of the processes that, like urbanization for Tönnies, are frequently signalled as in some way or another *threatening* community (though it might be less scare-mongering for us to say that they are *transforming* community). A lot of these are conceived as symbolic or symptomatic of late-modern (or postmodern) societies (Giddens 1991). I've already listed a couple of these, so let's return to them and flesh them out a bit. The first concept is *detraditionalization,* or the shift towards a "post-traditional" society. The erosion of tradition is itself associated with another key transformation, *disembedding*—in turn linked with a third process, *globalization.* We need to discuss these together, as they are centrally implicated in changes to ideas of community.

Globalization can be thought of as the sum of a series of processes that have forged a sense of increasing connectedness between people and places dispersed around the world. It is defined quite neatly by Malcolm Waters (1995: 3) as "a social process in which the constraints of geography on social and cultural arrangements recede and in which people become increasingly aware that they are receding." Innovations in transport and communication have effectively shrunk the world—a process sometimes called "time–space compression" (Harvey 1989). All kinds of things now move speedily around the world, criss-crossing it in complex, disjunctive ways: people, ideas, images, commodities, technologies, money (Appadurai 1996). All of these things, and our experience of them, are thus *disembedded*—no longer rooted in place, but characterized as global *flows.*

10   As Waters' definition makes clear, an important aspect of globalization is our *experience* or perception of this reshaping and shrinking of the world. Late-modernity, it has been argued, is marked by heightened *reflexivity* (Giddens 1991)—by a kind of self-scrutiny and self-consciousness, by which we rework our sense of who we are in the face of the global flows we come into contact with. Part of this reflexivity involves making choices about our identities and our politics; since we are *disembedded,* and able to access global flows of ideas and information, we can choose who we want to be (within certain structural limitations, of course!). And this disembeddedness and reflexivity enables us to question and transform the taken-for-granted, leading to *detraditionalization* (Heelas *et al.* 1996)—a chance to make over the social fabric anew and, in terms of our focus here, to *imagine* new forms of community.

Now, while all this sounds quite exhilarating, some critics argue that it has severe negative impacts for us all, for example by making us "schizophrenic," and giving us a "depthless" existence (Jameson 1991). Moreover, these processes may have transformed the forms and functions of community, but they have not led to an erosion of the *ideal* of community—in fact, many commentators have argued that the "*uncertainization*" of late-modern societies actually strengthens our need to "belong" (Slevin 2000). As we shall see, in many such accounts there emerges a problematic *essentializing* of this need, which theorizes community as a "natural" manifestation of an "innate" human desire for association and identification—and this motif resurfaces in discussions of online communities, too.

Added to these concerns about late-modern or postmodern life are analyses of the intensification of the "problems" of urban living under late modernity. As cities sprawl and fracture, and become the battleground for forms of social, economic and political struggle, so they become increasingly characterized as landscapes of alienation and foreboding. Ziauddin Sardar (CR: 743) writes that cities have come to be seen as "little more than alien perpendicular tangles," adding that "inner cities resemble bomb sites and fear and loathing stalk the streets." "White flight" and "fortressing"—the paranoid emptying-out of cities as middle-class citizens retreat to gated suburban and exurban "planned communities"—can thus be read as responses to this particular city vision (Goldberg 2000). (Of course, the flipside to this formulation—as we shall see—is cities as spectacular sites of difference and cosmopolitan syncretism; see Young 2000.)

All of this, it should now be clear, has tremendous implications for how we think about community, and is useful for our discussion of online community. The notion of imagined community means that we can rethink how we conceptualize (and create) communities—and the Internet is an imaginative space to do this. Globalization can be argued to open up the whole world as a potential source of community—and the Internet has been seen as key to this. Disembedding allows us to choose our communities—and the Internet gives us a vast reservoir of choices. Reflexivity allows us to think about who we are and who we want to be—and the Internet is the ideal site to "play" with our identities. Detraditionalization frees us from old obligations, and lets us give community a postmodern make-over—and again the Internet offers possibilities to substantially re-imagine the very notion of community. Cities have become too big, too fractured, too scary—and the Internet offers a safe space to build new communities in. In sum, in the face of all this disembedding, detraditionalizing, globalizing uncertainty, we need to find new way to belong—and the Internet is on hand to provide exactly that.

There is, however, an important paradox to be recognized here, summed up by this question: *is the Internet the solution or part of the problem?* As Heather Bromberg puts it:

> It does seem clear that people make use of this technology to combat the symptoms that are characteristic of. . . the "postmodern condition." The technologies themselves are highly characteristic of the postmodern by virtue of their fluidity and malleability. Ironically, however, it is their fluid and malleable nature which leads them to be used to combat that "condition."
>
> (Bromberg 1996: 147)

As we shall see, there are different perspectives on this matter. What should now be apparent, then, is that cyberspace is certainly seen to be *intensifying* the transformations in late-modern (or postmodern) conceptions and uses of community. It is not unique—as Wellman and Gulia (1999) remind us—but its role cannot be denied, and shouldn't be downplayed. Ultimately, however, we return to the central questions fought over by those "duelling dualists" of online community: *Are these transformations in community a good thing or a bad thing? Are virtual communities ameliorating or exacerbating these transformations in the forms and meanings of community?* We need to turn our attention to those questions now.

Arguments About Online Community

Cyberspace is already the home of thousands of groups of people who meet to share information, discuss mutual interests, play games, and carry out business. Some of these groups are both large and well developed, but critics argue that these groups do not constitute *real* communities. Something is missing, they argue, that makes these online communities pale substitutes for more traditional face-to-face communities. Other respond that not only are online communities real communities, but also that they have the potential to support face-to-face communities and help hold local communities together.

(Kollock and Smith 1999: 16)

15   In order to get a fix on arguments around online community, I want to begin by looking at the writings of Howard Rheingold, often cited as among the most enthusiastic proponents of the individual and social benefits of online community life. I will draw on the ideas he presents in an essay called "A slice of life in my virtual community," first published in 1992 (Rheingold 1999)—ideas that recur in his book-length argument *for* online community, *Virtual Community: homesteading on the electronic frontier* (Rheingold 1993). Already, the title of that book might give us a hint at Rheingold's position—something which has also been seized upon by those who criticize his vision, as we shall see. The use of the terms "homesteading" and "frontier" give us a particular imagining of community, typical of what Wellman and Gulia (1999) identify as a nostalgic, pastoralist "myth" of community. Rheingold is unapologetic about this, describing virtual community as "a bit like a neighborhood pub or coffee shop" (422) and comparing its spirit of mutuality with "barn-raising" (425). So, what is his version of online community like? He describes it thus:

In cyberspace, we chat and argue, engage in intellectual intercourse, perform acts of commerce, exchange knowledge, share emotional support, make plans, brainstorm, gossip, feud, fall in love, find friends and lose them, play games and metagames, flirt, create a little high art and a lot of idle talk. We do everything people do when they get together, but we do it with words on computer screens, leaving our bodies behind. Millions of us have already built communities where our identities commingle and interact electronically, independent of local time or location.

(Rheingold 1999: 414)

This process is, for Rheingold, simultaneously surprising and inevitable. It's inevitable for two reasons. First, it's inevitable because folks "are going to do what people always do with a new communication technology: use it in ways never intended or foreseen by its inventors, to turn old social codes inside out and make new kinds of communities possible" (415). Second, it's inevitable because virtual communities are a natural response to "the hunger for community that has followed the disintegration of traditional communities around the world" (418). In the place of these communities, we are left with the "automobile-centric, suburban, highrise, fast food, shopping mall way of life" (421), which is lonely, isolated, empty. There's the logic of this kind of thesis on online communities: "traditional communities" have disintegrated (an interesting choice of word, implying they have fallen apart and *dis-integrated,* i.e. become too heterogeneous), and human ingenuity, combined with a "hunger" for community, can rewire CMC to rebuild those "lost" communities in cyberspace—which is itself presented as virgin terrain, as a new "frontier" ripe for barn-raising and communo-genesis.

Online communities are therefore thought of here as growing "organically" to fill the space left by the demise of "traditional" communities; at its simplest, online community-formation occurs "when enough people bump into each other often enough in cyberspace" (413). *Virtual Community* expands this organic metaphor:

> In terms of the way the whole system is propagating and evolving, think of cyberspace as a social petri dish, the Net the agar medium, and *virtual communities, in all their diversity, as colonies of microorganisms that grow in petri dishes.* . . . Whenever CMC technology becomes available to people anywhere, they *inevitably* build virtual communities with it, just as microorganisms inevitably create colonies.
>
> (Rheingold 1993: 6; my emphasis)

There's a lot to think about in this formulation of cyberspace-as-petri-dish (as a kind of "growth medium") and online communities as microorganisms that *inevitably* grow in the medium. It's troublesome in its essentializing of community-formation, for one thing; it also conjures particular images of communities as mould- or germ-like.

Rheingold fleshes out online community life by walking us through his "virtual neighborhood" on the WELL—the Whole Earth 'Lectronic Link, a pioneering Bay Area based virtual community that grew out of the productive intersection in San Francisco of 1960s *Whole Earth* counterculture, computer hackers and hobbyists, and "deadheads" (Grateful Dead fans) (on the "secret history" of this melding, see Davis 1998). In the increasingly complex and heterogeneous world of the WELL, Rheingold indentifies those "places" he most often visits as his "customized neighborhood" (431); added together, these "places" make a mosaic of his interests, intersecting with the interests of fellow WELLers. That the community condenses out of individuals" interests is made clear by Rheingold himself, in a passage where he compares the possibilities for finding likeminds in cyberspace with the difficulties of doing that through other media:

> You can't simply pick up a phone and ask to be connected with someone who wants to talk about Islamic art or California wine, or someone with a three year old daughter or a 30 year old Hudson; you can, however, join a computer conference on any of those topics, then open a public or private correspondence with the previously-unknown people you find in that conference.
>
> (Rheingold 1999: 423)

So, the possibility of community arises from shared interests—these then catalyse the social bonds that extend beyond the narrow focus of those interests. But how does a sense of community develop from that? Rheingold answers this question by discussing shared social codes ("netiquette") and reciprocity ("knowledge-potlatching") as social cement to bind those interest-groups as communities. In *Virtual Community,* he adds longevity, critical mass and "sufficient human feeling" as the bonding material that turns association into community (Rheingold 1993: 5).

Now, I was mulling this over last night, as I drove home from work, and an analogy came to me. It was prompted by Steve Jones' (1995) comparison of the building of highways across America and the construction of the information superhighway, and by Rhiengold's mention of his "30 year old Hudson", and by a discussion by Wellman and Gulia (1999) about a BMW aficionados' online discussion group—and by sitting in my car. As a bridge between virtual community (above) and its discontents (below), then, I'd like to think this through. The analogy is this: I drive a car. *To what extent could I argue that I belong to a "community of car drivers"?* Let's work it up. Part of my identity is as a "car driver"—institutionalized by things like my driving licence (which gives me certain privileges, and functions as a broader "badge" of my identity, to prove who I am). In that, I share part of my identity with other car drivers—it is something we have in common. This can itself be formalized or deepened (by joining an owner's club for my model of car, for example). Also, I might talk to another car driver about cars or driving, and through that build up a broader "friendship" with them. I have a set of knowledges that all car drivers have to varying degrees: knowledge about driving, and about cars (though this has its limits—like my knowledge about computers—and I sometimes have to turn to "experts" for help). Moreover, the "community of car drivers" has a set of social conventions, some of them formalized (the Highway Code), some of them tacit (driving etiquette, like letting someone pull out in front of me at a junction). There's a broad reciprocity to this. If I let someone pull out in front of me, she or he might do the same favour for another driver. Likewise, if I break down at the side of the road, I hope that a passing driver might stop to help me out, just as I would assist a stranded fellow traveller. The community informally polices the transgression of this social code—by honking the horn, for example (and at its most extreme, by road rage). And my car also facilitates my membership of "off-road" communities: when I drive to visit my family, or car-share with a colleague, or give a neighbour a ride home, or pick up a hitch-hiker. So, I return to my question: *does that make me part of a car driving community?* Whether the answer is "Yes" or "No" has, I think, implications for the question of online community. I think for now, however, my best answer is an unemphatic "Maybe." In order to transpose this conundrum to cyberspace, I'd like now to map out the ways in which online communities are "made."

What Makes an Online Community?

20   Let me start here by sharing another of my conundrums: I have been worrying about the distinction between a "community" and a "subculture"—especially since some of the groups I discuss as cybersubcultures . . . have been named as communities

by other researchers. For example, Nancy Baym (1998) discusses online soap opera fans as a "community," and Nessim Watson (1997) describes fans of "jam rock" band Phish as a virtual community, even as he debates the usefulness of the very term "online community." On the other hand, right at the start of *Virtual Community,* Howard Rheingold (1993: 2) calls the WELL a "full-scale sub-culture," and Catherine Bassett (1997: 538) describes LambdaMOO as composed of "subcultural spaces." Clearly, in some instances, there's merely a slippage between the two words, both taken to mean the same thing—Baym's own work has used both to describe the same group of online soap fans, for example. But I think that the two words have very different *connotations,* so I started to wonder where the boundary between terms like these lies. I thought that maybe researchers looking at online social formations might more readily describe their study groups as communities than those who look at offline groups. Ziauddin Sardar expresses his exasperation at the misuses of "community" in cyberspace:

> Belonging and posting to a Usenet group, or logging on to a bulletin board community, confirms no more an identity than belonging to a stamp collecting club or a Morris dancing society. . . . On this logic, the accountants of the world will instantly be transformed into a community the moment they start a newsgroup: *alt.accountants* (with *alt.accountants.spreadsheets* constituting a sub-community).
>
> (Sardar CR: 743)

I think we can guess from this that Sardar wouldn't see car drivers as a community, then! But his point is a valid one; some online groups aren't communities, and neither do they self-identify as communities. They may be too "task-oriented" (and therefore not "social" enough), or might not stimulate sufficient interaction to develop "group-specific meanings," or they might be too divided and divisive to coalesce (Baym 1998). Shawn Wilbur (CR: 55) raises this question, too, when he asks if we can tell the difference between "a community and a market segment, or a culture of compatible consumption?" I'd like to add my own question to his: why is it that commentators are so keen to see *communities* (rather than market segments or cultures of compatible consumption) in cyberspace?

Could it be that the technology effectively turns a subculture into a community? Bruno Latour (1991) once wrote that "technology is society made durable," which we could maybe see as a way of thinking about how computers might make a subculture into a community. Or, does the technology merely give us a silicon-induced *illusion* of community? The "aura" of cybertechnology—which we'll pick up on again later—might in fact be the cement that binds these communities together, just as earlier "communications communities" were seen to form around the telegraph, the radio and the television (Stone CR). Paradoxically, of course, technologies such as the car are seen as moving us in the opposite direction—atomizing individuals in their "metal cocoons" (Lupton 1999). Some technologies are seen as collectivizing, others as individuating, therefore. Computers presently sit uneasily in this formulation, potentially able to go either way, or pulling both ways simultaneously. Which direction you prioritize, it seems, depends on your perspective on and experience of computers and communities.

Baym (1998) gets round this issue by arguing that an online community is a community if participants *imagine* themselves as a community. And given the positively-invested rhetoric of community, it's understandable why there might indeed be a "will-to-community." In that sense, car drivers *might* imagine themselves as a community—for example when their "right" or "freedom" to enact their identities is threatened (by car tax or fuel prices), but in that kind of context community is a *defensive* concept, bringing people together only when they feel under collective threat. Maybe the "ambient fear" of the death of community is the threat that prompts defensive communo-genesis in cyberspace, then? I doubt we can resolve this question here, but it's worth keeping in mind as we move now to look the "stuff" of virtual communities.

Latour's aphorism about technology being society made durable refers to technology in its broadest sense, to the material traces left by social interaction (texts, tools, etc.) that "carry" the society beyond the face-to-face. In the immaterial world of cyberculture, there are material traces, too—the texts that constitute the shared space of community: "[s]table patterns of social meanings, manifested through a group's on-going discourse, . . . enable participants to *imagine themselves part of a community*" (Baym 1998: 62; my emphasis). Analysing these discursive patterns has been a central strategy for getting inside online communities, and "talk-and-text" type readings of online interactions are commonplace in the literature (see Watson 1997; Baym 1998, for examples discussed in this chapter).

25   The discursive patterns that most interest me are the social codes developed within online communities; the ways in which members of communities establish group norms and find ways to put these in place. These are interesting stories for a number of reasons. They reveal the implicit assumptions about what makes a community (what things are needed: money? laws? guns?), and they reveal the *limits* of the community. In order to explore these issues, I want to begin by looking at work on the kinds of social contracts drawn up in MUDs, and then move over to a virtual "city," Lucasfilm's Habitat.

Kollock and Smith (1999) provide a summary of forms of social control in MUDs. It should be remembered that MUDs are particular kinds of online communities, with their origins in the fantasy role-playing world of Dungeons and Dragons. There has been a branching into two distinct types, "social MUDs" and "adventure MUDs," with the latter retaining most prominently the "sword and sorcery" motifs (although this can still be traced in "social MUDs" like LambdaMOO). The social codes therefore reflect the virtual world created—a world of magic and mayhem, where characters might kill or be killed, or use "voodoo" to "rape" each other (Dibbell 1999). Even when behaviour isn't that dramatic, the "disinhibition" experienced online allows participants to behave in ways they wouldn't dream of doing IRL (Slevin 2000).

The list of modes of social control in MUDs picked out by Kollock and Smith includes eliminating specific commands in the software (such as the "shout" command, to stop rowdiness); instituting "gag" commands to silence miscreants; restricting the "rights" of troublesome participants; public shaming; banishment;

introducing admission policies (to vet potential participants); registering participants" identities (to increase accountability and prohibit anonymity); forming regulatory committees; establishing frameworks for mediation; and vigilante action. The less "extreme" end of this spectrum includes elements of "netiquette", which covers minor transgressions such as shouting, cross-posting, lurking and flaming. However, Elizabeth Reid's (1999) work on adventure MUDs refers to the prominence of public displays of punishment there as a return to "Medieval" forms of social control, reversing Foucault's (1986) famous discussion of the historical move from punishment to discipline—an analysis at odds with the supposed "freedom" on offer in cyberspace.

In his widely-known discussion of online "rape," Julian Dibbell (1999) shows how the crisis brought about by Mr Bungle's use of "voodoo" in LambdaMOO galvanized the community into a heated debate about appropriate modes of intervention and sanction. The fall-out from that singular event radically transformed the structure of LambdaMOO, ushering in universal suffrage, an arbitration system, and the facility to eject troublesome visitors (the "@boot" command). As for Mr Bungle, perpetrator of the virtual "rape," he was "killed" by one of the MUD's wizards (though he soon returned under a new name, Dr Jest). For Dibbell, this incident "turned a database into a society." Against this, Kolko and Reid read instances like this as moments of "breakdown," in which "the inability of the community to collaborate effectively interrupted daily routines" (Kolko and Reid 1998: 225)—the "consensual hallucination" of cyberspace has to be matched by "consensual discourse" if communities are going to be sustainable. Importantly, Kolko and Reid stress the problem for communo-genesis posed by the multiplicity of on-line identities—or, more accurately, from the way that multiplicity is re-singularized online. As people fracture their sense of self into multiple online selves, they paradoxically produce a portfolio of singularities, rather than recognizing that multiplicity dwells within an individual self. As they write, "it has been all too easy for virtual communities to encourage multiplicity but not coherence, with each individual persona having a limited, undiversified social range" (227). This compartmentalization stands in the way of community-building in that it produces rigid online identities, making conflict-resolution and accommodation difficult. As we shall see later in this chapter, this issue is linked to the problematic of online community's dealings with otherness.

My second story of online social contract comes from Lucasfilm's Habitat, an early experiment in virtual cityscaping (see Ostwald and Stone CR). The evolution of a "community" or "society" in Habitat—different from LambdaMOO in that it is a graphical computer environment complete with buildings and avatars (cartoon-like depictions of Habitat's inhabitants, who can move around, and "talk" to each other in speech-bubbles)—gives us another interesting set of insights into online community. Ostwald (CR) plots the story of Habitat, which also has part of its ancestry in role-play gaming, describing how inhabitants made a virtual community come to life on screen. As with Dibbell's reading of LambdaMOO, the first incidents to turn this software environment into a society were crimes, though in this case they were robberies. The "Gods" who programmed Habitat refused to intervene, leaving the residents to sort the problem out—the crime-wave was meantime escalating, as the robbers now had guns (weapons were already in place in Habitat, as part of its gaming ancestry). Murders were committed, and gangs went on killing sprees (although avatars would rise from the dead next day). A meeting was called, a sheriff appointed, and some basic laws were hastily drawn up. Once these bedrocks had been established, Habitat grew in a recognizable way—like a town from the Old West. A church and a newspaper were established; the economic system stabilized and some folks got rich; formalized forms of government, with elections, were put in place. Before it was closed down (due largely to external factors), Habitat had become a simulation of smalltown America—showing us, I think, that self-organized communities in cyberspace can indeed perform a Rheingold-like act of homesteading. Of course, that they *needed* to perform homesteading is equally revealing—that a settled political, legal and economic system had to emerge to stem the tide of anarchy and lawlessness. We might say that the Habitat social experiment therefore failed, in that it produced a conservative virtual community. That's one prominent criticism levelled at online communities, and I want now to turn to this and other arguments *against* online community.

Arguments Against Online Community

30   To begin with—and I know this might seem unfair, or biased—I want to look specifically at arguments against Howard Rheingold. In his essay "Cyberspace and the world we live in," Kevin Robins (in Bell and Kennedy 2000) gives Rheingold's virtual community thesis a thorough working over. Robins begins his critique by reminding us that any thinking we might do about cybercommunities has to be located in "the world we live in": "virtual communities do not exist in a different world. They must be situated in the context of [the] . . . new cultural and political geographies" of our time, he writes (CR: 86). What particularly concerns Robins, in fact, is the way in which the relationship between online life and RL is framed by writers like Rheingold. As he puts it, we can see in arguments for virtual community "the sense of virtual reality as an alternative reality in a *world gone wrong*. Technosociality is seen as the basis for developing new and *compensatory* forms of community and conviviality" (87; my emphasis). In this "world gone wrong", community has become a "lost object," nostalgized and looked-for (or longed-for) in cyberspace. In particular, Robins argues, the sense of "community" mobilized in accounts like Rheingold's "freezes" history, and turns away from broader questions of society and polities: "what we have is the preservation through simulation of old forms of solidarity and community. In the end, not an alternative society, but an alternative to society" (89). And, in its desire for a kind of smalltown, *Gemeinschaft*-like community, Rheingold's vision neutralizes difference, producing a virtual version of the American "fortress communities" that Mike Davis (1990) describes. For all their proponents' chatter about inclusion and heterogeneity, the space of online community is, rather, a "domain of order, refuge, withdrawal" (Robins CR: 91). As he writes in another essay,

"virtual culture is a culture of retreat from the world" (Robins 1999: 166). Arthur and Marilouise Kroker describe the withdrawal into VR as "bunkering in":

> bunkering in is about something really simple: being sick of others and trying to shelter the beleaguered self in a techno-bubble. . . . Digital reality is perfect. It provides the bunker self with immediate, universal access to a global community *without people:* electronic communication without social contact, being digital without being human, going on-line without leaving the safety of the electronic bunker.
>
> (Kroker and Kroker CR: 96–7)

Being "sick of others" reminds us that membership of online communities is elective and selective, as is withdrawal: "cyberspace community is self-selecting; . . . it is contingent and transitory, depending on a shared interest of those with the attention-span of a thirty-second soundbite" (Sardar CR: 744). Moreover, "bunkering in" means cocooning oneself from the "contamination of pluralism" found in the RL city (*Ibid*): being "sick of others" thus also implies being sick of *otherness*—a point we shall return to later. Ultimately, Robins reads virtual life as regressive, infantile and Edenic (the second VR life-strategy the Krokers highlight is "dumbing down"), and its will-to-community as manifesting a "familial communitarianism" (Robins CR: 92; see also Robins 1999). (This should also remind us that in RL, too, similar sentiments are expressed in communitarian rhetoric seen, for example, in New Labour; see Driver and Martell 1997.)

Steve Jones also does some deconstructive work on visions of virtual community, and his comments are equally insightful and useful to us here. For example, he argues that:

> The situation in which we find computer-mediated communities at present is that their very definition as communities is perceived as a "good thing," creating a solipsistic and self-fulfilling community that pays little attention to political action outside of that which secures its own maintenance. Community and power do not necessarily intersect, but such solipsism is a form of power, wielded by those who occupy the community.
>
> (Jones 1995: 25)

Moreover, Jones questions the entire "community ideal," asking why we continue to hold up face-to-face interaction (or interface-to-interface interaction in cyberspace) as the best way to relate to one another and as the building-block of community. However, he argues that we always experience something lacking in the online simulacra of face-to-face interaction—and it might be that this "gap" or "lack" itself feeds the yearning for community: we're looking for that "lost object", and will it into being on our screens.

Jones' point about the fetish of community is interesting, in that we need to contest the notion of community as a "good thing." Whenever I've talked with students about *Gemeinschaft*-like communities, the tales they tell of their experiences are equally ambivalent: the strong ties matched with small minds, community spirit matched with oppressive regulation, safety matched with surveillance. *The place where everybody knows your name is also the place where everyone knows your business.* Small, tight-knit communities are fine if you fit in, but are incredibly exclusive and uncomfortable places if you don't—witness the mass migrations of "outcasts" such as sexual minorities from the country to the city (Bell and Binnie 2000). However, as Wellman and Gulia (1999) write, most RL communities are no longer like that—so why are online communitarians trying to reclaim a virtual *Gemeinschaft?* Are there no other ways of thinking about online sociality?

Beyond Online Community?

35   In his book on new social movements, *Expressions of Identity,* Kevin Hetherington (1998) revisits Tönnies' work in the context of "neo-tribes," also drawing on the notion of the *Bund,* or communion—partly because it offers a better way to think through the kinds of groups he's interested in. As he says, "[t]he term community is far too vague and its association with the organic, traditional and ascriptive ideas of a past way of life is too inaccurate when trying to account for . . . elective identifications and groupings" (Hetherington 1998: 83). Gordon Graham (1999: 131) also highlights the increasing conceptual meaninglessness of the term, arguing that "it seems that we cannot fail to be members of some community or other." Given the inaptitude of community as a term to describe online groupings, as noted by both Hetherington and Graham, might Hetherington's revival of the *Bund* offer us a new way of thinking about what people do together in cyberspace?

A now-neglected sociological concept, *Bund* was partly conceived (by Herman Schmalenbach, in the 1920s) as a "third term" to add to Tönnies' dichotomy— and Hetherington reintroduces it in a way that, I think, is incredibly useful for thinking about online sociality. (Hetherington never turns his attention to online life, though he ponders in a footnote the possibility of exploring *Bünde* in cyberspace.) It might be, even, that talking of the "virtual *Bund*" can lead us out of the impasse of arguments for or against virtual community.

Hetherington quotes from Freund (1978), who was busy dismissing the term *Bund* as "a place for the expression of enthusiasms, of ferment, of unusual doings" (quoted in Hetherington 1998: 88)—to me, that sounds a lot like descriptions found in texts like *Virtual Community.* A *Bund,* then, is an elective grouping, bonded by affective and emotional solidarity, sharing a strong sense of belonging. Schmalenbach also identified the presence of "charismatic governance" in *Bünde* (as a corrective to Weber); while this might imply a charismatic leader, Hetherington argues than charisma can also be collective: "[t]erms like "energy" and "commitment", describing characteristics that all members are expected to exhibit, are the means by which this generalized charisma is likely to be expressed" (93). In terms of cyberspace, we might add a notion of "techno-charisma"—the aura of new technologies that lends them a charismatic appeal (Davis 1998). What's useful about this notion, then, is it allows us to disentangle ourselves from the Manichean, presentist, unscholarly and parochial arguments about online community; by recognizing that the problem is at least in part the over-freighted term "community" itself. Ananda Mitra (CR: 677) spots this, too—as the trouble with "the way we have been naturalized to think of communities."

Hetherington also fleetingly discusses ways of re-evaluating *Gesellschaft*-like sociality, drawing principally on Georg Simmel's work on the ways in which individuals manage the heterogeneity and ephemerality of urban life (see Simmel 1995; originally published 1903). As Hetherington describes, Simmel's writings show how "the individual uses the alienating experiences of modern life to promote a more cosmopolitan form of individuality" (Hetherington 1998: 95). This expressive individual, who wears his or her identity on the surfaces of his or her body, performs a new mode of communication based on signs. A similar manoeuvre—to turn urban anomie into something productive—can be found in other accounts, too. In terms of online communities, for example, Wellman and Gulia (1999) describe online life as city life; or, more accurately, as living "in the heart of densely populated, heterogeneous, *physically safe,* big cities" (172; my emphasis)—note the stress on "virtual safety", which marks cyberspace as preferable to cityspace.

Simmel's emphasis on making individuality work on the stage of the city streets also reminds me of Henning Bech's (1997) up-beat account of gay men's urban lives: of cruising, the gaze, the endless passage of strangers, the brief encounters. Anonymity, heterogeneity and ephemerality are here celebrated, even fetishized. Now, while I have a lot of sympathy for Bech's thesis, the introduction of homosexuality also makes me mindful of the exclusions and prohibitions played out in urban space (and not just for "sexual dissidents"). Cities of difference are also spaces of exclusion. This rejoinder ushers in the final question for this chapter.

Whose Online Community?

While Internet use may hold out the possibility of emancipation, we must at the same time be aware of how it might create new mechanisms of suppression.

(Slevin 2000: 109)

40   In order to think about inclusion and exclusion in online communities, I need to remind readers of the issues of information inequality. . . . Joining an online community is, in many accounts, described as unproblematic or "easy"—*all you need is a computer and a modem.* Considering the question of who can find a "home" in cyberspace, Susan Leigh Star in fact listed these minimal requirements (CR): having sufficient money to buy the equipment, and living in a "traditional home" with the telecommunications infrastructure needed for connection (or access to these facilities at work); having access to "maintenance people" to help out and to facilitate getting "plugged in"; possessing the requisite physical and educational abilities (being literate, being able to sit at a computer and type—or being aided in that process); and having the time, inclination and ability to build up a social network, to make and sustain membership of a "community." Stacked up like that, we can see the many obstacles that stand in a lot of people's way.

Even assuming those obstacles can be overcome, things needn't be plain sailing from here on in. All kinds of social and cultural barriers are also in place. Most online communities beyond the scale of the national are still usually run in English, for one thing. Then there are the ways in which "appropriate" criteria for membership might put up blocks, or lead to expulsion. Stone (CR) discusses an early San Francisco-based BBS known as CommuniTree, which worked as a homogeneous online community until it became too widely accessible (when Apple began giving computers to schools). The orderly community became rapidly "choked to death" by the volume of postings, mainly from adolescent schoolkids. The "Gods" who operated the system hadn't factored this kind of material into their vision of CommuniTree. In the end, as Stone writes, "unlimited access to all conferences did not work in the context of increasing availability of terminals to young men who did not necessarily share the Tree gods' ideas of what counted as community. As one Tree veteran put it, "The barbarian hordes mowed us down" (Stone CR: 511). What this example shows us is one particular limit of one BBS—that it couldn't cope with the *"barbarian hordes,"* the undesirable others. As in Rheingold's writing of online community, the ideal-type is a friendly neighbourhood or coffee bar, where difference is contained.

Moreover, the broader question of difference online needs to be added to this mix. . . . [T]he possibilities for "identity-play" in cyberspace have complex implications for how otherness is produced and consumed online. MUDs like LambdaMOO, which allow participants to construct fantastical new identities, tend towards forms of self-presentation that suppress RL axes of difference in favour of mystical hybrids and shapeshifters. Where RL identities are mobilized—notably gender identities—these tend to be stereotypical "hyper-genderings" (Bassett 1997). So, some kinds of difference are fetishized, while others are invisibilized. Online disembodiment (or re-embodiment), held as liberatory, therefore raises intensely problematic questions about otherness in cybercommunities. As Sardar (CR: 744) laments, "the totalizing on-line character of cyberspace ensures that the marginalized stay marginalized."

Michele Willson's "Community in the abstract" (CR) is insightful in this regard, especially in its discussion of online community membership as essentially self-serving: the benefits of membership are often described in terms of the individual member's quality of life, rather than in the quality of *relations between subjects.* Drawing on Jean-Luc Nancy's philosophical ponderings on community, Willson asks that we pay more attention to the sharing of the relationship between beings as constitutive of community. Insights from Emmanuel Levinas, provided by Tony Gorman's work on cities, similarly provide us with a rewriting of community, in this case as "reciprocal alterity", or as "a freely constituted ethical association founded on the indirect absolute recognition of all by each" (Gorman 2000: 225). Squaring these kinds of formulations with the evidence from online communities brings the question of otherness (alterity) in cyberspace into stark relief.

Dealing with difference online is partly a matter of boundary-drawing. As we've already seen, compartmentalizing the heterogeneity of cyberspace into "neighbourhoods" of shared interests has become one important way in which communities are coalesced. Cohesion within the community is therefore sustained by bounding-out other communities (as well as individuals)—although there are overlaps between communities embodied in the mosaic of groups any member belongs to. Cross-posting between the communities someone belongs to can bring different communities into textual contact with one another. While this can be a productive cross-fertilization process, it can sometimes have antagonistic outcomes, as Ananda Mitra shows in his work on soc.culture.indian (CR).

55   What these few examples have in common, then, is that they serve as a reminder of the problematic relationship between community and exclusion. Finding ways to enlarge community (as a concept) and communities (as practised), as Willson and Gorman both propose, is one way to deal with this problem. Jettisoning the whole concept, and replacing it with something more suitable—*Bund,* maybe—is another strategy. I don't think we can resolve the question here; but we will need to keep a close eye on cybercommunities *and* our ways of understanding them, as both evolve symbiotically. Being mindful of the ways communities deal with difference, rather than merely celebrating their inclusivity, must be high on the agenda of everyone involved in thinking about communities in cyberspace.

Summary

This chapter has outlined some key arguments about online communities, setting these in the context of transformations in the forms and meanings of community brought about by broader social, economic, political and cultural processes. Cyberspace is located at the heart of these processes. However, some people argue that cyberspace is the solution to the "problem" of community (where real-life communities are seen to by "dying"), while others suggest that cyberspace is in fact making thing worse (by encouraging further withdrawal from "real-life"). In order to explore both sides of this debate, I worked through Howard Rheingold's writing, which seeks to promote online community-formation, and then looked at a number of critical responses to online community. In order to narrow the focus, the chapter discussed the "social contracts" that bind members of particular online communities together, and related this to issues of exclusion and otherness in online groups. I also considered whether alternative ways of thinking about virtual social relations might offer a way out of the gridlock of the arguments about online community, and drew on Kevin Hetherington's discussion of the *Bund* as a different way of conceptualizing how CMC-based social groups work. Taken together, I hope that these aspects of the online community debate have assisted in thinking and rethinking the reasons why there has been so much interest in, and argument about, communities in cyberspace.

Hot Links

Chapters from The Cybercultures Reader

Arthur Kroker and Marilouise Kroker, "Code warriors: bunkering in and dumbing down" (Chapter 5: 96–103).
Ananda Mitra, "Virtual commonality: looking for India on the Internet" (Chapter 44: 676–94).

Further reading

Peter Ludlow (ed.) (1999) *High Noon on the Electronic Frontier: Conceptual Issues in Cyberspace,* Cambridge MA: MIT Press (section V: self and community online)
Howard Rheingold (1993) *Virtual Community: Homesteading on the Electronic Frontier,* Reading MA: Addison Wesley.
Marc Smith and Peter Kollock (eds) (1999) *Communities in Cyberspace,* London: Routledge.

Websites

http://www.well.com
The WELL's homepage, with lots of info, links, instructions on how to join, etc.
http://www.rheingold.com
Howard Rhiengold's homepage, with articles, archives, links.
http://www.moo.mud.org
General homepage for MOOs, with lots of links and ways to start MOOing.
http://www.fortunecity.com/bally/skull/100/lambdamooers.html
Rusty's LambdaMOO Web index, listing all Lambdans, and linking to sites and information on LambdaMOO.

References

Anderson, B. *Imagined Communities: reflections on the origin and spread of nationalism,* London: Verso.
Appadurai, A. (1996) *Modernity at Large: cultural dimensions of globalization,* Minneapolis: University of Minnesota Press.
Bassett, C. (1997) "Virtually gendered: life in an online world," in K. Gelder and S. Thornton (eds) *The Subcultures Reader,* London: Routledge.
Baym, N. (1998) "The emergence of an online community," in S. Jones (ed.) *Cybersociety 2.0: revisiting computer-mediated communication and community,* London: Sage.
Bech, H. (1997) *When Men Meet: homosexuality and modernity,* Cambridge: Polity Press.
Bell, D. and Valentine, G. (1997) *Consuming Geographies: we are where we eat,* London: Routledge.

Bell, D. and Binnie, J. (2000) *The Sexual Citizen: queer politics and beyond,* Cambridge: Polity Press.

Bromberg, H. (1996) "Are MUDs communities? Identity, belonging and consciousness in virtual worlds," in R. Shields (ed.) *Cultures of Internet,* London: Sage.

Davis, E. (1998) *TechGnosis: myth, magic and mysticism in the age of information,* London: Serpent's Tail.

Davis, M. (1990) *City of Quartz: excavating the future in Los Angeles,* London: Verso.

Dibbell, J. (1999) "A rape in cyberspace; or how an evil clown, a Haitian trickster spirit, two wizards, and a cast of dozens turned a database into a society," in P. Ludlow (ed.) *High Noon on the Electronic Frontier,* Cambridge, MA: MIT Press.

Driver, S. and Martell, L. (1997) "New Labour's communitarianisms," *Critical Social Policy* 52: 27–46.

Edensor, T. (2001) *National Identities and Popular Culture,* Oxford: Berg.

Foucault, M. (1986) *The Care of the Self: the history of sexuality volume three,* Harmondsworth: Penguin.

Freund, J. (1978) "German Sociology in the time of Max Weber," in T. Bottomore and R. Nisbet (eds) *History of Sociology Analysis,* London: Heinemann.

Giddens, A. (1991) *Modernity and Self-Identity: self and society in the late modern age,* Cambridge: Polity Press.

Goldberg, D. T. (2000) "The new segregation," in D. Bell and A. Haddour (eds) *City Visions,* Harlow: Prentice Hall.

Gorman, A. (2000) "Otherness and citizenship: towards a politics of the plural community," in D. Bell and A. Haddour (eds) *City Visions,* Harlow: Prentice Hall.

Graham, G. (1999) *The Internet: a philosophical inquiry,* London: Routledge.

Harvey, D. (1989) *The Condition of Postmodernity: an enquiry into the origins of cultural change,* Oxford: Blackwell.

Heelas, P., Lash, S. and Morris, P. (eds) (1996) *Detraditionalization: critical reflections on authority and identity,* Oxford: Blackwell.

Hetherington, K. (1998) *Expressions of Identity: space, performance, politics,* London: Sage.

Jameson, F. (1991) *Postmodernism, or, the Cultural Logic of Late Capitalism,* London: Verso.

Jary, D. and Jary, J. (eds) (1991) *Collins Dictionary of Sociology,* London: HarperCollins.

Jones, S. (1995) "Understanding community in the information age," in S. Jones (ed.) *Cybersociety: computer-mediated communication and community,* London: Sage.

Kolko, B. and Reid, E. (1998) "Dissolution and fragmentation: problems in online communities," in S. Jones (ed.) *Cybersociety 2.0: revisiting computer-mediated communication and community,* London: Sage.

Kollock, P. and Smith, M. (1999) "Communities in Cyberspace," in M. Smith and P. Kollock (eds) *Communities in Cyberspace,* London: Routledge.

Latour, B. (1991) "Technology is society made durable," in J. Law (ed.) *A Sociology of Monsters,* London: Routledge.

Lupton, D. (1999) "Monsters in metal cocoons: 'road rage' and cyborg bodies," *Body & Society,* 5: 57–72.

Reid, E. (1999) "Hierarchy and power: social control in cyberspace," in M. Smith and P. Kollock (eds) *Communities in Cyberspace,* London: Routledge.

Rheingold, H. (1991) *Virtual Reality,* London: Secker & Warburg.

Rheingold, H. (1993) *Virtual Community: homesteading on the electronic frontier,* Reading, MA: Addison Wesley.

Rheingold, H. (1999) "A slice of life in my virtual community," in P. Ludlow (ed.) *High Noon on the Electronic Frontier: conceptual issues in cyberspace,* Cambridge, MA: MIT Press.

Robins, K. "Against virtual community: for a politics of distance," *Angelaki: Journal of the Theoretical Humanities,* 4: 163–70.

Simmel, G. (1995) "The metropolis and mental life," in P. Kasinitz (ed.) *Metropolis: centre and symbol of our times,* Basingstoke: Macmillan.

Slevin, J. (2000) *The Internet and Society,* Cambridge: Polity Press.

Tönnies, F. (1955) *Community and Association,* London: Routledge and Kegan Paul.

Waters, M. (1995) *Globalization,* London: Routledge.

Watson, N. (1997) "Why we argue about virtual community: a case study of the Phish.net fan community," in S. Jones (ed.) *Virtual Culture: identity and community in cybersociety,* London: Sage.

Wellman, B. and Gulia, M. (1999) "Virtual communities as communities:net surfers don't ride alone," in M. Smith and P. Kollock (eds) *Communities in Cyberspace,* London: Routledge.

Young, I. M. (2000) "A critique of integration as the remedy for segregation," in D. Bell and A. Haddour (eds) *City Visions,* Harlow: Prentice Hall.

QUESTIONS FOR INQUIRY AND ACTION

1. Bell summarizes several key conversations circulating around virtual communities. Discuss where your views would fit in relation to each of these conversations.

2. Bell's chapter is an excellent model of academic research writing. In what ways does it differ from other works in this chapter, like Jon Katz's "Birth of a Digital Nation"?

3. Bell defines a *Bund* as a voluntary grouping of people who share a strong sense of camaraderie; he suggests the *Bund* might offer an alternative way to talk about online communities. Explore three different online communities; are they better described by the *Bund* idea or by the ideas of *community* that we've been exploring throughout the book?

4. At the end of his chapter, Bell provides "hot links" for further research. Take up his offer and read one of the suggested print or online works. What does the work add to your understanding of online communities and of Bell's work?

CASE
STUDY

THE NETIZEN AND CITIZEN ACTION: DOES
THE INTERNET PROMOTE DEMOCRACY?

JON KATZ Birth of a Digital Nation

> *Jon Katz is a journalist, the columnist of "Media Rants" for* Wired's *online magazine* HotWired, *former executive producer of* CBS Morning News, *a writer of mystery novels, and the author of* Virtuous Reality: How America Surrendered Discussion of Moral Values to Opportunists, Nitwits, and Block-heads like William Bennett *(1997) and* Geeks: How Two Lost Boys Rode the Internet Out of Idaho *(2000). "Birth of a Digital Nation" appeared in his "Netizen" column on* Wired *(April 5, 1997).*

First Stirrings

On the Net last year, I saw the rebirth of love for liberty in media. I saw a culture crowded with intelligent, educated, politically passionate people who—in jarring contrast to the offline world—line up to express their civic opinions, participate in debates, even fight for their political beliefs.

I watched people learn new ways to communicate politically. I watched information travel great distances, then return home bearing imprints of engaged and committed people from all over the world. I saw positions soften and change when people were suddenly able to talk directly to one another, rather than through journalists, politicians, or ideological mercenaries.

I saw the primordial stirrings of a new kind of nation—the Digital Nation—and the formation of a new postpolitical philosophy. This nascent ideology, fuzzy and difficult to define, suggests a blend of some of the best values rescued from the tired old dogmas—the humanism of liberalism, the economic opportunity of conservatism, plus a strong sense of personal responsibility and a passion for freedom.

I came across questions, some tenuously posed: Are we living in the middle of a great revolution, or are we just members of another arrogant élite talking to ourselves? Are we a powerful new kind of community or just a mass of people hooked up to machines? Do we share goals and ideals, or are we just another hot market ready for exploitation by America's ravenous corporations?

5   And perhaps the toughest questions of all: Can we build a new kind of politics? Can we construct a more civil society with our powerful technologies? Are we extending the evolution of freedom among human beings? Or are we nothing more than a great, wired babble pissing into the digital wind?

Where freedom is rarely mentioned in mainstream media anymore, it is ferociously defended—and exercised daily—on the Net.

Where our existing information systems seek to choke the flow of information through taboos, costs, and restrictions, the new digital world celebrates the right of the individual to speak and be heard—one of the cornerstone ideas behind American media and democracy.

Where our existing political institutions are viewed as remote and unresponsive, this online culture offers the means for individuals to have a genuine say in the decisions that affect their lives.

Where conventional politics is suffused with ideology, the digital world is obsessed with facts.

10   Where our current political system is irrational, awash in hypocritical god-and-values talk, the Digital Nation points the way toward a more rational, less dogmatic approach to politics.

The world's information is being liberated, and so, as a consequence, are we.

My Journey

Early last year, writer John Heilemann and I set out on parallel media journeys for HotWired's *The Netizen,* originally created to explore political issues and the media during the election year. One concept behind *The Netizen*—a conceit, perhaps—was that we would watch the impact of the Web on the political process in the first wired election. Heilemann was to cover the candidates, the conventions, and the campaigns. I would write about the media covering them.

Things didn't turn out quite as we'd expected at *The Netizen.* The year of the Web was not 1996—at least not in terms of mainstream politics. The new culture wasn't strong enough yet to really affect the political process. The candidates didn't turn to it as they had turned in 1992 to new media like cable, fax, and 800 numbers.

And the election was shallow from the beginning, with no view toward the new postindustrial economy erupting around us and no vision of a digital—or any other kind of—future. By spring '96, it seemed clear to me that this campaign was a metaphor for all that doesn't work in both journalism and politics. I couldn't bear *The New York Times* pundits, CNN's politico-sports talk, the whoring Washington talk shows, the network stand-ups.

15   Why attend to those tired institutions when what was happening on the monitor a foot from my nose seemed so much more interesting? Fresh ideas, fearsome debates, and a brand-new culture were rising out of the primordial digital muck, its politics teeming with energy. How could a medium like this new one have a major impact on a leaden old process like that one? By focusing so obsessively on Them, we were missing a much more dramatic political story—Us.

So I mostly abandoned Their campaign, focusing instead on the politics of Ours—especially interactivity and the digital culture. I was flamed, challenged, and stretched almost daily. The Web became my formidable teacher, whacking me on the palm with a ruler when I didn't do my homework or wasn't listening intently enough; comforting me when I got discouraged or felt lost.

I argued with technoanarchists about rules, flamers about civility, white kids about rap, black kids about police, journalists about media, evangelicals about sin. I was scolded by scholars and academics for flawed logic or incomplete research. I was shut down by "family values" email bombers outraged by my attacks on Wal-Mart's practice of sanitizing the music it sells.

I saw the strange new way in which information and opinion travel down the digital highway—linked to Web sites, passed on to newsgroups, mailing lists, and computer conferencing systems. I saw my columns transformed from conventional punditry to a series of almost-living organisms that got buttressed, challenged, and altered by the incredible volume of feedback suddenly available. I lost the ingrained journalistic ethic that taught me that I was right, and that my readers didn't know what was good for them. On the Web, I learned that I was rarely completely right, that I was only a transmitter of ideas waiting to be shaped and often improved upon by people who knew more than I did.

Ideas almost never remain static on the Web. They are launched like children into the world, where they are altered by the many different environments they pass through, almost never coming home in the same form in which they left.

20   All the while, I had the sense of Heilemann cranking along like the Energizer Bunny, responsibly slugging his way through the torturous ordeal of campaign coverage, guiding the increasingly-exasperated people who actually wanted to follow the election. What Heilemann learned and relayed was that the political system isn't functioning. It doesn't address serious problems, and the problems it does address are not confronted in a rational way. It doesn't present us with the information we need or steer us toward comprehension—let alone solution.

Over the course of 1996, the ideologies that shape our political culture seemed to collapse. Liberalism finally expired along with the welfare culture it had inadvertently spawned. Conservatism, reeling from the failure of the so-called Republican revolution, was exposed as heartless and rigid. The left and the right—even on issues as explosive as abortion and welfare—appeared spent. While they squabbled eternally with one another, the rest of us ached for something better. In 1996, we didn't get it.

The candidates didn't raise a single significant issue, offer a solution to any major social problem, raise the nation's consciousness, or prod its conscience about any critical matter. The issues the candidates did debate were either false or manipulative, the tired imperatives of another time.

"Nineteen ninety-six was the year that Old Politics died," wrote Heilemann. "For outside this bizarre electoral system that's grown and mutated over the past 40 years—this strange, pseudo-meta-ritual that, experienced from the inside, feels like being trapped in an echo chamber lined with mirrors—there are profound, paradigm-shifting changes afoot."

There are paradigm-shifting changes afoot: the young people who form the heart of the digital world are creating a new political ideology. The machinery of the Internet is being wielded to create an environment in which the Digital Nation can become a political entity in its own right.

25   By avoiding the campaign most of the time, I ended up in another, unexpected place. I had wandered into the nexus between the past and the future, the transition from one political process to a very different one.

While Heilemann came to believe he was attending a wake, I began to feel I was witnessing a birth—the first stirrings of a powerful new political community.

The Nascent Nation

All kinds of people of every age and background are online, but at the heart of the Digital Nation are the people who created the Net, work in it, and whose business, social, and cultural lives increasingly revolve around it.

The Digital Nation constitutes a new social class. Its citizens are young, educated, affluent. They inhabit wired institutions and industries—universities, computer and telecom companies, Wall Street and financial outfits, the media. They live everywhere, of course, but are most visible in forward-looking, technologically advanced communities: New York, San Francisco, Los Angeles, Seattle, Boston, Minneapolis, Austin, Raleigh. They are predominantly male, although female citizens are joining in enormous—and increasingly equal—numbers.

The members of the Digital Nation are not representative of the population as a whole: they are richer, better educated, and disproportionately white. They have disposable income and available time. Their educations are often unconventional and continuous, and they have almost unhindered access to much of the world's information. As a result, their values are constantly evolving. Unlike the rigid political ideologies that have ruled America for decades, the ideas of the post-political young remain fluid.

30   Still, some of their common values are clear: they tend to be libertarian, materialistic, tolerant, rational, technologically adept, disconnected from conventional political organizations—like the Republican or Democratic parties—and from narrow labels like liberal or conservative. They are not politically correct, rejecting dogma in favor of sorting through issues individually, preferring discussions to platforms.

The digital young are bright. They are not afraid to challenge authority. They take no one's word for anything. They embrace interactivity—the right to shape and participate in their media. They have little experience with passively reading newspapers or watching newscasts delivered by anchors. They share a passion for popular culture—perhaps their most common shared value, and the one most misperceived and mishandled by politicians and journalists. On Monday mornings when they saunter into work, they are much more likely to be talking about the movies they saw over the weekend than about Washington's issue of the week. Music, movies, magazines, some television shows, and some books are elementally important to them—not merely forms of entertainment but means of identity.

As much as anything else, the reflexive contempt for popular culture shared by so many elders of journalism and politics has alienated this group, causing its members to view the world in two basic categories: those who get it, and those who don't. For much of their lives, these young people have been branded ignorant, their culture malevolent. The political leaders and pundits who malign them haven't begun to grasp how destructive these perpetual assaults have been, how huge a cultural gap they've created.

Although many would balk at defining themselves this way, the digital young are revolutionaries. Unlike the clucking boomers, they are not talking revolution; they're making one. This is a culture best judged by what it does, not what it says.

In *On Revolution,* Hannah Arendt wrote that two things are needed to generate great revolutions: the sudden experience of being free and the sense of creating something. The Net is revolutionary in precisely those ways. It liberates millions of people to do things they couldn't do before. Men and women can experiment with their sexual identities without being humiliated or arrested. Citizens can express themselves directly, without filtering their views through journalists or pollsters. Researchers can get the newest data in hours, free from the grinding rituals of scientific tradition. The young can explore their own notions of culture, safe from the stern scrutiny of parents and teachers.

35   There's also a sense of great novelty, of building something different. The online population of today has evolved dramatically from the hackers and academics who patched together primitive computer bulletin boards just a few years ago—but the sensation of discovery remains. People coming online still have the feeling of stepping across a threshold. Citizenship in this world requires patience, commitment, and determination—an investment of time and energy that often brings the sense of participating in something very new.

It's difficult to conceive of the digital world as a political entity. The existing political and journalistic structures hate the very thought, since that means relinquishing their own central place in political life. And the digital world itself—adolescent, self-absorbed—is almost equally reluctant to take itself seriously in a political context, since that invokes all sorts of responsibilities that seem too constraining and burdensome.

This is a culture founded on the ethos of individuality, not leadership. Information flows laterally, or from many to many—a structure that works against the creation of leaders.

Like it or not, however, this Digital Nation possesses all the traits of groups that, throughout history, have eventually taken power. It has the education, the affluence, and the privilege that will create a political force that ultimately must be reckoned with. . . .

SIMON DAVIES AND IAN ANGELL Double Clicking on Democracy

Ian Angell is a professor in the Department of Information Systems at the London School of Economics and Political Science. Simon Davies is a research fellow at the LSE and director of Privacy International, a London-based advocacy group. Their article "Double Clicking on Democracy" first appeared in the LSE Magazine *(Summer 2000) of the London School of Economics and Political Science, and was republished on the Web site* Fathom.com.

When did democracy don the mantle of morality? For how much longer can we keep up the pretence that democracy is a stepping-stone to a global social utopia? When will it be seen for what it really is: a body count of the manipulated mob, to be abused by any determined control freak; an alliance of cronyism, corruption and self-interest. Steered by a concoction of vox-pops and pick 'n' mix marketeering, governments ram through ever more pointless and dangerous legislation—proclaiming, invariably, that they are acting for the "public good."

Iceland's government has sold the medical records of its population to deCODE Genetics, a private company. The UK population is forced to register names and addresses on the electoral roll; the roll is exempt from the Data Protection Act and is sold to whoever will pay. Burglars cross-reference likely targets against directories on compact disks and then telephone to check that their victims are out before breaking and entering.

A democratic vote is an excellent way to justify trampling on individual privacy. Tony Blair wants every police force to follow the example of the Lothian and Borders police, who are archiving DNA data from everyone arrested. Apparently, 75 per cent of the local population supports this action. But did the people of Edinburgh realise that a motoring offence would place them in the database? Elsewhere in the UK, 92 per cent of the citizens of the London Borough of Newham want CCTV cameras to watch over their town centre. Newham is at the forefront of new technology; it uses face-recognition software. The movement of individuals can now be tracked around the borough. The odd few per cent who want anonymity will just have to shop elsewhere. Plato claimed that democracy always leads to despotism and tyranny. Big Brother turns out to be the manipulated voice of the tyrannical masses insisting on a state-led invasion of privacy.

What do we get in return for abandoning our privacy? An insignificant input into an inconsequential national election of a nanny-state, every four or five years, that has little or no influence on the general scheme of things. But do we care? The BBC extended its nine o'clock news bulletin by 20 minutes to report the 1997 General Election. Its normal viewing figures of 5.5 million dropped to less than 4 million. The cost of administering the same election on the remote Atlantic islands of St. Kilda would have cost the 29 adults living there a total of £ 5,000. They decided not to bother and save the money.

5   Meanwhile, pious words abound concerning "extending democracy" in an "information society." The United States administration has placed more than 100,000 documents on the Internet. However, a snowstorm of selected information from Washington (or Brussels, or Westminster) changes nothing. True, cable, telephone and the Internet will enable the public to receive far more relevant and in-depth explanations of political issues. But will they participate more intelligently in the political process?

They won't need to. The new generation of interactive television will monitor customer habits, viewing patterns, spending profiles and opinions, and offer a quick and easy online democracy, complete with personalised prompts.

But governments won't have it all their own way. Far from allowing the manipulated voter into the policy and decision-making process, technology actually spreads "demosclerosis" (Jonathan Rauch), a disease of government. Mass lobbying by vested interests causes stalemates on every issue and forces through economically insane proposals, thereby driving government to its knees. On 5 November 1996, voters in California approved Proposition 218. All property-related assessments, fees and charges have to be approved (but more likely disapproved) by the vote of property owners. Consequently, Moody's lowered the ratings on the various bonds of the City of Los Angeles, completing a self-fulfilling prophecy that the city would lose tens of millions of dollars in revenue.

The old cosy relationship between lobbyists and politicians, riding the gravy train of public money, is coming off the rails. So should individuals be worried about the rabble-rousers in government? Modern technology extends the opportunity for any self-appointed control freak to mobilise the masses. Anyone with deep pockets can manipulate the bigoted moral majority and call for support on single-issue campaigns. They will disseminate blacklists of names of those who dare stand out against them.

Perhaps the difference these days is that not only are desperate governments more willing to succumb to such tactics, but the exposed politician has become a rabbit caught in the headlights, needing to please all of the people, all of the time, on every single issue, or else face their wrath come re-election time. Adding to the paranoia are advertisements, opinion polls, talk-radio spots, and mass telephone calls funnelled through toll-free numbers. Astronomical sums of money will be needed for mass propaganda. In a democracy, like everywhere else, money talks.

10   Self-serving politicians will promise a wish list of jam today and jam tomorrow. The hell of a collectivist heaven will poll the opinions of the herd to reinstate capital punishment, to ban homosexuality and immigration, and to insist on a fair distribution of wealth by stealing from the few rich. However, as Alexander Tytler suggests, "a democracy cannot exist as a permanent form of government. It can only exist until a majority of voters discover that they can vote themselves largesse out of the public treasury."

Today, that largesse is free welfare, medical payouts and other social-security safety nets. But no society can vote itself into an economic utopia. The invisible hands of untamed economic forces are at play. Individuals, companies and countries can only steer within the limits allowed by the flow of self-organising trends of the global economy. Going against the flow is futile. If a society doesn't earn its wages, then economic reality can be kept at bay for only a little while.

Ultimately, by insisting that society can pay itself unreasonable salary levels, or set excessive levels of taxation, either inflation or recession will return, and jobs will disappear. Nevertheless, to get elected, democratic governments will be forced to play this game. The needs of the masses will justify the invasion of individual privacy to check that everyone is paying their fair share. However, the rich, their wealth and their privacy will emigrate, as Christopher Lasch predicted in *The Revolt of the Elites*. In the Information Age, the politics of envy is suicide. The big political question of the coming decades is how to find a socially acceptable means of dismantling democracy.

STOP AND THINK

THE INTERNET AND WORLD HUNGER

One way people have tried to alleviate the perpetual problem of hunger around the world is through the establishment of charitable relief agencies. These agencies solicit money from governments and individuals, and then use that money to buy food and distribute it to the people who need it. Traditionally, these agencies have advertised in magazines and on television, and solicited their contributors by mail or phone call.

Recently, hunger relief activists have taken their mission online. The most popular Web site is *The Hunger Site* http://www.thehungersite.com/, which was founded in 1999. On it, visitors are asked to click a button in order to donate cups of food. Unlike with other charities, there is no cost to the donor; the donor has only to visit the Web site and click the button. The food is paid for by businesses who advertise on *The Hunger Site* and provide links to their sites so that visitors can patronize them. (There are other hunger relief sites, such as one focused on hunger in the United States sponsored by the Second Harvest organization, *Stop the Hunger*: http://www.stopthehunger.com/hunger/.)

In what ways is giving to an online charity a form of citizen action? Visit *The Hunger Site* and the Second Harvest *Stop the Hunger* site. How do you feel when you read their text and view their maps? Do you find yourself emotionally moved and concerned by the weightiness and urgency of the problem? Or, conversely, do you feel optimistic that world hunger will be easily taken care of through online contributions?

Make a contribution. Then reflect upon your action. Does visiting a Web site and donating food make you feel like a responsible Netizen? Do you feel empowered and feel as if you are doing your part to alleviate world hunger when you click the button? Compare this to how you have felt in the past when you donated your time and money to a charitable organization. When you contributed online, did you feel the same as if you gave to an organization that contacted you through the mail, or one that you interacted with personally in your community? Did you feel needed, for instance? Did you feel responsible for helping to change the situation?

Survey others to get their responses to online charitable donating. Research the success rate of *The Hunger Site* and other organizations to see whether this form of activism is effective.

CASS SUNSTEIN Exposure to Other Viewpoints Is Vital to Democracy

Cass Sunstein is Karl N. Llewellyn Distinguished Service Professor of Jurispru-
dence at the University of Chicago Law School and the Department of Polit-
ical Science. He is the author of many books, including Democracy and the
Problem of Free Speech *(1993) and* Designing Democracy: What Constitutions
Do *(2001). "Exposure to Other Viewpoints is Vital to Democracy" appeared*
in the Chronicle of Higher Education *(March 16, 2001) and is adapted from*
his book Republic. com *(Princeton University Press, 2001).*

It is some time in the future. Technology has greatly increased people's ability to "filter" what they want to read, see, and hear. General-interest newspapers and magazines are largely a thing of the past. The same is true of broadcasters. The idea of choosing "Channel 4" instead of "Channel 7" seems positively quaint. With the aid of the Internet and a television or computer screen, you are able to design your own newspapers and magazines. Having dispensed with broadcasters, you can choose your own video programming, with movies, game shows, sports, shopping, and news of your choice. You mix and match. You need not come across topics and views that you have not sought out. Without any difficulty, you are able to see exactly what you want to see, no more and no less.

Maybe you want to focus on sports all the time, and to avoid anything dealing with business or government. It is easy for you to do exactly that. Perhaps you choose replays of famous football games in the early evening, live baseball from New York at night, and college basketball on the weekends. If you hate sports, and want to learn about the Middle East in the evening and watch old situation comedies late at night, that is easy, too. If you care only about the United States, and want to avoid international issues entirely, you can restrict yourself to material involving the United States. So, too, if you care only about New York City, or Chicago, or California, or Long Island.

Perhaps you have no interest at all in "news." Maybe you find news impossibly boring. If so, you need not see it at all. Maybe you select programs and stories involving only music and weather. Or perhaps you are more specialized still, emphasizing opera, or Beethoven, or the Rolling Stones, or modern dance, or some subset of one or more of the above.

If you are interested in politics, you may want to restrict yourself to certain points of view, by hearing only from people you like. In designing your preferred newspaper, you choose among conservatives, moderates, liberals, vegetarians, the religious right, and socialists. You have your favorite columnists; perhaps you want to hear from them and from no one else. If so, that is entirely feasible with a simple "point and click." Or perhaps you are interested in only a few topics. If you believe that the most serious problem is gun control, or global warming, or lung cancer, you might spend most of your time reading about that problem—if you wish, from the point of view that you like best.

5   Of course, everyone else has the same freedom that you do. Many people choose to avoid news altogether. Many people restrict themselves to their own preferred points of view—liberals watch and read mostly, or only, liberals; moderates, moderates; conservatives, conservatives; neo-Nazis, neo-Nazis. People in different states, and in different countries, make predictably different choices.

The resulting divisions run along many lines—of race, religion, ethnicity, nationality, wealth, age, political conviction, and more. Most white people avoid news and entertainment options designed for African-Americans. Many African-Americans focus largely on options specifically designed for them. So, too, with Hispanics. With the reduced importance of the general-interest magazine and newspaper, and the flowering of individual programming, different groups make fundamentally different choices.

The market for news, entertainment, and information has finally been perfected. Consumers are able to see exactly what they want. When the power to filter is unlimited, people can decide, in advance and with perfect accuracy, what they will and will not encounter. They can design something very much like a communications universe of their own choosing.

Our communications market is rapidly moving in the direction of this apparently utopian picture. As of this writing, many newspapers, including *The Wall Street Journal,* allow subscribers to create "personalized" electronic editions, containing exactly what each reader wants, and excluding what each does not want. If you are interested in getting help with the design of an entirely personalized paper, you can consult an ever growing number of Web sites, including <http://www.individual.com> (helpfully named!) and <http://www.crayon.net> (a less helpful name, but evocative in its own way).

In reality, we are not so very far from complete personalization of the entire system of communications.

10   If you put the words "personalized news" in any search engine, you will find vivid evidence of what is happening. And that is only the tip of the iceberg. Thus Nicholas Negroponte, director of the Media Laboratory at the Massachusetts Institute of Technology, prophesies the emergence of the "Daily Me"—a communications package that is personally designed, with each component chosen in advance. Many of us applaud those developments, which obviously increase individual convenience and entertainment.

But in the midst of the applause, we should insist on asking some questions. How will the increasing power of private control affect democracy? How will the Internet, the new forms of television, and the explosion of communications options alter the capacity of citizens to govern themselves? What are the social preconditions for a well-functioning system of democratic deliberation, or for individual freedom itself? We need to ensure that new communications technologies serve democracy, rather than the other way around.

Perhaps above all, the growing power of consumers to filter what they see demands a better understanding of the meaning of freedom of speech in a democratic society. To obtain that understanding, we must explore what makes for a well-functioning system of free expression. Such a system requires far more than restraints on government censorship and respect for individual choices. For the last few decades, those topics have been the preoccupation of American law and politics, and the law and politics of many other nations as well, including England, Germany, France, and Israel. Censorship is indeed a threat to democracy and freedom. But an exclusive focus on government censorship produces serious blind spots. In particular, a well-functioning system of free expression must meet two distinctive requirements.

First, people should be exposed to materials that they would not have chosen in advance. Unplanned, unanticipated encounters are central to democracy itself. Such encounters often involve topics and points of view that people have not sought out and, perhaps, find quite irritating; they are important because they ensure against fragmentation and extremism, which are predictable outcomes of any situation in which like-minded people speak only with each other. I do not suggest that government should force people to see things that they wish to avoid. But I do contend that, in a democracy deserving the name, people often come across views and topics that they have not specifically selected.

Second, many—or most—citizens should have a range of common experiences. Without shared experiences, a heterogeneous society will have a much more difficult time in addressing social problems. People may even find it hard to understand one another. Common experiences, emphatically including the common experiences made possible by the media, provide a form of social glue. A system of communications that radically diminishes the number of such experiences will create numerous problems, not least an increase in social fragmentation.

15   As preconditions for a well-functioning democracy, these requirements hold in any large nation. They are especially important in a heterogeneous nation, which is bound to face an occasional risk of fragmentation. They have all the more importance as each nation becomes increasingly global, and each citizen becomes, to a greater or lesser degree, a "citizen of the world."

An insistence on these two requirements should not be rooted in nostalgia for some supposedly idyllic past. With respect to communications, the past was hardly idyllic. Compared with any other period in human history, we are in the midst of many extraordinary gains, particularly from the standpoint of democracy itself. For us, nostalgia is not only unproductive but also senseless.

Nor should anything here be taken as a reason for "optimism" or "pessimism," two great obstacles to clear thinking about new technological developments. If we must choose between them, by all means let us choose optimism. But, in view of the many potential gains and losses inevitably associated with massive technological change, any attitude of optimism or pessimism is far too general to make sense. What we need to have is not a basis for pessimism, but a lens through which we might understand, a bit better than before, what makes a system of freedom of expression successful in the first place. That improved understanding will equip us to appreciate a free nation's own aspirations, and thus help in evaluating continuing changes in the system of communications. It will also point the way toward a clearer understanding of the nature of citizenship, and toward social reforms if emerging developments disserve our aspirations, as they threaten to do.

To make progress on this issue, we must take a stand on some large questions in democratic theory. Some political theorists are pure populists. They focus on improving people's ability to influence government directly. Pure populists tend to welcome the Internet as a wonderful boon, and for one simple reason: For the first time in the history of the world, millions of people can make their views known, immediately, to elected representatives. Indeed, considerable academic thinking about democracy celebrates the technological capacity of the Internet to provide stronger citizen control over government.

But many other theorists are nervous about populism. Following Edmund Burke, they believe that representatives should be largely insulated from the ebb and flow of public opinion, to ensure that elected officials can deliberate wisely on the issues of the day. For faithful Burkeans, the Internet is, in many ways, a threat to wise rule.

20   In American constitutional thought, and to a significant extent in modern political theory, a distinctive conception of democracy has risen to prominence in the past decade. According to this conception, it is best to have a deliberative democracy—one that combines elements of accountability and inclusiveness with a commitment to reflection and providing reasons. Deliberative democrats reject populism on the ground that it is likely to give too little space for deliberation, but they reject Burkeanism, too, on the ground that, in most forms, it devalues the importance of ensuring public checks on official behavior—and even on official thought. The influential German philosopher Jürgen Habermas, for one, has developed the argument for deliberative democracy in particular detail.

From the standpoint of deliberative democracy, the Internet is both a promise and a threat. It is a promise insofar as it allows so many diverse people to learn and to reflect and to exchange reasons with each other. But it is a threat insofar as it allows instantaneous reactions to have a large influence on policy—and even more insofar as it promotes the "Daily Me," allowing so many people to create communications universes of their own choosing.

As Habermas has stressed, one of the preconditions of a deliberative democracy is a large set of "public forums" (including streets and parks) in which diverse people encounter each other, often by chance. If public forums become increasingly specialized, many people might substitute technological echo chambers for the streets and parks in which diverse people meet. In fact, that is already happening.

It follows that, in the long run, the most serious "digital divides" that we will face might not involve the exclusion of poor people from communications technologies, but the creation of numerous free-speech enclaves, in practice walled off from each other. A great advantage of general-interest newspapers and magazines is that they ensure that people will see topics and ideas that they might not have specifically chosen in advance. If the role of such media diminishes, democracy may be impoverished, if only because people will understand their fellow citizens less well—and possibly not at all.

If this is right, there is all the reason in the world to reject the view that free markets, as embodied in the notion of "consumer sovereignty," are the appropriate foundation for communications policy. Free markets have many virtues, but, in the area of communications, they will serve democracy imperfectly. They might even compromise the preconditions for citizenship.

25   Above all, it is important to see that, in well-functioning democracies, public forums of various stripes—from streets and parks to daily newspapers—expose people to a variety of (sometimes unexpected) ideas and topics. Unanticipated, chance encounters—with people and ideas—are fundamental to democracy. This is not the place to set out a specific agenda, but we might consider the possibility of building on the precedents we already have and providing creative links among Web sites; or, perhaps, of setting up, under public or private auspices, deliberative forums on the Internet for people who would not otherwise "meet."

The crucial step will be to recognize the problem. The imagined world of the "Daily Me" is the farthest thing from a utopian dream, and it would create serious problems from the democratic point of view.

QUESTIONS FOR INQUIRY AND ACTION

1. Discuss how much technologies (telephones, computers, the Internet, television, video games) have shaped how you live and interact with others. Go into detail on how you use these technologies, when you use them, how often, and with whom you interact. Then, speculate on how technology has strengthened or weakened your connection to others in your various communities.

2. Interview someone of a different generation (e.g., your grandparents) to learn about their attitudes toward technology. Do they understand it? Do they like or dislike it? What were the new technologies when they were your age? How did they respond to them? Next, compare and contrast their views of technology with your own. Then, explain why these views are similar or different. Does a different generation's perspective help us form a more critical view of our own time?

3. Using different technologies, search out new opportunities to connect with others. You might call people you wouldn't normally call, join online discussion groups, even email new people. Do this for one week and then discuss how these technologies enhanced or detracted from your ability to create communities.

4. Determine which technologies you use the most and then give them up for one week. Each time you feel like calling someone, watching television, or playing a video game, write in your writer's notebook. When did you want to use the technology and why? At the end of a week, discuss how the absence of this technology affected your quality of life. Was it affected in a positive or negative way?

5. Using Internet search engines, seek out resources that would help someone going into your field of study. (For example, a future lawyer might find the *American Bar Association Network*, <http://www.abanet.org/>, a useful site for meeting other attorneys, learning of new developments in the field, and keeping track of new ABA rules.) Describe why the resources would be useful for students of your field. In what ways do you think technology improves or harms the work in your field?

6. See how many Web sites you can find that promote democratic discussion and social change, or provide alternative views on mainstream issues. How many of them do more than talk? Which ones provide practical ways to get involved in issues that concern you?

CREDITS

A Citizen's Guide to the World Trade Organization, published by the Working Group on the WTO/MAI, July 1999. All rights reserved.

"Our Greatest Need" (A testimonial given to the Subcommittee on Crime of the House Judiciary Committee) by Darrell Scott, as found on Website www.thecolumbineredemption.com. All rights reserved.

"We Called It 'Littlefun,'" by Jeff Stark, from *Salon.com*, April 21, 1999. Copyright © 1999. Reprinted by permission of Salon.com.

"Beliefs about Families," from *The Shelter of Each Other* by Mary Pipher, Ph.D, copyright ©1996 by Mary Pipher, Ph.D. Used by permission of G.P. Putnam's Sons, a division of Penguin Putnam Inc.

Editorial from the *Orlando Sentinel*, April 21, 1999. Copyright © 1999. Reprinted with permission of the *Orlando Sentinel*.

From *Decolonising the Mind: The Politics of Language in African Literature* by Ngugi wa Thiong'o. Copyright ©1986 by Ngugi wa Thiong'o. Published in North America by Heinemann, a division of Reed Elsevier Inc., Portsmouth, NH. Reprinted by permission of the publisher.

"Massacre at Columbine High" by Mark Obmascik, from *The Denver Post*, April 21, 1999. Copyright 1999. Reprinted by permission of *The Denver Post*.

"Take Up Quayle's Call" as first appeared in *The Christian Science Monitor*, May 26, 1992 and is reproduced with permission. Copyright © 1992 the *Christian Science Monitor* (csmonitor.com). All rights reserved.

From "Somehow Form a Family" by Tony Earley. Copyright © 2001 by the author. Reprinted by permission of Algonquin Books of Chapel Hill, a division of Workman Publishing.

"School Shootings and White Denial" by Tim Wise, from *hip Mama*, as appeared in Number 25, "The Connections Issue" 2001. Copyright © 2001 Tim Wise. Reprinted by permission of the author.

"Cheating" from *Beer and Circus: How Big-Time College Sports is Crippling Undergraduate Education* by Murray Sperber, Copyright © 2000. Reprinted by permission of Henry Holt and Company, LLC.

"Where Was the Color in Seattle?" by Elizabeth (Betita) Martinez, from *ColorLines*, Spring 2000. Copyright © 2000. Reprinted by permission.

Excerpt from Act Two from *The Night Thoreau Spent in Jail* by Jerome Lawrence and Robert E. Lee. Copyright © 1970 by Lawrence & Lee, Inc. Reprinted by permission of Hill and Wang, a division of Farrar, Straus and Giroux, LLC.

BIBLIOGRAPHY

Ballenger, Bruce. *The Curious Researcher: A Guide to Writing Research Papers.* 2nd ed. Boston: Allyn and Bacon, 1998.

Bly, Carol. *Beyond the Writers' Workshop: New Ways to Write Creative Nonfiction.* New York: Alfred A. Knopf, 2001.

Buzan, Tony. *The Mind Map Book: How To Use Radiant Thinking to Maximize Your Brain's Untapped Potential.* New York: Plume, 1993.

Cheadle, Allen. "The Community Research Partnership: Trying to Build Better Relations Between Community Groups and Researchers in Seattle." *Doing Community-Based Research.* Ed. Danny Murphy, Madeleine Scammell, and Richard Sclove. Amherst: The Loka Institute, 1997. 7–9.

Creedon, Jeremiah. "God with a Million Faces." *Utne Reader* July–August 1998.

Culler, Jonathan. "Reading as a Woman." *On Deconstruction: Theory and Criticism after Structuralism.* Ithaca, NY: Cornell University Press, 1982.

Damasio, Antonio R. *Descartes' Error: Emotion, Reason, and the Human Brain.* New York: G. P. Putnam's Sons, 1994.

Didion, Joan. "Why I Write." *New York Times Magazine.* December 5, 1976.

Ferreira, Eleonora Castaño and Jaño Castaño Ferreira. *Making Sense of the Media: A Handbook of Popular Education Techniques.* New York: Monthly Review Press, 1997.

Freire, Paulo. *Pedagogy of the Oppressed.* New York: Continuum, 2000.

Geertz, Clifford. *The Interpretation of Cultures.* New York: Basic Books, 1977.

Gelb, Michael J. *How to Think Like Leonardo Da Vinci.* New York: Bantam Doubleday, 1998.

Hansen, Kristine. *A Rhetoric for the Social Sciences: A Guide to Academic and Professional Communication.* Upper Saddle River, NJ: Prentice Hall, 1998.

Ickes, William, ed. "Introduction." *Empathic Accuracy.* New York: Guilford Press, 1997. 1–16.

Issac, Katherine. *Ralph Nader's Practicing Democracy 1997: A Guide to Student Action.* New York: St. Martin's Press, 1997.

Ives, Edward. *The Tape-Recorded Interview.* Knoxville: University of Tennessee Press, 1995.

Johnson, Mark. *Moral Imagination: Implications of Cognitive Science for Ethics.* Chicago and London: The University of Chicago Press, 1993.

King, Larry. *How to Talk to Anyone, Anytime, Anywhere: The Secrets of Good Communication.* New York: Random House, 1995.

King, Stephen. *On Writing.* New York: Simon and Schuster, 2000.

Lamott, Anne. *Bird by Bird: Some Instructions on Writing and Life*. New York: Anchor Books, 1994.

Lasch, Christopher. *The Revolt of the Elites and the Betrayal of Democracy*. New York: W. W. Norton, 1994.

Leopold, Aldo. *A Sand Country Almanac*. New York: Ballantine Books, 1970.

Loeb, Paul Rogat. *Soul of a Citizen: Living with Conviction in a Cynical Time*. New York: St. Martin's, 1999.

Maner, Martin. *The Research Process: A Complete Guide and Reference for Writers*. Mountain View, CA: Mayfield, 2000.

McLuhan, Marshall. *The Gutenberg Galaxy: The Making of Typographic Man*. Toronto: University of Toronto Press, 1962.

Putnam, Robert. *Bowling Alone: The Collapse and Revival of American Community*. New York: Simon and Schuster, 2000.

Salinger, J. D. *The Catcher in the Rye*. New York: Little, Brown, 1991.

Schweickart, Patrocinio P. "Reading Ourselves: Toward a Feminist Theory of Reading." *Gender and Reading: Essays on Readers, Texts, and Contexts*. Eds. Elizabeth A. Flynn and Patrocinio P. Schweickart. Baltimore: Johns Hopkins University Press, 1986.

Shapiro, Jeremy J. and Shelley K. Hughes. "Information Literacy as a Liberal Art." *Educom Review* 31:2 (March/April 1996) 12 Feb. 2002. (http://www.educause.edu/pub/er/review/reviewarticles/31231.html)

Shermer, Michael. *Why People Believe Weird Things: Pseudo-Science, Superstition, and Bogus Notions of Our Time*. New York: MJF Books, 1997.

Sommers, Nancy. "Revision Strategies of Student Writers and Experienced Adult Writers." *College Composition and Communication* 31 (1980).

Steinberg, Eve P. *How to Become a U.S. Citizen*. New York: Macmillan, 1998.

Tannen, Deborah. *The Argument Culture: Moving from Debate to Dialogue*. New York: Random House, 1998.

Woolf, Virginia. *A Writer's Diary*. New York: Harcourt, 1973.

INDEX